LINKING AMERICA'S SCHOOLS AND COLLEGES

GUIDE TO PARTNERSHIPS & NATIONAL DIRECTORY

2ND EDITION

by

Franklin P. Wilbur

Leo M. Lambert

Published by

American Association for Higher Education
Washington, DC

Anker Publishing Company, Inc.
Bolton, MA

About the authors

FRANKLIN P. WILBUR is the associate vice president for undergraduate studies at Syracuse University, where for many years he has also administered Project Advance, a nationally known school-college partnership serving schools throughout the Northeast. As an associate professor in Syracuse's Graduate School of Education, he has taught courses on instructional development, planning and managing change and innovation, project management, and educational administration. A frequent speaker at national and regional meetings, Dr. Wilbur has consulted and served as a program evaluator with schools and colleges throughout the country. He has written extensively in the areas of educational reform and ways of fostering interinstitutional relationships, including coauthoring (with Leo M. Lambert) two previous books on school-college partnerships.

LEO M. LAMBERT is the associate vice chancellor and dean of graduate studies at the University of Wisconsin-La Crosse, where he also holds an appointment as professor in the Department of Foundations of Educational Policy and Practice. He has coedited several other AAHE volumes, including *Preparing Graduate Students to Teach* (with Stacey Lane Tice). He is also the coeditor of *University Teaching: A Guide for Graduate Students,* which is forthcoming from the Syracuse University Press. Dr. Lambert is a member of the advisory board for the Undergraduate Teaching Improvement Council of the University of Wisconsin System and consults with universities throughout the United States in the areas of faculty development and the preparation of graduate students for university teaching responsibilities.

About AAHE

The American Association for Higher Education (AAHE) is a national organization of 8,500+ individuals dedicated to the common cause of improving the quality of American higher education. AAHE is higher education's "citizen's organization," where faculty, administrators, and students from all sectors, plus policy makers and leaders from foundations, government, accrediting agencies, and business can address collectively the challenges higher education faces. AAHE members share two convictions: that higher education should play a more central role in national life, and that each of our institutions can be more effective. AAHE helps members translate these convictions into action through its conferences, publications, and special programs. For more, contact : American Association for Higher Education, One Dupont Circle, Suite 360, Washington, DC 20036-1110; 202/293-6440, fax 202/293-0073.

LINKING AMERICA'S SCHOOLS AND COLLEGES: Guide to Partnerships & National Directory, 2nd ed.
by Franklin P. Wilbur and Leo M. Lambert

ISBN 1-882982-10-X

Cover design by Pamela Thompson

Anker Publishing Company, Inc.
176 Ballville Road
PO Box 249
Bolton, MA 01740

CONTENTS

□ □ □

FOREWORD

by Russell Edgerton
President, American Association for Higher Education

The American Association for Higher Education is deeply grateful to the authors of this second edition of *Linking America's Schools and Colleges*, Franklin Wilbur, associate vice president for undergraduate studies at Syracuse University, and Leo Lambert, dean of graduate studies at the University of Wisconsin-La Crosse, for their untiring commitment to this research and writing effort. Despite multiple other professional responsibilities, Wilbur and Lambert have, once again, made a major contribution to the literature on school-college-university partnerships.

Linking America's Schools and Colleges provides detailed information on more than 1,100 school-college-university partnerships and directory data on another 1,000+ — information that tells the story of a sophisticated and growing movement. As Wilbur and AAHE vice president Louis Albert report in their opening chapter, "The Partnership Terrain," more than 1,000 of the programs report startup dates of 1990 or later.

The partnerships involve every level of elementary and secondary education . . . and every sector of the college and university world. The largest number of these interinstitutional arrangements provide direct services for K-12 students. Others are organized to meet the professional development needs of faculty and/or administrators. Still others involve efforts to restructure the curriculum. This second edition of *Linking* also describes an expanding number of community-wide partnership initiatives that focus on K-16 systemic education reform.

Whether your school, college, or university is already involved in building linkages with K-12 education or is just getting started, *Linking America's Schools and Colleges* will provide you with vital information about successful programs and put you in touch with colleagues throughout the country who can be of help to you and your institution.

It is with pride that AAHE sponsors this effort, and we commend the volume to your use. ☐

PREFACE

The programs described in this book address one or more of the important, complex questions facing contemporary education in this country: how to prepare disadvantaged and at-risk youth for higher education; how to challenge and foster the most precocious and talented of our youth; how to keep teachers intellectually invigorated and enthusiastic about teaching; how to best train new teachers for the profession; and how to effectively manage resources for education in the face of sagging federal and state funding for education. These fundamental questions bridge the mysterious chasm that separates K-12 from higher education. The programs described here are testimony to the fact that these questions can best be addressed when educators from schools and colleges regard each other as equal partners having overlapping missions.

This second edition of *Linking America's Schools and Colleges* is the product of the third National Survey of School-College Partnerships, which was initiated in November 1993 and continued with a follow-up survey mailing in spring 1994. As with the earlier studies in 1986 and 1989, survey instruments were mailed to the chief academic officers of all two- and four-year colleges and universities in the United States, excluding proprietary, rabbinical, and theological institutions. The survey instrument used in the study, in slightly modified form, is included in Appendix A. The chief academic officers were asked to forward the survey, making duplicates as needed, to those faculty and administrators on their campuses involved in school-college collaborative activities. Surveys were also mailed directly to all of the programs identified in the 1989 survey and to approximately 100 programs identified as "outstanding" by a panel of experts. In addition to basic demographic and descriptive information regarding both the partnership and the collaborating institutions, the survey called for respondents to compose abstracts of approximately 100 words describing their programs in narrative form. Both the fall survey and the spring follow-up survey continued to elicit responses well into 1995. All survey data, including the abstracts, were entered into a computer database on school-college partnerships, which is more fully described in Appendix B.

In this volume's introductory chapter, "The Partnership Terrain," Louis Albert, vice president of the American Association for Higher Education, and Franklin Wilbur, associate vice president at Syracuse University, provide an overview of the data collected in the 1994 survey and a context for the sections of the book that follow. In this opening statement, Drs. Albert and Wilbur comment on the vitality and growth of the partnership movement, summarize the National Survey data, and point out emerging trends.

The main portion of this book is divided into five parts, each focusing on a major group of partnerships: (1) Programs and Services for Students; (2) Programs and Services for Educators; (3) Articulation, Development, and Evaluation of Curriculum and Instruction; (4) Restructuring; and (5) Learning Technologies and New Alliances. Each part begins with a brief introduction, followed by a selection of abstracts that captures the depth and variety of partnership activities. Selecting the approximately 1,100 abstracts to be included in these five chapters from the more than 2,300 submitted in the surveys required making some hard choices. Many excellent programs were not included because their goals and activities were too similar to other programs; some were excluded in striving for representation across geographic regions, higher education sectors (public, independent, two-year, four-year), discipline foci, and scope of activity (national, regional/state, local). The intent of the abstract chapters is to present a sample of a wide array of creative links, an "idea" book, to motivate readers to consider the possibilities for collaboration in their community or region.

Following these five parts is a comprehensive national directory to all 2,300+ programs contained in the National School-College Partnership Database. For each partnership program the directory lists the name of the higher education institution; name of the partnership; name, job title, address, phone number, and e-mail address of the higher education contact person; an 11-digit database reference number; and the program's primary focus. The "▶" character denotes those programs abstracted in Parts 1-5; brackets enclose the pertinent page number. It is our intent and that of the American Association for Higher Education that this national directory facilitate the sharing of information about school-college partnerships from institution to institution.

The two appendixes are also noteworthy. Appendix A provides a blank survey form for readers interested in submitting new entries to the database or updating existing information. Institutions absent from this edition's directory section are encouraged to return surveys now, which will enable them to be considered for inclusion in future publications, as well as ensure their receiving important announcements about upcoming partnership conferences and publications. Appendix B describes the national partnership computer database administered at Syracuse University's Center for Research and Information on School-College Partnerships. The database was structured to make the information accessible to researchers, practitioners, students, administrators, corporate representatives, foundation heads, and others, filtered, sorted, and presented in a manner consistent with individual needs. In addition to information fields such as partnership focus, subject-matter orientation, and school/college locations, the database can be filtered and sorted by Carnegie classification code, public/private, year established, program scope (local, regional, national), size (number of schools involved), funding, geographic region, and whether or not participants believe they are involved in the business of systemic reform. For example, a school superintendent might want to become familiar with partnerships targeting middle school minority females that focus on science and technology involving community colleges in the Southwest. A state or regional office charged with facilitating partnership activities might find a regional mailing list helpful in the process of organizing a conference. The order form to be completed to request a search of the database is included in Appendix B, as are samples of report format options.

The school-college partnership movement grew extraordinarily during the 1980s and the first half of the 1990s. We hope that this second edition of *Linking America's Schools and Colleges* will contribute to the increased vitality and strength of the movement throughout the remainder of this decade and into the next century. □

ACKNOWLEDGMENTS

The second edition of *Linking America's Schools and Colleges* is the product of many talented individuals, both on the national scene and at Syracuse University, committed to the ideas and ideals of the school-college partnership movement. We are indebted to the staff of Syracuse University's Project Advance, without whose support this undertaking would have been impossible to complete. Bill Newell worked on every phase of the survey, database construction, and data analysis. Cindy Purtell, with assistance from Debra LaVine, coordinated the movement of the survey data into text format and took major responsibility for the layout of the document. Bill and Cindy also responded to our requests for comparative and descriptive information with the attractive charts and graphs included in this publication. Bette Gaines worked tirelessly on a wide variety of editorial tasks, including preparing the database's more than 2,300 program abstracts. For any errors or omissions that might remain despite the competence of these individuals, we hold ourselves fully responsible.

We particularly want to thank all of our wonderful colleagues at the American Association for Higher Education for championing school-college partnerships and playing a primary role in placing the partnership movement high on the nation's higher education agenda. AAHE's sponsorship of this book and previous related publications, and its conferences on school-college collaboration, demonstrate the organization's intellectual leadership on this topic — one that is increasingly important to the overall vitality of our troubled education system. Specifically, we wish to thank our AAHE friends Russ Edgerton, Lou Albert, Bry Pollack, Nevin Brown, Kati Haycock, and Carol Stoel for their continuing encouragement and ongoing editorial comments.

The patience of our families in allowing us to devote so many evenings and weekends to this book is yet another important reason why projects like this one ever get finished. We reserve our most heartfelt thanks and love for Cheryl, Jeff, and Tim Wilbur and Laurie, Callie, and Mollie Lambert.

F.P. Wilbur
L.M. Lambert

THE PARTNERSHIP TERRAIN

An overview of the 1994 National Survey data.

by

Louis S. Albert
Vice President
American Association for Higher Education

Franklin P. Wilbur
Syracuse University

This second edition of *Linking America's Schools and Colleges* is the product of a third national study of school-college-university partnerships. The study, like its predecessors in 1986 and 1989, is based on the results of a survey mailed to the approximately 2,600 chief academic officers of all U.S. colleges and universities, excluding rabbinical, theological, and proprietary institutions. In addition, the survey was sent to more than 125 partnerships nominated by a national panel as being highly significant, and to all partnerships identified in the 1989 survey.

The database compiled by the research team includes information on some 2,300+ partnerships identified by collaborating colleges and universities, covering every region in the country. In comparison, the 1989 study yielded data on 1,286 partnerships, and the 1986 study identified 750. A major portion of the increased response can be attributed to the wide visibility achieved by the 1991 edition of *Linking America's Schools and Colleges.* Following its publication, many institutions wrote to the study's sponsors, Syracuse University and the American Association for Higher Education, and asked that their partnership programs be included in the next edition. The improved response rate can also be attributed to a more sophisticated survey methodology, which included follow-up with nonrespondents, and active support by some local and regional agencies (e.g., the Middle States Association of Colleges and Schools). We believe, however, that a major reason for the increasing numbers is that the partnership movement continues to grow. More than 1,000 of the responding programs reported start dates of 1990 or later.

The survey paints a picture of a complex and vibrant movement that involves collaborative efforts between K-12 schools and all sectors of higher education. As was the case in 1986 and 1989, most of these partnerships are local, grassroots efforts that place school professionals into new and very different working relationships with their colleagues from universities and colleges. Some are based in colleges and schools of education, but most are not. They also involve traditional academic departments in research universities, liberal arts colleges, and community colleges in both the public and independent sectors. In contrast to the more traditional ways in which colleges and universities relate to schools, these partnership programs tend to be less one-directional, less hierarchical. Schools and postsecondary institutions both report a variety of benefits from their participation in partnerships.

This introduction summarizes the results of the 1994 survey and provides a context for the abstracts of Parts 1-5 and the National Directory that follow.

Who are the higher education partners?

Of the 2,594 colleges and universities sent surveys, 861 institutions responded by reporting one or more active partnership programs each, for a total of 2,322 programs. Fifty-two institutions took the time to report that they have no partnerships currently active. Of those institutions responding, 66% (568) are public and 34% (293) are independent.

The partnerships involve every kind of higher education institution. The largest numbers of the

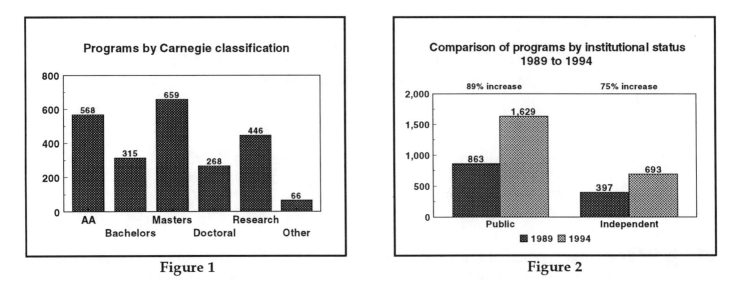

Figure 1

Figure 2

partnerships are associated with master's degree-granting institutions, community colleges, and research universities (see Figure 1). Seventy (70) percent of the programs (1,629) are involved with public institutions and 30% (693) with independent institutions (see Figure 2).

Who are the school partners?

Apart from its stated purposes, each partnership program was asked: If it serves students directly, which grade level(s) are served? Because many partnerships reported serving more than one grade level, the total in this category exceeds the number of partnerships responding.

High schools are partners in nearly 60% (1,362) of the programs, 33% (775) of the programs aim at middle schools, and 26% (601) aim at elementary schools. Most partnerships involve one college or university and ten or fewer schools. A smaller number of partnerships, especially those of national or regional scope, reported relationships between one college or university and more than ten schools; of those, a still smaller group involve more than 100 schools (see Figures 3 and 4).

When were the programs formed?

More than 50% of the responding partnerships reported start dates within the past five years. More than 75% of the partnerships had been established within the last ten years. A relatively small number of

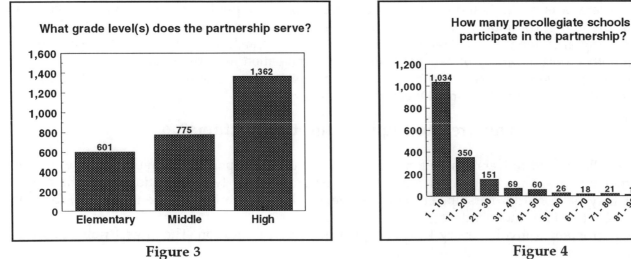

Figure 3

Figure 4

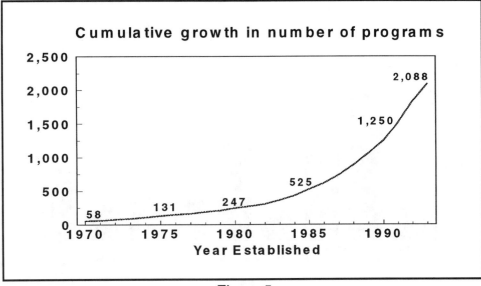

Figure 5

programs, such as Syracuse University's Project Advance, LaGuardia Community College's Middle College High School, and the Yale-New Haven Teachers Institute, have been operating for more than 20 years and clearly have reached "institutionalized" status.

As the 1989 survey observed, the mid-1980s marked the beginning of a period of rapid growth in the number and variety of partnerships. Some observers credit national school reform reports, especially the 1984 publication *A Nation At Risk*, with driving the expansion of collaborative programs. In the 1990s the pace and intensity of the school reform movement increased, leading to a second wave of partnership programs. Figure 5 shows the cumulative growth of the partnerships by year established. (Not all respondents reported their start date.)

Where are the programs and higher education partners located?

Programs in the study database cover every state in the nation. While the preponderance of colleges and universities participating in partnerships are located in urban areas, the data show a more even program distribution by *school* location, suggesting that colleges and universities are embracing as partners schools outside their immediate areas. Figures 6, 7, and 8 indicate the distribution of the partners by location

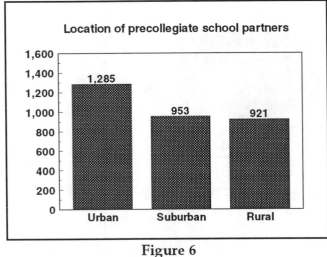

Figure 6

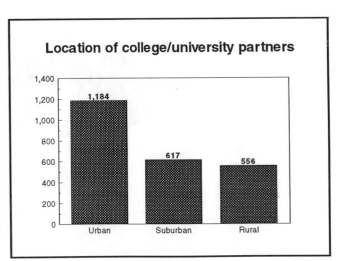

Figure 7

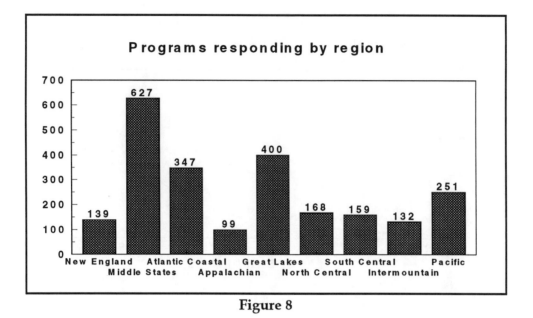

Figure 8

(urban, suburban, and rural) and by region. The regional distributions shown in Figure 8 were affected by several factors, including a disproportionate concentration of higher education institutions in certain areas and active encouragement of survey responses by particular regional accreditation associations and state higher education offices.

What are the general classifications of partnership programs?

The three most significant general classification categories were (1) programs and services for students, (2) professional development for faculty, and (3) curriculum development and articulation.

Fifty-one (51) percent of the respondents described the primary purpose of their program as providing direct services for students. They include a large number of early identification and

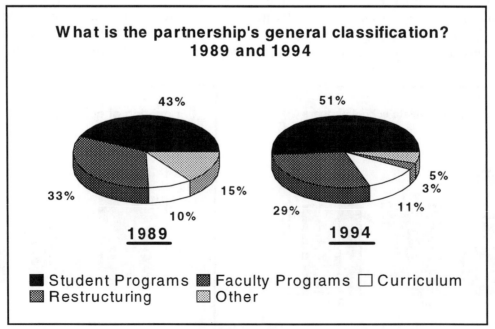

Figure 9

intervention programs, and programs that bring K-12 students to college and university campuses for academic enrichment and/or skill building. The programs take place after school, on weekends, and during the summer; many connect students' achievement with the promise of college scholarships.

Programs aimed at the professional development of faculty, and to a lesser extent administrators, account for 29% of the total. As in 1989, "academic alliances" were reported in this response category. The category also includes a variety of continuing education opportunities for school faculty, ranging from graduate work to funded summer institutes in their disciplines.

Articulation and curriculum development was the reported primary purpose of 11% of the responding programs; 8% of programs reported school restructuring, facilities and resource sharing, and other miscellaneous efforts as their primary purpose. Figure 9 shows the general classification of the programs contained in the 1989 and 1994 databases.

What is the primary programmatic focus of the partnerships?

Each partnership also was asked to describe the primary focus of its work. Of the 2,322 programs responding to the survey, the largest number of programs (22%) reported a primary focus on the needs of underrepresented or at-risk populations, often urban poor and minority students. The second-largest response was the professional development of teachers and administrators (20%). Smaller numbers were reported for student academic enrichment programs (10%) and credit-bearing college courses for high school students (9%). The emergence of the tech-prep programs under the Perkins Act accounted for 8% of the reported primary foci. Figure 10 provides data on the top ten primary focus classifications. It is

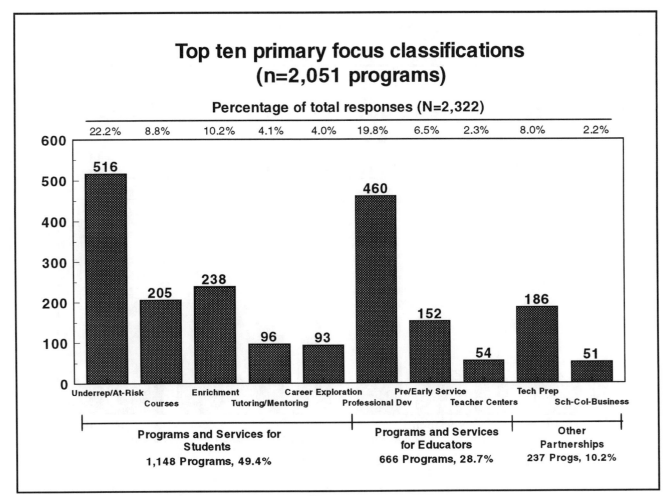

Figure 10

notable that just these ten of the 38 available primary focus classifications describe more than 88% of *all* the responding programs.

What subject areas do the partnerships focus on?

Respondents were asked to indicate their partnership's specific content orientation, where applicable. The most frequently reported general content areas were mathematics (18%), science (16%), and writing (16%). Figure 11 indicates the subject area emphasized, comparing 1989 and 1994 surveys. (Programs frequently reported more than one subject focus.) In addition, 1,271 (55%) indicated they focus on content outside traditional disciplines of math, science, humanities, and the arts; these nontraditional foci are shown collectively as "miscellaneous." By contrast, in 1989 only 14% of programs focused on such nontraditional content. The "miscellaneous" foci were a significant factor for several primary classifications.

On this question of subject focus, the responses of the 516 partnerships serving underrepresented and at-risk populations, including poor and minority students, are interesting. This group of partnerships reported a particularly large "miscellaneous" category. As indicated on Figure 12, a significant number of those programs focus on basic/study skills (47%), parental/community involvement (40%), critical thinking (39%), leadership skills (35%), financial aid (29%), and cultural pluralism (27%).

How many programs receive outside financial support?

Fifty-four (54) percent of the 2,322 partnerships reported they receive external funding (i.e., from sources other than the collaborating schools or colleges). Of those 1,250 receiving outside financial support, government, private foundations, and businesses are the three primary sources. Figure 13 indicates the sources of external financial support reported by the partnerships.

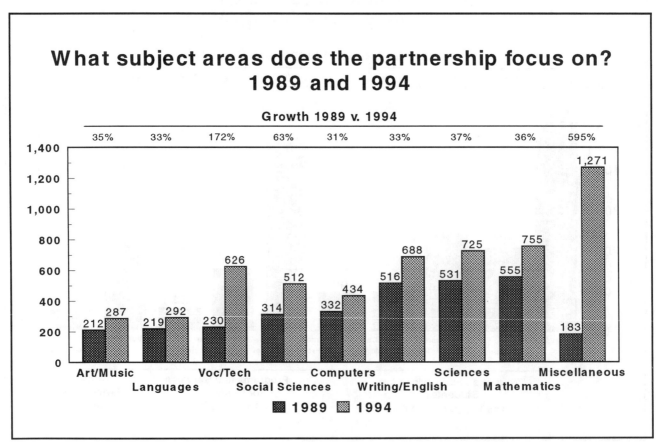

Figure 11

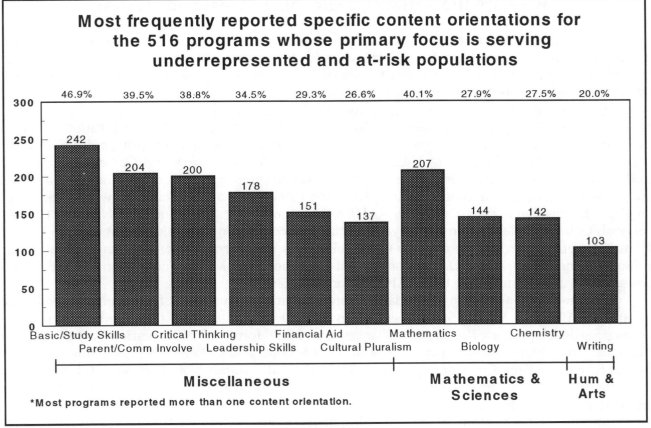

Figure 12

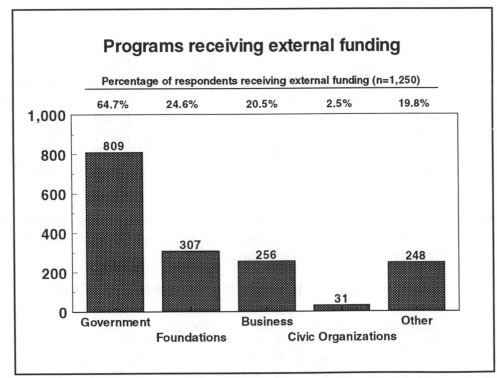

Figure 13

Who are the national, regional, and state advocates?

While most partnerships are clearly local in origin and scope, a number of national, regional, and statewide organizations are important contributors to the partnership movement. These advocates for collaboration, as part of their larger efforts to improve students' achievement by improving teaching and learning at all levels, often support local collaborative programs.

At the national level, the advocates include The College Board, the National Association of Secondary School Principals, the Council of Chief State School Officers, and the Education Commission of the States, plus a number of higher education associations, among them principally the American Association for Higher Education (AAHE). With funding from the John D. and Catherine T. MacArthur Foundation, AAHE conducted, from 1988 to 1992, a national project in support of academic alliances — local groups of school and college faculty from the same or related disciplines who meet regularly throughout the academic year. Currently, AAHE's Education Trust runs an annual National Conference on School/College Collaboration and several initiatives focused on systemic reform of K-16 education, with major support provided by the Pew Charitable Trusts, the Carnegie Corporation of New York, and the Fund for Innovation of the U.S. Department of Education. The Knight Foundation annually supports representation of its grantees at that AAHE national conference.

Some regional accrediting associations are also in the business of encouraging collaborative programs. In 1989, the Middle States Association of Colleges and Schools (MSA) adopted a resolution encouraging development of academic alliances and other forms of collaboration within its member institutions. In 1990, the New England Association of Schools and Colleges (NEASC) started a full-time Office of School/College Collaboration. NEASC, MSA, and a number of other accrediting associations are discussing how to encourage colleges and schools to include collaborative activities in their accreditation self-studies.

Support for partnerships is also growing at the state level. Since the mid-1980s, the California Academic Partnership Program has funded a large number of innovative projects. New Jersey, Tennessee, Arkansas, Iowa, Virginia, Wisconsin, Ohio, Georgia, Texas, North Dakota, Minnesota, New York, Pennsylvania, Utah, Oregon, and Massachusetts, among others, have supported partnership programs or mandated particular collaborative activities or partnership programs at the state level.

Who else supports partnerships?

No list of advocates for collaboration would be complete without mentioning the discipline-based faculty professional societies. The American Physical Society is an active supporter of academic alliances and other collaborative activities. In addition, a variety of programs and/or statements of support have been developed under the auspices of the American Historical Association, the Mathematics Association of America, the American Chemical Society, the National Geographic Society, the National Science Teachers Association, and the Modern Language Association.

Foundations also have played a major role in shaping the partnership movement. Many programs owe their origins to the Ford Foundation, the Rockefeller Foundation, the John D. and Catherine T. MacArthur Foundation, or the Carnegie Corporation of New York. Government-sponsored foundations, such as the National Science Foundation and the National Endowment for the Humanities, have played similar supportive roles. More recently, the Pew Charitable Trusts have led the way toward the creation of more systemic connections between K-12 and higher education.

Where is the partnership movement headed?

The data describe a partnership movement that is growing in number, variety, and complexity. Partnerships are usually seen not as an end in themselves but as a way to improve educational opportunities for students and to enhance students' performance. Increasingly, school-college-university partnerships are developing connections to the business sector. Many states and/or local communities have turned to comprehensive umbrella structures to serve as central coordinating agencies for particular partnership activities.

Most important, the faculty, administrators, and community leaders who work collaboratively with one another are redefining the education profession. They tend to see themselves as part of a single system of education stretching unbroken from kindergarten through graduate school. They are gaining new respect for the sophistication and complexities of the teaching-learning process at all levels. And they have formed new professional relationships with one another based on a sense of interdependence and shared mission. A transformed education profession should prove, in the long run, to be one of the most important contributions of the partnership movement. □

Part One
PROGRAMS AND SERVICES FOR STUDENTS

Introduction

The majority of school-college partnerships identified by the 1994 national survey are focused on providing instruction, career exploration experiences, mentoring, and other forms of support directly to students. While the range of activities and goals being pursued by these partnerships is impressive, what is even more stirring is the mobilization of a vast array of community resources aimed at helping children and young adults achieve their fullest potential. While these community resources always include college and university faculty, they also often include other "people resources" — parents, community volunteers, clergy, business and corporate leaders, private industry councils, for example — as well as facilities and equipment resources, such as research labs, computers, and, increasingly, means to electronically link America's schools and colleges using the information superhighway.

The breadth of programs featured in Section One, "Serving Underrepresented or At-Risk Populations," is extraordinary. Many partnerships focus on bringing underrepresented groups into academic and professional fields, such as education, law, health and medicine, science, engineering, and information technology. Other programs, such as Maryland's Tomorrow Program, emphasize retention in the secondary grades. Many partnerships in this section emphasize school-to-work options by providing increased access to vocational and technical training in cooperation with local industries. Some postsecondary institutions, such as Southern Maine Technical College, have not only promised college tuition scholarships to at-risk youth in the community but also have upped the ante by providing mentoring, tutoring, cultural awareness, and attendance incentive programs. Still other programs, such as Access 2000 Chicago Partnership of Loyola University of Chicago, aim for more systemic reform by providing "a continuous pipeline of out-of-school activities that enable students to learn mathematics and science in enriched environments and provide opportunities for their teachers to learn new instructional methods." That partnership won the 1993 Robert Anderson Medal, awarded by the Business-Higher Education Forum.

Section Two, "College Courses for High School Students," describes the range of opportunities for high school students to begin college-level studies early. Minnesota's Postsecondary Enrollment Options Act and Florida's Dual Enrollment statute both provide models for time-shortened degrees, broaden curricular choices for students, and/or increase the depth of study in a particular field. Cornell University's Summer College helps junior and senior high school students adjust to the rigors of university studies by participating with undergraduates in seminars that earn college credits. Increasingly, universities are turning to technology to offer college-level studies in the high schools, especially in rural areas. St. Cloud State University, for example, uses two-way television to reach partner schools; many other universities use audio graphics to teach subjects, such as calculus, that would otherwise be unavailable to geographically isolated students. Courses in many programs are taught by well-qualified and specially prepared high school teachers in the schools, but in other instances they are led by college faculty in the schools or on campus. College credit earned through these programs is generally transferable to most postsecondary institutions, but, more important, the programs combat "senioritis" by offering students a sample of the challenges and demands of the college curriculum.

Section Three, "Enrichment and Gifted-and-Talented Programs," provides examples of exciting partnerships focused on high-achieving students and/or supplementing the curriculum with career exploration experiences, academic olympics, theater and the arts, summer academic enrichment, and a myriad of other programs. Educational partnerships focusing on gifted and talented students range from Johns Hopkins University's nationally prominent Center for Talented Youth, to the Georgia Institute of Technology's CHIPS program, an introduction to computer-aided design for middle school students.

Section Four, "Middle Colleges and Early Colleges," describes 13 varying approaches to allowing students to begin collegiate studies early. The Clarkson School's Bridging Year Program (Clarkson University) offers early admission for students after their junior year of high school, demonstrating that "talented students can benefit from early admission and avoid wasting an academically unchallenging senior year by getting a head start on university courses." City University of New York's Middle College High School takes a different approach, focusing on students at risk of not completing high school and providing an instructional program that emphasizes small classes, counseling, and internships in the community.

Sections Five and Six are new to this second edition. Section Five, "Tutoring, Mentoring, and Counseling Programs," describes programs like Howard University's partnership with J.C. Nalle Elementary School, which focuses on building students' self-esteem and raising at-risk students' scores on the California Test of Basic Skills by providing after-school tutorials. Section Six, "Career Exploration, Internships, or Apprenticeships," describes many efforts focusing on exploring new career paths. George Washington University's Science and Engineering Apprenticeship Program links high school students with paid apprenticeships in the U.S. Department of Defense. Another example is the Women Making Strides program of Manhattan Community College, which focuses on women enrolled in schools for pregnant women and parenting services, providing them with career experiences, information about nontraditional career paths, and job readiness skills.   □

Section One
Serving Underrepresented or At-Risk Populations

ALASKA

University of Alaska-Fairbanks (DOC II)
Rural Alaska Honors Institute

Grades served: HS	Schools served: 118	Year established: 1982
Location of schools served: RU	Type of schools served: PUB, PRI	

The Rural Alaska Honors Institute (RAHI) of the University of Alaska - Fairbanks links the university with all rural Alaska secondary schools and districts. RAHI's primary mission is to offer qualified college-bound Alaska Native students the opportunity for a head start in college. The students sharpen academic skills, especially in mathematics and writing, examine career possibilities, and learn to live and work together on a large urban campus. The seven-week program for students finishing their junior or senior years is primarily enrichment rather than remediation. Students are selected from applicants on the basis of academic achievement and desire to earn a college degree. Full-cost scholarships and travel support are provided.

ARIZONA

Northern Arizona University (DOC I)
Project ASSIST, Educational Psychology, Center for Excellence in Education

Grades served: M, HS	Schools served: 23	Year established: 1992
Location of schools served: RU	Type of schools served: NR	

Project ASSIST in the Educational Psychology area of the Center for Excellence in Education is a program linking Northern Arizona University with middle and high schools serving Native American children living on Arizona reservations. The goal of Project ASSIST is to strengthen the existing school-based drug and alcohol programs and student services. Ongoing consultation is provided to school personnel to establish Student Assistance Programs (SAP's), which are comprehensive systems focusing on early identification and intervention with high-risk children in collaboration with school and community-based treatment services.

Note: Each institution's Carnegie class is given in parentheses. **Key:** E=elementary school, HS=high school, M=middle school, NR=not reported, PRI=private, PUB=public, RU=rural, SU=suburban, UR=urban

University of Arizona (RES I)
Educational and Community Change Project

Grades served: E   Schools served: 2   Year established: 1990
Location of schools served: NR   Type of schools served: PUB

The foundation-funded Educational and Community Change (ECC) Project explores conditions necessary to change school curricula, structures, and practices. Its ultimate goal is to enhance the educational and societal opportunities for poor, multicultural students whose dominant language is not English. The project began in 1990 in one urban elementary school and expanded to a second school in 1992. The area served by schools is populated predominantly by Spanish-speaking residents, and about 55% of the families live at or below the poverty level. An adjunct of the school's efforts is a community coalition that strives to transform educational, economic, societal, and other aspects of the total school-community ecology.

CALIFORNIA

California Institute of Technology (RES I)
The W.M. Keck Foundation High School Outreach Program at Caltech

Grades served: HS   Schools served: 30   Year established: 1991
Location of schools served: UR, SU Type of schools served: PUB, PRI

The W.M. Keck Foundation High School Outreach Program at Caltech provides public school students in the Los Angeles area with the opportunity to perform biotechnology experiments that are not usually part of a high school program. Each summer teachers are selected to participate in an intensive five-day workshop on the Caltech campus, where they learn the experiments. During the school year, teachers are loaned kits containing all the equipment and supplies necessary to take the laboratory exercises to their schools. The experiments include state-of-the-art techniques, such as DNA fingerprinting and polymerase chain reaction.

California State University-Fresno (MA I)
California Mini-Corps Enhancement

Grades served: E, M, HS   Schools served: 20   Year established: 1994
Location of schools served: UR, RU Type of schools served: PUB

California Mini-Corps is a component of the state's migrant program established in 1967 that was designed to provide direct categorical services to migrant students and to develop a corps of professional educators especially sensitive to the needs of migrant children. Currently serving 80 students, Mini-Corps Program 4 is a true collaboration involving CSUF's School of Education and Human Development, California Mini-Corps, Fresno County's Office of Migrant Education, and the local public schools. The university contributes facilities and personnel for administration of the program; the Office of Migrant Education contributes secretarial support; California Mini-Corps contributes office equipment and resources for student support, and the public schools contribute supervisory staff.

California State University-Hayward (MA I)
College Readiness Program

Grades served: M   Schools served: 3   Year established: 1986
Location of schools served: NR   Type of schools served: PUB

The College Readiness Program, a partnership of California State University and the California Department of Education, links CSU-Hayward and three middle schools in its service area in a program designed to enrich academic programs of African-American and Latino students. Tutoring sessions are conducted after school and on Saturdays. Hayward student interns are trained by teacher education faculty to work with middle grade students in problem solving, higher order thinking skills, analytical reasoning, computational skills, written and oral communication, and reading and writing. The program's overall goal is to encourage students to enroll in college preparatory classes and to increase the college matriculation of minority students.

California State University-Long Beach (MA I)
Long Beach Access Program
Grades served: M   Schools served: 15   Year established: 1991
Location of schools served: UR   Type of schools served: PUB

The Long Beach Access Program, a partnership of California State University, Long Beach and the Long Beach Unified School District, works with middle schools by providing a mobile science van that travels to district middle schools to provide hands-on experience for sixth and seventh grade students. During the summer, a residential academy (Summer Intensive Math and Science) for seventh and eighth grade girls is housed on campus. Participants are provided an enriched curriculum and a social network with follow-up during the year. The combined efforts are increasing the pool of women and underrepresented minorities staying in the educational pipeline and entering the university.

California State University-Los Angeles (MA I)
Improving School and Community Services to Children and Families in the Inner City
Grades served: E   Schools served: 5   Year established: 1991
Location of schools served: NR   Type of schools served: PUB

Murchison Street School, in partnership with CSU-Los Angeles, established a school-based integrated services center to help manage the problems of inner-city students and their families. The center is the primary agency (the hub), which is linked with other agencies to meet specific needs. Students and families are referred to the center by teachers and other school staff or by parents. On-site services, such as short-term counseling and limited health care, are provided by county and nonprofit community agencies. Resource and referral services are also available to parents through case management.

California State University-San Bernardino (MA I)
Reading Recovery™
Grades served: E   Schools served: NR   Year established: NR
Location of schools served: UR, SU, RU   Type of schools served: PUB

The Reading Recovery™ program, an early intervention program for young readers who are experiencing difficulty in the first grade, links CSU-San Bernardino, and schools in Riverside and San Bernardino Counties. Based on a whole-language approach to reading, it uses exciting and age-appropriate literature for children. Built into the program is an evaluation process so that the teacher will know the students' progress. "Super trainers" take a year-long course to ensure that they can teach others; they then go back to county and district offices to train future Reading Recovery™ specialists.

California State University-San Bernardino (MA I)
Community Service in Tutoring At-Risk Adolescents (Student Literacy Corps Project)
Grades served: HS   Schools served: NR   Year established: NR
Location of schools served: NR   Type of schools served: PUB

San Bernardino High School, community agencies, EOP, SAIL, and CSU's Learning Center work together in this project. A university course trains undergraduates and others in tutoring adolescents; it requires at least six hours a week of tutoring during the semester. Trainees are matched with at-risk ninth graders. The course is taught by CSU faculty in bilingual education, special education, reading and writing, and technology. Additionally, literacy coordinators from the California Literacy Campaign assist in conducting some of the sessions in family literacy and emergent reading. The U.S. Department of Education has selected the project as one of 15 outstanding Student Literacy Corps projects.

Note: Each institution's Carnegie class is given in parentheses. **Key:** E=elementary school, HS=high school, M=middle school, NR=not reported, PRI=private, PUB=public, RU=rural, SU=suburban, UR=urban

De Anza College (AA)
Middle College Program
Grades served: HS
Location of schools served: SU

Schools served: 5
Type of schools served: PUB

Year established: 1989

Middle College, a collaborative effort between Fremont Union High School and De Anza College, is an alternative program located on the De Anza campus. The program is designed for students who are academically very capable but for a variety of reasons are not performing up to their potential. By interacting with more mature role models and taking advantage of advanced courses, students with previous attendance and study problems develop responsibility and a sense of self-direction, benefiting from teaching and support services of both institutions. Middle College is a program for juniors and seniors.

Dominican College of San Rafael (MA II)
Communities in Schools
Grades served: E, M, HS
Location of schools served: NR

Schools served: 4
Type of schools served: PUB

Year established: 1991

Communities in Schools assesses students' needs and matches them with individuals, businesses, and social service agencies to provide what the schools cannot. Communities in Schools, a project in wealthy Marin County, provides an opportunity for children who have difficulty learning because of language barriers, drug abuse, teen pregnancy, family problems, health needs, low income, or other problems. It engages the residents of Marin County to make a difference in their own community by tutoring, mentoring, counseling, providing health services or job training, and much more.

Harvey Mudd College (ENGR)
Mathematics, Engineering, Science Achievement
Grades served: M, HS
Location of schools served: NR

Schools served: 14
Type of schools served: PUB, PRI

Year established: 1973

The purpose of Harvey Mudd College's (HMC) precollege Mathematics, Engineering, Science Achievement (MESA) Center is to increase the number of minority students who are prepared for a math-based career and to improve the academic preparation of students intending to pursue a math-based college major. The center serves approximately 500 underrepresented minority high school students at seven participating schools and 200 underrepresented middle school minority students at seven participating schools. During the summer, the center also serves approximately 75 eighth and ninth grade MESA students in a pre-MESA summer enrichment program at the college. Ethnic minority students are chosen on the basis of their preparation and commitment to explore math-related career opportunities.

Holy Names College (MA I)
Holy Names-Oakland High School Upward Bound
Grades served: M, HS
Location of schools served: NR

Schools served: 3
Type of schools served: PUB

Year established: 1992

Upward Bound links Holy Names College, Oakland High School and its three feeder schools, the Oakland Unified School District, the Oakland business community, and postsecondary institutions in a program designed to serve students classified as educationally disadvantaged. Upward Bound is an early intervention program that offers assessment, instruction, curricular enrichment, and a basic instructional program in English and mathematics. Advising, tutoring, and other support services complement instruction in computer competency, multicultural education, and career/college awareness.

Humboldt State University (MA I)
Project PARITY (Promoting Academic Retention for Indian Tribal Youth)

Grades served: E, M, HS   Schools served: 2   Year established: 1989
Location of schools served: RU   Type of schools served: PUB

PARITY is a partnership involving Humboldt State University and two Indian Reservation School Districts (K-12), students' families, and local businesses. Its primary focus is to increase interest and skills in mathematics and science. Faculties work in teams to develop new courses incorporating Native American social, cultural, and historical contributions and building on students' experiential knowledge through studying outdoors and developing a greater understanding of the students' surroundings and their relation to the larger world of learning, academic adventure, and exploration.

Monterey Peninsula College (AA)
Upward Bound

Grades served: HS   Schools served: 2   Year established: 1989
Location of schools served: UR   Type of schools served: PUB

Monterey Peninsula College's federally funded Upward Bound program provides academic support, college experiences, and opportunities for personal growth for low-income, potential first-generation college students attending district high schools. Working collaboratively with the area's four-year colleges, universities, and the community, Upward Bound offers after-school tutoring, Saturday study skills classes, career/college workshops, and field trips to West Coast colleges and universities. Participants attend a rigorous six-week academic study program on the main campus, focusing on math, science, English, foreign languages, and critical thinking skills.

Mount St. Mary's College (MA II)
STEP (Strides Toward Educational Proficiency)

Grades served: HS   Schools served: 6   Year established: 1985
Location of schools served: UR   Type of schools served: PRI

Mount St. Mary's College introduced its STEP program to motivate economically disadvantaged students in inner-city high schools to attend college. A three-week summer workshop focuses on strengthening reading, writing, mathematics, and study skills; provides career and financial aid counseling; and introduces students to museums, galleries, plays, and concerts. During the school year, STEP's coordinator regularly visits the high schools to meet with students and consult with their counselors. College students serve as tutors and help keep the STEP students motivated for college.

Mt. San Antonio College (AA)
Links: Women in Math, Science & Technology

Grades served: HS   Schools served: 2   Year established: 1993
Location of schools served: UR   Type of schools served: NR

Mt. San Antonio College's Links: Women in Math, Science, and Technology is a partnership linking the college, secondary schools, and the local CSU campus (Cal Poly, Pomona). Women are recruited for nontraditional careers targeting four applied science and technology programs: air conditioning and refrigeration, airframe maintenance technology, computer-aided drafting, and electronics. Students enroll in a vocational class, an appropriate math class, and a course in career options for women. Participants are provided a stipend for child care, if needed, tutoring, and the support of a mentor.

Note: Each institution's Carnegie class is given in parentheses. **Key:** E=elementary school, HS=high school, M=middle school, NR=not reported, PRI=private, PUB=public, RU=rural, SU=suburban, UR=urban

Rancho Santiago College (AA)
Networks
Grades served: E, M, HS   Schools served: 30   Year established: 1983
Location of schools served: UR Type of schools served: PUB

Rancho Santiago's Networks is an outgrowth of two powerful and broad-based local collaboratives: STEP (Student and Teacher Educational Partnership) and Santa Ana 2000. Funded by the Ford Foundation under the auspices of the Urban Partnership program, the initiative unites educational, business, and civic partners with the communities they serve to improve the educational success of at-risk urban youth. The program includes direct services to students (through cohort classes, targeted counseling/support services, and the Summer Scholars Transfer Institute), professional inservice/staff development, and community events.

San Diego State University (DOC II)
College of Professional Studies & Fine Arts/National City Middle School
Grades served: M   Schools served: 1   Year established: 1989
Location of schools served: NR Type of schools served: PUB

Ninety-three (93) percent of National City Middle School's culturally enriched student body of 762 students is of ethnic origins. Students' educational continuation rates of these students are low, and this partnership between the university and the school has the shared goal of encouraging educational progress among underrepresented youth. The partnership's goals include providing positive role models for students, promoting exposure to visual and performing arts, demystifying college, and awarding university scholarships. Students are provided opportunities to visit campus, attend university and community visual and performing arts events, and explore related careers/academics.

San Diego State University (DOC II)
Auditory Discrimination in Depth Project
Grades served: NR   Schools served: 1   Year established: 1983
Location of schools served: UR Type of schools served: PUB

The Auditory Discrimination in Depth (ADD) Project to assess whether Granger Junior High School students identified as having auditory problems would benefit from therapy to improve their skills in discriminating sounds and thereby improve their reading skills. The project is funded by the Sweetwater Union High School District and staffed at Granger Junior High School by high school and college professionals specializing in the subject area. Graduate students, trained to conduct the program with the identified students, are paid for their services. Results to date indicate that the grade-equivalent reading scores of participating Granger students have significantly increased.

San Francisco State University (MA I)
Women and Girls in Science, Engineering, and Mathematics (WGSEM)
Grades served: E, M, HS   Schools served: 5   Year established: 1993
Location of schools served: UR, SU Type of schools served: PUB, PRI

WGSEM provides assistance at precollege and undergraduate levels so girls and women can succeed in math-based studies. Precollege students are offered workshops, competitions, advising, and outreach. Undergraduate women are offered workshops, summer research opportunities, career advising, scholarships, and employment. The School of Science at San Francisco State University established WGSEM in collaboration with the Center for Underrepresented Engineering Students (CUES) at the University of California-Berkeley.

San Francisco State University (MA I)
NASA SHARP PLUS

Grades served: HS

Schools served: NR

Year established: 1994

Location of schools served: UR, SU

Type of schools served: PUB, PRI

NASA SHARP PLUS is a research-based mentor program offering the opportunity to conduct research in industry or laboratories at host universities. The program establishes working relationships between students and active researchers in aerospace-related fields, offering researchers and other science and engineering professionals the opportunity to serve as mentors to minority students (16 or older) who are entering 11 or 12 grade and exhibit interest and potential in math, science, and engineering. The apprenticeships aim to recruit and sustain minority students in science and engineering fields.

San Francisco State University (MA I)
On the Right Track

Grades served: M, HS

Schools served: 3

Year established: 1992

Location of schools served: UR

Type of schools served: PUB

On the Right Track serves high-risk Asian youth who have been targeted for gang activities and adjustment difficulties in Oakland and Union City public school classrooms. Thirty boys and girls from the Hmong, Mien, and Cambodian communities who attend East Oakland middle schools and 15 Philippine Logan High School students were referred by counselors or street workers to join the on-site program in East Oakland. Counselors are from the communities and speak the native dialects. The school-college partnership deploys college students as counselors and tutors; one faculty member conducts the research and evaluates the program. Preventive services are provided for the high-risk youth.

San Francisco State University (MA I)
Graduate Program in Physical Therapy Outreach Program to Grade Schools

Grades served: E

Schools served: 3

Year established: 1992

Location of schools served: UR

Type of schools served: PUB, PRI

This program in was created to recruit minority students to the physical therapy profession by strengthening their preparation and skills in mathematics, science, reasoning, and communication. The second-year pilot project places graduate students in four urban grade schools serving primarily children from African and Mexican heritage (grades 5-8) to guide the students through discussions of what it means to be disabled, rehabilitation, and the applied science background needed to become a physical therapist. Videotapes, discussion, and hands-on experience in laboratory settings (anatomy, human performance) are used in instruction. Teaching materials and models are left at the site for use in science classes.

University of California-Davis (RES I)
The UC-Davis Early Academic Outreach Program

Grades served: M, HS

Schools served: 76

Year established: 1976

Location of schools served: UR, SU, RU

Type of schools served: PUB, PRI

The UC-Davis Early Academic Outreach Program links the university with middle school/junior high and high schools. Its primary mission is to motivate underrepresented students to pursue a postsecondary education, specifically to increase the number of underrepresented students eligible to attend schools in the University of California system. Target groups are African-Americans, Chicanos/Mexican-Americans, Latinos, Native Americans, and economically disadvantaged seventh through 12th graders. The program primarily provides college advising directly to the targeted students, but also it provides necessary information to school personnel and parents.

Note: Each institution's Carnegie class is given in parentheses. **Key:** E=elementary school, HS=high school, M=middle school, NR=not reported, PRI=private, PUB=public, RU=rural, SU=suburban, UR=urban

University of California-Davis (RES I)
Engineering Summer Residency Program
Grades served: HS   Schools served: 34   Year established: 1975
Location of schools served: NR   Type of schools served: PUB

The Engineering Summer Residency Program is a partnership linking the university and secondary schools that helps to promote the entrance of women and minorities into science and engineering careers. The purpose of the week-long program is to give qualified minority and disadvantaged high school students the opportunity to explore engineering education through first-hand university instruction and laboratory experience. Eleventh and 12th graders live in university residence halls with upper-division minority engineering student advisers and participate in laboratories, lectures, design competitions, writing exercises, workshops, and field trips.

University of California-Irvine (RES I)
PRISM (Partnership for Reform in Science and Mathematics)
Grades served: E, M, HS   Schools served: 13   Year established: 1992
Location of schools served: UR   Type of schools served: PUB

PRISM is a teacher-driven academic partnership designed to increase the enrollment and retention of ethnic minority students in college preparatory courses in the Santa Ana Unified School District by encouraging them to seek careers as science, engineering, and mathematics professionals. Partners include the students, parents, faculty, and administrative leadership of the district and four surrounding college campuses associated with Project STEP, role models from the community and corporate/business sector, and the National Science Foundation.

University of California-Irvine (RES I)
KIDS (Kids Investigating and Discovering Science)
Grades served: M, HS   Schools served: 8   Year established: 1989
Location of schools served: NR   Type of schools served: PUB

Kids Investigating and Discovering Science began at the University of California-Irvine to establish a national model program of elementary science instruction for at-risk elementary students. The three-week annual summer program brings 120 to 150 elementary students with limited proficiency in English to the campus, where the KIDS staff has developed and implemented innovative curricula to teach concepts in the physical, biological, and environmental sciences. KIDS implements and disseminates a science program for grades K-8, develops new physical, environmental, and biological science curricula, institutes a training program for science educators, and conducts related longitudinal research. Lessons are taught bilingually, during the summer and in after-school and weekend sessions during the academic year.

University of Southern California (RES I)
Educational Talent Search Program
Grades served: M, HS   Schools served: 13   Year established: 1991
Location of schools served: UR   Type of schools served: PUB, PRI

The purpose of the Educational Talent Search Program is to assist participants in developing the academic and motivational skills necessary to become better students, graduate from high school or obtain a GED, and enroll in college. The program will serve 1,200 students from South Central Los Angeles and Inglewood. Participation in the program, funded by the U.S. Department of Education, is free. Students must be from low-income families and/or be potential first-generation college students.

University of Southern California (RES I)
Joint Educational Project
Grades served: E, M   Schools served: 10   Year established: 1972
Location of schools served: UR   Type of schools served: PUB

USC's Joint Educational Project is a service-learning program linking undergraduates from the College of Letters, Arts, and Sciences with local schools, agencies, clinics, and hospitals in Latino and African-American neighborhoods. In the schools, university students mentor, assist teachers and other professionals, teach minicourses, and provide enrichment activities for children aged 3 to 18. University students, drawn from 65 general education and upper-division courses, are required to apply course-related knowledge through teaching or participant observation. The program includes very stringent requirements for written reflection.

University of Southern California (RES I)
Education Consortium of Central Los Angeles (ECCLA)
Grades served: E, M, HS   Schools served: 49   Year established: 1988
Location of schools served: UR   Type of schools served: PUB, PRI

ECCLA seeks to enhance the opportunities for quality education for approximately 65,000 students enrolled in 49 K-12 public and parochial schools in central Los Angeles near the University of Southern California/Exposition Park area. The consortium includes four higher education institutions, three museums, the Los Angeles Unified School District, and the Education Department of the Archdiocese of Los Angeles. The programs offers teacher recognition awards, student scholarships, intersession programs, a newsletter, summer work programs, human relations minigrants, and art and composition contests. The board of directors includes representatives of the nine organizations and at-large representatives from the community (teachers, administrators, parents, and residents).

University of Southern California (RES I)
Upward Bound Project
Grades served: HS   Schools served: 11   Year established: 1977
Location of schools served: UR   Type of schools served: PUB

The Upward Bound Project has two components. The first, an intensive six-week summer residential program, includes needs assessment, academic tutoring, and instruction in English, reading, writing, mathematics, and laboratory sciences; culturally enhancing and recreational programs; college guidance; and career and personal development. The second, an academic year component, provides such services as advising on college admissions and financial aid, preparation for College Board tests, and academic advisement. Students participate in culturally diverse activities. The program involves low-income, first-generation students, aged 13 to 19, from 11 high schools.

University of Southern California (RES I)
Peer Counseling Program
Grades served: HS   Schools served: 10   Year established: 1992
Location of schools served: UR   Type of schools served: PUB, PRI

USC's Peer Counseling Program, funded through the Office of Admissions, focuses on recruiting students from strategically targeted high schools in neighborhoods contiguous to the USC campus. USC students spend ten to 20 hours weekly assisting minority and nontraditional college-bound students to apply to college, helping them identify and apply for financial aid. Peer counselors interact with high school college counselors to provide information to the high school students about entering the University of California, California State University, private colleges and universities in California, and the California community colleges.

Note: Each institution's Carnegie class is given in parentheses. **Key:** E=elementary school, HS=high school, M=middle school, NR=not reported, PRI=private, PUB=public, RU=rural, SU=suburban, UR=urban

University of Southern California (RES I)
USC Mobile Dental Clinic

Grades served: E   Schools served: 70   Year established: 1966
Location of schools served: NR   Type of schools served: PUB

Since 1966, USC's Mobile Dental Clinic has provided free dental care to more than 60,000 lower-income children in 50 communities throughout Southern California. Four equipped mobile units are in service, staffed by volunteer dental and hygiene students from USC, who provide care under the supervision of faculty members, many of whom also volunteer their services.

University of Southern California (RES I)
National Youth Sports Program

Grades served: E, M, HS   Schools served: NR   Year established: 1968
Location of schools served: UR   Type of schools served: PUB, PRI

The National Youth Sports Program is a cooperative partnership developed and operated by the federal government, the National Collegiate Athletic Association (NCAA), and 175 selected institutions of higher education. It introduces youngsters from economically disadvantaged areas to an instructive environment to inspire new ideas and personal goals. Children aged 10 to 16 are involved in a competitive sports program intended to motivate them toward self-improvement and self-awareness, resulting in constructive and lasting emotional and social experience. The program assists at-risk youth in building positive attitudes, and achieving career and personal goals. Activities include field trips to the beach and to museums, nature hikes, and math/science programs.

University of Southern California (RES I)
MESA (Mathematics, Engineering, Science Achievement)

Grades served: M, HS   Schools served: 12   Year established: 1977
Location of schools served: UR   Type of schools served: PUB

MESA was initiated to motivate and prepare high school and junior high school students to pursue math-based college education and careers. MESA is a highly academic program with a strong focus on enrichment. Student services are provided at school sites and at the university. Activities include regular student meetings at each school, hands-on math and science activities, guest speakers, field trips, SAT preparation, tutorial and study group assistance, and summer, Saturday, and intersession enrichment programs at USC. Services include counseling, personal and family assistance, staff development, and statewide conferences for teachers.

University of Southern California (RES I)
EEXCEL (Educational Excellence for Children With Environmental Limitations)

Grades served: E, M, HS   Schools served: 15   Year established: 1991
Location of schools served: UR, SU   Type of schools served: PUB, PRI

EEXCEL is a partnership combining the expertise available at USC with a private developer and local schools. The program combines educational and family development in specially designed, affordable housing. Resident students receive private tutoring and may attend an evening study hall for additional assistance. All programs take place in the on-site classroom, which is equipped with computers, books, and other resources to enrich learning. Full four-year tuition scholarships to the University of Southern California are also offered to students graduating from high school and meeting admission requirements.

University of Southern California (RES I)
Precollege Summer Art Program

Grades served: HS
Location of schools served: UR

Schools served: 15
Type of schools served: PUB

Year established: 1993

USC's School of Fine Arts Precollege Summer Art Program is geared toward talented high school students within a ten-mile radius of USC. The program focuses on challenging students artistically and intellectually and encouraging them toward a college education. The program is open only to public high schools from the economically disadvantaged area around USC.

COLORADO

Community College of Denver (AA)
Youth Fair Chance

Grades served: E, HS
Location of schools served: UR

Schools served: 2
Type of schools served: PUB

Year established: 1992

Youth Fair Chance, a partnership of the Community College of Denver (CCD), the Mayor's Office of Employment and Training (MOET), and Denver Public Schools, is designed to establish a community learning center to assist in encouraging youth to remain in high school and to offer an opportunity for dropouts to complete the GED and a college education. MOET and CCD cooperate with the Denver Police Department, the juvenile court system, and juvenile probation officers to offer scholarships (alternative sentencing) to youthful offenders and high-risk youth involved in gangs or substance abuse. Social service agencies offer services to teen mothers and provide a child development center, parenting workshops, and family and career planning services.

Community College of Denver (AA)
Hispanic Entrepreneurship Program

Grades served: HS
Location of schools served: UR

Schools served: 1
Type of schools served: PUB

Year established: 1991

The Hispanic Entrepreneurship Program (HEP) is a partnership linking the Community College of Denver and West High School/Denver Public Schools with the Hispanic community. Its primary mission is to offer qualified high-risk Hispanic youth (economically disadvantaged youth aged 17 to 30) and displaced workers (21 years old or older) the opportunity to enroll in a challenging entrepreneurship program at the college. HEP also recruits students and provides group registration, Hispanic instructors, blocked scheduling, mentors from business, and internships.

Community College of Denver (AA)
Denver Education Network

Grades served: E, M, HS
Location of schools served: UR

Schools served: 18
Type of schools served: PUB

Year established: 1992

The Denver Education Network is a collaborative partnership of Community College of Denver, Denver Public Schools, Metropolitan State College, University of Colorado at Denver, Colorado Alliance of Business, Clayton Foundation, Greater Denver Chamber of Commerce, Colorado VIP Student Program, Junior Achievement, LARASA, community organizations, and the Mayor's Offices of Social Services and Employment and Training. It is one of the 17 urban projects funded by the Ford Foundation to increase the participation and advancement rates of minority students in two- and four-year colleges, primarily through systemic change in the public school system.

Note: Each institution's Carnegie class is given in parentheses. **Key:** E=elementary school, HS=high school, M=middle school, NR=not reported, PRI=private, PUB=public, RU=rural, SU=suburban, UR=urban

Community College of Denver (AA)
Mentoring Girls for Careers in Science & Technology
Grades served: HS   Schools served: 30   Year established: 1992
Location of schools served: UR, SU   Type of schools served: NR

The Mentoring Girls for Careers in Science & Technology partnership, a collaboration of the Community College of Denver (CCD) and the University of Colorado at Denver (UCD), is designed to provide selected high school girls in the Denver metropolitan area with hands-on exposure to the kinds of tasks associated with careers in science or technology. Mentors for technology are Associate of Applied Science degree women students at CCD. Mentors for science are UCD women graduate students in the natural sciences, computer science, mathematics, or engineering. On Saturdays girls are invited to campus, where they work with a mentor in tasks related to their areas of interest.

University of Colorado System (OTHER)
CU Systemwide Precollegiate Development Program
Grades served: HS   Schools served: 40   Year established: 1983
Location of schools served: UR, SU   Type of schools served: PUB

The University of Colorado's Systemwide Precollegiate Development Program is designed to motivate minority high school students (grades 9-12) to pursue successful postsecondary education. It involves 350 students from 38 front-range schools who are identified by their counselors or other community representatives as academically able and who meet the criteria established. During the school year, students attend required monthly Saturday Academies, where basic and interpersonal skills are stressed. Students are provided an academically intense five-week summer residential or commuter-type program on a CU campus, exposing them to college-relevant academic courses that augment their high school studies. Advising, counseling, tutoring, and mentoring are provided throughout the program as needed.

University of Denver (DOC I)
VIP Program
Grades served: HS   Schools served: 1   Year established: 1990
Location of schools served: UR   Type of schools served: PUB

The VIP Program brings together the University of Denver and the Community College of Denver as sponsors of West High School in a program designed to encourage high school students to remain in school, to learn the importance of completing high school, and to structure the essential bridge between high school and higher education. The VIP Program is designed for at-risk high school students who come from families that have virtually no college and often no high school graduation in their backgrounds. The program provides counseling, mentoring, career information, and assistance in reaching their academic, career, and life goals.

CONNECTICUT

Albertus Magnus College (BA II)
AM Bassetters Go to College
Grades served: E   Schools served: 1   Year established: 1989
Location of schools served: UR   Type of schools served: PUB

The AM Bassetters Go to College is a partnership linking Albertus Magnus College and Lincoln Bassett Elementary School. Its main goal is to further enrich the schooling of urban youth and to promote an interest in higher education. Partnership activities include an after-school program, a series of six-week, one-hour classes in science and art, Newspapers in the Schools, which sponsors daily newspaper delivery, and Turn on to Learning, a four-week summer program.

Connecticut College (BA I)
High School Students Advancement Program
Grades served: HS
Location of schools served: UR

Schools served: 30
Type of schools served: PUB

Year established: 1989

The High School Students Advancement Program (HSSAP) was created to increase the number of minority students who graduate from high school and attend college. The program focuses on those students in the 20th to 50th percentiles who have the potential to succeed, given extra encouragement. HSSAP supports inservice education, faculty development, and academic alliances designed to strengthen the teaching and learning of academic subjects; it also supports research related to teaching and learning and encourages disadvantaged minority students through a college awareness/mentoring project.

Fairfield University (MA I)
GTE Math/Focus Program
Grades served: E, M
Location of schools served: NR

Schools served: NR
Type of schools served PUB, PRI

Year established: 1991

The GTE Math/Focus Program was developed by Fairfield University and the Bridgeport schools to improve the recruitment and retention of underrepresented minority students in the field of mathematics. The dynamic, multitiered program involves middle school students and teachers as well as Fairfield University students and math faculty in a three-week summer seminar plus academic-year workshops for math teachers, weekly coaching of middle school pupils by university students (culminating in a Math Challenge at the university), and one major teachers' conference each year.

Saint Joseph College (MA I)
Adventures in Science
Grades served: E, M
Location of schools served: UR, SU

Schools served: 12
Type of schools served: PUB, PRI

Year established: 1985

A Merck Award enabled Saint Joseph College to expand the Adventures in Science program with middle grade girls of the West Hartford schools to the predominantly African-American and Hispanic students of the Hartford schools. Twelve episodes of Adventures in Science developed explicitly for middle grade science explorers have been published, and more than 100 copies are being field tested in area schools. A video introduction for students of this new way of approaching science problems and of the students working on the problem is also available. Emphasis is on hands-on, laboratory-oriented science instruction.

Teikyo Post University (BUS)
Proyecto METAS
Grades served: M, HS
Location of schools served: UR

Schools served: 5
Type of schools served: PUB

Year established: 1992

Teikyo Post University, in collaboration with Waterbury School Department's Migrant Program, sponsors Proyecto METAS (Project Goals), a weekly program on the university campus designed to provide migrant students with different opportunities to assist them in strengthening their self-images, raise their aspirations, and learn how to make choices in life. Students discuss careers with professionals in the field; form international partnerships with Japanese college students; and are trained as leaders after one year in the program. METAS means "Mas Educacion, Triunfo, Anhelos, Superacion," or "more education for success, desires, achievement."

Note: Each institution's Carnegie class is given in parentheses. **Key:** E=elementary school, HS=high school, M=middle school, NR=not reported, PRI=private, PUB=public, RU=rural, SU=suburban, UR=urban

Trinity College (BA I)
Connecticut Pre-Engineering Program (CPEP)

Grades served: M, HS
Schools served: 8
Year established: 1986
Location of schools served: UR
Type of schools served: PUB

The program is a collaboration of eight Hartford public middle/high schools and Trinity College that emphasizes multidisciplinary learning with a hands-on curriculum that includes language arts, guidance, science, math, and computer studies. CPEP involves outstanding public school teachers, and Trinity faculty present lectures and demonstrations. The program stresses active learning, requiring students to develop verbal and writing skills and to work cooperatively in labs. Saturday programs throughout the academic year reinforce summer learning and provide additional enrichment.

Trinity College (BA I)
National Youth Sports Program (NYSP)

Grades served: E, M
Schools served: 1
Year established: 1970
Location of schools served: NR
Type of schools served: PUB

Trinity College is one of 175 sites for NYSP. The program uses the facilities of universities, colleges, and junior colleges to provide supervised sports training and competition for young people who could not otherwise secure them. Participants acquire skills and health knowledge, improve their physical fitness, and are acquainted with career and educational opportunities. Principal partners are selected institutions of higher education, the National Collegiate Athletic Association, and the Office of Community Services. Funding comes from federal and college sources. Transportation to the facility, hot lunches, accident-medical-dental insurance, and drug and alcohol abuse education are offered to the participants.

University of Hartford (MA I)
Hartford Urban Education Network

Grades served: M, HS
Schools served: 3
Year established: 1992
Location of schools served: UR
Type of schools served: NR

The Hartford Urban Education Network is a partnership of school, college, business, and community interests designed to transform the conditions under which Hartford's youth prepare for their educational futures. The program fosters systemic change in the three high schools and middle schools by bringing key stakeholders and institutions into the network, creating the broad-based Student Success Corps within the secondary schools, and collecting and analyzing data about students' success. Tutoring, mentoring, and counseling are provided.

University of Hartford (MA I)
Aetna/Ward Career Ladder Scholarship Program

Grades served: HS
Schools served: 4
Year established: 1974
Location of schools served: UR
Type of schools served: PUB

The Aetna/Ward Career Ladder Scholarship Program is a partnership between the University of Hartford's Samuel I. Ward College of Technology and the Aetna Life and Casualty Company. The endowment provided by Aetna furnishes tuition and fees to students from traditionally underrepresented minorities in the four Hartford high schools to study architectural, audio, computer, electronic, and mechanical engineering technologies in an academic and well-equipped laboratory setting.

Wesleyan University (BA I)
Upward Bound/Conncap

Grades served: M, HS	Schools served: 6	Year established: 1968
Location of schools served: UR	Type of schools served: PUB	

Upward Bound/Conncap is a year-round program serving 125 students in grades 9-12 from Middletown, Meriden, and Portland, Connecticut. The program begins in grade 8 at the university's Great Hollow Wilderness School. All students participate in a six-week nonresidential summer program designed to prepare them academically and socially for the coming school year. They learn courtesy and manners, and discuss issues facing teens, such as AIDS, pregnancy, drugs, and alcohol. The teens acquire self-confidence and learn to set goals and work in teams by rock climbing, canoeing, caving, backpacking, and navigating a ropes course.

DISTRICT OF COLUMBIA

Gallaudet University (MA I)
Young Scholars Program

Grades served: HS	Schools served: 18	Year established: 1985
Location of schools served: UR, SU, RU	Type of schools served: PUB, PRI	

This four-week program is for talented and gifted hard-of-hearing and deaf individuals aged 14 and older. During summer 1994, for instance, the YSP provided an opportunity to study the performing arts. Participants took classes in character development and creative sign language. Course work is supplemented by day trips to various Washington, D.C., attractions, including theaters, museums, and recreation areas.

George Washington University (RES II)
BOOKS Project

Grades served: E, M	Schools served: NR	Year established: 1989
Location of schools served: UR, SU	Type of schools served: PUB	

The Human Services Department of George Washington University is engaged in a pilot project to improve literacy and international cross-cultural communication and to promote educational exchange between Spanish-speaking refugee students (primary and secondary schools) in the D.C. area and Central American students through writing, illustrating, and publishing books. BOOKS helps to reestablish a connection with the author's country, fostering cultural pride and building self-esteem. The best books will be published and presented to teachers and pupils in El Salvador. Teachers in the schools work with George Washington faculty and staff.

Howard University (RES I)
Upward Bound

Grades served: M, HS	Schools served: 9	Year established: 1965
Location of schools served: NR	Type of schools served: PUB	

Upward Bound links Howard University with nine area schools. It is designed to provide low-income, first-generation college-bound students with the skills and motivation to successfully complete high school and enter and complete a program of postsecondary education. Classes are offered in English, mathematics, reading, science, study skills, and SAT Prep. Individual tutoring is provided in major subject areas, and each student receives individual and group counseling. Field trips to colleges, institutions, and organizations promote cultural development. Career shadowing provides exemplary role models, and resource persons provide workshops and seminars on issues crucial to students' development.

Note: Each institution's Carnegie class is given in parentheses. **Key:** E=elementary school, HS=high school, M=middle school, NR=not reported, PRI=private, PUB=public, RU=rural, SU=suburban, UR=urban

Florida Atlantic University (DOC II)
WISE Speakers' Bureau

Grades served: M, HS   Schools served: NR   Year established: NR
Location of schools served: UR   Type of schools served: PUB

The Women In Science and Engineering (WISE) Speakers' Bureau, developed by FAU's Office of Precollegiate Programs, aims to help students reach their full potential through planning, goal setting, and career awareness. Based on the South Eastern Consortium for Minorities in Engineering (SECME) model, engineers serving as role models go into the schools, helping students by example and through interaction. SECME and the speakers' bureau provide opportunities that help students to keep their options open while protecting them from the erosive effects of gender and racial stereotyping.

Florida Atlantic University (DOC II)
Expanding Horizons

Grades served: M   Schools served: NR   Year established: NR
Location of schools served: NR   Type of schools served: NR

Expanding Horizons, Broward, is an interagency program that specifically seeks to increase the awareness of middle school students, especially girls, and their parents to high-tech and nontraditional occupations and to increase the awareness, interest, and participation of girls in upper-level science and math courses at the high school level. The program also emphasizes the importance of developing and setting career goals at an early age. In addition, various activities focus on those high-salaried careers that offer increased opportunity for economic independence and greater earning potential.

Florida International University (MA I)
PIP (Partners In Progress)

Grades served: HS   Schools served: 16   Year established: 1982
Location of schools served: UR, SU, RU Type of schools served: PUB, PRI

Partners in Progress, a cooperative program between Florida International University and the Dade County Public School System, identifies promising minority tenth graders to participate in academic enrichment and career counseling. The program has two phases. During the first summer, participants are prepared for college entrance exams, and instructed in critical thinking, creative writing, and mathematics. During the second phase, which is scheduled the subsequent summer, participants enroll in college courses. All students receive counseling to assist in college planning. Full-tuition scholarships are provided to previous participants who matriculate at Florida International University.

Lake-Sumter Community College (AA)
Nursing Department and Lake County Adult Education

Grades served: HS   Schools served: 2   Year established: 1987
Location of schools served: NR   Type of schools served: PUB

A partnership between Lake-Sumter Community College's Nursing Program and Lake County Adult Education for Teenage Parents (ETP) program allows second-year RN students to rotate to the ETP program each week for a semester and to teach classes covering such topics as child growth and development, labor and birthing strategies, prenatal health care, parenting skills, and future aspirations. Through the partnership, many teenagers have been motivated to finish high school and to seek careers in nursing.

Tallahassee Community College (AA)
Panhandle College Reach-Out Program (CROP) Consortium

Grades served: M, HS   Schools served: 20   Year established: 1989
Location of schools served: UR, SU, RU   Type of schools served: PUB

Tallahassee Community College's CROP participates in a cooperative educational consortium with three other North Florida public colleges and seven public school districts. The primary mission of the consortium is to provide low-income middle and high school students who are potential first-generation college students with continuous contact, supplemental academic education, and financial and career planning. Among the services provided are daily instruction in study skills for middle school students, ACT/SAT preparation workshops, weekly tutoring, motivational seminars, educational field trips, dual enrollment, and financial aid assistance.

University of Miami (RES I)
Restructuring Education for All Learners (REAL)

Grades served: E   Schools served: 3   Year established: 1993
Location of schools served: NR   Type of schools served: PUB

Project REAL is designed to incorporate effective practices for individuals with disabilities into broader school-based educational reform and restructuring in three elementary schools in Dade County. Through professional development and curricular and instructional restructuring, REAL seeks to achieve a collaborative school-based effort that infuses special education into the total school structure to consider the needs of all learners, including those with disabilities or those who are likely to be referred for special education.

University of South Florida–St. Petersburg Campus (RES II)
Accelerated Literacy Learning (ALL)

Grades served: E   Schools served: 105   Year established: 1990
Location of schools served: UR, SU   Type of schools served: PUB

The ALL program, developed at USF, Tampa, is a one-on-one literacy program for at-risk first grade students. Thirteen counties have partnership agreements with USF designed to accelerate the reading progress of ALL students to a level at or above the norm and to lower the number of referrals for special education. The program includes year-long training for teachers who implement the program and follow-up with trainees to ensure quality. ALL has expanded to an experimental design for a second grade, small-group model.

GEORGIA

Albany State College (MA I)
Albany State College/Southside Middle School/Professional Development School

Grades served: M   Schools served: 1   Year established: 1991
Location of schools served: UR   Type of schools served: PUB

The purpose of this program is to create a positive community environment to foster and promote equally positive relationships among students, parents, teachers, and members of the community. The program provides inservice training for teachers in integrated thematic teaching and curriculum planning in mathematics and science. Opportunities are provided for parents to understand the curriculum and to appreciate how their children are taught and how to encourage them at home. Parents participate in hands-on activity workshops that offer activities to be completed at home.

Note: Each institution's Carnegie class is given in parentheses. **Key:** E=elementary school, HS=high school, M=middle school, NR=not reported, PRI=private, PUB=public, RU=rural, SU=suburban, UR=urban

Bainbridge College (AA)
Mentor Program
Grades served: M, HS   Schools served: 3   Year established: 1988
Location of schools served: NR   Type of schools served: PUB

The Bainbridge/Decatur County Chamber of Commerce Mentor Program is a partnership linking area businesses and Bainbridge College with support from the Chamber of Commerce. The program's primary mission is to provide a support system for at-risk high school and middle school students. Community volunteers are assigned as mentors. The college coordinates several special programs for the mentors and students during the year, such as study skills seminars, and provides administrative support and faculty volunteers.

Columbus College (MA I)
Bridges Pre-College Program
Grades served: M, HS   Schools served: 3   Year established: 1990
Location of schools served: UR   Type of schools served: PUB

The Bridges Pre-College Program is designed to improve high school graduation rates among high-risk pupils. The program is concentrated around academic assistance, cultural growth, career planning, and parent-family involvement. The target group of disadvantaged students is selected from two local middle schools that feed into one high school. The components are designed to aid pupils in basic skills; to promote parental support of academic, career, and cultural growth of pupils' families; and to provide direct, positive, and meaningful connections of targeted pupils and their families through its faculty and student mentors.

Darton College (AA)
Adventures in Science
Grades served: E, M, HS   Schools served: 26   Year established: 1989
Location of schools served: UR, RU   Type of schools served: PUB

The Darton College Adventures in Science program is a partnership with regional schools that allows K-12 students and their teachers to explore science through hands-on activities. Each activity emphasizes students' and teachers' exploration and problem solving through scientific investigation. The program currently offers educational modules in mammal studies, chemistry, physics, oceanography, and nature studies. Individual modules are presented to students and teachers, either on or off campus. Teacher training workshops are also provided to train teachers in the use of modules. Several modules are portable for teachers to check out and use in their classrooms.

Georgia Institute of Technology (RES I)
Playing and Inventing
Grades served: HS   Schools served: NR   Year established: NR
Location of schools served: NR   Type of schools served: NR

During five consecutive summers, ninth graders will design new products using engineering principles and tools that apply math/science and design methodology in solving simple problems. Students conduct real-world research (using their peers as clients), propose alternative solutions to problems, build and test their designs, and write out and present their inventions to their clients. They will also learn college application procedures from SAT strategies for obtaining scholarships. High school teachers will be helped to plan courses using playing and inventing strategies to organize design laboratories that benefit all students. A team of professors and engineers (mentor pairs) works with the teachers to develop sensory-oriented exercises that involve students in their own education and prepare underrepresented students for engineering careers.

<u>ILLINOIS</u>

Loyola University of Chicago (DOC I)
Project Enrichment

Grades served: HS   Schools served: 20   Year established: 1991
Location of schools served: UR   Type of schools served: PUB, PRI

Project Enrichment recruits disadvantaged and minority high school students from the inner city who have achieved an overall GPA of 3.0 or better. Key elements include enrichment courses offered during the summer, which could be credit-bearing at the high school or college level; a tutorial program; career orientation workshops; field trips to research laboratories; and social activities designed to foster group spirit. The goal is to increase minorities' participation in college-level mathematics and sciences. A significant number of students have enrolled and majored in these fields as a result of the program.

Loyola University of Chicago (DOC I)
Access 2000 Chicago Partnership

Grades served: E, M, HS   Schools served: 551   Year established: 1989
Location of schools served: UR   Type of schools served: PUB

Access 2000 Chicago Partnership administers an array of educational programs for precollege students and their teachers. These programs provide a continuous pipeline of out-of-school activities that enable students to learn mathematics and science in enriched environments and provide opportunities for their teachers to learn new instructional methods. By 1992 the partnership had directly or indirectly served 44,000 students from the Chicago Public Schools. Access 2000 is the winner of the 1993 Robert Anderson Medal, awarded by the Business-Higher Education Forum in recognition of exemplary partnerships of higher education, business, and public schools.

Northeastern Illinois University (MA I)
Dropout Prevention Program/Chicago Teachers' Center

Grades served: E, M, HS   Schools served: 12   Year established: 1991
Location of schools served: UR   Type of schools served: PUB

The Dropout Prevention Program, a partnership with six community-based organizations, is a national demonstration project in Chicago funded by the U.S. Department of Education at Northeastern Illinois University's Chicago Teachers' Center to address the needs of 650 targeted at-risk youth in three predominantly Hispanic high schools and nine elementary feeder schools. To reduce the dropout rate, the project focuses on restructuring the curriculum in partnership with teachers at the high schools (e.g., school-within-a-school programs) to provide more engaging educational experiences for students and assist elementary school students in making the transition to high school.

Note: Each institution's Carnegie class is given in parentheses. **Key:** E=elementary school, HS=high school, M=middle school, NR=not reported, PRI=private, PUB=public, RU=rural, SU=suburban, UR=urban

Northeastern Illinois University (MA I)
University Scholars Program

Grades served: E   Schools served: 4   Year established: 1991
Location of schools served: NR   Type of schools served: PUB

The University Scholars Program serves 220 college-bound students from two inner-city elementary schools and two feeder elementary schools. Its primary goal is to involve high school and college students, HS and university teachers, parents, and the local business and professional communities in promoting college as a viable option for minority students and laying the groundwork for success among minority students who aspire to college. Saturday classes and interactive workshops for students and parents, in-school tutoring, ACT preparation, a Career Exploration Internship, and cultural field trips and college visits are the key ingredients in the program's success.

Northeastern Illinois University (MA I)
Writing From the Source

Grades served: E, HS   Schools served: 14   Year established: 1993
Location of schools served: UR   Type of schools served: PUB

The Writing from the Source program of the Chicago Teachers' Center works in 14 inner-city schools serving 300 teachers, 1,000 students, and 40 parents. Through classroom demonstrations, after-school programs, and on- and off-site parent and teacher workshops, the program supports literacy empowerment, by providing professional development in writing methodologies and strategies that stress the natural connection between speech and writing. It uses image- and person-centered stories, and effective ways of imaginative, cognitive, and editorial engagement. Instructors draw on the services of writer-teachers, matching their ethnic and teaching orientations to support individual schools, creating needs-based curricula, classroom support, professional development programs, and university-community school partnerships.

Northeastern Illinois University (MA I)
Neighborhood Arts Partnership

Grades served: E, M, HS   Schools served: 3   Year established: 1993
Location of schools served: PUB   Type of schools served: PUB

The Neighborhood Arts Partnership links Northeastern Illinois University, two elementary schools and a high school, a theater, a gallery, a regional library, and the local Chamber of Commerce. Its mission is to actively engage students in learning by integrating a range of art forms into the daily classroom curriculum. Initially focusing on 350 students in grades 6-9, forty educators and artists, parents, and community members plan sequential units, reflect on their work, and document new perspectives on teaching, learning, and authentic means of assessing students' achievement. The project will expand each year until a K-12 program is in place.

Northeastern Illinois University (MA I)
Future Teachers of Chicago

Grades served: M, HS   Schools served: 43   Year established: 1993
Location of schools served: UR   Type of schools served: PUB, PRI

Future Teachers of Chicago is a partnership of 45 public and nonpublic schools and six community organizations formed to recruit and support minority students in teaching and educational leadership in Chicago. Through Future Teachers programs in all program schools (grades 7-university), 1,500 students gain knowledge, skills, and experience, and share ideas about teaching and learning. Students receive academic and moral support, training, and placement in paid tutoring and mentoring programs by exemplary classroom teachers. They participate in hands-on career exploration activities, interact with teachers inside and outside classrooms, and learn about current issues in education.

Southern Illinois University at Edwardsville (MA I)
Project CARING (Children at Risk: Initiating New Gateways)

Grades served: M
Schools served: 2
Year established: 1991

Location of schools served: NR
Type of schools served: PUB

Project CARING is a consortium of Southern Illinois University at Edwardsville, St. Louis University, Lessie Bates Davis Neighborhood House, Hoyleton Youth and Family Services, the Lansdowne Improvement Association, the Leadership Council of Southern Illinois, and the cities and school districts of East St. Louis (IL), and St. Louis (MO). It is designed to reduce the odds against children at risk by combining health care, competence in school, and family services into a comprehensive program for children and their parents.

University of Illinois at Chicago (RES I)
Early Outreach Health/Science Enrichment Program (H/SEP)

Grades served: HS
Schools served: NR
Year established: 1993

Location of schools served: UR, SU, RU
Type of schools served: PUB, PRI

The Early Outreach Health/Science Enrichment Program is a four-week summer residential and school-year mentoring program for rising tenth graders. The program identifies students from Illinois and Indiana who are interested in careers in health professions, science, mathematics, or biomedical research. During the summer, students live on campus at UIC and study biology, data analysis, and technical writing. In addition, they are linked with mentors and work on research projects under their guidance. During the school year, the students continue work with their mentors.

University of Illinois at Chicago (RES I)
Early Outreach Saturday College Program

Grades served: M, HS
Schools served: 155
Year established: 1979

Location of schools served: UR, SU
Type of schools served: PUB, PRI

Saturday College, a long-term developmental program for students in grades 7-12, serves students citywide from Chicago's public and parochial schools. The program convenes on campus at UIC each Saturday during the school year and helps to prepare minority students at an early age for college and career options by providing academic enrichment in mathematics, science, reading, and writing; academic, college, and career counseling; exposure to diverse careers; and early socialization to a college environment. Students also participate in summer preceptorships at the university and/or community-based agencies. Parents' participation in the Early Outreach Parent Network is a requisite for students' participation.

University of Illinois at Chicago (RES I)
Summer Enrichment Program for Sixth Graders Attending Project CANAL Schools

Grades served: M
Schools served: 17
Year established: 1989

Location of schools served: UR
Type of schools served: PUB

The Summer Enrichment Program for Sixth Graders Attending Project CANAL (Creating a New Approach to Learning) Schools is a collaboration of the Chicago Public Schools' Department of Equal Educational Opportunity Programs and UIC's Early Outreach Program. The four-week summer program provides students with opportunities to enhance their reading, writing, and mathematical skills; explore careers; refine socialization skills; broaden cultural awareness; explore self-expression through art; enhance self-confidence; and develop team skills and discipline through sports and academic activities. During the fourth week of the program, sixth graders are housed on campus in the dormitory with Early Outreach college students.

Note: Each institution's Carnegie class is given in parentheses.   **Key:** E=elementary school, HS=high school, M=middle school, NR=not reported, PRI=private, PUB=public, RU=rural, SU=suburban, UR=urban

University of Illinois at Urbana-Champaign (RES I)
Principal's Scholars Program
Grades served: E, M, HS   Schools served: 38   Year established: 1975
Location of schools served: NR   Type of schools served: PUB

The Principal's Scholars Program is a statewide interactive partnership linking the University of Illinois at Urbana-Champaign, 38 high schools, their elementary/middle feeder schools, and private industry. The program is designed to increase the pool of minority students entering mathematics- and science-based academic programs. Through grade-level-specific activities such as hands-on research sessions, academic competitions, workshops, cultural and field experiences, and parent-teacher seminars, the program seeks to promote interest in math, science, and communications; develop critical/analytical thinking skills; enhance self-esteem and academic confidence; and prepare students to compete in the global economy.

University of Illinois at Urbana-Champaign (RES I)
Young Scholars in Agriculture Program
Grades served: HS   Schools served: 64   Year established: 1989
Location of schools served: UR, SU, RU   Type of schools served: PUB, PRI

The Young Scholars in Agriculture Program (YSAP) is a six-week intensive academically enriching experience offered by the College of Agriculture for incoming freshmen who plan to pursue an undergraduate major in the sciences at the university. Its primary mission is to prepare students (members of underrepresented ethnic groups) for the freshman-year experience. Young scholars learn skills in critical thinking and quantitative reasoning. Educators from the university and schools are provided an opportunity for dialogue regarding the academic preparation of students entering science-based curricula.

INDIANA

Indiana University Purdue University at Fort Wayne (MA I)
Future Academic Scholar's Track (FAST)
Grades served: M, HS   Schools served: 32   Year established: 1987
Location of schools served: UR, SU   Type of schools served: PUB, PRI

The FAST program is a long-term, comprehensive program designed to encourage African-American, Hispanic, and at-risk students to attend postsecondary schools, preferably four-year colleges. Students remain in the program from sixth grade through high school graduation. Students attend a three-week summer session and Saturday Academies two times per month during the school year. They receive academic instruction in English, math, and science, personal development, and precollege planning. Other important components of the program include parental involvement, school visits, faculty/staff training, partnerships with business, and research and evaluation of the program.

Indiana Vocational Technical College-Southcentral (AA)
Region 14 Vocational Education Planning-Communications Group
Grades served: HS   Schools served: 25   Year established: 1972
Location of schools served: SU, RU   Type of schools served: PUB, PRI

The Region 14 Vocational Education Planning-Communications Group is a partnership linking Ivy Tech State College, secondary schools, and the Hoosier Falls Private Industry Council. Through joint planning, the partnership responds to regionwide requests for applications by providing funding for a variety of projects related to serving underrepresented minorities and guiding at-risk populations seeking access to vocational/technical education and training before entry into the Region 14 workplace. The partnership has also initiated educator renewal internship projects for instructors, counselors, and administrators with business/industry, public/private entities in Region 14.

Valparaiso University (MA I)
PRISMS (Precollege Research in the Sciences for Minority Students)

Grades served: HS

Schools served: NR

Year established: 1989

Location of schools served: UR, SU

Type of schools served: PUB, PRI

PRISMS is a four-week summer science program for minority juniors and seniors in high school whose goal is to encourage more minority students to attend college and select one of the sciences as a profession. Each student is assigned a research project in a field of science or engineering. The student carries out the project under the supervision of a Valparaiso University science professor. The students live on campus during the four weeks and take part in various cocurricular activities and field trips.

IOWA

Iowa Lakes Community College (AA)
Success Alternatives High School

Grades served: HS

Schools served: 13

Year established: 1992

Location of schools served: NR

Type of schools served: PUB

Success Alternatives High School is a joint partnership between the community college, local high schools, and JTPA. The goal of Success Alternatives is to provide the setting, opportunity, support, and encouragement needed for students to acquire the knowledge, attitudes, and habits of mind needed to become productive, happy members of society. Students enrolled in the program work toward high school completion. Students at risk of dropping out or who have dropped out are referred by local schools to the alternative high school, which offers basic academic courses, counseling services, job-seeking and job-keeping skills, and the opportunity to attend the community college for Course work.

Iowa Lakes Community College (AA)
Educational Talent Search

Grades served: M, HS

Schools served: 18

Year established: 1987

Location of schools served: RU

Type of schools served: NR

The Iowa Lakes Educational Talent Search links low-income, potential first-generation college students with higher education programs. The ultimate purpose of the program is to generate the skills and motivation necessary for students to successfully complete high school and enroll in a postsecondary program. Talent Search is a comprehensive educational planning program that works with students in grades 6-12 and with adults throughout a five-county area. Program services include weekly tutoring, career assessment and advising, ACT test preparation, study skills instruction, campus visits, goal setting, college application, and financial aid information.

Iowa State University (RES I)
Science Bound

Grades served: M, HS

Schools served: 15

Year established: 1989

Location of schools served: UR

Type of schools served: PUB

Science Bound provides science and mathematics enrichment and career and academic guidance for ethnic minority students in the Des Moines public middle and high schools. Students selected are those whose standardized test scores and teacher recommendations indicate ability to achieve in mathematics and science but whose grades indicate lack of motivation. The program uses a three-way partnership with private-sector scientists, public school teachers, and Iowa State university faculty. ISU will provide tuition scholarships to students who are admitted to the University in good standing and enter a science, mathematics, or engineering program.

Note: Each institution's Carnegie class is given in parentheses. **Key:** E=elementary school, HS=high school, M=middle school, NR=not reported, PRI=private, PUB=public, RU=rural, SU=suburban, UR=urban

University of Northern Iowa (MA I)
Minorities in Teaching (MIT)

Grades served: E, M, HS   Schools served: NR   Year established: 1989
Location of schools served: UR   Type of schools served: PUB

The University of Northern Iowa's MIT program is a partnership linking the university with Iowa school districts that have a significant minority student population. The MIT program involves the collaborative efforts of parents, school personnel, community members, and UNI faculty in identifying, recruiting, and graduating students in grades 6-12 who are interested in pursuing teaching as a career. Each cohort group of students is provided both cognitive and affective experiences to help them be successful in school and prepare for entrance to the university and the teacher education program. The MIT program also provides opportunities for communication, professional growth, and research that will enhance students' success and the quality of teaching in both school and university settings.

KENTUCKY

Centre College (BA I)
M²SE (Minorities in Math, Science & Engineering)

Grades served: M, HS   Schools served: 50   Year established: 1992
Location of schools served: UR   Type of schools served: PUB, PRI

M²SE is a nonprofit, Cincinnati-based partnership involving an expanding consortium of business and industry, institutions of higher leaning, and public school systems. Its mission is to significantly increase the number of minority students who are motivated, prepared for, and enter careers in mathematics, science, and engineering and technology. The model incorporates student enrichment, teacher development, parent involvement, links with college admissions, bridge programs, and opportunities for research, co-op, and internships. School-based and summer programs provide services for students in grades 4-12.

University of Louisville (DOC I)
Young Minority Scholars Program

Grades served: HS   Schools served: 35   Year established: 1983
Location of schools served: UR, SU   Type of schools served: PUB, PRI

The Young Minority Scholars Program offers 15 minority high school students each summer the opportunity to conduct research projects under the mentorship of professors from the College of Arts and Sciences at the University of Louisville. In addition to their one-on-one work with their faculty mentors, students meet daily over a five-week period with a writing consultant to develop the skills required in college research, writing, and oral presentations. Students receive a broad introduction to campus life and resources through the program. The results of their research projects are presented at a symposium to which faculty and families are invited.

LOUISIANA

Louisiana State University at Alexandria (AA)
STARS (Summer Tutorial for At-Risk Students)

Grades served: M, HS   Schools served: 20   Year established: 1984
Location of schools served: UR, SU, RU Type of schools served: PUB

Louisiana State University at Alexandria offers a nine-week summer program for high school juniors identified as at-risk by their high school principals and guidance counselors. The program seeks to reduce the dropout rate by improving academic performance, improving the students' self-concepts, and enhancing college and career options by helping students reach their potential. The program uses peer models, enriched classes in reading, mathematics, and study skills; on-campus jobs; and personal and career counseling. Students receive credit for mathematics taken during the summer. The programs have been funded by a Job Training Partnership Act grant each year.

MAINE

Southern Maine Technical College (AA)
Students of the 21st Century

Grades served: M, HS   Schools served: 11   Year established: 1989
Location of schools served: UR   Type of schools served: PUB

In 1989, Southern Maine Technical College adopted 26 first graders (the high school graduating class of 2000) and promised them 12 years of continued academic services, including free tuition to the college if they graduated from high school; mentoring and tutoring; career and cultural awareness activities; and annual attendance incentives (U.S. savings bonds for perfect or near-perfect attendance). The program is intended to raise the aspirations of identifiable at-risk students, many of whom might become first-generation college graduates, and to enlist the participation of parents in supporting their children's aspirations.

University of Maine at Machias (BA II)
Mawioyne Partnership

Grades served: E   Schools served: 1   Year established: 1992
Location of schools served: RU   Type of schools served: NR

This partnership between the university's Education Division and the Indian Township School (a unit of the Indian Education School Union) at Peter Dana Point, Princeton, Maine, aims to provide for continuous, cooperative needs assessment and study of organization, curriculum, instruction, and school-community relationships as they affect students' development. The partnership also provides a field site for prospective teachers in preparatory programs and provides for professional growth for faculty through informal and formal delivery of courses, seminars, and workshops.

MARYLAND

Goucher College (BA I)
Science Mentoring to Achieve Rewarding Transition (SMART)

Grades served: HS   Schools served: 1   Year established: 1992
Location of schools served: UR   Type of schools served: PUB

Goucher College's SMART program is a partnership with Northern High School in Baltimore City. Its primary goal is to spark interest in science education through shared experience in science-related activities. Goucher science students are paired with Northern High students in their junior and senior years, and on-campus training is provided to Northern's teachers to help them adapt to new, mandated curricular changes and to develop hands-on laboratory experiences that will excite students about science.

Johns Hopkins University (RES I)
Hopkins/Dunbar Health Professions Program

Grades served: HS   Schools served: 1   Year established: 1985
Location of schools served: NR   Type of schools served: PUB

Hopkins/Dunbar Health Professions Program is a cooperative effort to prepare high school students for admission to college and for careers in the health professions. Students in grades 9-12 are enrolled in the Advanced College Prep Course. The Johns Hopkins Medical School, Hospital, and University provide support services, including site experiences, summer internships, equipment, faculty development, scholarships, mentors, and lecturers.

Note: Each institution's Carnegie class is given in parentheses. **Key:** E=elementary school, HS=high school, M=middle school, NR=not reported, PRI=private, PUB=public, RU=rural, SU=suburban, UR=urban

Johns Hopkins University (RES I)
Peabody Preparatory/Baltimore City Schools Partnership Program

Grades served: E   Schools served: 2   Year established: 1985
Location of schools served: UR   Type of schools served: PUB

Officially titled the Peabody Institute Outreach Program, this partnership was created by the Peabody staff for early elementary students in Baltimore City schools. Basic music concepts and skills are presented through activities such as singing, playing rhythm instruments, dancing, and street games and rhymes. The program focuses on guiding the critical thinking skills, perceptivity, and skills development of children through music rather than teaching music to children, keeping a balance between structure and freedom. The program provides 900 to 1,000 children in grades preK-2 in two elementary schools with 50 minutes of instruction per week by Peabody staff.

Johns Hopkins University (RES I)
Teach Baltimore

Grades served: E, HS   Schools served: NR   Year established: 1993
Location of schools served: UR   Type of schools served: PUB

Based in the Johns Hopkins Office of Volunteer Services, Teach Baltimore's primary mission is to design and implement innovative education programs that promote the academic and personal advancement of Baltimore's public school students. Through its programs, Teach Baltimore seeks to transform community resources — such as university students — into effective educational action, to empower Baltimore's students to recognize and develop their talents and potential, and to explode the negative myths and stereotypes that surround urban education. Teach Baltimore's approach is premised on a philosophy that no student will slip through the cracks.

Johns Hopkins University (RES I)
Center for Technology in Education

Grades served: NR   Schools served: 30   Year established: 1986
Location of schools served: UR, SU, RU   Type of schools served: PUB

The Center for Technology in Education, a partnership between the university's Division of Education and the Maryland State Department of Education, is designed to explore ways computers and related technology can serve children with special needs. The center's activities include staff development for regular and special educators, parent training, research, dissemination of research findings and best practices, and graduate training through the Division of Education.

Johns Hopkins University (RES I)
Maryland's Tomorrow Program

Grades served: HS   Schools served: 76   Year established: 1988
Location of schools served: UR, SU, RU   Type of schools served: PUB

Maryland's Tomorrow Program is a year-round program for students in grades 9-12 who are identified in grade 8 as at risk of dropping out of school. Beyond keeping these students in school, the program helps them to make a successful transition to the workplace or to postsecondary education. Students continue to participate for one year after graduation. The program involves students in orientations, work experience, community service, remediation, enrichment, and preparation for tests required for high school graduation. The partnership responsible for this statewide program includes the Maryland State Department of Education, the Johns Hopkins University Institute for Policy Studies, the Department of Economic and Employment Development, local private industry councils, and the state's school systems.

Towson State University (MA I)
Kenwood Adolescent Parenting Project

Grades served: HS

Location of schools served: UR

Schools served: 2

Type of schools served: PUB

Year established: 1992

The Kenwood Adolescent Parenting Project is a collaborative project among Baltimore County Public Schools, Baltimore County government, Towson State University, Franklin Square Hospital, and Open Door, Inc., to provide services for adolescent parents attending Kenwood High School in Baltimore County and their infants or toddlers. Services include providing opportunities for adolescent parents to complete their high school requirements; on-site child care; parenting, career, and health care seminars/workshops; and paid summer internships.

University of Maryland at Baltimore (DOC I)
Lexington Terrace Elementary School/UMAB Partnership

Grades served: E

Location of schools served: UR

Schools served: 1

Type of schools served: PUB

Year established: 1993

The Lexington Terrace Elementary School/UMAB Partnership matches university resources with this inner-city public school. UMAB's School of Social Work has established a satellite operation for community outreach at the elementary school. Each of two graduate student interns spends 20 hours a week responding to the social service needs of students and their parents. The social work students and their cases are supervised by university faculty. Cases include counseling for depression, referral for child abuse, and referral for substance abuse. UMAB's law student interns are involved when advocacy is required in such cases as expulsion from school or tenants' issues.

University of Maryland-College Park (RES I)
Team Maryland

Grades served: E, M, HS

Location of schools served: UR, SU

Schools served: 40

Type of schools served: PUB, PRI

Year established: 1991

Team Maryland is a joint project of the Department of Intercollegiate Athletics and the Center for Political Leadership and Participation that brings together members of the university athletic teams in good academic standing and public school students in 40 Maryland middle schools and high schools. The athletes receive voice-intensive professional speech and leadership training to prepare them to speak about topics of interest to young people, serving as role models in the community while emphasizing the theme "You Can Make It Happen." Team Maryland helped to organize and direct the UMCP Rising Stars Leadership Conference.

University of Maryland-College Park (RES I)
Equity 2000

Grades served: M

Location of schools served: NR

Schools served: 26

Type of schools served: NR

Year established: 1991

Equity 2000 is a project initiated by The College Board in the Prince George's County public schools and at the University of Maryland-College Park to enable historically underrepresented groups to enter and successfully complete college. With improved mathematics instruction and a new curriculum, and improved guidance services for middle and high schools, university faculty have collaboratively planned and participated in mathematics and guidance institutes with the Prince George's County schools and the College Board. Mathematics curriculum development and teaching demonstrations, a symposium for middle-school guidance counselors, campus academies and summer institutes for middle school students, and research opportunities highlight the university's participation in Equity 2000.

Note: Each institution's Carnegie class is given in parentheses. **Key:** E=elementary school, HS=high school, M=middle school, NR=not reported, PRI=private, PUB=public, RU=rural, SU=suburban, UR=urban

University of Maryland-College Park (RES I)
Empowering Schools and Families

Grades served: E   Schools served: 2   Year established: 1989
Location of schools served: NR   Type of schools served: PUB

Empowering Schools and Families is a collaborative project of the Prince George's County Public Schools' Office of Drug Education and the University of Maryland-College Park's Department of Psychology. Located in two Prince George's County elementary schools, the project's goal is to design, implement, and evaluate a school/community approach to reducing the risk for alcohol and other drug use by children growing up in communities characterized by pervasive violence, economic disadvantage, and high levels of substance abuse. Project activities include supplemental tutoring, family support, after-school and summer camps, and in-school aid for selected children.

University of Maryland-College Park (RES I)
Rising Stars Leadership Conference

Grades served: HS   Schools served: 400   Year established: 1990
Location of schools served: UR, SU, RU   Type of schools served: PUB, PRI

The Rising Stars Leadership Conference is a one-day annual conference for Maryland high school students sponsored by the Center for Political Leadership and Participation and the Student Government Association. Invited by the governor and nominated by their principals, more than 400 student leaders and 80 principals/advisers attend the conference at the University of Maryland. Experts provide instruction in leadership skills, public speaking, and motivation.

MASSACHUSETTS

Bunker Hill Community College (AA)
Community Compact for Student Success

Grades served: M, HS   Schools served: 7   Year established: 1993
Location of schools served: UR   Type of schools served: PUB

Boston's Community Compact for Student Success involves Bunker Hill Community College, ten other area colleges and universities, four of Boston's high schools, and three of Boston's middle schools in a broad-based effort to foster systemic changes in K-16 education. The program is aimed at increasing the number of students gaining access to and succeeding in higher education. Key features of the higher education involvement include the development of in-depth understanding of the Boston public school students' experience in relation to the participating colleges and, consequently, the development of policy recommendations and intervention that would contribute to raising degree completion rates and to the guarantee of admission with adequate financial aid to at least one of the participating institutions.

Springfield Technical Community College (AA)
METRICS (Mentorship, Experimentation, and Tutoring Resources for Increasing Competence in Science)

Grades served: M, HS   Schools served: NR   Year established: 1987
Location of schools served: UR   Type of schools served: PUB

Springfield Technical Community College's METRICS program is a collaborative effort with Springfield and Chicopee public and private middle and high schools to provide support and enrichment in math, science, and technology. Up to 90 students attend weekly after-school science club meetings, and they are bused to STCC for at least eight hands-on labs under the supervision of STCC faculty, who also serve as instructors and mentors. The program is funded in part by the Dwight D. Eisenhower Math and Science Act and the Higher Education Coordinating Council. The program has been cited for exemplary excellence by NEASC and AAHE.

University of Massachusetts at Amherst (RES I)
The TEAMS Project

Grades served: E, M, HS   Schools served: 12   Year established: 1984
Location of schools served: UR, SU, RU   Type of schools served: PUB

The TEAMS (Tutoring Enrichment Assistance Models for Schools) Project is an 11-year partnership connecting the university with public schools and alternative education programs in local communities. College students provide one-on-one and small-group tutoring in mathematics, science, social studies, reading, and writing to African-American, Latino, Asian, and other culturally and linguistically diverse elementary and secondary students and adult learners. The goal is to offer additional academic support for students who seek assistance while creating an environment where tutors and tutees can effectively learn, develop a sense of social concern, and work to bring about constructive change.

University of Massachusetts-Lowell (DOC I)
College Prep Program

Grades served: HS   Schools served: 1   Year established: 1985
Location of schools served: UR   Type of schools served: PUB

College Prep, a collaboration of the University of Massachusetts-Lowell and Lawrence High School, provides 240 hours of academic, social, artistic, and cultural activities to a diverse group of inner-city students: high achievers and at-risk youth, students whose native language is English and those with limited English proficiency. Almost all program participants come from poor families and have not thought seriously about the possibility of college enrollment. The program concentrates on developing students' academic confidence and competence to make college admission a reality. Annually, more than 90% of College Prep's seniors are accepted into two- or four-year colleges.

MICHIGAN

Charles S. Mott Community College (AA)
One and One and All Together Project

Grades served: HS   Schools served: 17   Year established: 1993
Location of schools served: UR   Type of schools served: PUB

One and One and All Together Project is a partnership of Mott Community College's Child Development Program, Mott Children's Health Center Family Ties Program, and 17 school districts. Its primary mission is to offer parenting classes for teen parents (17-19 years of age). The project provides transportation by taxi, child care for the teens' children, incentives, and 12 college credits in child development. The project is funded by a two-year grant from the Community Foundation to support parenting skills and motivate at-risk high school students to attend college.

Kalamazoo Valley Community College (AA)
Project Success: Eighth Grade Academic Summer Camp

Grades served: M, HS   Schools served: 3   Year established: 1991
Location of schools served: UR   Type of schools served: PUB

The Eighth Grade Academic Summer Camp is a partnership between the Kalamazoo public schools and Kalamazoo Valley Community College (KVCC). The camp helps at-risk students make the transition from middle to high school. Students participate in a four-week summer program at the college based on integrated learning theory. Classes and activities are designed to optimize positive thinking, active learning, and ownership of actions. Each summer one of the three middle schools refers students to the program; however, KVCC tracks and provides workshops to the students throughout their high school careers.

Note: Each institution's Carnegie class is given in parentheses. **Key:** E=elementary school, HS=high school, M=middle school, NR=not reported, PRI=private, PUB=public, RU=rural, SU=suburban, UR=urban

Kalamazoo Valley Community College (AA)
Kalamazoo Academic Partnership
Grades served: E, M   Schools served: 4   Year established: 1990
Location of schools served: UR, SU   Type of schools served: PUB

Kalamazoo Academic Partnership is a project linking three colleges and one university with the Kalamazoo public schools. Its mission is to enable public school students in the community to achieve educational success and to promote communication and professional development among faculty members at all levels. The primary objective of this effort is to promote, by means of a broad array of services and activities, the involvement of parents of elementary school students in their children's educational opportunities. Other programs include College Visitation Day, Faculty Partnerships, and On-To-College.

Lake Michigan College (AA)
Winner Within Program
Grades served: HS   Schools served: NR   Year established: 1986
Location of schools served: NR   Type of schools served: PUB

The Winner Within Program involves adopting students and tracking their academic success through grade 12 and beyond. Once students have completed high school, they receive a full two-year scholarship. Each student is sponsored by an adult from the college, who serves as a mentor for the student and supports and encourages him or her throughout the program. The college provides educational preparatory workshops as well as opportunities for the students, parents, and sponsors to attend plays, art exhibits, sporting events, and various other college activities.

Oakland University (MA I)
Preprimary Impaired Program
Grades served: E   Schools served: 1   Year established: 1989
Location of schools served: SU   Type of schools served: PUB

The Preprimary Impaired Program at Lowry Early Childhood Center of Oakland University is a collaboration between Rochester Community Schools Special Education Department and the university staff and administrators of the Early Childhood Center. Rochester preschool-age children with special needs are offered the opportunity to participate in the university's community-based preschool program with age-appropriate nonhandicapped peers. The staff of the Lowry Center and the special education teacher and ancillary staff from Rochester schools work together to adapt materials and strategies to facilitate hands-on experiences and social interactions, to offer individual instruction, and to provide for a developmentally appropriate curriculum.

University of Michigan-Ann Arbor (RES I)
Wade H. McCree, Jr., Incentive Scholarship Program
Grades served: HS   Schools served: NR   Year established: 1986
Location of schools served: NR   Type of schools served: PUB

The Wade H. McCree, Jr., Incentive Scholarship Program is part of an ongoing effort to increase the number and proportion of underrepresented populations who will reach high levels of academic achievement. In 1989 the Presidents' Council of State Universities endorsed a statewide commitment on the part of its member institutions to offer guaranteed, full-tuition scholarships to selected students. Scholarship recipients are selected by participating schools throughout the state of Michigan; they have the opportunity to participate in various programs presented by their sponsoring university.

University of Michigan-Ann Arbor (RES I)
Martin Luther King/Cesar Chavez/Rosa Parks–Career Exploration Program

Grades served: HS	Schools served: 50	Year established: 1987
Location of schools served: UR, SU, RU	Type of schools served: PUB	

The Martin Luther King/Cesar Chavez/Rosa Parks Career Exploration Program is a free one-week residential summer session at the University of Michigan for more than 250 tenth and 11th grade public school students selected from various southeastern Michigan schools. Activities include workshops, laboratory demonstrations, campus tours, and multicultural activities conducted by university faculty and staff. Each week a different career theme is offered (law, business, communication, and so on), and students concentrate on their particular area of career interest. Participants are supervised by University of Michigan students 24 hours a day. The University of Michigan students are trained in group dynamics, team building, diversity, counseling, and motivation.

MINNESOTA

Minneapolis Community College (AA)
Minneapolis Pathways

Grades served: M, HS	Schools served: 8	Year established: 1992
Location of schools served: UR	Type of schools served: PUB	

Minneapolis Pathways is funded by the Ford Foundation. Its goals are to integrate the higher education systems into an already active multisector collaboration called New Workforce, which is facilitated by Minneapolis Youth Trust. Immediate objectives are to create networks of public and private institutions in a formal partnership, to develop a strategic plan for evaluating current endeavors for identifying strategic actions to be taken, and to assess the success of activities aimed at enhancing success rates of underserved students in the K-12 and postsecondary systems of Minneapolis. Data gathering and assessment will use the research capabilities of the eight institutions of higher education engaged in the partnership.

MISSOURI

Avila College (MA I)
PASS (Project Avila — Stay in School)

Grades served: E	Schools served: 2	Year established: 1993
Location of schools served: UR	Type of schools served: PUB, PRI	

Developed by the Avila College chapter of Students in Free Enterprise, the PASS program uses Avila's intercollegiate student-athletes as role models for third and fourth graders to deliver the message, "Stay in school, and stay off drugs." The student-athletes provide a motivational support system through classroom presentations, role playing and discussions of real-life situations, and educational and recreational minicamps on the college campus. PASS helps youngsters understand and accept the importance of education to eventually affect the school dropout rates and overall educational background of children from the urban core.

Note: Each institution's Carnegie class is given in parentheses. **Key:** E=elementary school, HS=high school, M=middle school, NR=not reported, PRI=private, PUB=public, RU=rural, SU=suburban, UR=urban

St. Charles County Community College (AA)
Project YES (Youth Experiencing Success)

Grades served: HS   Schools served: 7   Year established: NR
Location of schools served: SU   Type of schools served: PUB, PRI

St. Charles County Community College, in conjunction with the St. Charles School District, the Office of Employment and Training Programs, and Lewis and Clark Area Vocational Technical School, sponsors the countywide Project YES for at-risk youth. This school-to-work program is aimed at keeping potential dropouts in school to complete their diplomas. The program encompasses an alternative high school where college personnel assist students in completing high school credits, career development, mentoring and shadowing programs, study skills classes, and counseling.

University of Missouri-Columbia (RES I)
Mid-Missouri Diagnostic and Prescriptive Clinic

Grades served: E, M, HS   Schools served: 9   Year established: 1988
Location of schools served: RU   Type of schools served: PUB

As an extension of the Department of Educational and Counseling Psychology's graduate mission in teaching, research, and service, the Specific Learning Disabilities (SLD) Assessment and Consultation Clinic provides extensive diagnostic and prescriptive services for adolescents and adults with learning disabilities. The goal is to reduce the risk of failure in school or dropping out, unemployment or underemployment, and personal, social, and emotional difficulties among SLD individuals. Functional strengths and limitations are identified, and clients are actively involved in planning and implementing accommodation strategies.

University of Missouri-St. Louis (DOC I)
Access to Success

Grades served: M   Schools served: 13   Year established: 1988
Location of schools served: UR   Type of schools served: PUB

Access to Success was instituted as a joint effort of the University of Missouri-St. Louis and the General Dynamics Corporation to encourage sixth, seventh, and eighth graders to consider careers in science and mathematics. Three school districts with high minority populations were selected to participate. A Partnership for Progress committee includes representatives from the university, General Dynamics, and major community corporations; a planning committee includes the project director and 12 classroom teachers who are science/math club coordinators. Program components include tutoring, teacher aides, field trips, and a summer camp; UM-St. Louis education majors gain practical experience in teaching students in multicultural settings.

University of Missouri-St. Louis (DOC I)
Regional Science and Technology Career Access Center

Grades served: M, HS   Schools served: 25   Year established: 1987
Location of schools served: UR   Type of schools served: PUB

The St. Louis Regional Science and Technology Career Access Center is a collaboration of the University of Missouri-St. Louis, the University of Missouri-Rolla, the St. Louis Community College, Harris-Stowe State College, and the St. Louis Public School System. Its mission is to develop and coordinate school-based and external strategies that result in the academic preparation of urban minority students to enter undergraduate studies in the sciences, mathematics, and engineering. The center provides opportunities to involve students in formal and informal science and mathematics enrichment, scientific research, inquiry-based learning experiences, and career orientation.

NEBRASKA

Metropolitan Community College (AA)
Project FREE (Family Reading Encourages Education)

Grades served: E	Schools served: NR	Year established: 1992
Location of schools served: UR	Type of schools served: PUB	

Project FREE provides literacy training, life skills instruction, and language experiences for parents and children of broadly diverse socioeconomic groups and multicultural backgrounds. The curriculum is based on expanded adult basic education instruction to include intensive parenting skills, a separate prereading/language experience component for children, and a parent/child interactive learning component using children's books as topical units. Volunteer grandparents assume essential support roles in assisting children and teachers with project tasks.

NEW HAMPSHIRE

New Hampshire College (BUS)
Partnership for the 21st Century

Grades served: HS	Schools served: 2	Year established: 1992
Location of schools served: UR, SU	Type of schools served: PUB	

This New Hampshire College/Manchester School District partnership seeks to provide college opportunities to students who would not view college as possible. Students selected from the middle third of the sophomore, junior, and senior classes show potential but have mixed academic performances and limited finances. School-year activities include tutoring, career counseling, parent/student meetings, SAT preparation, and two hours of volunteer community service weekly. Summer activities include English, math, social science, and computer classes at NHC and 20 hours of paid community service per week at nonprofit organizations in Manchester.

NEW JERSEY

Essex County College (AA)
Newark Educational Partnership

Grades served: NR	Schools served: 12	Year established: 1993
Location of schools served: NR	Type of schools served: PUB	

The Newark Educational Partnership is a comprehensive collaboration of public, private, and nonprofit agencies designed to bring about systemic change in public education. The approach is incremental, with the primary foci curricular reform and faculty development at both the K-12 and college levels. The long-range goal is to create an integrated K-12 educational system characterized by strong, school-based management and comprehensive high schools that serve as complete community centers.

Note: Each institution's Carnegie class is given in parentheses. **Key:** E=elementary school, HS=high school, M=middle school, NR=not reported, PRI=private, PUB=public, RU=rural, SU=suburban, UR=urban

Jersey City State College (MA I)
Linkages
Grades served: E, M

Schools served: 10

Year established: 1990

Location of schools served: UR

Type of schools served: PUB, PRI

Linkages is an after-school intervention program that offers instructional services to students in grades 5-8 in math, reading, language arts, English as a second language, and science. Paid and volunteer college students serve as peer counselors and coordinate recreational activities and community projects offered at the Linkages sites. College faculty train and supervise the peer counselors. Field trips to college cultural and sports activities familiarize students with campus life and the institution's facilities. Special workshops on career choices are offered in conjunction with these field experiences.

New Jersey Institute of Technology (DOC II)
The Center for Pre-College Programs
Grades served: E, M, HS

Schools served: NR

Year established: 1978

Location of schools served: NR

Type of schools served: NR

The New Jersey Institute of Technology's Center for Pre-College Programs administers several programs designed to interest public school students in pursuing careers in science and engineering. The programs create new learning opportunities for students in New Jersey's public and private schools and for the teachers and guidance counselors who advise them. Programs are offered by hand-picked, experienced, and motivated faculty and graduate students, who work in one or more of 35 different programs funded by corporations, private foundations, municipal, state, and federal agencies, and the New Jersey Institute of Technology. Programs are offered on weekends, after school, and during the summer.

University of Medicine and Dentistry of New Jersey-New Jersey Medical School (MED)
Project 3000 by 2000
Grades served: HS

Schools served: 3

Year established: 1992

Location of schools served: NR

Type of schools served: PUB, PRI

Project 3000 by 2000 is a partnership between the New Jersey Medical School and three area magnet schools. The project is linked with an initiative of the American Association of Medical Colleges designed to increase the enrollment of underrepresented minorities in the nation's medical schools to 3,000 by the year 2000. The New Jersey initiative uses existing academic outreach and enrichment programs targeting minority students and their teachers from high school through college. Systemic reform in science education is facilitated by instructional development and curriculum enhancement.

University of Medicine and Dentistry of New Jersey-New Jersey Medical School (MED)
Minority High School Student Research Apprentice Program
Grades served: HS

Schools served: 1

Year established: 1981

Location of schools served: UR

Type of schools served: PUB

This program links the New Jersey Medical School and the Newark Science High School to promote students' interest in biomedical research and to make participants aware of opportunities in various types of medical careers. The program serves minority students who are underrepresented in biomedical research and their teachers. Teachers are given practical experience in a biomedical research lab, and participants also meet in seminars and skill development classes.

<u>NEW YORK</u>

Binghamton University (DOC I)
Home and School Partnerships

Grades served: E   Schools served: 9   Year established: 1986
Location of schools served: UR, RU   Type of schools served: PUB

Home and School Partnerships are early intervention/prevention models involving a consortium of Binghamton University and five school districts. The focus of the intervention is an outreach program designed to assist families and teachers of children in grades K-5 who are experiencing difficulties in school. The model is designed to develop an ongoing positive relationship between home and school through parent and teacher visits, building change awards, forums, portable staff development materials, and parenting programs.

Binghamton University (DOC I)
Binghamton Liberty Partnership Project

Grades served: M, HS   Schools served: 6   Year established: 1989
Location of schools served: UR, SU   Type of schools served: PUB

The Binghamton Liberty Partnership Project links Binghamton University and the school districts of Binghamton, Newark Valley, and Whitney Point in an alliance to serve the educational and developmental needs of students at risk of dropping out of school. School coordinators working within the school buildings develop relationships with identified students to remedy motivational issues related to family, institutional constraints, and structures that are obstacles to educational and personal achievement. Activities take place within the students' school program and in weekend and summer programs using community and postsecondary institutional resources.

Binghamton University (DOC I)
More Math for More Females Project

Grades served: E, M, HS   Schools served: 15   Year established: 1985
Location of schools served: UR, SU, RU   Type of schools served: PUB, PRI

The More Math for More Females Project links the School of Education and Human Development at Binghamton University and 15 local school districts in providing activities to encourage women to continue studying mathematics throughout high school. The program began as a service to local grade 4-12 students and teachers, and now includes participants from several surrounding counties. Major activities include a graduate course for teachers, Improving Gender Equity in Mathematics Classrooms, and an annual career conference, "Females + Math = Exciting Careers," to educate girls and their parents about the importance of mathematics for future career options.

Cayuga County Community College (AA)
Nontraditional Careers for Women: Role Models & Networking

Grades served: M   Schools served: 18   Year established: 1994
Location of schools served: RU   Type of schools served: PUB, PRI

Cayuga County Community College's Nontraditional Careers for Women: Role Models & Networking project aims to inspire both college women and middle school girls to pursue nontraditional careers. Selected college women students and faculty are trained in the concept of career networking; highly successful women role models in nontraditional areas present motivational lectures to trainees and to middle school girls. Finally, M school girls, trainees, and area career women engage in informal discussions about careers at networking luncheons. The goal is to promote career skills in the college women while keeping options open for the middle school girls.

Note: Each institution's Carnegie class is given in parentheses. **Key:** E=elementary school, HS=high school, M=middle school, NR=not reported, PRI=private, PUB=public, RU=rural, SU=suburban, UR=urban

City University of New York Borough of Manhattan Community College (AA)
Sex Equity Math/Science Project
Grades served: M, HS Schools served: 33 Year established: 1991
Location of schools served: UR Type of schools served: PUB

The Sex Equity Math/Science Project links 33 middle schools and high schools in an effort to provide 800 young women in grades 7 through 12 with the services and activities needed to make sound career and educational decisions, increase their awareness of new career opportunities, and acquire the information they will need to overcome sex bias and sex role stereotyping. Activities include two eight-week Saturday programs integrating science, math, and occupational exploration; a four-week summer instructional program integrating science, mathematics, language arts, and career exploration; an annual career fair focusing on nontraditional careers and training/education for women. Inservice training is offered for school guidance counselors as well as the college staff.

City University of New York College of Staten Island (MA I)
The Liberty Partnership Program
Grades served: M, HS Schools served: 4 Year established: 1989
Location of schools served: UR Type of schools served: PUB

The Liberty Partnership Program is a collaborative school-college-community project that links the college, Brooklyn and Staten Island High School, and the Staten Island branch of the New York Urban League to improve attendance, academic performance, and retention of at-risk students by providing a broad range of instruction, enrichment, and support services to students and their parents. The program also provides professional development for teachers and staff who work with this population. The program increases students' motivation, builds self-confidence, and improves the skills needed for college entry or for employment.

City University of New York Herbert H. Lehman College (MA I)
PRISMMS (Program to Increase Student Mastery in Mathematics & Science)
Grades served: E Schools served: 3 Year established: 1985
Location of schools served: UR Type of schools served: PUB

PRISMMS assists students in grades 4-6 to acquire the prerequisite skills needed to succeed in science and mathematics (progressing to the Science and Technology Entry Program). Students engage in a project-based program to improve skills and attitudes related to mathematics and science. In the summer and on Saturdays during the school year, students work in small groups, on hands-on projects, and become familiar with grade-appropriate computer software; a demonstration program is provided for teachers. College and high school preteachers serve as assistant teachers. The summer and academic year programs culminate in science fairs.

City University of New York Herbert H. Lehman College (MA I)
STEP (Science and Technology Entry Program)
Grades served: M, HS Schools served: 3 Year established: 1985
Location of schools served: NR Type of schools served: PUB

The Science and Technology Entry Program is designed to assist students in grades 7-9 who are economically disadvantaged and underrepresented in programs of study and careers in scientific/mathematical, technical, and health-related fields to acquire the prerequisite skills these areas require. Summer and academic year activities are thematic in concept and stress hands-on projects integrating science, mathematics, and language arts, and incorporating computer applications. Students are encouraged to formulate hypotheses, develop research protocols, collect and analyze data, write comprehensive project reports, and present their projects at a science fair. College and high school preteachers serve as assistant teachers.

City University of New York Herbert H. Lehman College (MA I)
Hughes Biological Science Program

Grades served: HS   Schools served: 5   Year established: 1993
Location of schools served: UR   Type of schools served: PUB

The Hughes Biological Science Program builds upon Lehman's academic strengths and on its existing K-16 collaborative programs. It is a bridge-to-college program that serves students from the 11th grade to the sophomore year of college and seeks to increase the number of African-American, Latino, and women high school graduates prepared to succeed in college-level science and mathematics courses; it also seeks to attract more qualified students by improving undergraduate laboratories and providing earlier opportunities for meaningful research. Activities are designed to strengthen teacher-student mentoring, strengthen students' cooperation, provide early research experiences, and improve academic achievement.

City University of New York LaGuardia Community College (AA)
Northeast Consortium

Grades served: M, HS   Schools served: 7   Year established: 1990
Location of schools served: NR   Type of schools served: PUB

The Northeast Consortium is a regional coalition that links Clarkson University, Brookhaven National Laboratory, and LaGuardia, Monroe and North Shore Community Colleges. It is designed to increase minority participation in science and to offer eighth grade students a continuum of science education opportunities in the summer and during the academic year. The program includes a half-day orientation to LaGuardia, a one-day program at Brookhaven, a four-week summer science program at each participating community college campus, and a three- to-four-week summer program at Clarkson in the senior year.

College of New Rochelle (MA I)
CNR Sisters

Grades served: E   Schools served: 1   Year established: 1988
Location of schools served: UR   Type of schools served: PUB

CNR Sisters is a mentoring organization for undergraduate students of the College of New Rochelle. Each college student is paired with an elementary school child from the neighboring Jefferson Elementary School and volunteers a minimum of one hour per week to interact with the child. Activities might include playing a game, reading a book, helping with homework, or engaging in an activity suggested by the public school classroom teacher. Children selected to have a big sister are identified by the principal of the school as underprivileged or having a particular need. A one-year commitment is required of each CNR Sister.

College of New Rochelle (MA I)
BIZKIDS

Grades served: HS   Schools served: 2   Year established: 1992
Location of schools served: SU   Type of schools served: PRI

BIZKIDS is an entrepreneurial program initiated by Russell Taylor, founder of the college's Taylor Institute for Entrepreneurial Studies. The program is designed to motivate at-risk students to complete their education by teaching them how to start a successful business. Modeled after a similar program for street kids in the South Bronx, the program helps these high school students to develop self-esteem, confidence, and responsibility in reaching a goal. The program is being integrated into the business curriculum of several area high schools.

Note: Each institution's Carnegie class is given in parentheses. **Key:** E=elementary school, HS=high school, M=middle school, NR=not reported, PRI=private, PUB=public, RU=rural, SU=suburban, UR=urban

Cornell University (RES I)
Cornell ON-TOP (Opportunities in Non-Traditional Occupations Program)
Grades served: HS   Schools served: 4   Year established: 1990
Location of schools served: UR, RU   Type of schools served: PUB

Cornell ON-TOP is a collaboration of the Maintenance and Service Operations/Facilities and Campus Planning unit of Cornell University, the Ithaca Youth Bureau, the Learning Web, and Ithaca and area high schools, whose representatives make up the steering committee for the program. It encourages and develops the interest of minority students and girls in the skilled trades, connects high school education through graduation with continuing education in work and the trades, and offers a paid summer work experience and mentored exposure to the trades in maintenance and service operations. The steering committee selects 12-15 students from the applicants each spring.

Cornell University (RES I)
Exploring Careers in Information Technologies
Grades served: HS   Schools served: 1   Year established: 1990
Location of schools served: UR   Type of schools served: PUB

Exploring Careers in Information Technologies is an outreach program for minority youth interested in an introduction to information technologies, a diverse field encompassing the tools, applications, and services pertaining to computer systems, personal computers and work stations, network systems, databases, and software. The program's goals are to help participants develop their full potential, explore career paths available in information technologies while obtaining on-the-job experience, and obtain the education required to pursue their chosen careers. The program is sponsored by Cornell Information Technologies, the Office of Equal Opportunity, Ithaca City School District, Tompkins-Cortland Community College, and several community organizations.

Cornell University (RES I)
Expanding Your Horizons in Math, Science & Engineering
Grades served: M   Schools served: 19   Year established: 1987
Location of schools served: UR, SU, RU   Type of schools served: PUB, PRI

Expanding Your Horizons is a conference for sixth to eighth grade girls and their parents that is designed to stimulate interest in math, science, and engineering. Cornell women graduate and undergraduate students, faculty, and staff work with Ithaca schools to offer a variety of hands-on workshops using math, science, and engineering. The girls hear the messages over and over throughout the conference that they should take math and science in junior and senior high school and that women can be successful mathematicians, scientists, and engineers, communicated through the enthusiasm and excitement of the many role models (all women).

Cornell University (RES I)
Sidney High School Partnership
Grades served: HS   Schools served: 1   Year established: 1989
Location of schools served: RU   Type of schools served: NR

The Sidney High School Partnership with Cornell University enables a high school instructor and two to five students entering their senior year in high school to work in the chemistry laboratories with various professors during the summer. Their work with professors, postdoctoral graduate students, and undergraduates covers various aspects of chemical research from biochemical assays to laser-induced reactions. The university has also worked with the high school in developing a mobile chemistry lab using sophisticated analytical chemical instrumentation located in a specially designed 45-foot trailer. The mobile unit is used to teach high school teachers and their students to use scientific instrumentation, perform laboratory experiments, and initiate research.

Fashion Institute of Technology (ART)
High School Partnership Program for Design Arts Students

Grades served: HS   Schools served: 1   Year established: 1988
Location of schools served: UR   Type of schools served: PUB

This joint program with the High School for Fashion Industries and Washington Irving High School combines academics and art education, mentoring, and career development to assist, each year, 40 artistically talented junior students who are at risk of not graduating from high school. A senior program assists students with college applications and continues their mentoring and art education. The program is designed to encourage students to finish high school and go to college to prepare for design careers.

Fordham University (DOC I)
Science and Technology Entry Program (STEP)

Grades served: M, HS   Schools served: 20   Year established: 1986
Location of schools served: UR   Type of schools served: PUB, PRI

Fordham University's Science and Technology Entry Program joins Fordham and 20 secondary schools. The program is designed to motivate and better prepare academically able minority and disadvantaged secondary school students for careers in science, technology, health, and the licensed professions in New York State. The program emphasizes academic preparation and career awareness through academic enrichment classes and laboratories, paid internships, an on-campus summer program, preparation for standardized tests, and teacher training workshops.

Ithaca College (MA I)
Access to College Education (ACE)

Grades served: HS   Schools served: 14   Year established: 1989
Location of schools served: UR, SU, RU   Type of schools served: PUB

ACE is a partnership linking four higher education institutions (Ithaca, Cornell, Cortland, Tompkins-Cortland Community College) and 14 public schools in a multicounty area of upstate New York. The program identifies eighth graders who have the aptitude for college-level work but for reasons of poverty, lack of role models, or other socioeconomic reasons probably will not pursue a college education. The colleges provide conferences for students and parents, summer writing workshops, regional institutes, and career, financial aid, and admissions counseling. A monthly newsletter maintains communication. College students provide mentoring and a homework help line to support academic efforts.

Ithaca College (MA I)
Special Children's Center Swim/Gym Program

Grades served: E   Schools served: 1   Year established: 1976
Location of schools served: UR   Type of schools served: NR

Ithaca College's School of Health Sciences and Human Performance, in partnership with the Ithaca Special Children's Center, sponsors this program, whose primary goal is to allow college students and preschool children with disabilities to interact with each other weekly in a one-to-one swim/gym program. College students learn to interact with young children, and the preschool children increase their abilities physically, cognitively, and socially.

Note: Each institution's Carnegie class is given in parentheses. **Key:** E=elementary school, HS=high school, M=middle school, NR=not reported, PRI=private, PUB=public, RU=rural, SU=suburban, UR=urban

Manhattan College (MA I)
Project CHAMP (Children Having Additional Motor Power)

Grades served: E, M, HS
Location of schools served: UR

Schools served: 22
Type of schools served: PUB, PRI

Year established: 1985

Project CHAMP is a joint program of Manhattan College and the Miriam de Soyza Learning Center, funded by the New York City Department of Mental Health and Mental Retardation Services. The project serves children with developmental disabilities from 22 schools in Bronx County. The major emphasis is on developing motor skills, self-concept, and muscular coordination for children who have difficulty keeping pace with their peers. Activities take place in Manhattan College's field house, fitness and rehabilitation center, and swimming pool. Specific goals are to reduce risk factors associated with coronary heart disease, build the muscular system, and develop coordination to build children's self-esteem and enable them to successfully participate in appropriate physical activities with peers.

Nazareth College of Rochester (MA I)
D.D. Eisenhower Grant

Grades served: HS
Location of schools served: UR

Schools served: 2
Type of schools served: NR

Year established: 1991

This grant is dedicated to strengthening the competitiveness of students in grades 9-12 by improving their knowledge, skills, and performance in mathematics and science. Laboratory games, information, and books are developed in the cooperating schools for use by nonprogram colleagues, and the site coordinator shares handouts during citywide math meetings. A professional development program for teachers of math and science in the site schools supports their efforts to improve their skills and the quality of instruction.

Rochester Institute of Technology (MA I)
Edison Tech/RIT Enrichment Program

Grades served: HS
Location of schools served: UR

Schools served: 1
Type of schools served: PUB

Year established: 1992

The purpose of the Edison Tech/RIT Enrichment Program is to keep students (grades 9-12) in school and to assist them academically by providing on-site tutoring by RIT graduate students and current seniors during the school day. Faculty exchanges provide information about academic programs and about how RIT faculty can assist Edison Tech. Edison Tech's Guidance Department offers admissions information, and career seminars start with seniors and work through every class through ninth grade making students aware of work and post-high school academics, including part-time study evenings, potential careers and requirements, and realistic goals.

Rochester Institute of Technology (MA I)
Partnership-School #4

Grades served: E
Location of schools served: UR

Schools served: 1
Type of schools served: PUB

Year established: 1987

RIT's partnership links the college with School #4, an inner-city elementary school in Rochester. This liaison focuses on building partnerships between individual students and teachers by providing opportunities for college students to mentor and tutor, renovate the facility, and host the children on campus at an annual event called Love Day. At this afternoon-long event, children are grouped with RIT students for campus activities and an introduction to college life as a way of encouraging them to persist and succeed in school.

State University of New York at Albany (RES II)
Model for Social Work Intervention in Schools

Grades served: E   Schools served: 4   Year established: 1991
Location of schools served: UR   Type of schools served: PUB

The Model for Social Work Intervention in Schools is a partnership between SUNY at Albany's Rockefeller College and the Albany Public School System, for which its designer has received recognition for excellence in social work research from the National Association of Social Workers. The model is task-centered. A School of Social Work intern forms a case management team with parents, the student, and teachers. A contract is developed setting goals and a strategy for reaching them. A weekly home visit is also a part of each intern's agenda. The goal is to help academically troubled children get back on the right track.

State University of New York College at Old Westbury (BA II)
Dwight D. Eisenhower Title IIA Cooperative Demonstration Program

Grades served: M, HS   Schools served: 11   Year established: 1991
Location of schools served: SU   Type of schools served: PUB, PRI

This program, designed to serve students from groups presently underrepresented in science and technology careers, motivates and prepares students from neighboring schools to pursue such careers. The summer program provides courses in English, math, computers, biology, and chemistry. Cultural activities, recreation, special workshops, field trips, and guest speakers are also provided. The academic year program offers tutoring in science and math, multicultural workshops, SAT prep classes, college/career planning, science project workshops, field trips, and parent involvement meetings. Teacher training workshops illustrate useful strategies for participants.

State University of New York College at Potsdam (MA I)
Very Special Arts Festival

Grades served: E, M, HS   Schools served: 30   Year established: NR
Location of schools served: RU   Type of schools served: PUB

The Very Special Arts Festival is part of a nationwide effort designed to bring quality programs in the arts to disabled children and adults and to give them a chance to celebrate and share their own accomplishments in the visual and performing arts. Potsdam College faculty and students present art, music, and drama activities and assist in the organization and setup of the festival. Area teachers bring their classes, and community residents participate as well. Money raised is used to send representative classes to the All-State Very Special Arts Festival at the Governor's mansion in Albany each spring.

State University of New York College of Agriculture and Technology at Cobleskill (AA)
Project Quest

Grades served: M, HS   Schools served: 7   Year established: NR
Location of schools served: RU   Type of schools served: PUB

Project Quest links middle, HS, and postsecondary educators; students and parents; and local business owners. One of the activities sponsored by the project is the Schoharie County Gender Equity Task Force, which involves middle, HS, and postsecondary educators in a continuous effort to address equity in school curricula and policy. The project sponsored Discovering Careers in Science and Technology summer camp (grades 8-10, girls), Expanding Your Horizons in Science and Mathematics conferences, and mentoring and job-shadowing, bringing together female role models from nontraditional fields. Other seminars, workshops, and conferences for educators, parents, students, and businesses respond to needs.

Note: Each institution's Carnegie class is given in parentheses. **Key:** E=elementary school, HS=high school, M=middle school, NR=not reported, PRI=private, PUB=public, RU=rural, SU=suburban, UR=urban

State University of New York Institute of Technology at Utica/Rome (MA II)
Today's Women in Science and Technology (TWIST)

Grades served: M

Schools served: NR

Year established: NR

Location of schools served: UR, SU, RU

Type of schools served: PUB, PRI

Today's Women in Science and Technology is a partnership between SUNY-Utica/Rome and Upper Mohawk Valley schools that is designed to encourage middle and junior high school girls to continue studies in math and science throughout high school and to consider future careers in science and technology. In addition to developing programs for the students, TWIST seeks to sensitize public school teachers and counselors to the great untapped potential among young girls in math and science and to consider the growing number of rapidly emerging careers in technology.

Syracuse University (RES II)
Maxwell School/High School for Leadership and Public Service

Grades served: HS

Schools served: 1

Year established: 1993

Location of schools served: UR

Type of schools served: PUB

This partnership between Syracuse University' Maxwell School and the High School for Leadership and Public Service is an attempt to better prepare students for college The high school and the university work together to design the high school curriculum, and the university assists the high school in applying contemporary educational technologies. The high school receives volunteer assistance from area SU alumni and contacts for additional financial and human resources for projects. SU undergraduates earn a full semester's credit by studying urban education and working as tutors, teaching assistants, and research analysts for the staff of the high school.

Syracuse University (RES II)
TechReach®

Grades served: E, M, HS

Schools served: 25

Year established: 1990

Location of schools served: UR, SU, RU

Type of schools served: PUB, PRI

TechReach® is an outreach program of the L.C. Smith College of Engineering at Syracuse University concerned with recruiting and retaining women and minority students in engineering to meet the nation's need for engineers. The program involves approximately 25 schools from elementary through high school, engineering firms, the corporate community, other community groups and leaders, the College of Engineering Advisory Board, and its faculty, students, and alumni in efforts to provide support for curriculum development, tutoring, and inservice training.

Syracuse University (RES II)
University Reach

Grades served: HS

Schools served: 8

Year established: 1990

Location of schools served: UR

Type of schools served: PUB

The program links undergraduates with at-risk youth through community organizations such as the Boys and Girls Clubs and, more recently, the local public high schools. The program has undergraduates working as coaches and supervisors with a small number of at-risk youth on research and action projects to solve community problems. The director works with a teacher to set up a six-week internship, either at the school or the university, where each undergraduate coaches a team of four or five teens to produce a service or product.

Union College (BA I)
G.E. Scholars

Grades served: HS	Schools served: 2	Year established: 1992
Location of schools served: NR	Type of schools served: PUB, PRI	

Union College's link with G.E. Scholars involves several components: the placement of interns, for a year, with teachers for their student teaching experience; mentoring by undergraduate mathematics and science majors of junior high and high school students in the COMPASS program sponsored by General Electric and Union's mathematics department; invitations to G.E. Scholars faculty to attend education workshops and lectures at the college; and encouragement of G.E. Scholars to attend Summer Skill/Summer High Enrichment programs and to take advanced science and mathematics courses at Union College during their senior year. The program serves talented students from underrepresented, minority, and at-risk populations.

University of Rochester (RES I)
School #37

Grades served: E	Schools served: 1	Year established: 1993
Location of schools served: UR	Type of schools served: PUB	

The University of Rochester and School #37 in the Rochester City School District are partners in an effort to enhance educational opportunities for the elementary school children and their families. University students tutor individual school children on site after school, and a Partners in Reading Program brings university students to the school several times a semester to read with a primary grade child who is his or her partner for the year. Activities include an evening of activities on campus for sixth grade students and their parents and an overnight stay for the students. Special classes, tours, and activities the next day link university students and sixth graders.

Utica College of Syracuse University (BA II)
Young Scholars Program

Grades served: M, HS	Schools served: 3	Year established: 1993
Location of schools served: UR	Type of schools served: PUB	

The Young Scholars Program is a collaboration between Utica College and the Utica City School District. The program serves students in grades 7-12 who have been identified as potentially capable of earning a NYS Regents diploma and going on to postsecondary education but are at risk of failure or attrition as a result of socioeconomic factors. Students attend a summer session at Utica College, attend other college events, and receive academic support as needed during the school year. Successful graduates are guaranteed admission to the college.

NORTH CAROLINA

Cape Fear Community College (AA)
Alliance for Achievement

Grades served: M, HS	Schools served: 3	Year established: 1992
Location of schools served: UR	Type of schools served: PUB	

The Wilmington Alliance for Achievement is a partnership of Virgo and Williston Middle Schools, New Hanover High School, Cape Fear Community College, and the community and businesses designed to develop greater understanding among young adolescents of the connection between academic achievement and success in the labor market; to increase students' and families' awareness of opportunities provided by careers in critical fields, in nontraditional occupations, and emerging technical fields; and to keep postsecondary educational and vocational options open for all students. Strategies include inservice training for faculty, expanded career awareness, increased minority enrollment in gatekeeper courses, family involvement, and curriculum modification.

Note: Each institution's Carnegie class is given in parentheses. **Key:** E=elementary school, HS=high school, M=middle school, NR=not reported, PRI=private, PUB=public, RU=rural, SU=suburban, UR=urban

Central Piedmont Community College (AA)
Even Start Families Learning Together for Success
Grades served: E   Schools served: 3   Year established: 1993
Location of schools served: UR   Type of schools served: PUB

Even Start Families Learning Together for Success is a program linking Central Piedmont Community College and elementary and preschools. Its primary mission is to improve children's and adults' educational opportunities and literacy by creating a collaborative, family-centered education program that provides adult education, early childhood education, and parenting education. The project involves parents, children, educators, and community members in a coordinated effort to help parents become full partners in their children's education.

Cleveland Community College (AA)
Inservice Program for Underrepresented Students in the Middle Schools and High Schools of Cleveland County
Grades served: NR   Schools served: 6   Year established: 1993
Location of schools served: NR   Type of schools served: PUB

This program is designed to increase the number of minorities and underrepresented students in science and mathematics courses by facilitating career exploration in these fields; effecting instructional improvement in science and mathematics; fostering an improved understanding of cultural diversity and its effect on career choices, learning, and social, intellectual, and personal development for minorities; and improving articulation among educators and business and industry involved in science and mathematics. Inservice training for teachers includes related training in instruction, advisement, and community relationships during a 50-hour program and ten-hour follow-up directed by an operations committee.

OHIO

Bowling Green State University (DOC I)
Music Plus
Grades served: M, HS   Schools served: 7   Year established: 1986
Location of schools served: UR   Type of schools served: PUB

Music Plus is a music and academic enhancement program for economically disadvantaged Toledo Public School junior and senior high students from one district. Students are eligible to stay in the program through high school. The format of the project includes Wednesday night meetings during the university's academic year with students picked up and taken back to their homes. Wednesday night meetings include private music lessons, class keyboard lessons, and a creative experience module. Students attend a week-long summer camp as well as cultural events during the academic year.

Case Western Reserve University (RES I)
Case Early Exposure to Engineering for Minority Students (CE³MS)
Grades served: HS   Schools served: 27   Year established: 1975
Location of schools served: UR, SU, RU   Type of schools served: PUB, PRI

The Case Western Reserve University CE³MS program is designed to introduce ninth and tenth grade students and their parents, teachers, and counselors to the various fields of engineering. Selected students, who have demonstrated interest and ability in mathematics and science, attend a five-week summer session consisting of classes in mathematics, chemistry, and computer science. A variety of activities familiarize students with the field and inform participants about course prerequisites for students seeking admission to engineering schools: lectures by Case faculty and local minority engineers, hands-on laboratory experiences, and field trips to industrial and research facilities.

Case Western Reserve University (RES I)
Upward Bound: Special Program for Preprofessional Students in the Health Sciences
Grades served: HS   Schools served: 16   Year established: 1966
Location of schools served: UR   Type of schools served: PUB

This program at Case Western Reserve University was established to prepare inner-city minority and other high school students for successful postsecondary studies toward professional health careers. Students in grades 9-12 attending Cleveland and East Cleveland public schools are eligible to participate in the six-week summer residential and well-developed academic year components, including intensive instruction in mathematics, natural sciences (with laboratory), English, reading, study skills, computer science, and foreign language, and to participate in summer internships at local health facilities. Counseling in college and career exploration and application procedures is offered for individuals and groups.

Case Western Reserve University (RES I)
Minority Engineers Industrial Opportunity Program
Grades served: HS   Schools served: 27   Year established: 1974
Location of schools served: UR, SU   Type of schools served: PUB, PRI

The Minority Engineers Industrial Opportunity Program recruits academically talented students who have completed 11th grade and maintained a GPA of at least 3.0. Students attend a five-week summer program that includes special college preparatory classes in mathematics, physics, expository writing, and speech. During the academic year, Saturday morning classes help students to develop their mathematics and verbal skills in preparation for SAT and ACT exams. The program enables students to gain hands-on engineering laboratory experiences and, when possible, places students as research apprentices in engineering and science laboratories on campus.

Kenyon College (BA I)
Kenyon Summer Seminars
Grades served: HS   Schools served: 4   Year established: 1986
Location of schools served: NR   Type of schools served: PUB

Kenyon Summer Seminars are intensive three-week seminars that are an extension and reinforcement of the School-College Articulation Program (SCAP) designed to prepare promising, gifted, Ohio public school students, mostly from minority backgrounds, to enter a regular SCAP course at their schools and thus broaden their intellectual and cultural horizons. Seminars have two components: English/history, and mathematics/science. Students produce work for college faculty, participate in tutorials with college students, and live with both in the college dormitory. Faculty and tutors give help and support as needed.

The Ohio State University-Mansfield Campus (BA II)
Richland County Collaborative Integrated Preschool
Grades served: E   Schools served: 9   Year established: 1990
Location of schools served: NR   Type of schools served: NR

The Richland County Collaborative Integrated Preschool is a joint effort by the Ohio State University at Mansfield, nine local school districts, and many regional service agencies to provide an integrated preschool for the area that serves all children (disabled, at risk, typically developing) in a developmentally appropriate and exceptionality-appropriate learning environment. Originally funded by the Ohio Department of Education through a dropout prevention grant, the preschool also serves as a preservice education field experience site and as a model program for observation by early childhood educators.

Note: Each institution's Carnegie class is given in parentheses. **Key:** E=elementary school, HS=high school, M=middle school, NR=not reported, PRI=private, PUB=public, RU=rural, SU=suburban, UR=urban

Clackamas Community College (AA)
Vocational Options Program
Grades served: HS
Location of schools served: SU

Schools served: 11
Type of schools served: PUB

Year established: 1984

The Vocational Options Program is a partnership involving Clackamas Community College, the Private Industry Council, and local high schools designed to focus on 16- to 21-year-old youth who need a vocational training program (special education and high-risk youth usually exiting high school without a diploma or job skills). VOP students spend half the day in school and attend the program for the other half, moving from affective skills to individual work experience and job placement in a four-step program. Community college staff teach affective and crew skills. Contracts with the school districts regulate student referrals, and schools purchase slots for their students.

Reed College (BA I)
HHMI Summer Science Program for Under-Represented High School Students
Grades served: HS
Location of schools served: UR

Schools served: 2
Type of schools served: PUB

Year established: 1992

This program is specially designed to persuade underrepresented high school students to follow an education in mathematics, biology, physics, or chemistry. Twenty-five students from Grant High School spend two weeks on the Reed campus in courses taught by faculty from the mathematics, biology, and physics departments. The program, made possible by a grant from the Howard Hughes Medical Institute, attracts students with a variety of interests and achievement levels. Faculty make themselves informally available to the students throughout the school year to offer encouragement and information to students who are considering applying to college.

Edinboro University of Pennsylvania (MA I)
Partnership for Academic Progress
Grades served: HS
Location of schools served: UR

Schools served: 3
Type of schools served: PUB

Year established: 1989

Partnership for Academic Progress is designed to increase the number of university-bound minority students who are classified as economically disadvantaged. The partnership is a multifaceted program focusing on cognitive, emotional, social, educational, and career development needs of the participating students. Communication, mathematics, scientific reasoning, decision making, time and stress management, learning strategies and study skills, interpersonal relationships, critical thinking, and responsible citizenship skills are emphasized. The goal of the program is to create a support system for each student composed of volunteer mentors, counselors, parents, and Edinboro University faculty and students.

Pennsylvania State University-McKeesport Campus (AA)
PEPP (Penn State Educational Partnership Program)
Grades served: M, HS
Location of schools served: UR, SU

Schools served: 24
Type of schools served: NR

Year established: 1988

The primary foci of PEPP are to provide mentoring and tutorial assistance, academic survival skills, career awareness and educational enhancement opportunities. Field trips to Penn State campuses familiarize students with campus faculty, students, and facilities. Penn State students, acting as PEPP learning assistants at the PEPP Academy for middle school students and the PEPP Institute for high school students, offer tutoring. Summer experiential opportunity programs are sponsored by Penn State's Minority Teachers for the 21st Century (education), and Bridges to the Future (liberal arts). The program also works with parents and provides professional development workshops and seminars for teachers.

Reading Area Community College (AA)
Even Start Family Literacy Program

Grades served: E　　　　　　　　Schools served: 7　　　　　　Year established: 1989
Location of schools served: UR　　Type of schools served: PUB

The Even Start Family Literacy Program links Reading Area Community College and the Reading School District. The program is intended to increase the literacy and parenting skills of parents so that they can help their children succeed in school. The program has four major components: adult education, parenting education, early childhood education, and home visitations. Even Start builds on existing community services.

Slippery Rock University of Pennsylvania (MA I)
Head Start

Grades served: E　　　　　　　　Schools served: NR　　　　　Year established: NR
Location of schools served: NR　　Type of schools served: PUB

Head Start is an active working partnership between Slippery Rock University's Child Education Department and the local Head Start agency. Designed to enhance the quality of education for Head Start children, it provides a wide variety of activities developed and implemented by closely supervised university students and increases training opportunities for and knowledge base of Head Start staff. The program provides university students with a strong field experience. In addition, the university conducts an annual symposium, and the university's dance department provides a structured, scheduled movement program for children taught by university preservice dance education students.

Temple University (RES I)
Teaching Opportunities Program for Students (TOPS)

Grades served: HS　　　　　　　Schools served: 3　　　　　　Year established: 1987
Location of schools served: NR　　Type of schools served: PUB

TOPS is a three-year mentoring program that encourages minority students from Olney, Gratz, and Martin Luther King High Schools to consider teaching as a career. In their sophomore through senior years, students receive academic support and career exposure and participate in enrichment programs. Students who successfully complete the program and are accepted at Temple enroll in the five-year CAS/ED Extended Teacher Education program funded by Provident National Bank.

University of Pennsylvania (RES I)
Say Yes to Education

Grades served: NR　　　　　　　Schools served: NR　　　　　Year established: 1987
Location of schools served: UR　　Type of schools served: NR

Say Yes to Education is a cooperative program between the University of Pennsylvania and Belmont Elementary School designed to provide support and enrichment to help each child in 1987's sixth grade class toward graduation, to develop expanded career choices and an understanding of how to achieve them, and to promote active and responsible participation in learning and expanded ability to write and speak effectively. The program includes tutorial assistance from university student volunteers, sex and substance abuse education, personal contacts with students' families, summer programs, monthly informational meetings with parents, home visits, and career exploration field trips. Scholarships for successful high school graduates are provided by university trustees George and Diane Weiss.

Note: Each institution's Carnegie class is given in parentheses. **Key:** E=elementary school, HS=high school, M=middle school, NR=not reported, PRI=private, PUB=public, RU=rural, SU=suburban, UR=urban

Ursinus College (BA I)
Ursinus College Partnership Scholarships

Grades served: HS
Location of schools served: UR

Schools served: 22
Type of schools served: PUB

Year established: 1991

Five Philadelphia Collaborative Science Scholar awards, total grants equal to full tuition at Ursinus College, are given annually to students from the 22 participating high schools. In addition, 100% of demonstrated financial need beyond the full-tuition scholarship is met. All Scholars participate in the Ursinus College Bridge Program, a four-week program that includes a four-credit course, a study skills workshop, a computer workshop, and science research. The program also includes field trips, guest speakers, athletic activities, and discussions with faculty and alumni. All costs are covered in the award.

RHODE ISLAND

Brown University (RES I)
MEDAC Program

Grades served: HS
Location of schools served: UR

Schools served: 5
Type of schools served: PUB

Year established: 1992

MEDAC (Access to Medical Careers) is an early identification program to facilitate minorities' representation in biomedical education by linking and building on an existing base of high school and college programs encouraging students' interest in the sciences, particularly in the health professions. In partnership with Tougaloo College, the University of Rhode Island, Providence College, Rhode Island College, and public high schools in Providence, Brown University's School of Medicine proposes to expand and enhance its existing early identification network by identifying prospective candidates in middle school and preparing them academically and personally for careers in the health profession, particularly medicine, through a longitudinal program of instruction, motivational activities, counseling, and mentoring.

SOUTH CAROLINA

College of Charleston (MA I)
Project SEARCH (Selection, Enrichment, and Acceleration of Rural Children)

Grades served: E
Location of schools served: RU

Schools served: 3
Type of schools served: PUB

Year established: 1992

Project SEARCH (the Javits Program for Gifted & Talented) is a three-year collaboration among the South Carolina Department of Education, Charleston County School District, and the College of Charleston. It is designed to identify and serve potentially gifted children in grades K-3 from economically disadvantaged rural populations. Although the primary purpose of the project is to explore nontraditional methods of identifying potential, the project also includes a major teacher training component that supports program development for the identified children.

College of Charleston (MA I)
South Carolina Accelerated Schools Project

Grades served: E
Location of schools served: UR, SU

Schools served: 7
Type of schools served: PUB

Year established: 1991

The South Carolina Accelerated Schools Project is designed to do for all children what it currently does for the gifted and talented: provide stimulating, challenging, and relevant learning. The goals of the project are to bring decision making to the school level, create a unity of purpose among everyone in the school community, and build on the strengths of children, school staff, parents, and the community. The project works primarily with schools serving at-risk children to ensure that children are at or above grade level when they leave elementary school.

Lander University (MA II)
Summer Smart Program

Grades served: HS   Schools served: 1   Year established: 1989
Location of schools served: NR   Type of schools served: PUB

The Lander University Summer Smart Program provides a stimulating four-week preview of college life. The program is designed to admit graduating high school seniors who fall just below the university's admissions standards and to help them structure a strong and comprehensive base on which to build a successful career. Students participate in an academic program offering six hours of college credit, the opportunity to participate in leadership and team-building activities, educational games, debates, and informal get-togethers.

Midlands Technical College (AA)
JTPA School-to-College Articulation Agreement

Grades served: HS   Schools served: 1   Year established: 1993
Location of schools served: NR   Type of schools served: PUB

The Midlands Technical College-Richland Northeast High School JTPA School-to-College Articulation Agreement is a pilot program designed to facilitate the successful transition of low-income, unemployed youth through counseling, development of employability skills, and follow-up to support tech-prep and school-to-work initiatives for this at-risk population who qualify for job training services. As part of the initiatives, JTPA (Job Training Partnership Act) counselors working with students in the high school provide support and follow-up, in coordination with the college counselor, during the student's first year of college.

Technical College of the Lowcountry (AA)
TCL Black Male Mentor Program

Grades served: HS   Schools served: 4   Year established: 1990
Location of schools served: NR   Type of schools served: PUB

This program is a specialized self-development program for selected African-American males. In addition to school day and weekend activities, the program offers college incentives for students who successfully complete a college preparatory curriculum. The student, his mentor, and his parents work with college faculty, the community, churches, and high schools to develop a mentoring relationship to assist with academics and other problems and to begin to prepare the student for college.

Winthrop University (MA I)
WINGS (Winthrop's Involvement in Nurturing and Graduating Students)

Grades served: M   Schools served: 5   Year established: 1990
Location of schools served: SU   Type of schools served: PUB

WINGS is one component of Winthrop University's initiatives for at-risk students. Thirty-six sixth, seventh, and eighth grade male Rock Hill (SC) students identified by their guidance counselors as at risk of dropping out of school are brought to campus for special sessions on self-esteem, goal setting, and broadening horizons. Project staff, guidance counselors, Winthrop University students, parents, and teachers work together on the project. Every summer the students live on campus for three weeks for intensive work in English, math, Spanish, and African-American history.

Note: Each institution's Carnegie class is given in parentheses. **Key:** E=elementary school, HS=high school, M=middle school, NR=not reported, PRI=private, PUB=public, RU=rural, SU=suburban, UR=urban

Winthrop University (MA I)
Phone Friend

Grades served: E
Location of schools served: SU, RU

Schools served: 20
Type of schools served: PUB, PRI

Year established: 1984

Phone Friend is a component of Winthrop University's initiatives for at-risk students. It is an after-school talk line for elementary school children in York County. Students majoring in education are responsible for answering the phone daily from 2:30 to 5:30 PM. The college students gain valuable experience in empathic listening, and the children know that someone is always available to talk when their parents are not. Phone Friend is patterned after the program at Penn State and seeks to expand to other colleges and universities across South Carolina.

Winthrop University (MA I)
Child Abuse Awareness and Prevention Project

Grades served: E, M, HS
Location of schools served: UR, SU, RU

Schools served: NR
Type of schools served: PUB, PRI

Year established: 1985

This project is a component of Winthrop University's initiatives for at-risk students. Seventeen curriculum units and accompanying videotapes are provided to all of the school districts in South Carolina as well as to almost 30 independent and federal schools. Throughout the year, the office provides inservice programs, technical assistance, and assistance in curriculum development and presentations. Project representatives participate in two annual conferences, where materials are distributed and guest speakers deal with issues such as attention deficit disorder, drug abuse, and conflict resolution.

Winthrop University (MA I)
Governor's Remediation Initiative

Grades served: HS
Location of schools served: NR

Schools served: 69
Type of schools served: PUB

Year established: NR

The Governor's Remediation Initiative is a partnership linking Winthrop University and 69 public South Carolina high schools. The primary objective is to enhance the basic skills of 7,000 students in grades 8-12 who have scored below standard on state standardized tests. Winthrop provides a nine-day classroom-management training session each summer for teachers newly assigned to initiative classrooms. The students are placed in individualized prescriptive programs within the curriculum, which incorporates a combination of computer, whole class, and individual instruction. Program funding is provided by the state through the Job Training Partnership Act.

York Technical College (AA)
Learning Enhanced Achievement Program (LEAP)

Grades served: HS
Location of schools served: RU

Schools served: 12
Type of schools served: PUB

Year established: 1987

LEAP is designed to make educational opportunities accessible to students with learning disabilities who show the ability and motivation to succeed in a postsecondary course of study. The program offers participating students a range of services designed to assess individual learning needs and to provide reasonable educational accommodations, such as auxiliary aids, modified nondiscriminatory academic requirements, and appropriate evaluation methods. Through integrated program planning and evaluation, students increase self-awareness of their learning styles and develop effective strategies to fit them.

York Technical College (AA)
The Women's Center
Grades served: M, HS

Schools served: 20

Year established: 1987

Location of schools served: NR

Type of schools served: PUB

The Women's Center at York Technical College provides services to displaced homemakers, women who are single parents, those who have dropped out of school as a result of pregnancy, women in nontraditional fields of study, and others in transition. The center seeks to help women become self-sufficient by exploring training and job opportunities in the community, and support services needed for success in education and employment. Services include tuition and/or books, child care assistance, transportation allowance, career assessment, financial and personal counseling, special seminars, workshops, support groups, and job development.

SOUTH DAKOTA

South Dakota School of Mines and Technology (ENGR)
Scientific Knowledge for Indian Learning and Leadership (SKILL)
Grades served: E, M, HS

Schools served: 87

Year established: 1989

Location of schools served: SU, RU

Type of schools served: PUB, PRI

The SKILL program's mission is to develop and support academic training emphasizing mathematics, science, and engineering and thus enable minority students, principally American Indians, to enroll in and graduate from postsecondary institutions. SKILL provides enrichment activities to students beginning in the fourth grade and extending to college bridge programming. A major emphasis of the program has been residential summer academic programs for extremely rural American Indian students. SKILL supported 100 Family Math facilitators in sponsoring the American Indian Science and Engineering Society student chapter, which provided tutoring to area high school students.

TENNESSEE

Meharry Medical College (MED)
Summer Biomedical Sciences Program (SBSP)
Grades served: NR

Schools served: 1

Year established: 1969

Location of schools served: UR, SU, RU

Type of schools served: PUB, PRI

The SBSP began as an eight-week summer enrichment activity designed to increase the number of minority students, particularly African-Americans, who enter health professions. The major emphasis is on academic coursework: mathematics, biology, chemistry, and reading/study skills. Other activities include acquainting students with undergraduate and postgraduate medical curricula, requirements, financial aid information, and interactions with clinical faculty (hospital tours, emergency room visits, clinical seminars, faculty as role models, for example), helping to prepare students for the rigors of a health profession education.

Meharry Medical College (MED)
P.M. Scientists Program
Grades served: M

Schools served: 1

Year established: 1990

Location of schools served: NR

Type of schools served: PUB

The community-based P.M. Scientists Program focuses primarily on seventh graders at the Martin Luther King, Jr., Magnet School for Health Sciences and Engineering; it operates after regular school hours. Meharry faculty and graduate students present informal lectures each month on research directions within their respective departments and lead discussions on career opportunities in the sciences. These sessions are followed by hands-on scientific experiments and activities designed to enhance and challenge reasoning powers and to stimulate interest in science. Twenty-five students participate annually in the program.

Note: Each institution's Carnegie class is given in parentheses. **Key:** E=elementary school, HS=high school, M=middle school, NR=not reported, PRI=private, PUB=public, RU=rural, SU=suburban, UR=urban

Meharry Medical College (MED)
Science Motivation Program (SMP)

Grades served: M, HS   Schools served: 17   Year established: 1987
Location of schools served: UR, SU   Type of schools served: PUB, PRI

SMP is designed to provide participants six weeks of exposure to science role models and to cell and biomedical research laboratories. The program is designed for junior high and high school students and high school teachers. The goals for the program are to heighten students' awareness of research opportunities through strategic exposure to MRCE (Minority Research Center of Excellence) research programming and to increase the development of minority students who pursue research careers in science. Students develop an appreciation for basic sciences research and learn the value of scientific approaches to problem solving.

Meharry Medical College (MED)
Saturday Scientists Program

Grades served: HS   Schools served: 13   Year established: 1990
Location of schools served: NR   Type of schools served: PUB

The Saturday Scientists Program provides laboratory exposure for African-American high school students two Saturdays per month on the Meharry campus. Program features include mathematics and enrichment workshops coordinated by the Nashville chapter of The Links, Incorporated, and five basic science laboratory rotations. These monthly laboratory rotations use Meharry faculty and graduate students to conduct experiments illustrating aspects of the respective departments' research. Career awareness and exploration sessions are interwoven on both Saturdays. Twenty-five students participate annually in the program.

University of Memphis (DOC I)
Memphis Center for Urban Partnerships (MCUP)

Grades served: E, M, HS   Schools served: 8   Year established: 1992
Location of schools served: UR   Type of schools served: PUB

Memphis Center for Urban Partnerships is a Ford Foundation-sponsored National Center for Urban Partnerships projects. MCUP links the university, LeMoyne College, and Shelby State Community College with the Memphis City Schools to serve as a catalyst in providing access, resources, and opportunities for students to realize their potential and achieve success by increasing college preparedness, matriculation, retention, and graduation from postsecondary institutions. Activities include a computerized system for locating volunteers and other resources for K-12 schools, college and career awareness, college and K-12 student connections, summer institute for students, a collaborative academy for college and K-12 faculty, and mentoring programs.

TEXAS

Northeast Texas Community College (AA)
Communities in Schools/PASS (Positive Alternatives for SuccesS)

Grades served: E, M, HS   Schools served: 16   Year established: 1988
Location of schools served: SU, RU   Type of schools served: PUB

The Northeast Texas Communities in Schools is a dropout prevention program funded by federal, state, and local sources. Its primary mission is to assist the public schools in reducing dropouts and increasing retention of at-risk students. The program uses case management to provide academic enhancement, supportive guidance counseling, parental involvement, enrichment, health and social service agency referrals, and preemployment career training. In addition to placing case managers in the local schools as adjunct staff, the program operates an alternative high school, PASS, on the campus of Northeast Texas Community College as a dropout prevention and recovery program.

San Jacinto College (AA)
Middle School Math and Science Project [(MS)²]

Grades served: M, HS
Schools served: 20
Year established: 1992

Location of schools served: SU
Type of schools served: PUB

$(MS)^2$, a partnership between San Jacinto College and area middle schools, encourages students to take more courses in science, computer science, or mathematics and to pursue professional fields that require such strong backgrounds. Key personnel at the middle schools select eligible seventh grade minority students with some interest in these areas. Students engage in a five-year summer project at the college that provides hands-on involvement and experiences designed initially to instill knowledge and interest in science and mathematics and in later summers to improve their understanding of these areas.

Southwest Texas State University (MA I)
Spruce Cluster Partnership

Grades served: M, HS
Schools served: 14
Year established: 1991

Location of schools served: UR
Type of schools served: NR

The Spruce Cluster Partnership, a collaboration between Southwest Texas State University and the Dallas Independent School District, implements restructuring activities in a cluster of 14 schools. With the goals of increasing high school completion and student participation in postsecondary education, school programs are being redesigned within the context of local governance, collaborative professional interaction, shared decision making, increased parental involvement, and social support. The partnership facilitates students' transitions from elementary to junior high school and from junior high to high school. Additionally, it uses innovative curricula, operates school-based adolescent health clinics, and provides day care.

Southwest Texas State University (MA I)
Southwest Texas Summer Science Camp

Grades served: M
Schools served: 10
Year established: 1993

Location of schools served: RU
Type of schools served: PUB

Southwest Texas Summer Science Camp is a partnership linking the National Science Foundation, the university, and ten rural middle schools. Its primary missions are to offer minority middle school students (seventh graders) the opportunity to participate in a hands-on science program; meet successful minority scientists in industry and education; work with tutors, mentors, and counselors; and explore career opportunities in the sciences. The university will maintain contact with all participating students throughout their academic years.

St. Edward's University (MA II)
State Migrant Program

Grades served: HS
Schools served: 15
Year established: 1973

Location of schools served: RU
Type of schools served: NR

The State Migrant Program is geared to assist migrant secondary students in gaining academic credit and job experience in an eight-week summer residential program. Participants are selected from various areas of Texas in cooperation with private industry councils and the Texas Education Agency, which jointly fund the program. All participants must qualify as eligible migrants under TEA guidelines and meet certain other requirements for certification. Academic instruction in English and mathematics, a well-rounded health and physical education program, counseling and special remedial assistance for study skills are provided. Students work 15 hours per week in state or nonprofit agencies in the Austin area.

Note: Each institution's Carnegie class is given in parentheses. **Key:** E=elementary school, HS=high school, M=middle school, NR=not reported, PRI=private, PUB=public, RU=rural, SU=suburban, UR=urban

University of Texas at Dallas (DOC I)
Region 10 Consortium for Education of Homeless Children & Youth

Grades served: E, M, HS   Schools served: NR   Year established: 1988
Location of schools served: UR, SU   Type of schools served: PUB

This consortium is cosponsored by the University of Texas at Dallas, five school districts, and several shelters to provide tutoring before or after school, summer educational enrichment, parent training, enrollment and resource information, special cocurricular and extracurricular activities as appropriate, necessary transportation, school supplies, and apparel. A network of referral sources for health needs, awareness of domestic violence and its relationship to homeless students, and staff development are designed to make school personnel aware of and sensitive to the needs and rights of these homeless students.

University of Texas at Dallas (DOC I)
Hispanic Mother Daughter Program

Grades served: M, HS   Schools served: 14   Year established: 1991
Location of schools served: NR   Type of schools served: PUB

This program is a collaborative of four University of Texas System academic components and selected middle and high schools in the Dallas, Austin, San Antonio, and Rio Grande Valley areas. It is designed to increase high school completion and college enrollment rates. The program targets 50 female Hispanic eighth graders annually to provide academic assistance and family support through a series of meetings that provide a forum for leadership training, academic support, career exploration, development of self-esteem, family communication skills, goal setting, and health issues. The program monitors participants through high school graduation and into the first year of college.

University of Texas at San Antonio (MA I)
Texas Prefreshman Engineering Program (TexPREP)

Grades served: M, HS   Schools served: 400   Year established: 1979
Location of schools served: UR, SU, RU   Type of schools served: PUB, PRI

Texas PREP is an eight-week summer mathematics-based academic enrichment program designed to reinforce middle school and high school students in the pursuit of science or engineering careers. It emphasizes the development of abstract reasoning and problem-solving skills. Participants, most of whom come from low-income minority families, may return for a second and third summer. The high school graduation rate has been 100%, while the college graduation rate has been 80%. Fifty-nine (59) percent of the college graduates are engineering or science majors. The program is conducted in 11 Texas cities on 18 college campuses.

University of Texas Medical Branch at Galveston (MED)
Saturday Biomedical Sciences Forum

Grades served: E   Schools served: 10   Year established: 1983
Location of schools served: NR   Type of schools served: PUB

The Saturday Biomedical Sciences Forum was introduced to local fourth, fifth, and sixth graders to increase the number of underrepresented minorities and disadvantaged persons in health professions and to provide a vehicle to bridge the gap between the university and the community. Participants are given an opportunity to interact with health profession students and health care professionals, including physicians, basic medical scientists, nurses, physical therapists, and medical technicians. The students engage in simple but exciting activities, which include hands-on experiences in with elementary research procedures, equipment, and techniques used in the various health fields.

VERMONT

Middlebury College (BA I)
Dewitt Clinton High School/Middlebury College

Grades served: HS

Schools served: 1

Year established: 1989

Location of schools served: UR

Type of schools served: PUB

The Dewitt Clinton High School/Middlebury College Partnership links the Vermont college and a Bronx (NY) high school. The program involves visits of faculty and staff from the college to the high school to present information designed to familiarize students with the academic, admissions, and financial aid opportunities Middlebury offers. A field trip and winter term internship bring Middlebury students to Clinton High School, and faculty workshops and the Breadloaf Young Writers' Conference bring Clinton faculty and students to the college. Scholarship assistance allows Clinton faculty to attend Middlebury summer programs or to participate in a research assistanceship in science.

Vermont Technical College (AA)
Women In Technology (WIT) Project

Grades served: E, M, HS

Schools served: 450

Year established: 1986

Location of schools served: UR, SU, RU

Type of schools served: PUB, PRI

The WIT Project at Vermont Technical College is a partnership to encourage young women to study advanced math and science courses in high school and to pursue technical careers. Residential summer camps, a speakers bureau, and computer workshops provide a hands-on approach to show the relevance of math and science to technology professions, and expose students to women scientists, engineers, mathematicians, and technicians to discourage stereotyping and increase the sensitivity of students and teachers to the importance of gender equity. Grants fund the project, with little or no cost to participating girls.

VIRGINIA

George Mason University (DOC II)
Early Identification Program

Grades served: M, HS

Schools served: 17

Year established: 1987

Location of schools served: NR

Type of schools served: PUB

The Early Identification Program targets academically at-risk minority secondary school students who possess the ability to succeed in college. Students participate from grade 8-12 in a year-round program that combines leadership training, academic skills development, and special activities. A three-week summer academy on the university campus addresses writing and communication skills, mathematics, and lab sciences, and develops confidence as the students form life plans. Parental involvement, tutorial sessions, and continuous monitoring and counseling are stressed during the school year. Successful completion of the program and high school graduation guarantee admission to GMU.

Note: Each institution's Carnegie class is given in parentheses. **Key:** E=elementary school, HS=high school, M=middle school, NR=not reported, PRI=private, PUB=public, RU=rural, SU=suburban, UR=urban

J. Sargeant Reynolds Community College (AA)
Urban Community College Transfer Opportunities Program
Grades served: M, HS
Schools served: 7
Year established: 1984
Location of schools served: UR
Type of schools served: PUB

The Urban Community College Transfer Opportunities Program began at J. Sargeant Reynolds Community College as part of a national pilot project funded by the Ford Foundation to increase the number of minority students transferring from community colleges to senior institutions. The program includes a high school recruiting effort in which alumni serve as role models and speakers in the high schools they attended. Speakers emphasize the need to include college preparatory courses in students' schedules and provide information about financial aid. Specific counselors are designated to help parents and students complete admission and financial aid forms, and students are invited to tour the downtown campus.

WASHINGTON

University of Washington (RES I)
Washington MESA (Mathematics, Engineering, Science Achievement)
Grades served: M, HS
Schools served: 47
Year established: 1982
Location of schools served: UR, RU
Type of schools served: PUB

MESA's mission is to assist the state and the nation to achieve a citizenry who can compete globally and are individually competent in mathematics, engineering, and science. It seeks full participation of African-Americans, Hispanics, Native Americans, and women through a partnership of higher education, school districts, business and industry, community organizations, families, and alumni. MESA programs for students include the MESA Engineering Projects Class, integrated middle-level curriculum, study groups, summer enrichment and employment programs; field trips; tutoring; academic, college, and career advising; and scholarship incentive awards. In 1993-94 MESA provided classes for 3,289 Washington students.

WEST VIRGINIA

Marshall University (MA I)
Parent Involvement Program
Grades served: E
Schools served: 1
Year established: 1992
Location of schools served: RU
Type of schools served: PUB

Marshall University, Atenville Elementary School, and the Institute for Responsive Education are joined in a collaboration to develop a model of how parents, teachers, and community leaders can provide education in school and at home. Based on an African proverb — "It takes a village to [educate] a child" — this program has major implications for how schools and parents educate children and how colleges of education should prepare teachers to develop teacher/parent teams.

Marshall University (MA I)
External Diploma Program
Grades served: HS
Schools served: 1
Year established: 1993
Location of schools served: UR, RU
Type of schools served: PUB

Marshall University, Cabell County Schools, Steel of West Virginia, and the West Virginia State Department of Education are collaborating to establish a mechanism for adults (25 years or older) to obtain a high school diploma through an applied performance assessment process. The External Diploma Program is an alternative to the more traditional GED. Employees of Steel of West Virginia who do not have a high school diploma will participate in this pilot project at the Family Learning Center, located on the company's grounds, to develop postsecondary education opportunities using distance learning technologies and multiple centers. Plans are eventually to serve the entire West Virginia work force.

WISCONSIN

Mount Mary College (BA II)
A Healthy Head Start

Grades served: E	Schools served: 10	Year established: 1993
Location of schools served: UR	Type of schools served: PUB	

A Healthy Head Start is a partnership of the Milwaukee Area Health Education Center, health professions training programs at Mount Mary College, and the Head Start Program of the Social Development Commission of Milwaukee. The partnership enables Mount Mary College students enrolled in the dietetics, social work, and occupational therapy programs to gain clinical experience in culturally diverse Head Start programs, which benefit from students' services. To date these services have included leading classroom activities, writing newsletter articles, curriculum planning, and assessment of and advocacy for children and families at risk.

Saint Norbert College (BA II)
AISES-St. Norbert College American Indian Summer Math Camp

Grades served: M	Schools served: 25	Year established: 1989
Location of schools served: UR, SU, RU	Type of schools served PUB, PRI	

The AISES-St. Norbert College American Indian Summer Math Camp is a residential enrichment project for 30 eighth grade students from American Indian tribes throughout the United States. Activities at the camp include conducting experiments, making measurements, analyzing data, and working with computers. Students work closely with college faculty, local secondary school educators, and Native American mathematicians and scientists to integrate career exploration and problem-solving skills in classroom, laboratory, and field settings. Follow-up experiences include a project during the academic year with local teachers and college faculty mentors.

University of Wisconsin Centers (AA)
University Camp/Math-Science Project

Grades served: M, HS	Schools served: 5	Year established: 1987
Location of schools served: UR, SU	Type of schools served PUB, PRI	

University Camp was initiated to introduce minority students to college and to maintain contact with them through their high school years. Students selected have completed grades 5-8 and are identified by school counselors, principals, and teachers as potential college students. They attend a one-week summer program where college faculty introduce them to college academics, college students and graduates act as role models, and they are helped to develop confidence in their academic and career potential. Students come from Waukesha and Milwaukee schools.

University of Wisconsin-La Crosse (MA I)
Milwaukee South Division High School/College of HPER Partnership

Grades served: HS	Schools served: 1	Year established: 1989
Location of schools served: UR, RU	Type of schools served: PUB	

The College of Health, Physical Education, and Recreation at the University of Wisconsin-La Crosse and South Division High School are engaged in a formal partnership to narrow the gap between high school and college. The program is a natural link between the college's health, physical activity, and recreation programs and school district's career specialty in sports, health, and recreation management. Several formal activities are implemented each year to assist students with preparation for postsecondary education. The partnership assists the promotion of the University of Wisconsin's Design for Diversity and the Milwaukee Public Schools' goal of promoting postsecondary education.

Note: Each institution's Carnegie class is given in parentheses. **Key:** E=elementary school, HS=high school, M=middle school, NR=not reported, PRI=private, PUB=public, RU=rural, SU=suburban, UR=urban

Section Two
College Courses for High School Students

ARIZONA

Cochise College (AA)
Honors-Dual Credit Program

Grades served: HS	Schools served: 4	Year established: 1985
Location of schools served: NR	Type of schools served: PUB	

Cochise College's Honors-Dual Credit Program is a partnership linking the college and local Cochise County high schools. Its primary goal is to offer gifted high school students the opportunity to receive college credit for high school honors courses. The partnership allows the high school instructors to work with and become knowledgeable about the college, to become college certified, and sometimes to teach at night on the local campuses. Students become familiar with the registration process at the college, and they could go on to a local college or university with up to 15 transferable college credits already on their transcripts.

CALIFORNIA

American River College (AA)
American River College/Grant Union/San Juan Unified/Center Unified Articulation Council

Grades served: M, HS	Schools served: 30	Year established: 1988
Location of schools served: SU	Type of schools served: PUB	

This regional partnership links the community college and its three feeder high school districts. Its primary mission is to facilitate the flow of high school students to the college by offering college courses on high school campuses, developing Tech-Prep and 2+2 curricula, developing recruiting programs, offering summer academics for at-risk students, providing middle school tours, facilitating fund-raising, and promoting first-name relationships among K-12 and community college faculty, administrators, and staff.

California State University-Los Angeles (MA I)
College Credit Program

Grades served: HS	Schools served: 1	Year established: 1987
Location of schools served: UR	Type of schools served: PUB	

CSU-Los Angeles and the Los Angeles County High School for the Arts (LACHSA) jointly established the College Credit Program. Students enrolled in a course for both college and high school credit take a competency exam developed by CSU-LA and LACHSA faculty upon completion of the course. If students score above a predetermined level, they receive college credit. Some students have earned up to a year of college credit by the time they graduated from LACHSA.

Foothill College (AA)
Foothill Summer Youth College
Grades served: M, HS   Schools served: NR   Year established: 1984
Location of schools served: UR, SU, RU   Type of schools served: PUB, PRI

Foothill College invites able students from junior and senior high schools to attend college for summer enrichment. Students enroll in one or two academic classes and a sport. The college classes give the students experiences not available at their schools. Many of the classes are for the academically gifted, so students also enjoy the stimulation of bright, ambitious classmates. Instructors include selected, talented teachers from Foothill College, honors class teachers in public and private schools, and scientists from local industries and universities. All classes are part of the college curriculum and carry credit from the college. Most meet for two hours daily, Monday through Thursday, for six weeks.

DELAWARE

Delaware Technical and Community College Southern Campus (AA)
Academic Challenge Program
Grades served: M, HS   Schools served: 14   Year established: 1986
Location of schools served: UR, SU, RU   Type of schools served: PUB, PRI

Eight school systems with 14 schools are involved in the Academic Challenge Program, which is designed to nurture the scholastic and creative abilities of highly motivated, academically talented students in mathematics and English. The program provides a five-year accelerated program of instruction in mathematics and English, provides activities that enhance the academic experience, fosters independent learning, and provides a model that promotes the value of education in a changing society.

University of Delaware (RES II)
Summer College
Grades served: HS   Schools served: 15   Year established: 1984
Location of schools served: UR, SU, RU   Type of schools served: PUB, PRI

Summer College is a five-week residential program for academically advanced rising high school seniors. Students enroll in two courses, for which they can earn university credit. They live in supervised coed residence halls. Many recreational/social programs are planned, and the students learn time management. Summer College receives financial support from the Department of Public Instruction which subsidizes Delaware students. Each course is team-taught by a university faculty member and a Delaware high school teacher.

DISTRICT OF COLUMBIA

The American University (DOC I)
High School/College Internship Program (HI/SCIP)
Grades served: HS   Schools served: NR   Year established: 1987
Location of schools served: UR   Type of schools served: PUB

This program offers high school seniors the opportunity to maintain their high school status while enrolled part-time at the university. In addition to adjusting to college, many participants are advanced college freshmen by the time they graduate from high school. The university's Office of Multicultural Affairs provides orientation, academic counseling, and tutorial assistance for HI/SCIP participants.

Note: Each institution's Carnegie class is given in parentheses. **Key:** E=elementary school, HS=high school, M=middle school, NR=not reported, PRI=private, PUB=public, RU=rural, SU=suburban, UR=urban

George Washington University (RES II)
Anacostia High School College Bound Program
Grades served: HS

Schools served: 1

Year established: 1990

Location of schools served: UR

Type of schools served: PUB

Anacostia High School's College Bound Program assists students in making successful transitions from high school to college by teaching basic library research and guiding students through a process of applying these skills. In a university library, they collect and assess information and write a library-based research paper. University personnel work with the Anacostia librarian and faculty to develop a course-related program that students use while doing research for their English class. Instruction and transportation are provided by the high school.

FLORIDA

Barry University (MA I)
Barry Early Credit Program
Grades served: HS

Schools served: 12

Year established: 1980

Location of schools served: UR, SU

Type of schools served: PUB, PRI

The Barry Early Credit Program is a partnership linking the university and secondary schools. Its primary mission is to offer qualified high school students the opportunity to enroll in challenging university courses during their junior and senior years of high school. The program also provides the opportunity for the high school students to be part of the university's academic environment, participating in lectures and colloquia. The program provides inservice training for high school faculty and a forum for communication between faculty from the schools and the university.

Central Florida Community College (AA)
Legacies From Our Past: Florida Archaeology
Grades served: HS

Schools served: 10

Year established: 1993

Location of schools served: UR, SU, RU

Type of schools served: PUB, PRI

Legacies From Our Past was designed for Marion, Levy, and Citrus County students completing grades 8-11 with an interest in archaeology, history, social sciences, and the humanities. The program provides an overview of prehistoric Florida Indian art, religion, technology, and social organization, as well as the fundamentals of archeology and how this science contributed to the discovery and interpretation of the Florida Indian legacy. In 1993, students also were taught to create facsimiles to understand more about Native American technology and visited two major archaeological sites. The 1994 focus was on Florida's historic architecture.

Florida Atlantic University (DOC II)
FAU-Ely Partnership
Grades served: HS

Schools served: 1

Year established: 1988

Location of schools served: UR

Type of schools served: PUB

Ely is a magnet high school specializing in math and science education in Broward County. The high school's faculty and administration developed college-level courses to be taught by their teachers who qualify for adjunct status at FAU. Participating students receive college credit upon successful completion of a course. Tuition is waived, and books are supplied by the state of Florida. Earned credits can be used at most colleges and universities for advanced standing. Each year FAU offers one full four-year tuition-free scholarship to a qualified program graduate and six free graduate credits to participating teachers.

Lake-Sumter Community College (AA)
Dual Enrollment Program

Grades served: HS | Schools served: 12 | Year established: 1989
Location of schools served: SU, RU | Type of schools served: PUB, PRI

Dual Enrollment is an ongoing articulation program between Lake-Sumter Community College and the Lake and Sumter County School Districts. Its primary mission is to provide qualified high school students with opportunities for acceleration through enrollment in general education and occupational college courses. The program offers an early introduction to college life and studies at no cost to students. Dual Enrollment also provides an array of important links: direct liaison between high school and college faculty, placement testing and counseling services for high school students, and extensive input for curriculum development and review.

Ringling School of Art and Design (ART)
Pre-College Perspective

Grades served: HS | Schools served: NR | Year established: 1992
Location of schools served: UR, SU, RU | Type of schools served: PUB, PRI

Ringling School of Art and Design's Pre-College Perspective provides students with an intensive and exciting opportunity to experience learning at a professional art and design college. Students gain proficiency in visual and verbal vocabularies of art and design while learning a wide variety of techniques. All students participate in the major concentrations of Color and 2-D Design, Drawing and Life Studies, 3-D Design, and Art History. Other courses include The Computer as an Artistic Tool and a performance art workshop. Classes are taught by Ringling's degree-program faculty.

Rollins College (MA I)
Florida Interacademic Consortium (FLIC)

Grades served: HS | Schools served: 5 | Year established: 1988
Location of schools served: UR | Type of schools served: PUB

FLIC is a partnership offering college courses to secondary students and additional training to secondary teachers. The program is intended to improve the transition from high school to college, whereby qualified high school seniors and juniors are offered college courses for credit and access to the academic resources of the college to increase their academic confidence. Secondary teachers collaborate with college faculty in course development and content, teaching techniques, and evaluation through summer workshops and seminars during the academic year. FLIC courses are offered at participating schools under faculty supervision to ensure that collegiate standards are maintained.

Valencia Community College (AA)
Dual Enrollment

Grades served: HS | Schools served: 14 | Year established: NR
Location of schools served: SU | Type of schools served: PUB

Dual Enrollment is an articulation agreement mandated by the Florida State Legislature for county public schools and the community colleges. The plan makes possible time-shortened degrees, broadens the scope of curricular options for students, and permits greater depth of study in some subjects. Valencia and the county public schools jointly sponsor approved college credit courses for students before, during, and after normal school hours, and during the summer term when requested by the principal. Courses might include art, music, humanities, communications, mathematics, science, social sciences, foreign languages, theater/drama, or vocational studies. Dual Enrollment students earn dual credit.

Note: Each institution's Carnegie class is given in parentheses. **Key:** E=elementary school, HS=high school, M=middle school, NR=not reported, PRI=private, PUB=public, RU=rural, SU=suburban, UR=urban

GEORGIA

Augusta College (MA I)
Joint Enrollment
Grades served: HS

Schools served: 7

Year established: NR

Location of schools served: UR, SU, RU

Type of schools served: PUB, PRI

The Augusta College Joint Enrollment program is designed to give qualified high school students the opportunity to earn college credit before graduating from high school. Applicants must be at least juniors in good standing with regard to state College Preparatory Curriculum requirements and earn at least 1000 on the SAT. Recommendation from the student's high school guidance counselor or principal and permission from a parent or guardian are also required. Under Georgia's Post Secondary Options program, a qualified Joint Enrollment applicant enrolled in a public school can attend a Georgia public university at no charge for admission.

HAWAII

Hawaii Pacific University (MA I)
Collegiate Advanced Placement (CAP)
Grades served: HS

Schools served: 2

Year established: 1993

Location of schools served: NR

Type of schools served: PRI

CAP is a collaboration of Hawaii Pacific University, Hawaii's largest independent university, and St. Andrew's Priory School, a 127-year-old private school for girls. The primary mission of the program is to offer selected freshman-level courses at Hawaii Pacific University to qualified junior and senior students at St. Andrew's Priory School. In addition, the CAP program provides reduced tuition scholarships at the graduate level for St. Andrew's Priory teachers, and the two institutions share staff, facilities, and other resources.

ILLINOIS

Loyola University of Chicago (DOC I)
College Option Program (COP)
Grades served: HS

Schools served: 15

Year established: 1971

Location of schools served: UR, SU

Type of schools served: PUB, PRI

The College Option Program is a partnership linking the university with local secondary schools. Its primary mission is to offer qualified high school seniors the opportunity to enroll in challenging and enriching courses at Loyola University. These introductory-level courses are selected from a wide range of academic disciplines and are intended to expose students to fundamental concepts and lines of intellectual inquiry, while enabling them to earn college credit. The courses also introduce students to college life: types of assignments, campus resources, and student/faculty relationships.

Western Illinois University (MA I)
Satellite-Delivered Interactive AP Calculus
Grades served: HS

Schools served: 38

Year established: 1992

Location of schools served: UR, SU, RU

Type of schools served: PUB

Advanced Placement Calculus is broadcast live via satellite in a one-way video, two-way audio format five times each week from the campus of WIU to downlink sites throughout the United States belonging to the TI-IN Satellite Network. Students can call in from their home school to the broadcast center to ask questions or to get help.

Indiana University at Bloomington (RES I)
Advance College Project (ACP)

Grades served: HS	Schools served: 48	Year established: 1981
Location of schools served: UR, SU, RU	Type of schools served: PUB	

The Indiana University Advance College Project is a cooperative program of Indiana University and selected high schools within Indiana. The project offers dual credit to high school seniors who enroll in IU courses offered as part of their high school curriculum. The ACP high school instructors enjoy a collegial relationship with university faculty members, which includes summer seminars, inservice training, and visitations. The courses taught by each participating high school are determined by that school's curricular needs. The courses are appropriate for the top 20% of students, although they are not limited to that population.

University of Evansville (MA I)
University of Evansville-Evansville Day School Alliance

Grades served: HS	Schools served: 1	Year established: 1993
Location of schools served: UR, SU	Type of schools served: PRI	

This alliance offers junior and senior students the opportunity to take college-level courses in a variety of fields. Special emphasis is given to the lesser-taught foreign languages and to advanced courses in French and Spanish. Students may also take college algebra and certain literature and interdisciplinary courses. The alliance also gives students access to the university library and to special international events. During the summer, HS students may take advantage of the university's campus in England, Harlaxton College. Appropriate courses may be applied for credit toward a degree at the University of Evansville.

Ellsworth Community College (AA)
Postsecondary Enrollment Act

Grades served: HS	Schools served: NR	Year established: 1987
Location of schools served: NR	Type of schools served: PUB	

The Postsecondary Enrollment Act permits students in grades 9-12 who have been identified by district criteria as gifted and/or talented to enroll in postsecondary institutions and take college courses under strictly defined conditions and limitations. School districts are responsible for informing their populations of eligibility and conditions under which they may enroll in part-time college study.

Johnson County Community College (AA)
College Now

Grades served: HS	Schools served: 19	Year established: 1984
Location of schools served: SU, RU	Type of schools served: PUB, PRI	

College Now is a dual-enrollment program in which high school students enrolled in selected junior- or senior-level honors or advanced placement classes can also earn college credit. Courses that follow the college's content, objectives, and assignments are taught on the high school campus by qualified high school teachers. The college regularly conducts follow-up studies of College Now graduates.

Bellarmine College (MA I)
ACCP (Advanced College Credit Program)

Grades served: HS
Location of schools served: UR, SU, RU

Schools served: 30
Type of schools served: PUB, PRI

Year established: 1971

Bellarmine College's Advanced College Credit Program is a dual-credit program for Louisville-area private and public high schools uniting the area's best young scholars, exemplary high school teachers, and college faculty. High school juniors and seniors meeting the program's rigorous academic admissions standards qualify to earn college credit for advanced courses taught by high school teachers who meet or exceed the minimum requirements for college faculty. Full-time Bellarmine faculty coordinators work with their school colleagues to maintain the program's academic quality and integrity. Courses and instructors are regularly evaluated.

University of Louisville (DOC I)
College School Cooperative Program

Grades served: HS
Location of schools served: UR, SU

Schools served: 22
Type of schools served: PUB

Year established: 1983

The College-School Cooperative Program links the College of Arts and Sciences at the University of Louisville with the 22 high schools of local Jefferson County Public Schools. By offering special sections of freshman-level courses, the program gives qualified high school students the opportunity to work with college faculty, experience the demands of college writing and research, use the university library and other facilities, and earn college credit. College faculty teach the courses as off-campus sections, collaborating with high school teachers.

University of Louisville (DOC I)
International Academy

Grades served: HS
Location of schools served: UR, SU, RU

Schools served: 35
Type of schools served: PUB, PRI

Year established: 1987

The International Academy at the University of Louisville's College of Arts and Sciences offers high schools students the opportunity to explore world cultures and international affairs. Students attend a five-week seminar on anthropology and cultural diversity and may elect enrollment in college courses on world history and governments, religions, literature, art, music, philosophy, and languages. Field trips to cultural centers, films, and lectures by faculty and community leaders supplement instruction. Students also spend a day with a career diplomat from the U.S. Department of State to discuss cultural affairs, foreign policy, and issues relating to careers in international business and law and the foreign service.

Harford Community College (AA)
ELI Project (Extended Learning Initiative)

Grades served: HS
Location of schools served: SU

Schools served: 4
Type of schools served: PUB

Year established: 1993

The ELI Project is a partnership linking Harford Community College and secondary schools in Harford County through programming that uses commercial cable. Its primary mission is to offer qualified high school students the opportunity to enroll in higher-level mathematics courses not available in the individual high schools. Students may earn dual credit, acquiring college credit while meeting the mathematics course requirements for high school graduation.

St. Mary's College of Maryland (BA I)
Charlotte Hall Fellows Program

Grades served: HS

Location of schools served: RU

Schools served: 4

Type of schools served: PUB

Year established: 1979

The Charlotte Hall Fellows Program provides distinguished high school students an opportunity to explore a liberal arts education while completing their secondary education. Chosen competitively on the basis of excellent academic performance, teachers' recommendations, and promise of success in college. Fellows are fully integrated into academic life at St. Mary's. The experience is intended to motivate the students chosen as Fellows to further develop their intellectual potential, thus enhancing their chances for academic success when they matriculate in the colleges of their choice.

MINNESOTA

Austin Community College (AA)
11th and 12th Grade Enrollment Program

Grades served: HS

Location of schools served: UR, SU, RU

Schools served: NR

Type of schools served: PUB

Year established: 1985

Minnesota law permits any 11th or 12th grade student to attend any public or private postsecondary institution in the state, full or part time, with free tuition and books and the opportunity to earn both high school and college credit. School foundation aid is apportioned accordingly. The program provides more options for high school students, broadens and supplements course offerings available in rural districts, and encourages the school districts to consider expanding their regular offerings. Approximately 3% of Minnesota high school juniors and seniors participate in the program.

Rochester Community College (AA)
Post Secondary Enrollment Options Program

Grades served: HS

Location of schools served: UR, SU, RU

Schools served: 20

Type of schools served: PUB

Year established: 1985

This program allows high school juniors and seniors to take full- or part-time courses at a liberal arts college, community college, technical college, or university for high school credit. The program provides students with a greater variety of class offerings and the opportunity to pursue challenging college coursework. Tuition, fees, and required textbooks are at no cost to eligible students. Any Minnesota public high school student classified as a junior with a 3.0 grade point average or senior with a 2.5 grade point average may enroll in a combination of high school and college nonsectarian courses equivalent to a full-time student schedule.

St. Cloud State University (MA I)
Postsecondary Option Program

Grades served: HS

Location of schools served: NR

Schools served: 6

Type of schools served: PUB

Year established: 1988

The Postsecondary Option Program is a statewide effort allowing high school students to take college courses during their junior and senior years; most students who have taken advantage of it have been in schools near colleges or universities. St. Cloud's program, however, makes the program accessible to rural students by connecting its classrooms to rural schools via two-way television. With more than 30 high schools within the range of the university and with networks expanding, this option increasingly will become available to more of the state's high schools.

Note: Each institution's Carnegie class is given in parentheses. **Key:** E=elementary school, HS=high school, M=middle school, NR=not reported, PRI=private, PUB=public, RU=rural, SU=suburban, UR=urban

University of Minnesota-Duluth (MA I)
Postsecondary Enrollment Options Act
Grades served: HS   Schools served: NR   Year established: 1985
Location of schools served: NR   Type of schools served: PUB

Minnesota's Postsecondary Enrollment Options Act allows advanced high school students the opportunity to attend college classes to fulfill high school requirements and get a head start on their college curriculum. Students may attend the college part time and continue with courses at their high school, or they may attend the college full time. At the University of Minnesota-Duluth, Continuing Education and Extension is the point of entry for students in the top 20% of their class with recommendations from their high school counselor and principal. Students receive both high school and college credits.

MISSOURI

University of Missouri-St. Louis (DOC I)
Advanced Credit Program
Grades served: HS   Schools served: 46   Year established: 1986
Location of schools served: UR, SU, RU   Type of schools served: PUB, PRI

The Advanced Credit Program provides enrichment for university-bound high school students who demonstrate an ability to benefit from enrollment in courses offered in their high schools for college credit. The program also creates and strengthens links between the university and regional high schools. Important benefits are professional development scholarships for teachers and adjunct faculty, student scholarships, and on-campus privileges, including access to the four-campus library system. University faculty work closely with the teachers to ensure instruction is comparable to that on campus.

NEBRASKA

Peru State College (BA II)
Early Entry
Grades served: HS   Schools served: 10   Year established: 1980
Location of schools served: UR, RU   Type of schools served: PUB

This program, offered in cooperation with area high schools, is designed to enrich the curriculum offerings available at the high schools. It now includes ten high schools with approximately 150 students. Courses include English composition, chemistry, precalculus, and calculus taught by high school faculty who meet the qualifications of the respective campus division. Enrolled students and their instructors visit the college campus once during the semester to attend a college section of the same course. A college pass provides entry to campus activities.

NEW MEXICO

Clovis Community College (AA)
Eastern Plains Instructional Television Cooperative
Grades served: HS   Schools served: 9   Year established: 1991
Location of schools served: RU   Type of schools served: PUB

The Eastern Plains Instructional Television Cooperative serves communities of 2,500 or fewer people, with Clovis Community College providing concurrent enrollment classes for high school students and general college classes for community members on the two-way interactive TV system. Initial equipment was provided by the Eastern New Mexico Rural Telephone Cooperative, which has continued to provide transmission facilities without charge during the project's pilot phase. The system is also used for inservice education courses for rural teachers and by the New Mexico Department of Labor to provide intake services and job training to rural clients.

NEW YORK

Cayuga County Community College (AA)
Cayuga Secondary Linkage

Grades served: HS	Schools served: 14	Year established: 1978
Location of schools served: SU, RU	Type of schools served: PUB	

The Cayuga Secondary Linkage was forged in the 1970s to provide eligible high school students the opportunity to earn college credit for selected college-level courses taught in their high schools. The program provides the opportunity to undertake advanced work in English, history, mathematics, and science. Courses are taught either by full-time Cayuga faculty or secondary school instructors who meet the requirements for appointment as Cayuga adjunct faculty. Frequent contact between Cayuga's division chairs and high school faculty; review of course outlines, assignments, tests, and texts; and a collegial and open approach to issues and concerns maintain the quality and success of the program.

City University of New York Bernard M. Baruch College (MA I)
Academy of Finance

Grades served: HS	Schools served: 10	Year established: 1985
Location of schools served: UR	Type of schools served: PUB	

Baruch College collaborates with the Academy of Finance, a National Academy Foundation partnership program in finance education. The Academy is a college preparatory program that exposes students to the study of finance as an academic discipline. Seniors in Academy schools take a tuition-free course in principles of finance at Baruch College, and students enrolled in the High School of Economics and Finance have the option of taking three additional courses at the Baruch satellite established at the high school. The college provides free use of its facilities for major conferences and weekly seminars.

City University of New York Borough of Manhattan Community College (AA)
Distance Learning Project

Grades served: HS	Schools served: 3	Year established: 1993
Location of schools served: UR	Type of schools served: PUB	

The Distance Learning Project is offered in cooperation with three New York City high schools: Humanities, Washington Irving, and Sarah J. Hale. It is designed to bridge the social and psychological distances separating inner-city youth from their more affluent contemporaries. Through the interactive capabilities of the Distance Learning Network, students in the three schools are able to see and talk with each other and engage in fully interactive dialogues for learning. Students participate in a college-level course in critical thinking, for example, offered through the BMCC Social Science Department. The program serves 60 students each semester.

City University of New York John Jay College of Criminal Justice (OTHER)
ASCENT (Advanced Standing for College Entrants)

Grades served: HS	Schools served: NR	Year established: 1976
Location of schools served: NR	Type of schools served: PUB, PRI	

ASCENT is a special project of John Jay College of Criminal Justice, approved and endorsed by the New York City Board of Education. The program offers high school juniors and seniors the opportunity to experience college classes and student life by taking courses at John Jay College after school. Full college credit is awarded for all successfully completed courses. Students have access to the college's clubs, interest groups, and sports events. They may use campus facilities, such as the library, bookstore, fitness center, athletic facilities, and cafeteria.

Note: Each institution's Carnegie class is given in parentheses. **Key:** E=elementary school, HS=high school, M=middle school, NR=not reported, PRI=private, PUB=public, RU=rural, SU=suburban, UR=urban

City University of New York Kingsborough Community College (AA)
College Now Program
Grades served: HS   Schools served: 17   Year established: 1984
Location of schools served: UR   Type of schools served: PUB

The purpose of College Now is to help high school seniors, especially those whose GPAs identify them as moderate achievers, to make a smooth transition to college. Serving more than 4,000 students annually, the program offers college-level instruction to precollege students, provides skills assessment and remediation where needed, holds freshman orientation seminars, and offers academic counseling. In 1992 the U.S. Department of Education cited the program as an exemplary partnership.

Cornell University (RES I)
Cornell University Summer College
Grades served: HS   Schools served: 605   Year established: 1961
Location of schools served: UR, SU, RU   Type of schools served: PUB, PRI

Summer College introduces academically talented high school juniors and seniors to the challenges of university study as a way of easing their transition into college. Students enroll in college courses with undergraduates and are able to earn college credit that can later be applied to an undergraduate degree. Summer College offers workshops in math, writing, and study skills, and the college admissions process. Students also enroll in one of 13 specially designed noncredit career exploration seminars that give a comprehensive look at a professional or academic field.

Genesee Community College (AA)
Genesee Community College Enrichment Program
Grades served: HS   Schools served: 21   Year established: 1990
Location of schools served: SU, RU   Type of schools served: PUB, PRI

This partnership provides high school students the opportunity to earn college credits while in high school. CEP benefits students by offering more challenging courses in high school, eliminating duplication of course work, saving money, developing self-confidence, and enabling them to enter college at an advanced level. The program fosters communication between the college and high school and enables high school instructors to participate in the college's professional staff development activities.

Long Island University-Brooklyn Campus (MA I)
Bridge Programs
Grades served: HS   Schools served: 2530   Year established: 1981
Location of schools served: UR   Type of schools served: PUB, PRI

Designed to help students make responsible educational choices, Bridge Programs operate out of the university's Honors Program. The Senior Bridge Program allows high school seniors with averages above 90 to take regular introductory courses, tuition-free. The College Project is designed to expose high-achieving, college-bound juniors to critical thinking and differences among disciplines in their approach to critical analysis through weekly seminars with college faculty. Successful students are encouraged to take college courses at LIU during their senior year. A summer program (BASIS), directed toward relatively unmotivated juniors, operates in cooperation with the New York City Board of Education; it selects 16 students each summer for a program that produces a communications project.

Long Island University-C.W. Post Campus (MA I)
SCALE (Secondary Collegiate Articulated Learning Experience)

Grades served: HS

Schools served: 35

Year established: 1974

Location of schools served: SU

Type of schools served: PUB, PRI

This program provides qualified high school students the opportunity to earn college credit for courses taken at their high schools. The program provides qualified students with the opportunity to accelerate their academic pursuits and enriches instruction in the secondary school. C.W. Post's faculty work directly with participating high school faculty as mentors and with the students directly. Students accepted in the SCALE program are considered fully matriculated students and have full use of the campus facilities.

Long Island University-Southampton Campus (MA II)
Accelerated College Entry (ACE)

Grades served: HS

Schools served: 40

Year established: 1982

Location of schools served: SU, RU

Type of schools served: PUB

ACE is a partnership between the Southhampton Campus of Long Island University and a network of secondary schools in the region. University-level freshman courses are offered to qualified high school students in their junior and senior years in high school. Syllabi, textbooks, and examinations are developed jointly by campus faculty and their colleagues in the high schools. Courses are reviewed by campus faculty visiting the high schools, and class visits to the campus are encouraged. Successful students earn college credits for their courses.

Rochester Institute of Technology (MA I)
Key Program

Grades served: HS

Schools served: 2

Year established: 1988

Location of schools served: RU

Type of schools served: PUB

RIT's Key Program is a distance learning partnership allowing rural high school students to take six first-year college courses for college credit or enrichment from their schools. RIT professors offer courses in American politics, economics, communications, literature, and calculus via a variety of distance learning technologies, including live two-way audiographic conferences, computer conferencing, electronic mail, and on-line research via the Internet. Students are supported locally by mentor teachers at their schools.

St. Lawrence University (BA I)
Modern Language Collaborative

Grades served: HS

Schools served: 4

Year established: 1992

Location of schools served: RU

Type of schools served: PUB

The goal of the Modern Language Collaborative is promoting excellence in the teaching and study of Spanish in secondary schools. The Spanish V syllabus was developed jointly by participating secondary school teachers and Spanish staff from St. Lawrence University. Teachers participate in campus seminars four times a year, while students gather at St. Lawrence once a year for a day of immersion activities. The project publishes a collection of student writing. Students taking the course can receive credit for the equivalent university class, and a St. Lawrence transcript is issued at the end of the year.

Note: Each institution's Carnegie class is given in parentheses. **Key:** E=elementary school, HS=high school, M=middle school, NR=not reported, PRI=private, PUB=public, RU=rural, SU=suburban, UR=urban

State University of New York at Albany (RES II)
University in the High School Program
Grades served: HS
Location of schools served: UR, SU, RU

Schools served: 70
Type of schools served: PUB, PRI

Year established: 1983

The University in the High School Program annually serves more than 2,200 students. Students earn college credit while they study art, biology, English, Spanish, mathematics, and other subjects offered by 12 SUNY at Albany departments in their own schools and with their own teachers. For each year-long, three-credit course, students receive temporary identification cards giving them university student privileges. Teachers are given adjunct appointments and receive a tuition waiver for a graduate course at Albany.

Syracuse University (RES II)
Project Advance®
Grades served: HS
Location of schools served: UR, SU, RU

Schools served: 102
Type of schools served: PUB, PRI

Year established: 1973

This partnership's primary mission is to offer qualified high school students the opportunity to enroll in challenging Syracuse University freshman courses during their senior year of high school. It also provides several other important services in working with the high schools: inservice training for high school instructors, a continuing forum for communication between educators from both school and university settings, and extensive research and evaluation to improve instruction systematically.

OHIO

Case Western Reserve University (RES I)
Pre-College Scholars Program
Grades served: HS
Location of schools served: UR, SU

Schools served: NR
Type of schools served: PUB, PRI

Year established: 1992

This program is designed to give highly motivated and able secondary school students the opportunity to enroll in challenging college courses during the junior or senior year of high school. Pre-College Scholars attend regularly scheduled classes with CWRU undergraduates and must be able to work well independently at the college level. Students enrolling independently as Pre-College Scholars are charged regular part-time tuition. Students enrolling under the Post-Secondary Enrollment Options program (Ohio Senate Bill 140) are not charged tuition.

Kenyon College (BA I)
School-College Articulation Program (SCAP)
Grades served: HS
Location of schools served: UR, SU, RU

Schools served: 13
Type of schools served: PUB, PRI

Year established: 1979

SCAP is an early college program through which a number of central and northern Ohio public and independent secondary schools offer selected Kenyon College freshman courses on their own campuses for credit at Kenyon. Course standards are maintained by the college's control of appointments. Departmental representatives from the college visit the classes in the schools, course materials and methods are developed jointly by college and high school faculty, and students' work is cross-graded. The courses are open to juniors and seniors approved by the college.

OREGON

Portland State University (DOC II)
LINK Program

Grades served: M, HS   Schools served: 8   Year established: 1990
Location of schools served: NR   Type of schools served: PUB, PRI

The LINK Program is a partnership between the university and secondary schools in the greater Portland metropolitan area that makes it possible for selected gifted students to attend the university for part-time advanced study in a particular academic discipline. LINK also provides other partnership services: creating and enhancing articulation between participating schools and the university, providing a workable link with higher education for students who have exhausted advanced mastery courses in their high schools, and laying a foundation on which to build increased collegial relationships between secondary and university educators.

Portland State University (DOC II)
Challenge Program

Grades served: HS   Schools served: 16   Year established: 1976
Location of schools served: UR, SU, RU   Type of schools served: PUB, PRI

A partnership between the university and high schools in the greater Portland metropolitan area, the Challenge Program gives qualified high school students an option to enroll in freshman-level college courses during their senior year of high school. The program also provides a forum for continuing collaboration between the university and secondary school programs. Challenge instructors and campus departmental faculty participate together in curriculum workshops and seminars during the fall and spring semesters each academic year, and faculty from both schools and the university have a well-established ongoing link through which they share information.

Reed College (BA I)
Young Scholars

Grades served: HS   Schools served: 15   Year established: 1980
Location of schools served: UR, SU Type of schools served: PUB, PRI

The Young Scholars program permits gifted high school seniors to enroll in Reed College courses in mathematics, biology, physics, chemistry, foreign languages, and the humanities while they are completing their final year of high school. In addition, Reed faculty offer special one-day programs exclusively for high school students. This program, supported by private donors and the Portland Public Schools, was developed to meet the needs of students who have exhausted curricular options at their high schools.

PENNSYLVANIA

Thiel College (BA II)
Thiel Scholars Program

Grades served: HS   Schools served: 14   Year established: 1986
Location of schools served: SU, RU Type of schools served: PUB

This program provides the opportunity for outstanding juniors and seniors from area high schools to take college courses for credit, before high school graduation, at a substantially reduced tuition rate. The students not only benefit from the head start on their college education but are afforded all the privileges of part-time students, including full access to the library, computer labs, athletic facilities, and cultural events. They are expected to fulfill the same class requirements as full-time students.

Note: Each institution's Carnegie class is given in parentheses. **Key:** E=elementary school, HS=high school, M=middle school, NR=not reported, PRI=private, PUB=public, RU=rural, SU=suburban, UR=urban

University of Pittsburgh (RES I)
College in High School
Grades served: HS

Location of schools served: UR, SU, RU

Schools served: 78

Type of schools served: PUB, PRI

Year established: 1981

The University of Pittsburgh offers qualified high school students the opportunity to take eight different courses through the College in High School (CHS) program. Modeled after Syracuse University's Project Advance®, courses in mathematics, chemistry, computer science, communications, and statistics are given at the high school by high school teachers, who are qualified instructors for the university. Students complete a registration packet, pay a fraction of the normal tuition, and earn regular college credit upon successful completion of a course.

Wilkes University (MA I)
Wilkes Young Scholars Program
Grades served: HS

Location of schools served: UR, SU, RU

Schools served: 24

Type of schools served: PUB, PRI

Year established: 1986

This partnership between Wilkes University and 24 secondary schools in Luzerne County provides an opportunity for gifted juniors and seniors to take courses at the university at nominal cost. Students in the top 10% of their classes may be nominated by their school principal or guidance counselor. Wilkes Young Scholars are granted full library privileges and may participate in various cultural activities at the university. About 90 students in the area participate each semester.

SOUTH DAKOTA

South Dakota State University (MA I)
Teaching Russian in Rural America
Grades served: HS

Location of schools served: RU

Schools served: 4

Type of schools served: PUB

Year established: 1993

South Dakota State University's Television Through the Rural Development Television Network project offers high school students the opportunity to study a less commonly taught language while receiving college credit. Students are juniors or seniors, although qualified sophomores may also be accepted. The Russian language project is also being used to show that language learning via interactive television can be personalized, stimulating, and challenging.

TENNESSEE

King College (BA II)
Howard Hughes Medical Institute High School Science Scholars Program
Grades served: HS

Location of schools served: UR, SU, RU

Schools served: NR

Type of schools served: PUB, PRI

Year established: 1992

This program is a summer institute designed to attract capable students to research and teaching careers in medicine and biological sciences and to encourage more minority students and women to pursue these careers. The central focus of the four-week program is a course taken for college credit. The 25 participants are divided among three introductory laboratory courses. Special seminars, demonstrations, and visits to area laboratories are included.

University of the South (BA I)
Sewanee Summer Scholars Program

Grades served: E, M, HS   Schools served: 4   Year established: NR
Location of schools served: NR   Type of schools served: PUB, PRI

Designed to develop and promote learning skills in African-American students, this program is a cooperative venture linking the University of the South, Chattanooga City, and the Franklin County School Systems. Its focus is on oral and written English, mathematics, study and test-taking skills, and motivating interest in the sciences. The program provides full scholarships, textbooks, and a stipend for a four-week summer program for rising sophomores, juniors, and seniors. The university provides tutoring and mentoring, emphasizing the development of students' personal confidence in their ability to succeed in postsecondary education.

UTAH

Salt Lake Community College (AA)
Concurrent Enrollment

Grades served: HS   Schools served: 18   Year established: 1989
Location of schools served: NR   Type of schools served: PUB

Concurrent Enrollment offers challenging, high-quality college-level classes to high school juniors and seniors for high school and college credit. Both vocational and general education courses are offered, and students attend concurrent classes on the high school or college campus. Teachers may be college faculty or high school teachers who meet the college requirements for adjunct faculty, and students are dually enrolled in high school and college. High school teachers use the same syllabi, textbooks, and exams as the college faculty. Regular college credit earned is recorded on a college transcript.

Salt Lake Community College (AA)
Applied Technology Center for Secondary Students

Grades served: HS   Schools served: 31   Year established: 1992
Location of schools served: NR   Type of schools served: PUB, PRI

The Applied Technology Center for Secondary Students is a partnership linking Salt Lake Community College with five local school districts. Its primary mission is to offer high school juniors and seniors an opportunity to begin preparing for work in specific applied technology disciplines. Courses are offered at numerous instructional sites in a two-county area.

VIRGINIA

Mary Baldwin College (BA II)
Program for the Exceptionally Gifted (PEG)

Grades served: HS   Schools served: NR   Year established: 1985
Location of schools served: UR, SU, RU   Type of schools served: PUB, PRI

PEG is a residential program offering motivated students the opportunity to begin college one to four years early. Students who enroll as rising high school freshmen take a combination of high school and college courses and live in a supervised residence hall, where they receive the support necessary to adjust to college. By their second year, these students receive full-time college status. Students enrolling as rising sophomores, juniors, or seniors are generally exempt from the high school curriculum and begin as full-time college students. Age-appropriate activities are planned around students' interests. When they are ready, PEG students live independently on campus.

Note: Each institution's Carnegie class is given in parentheses. **Key:** E=elementary school, HS=high school, M=middle school, NR=not reported, PRI=private, PUB=public, RU=rural, SU=suburban, UR=urban

Seattle University (DOC II)
Matteo Ricci College Consortium

Grades served: HS   Schools served: 3   Year established: 1988
Location of schools served: UR, SU   Type of schools served: PRI

The Matteo Ricci College Consortium is a loose federation of several Catholic high schools and the nearby Matteo Ricci College at Seattle University. The consortium features jointly developed, school-specific, senior-year curricula that generate ten quarter credits from Seattle University and open MRC/SU to graduates of these schools. They join students entering from Seattle Preparatory School, cofounder of the program and the normal point of entry. Students from all participating high schools who complete the three-year MRC/SU program earn the Bachelor of Arts in Humanities. Cross-level collaboration focuses on mutually rewarding activities in faculty development and curriculum improvement.

University of Charleston (MA II)
Community Alliance to Support Education (CASE)

Grades served: HS   Schools served: 1   Year established: 1987
Location of schools served: RU   Type of schools served: PUB

CASE addresses the demographic and academic needs of Herbert Hoover High School. The program includes the opportunity to take accredited college courses in the high school, the use of the college library and Multimedia Educational Technology Center, one-on-one tutoring in mathematics and English, and a shadowing program for high school students to attend classes with a college student, visit dormitories, and tour the campus. At-risk students similarly spend time with staff, learning about alternatives for those not academically motivated. Teachers have access to the college athletic facilities as well.

Marian College of Fond Du Lac (MA II)
Post Secondary Enrollment Options (PSEO)

Grades served: HS   Schools served: NR   Year established: 1993
Location of schools served: UR   Type of schools served: PUB

The PSEO program provides public school students in the 11th or 12th grade the opportunity to enroll and take classes at approved institutions of higher education in the state. The program is administered jointly by the college and by the student's school board. Prospective students apply for admission to Marian College as special, part-time students. After being accepted, they take courses on the college campus with the approval and support of their local school boards. The school board pays tuition fees at established rates for courses approved for high school or high school/college dual credit.

Saint Norbert College (BA II)
St. Norbert College Credit Program

Grades served: HS   Schools served: 11   Year established: 1962
Location of schools served: SU   Type of schools served: PUB, PRI

St. Norbert College, in partnership with area high schools, offers college credit to qualified high school students who participate in various classes under college direction. The high school instructors, having received administrative recommendation from their high school and having qualified as adjunct faculty appointed by the college, follow the St. Norbert College syllabus, mirroring the courses, standards, and expectations found on the St. Norbert campus.

University of Wisconsin-Eau Claire (MA I)
Introduction to College Writing

Grades served: HS   Schools served: 6   Year established: 1992
Location of schools served: RU   Type of schools served: NR

Introduction to College Writing is a freshman-level college writing course offered through two-way audio-video distance learning to talented high school seniors meeting qualification standards. One section of the course originates from the UW-Eau Claire campus and involves students from three high schools; another section originates from one high school and involves students from two other high schools. The course is typically taught by both college and high school faculty. Full college credit is awarded to students who successfully complete the course.

University of Wisconsin-Oshkosh (MA I)
Cooperative Academic Partnership Program (CAPP)

Grades served: HS   Schools served: 30   Year established: 1975
Location of schools served: UR, SU, RU   Type of schools served: PUB, PRI

CAPP links the university and secondary schools in eastern Wisconsin. Its primary mission is to offer qualified high school students the opportunity to enroll in challenging UW-Oshkosh freshman courses during their junior and/or senior year of high school. CAPP provides several other important services to high schools: inservice training for high school instructors, a continuing forum for communication between educators from schools and the university, and the opportunity to jointly develop curricula.

WYOMING

Casper College (AA)
BOCES (Board of Cooperative Educational Services)

Grades served: HS   Schools served: 4   Year established: 1990
Location of schools served: UR   Type of schools served: PUB

Central Wyoming BOCES provides Natrona County and Central Wyoming quality educational services not readily provided by the Natrona County Schools or Casper College when offered independently. BOCES is designed to meet the educational needs of the community by training adult learners in programs leading to undergraduate and graduate education degrees earned in Casper, to meet the educational needs of high school students through articulated programs in technical and academic areas where high school students can earn college credit, and to serve as a catalyst for developing and implementing programs benefiting educational institutions, the business community, and the general citizenry.

Note: Each institution's Carnegie class is given in parentheses. **Key:** E=elementary school, HS=high school, M=middle school, NR=not reported, PRI=private, PUB=public, RU=rural, SU=suburban, UR=urban

Section Three
Enrichment and Gifted-and-Talented Programs

ALABAMA

University of Alabama at Birmingham (RES I)
Theatre Touring to Elementary and Secondary Schools

Grades served: E, M, HS   Schools served: 90   Year established: 1983
Location of schools served: UR, SU   Type of schools served: PUB, PRI

The University of Alabama, without an official partnership, sends educationally based touring theater companies into schools, primarily in central Alabama, consulting first with teachers and administrators. UAB Kids on the Block is a nationally franchised puppet troupe that teaches K-2 children that disabled children are not as different as they appear, UAB Bookends encourages children in grades 3-5 to develop good reading and thinking skills, the UAB Shakespeare Ensemble offers abridged performances of plays they are studying for middle and high school audiences, and the UAB Civil Rights Ensemble creates works based on speeches and events in the Civil Rights movement.

CALIFORNIA

Foothill College (AA)
Foothill College Summer Children's Program

Grades served: E   Schools served: NR   Year established: 1989
Location of schools served: UR, SU, RU   Type of schools served: PUB, PRI

The Foothill College Summer Children's Program provides many enriching educational experiences for children entering grades 1-7. Talented teachers design and implement an educational program that is often augmented by guest speakers, special performances, and field trips. Classes offer children the opportunity to participate in science, math, language arts, speed reading, Spanish language instruction, sports, and cooperative games. Programs are offered in three two-week sessions and are supported by fees. Enrollment can be for a single two-week session or for any combination of two-week sessions.

Occidental College (BA I)
OPTIMO

Grades served: M, HS   Schools served: NR   Year established: 1992
Location of schools served: UR   Type of schools served: PUB

OPTIMO is a four-week summer residential Young Scholars project in mathematics for 32 students in the northeast Los Angeles area entering grades 8-10 in the 11 public high schools nearest the college. Participants engage actively in the processes of mathematical development: seeking patterns, formulating conjectures, reasoning, writing, and speaking. Students use programmable graphing calculators to solve problems in chosen areas of discrete mathematics. Computer and science laboratories complement mathematics workshops. Academic year follow-up includes classes, lectures by local scientists, engineers, and other professionals, career and college admission workshops, field trips, and science fairs.

San Francisco State University (MA I)
Young Engineers and Scientists (YES)

Grades served: E, M   Schools served: 20   Year established: 1992
Location of schools served: UR, SU   Type of schools served: PUB, PRI

YES offers an intensive math and science enrichment summer program at the San Francisco State University campus. Two hundred twenty-five students from grades 4-8 participate in the commuter program for six weeks. They continue in a 32-week program during the academic year. YES introduces students to science, engineering, and math concepts in a multicultural context, discusses how science is relevant to students' day-to-day life, and helps parents to become more involved in education. YES was established in 1992 through a grant from the National Science Foundation.

San Francisco State University (MA I)
Alexander String Quartet Outreach Program

Grades served: M, HS   Schools served: 12   Year established: 1989
Location of schools served: UR, SU   Type of schools served: PUB, PRI

The Alexander String Quartet Outreach Program is part of a residency project at San Francisco State University. The program includes activities for both music and nonmusic students and is intended to provide experiences that will lead to a greater appreciation of music and potentially to a lifetime of involvement in the field as performers and audience members. The program consists of a series of live performances and discussions at inner-city schools, with ongoing humanities programs, workshops, and ensemble coaching for music students from high schools and youth orchestras throughout the San Francisco Bay area.

University of San Diego (DOC II)
Partnership in Education

Grades served: E, M, HS   Schools served: 4   Year established: 1986
Location of schools served: UR   Type of schools served: PUB

The University of San Diego has Partnerships in Education with four San Diego City schools: two elementary, one junior high, and one senior high. All of the schools are located in neighboring Linda Vista, a community with a very diverse, lower socioeconomic population. The partnership focuses primarily on providing after-school enrichment for youth, mentoring, tutoring, drama, sports, and art programs. Partnership school staff serve on an advisory committee to guide program development, and university students coordinate the specific projects.

COLORADO

University of Denver (DOC I)
University of Youth

Grades served: E, M   Schools served: 40   Year established: 1980
Location of schools served: UR, SU   Type of schools served: PUB

Intellectually oriented, University for Youth enrichment courses focus on conceptual development through productive thinking, aesthetic expression, and problem solving. Courses are presented at schools in the Denver metro area and on the university campus during weekends and in the summer, offering an opportunity for students with high interest levels and strong abilities to expand their knowledge and skills in a university environment.

Note: Each institution's Carnegie class is given in parentheses. **Key:** E=elementary school, HS=high school, M=middle school, NR=not reported, PRI=private, PUB=public, RU=rural, SU=suburban, UR=urban

University of Denver (DOC I)
Rocky Mountain Talent Search Program
Grades served: M, HS   Schools served: 1800   Year established: 1981
Location of schools served: UR, SU, RU   Type of schools served: PUB, PRI

The Talent Search Program identifies academically talented middle school students and provides opportunities for participation in a summer institute offering accelerated and highly rigorous academic courses along with supervised social activities in a university setting. Residential and commuter students may participate in two- and three-week sessions. Eligibility is based on qualifying scores on SAT or ACT tests.

University of Denver (DOC I)
Odyssey of the Mind
Grades served: E, M, HS   Schools served: 540   Year established: 1982
Location of schools served: UR, SU, RU   Type of schools served: PUB, PRI

Colorado Odyssey of the Mind (COM) is a chartered associate of OM Association, Inc., a school-based (K-12) program that promotes divergent thinking and creative problem solving. COM is sponsored by the Bureau of Educational Services at the University of Denver. It provides statewide program administration, facilitates training sessions for several hundred volunteer coaches and judges, coordinates state memberships, publishes newsletters, and coordinates the Colorado state tournament. Its board of directors consists of Colorado school district representatives. In addition, COM works with a community advisory board to promote awareness of the program and participation in Colorado.

CONNECTICUT

Trinity College (BA I)
Poet-In-Residence
Grades served: HS   Schools served: 3   Year established: 1977
Location of schools served: UR   Type of schools served: PUB

The Poet-In-Residence partnership offered through Trinity College involves students in Hartford Public, Bulkeley, and Weaver High Schools. Thirty-five selected student poets are bussed to Trinity College for ten days for four two-hour workshops with a major poet in residence at Trinity. Following the workshops, the poet conducts a luncheon-workshop on pedagogical issues with a group of the students' teachers. Poets who have participated in the program include W.D. Snodgrass, Lucille Clifton, Philip Levine, Marvin Bell, Sharon Olds, Gary Snyder, Margaret Gibson, Stephen Dunn, Marge Piercy, and Tess Gallagher.

Wesleyan University (BA I)
Center for Creative Youth (CCY)
Grades served: HS   Schools served: 70   Year established: 1977
Location of schools served: UR, SU   Type of schools served: PUB, PRI

The Center for Creative Youth is a national model of a public, independent school/university/corporation/foundation partnership. It was established to provide quality arts education in a precollege setting to prepare students for success in future education and careers. Emphasis is on multicultural and interdisciplinary learning, critical thinking, and leadership. Qualified students from a variety of economic and cultural backgrounds may participate in the program. A program of the Capitol Region Education Council, CCY is endorsed by the Connecticut State Department of Education.

<u>DISTRICT OF COLUMBIA</u>

George Washington University (RES II)
ARTS (Artistic Reinforcement for Talented Students)

Grades served: M

Schools served: 2

Year established: 1993

Location of schools served: UR

Type of schools served: PUB

The ARTS program links George Washington University, the Arts Club of Washington, and Hines and Lincoln Junior High Schools to provide students selected by the schools an opportunity to experience different facets of art and art careers. Group discussions, hands-on activities, and a variety of artistic techniques serve to prepare students for art majors. Students attend classes at GWU every third Saturday between February and May. Faculty, staff, and students volunteer time to provide instruction and facilitate group discussion, guidance, and expertise. The partnership also plans a museum trip.

George Washington University (RES II)
Summer Scholar Program

Grades served: HS

Schools served: NR

Year established: NR

Location of schools served: UR

Type of schools served: PUB

George Washington University's Summer Scholar Program allows exceptionally talented high school students to live and learn at George Washington during the summer before their junior or senior year. The five-and-a-half-week program involves 50 high school students and a program staff of five, plus regular interaction with the undergraduate faculty and residence hall associates. Summer Scholars may choose from among 20 undergraduate courses. Scholarships covering the cost of tuition for two courses are available for the most exceptional students, with no separate application required for these scholarships. GWU publicizes, recruits, advises, makes housing and meal arrangements, and monitors students' progress.

Howard University (RES I)
Mathematics/Science Initiative Program

Grades served: HS

Schools served: NR

Year established: 1990

Location of schools served: UR

Type of schools served: PUB

The Mathematics/Science Initiative Program provides high schools with an intensive six-week residential program designed to increase students' awareness and competence in science, mathematics, and technical areas. Students have the opportunity to take classes in engineering, laboratory science, mathematics, robotics, and computer science. Each student is assigned a mentor, who guides the student through a research project. Students take weekly field trips to scientific organizations and research centers. Participants are accepted from Virginia, West Virginia, Delaware, Pennsylvania, Maryland, and the District of Columbia.

Note: Each institution's Carnegie class is given in parentheses. **Key:** E=elementary school, HS=high school, M=middle school, NR=not reported, PRI=private, PUB=public, RU=rural, SU=suburban, UR=urban

Howard University (RES I)
Tubman 6th Graders Study/Poets Theater 208

Grades served: E   Schools served: 1   Year established: 1990
Location of schools served: UR   Type of schools served: NR

This project, designed to help sixth graders improve language skills through poetry, focuses on writing, reading, listening, speaking, and comprehension. In Phase I, "Learning About African-American, African, and Hispanic Poets and Their Poems," students select a poet, read about the poet's life, research what happened in the world and/or the United States during the time the poet lived, and select a short poem to commit to memory. Students present to the class, from memory, the information they have gathered and recite the chosen poem, with expression. Their classmates are asked to interpret the poem. In Phase II, students engage in creative writing; in Phase III, they perform in a poetry dramatization before the entire Tubman school body. Outreach activities take the student performers before other audiences.

FLORIDA

Chipola Junior College (AA)
Chipola Regional Science & Engineering Fair

Grades served: M, HS   Schools served: 31   Year established: 1989
Location of schools served: UR, RU Type of schools served: PUB

This partnership links the college with six county school districts. Its primary mission is to offer aspiring young scientists and engineers the opportunity to engage in the scientific method and to advance their winning projects to the state and international levels. Teachers received inservice training in the rules and guidelines, and then conduct workshops for parents and students. The program offers a continuing forum for science faculty from the schools and the college, and well-known scientists, as keynote speakers, provide timely information about their specialties.

Florida Atlantic University (DOC II)
TC-94, The Technology Connection

Grades served: M, HS   Schools served: NR   Year established: NR
Location of schools served: NR   Type of schools served: NR

TC-94 is a five-day residential program for two groups of 48 students featuring hands-on learning experiences in five engineering labs intended to create enthusiasm for learning and curiosity about engineering, science, and technology. The program includes industry tours, evening programs, and a mystery design contest. TC-94 is open to middle and high school students who express an interest in engineering, math, science, and technology and are recommended by their counselors. Full and partial scholarships for room and board are available based on need.

Florida State University (RES I)
Young Scholars Program

Grades served: HS   Schools served: 825   Year established: 1983
Location of schools served: UR, SU, RU Type of schools served: PUB, PRI

The Young Scholars Program is a six-week residential project for 50 rising 11th and 12th grade students in science, mathematics, and computer science. Each student elects a course in math, computer science, and science (biochemistry, physics, or science communication) and completes an individual research project in collaboration with a researcher at FSU. Evening seminars on science ethics and career exploration, and weekend field trips complete the summer program. The program is funded by grants from the National Science Foundation and the Florida Department of Education.

Florida State University (RES I)
Saturday-at-the-Sea

Grades served: M   Schools served: NR   Year established: 1984
Location of schools served: UR, SU, RU   Type of schools served: PUB, PRI

Saturday-at-the-Sea is a one-day environmental education program for middle school students that educates participants about the Gulf of Mexico and ignites their interest in science as a field of study and career. During the day, students actively explore a coastal salt marsh, an intertidal oyster bar, and, via pontoon boat, subtidal seagrass beds. While discovering these habitats, participants collect representative organisms and examine them more closely in a wet laboratory equipped with holding tanks, microscopes, and supplies for simple experiments.

Lake-Sumter Community College (AA)
Children's Theatre Series

Grades served: E, M   Schools served: 30   Year established: 1976
Location of schools served: SU, RU   Type of schools served: PUB, PRI

The Lake-Sumter Community College Children's Theatre Series has established an important cultural link with the area's younger school students. This curriculum-based program, which creates annual productions for thousands of elementary and middle school students, provides important early exposure to live theater. All performances and production activities are associated with college course work in acting, stagecraft, and technical aspects of performing arts. The Children's Theatre Series expands and reinforces college instruction while at the same time encouraging cultural enhancement.

GEORGIA

Augusta College (MA I)
Augusta College's Coca-Cola Young Writers Contest

Grades served: M, HS   Schools served: 50   Year established: 1972
Location of schools served: UR, SU   Type of schools served: PUB, PRI

Augusta College's Coca-Cola Young Writers Contest offers young people an opportunity to express themselves through creative writing. The contest, which includes short stories, poetry, and essays, encourages students in middle and high schools to write, rewards those who write well with scholarship funds, and brings about a closer working relationship among secondary schools, the business community, and the college. Coca-Cola funds the scholarships, school principals submit the entries, and English faculty at the college are the final judges.

Augusta College (MA I)
CSRA Science and Engineering Fair

Grades served: E, M, HS   Schools served: 209   Year established: NR
Location of schools served: UR, SU, RU   Type of schools served: PUB, PRI

The CSRA Science and Engineering Fair, Inc., is a volunteer organization of engineering, science, teaching, and medical professionals committed to enhancing science and math education in the public and private schools of the Central Savannah River area (CSRA). Volunteers judge each of the local fairs held every year in 18 Georgia and South Carolina counties. The organization also organizes and judges the culminating regional fair, comprising winning projects from the local fairs. It is one of more than 450 similar organizations affiliated through the International Science and Engineering Fair, an activity of the Science Service and Science Clubs of America.

Note: Each institution's Carnegie class is given in parentheses. **Key:** E=elementary school, HS=high school, M=middle school, NR=not reported, PRI=private, PUB=public, RU=rural, SU=suburban, UR=urban

Berry College (MA I)
Berry College Mathematics League

Grades served: M, HS

Location of schools served: UR, SU, RU

Schools served: 18

Type of schools served: PUB, PRI

Year established: 1972

The Berry College Mathematics League is a cooperative effort between the mathematics department of the college and the mathematics departments of 18 junior and senior high schools. The purpose of the league is to provide additional experience in competition through teams, to stimulate interest and pride in mathematics, to encourage students to pursue study in mathematics beyond high school, and to encourage all students to enjoy being on a team and competing. Preservice mathematics education students organize and administer two written and ciphering meets.

Georgia Institute of Technology (RES I)
Junior Toastmasters

Grades served: M

Location of schools served: NR

Schools served: 1

Type of schools served: PUB

Year established: NR

The Youth Development Program is an outreach program of Toastmasters International. Because Georgia Tech had already established a partnership with Walden Middle School, the GT Toastmasters Club joined other Georgia Tech personnel to provide additional services to students at Walden Middle School. The program seeks to develop the students' self-esteem and communication skills through a structured, participatory program devoted to the development of good oral communication skills. Students who complete the program are selected to volunteer at SciTrek and to serve as school ambassadors.

Georgia Institute of Technology (RES I)
Regional Science Olympiad

Grades served: M

Location of schools served: NR

Schools served: NR

Type of schools served: NR

Year established: NR

The Georgia Science Olympiad is an activity of the Georgia Academy of Science hosted regionally by Georgia Institute of Technology:. Approximately 20 faculty and 30 Georgia Tech students are involved in this all-day event for approximately 350 middle school students competing in 21 events, most of which are hands-on projects or require teamwork. This program is Georgia Tech's contribution to the statewide program.

Georgia Institute of Technology (RES I)
CHIPS

Grades served: M

Location of schools served: NR

Schools served: NR

Type of schools served: NR

Year established: NR

CHIPS, an introduction to computer-aided design, is open to open-minded and curious middle school students with a minimum average of 3.0. Prior knowledge of the computer is not necessary. The program's objectives are for students to gain experience in how to model ideas using the computer and by hand, to briefly introduce them to computers, to teach them the basic principles and modeling techniques used by engineers and architects, to explore the use of the computer as a tool in design, and to develop and improve their visual perception, creativity, special visualization skills, observation, and cognitive function. The student is responsible for daily transportation to and from the campus. Meals, activity fees, and costs of field-trips are provided.

Macon College (AA)
Reading and Writing Across the Curriculum at Southwest High School
Grades served: HS   Schools served: 1   Year established: 1991
Location of schools served: UR   Type of schools served: PUB

This project is a cooperative effort of Macon College and Southwest High School to enhance advanced placement and honors courses for high school students. Each quarter, Southwest teachers select a novel for three advanced classes in English, social studies, and science, which is provided for the students by the college's Center for Economic and Educational Development. College faculty lecture on the book after students have read it and meet with the class to discuss the ten best papers submitted. The writer of the best paper in each class receives a certificate. A small honorarium is provided for the three college faculty participating each quarter.

ILLINOIS

Northwestern University (RES I)
Center For Talent Development
Grades served: E, M, HS   Schools served: 3000   Year established: 1982
Location of schools served: UR, SU, RU   Type of schools served: PUB, PRI

The Center for Talent Development's mission is to provide leadership fir the Midwest in the education of the gifted and talented. The program includes regional talent-search testing programs for students in grades 4-8 and innovative academic programs for students preK-12. The center also provides seminars and training to parents and educators. A special focus is programs for underserved talented youth, especially minority and economically disadvantaged children. Programs and services are coupled with extensive research and evaluation.

Northwestern University (RES I)
Midwest Talent Search/Midwest Talent Search for Young Students
Grades served: E, M   Schools served: 3000   Year established: 1981
Location of schools served: UR, SU, RU   Type of schools served: PUB, PRI

Based on the philosophy of Talent Search that early and accurate identification of gifted and talented students using out-of-level tests enables appropriate and individualized curriculum and career planning, the Midwest Talent Search and the Midwest Talent Search for Young Students seek to identify fifth, sixth-, seventh-, and eighth-grade students with exceptional mathematical and verbal talents. Schools recommend students, who take tests designed for high school students. Students receive interpretive information about their scores, recommended course sequences, and a compendium of special educational opportunities for which they might qualify.

INDIANA

Anderson University (BA II)
Health, Safety, and Physical Education for Elementary Grades
Grades served: E   Schools served: NR   Year established: NR
Location of schools served: NR   Type of schools served: PRI

Anderson University conducts an 11-week teaching practicum involving elementary grades of home-schooled children each semester. The purpose of the program is twofold. First, university students plan and implement developmentally appropriate physical education lessons for an assigned age group. Second, the home-schooled children are afforded a structured, educationally sound activity program involving low-organized games, rhythmics, swimming, stunts and tumbling, fundamental skills, sport skills, games apparatus, and fitness.

Note: Each institution's Carnegie class is given in parentheses. **Key:** E=elementary school, HS=high school, M=middle school, NR=not reported, PRI=private, PUB=public, RU=rural, SU=suburban, UR=urban

Ball State University (DOC I)
Indiana Academy for Science, Mathematics, and Humanities

Grades served: HS   Schools served: NR   Year established: 1988
Location of schools served: UR, SU, RU   Type of schools served: PUB, PRI

Opened in fall 1990 and funded by the Indiana General Assembly, the Indiana Academy for Science, Mathematics, and Humanities fulfills a dual mission as a public residential school for 300 gifted and talented students throughout the state and as a resource for school corporations seeking to further advance their programs for gifted students. Interactive televised broadcasts of the academy's advanced courses via satellite complement curricular options across the state for students who cannot attend the residential program. Teaching fellowships in the academy, workshops, and curricular materials further support teachers.

University of Notre Dame (RES II)
Linkup

Grades served: M   Schools served: 5   Year established: 1983
Location of schools served: UR   Type of schools served: PUB

Linkup is a partnership between the University of Notre Dame and the South Bend Community School Corporation, which began with a two-year grant from Lilly Endowment. It offers enhancement of college preparatory skills and motivational activities to minority middle school students with high academic potential, many of whom are potential first-generation college students. An immediate goal of the program is to encourage and prepare participants for high school honors classes. The five-week summer program includes an intensive curriculum offered at Notre Dame. The academic year follow-up program takes place at the home schools.

MARYLAND

Johns Hopkins University (RES I)
Center for Talented Youth (CTY)

Grades served: E, M, HS   Schools served: NR   Year established: 1979
Location of schools served: NR   Type of schools served: NR

Johns Hopkins University's Center for Talented Youth began as the Center for the Advancement of Academically Talented Youth to meet the growing demand for a program that would accommodate adolescent youth who wished to advance according to their ability and level of performance. Students are selected for the program from a pool of applicants based on test scores and often on the recommendation of teachers and counselors. The program includes summer, winter, residential, and commuter courses at Johns Hopkins, at several other sites in the United States, and at one site in Geneva, Switzerland. CTY also offers a tutorial in expository writing by mail. The program offers courses in mathematics and writing. Services include assessment and evaluation of the child's reasoning ability in math, verbal, and abstract reasoning tasks, counseling, a training institute for educators and parents, and career education workshops. The program has been the model for programs at Duke, Northwestern, Denver, and Arizona State.

Johns Hopkins University (RES I)
CTY/Community School District 22 Project

Grades served: M   Schools served: 5   Year established: 1991
Location of schools served: UR   Type of schools served: PUB

The Center for Talented Youth (CTY) of Johns Hopkins University and Community School District 22 of Brooklyn (NY) have established a mathematics project in the district's intermediate schools based on CTY's pedagogy and philosophy. The project includes training teachers and adapting CTY's model of instruction to address the needs of individual schools. The CTY pedagogy, taking into consideration the prior knowledge, ability, learning style, and motivation of each individual student and tailoring instructional strategies to individual needs, is appropriate for a broad spectrum of ability. This project has demonstrated its validity beyond CTY's very selective environment.

Montgomery College-Rockville Campus (AA)
Summer Student Writing Institute
Grades served: E, M   Schools served: 200   Year established: 1987
Location of schools served: SU   Type of schools served: PUB, PRI

The Summer Student Writing Institute recognizes and encourages aspiring writers in grades 4-9 referred to the community college by their home schools. Groups of 25 students are team-taught by two instructors who have training in the Writing Project. The purpose of the institute is to immerse participants in the writing process used by professional writers. A variety of activities — directed instruction, free writing time, peer sharing and interviewing, and guest speakers — foster students' creativity and enjoyment of writing. Students are encouraged to write from their own experience. All institute participants contribute one original piece to a final publication.

United States Naval Academy (OTHER)
Anne Arundel County/USNA Gifted/Talented Program
Grades served: M, HS   Schools served: NR   Year established: 1978
Location of schools served: NR   Type of schools served: PUB

This partnership between the U.S. Naval Academy and Anne Arundel County Public Schools involves selected students from grades 6-12. The Naval Academy's military and civilian faculty offer courses in mathematics, computer science, chemistry, physics, biology, astronomy, geology, oceanography, meteorology, and engineering after school hours at the Naval Academy during fall, spring, and summer. Courses normally consist of five two-hour sessions, for which Anne Arundel County bears the costs. Classes involve 10 to 20 students, and approximately 200 students participate each semester.

University of Maryland-College Park (RES I)
High School Programming Contest
Grades served: HS   Schools served: 28   Year established: 1990
Location of schools served: UR, SU, RU Type of schools served: PUB

The High School Programming Contest is available to students in grades 9 - 12 from Maryland. Teams of students are required to solve four to five problems in Pascal during a four-hour period, and prizes are awarded to the top-ranked teams. IBM Corporation's Federal Sector Division provides hardware and software as well as much of the technical support for the contest.

University of Maryland-College Park (RES I)
Latin Day
Grades served: M, HS   Schools served: 40   Year established: 1977
Location of schools served: UR, SU, RU Type of schools served: PUB, PRI

Sponsored by the Department of Classics at the University of Maryland, Latin Day annually brings 1,300 students (grades 6-12) to campus for a program celebrating the language and culture of ancient Rome. The program is scripted as a drama based on ancient literary models and uses professional and student actors to educate students about aspects of Roman culture, such as politics, entertainment, history, and mythology. Students participate in various contests, and all students receive a T-shirt with an appropriate design. Teachers receive lesson plans in advance to prepare them for the program.

University of Maryland-College Park (RES I)
Chemathon

Grades served: HS

Schools served: 21

Year established: 1985

Location of schools served: UR, SU, RU

Type of schools served: PUB, PRI

The Chemathon is a one-day competition held annually at the University of Maryland for chemistry students attending high schools in Maryland, the District of Columbia, and Northern Virginia. Aimed at increasing students' interest in chemistry, the Chemathon is organized by a group of area high school chemistry teachers and university faculty. The events include both laboratory exercises and pencil-and-paper activities designed to be fun and to increase students' knowledge and skills in chemistry.

MASSACHUSETTS

Hampshire College (BA I)
Hampshire College Summer Studies in Mathematics

Grades served: HS

Schools served: 45

Year established: 1971

Location of schools served: UR, SU, RU

Type of schools served: PUB, PRI

Hampshire College Summer Studies in Mathematics is a National Science Foundation Young Scholars Program. It invites exceptionally talented and motivated students to a six-week program under the leadership of college or university mathematicians, assisted by talented graduate and undergraduate math students. Methods of discovery and communication are emphasized through the investigation of many significant problems outside secondary school and early college curricula, from rings and randomization to topology and tessellations.

Smith College (BA I)
Smith Summer Science Program (SSSP)

Grades served: M, HS

Schools served: 50

Year established: 1990

Location of schools served: UR, SU, RU

Type of schools served PUB, PRI

SSSP brings 48 nationally recruited girls (grades 9-12) with strong interests in science to campus for the month of July to do hands-on research with Smith science faculty. Students work on relevant research projects in a state-of-the-art science facility. They also participate in college and career workshops, meet women in science-based careers, and enjoy a wealth of recreational, sporting, and cultural activities. Through the SSSP, students form connections with Smith faculty, students, and science professionals, all of whom are committed to helping them gain confidence and define and achieve their goals.

University of Massachusetts-Dartmouth (MA I)
Projects for High Learning Potential (PHLP)

Grades served: HS

Schools served: 16

Year established: 1980

Location of schools served: UR, SU, RU

Type of schools served: PUB, PRI

PHLP has facilitated formation of the University/Westport Community Schools Partnership, which addresses such systemic restructuring issues as authentic learning, life skills planning, sharing resources, organizational restructuring, and learning technology. The programs, serving mostly high schools, but occasionally lower schools, has offered summer workshops for teachers directed toward educating students with high potential. Central to the project is the Spotlight Program, an enrichment program serving high-potential students in 16 to 18 schools in southeastern Massachusetts and Rhode Island. Approximately 100 students meet on campus each Thursday afternoon throughout the academic year.

Hope College (BA I)
Program for the Academically Talented at Hope (PATH)

Grades served: M, HS   Schools served: 20   Year established: 1986
Location of schools served: UR, SU, RU   Type of schools served: PUB, PRI

PATH provides a two-year sequence of fast-paced accelerated instruction in mathematics and writing for academically talented seventh, eighth, and ninth grade students from greater Ottawa County. Students come to Hope College one afternoon a week throughout the school year for instruction. Math students complete the equivalent of four years of high school mathematics (algebra I and II, geometry, and functions statistics and trigonometry). Writing students focus on the process of writing, with instruction at a level comparable to a high school honors course in composition.

Wayne State University (RES I)
Advanced Studies

Grades served: HS   Schools served: 27   Year established: NR
Location of schools served: NR   Type of schools served: PUB

This program was established for 11th and 12th graders with an excellent academic record and above-average scores on national standardized tests. Its purpose is to give students academic experience in a college environment to motivate them to higher academic achievement. The classes are offered on Saturday mornings on Wayne State's campus. Departments supporting the program include Art and Art History, Biology, Chemistry, Computer Science, History, Mathematics, Romance Languages and Literatures, and Speech. The program, focusing on special needs of underrepresented, minority, and at-risk populations, provides enrichment, tutoring, mentoring, and counseling regarding career options and requirements.

Rust College (BA II)
John Lennon Pre-College Summer Arts Award Program

Grades served: E, M, HS   Schools served: 6   Year established: 1993
Location of schools served: RU   Type of schools served: PUB, PRI

This partnership involves Rust Colleges and six surrounding area schools in Marshall County, Mississippi. The program invites students in grades 6-12 with high aptitudes for art and fine art to attend a six-week planned program of study in art, music, and literature. A two-year follow-up program monitors participants to ensure their enrollment and satisfactory academic progress in college preparatory art, fine art, music, and literature. Seminar topics focus on improving self-image and study habits, careers, occupations, and licensing requirements.

Note: Each institution's Carnegie class is given in parentheses. **Key:** E=elementary school, HS=high school, M=middle school, NR=not reported, PRI=private, PUB=public, RU=rural, SU=suburban, UR=urban

University of Southern Mississippi (DOC I)
Foreign Language Exploratory Program
Grades served: E, M   Schools served: 6   Year established: 1992
Location of schools served: NR   Type of schools served: PUB

The Foreign Language Exploratory Program at the University of Southern Mississippi is designed to provide instruction in Spanish, French, and Japanese to elementary and middle school students in the surrounding counties. Instructors are graduate teaching assistants enrolled in the Master of Arts in Teaching Languages program at USM. Instructors are paid a stipend and receive a full waiver of university tuition, allowing them to support their graduate education while providing inexpensive, part-time instruction to area school districts. All participating teaching assistants are supervised by USM faculty.

MISSOURI

Central Missouri State University (MA I)
Young Authors' Conference
Grades served: E   Schools served: 30   Year established: 1983
Location of schools served: NR   Type of schools served: PUB

The Young Authors' Conference is a collaboration of Central Missouri State University and the West Central Council of the International Reading Association, an organization of area teachers. The conference encourages elementary students' creative writing by providing information and incentives for teaching writing, and recognition and encouragement for individual students whose compositions are selected for publication in the conference book. The annual conference draws approximately 500 students, parents, and teachers.

Columbia College (BA II)
Partners-In-Education
Grades served: E   Schools served: NR   Year established: 1987
Location of schools served: UR   Type of schools served: PUB

The partnership between Columbia College and Field Elementary School provides a wide variety of activities designed to enrich the educational experiences of students and encourage their pursuit of a college education. Activities include a monthly academic recognition program, a career interest day, and employees and students from the college serving as volunteers and mentors in classrooms. In addition, each grade is brought to the campus each year for events ranging from Easter egg hunts and trick-or-treating, for the lower grades, to shadowing an employee or college student, for the upper grades.

University of Missouri-St. Louis (DOC I)
George Engelmann Mathematics & Science Institute
Grades served: HS   Schools served: 104   Year established: 1988
Location of schools served: UR, SU, RU Type of schools served: PUB, PRI

The George Engelmann Mathematics & Science Institute stimulates high-ability students in the St. Louis metropolitan area to pursue careers in science, mathematics, and engineering. Integrating scholarly, social, and applied experiences developed through a partnership among schools, universities, businesses, governmental agencies, and institutions of higher learning, the institute provides opportunities for students to work with university faculty, private researchers, and mentor teachers in an interdisciplinary approach to learning. The institute is composed of five programs serving more than 400 students annually through a systematic sequence of activities that provide for students' academic and socialization growth from the high school sophomore through college senior years.

Washington University (RES I)
Magnet School-Art School Experience

Grades served: HS   Schools served: 1   Year established: 1992
Location of schools served: NR   Type of schools served: PUB

Each semester, selected visual art students meet at the School of Fine Arts for six Friday mornings. In addition to drawing classes taught by their teachers in WU's fine arts classrooms, students tour the school and visit the two galleries on campus. They meet with a faculty member and/or students to learn about their work and their university experience. Students in their first and second year of high school are included to encourage them to see art school as a possibility and to help them see the importance of their high school work if they want to continue with an education in art.

Washington University (RES I)
High School Art Competition

Grades served: HS   Schools served: 60   Year established: 1976
Location of schools served: UR, SU, RU   Type of schools served: PUB, PRI

Since 1976, WU's School of Fine Arts has hosted an annual art competition for some 40 high school students in Missouri and Illinois. The competition has two categories of entry: portfolio and individual. Portfolio entrants are seniors who submit from eight to 12 slides of their work, and finalists receive bronze medals and are eligible for scholarship offers from Washington University and other participating art schools. Juniors and seniors may submit up to three slides in the individual category. A public opening reception and certificates of participation recognize students' achievements.

NEVADA

Sierra Nevada College (BA II)
DOE Pre-Freshman Enrichment Program

Grades served: M, HS   Schools served: 100   Year established: 1993
Location of schools served: UR, SU, RU   Type of schools served: PUB

Sierra Nevada College, as a partner with the Washoe County School District, received a grant from the U.S. Department of Energy's Pre-Freshman Enrichment Program to encourage females to enter the fields of math and science. The program serves gifted and talented female students with a strong aptitude in math and science who are entering grades 6-10. The course is designed to integrate the use of science and mathematics in extensive individual and group research in and around the Lake Tahoe basin.

NEW JERSEY

Middlesex County College (AA)
Vanguard: A Symposium for Future Leaders

Grades served: HS   Schools served: 1   Year established: 1992
Location of schools served: UR, SU   Type of schools served: PUB

Vanguard links Middlesex County College and John F. Kennedy High School in Woodridge (NJ) in a program designed to inform gifted and talented high school juniors about the problems they will need to solve in the future. Students have an opportunity to meet and interact with current leaders from various county high schools to discuss issues related to current public concern, such as information technology, health care, energy sources, government spending, the environment, multiethnic culture, education, and gender issues. Corporate sponsors cover the costs of lunches for the two-day meetings.

Ramapo College of New Jersey (BA II)
THE RECORD Debate Classic

Grades served: HS   Schools served: 24   Year established: 1978
Location of schools served: NR   Type of schools served: PUB, PRI

Funded by THE RECORD, the leading newspaper in northern New Jersey, the Debate Classic is the culminating event of year-long competitions among high school teams on the annual topic for debate chosen by the National Forensic League. Four rounds are followed by the championship round, and scholarships of $1,000 and $500 are awarded to first- and second-place teams, respectively. The event is orchestrated by Ramapo College with a steering committee drawn from Bergen County high school faculty. Attorneys from the Bergen Bar Association and Women Lawyers of Bergen County serve as judges for the annual competition.

NEW MEXICO

New Mexico State University-Main Campus (RES I)
Master Environmentalist Program

Grades served: E, M, HS   Schools served: NR   Year established: 1991
Location of schools served: NR   Type of schools served: PUB

The Master Environmentalist program provides volunteers to present information on the environment to all levels of the public school system in New Mexico. To date more than 150 presenters have been trained under the program and, in turn, have reached more than 7,500 students with their presentations. This ongoing statewide program has been adopted by the National 4-H Environmental Stewardship Program. Originally funded through a one-time grant, the program relies heavily on volunteer faculty. Its goal is to continue to train Master Environmentalists so that they, in turn, can teach young people about the environment.

New Mexico State University-Main Campus (RES I)
Citizen Bee

Grades served: HS   Schools served: NR   Year established: NR
Location of schools served: NR   Type of schools served: NR

Citizen Bee, a contest for high school students, is conducted every March on the NMSU campus. Finalists in this regional competition compete in the national contest, which tests their knowledge of government, history, and current events. This program, established under the auspices of the Close-Up Foundation, is designed to enrich the academic lives of students, encourage their interest in the field of government, increase their self-esteem, and interest them in the study of government at NMSU.

New Mexico State University-Main Campus (RES I)
Summer Sports Camp/Sport Education Institute

Grades served: E   Schools served: NR   Year established: 1983
Location of schools served: NR   Type of schools served: NR

NMSU's College of Education and the Department of Physical Education, Recreation, and Dance sponsor an annual summer coed Sports Camp, a six-week program for children aged 4-11. The camp is designed to facilitate cognitive, social, psychomotor, and fitness growth of children and to provide supervised experience for prospective physical education and classroom teachers working with children. The program has expanded to include the Sport Education Institute, which is designed to use movement as a vehicle for conveying academic content to fourth- and fifth-grade children.

New Mexico State University-Main Campus (RES I)
High School Chemical Olympics

Grades served: HS
Location of schools served: NR

Schools served: 15
Type of schools served: PUB

Year established: 1989

The goals of the annual High School Chemical Olympics are to promote chemistry and science education, provide needed funds through awards of cash prizes to schools, recognize excellence in schools and individual students, and assist science programs in public schools. Three-member teams from schools of all sizes from all over the state compete for cash prizes for the schools. Medals and trophies are awarded to competing individuals and teams. The program affects 15 schools, 20 teachers, and more than 120 students annually.

NEW YORK

City University of New York College of Staten Island (MA I)
Mathematics/Computer Science Olympics

Grades served: HS
Location of schools served: UR

Schools served: 18
Type of schools served: PUB, PRI

Year established: 1987

The College of Staten Island, in conjunction with the Staten Island Guild of Mathematics Associates, sponsors the annual Math/Computer Science Olympics, in which the brightest mathematics and computer science students compete in varying levels of events. College faculty and high school teachers design the competitive examinations. An awards ceremony, attended by faculty, teachers, parents, and students, features a guest speaker in mathematics or computer science, awards of individual and team trophies, and a scholarship to a senior student nominated by the winning high school.

City University of New York College of Staten Island (MA I)
Science Olympics

Grades served: HS
Location of schools served: UR

Schools served: 18
Type of schools served: PUB, PRI

Year established: 1988

Staten Island's brightest high school science students compete in the annual Science Olympics, sponsored by the College of Staten Island in conjunction with the Staten Island Science Teachers Association. School teams compete in varying levels of biology, chemistry, and physics events. College faculty and high school teachers design the competitive examinations. An awards ceremony, attended by faculty, teachers, parents, and students, features a scientist as guest speaker, presentations of individual and team trophies, and a scholarship to a senior student nominated by the winning high school.

City University of New York Herbert H. Lehman College (MA I)
MASTER (Mathematics and Science Through Excellence and Research)

Grades served: HS
Location of schools served: UR

Schools served: 5
Type of schools served: PUB

Year established: 1985

The MASTER program provides a high level of mathematics and science enrichment for high school students through applied laboratory research in environmental science, water ecology, forensics, anatomy and physiology, and mechanical design and drawing. Teams of high school and college faculty offer formal laboratory and class sessions supplemented by daily elective sessions with trained group leaders, intragroup cooperation, and intergroup competition in weekly academic Olympics. Intergroup competition develops motivation and provides a means of encouraging strong students to assist weaker students to benefit the group.

Note: Each institution's Carnegie class is given in parentheses. **Key:** E=elementary school, HS=high school, M=middle school, NR=not reported, PRI=private, PUB=public, RU=rural, SU=suburban, UR=urban

Clarkson University (DOC II)
High School of Excellence

Grades served: HS   Schools served: 15   Year established: 1992
Location of schools served: RU   Type of schools served: PUB

Area high schools are invited to send two of their top students to Clarkson University's High School of Excellence to participate in a week-long exploration of some problem from the perspectives of engineering, management, and social/ethical implications. Teams develop a variety of solutions to the problem, which are exhibited to local professional people at the end of the week. The program is designed to give students a broad-based perspective on creative problem solving.

Cornell University (RES I)
Graduate Student Outreach Project

Grades served: E, M, HS   Schools served: 11   Year established: 1993
Location of schools served: UR, SU   Type of schools served: PUB, PRI

The purpose of the Graduate Student Outreach Project is to share the university's resources with area schools through minicourses taught in the schools' classrooms by Cornell graduate students who desire to collaborate with teachers to share their knowledge and experience. The teachers host the graduate student an hour per week for eight to ten weeks, and they attend pre- and postprogram meetings.

Cornell University (RES I)
H.F. Johnson Museum of Art Education Dept.

Grades served: E, M, HS   Schools served: 23   Year established: 1974
Location of schools served: UR, SU, RU   Type of schools served: PUB, PRI

Cornell University's Johnson Museum offers a variety of programs that currently serve schools in Ithaca and outlying rural communities. Programs include thematic tours of the global collection, tours of special exhibitions, weekend programs for children and families, and a series of grade-specific, curriculum-based learning units called OMNI (Objects and Their Makers: New Insights). These interdisciplinary units examine cultures of the Dogon of Mali (Africa), China, pre-Colombian, Japan, Native American (Hopi, Kwakiutl, and Iroquois), and Southeast Asia.

Hudson Valley Community College (AA)
Summer Technology Enrichment Program (STEP)

Grades served: M   Schools served: 1   Year established: 1993
Location of schools served: SU   Type of schools served: PUB

Hudson Valley Community College and Bethlehem Central School District are partners in the Summer Technology Enrichment Program, designed to provide children in grades 5-8 with a summer learning experience that exposes them to the latest state-of-the-art technology. The program exposes students to the technology-related fields and prepares them to make decisions about curricula in middle and high school that will prepare them for appropriate postsecondary study and careers. The summer program provides a broad overview of these fields and in-depth study in specific areas.

Onondaga Community College (AA)
College for Kids
Grades served: E, M   Schools served: 20   Year established: 1984
Location of schools served: UR, SU, RU   Type of schools served: PUB, PRI

The primary mission of College for Kids is to provide an enrichment program for students aged 8-12. The program is offered during the summer for three weeks with half-day and full-day options, and during the fall and spring on weekends and weekday nights. Students choose from a wide variety of courses and build a schedule based on their interests and needs.

Onondaga Community College (AA)
Leaders of Tomorrow
Grades served: HS   Schools served: 20   Year established: 1986
Location of schools served: UR, SU, RU   Type of schools served: PUB, PRI

The primary mission of Leaders of Tomorrow is to provide training in leadership to high school students who are in leadership positions in their schools, recognizing that students often do not have the skills necessary to be a successful leader. Leaders of Tomorrow focuses on developing skills such as problem solving, organization, motivation, creativity, and public speaking.

State University of New York at Albany (RES II)
Geography and the Capital Region
Grades served: HS   Schools served: 3   Year established: 1990
Location of schools served: UR   Type of schools served: PUB

Geography and the Capital Region works on the premise that geography is a vital school discipline. The program helps to familiarize high school students with their environment. University professors and graduate students lecture at area schools and assist teachers in planning classroom activities and field trips that emphasize studies of the environment, places and peoples, spatial organization, and geographic information systems. Geography Department faculty and graduate students visit elementary schools to give informal talks on related topics. They also devise lesson plans and exercises for teachers' use.

State University of New York College at Cortland (MA I)
High School Leadership Conference
Grades served: HS   Schools served: 12   Year established: 1989
Location of schools served: RU   Type of schools served: PUB

The High School Leadership Conference is a one-day program for approximately 150 students and advisers from area schools that is coordinated by the Center for Educational Exchange in cooperation with area high school principals, students, and advisers. Workshops are facilitated by college faculty and staff, local administrators, teachers and students, and community leaders. The program is designed to help students develop leadership skills and to give area students and advisers opportunities to share ideas, resources, and enthusiasm. The college plans, coordinates, and evaluates the program; schools provide transportation, release time for faculty, and a small registration fee to cover the cost of food and materials.

Note: Each institution's Carnegie class is given in parentheses. **Key:** E=elementary school, HS=high school, M=middle school, NR=not reported, PRI=private, PUB=public, RU=rural, SU=suburban, UR=urban

State University of New York College at Potsdam (MA I)
County-Wide Science Fair

Grades served: E, M

Schools served: 12

Year established: 1988

Location of schools served: RU

Type of schools served: PUB

The County-Wide Science Fair for St. Lawrence County students in grades preK-6 was instituted to stimulate interest in science, to help children pursue scientific areas of interest, to provide a forum for sharing children's scientific accomplishments, and thus encouraging parent/child cooperation in a scientific endeavor, and to encourage cooperation between college faculty and elementary school students and teachers. Teachers are trained in the use of NY State's mandated problem-solving model. The partnership includes cooperating faculty from the area's Associated Colleges, who work with industrial, service, and nature organizations in the community.

NORTH CAROLINA

Wake Forest University (DOC II)
North Carolina Writing Awards Program

Grades served: HS

Schools served: NR

Year established: 1992

Location of schools served: UR, SU, RU

Type of schools served: PUB, PRI

This program was created to encourage high school students to write by offering a competition culminating in scholarships and publication. It is jointly sponsored by the North Carolina Writing Project and the North Carolina English Teachers Association. All high school juniors are invited to submit their best writing to their school, which selects the best submissions. The best writer from each of the local competitions is invited to participate in a timed essay. Authors of the top three essays become eligible for scholarships.

NORTH DAKOTA

University of North Dakota-Main Campus (DOC II)
Suitcase Shakespeare

Grades served: HS

Schools served: 30

Year established: 1991

Location of schools served: UR, SU, RU

Type of schools served: PUB

Suitcase Shakespeare, an acting company touring to secondary schools, is a partnership between the public schools and the University of North Dakota's Theatre Arts Department. It is designed to inspire North Dakota students to read and further explore Shakespeare's plays. Teachers are provided packets with games, improvisational activities, discussion topics, and lists of books, videos, and audiotapes. The energetic and innovative performances are followed by a period during which the performance and materials are evaluated and secondary schools are asked for information that will guide future scripts or performance styles.

OHIO

Art Academy of Cincinnati (ART)
High School Workshop Program

Grades served: HS

Schools served: 16

Year established: 1988

Location of schools served: UR, SU, RU

Type of schools served: PUB, PRI

This program supports outstanding high school art programs by providing free workshops for juniors and seniors in the academy's studios and adjacent galleries of the Cincinnati Art Museum. The program's chief goals are to provide stimulating field trips and hands-on workshops that introduce art media usually not available in high schools, to help smooth the transition between high school classes and college-level programs, to give students realistic expectations of the demands of art school life; and to encourage students who choose to pursue art as a career.

Case Western Reserve University (RES I)
LTV Steel Science & Technology Institute

Grades served: HS

Schools served: NR

Year established: 1992

Location of schools served: UR

Type of schools served: PUB

The LTV Steel Science & Technology Institute is a summer program designed to enhance and enrich students' lifelong interest in mathematics and science. Classes are held at Case Western Reserve University, with lectures by college professors, master teachers, and local engineers; hands-on laboratory experiences; field trips to industrial and research facilities; tours of LTV Steel; and instruction in integrated process control (a quality assurance system at LTV). Thirty tenth graders from Cleveland Public Schools are selected annually and recruited for the program, based on interest and ability in mathematics and science.

Cleveland Institute of Art (ART)
Summer Scholars Program

Grades served: HS

Schools served: 18

Year established: 1987

Location of schools served: UR

Type of schools served: PUB

The Summer Scholars Program is designed to give selected students from the Cleveland Public Schools an opportunity to become involved in the Institute's Young Artist Summer Program. Students choose a specialized visual arts program for a four-week period during the mornings and attend special activities in the afternoons. Activities might include field trips to museums, art galleries, and artists' studios, including some focusing on sculpture, computer graphics, and fiber arts. Students are encouraged to discuss their work and their experiences in an institution of higher learning.

Ohio Northern University (BA II)
Street Law

Grades served: HS

Schools served: 4

Year established: 1985

Location of schools served: UR, SU, RU

Type of schools served: PUB

The Street Law program is a community service of the Claude W. Pettit College of Law. Each year law students teach high school students about legal issues, including basic constitutional law, family law, consumer law, criminal law, and the juvenile justice system. Street Law classes meet once a week for 12 weeks as part of high school history or social studies classes. The program culminates with an interschool competition and mock trial. The university serves groups from college prep to remedial classes in schools ranging from predominantly African-American urban schools to predominantly white rural schools.

Shawnee State University (BA II)
Scioto River Water Quality Project

Grades served: E, M, HS

Schools served: 13

Year established: 1993

Location of schools served: UR, SU, RU

Type of schools served: PUB, PRI

The Scioto River Water Quality project involves the 13 southern Ohio school districts that border the Scioto River. In each district, one class takes responsibility for weekly monitoring of water quality at a sample location along the river. The data collected are shared on an electronic bulletin board. A grant covers the cost of necessary equipment for the tests, provides inservice training on testing procedures for participating teachers, and coordinates the ongoing communication of test results. Cooperating agencies include Shawnee State University, Ohio University-Chillicothe, the Ohio EPA, The Mead Corporation, and Martin-Marietta Energy Systems.

Note: Each institution's Carnegie class is given in parentheses. **Key:** E=elementary school, HS=high school, M=middle school, NR=not reported, PRI=private, PUB=public, RU=rural, SU=suburban, UR=urban

University of Findlay (BA II)
Mazza School Extension Program
Grades served: E, M

Schools served: 32

Year established: 1983

Location of schools served: UR, SU, RU

Type of schools served: PUB, PRI

The Mazza Collection includes original artwork by the most distinguished and honored illustrators of children's books. It has the distinction of being the only teaching gallery in the world specializing in such art. The Mazza School Extension Program is a partnership linking the University of Findlay, through the Mazza Collection, and elementary and middle schools. Students at participating schools study the art and books of several featured artists, then vote for their favorite. Winning artists often respond with letters, autographed books, and posters and/or taped messages to the respective schools.

OKLAHOMA

Southeastern Oklahoma State University (MA I)
Children's Theatre
Grades served: E

Schools served: 25

Year established: 1967

Location of schools served: RU

Type of schools served: PUB

The objective of this program is to educate elementary students in the theater arts. It also trains university students and public school teachers in children's theater by placing them as educational assistants within the program. All daily activities are geared toward the education and self-expression of children and the final artistic product, a one-hour children's musical. The majority of participants do not experience theater in their public school; therefore, this program is their first exposure to combining creative role playing, music, dance, and spoken word for presentation.

OREGON

Reed College (BA I)
Super Quest
Grades served: HS

Schools served: 4

Year established: 1992

Location of schools served: UR, SU, RU

Type of schools served: PUB, PRI

Reed College is one of four national sites for Super Quest, the national computational science contest funded by the National Science Foundation for high school students and their teachers. The program is designed to encourage high school students to study and use advanced computing resources in current research. Fourteen students and their teacher-coaches from across the country are assisted in their projects by mentors from Reed, Oregon Graduate Institute of Science and Technology, and Intel Supercomputer Systems Division. Projects can explore any area of mathematics, sciences, or other disciplines, but the research must require computational technology for analysis, visualization, or modeling.

PENNSYLVANIA

Temple University (RES I)
PRIME Universities Program (PUP)
Grades served: M, HS

Schools served: NR

Year established: 1978

Location of schools served: UR

Type of schools served: PUB, PRI

The PRIME Universities Program consists of four consecutive years of sequential summer enrichment beginning after eighth grade. It provides intensive instruction in mathematics, communication skills, and computer applications. Students may choose to follow one track of three: engineering, actuarial science, or pharmacy and allied health. Students must take both an academic math and science course during the academic year, maintain at least a B average in all major subjects, indicate interest in a mathematics- or science-based career, and participate in PRIME activities.

PUERTO RICO

Universidad del Turabo (MA I)
Pre-Engineering Preparatory Program

Grades served: HS

Schools served: 25

Year established: 1991

Location of schools served: UR, SU, RU

Type of schools served: PUB, PRI

The Pre-Engineering Preparatory Program is a partnership linking the University of Turabo, Sistema Educativo Ana G Mendez with NASA, CRCM, and the high school students classified as gifted and/or talented in public and private schools. The program's objective is to prepare future engineers with the necessary skills in mathematics, English, computers, chemistry, and physics to successfully undertake university study upon graduation from high school. The program also provides a Summer Research Program at national labs, field trips to industries employing engineers, and participation in science fairs. Evaluation includes attitudinal and academic measures, recordings, and a follow-up of program participants who went on to engineering study in college.

SOUTH CAROLINA

Medical University of South Carolina (MED)
Summer Research Program

Grades served: HS

Schools served: 26

Year established: 1993

Location of schools served: UR, SU, RU

Type of schools served: PUB, PRI

The Medical University of South Carolina's Summer Research Program for rising high school seniors is designed to provide opportunities for students, particularly minority students, to be involved in investigative research. In 1990 the South Carolina Governor's School for Science and Mathematics (GSSM) began the Research Mentor Program to place rising seniors in the laboratories of university and government scientists for four to ten weeks during the summer to conduct research. Additional grant support has expanded the program to other schools. Students present their work at the GSSM Research Colloquium, and many will also present it at the South Carolina Junior Academy of Science.

University of South Carolina-Columbia (RES II)
Odyssey of the Mind State Competition

Grades served: E, M, HS

Schools served: 60

Year established: 1992

Location of schools served: UR, SU, RU

Type of schools served: PUB

Odyssey of the Mind's state competition is an annual event hosted and coordinated by South Carolina Honors College at the University of South Carolina in Columbia and by the South Carolina Odyssey of the Mind board of directors. Its primary purposes are to provide gifted and talented students with team-building experience to develop cooperation, leadership, and problem-solving and critical thinking skills, and to promote partnerships and cooperation between the university and public schools. Students, parents, coaches, and judges whose teams have won regional Odyssey competitions come to Columbia for one day to participate in the state OM competition, with the winner sent to the national finals.

Note: Each institution's Carnegie class is given in parentheses. **Key:** E=elementary school, HS=high school, M=middle school, NR=not reported, PRI=private, PUB=public, RU=rural, SU=suburban, UR=urban

University of South Carolina-Columbia (RES II)
Adventures in Creativity
Grades served: HS   Schools served: NR   Year established: 1988
Location of schools served: UR, SU, RU   Type of schools served: PUB

Adventures in Creativity is a residential two-week interdisciplinary summer program for rising tenth and 11th grade South Carolina Junior Scholars. A group of the most creative and dynamic teacher/scholars at the University of South Carolina, representing disciplines as diverse as art and physics, guide the students as they develop creativity. This across-the-spectrum approach is intended to demonstrate to the students that creativity is at the heart of the pursuit of knowledge in all fields: science as well as art, philosophy no less than music. The adventures comprise both classes and extracurricular activities.

University of South Carolina-Columbia (RES II)
Carolina Journalism Institute (CJI)
Grades served: M, HS   Schools served: 90   Year established: 1960
Location of schools served: UR, SU, RU   Type of schools served: PUB, PRI

The Carolina Journalism Institute is a partnership linking the University of South Carolina with public and private, middle and secondary schools throughout the country, but primarily in the Southeast. CJI is a one-week scholastic journalism workshop sponsored by the Southern Interscholastic Press Association and supported by the university's College of Journalism and Mass Communications. The workshop covers specialized areas, including broadcast journalism, desktop publishing, and magazine, newspaper, yearbook, or photojournalism. CJI assists advisers and students in enhancing journalistic offerings at their school.

University of South Carolina-Columbia (RES II)
Benjamin E. Mays Academy for Leadership Development
Grades served: M, HS   Schools served: 30   Year established: 1988
Location of schools served: UR, SU   Type of schools served: PUB, PRI

The Benjamin E. Mays Academy for Leadership Development is designed to help outstanding youth develop leadership skills and achieve excellence in a number of scientific, literary, technological, mathematical, social, and cultural areas. Criteria for students' eligibility for the program include scholarship, leadership, citizenship, service, and character. Participants are required to have demonstrated positive leadership ability or to possess measurable leadership potential. Activities consist of lectures, discussions, practical experiences, and seminars by mentors who are talented academicians, professionals, and scholars as well as prominent personalities in South Carolina, the United States, and other countries.

University of South Carolina-Columbia (RES II)
Southern Interscholastic Press Association
Grades served: M, HS   Schools served: 250   Year established: 1924
Location of schools served: UR, SU, RU   Type of schools served: PUB, PRI

The Southern Interscholastic Press Association is a partnership linking the University of South Carolina and its College of Journalism and Mass Communications with public and private, middle and secondary schools throughout the Southeast. Member schools participate in critiques of their broadcasts, magazines, newspapers, and yearbooks; a spring convention; and a college scholarship competition. The association assists school broadcast, magazine, newspaper, and yearbook staffs to enhance their presentations.

Winthrop University (MA I)
Summer ST-ARTS Program (Summer Program for Special Students in the Arts)

Grades served: M   Schools served: 12   Year established: 1989
Location of schools served: UR, RU   Type of schools served: PUB

Sponsored jointly by Winthrop University's School of Visual and Performing Arts and its consortium of public schools, this three-week program offers a comprehensive arts program to 250 artistically gifted and talented middle school students. A faculty of 45 artists/teachers in dance, music, drama, and the visual arts includes national and regional performing artists, university faculty, and master public school teachers. Designed in accordance with the new South Carolina visual and performing arts framework, the curriculum emphasizes the process of creating art rather than the product alone. The program has been cited as a model for university/consortium cooperation.

TEXAS

University of Texas-Medical Branch at Galveston (MED)
Science Education

Grades served: E, M, HS   Schools served: 22   Year established: 1991
Location of schools served: UR, SU   Type of schools served: PUB, PRI

The objective of the UTMB Science Education program is to encourage students' interest in science, current technology, and scientific careers. Participation from all K-12 students is encouraged, but underrepresented minorities and females are principal target groups. The program's initiatives use university faculty, staff, and students to assist as telephone mentors, classroom or individual mentors, classroom speakers, and tour guides through specific research and/or health-related areas. A six-week Summer Science Camp for seventh and eighth grade students engages in hands-on laboratory experiences, and an eight-week Summer Research Program for high school students provides research experiences in specific labs.

UTAH

Weber State University (MA II)
Northern Utah Arts Consortium

Grades served: E   Schools served: NR   Year established: 1988
Location of schools served: NR   Type of schools served: PUB

The Northern Utah Arts Consortium is a joint venture of Weber State University's Departments of Performing Arts and Visual Arts and the Ogden City, Weber, Davis, and Morgan School Districts. The program is designed to make more efficient use of human and physical instructional resources, to generate new resources by enlisting the support of volunteer artists, and to promote the development of future artists and their audiences. Programs include music instruction, a piano preparatory school, a String Petting Zoo (enabling students to try a variety of stringed instruments), creative dramatics, art, and the Japanese language.

Weber State University (MA II)
Consortium for Academic Excellence

Grades served: HS   Schools served: 3   Year established: 1989
Location of schools served: NR   Type of schools served: PUB

The consortium's primary goals are to create cooperation and continuity between advanced placement teachers and WSU honors faculty; to introduce high school students to university-level work; to enhance AP subjects; and to familiarize both university and AP teachers with each other's expectations for students' performance. Costs are shared by the Honors Program, grants from a school district foundation, and university matching funds. The Davis School District Foundation's funding formula enables district students and teachers to participate as equal partners in the consortium.

Note: Each institution's Carnegie class is given in parentheses. **Key:** E=elementary school, HS=high school, M=middle school, NR=not reported, PRI=private, PUB=public, RU=rural, SU=suburban, UR=urban

VIRGINIA

Christopher Newport University (BA II)
Summer Institute for the Arts

Grades served: M, HS	Schools served: 11	Year established: 1986
Location of schools served: UR	Type of schools served: PUB	

The Summer Institute for the Arts is a partnership linking Christopher Newport University and the Newport News Public Schools to provide in-depth academic courses in the arts for selected high school students. Since its inception, 885 students have completed the program for high school credit in art, music, drama, or dance. Classes are taught on the university campus by professors, high schools instructors, and art professionals for seven hours a day, four days a week, for six weeks. Trips to galleries, museums, and theaters in Williamsburg, Norfolk, Richmond, and the District of Columbia enrich the curriculum.

Christopher Newport University (BA II)
Annual High School Theatre Festival

Grades served: HS	Schools served: 25	Year established: 1982
Location of schools served: UR, SU, RU	Type of schools served: PUB, PRI	

Christopher Newport University's Annual High School Theatre Festival offers live performances of classical drama to high school students throughout the Tidewater area of Virginia. Plays (e.g., *The Glass Menagerie, Tartuffe, Oedipus Rex*) coincide with the high school curricula. Annually 1,000-2,000 students visit the campus to watch a performance and take part in seminars with faculty members, cast members, and theater staff. Essay competitions are conducted for students in the four Newport News high schools; awards include publication and cash prizes.

WASHINGTON

Eastern Washington University (MA I)
International Field Study (IFS)

Grades served: HS	Schools served: NR	Year established: 1980
Location of schools served: UR, SU, RU	Type of schools served: PUB, PRI	

The International Field Study program involves Eastern Washington University; the College of Eastern Utah-San Juan Campus; Tver State University (Russia); the East Valley School District #361 of Spokane (WA); and many other cooperating schools. The program is based in the belief that high school students who actively participate in a global classroom field study tend to develop a better understanding of cultural diversity. IFS has developed secondary/university course work to support students' intercultural experiences. University course work and resources have also been developed for teachers' use.

WISCONSIN

Saint Norbert College (BA II)
Young Artist Workshops

Grades served: E, M, HS	Schools served: 1	Year established: 1989
Location of schools served: UR	Type of schools served: PUB	

Young Artist Workshops, sponsored by St. Norbert College and the Brown County Handicapped Children's Educational Board (Syble Hopp School), provide visual and performing arts workshops each summer for young people aged 3-22 with a variety of disabling conditions. The multifaceted program also sponsors year-round research and continuing education workshops and produces publications and video resources for educators. The three-week summer program serves as a practicum setting for students and special educators working on Adaptive Education Certification in Art, Music, Early Childhood, and Assistive Technology.

University of Wisconsin-Eau Claire (MA I)
WCATY (Wisconsin Center for Academically Talented Youth) Summer Program

Grades served: M, HS   Schools served: NR   Year established: 1992
Location of schools served: UR, SU, RU   Type of schools served: PUB, PRI

WCATY's Summer Program at the University of Wisconsin-Eau Claire is a three-week residential academic program for Wisconsin's brightest students aged 12-16. Students are accepted based on ACT or SAT scores. They choose one of ten courses to study in depth at a fast pace. Classes offered might include Japanese, geopolitics, writing, computer technology, anthropology, economics, and self-paced mathematics. Many of the students' home schools issue credit to the students based on their portfolios.

University of Wisconsin-Eau Claire (MA I)
Math Talent Development Project

Grades served: M   Schools served: NR   Year established: 1979
Location of schools served: UR, SU, RU   Type of schools served: PUB, PRI

The Math Talent Development Project takes middle school students through four years of high school mathematics in two years. Students qualify for the program through SAT or ACT scores and are identified and recommended largely by their schools. They come to the university for two hours of class on Saturday mornings, then complete assignments during the week. They do not take any math classes at their home schools during this time. The university communicates closely with students, parents, and the students' schools. Upon completion of the course, students are ready to begin college calculus.

University of Wisconsin-Eau Claire (MA I)
Distance Education and Gifted/Talented Project

Grades served: M   Schools served: 4   Year established: 1992
Location of schools served: UR, RU   Type of schools served: PUB

The Distance Education/Gifted Talented Project is a cooperative effort of area school districts, the Cooperative Educational Service Agency (CESA), and the university. Its purposes are to expose school personnel and students to the potentials of distance learning (live video and audio) and teach them how it works, to give gifted and talented students from different school systems a chance to network with students of similar abilities and interests, and to begin to introduce the concepts of differentiating curriculum and interdisciplinary, thematic approaches to the cooperating schools. The program uses new technology in new ways to use educators' and schools' time efficiently and effectively.

University of Wisconsin-Eau Claire (MA I)
Summer Institute for High-Potential Students

Grades served: E, M, HS   Schools served: NR   Year established: 1988
Location of schools served: UR, SU, RU   Type of schools served: PUB, PRI

The Summer Institute for High-Potential Students is a program of summer academic enrichment for K-12 students who live within 75 miles of the campus. Students can choose from about 50 classes in writing and literature, theater and arts, math and computer science, and science and technology for three 2-week sessions. Most classes are 16 hours. All classes use a hands-on approach. One local school district subsidizes its students' fees.

Note: Each institution's Carnegie class is given in parentheses. **Key:** E=elementary school, HS=high school, M=middle school, NR=not reported, PRI=private, PUB=public, RU=rural, SU=suburban, UR=urban

University of Wisconsin-Oshkosh (MA I)
NEWACE Social Action Theatre for Children & Youth

Grades served: E, M   Schools served: NR   Year established: 1992
Location of schools served: NR   Type of schools served: PUB

The NEWACE (Northeast Wisconsin Alliance for Continuing Education) Social Action Theatre for Children and Youth is a joint project of the University of Wisconsin-Oshkosh, the University of Wisconsin-Green Bay, and the Appleton Area School District. It employs educational drama to address issues of cultural diversity. The project's purpose is to develop the process, instructional guides, and supporting materials so teachers and school administrators in other school districts can undertake similar theater projects. Elementary and junior high school students, teachers, administrators, and NEWACE staff are participating in the development process.

University of Wisconsin-Whitewater (MA I)
Family Fun Math Nights

Grades served: E   Schools served: 6   Year established: 1992
Location of schools served: SU, RU Type of schools served: PUB

Family Fun Math Nights link current and prospective elementary teachers, with elementary students and their parents. University students prepare mathematical games and activities for students and their parents. The program's objectives are to promote alternative teaching strategies among university students, allow the elementary students to experience mathematics in an enjoyable setting, provide elementary teachers with an opportunity to stimulate mathematical thinking outside the classroom, and show parents how to incorporate mathematics-based activities into family life.

Section Four
Middle Colleges and Early Colleges

CALIFORNIA

Foothill College (AA)
Middle College

Grades served: HS   Schools served: 2   Year established: 1993
Location of schools served: SU   Type of schools served: PUB

Middle College is an alternative program located on the Foothill College campus. The program is designed for high school juniors and seniors who are academically very capable but for a variety of reasons are not performing up to their potential. By interacting with a more mature role group and taking advantage of advanced course work, students with previous problems in attendance and study develop responsibility and a sense of self-direction. Because Middle College is a collaboration of Palo Alto Unified School District, the Mountain View-Los Altos Union High School District, and Foothill College, students benefit from the teaching and support of all institutions.

MASSACHUSETTS

Bunker Hill Community College (AA)
BHCC/Fenway Middle College High School

Grades served: HS	Schools served: 1	Year established: NR
Location of schools served: UR	Type of schools served: PUB	

The Bunker Hill Community College/Fenway Middle College High School brings the high school program into the college. The program stresses the value of higher education and lifelong learning. Fenway students have access to the college's facilities and activities and a range of college courses, and BHCC students tutor the high school students. Joint cultural and social programs enhance the quality of collaboration.

Simon's Rock College of Bard (BA I)
Early College Partnership

Grades served: HS	Schools served: NR	Year established: 1966
Location of schools served: UR, SU, RU	Type of schools served: PUB, PRI	

Simon's Rock is a college devoted exclusively to meeting the intellectual, social, and emotional needs of younger scholars. Freshmen are typically 16 years old and have completed tenth or 11th grade, essentially skipping the last two years of high school to pursue full-time collegiate studies leading to the Associate and Bachelor of Arts degrees. Established in 1966, Simon's Rock merged with Bard College in 1979. The Simon's Rock campus, located in western Massachusetts, enrolls more than 300 students.

MISSOURI

Longview Community College (AA)
PACE (Program for Adult College Education)

Grades served: HS (adult)	Schools served: 2	Year established: 1981
Location of schools served: UR, SU	Type of schools served: PUB	

Longview Community College's Program for Adult College Education offers an Associate in Arts degree to rural high school students and urban working adults. The arrangement permits full-time status for students who attend class one evening a week, watch video tapes at home, and participate in an on-campus weekend conference once a month. A partnership with University of Missouri-Kansas City allows LCC graduates automatic admission to the UMKC College of Arts and Sciences and matriculation for the Bachelor of Liberal Arts. The two institutions work together in broadcasting classes live from UMKC's studio for transmission to homes and businesses via cablevision.

NEW JERSEY

Fairleigh Dickinson University (MA I)
Middle College

Grades served: HS	Schools served: 22	Year established: 1984
Location of schools served: UR, SU, RU	Type of schools served: PUB, PRI	

The Middle College program puts the university at the service of 22 secondary schools with relatively easy access to the three New Jersey campuses. More than 500 junior and senior honor students enroll in courses such as physics, calculus, Spanish, biology, and humanities taught by college and high school faculty. Activities include supplementary lectures, laboratory demonstrations, visits to theater and concert performances, art exhibits, and museum trips. The university's library and computer resources are open to participating students, who may attain advanced standing and/or college credit through the program.

Note: Each institution's Carnegie class is given in parentheses. **Key:** E=elementary school, HS=high school, M=middle school, NR=not reported, PRI=private, PUB=public, RU=rural, SU=suburban, UR=urban

City University of New York Bronx Community College (AA)
University Heights High School

Grades served: E, HS	Schools served: 1	Year established: 1989
Location of schools served: UR	Type of schools served: PUB	

University Heights High School, located on the campus of Bronx Community College, was initiated as an alternative school under the Coalition of Essential Schools directed by Theodore Sizer at Brown University. The school emphasizes shared governance and collaborative learning and the establishment of a functioning learning community. All seniors have advisers and receive assistance with applying to colleges and obtaining financial aid. In 1992-93, some 92% of participants went on to college, and the dropout rate was less than 3%.

City University of New York Herbert H. Lehman College (MA I)
Walton/Lehman Bridge to College

Grades served: HS	Schools served: 1	Year established: 1983
Location of schools served: UR	Type of schools served: NR	

The Walton/Lehman Bridge to College program seeks to increase preparedness for college and to ease the transition from high school to college; it also increases access to, retention in, and completion of postsecondary education. Activities include assessment of academic strengths and weaknesses, developmental courses (if needed), collaborative review and assessment of high school and college curricula and courses, mentoring and tutoring by college students, use of college facilities and services by the high school students, a program of joint professional development activities, team teaching, creation of a college planning class for tenth graders, and development of networks within and between the institutions.

City University of New York LaGuardia Community College (AA)
American Social History Project/Middle College High School Consortium National Project

Grades served: HS	Schools served: 10	Year established: 1993
Location of schools served: UR	Type of schools served: PUB	

This project expands the six-year-old New York City High School Collaboration Project to middle college high schools throughout the country. Teams of college and high school teachers engage in interdisciplinary teaching and promote collaborative learning in a high school classroom. The American Social History Project is the first cooperative curriculum project. It will be followed by math enrichment and science projects in an effort to enrich the education of at-risk students and to improve communication among the educators who work with them. The consortium sponsors national meetings for middle college administrators, teachers, and students.

City University of New York LaGuardia Community College (AA)
International High School

Grades served: HS	Schools served: 1	Year established: 1985
Location of schools served: UR	Type of schools served: PUB	

Jointly sponsored by the New York City Board of Education and the City University of New York, International High School is designed to develop students' linguistic, cognitive, and cultural skills necessary for success in high school and beyond. Study of all subject matter is combined with intensive study and reinforcement of English. The instructional program emphasizes interdisciplinary course work; the use of student learning communities; completion of an extensive personal and career development program, which includes three internships; enrollment in college-level courses, and small classes. Through Project PROPEL, International High School assists other schools to adopt key features of the program.

City University of New York LaGuardia Community College (AA)
Middle College High School

Grades served: HS   Schools served: 1   Year established: 1974
Location of schools served: UR   Type of schools served: PUB

Middle College High School is a joint project of the City University of New York and the New York City Board of Education. It seeks to improve the academic performance, self-concept, career planning, and higher education options of students who are perceived by referring counselors and teachers to be at risk of not completing high school. The instructional program emphasizes small classes; intensive daily group counseling, a specially adapted curriculum, completion of three work internships, and placements that range from hospitals to museums, schools, the courts, and social service agencies.

Clarkson University (DOC II)
The Clarkson School's Bridging Year Program

Grades served: HS   Schools served: 40   Year established: 1978
Location of schools served: UR, SU, RU   Type of schools served: PUB, PRI

This program allows talented high school students to enter college after their junior year in secondary school. Clarkson has attempted to remove misconceptions about early admission and encourage students to break out of the sequential approach behind most educational planning. The program demonstrates that talented students can benefit from early admission and avoid wasting an academically unchallenging senior year by getting a head start on university courses.

WASHINGTON

Seattle Central Community College (AA)
Middle College High School

Grades served: HS   Schools served: 14   Year established: 1990
Location of schools served: UR   Type of schools served: PUB

Seattle Central Community College's Middle College High School (MCHS) serves students who left high school before graduation by providing an opportunity for them to receive a high school diploma and take college classes for both high school and college credit in an adult atmosphere and college environment. MCHS teachers work with college instructors to develop a team-taught, coordinated curriculum incorporating multicultural components. The Career Education/Internship Program, for example, provides exposure to the professional working world, the Mentor Program provides role models other than a parent or peer, and a bilingual program assists bilingual students. Day care is free for the children of students.

Seattle University (DOC II)
Matteo Ricci College

Grades served: HS   Schools served: 1   Year established: 1975
Location of schools served: UR   Type of schools served: PRI

Matteo Ricci College at Seattle University is the final three-year phase of a six-year program that coordinates and integrates high and university studies, thereby enabling students to complete their post-elementary education in six or seven years rather than the traditional eight. The program includes collaboration among faculty, an interdisciplinary and coherent curriculum, active learning, and a spirit of community among teachers and learners. It was founded jointly by Seattle University and Seattle Preparatory School.

Note: Each institution's Carnegie class is given in parentheses. **Key:** E=elementary school, HS=high school, M=middle school, NR=not reported, PRI=private, PUB=public, RU=rural, SU=suburban, UR=urban

Section Five
Tutoring, Mentoring, and Counseling Programs

CALIFORNIA

California State University-Fresno (MA I)
Elementary Teacher Cadet Program

Grades served: E   Schools served: 8   Year established: 1991
Location of schools served: NR   Type of schools served: PUB

The School of Education and Human Development at California State University, Fresno, in collaboration with Fresno Unified School District, implemented the Elementary Teacher Cadet Program in 1991. More than 200 fifth and sixth grade students from eight elementary schools have participated in this project. The program focuses on training the students to be tutors at their school sites. Its principal objectives are to enhance self-esteem and academic skills of the tutors, to promote a strategic early-intervention plan to enhance the retention of students, and to establish collaborative efforts involving the university, school personnel, and parents.

University of California-Davis (RES I)
Mathematics Diagnostic Testing Program

Grades served: M, HS   Schools served: 374   Year established: 1982
Location of schools served: UR, SU, RU   Type of schools served: PUB, PRI

California State University and the University of California have jointly funded the test development activities of the Mathematics Diagnostic Testing Program (MDTP) since 1978. The tests are developed by a work group including faculty from both universities, community colleges, and high schools. The California Academic Partnership Program supports MDTP's direct services to junior and senior high schools. The project provides, without charge, tests and scoring services to individual students, teachers, schools, and districts in California. It also enables a number of university campuses to serve as regional resources for schools and teachers. UC-Davis is one of the resource sites.

COLORADO

Front Range Community College (AA)
Partners for Success

Grades served: M   Schools served: 2   Year established: 1992
Location of schools served: NR   Type of schools served: PUB

Partners for Success involves two student organizations at Front Range Community College and School District 14 in Commerce City. Mentors from the college provide friendship, role modeling, tutoring, and social, cultural, and/or recreational activities to at-risk eighth graders. Measurable outcomes are expected to be improved attendance, higher semester grade point average, improved persistence toward enrollment at Adams City High School, and enrollment in more college preparatory classes at ACHS. Achievement will be measured by comparing the group served with the total population and a control group of unserved students, and individuals with their previous performance.

Front Range Community College (AA)
Student Literacy Corps
Grades served: E, M, HS
Location of schools served: UR, SU

Schools served: 4
Type of schools served: PUB

Year established: 1993

The Student Literacy Corps, in partnership with the student organization Front Range Educational Empowerment (FREE) and Adams County School Districts 12 and 14, provides literacy tutoring to four schools. Two elementary schools, one middle school, and one high school were the focus of the 1994 program, and a student literacy coordinator was assigned to each school. The student coordinators, teachers, and principals design the specific elements of each school's program. A variable-credit course provides support for service-learning, which will promote understanding of community needs through voluntarism and the study of related topics.

CONNECTICUT

Trinity College (BA I)
Community Outreach Youth-At-Risk
Grades served: E
Location of schools served: UR

Schools served: 5
Type of schools served: PUB

Year established: 1985

Volunteers provide a variety of services to local schools through Trinity College's Community Outreach Youth-at-Risk program. The program is run by students and regularly enlists more than 350 student volunteers in approximately 18 projects, five of them tutoring. Two of the projects provide help within the classroom in whatever activities the teacher selects. The other three projects assist in established after-school projects as needed. All projects provide help within the classroom and individually as well.

Trinity College (BA I)
I Have A Dream
Grades served: E, M, HS
Location of schools served: UR

Schools served: 3
Type of schools served: PUB

Year established: 1987

The I Have A Dream (IHAD) program began with a promise to 57 sixth graders at Fred D. Wish Elementary School that in six years, upon graduation from high school, their college tuition would be paid. In addition to housing the IHAD offices, Trinity hosts the IHAD's summer employment program on campus, providing classroom space and work sites. During the academic year, Trinity students act as tutors and/or mentors for some of the Dreamers. The first class of Dreamers has graduated, and a new class chosen.

Trinity College (BA I)
Career Beginnings
Grades served: HS
Location of schools served: UR

Schools served: 3
Type of schools served: PUB

Year established: 1986

Career Beginnings is Trinity College's implementation of a national program in which the Hartford Consortium for Higher Education became involved in 1986. The program helps high school students from low-income families strengthen their chances for high school graduation, gain admission to college or a skills-training program, or obtain a full-time job with career potential. Individual Trinity faculty and administrators serve as mentors to local juniors and seniors. In addition, various departments offer special programs, such as financial aid workshops and tours.

Note: Each institution's Carnegie class is given in parentheses. **Key:** E=elementary school, HS=high school, M=middle school, NR=not reported, PRI=private, PUB=public, RU=rural, SU=suburban, UR=urban

DISTRICT OF COLUMBIA

George Washington University (RES II)
Slowe Elementary Mentoring Program

Grades served: E	Schools served: 1	Year established: NR
Location of schools served: UR	Type of schools served: PUB	

George Washington University's AKA sorority mentors children from Slowe Elementary School. Each AKA member has two young children with whom she keeps in contact. Activities include such events as trips to the National Museum of African Art, the movies, and George Washington and Howard University field trips. Mentors help students to form and express future goals and encourage them to include college plans. This year-long program involves 20 students from grades 3 to 10. Ten GWU students volunteer five hours a month to the program.

George Washington University (RES II)
Super Leaders

Grades served: HS	Schools served: 5	Year established: 1984
Location of schools served: UR, SU	Type of schools served: PUB	

George Washington University's School of Medical and Health Sciences's Super Leaders (SL) Program is a drug prevention, youth leadership program with five high schools in the District of Columbia and Maryland. Student Leaders meet at least twice a month for planning, evaluation, and training. Each spring, the medical school hosts the SL Parent-Student Summit, addressing such issues as substance abuse, HIV, teen pregnancy, and other health issues affecting youth. The program involves approximately 500 students from grades 9-12 in five high schools. The university arranges counseling, tutoring, demonstrations, and tours of the medical facility, and schools provide on-site counselors and tutors.

George Washington University (RES II)
DC Works

Grades served: HS	Schools served: NR	Year established: 1989
Location of schools served: UR	Type of schools served: PUB	

DC Works is a six-week summer program designed to encourage senior high school students to improve academically and to attend college. It combines employment with local corporations and academic instruction. Guidance counselors select ethnic minority students from New York, Baltimore, Philadelphia, and the District of Columbia. Thirty 11th and 12th graders are selected. The university academic instruction and mentor programs are managed by four staff members and two GWU students. The program includes workshops on financial aid, study skills, and career planning. DC Works and GWU personnel conduct ongoing evaluation of the program.

George Washington University (RES II)
Independent Living Program

Grades served: M, HS	Schools served: NR	Year established: 1991
Location of schools served: UR	Type of schools served: PUB	

This program is designed to help foster-care teenagers in grades 9 through 12 master the skills and knowledge necessary to achieve self-sufficiency after having lived as foster children and to help them make educational or career choices. George Washington staff and student volunteers provide support and counseling. A mentor program and workshops in study skills, financial aid, career planning, and social skills are offered, supplemented by academic and social counseling.

George Washington University (RES II)
Elementary School Partnership

Grades served: E   Schools served: 1   Year established: 1992
Location of schools served: UR   Type of schools served: PUB

George Washington University's Elementary School Partnership links the university's NROTC and Watkins Elementary School. During the school year, midshipmen act as tutors and mentors for about 30 students in grades 2-4, primarily during school hours at Watkins. The university students also assist with some extracurricular activities. Tutoring times are flexible to accommodate individual midshipmen's academic schedules. Teachers identify the Watkins students that need help and provide a location for tutoring.

Howard University (RES I)
Student to Student Substance Abuse Prevention Project

Grades served: E   Schools served: 1   Year established: 1991
Location of schools served: UR   Type of schools served: PUB

The goals of this project are to design a collaborative school-parent-community-university model program for drug and alcohol abuse education; to train students, parents, teachers, and community members in substance abuse education and prevention; to provide structures for after-school homework tutoring in reading and mathematics for at-risk elementary school students; to use their increased achievement in these areas to develop related activities for their peers; and to organize a traveling troupe of substance abuse educators to make presentations in the community. Partners include Howard University faculty and students, District of Columbia Public School teachers and administrators, and J.C. Nalle Elementary School students and their parents.

Howard University (RES I)
J.C. Nalle Elementary School Partnership in Education

Grades served: E   Schools served: 1   Year established: 1989
Location of schools served: UR   Type of schools served: PUB

This partnership is designed to increase self-esteem among all participating students and to raise at-risk students' scores on the California Test of Basic Skills to grade-level equivalency. The program implements an after-school tutorial/homework program and adjusts instructional activities/teaching techniques to address students' needs. Tutoring is provided in math, reading, and language arts. Teachers and staff members participate in staff development and a mentoring program. The partnership arrangement affords the school the opportunity to purchase computers, printers, television monitors, art supplies, and psychological services for the students.

FLORIDA

Florida International University (MA I)
Intergenerational Law Advocacy Program

Grades served: HS   Schools served: 19   Year established: 1989
Location of schools served: UR, SU   Type of schools served: PUB

The Intergenerational Law Advocacy Program, cosponsored by Florida International University's Institute for Public Policy and Citizenship Studies and the Dade County Public Schools, links high school students, many of whom are minority, at-risk students, with senior citizen mentors who are civic activists. The mentors use advocacy skills learned at an annual Intergenerational Public Policy Summer Institute to effect change in local and state government on issues of common concern, appearing, for example, before the Florida Legislature to support legislation assisting youth and the elderly.

Note: Each institution's Carnegie class is given in parentheses. **Key:** E=elementary school, HS=high school, M=middle school, NR=not reported, PRI=private, PUB=public, RU=rural, SU=suburban, UR=urban

University of Tampa (MA II)
Project SERVE

Grades served: E

Location of schools served: UR, SU

Schools served: NR

Type of schools served: PUB

Year established: 1988

Project SERVE links University of Tampa education students with elementary school students in the Hillsborough County School System. Students enrolled in Education 200, the entry-level course, and in elementary education methods and diagnostic reading courses, volunteer in elementary schools to assist teachers with instruction in reading. The teachers plan the methods and procedures, and the volunteer students carry out those instructions with individuals or small groups of children. The partnership provides needed assistance to both groups of participants: individual and small-group instruction for the elementary students, and a hands-on opportunity to evaluate their interest in teaching for the college students.

GEORGIA

Augusta College (MA I)
Augusta College Literacy in Action/Metro Adult Literacy Council

Grades served: E, M, HS

Location of schools served: UR, SU, RU

Schools served: NR

Type of schools served: PUB

Year established: 1989

Literacy in Action is designed to affect children and adults by creating and supporting highly effective literacy programs throughout the region. Diagnostic training, assessment, resource development, and instruction are a few of the many services offered. Campus-based community outreach programs for all levels of learners, including GED, and tutoring are available. Public school programs include offerings linking children's creative activities to literacy, and a homework center offered to the entire community at no charge.

Berry College (MA I)
Student Literacy Corps

Grades served: E

Location of schools served: NR

Schools served: 2

Type of schools served: PUB, PRI

Year established: 1993

Student Literacy Corps participants include approximately 40 undergraduate students, 15 graduate students, 20 elementary school teachers, and 50 disadvantaged elementary school children and their parents. The in-depth tutoring is longitudinal and focuses on children served under Chapter 1 programs and students with disabilities. The graduate and undergraduate tutors are expected to devote at least 60 hours a year to literacy tutoring in structured classroom settings in the Rome/Floyd County Schools and local agencies. The teachers participate in collaborative tutoring and workshops. Single parents and illiterate parents of the elementary school children participate in family literacy activities.

Georgia Institute of Technology (RES I)
Techwood Tutorial Project (TTP)

Grades served: E

Location of schools served: NR

Schools served: 2

Type of schools served: NR

Year established: 1964

Georgia Tech's oldest community service project, TTP pairs Georgia Tech students with children of elementary school age. Potential tutors interview with a member of the student committee that operates the program and must agree to tutor two hours per week for at least one year. Tutors attend a training session and are then paired with their children. Tutoring occurs at the child's school at a time agreeable to the teacher. Volunteers who do not want to commit to a single child may serve as a teacher's assistant for two hours per week. The TTP committee organizes from two to four outings per quarter for tutors and children. Staff advisement and office space, equipment, and supplies are provided in the Student Center.

Georgia Institute of Technology (RES I)
Meet-the-Mentor Day

Grades served: M, HS   Schools served: NR   Year established: NR
Location of schools served: NR   Type of schools served: NR

Meet-the-Mentor Day is held in the fall each year. Students in grades 6-12 who have already started research on their topics for a science fair are invited to Georgia Tech to meet with scientists, engineers, and mathematicians (mentors) from academe and industry. Students meet in small groups with a mentor in a specific area and discuss project ideas and career paths. Mentors are under no obligation to work with precollege students after the event but may do so if they wish. In addition, college students may offer to serve as long-term mentors for the precollege students as they work on their science fair projects.

ILLINOIS

Loyola University of Chicago (DOC I)
Loyola/Clemente Partners Program

Grades served: HS   Schools served: 1   Year established: 1982
Location of schools served: UR   Type of schools served: PUB

The Loyola/Clemente Partners Program, initiated in response to a Ford Foundation report documenting the educational needs of the Hispanic community in Chicago, is a collaboration between Loyola University of Chicago and Roberto Clemente Community Academy. Operating at the high school, the program, through peer tutoring and counseling, provides minority role models drawn from academically achieving college students, information about college financial aid workshops for college-bound high school students, field trips to the university, and student leadership development. The program serves more than 500 students yearly.

Northeastern Illinois University (MA I)
Bridges to the Future

Grades served: HS   Schools served: 4   Year established: 1991
Location of schools served: UR   Type of schools served: PUB, PRI

Bridges to the Future is a Chicago-based partnership of Northeastern Illinois University, four primarily Latino Chicago high schools, four community organizations, a business, and a foundation. Its primary focus is to help students successfully complete high school, plan for postsecondary education, explore career options, and prepare for employment and responsible citizenship. Support includes tutoring, mentoring, ongoing workshops, professional development for sponsoring teacher teams in cooperative learning, authentic assessment, and self-esteem, team building, and youth leadership retreats. More than 500 students and 20 teachers participate in the program annually.

INDIANA

Indiana University Purdue University at Indianapolis (DOC II)
Obesity in Children: Effectiveness of a School-Based Program

Grades served: E   Schools served: NR   Year established: NR
Location of schools served: SU   Type of schools served: PUB

The Department of Nutrition and Dietetics in the School of Allied Health Sciences has developed and implemented an interdisciplinary model program for obese children, aged 8 to 10, in two elementary schools in Lawrence Township. The goal is to improve self-esteem, body composition, and fitness through the development of life habits related to healthy eating and active lifestyles. The program includes physical fitness, nutrition education, cooking, and motivational dialogues for children and their parents.

Note: Each institution's Carnegie class is given in parentheses. **Key:** E=elementary school, HS=high school, M=middle school, NR=not reported, PRI=private, PUB=public, RU=rural, SU=suburban, UR=urban

Rose-Hulman Institute of Technology (ENGR)
Homework Hotline

Grades served: M, HS   Schools served: 10   Year established: 1991
Location of schools served: NR   Type of schools served: PUB

In partnership with the Vigo County School Corporation, the Homework Hotline uses the extensive science and mathematics expertise of its peer tutors to provide Terre Haute-area middle and high school students with assistance over the phone in their math and science homework. Rose-Hulman students serve as excellent role models for younger students. The program provides an invaluable opportunity for tutors to develop the communication skills required to adequately explain a new concept to a bewildered student. It also reinforces basic concepts and helps students and tutors to develop better problem-solving skills.

IOWA

St. Ambrose University (MA II)
Teens Teaching Youth

Grades served: E, HS   Schools served: 2   Year established: 1992
Location of schools served: UR   Type of schools served: PUB

Teens Teaching Youth is a partnership of St. Ambrose University, the Davenport Community Schools, and the city of Davenport designed to provide academic and social tutoring to at-risk children from local elementary schools. High school students can enroll in a half-credit elective course that provides the skills needed to meet children's needs. High school students commit three hours each week to tutoring. The tutoring is supervised by qualified staff from the university and the school district. A tutoring program involving training and supervision of parents and community volunteers is also a component of this partnership.

LOUISIANA

Louisiana Tech University (DOC II)
Student Literacy Corps

Grades served: E, M   Schools served: 1   Year established: 1993
Location of schools served: RU   Type of schools served: PUB

The Student Literacy Corps at Louisiana Tech University provides a graded elective course for three semester hours credit in the College of Education that provides undergraduate tutors with the skills and strategies necessary to instruct educationally disadvantaged children in reading. The project exposes college students to the problems of disadvantaged youth, particularly illiteracy. Based on their experiences in the Literacy Corps, participants are expected to continue their efforts to combat illiteracy.

MARYLAND

Harford Community College (AA)
Project PASS/Partnership for Learning

Grades served: M   Schools served: 1   Year established: 1991
Location of schools served: SU, RU   Type of schools served: PUB

Project PASS (Promoting Achievement in School and Society)/Partnership for Learning links Harford College and the public schools to provide academic support for at-risk sixth and seventh grade students and hands-on experience for college students studying teacher education. College students become tutors for the middle school students and provide direct assistance to teachers. Volunteers from the college and community supervise an after-school club. In addition to preparing students for eventual high school graduation and postsecondary education, the program works to develop self-esteem and to improve academic performance, social adjustment, classroom performance, and attendance.

Johns Hopkins University (RES I)
JHU Tutorial Project

Grades served: E

Schools served: 50

Year established: 1958

Location of schools served: UR

Type of schools served: PUB

For more than 30 years, the JHU Tutorial Project has sought to improve reading and mathematics skills of inner-city students through one-to-one personal tutoring, provided free of charge, and through the provision of social and cultural enrichment opportunities, such as concerts, films, and field trips. Tutors are volunteers, primarily from the university, but also from the surrounding community. Children are referred to the program by their parents and brought to the Hopkins Homewood campus by a shuttle bus provided by the Urban Services Agency of Baltimore.

University of Maryland-Baltimore County (DOC II)
Shriver Center Student Literacy Corps

Grades served: E, M, HS

Schools served: 40

Year established: 1990

Location of schools served: UR

Type of schools served: PUB

Shriver Center's Student Literacy Corps at the University of Maryland-Baltimore County involves undergraduate students as tutors working with elementary, middle, and high school youth from Baltimore City. UMBC students tutor in two community-based programs: The Choice Program, a center-operated program serving youth nine to 17, who are delinquent or at risk for out-of-home placement; and the East Baltimore Latino Organization (EBLO), a program for Hispanic children, six to eleven. The Student Literacy Corps allows UMBC students to learn firsthand about social problems through their direct involvement as tutors, while providing youth with one-to-one training in basic literacy skills and positive role models.

University of Maryland-Baltimore County (DOC II)
Choice Middle Schools Program

Grades served: M

Schools served: 9

Year established: 1993

Location of schools served: UR, RU

Type of schools served: PUB

The Choice Middle Schools Program links the University of Maryland-Baltimore County with nine middle schools in an effort to provide a strong support system for middle school youth at high risk of dropping out of school. Program staff maintain regular contact with each child, beginning in the sixth grade, seeing him or her two to five times a day and monitoring school attendance as well as in-school support. Each child receives additional support in areas such as behavior (evening curfew checks) and health. Development services for the students include life skills, tutoring, introduction to the world of art, and community service. These services, designed to develop the connection between home and school, continue during the seventh and eighth grades.

University of Maryland-College Park (RES I)
Literacy Internship Program

Grades served: HS

Schools served: 1

Year established: 1986

Location of schools served: SU

Type of schools served: PUB

The Literacy Internship Program allows University of Maryland students to gain college credit and to sharpen their own communication skills while serving nearby communities. Currently, interns are assigned to Northwestern High School, with the goal of improving the attendance and academic performance of at-risk students in grades 9-12. The interns work as tutors, one-on-one or in small groups, to high school students who are in danger of failing the Maryland Functional Reading Test and the Maryland Functional Writing Test, both of which are required for a high school diploma.

Note: Each institution's Carnegie class is given in parentheses. **Key:** E=elementary school, HS=high school, M=middle school, NR=not reported, PRI=private, PUB=public, RU=rural, SU=suburban, UR=urban

MASSACHUSETTS

Bunker Hill Community College (AA)
Tutoring for Literacy
Grades served: E, M, HS   Schools served: 10   Year established: 1988
Location of schools served: UR   Type of schools served: PUB

Tutoring for Literacy was begun to support needy individuals in learning. It operates with a Student Literacy Corps of interested college students, who tutor mainly elementary students. Under a broad definition of "literacy," the students work with public school students in appropriate supervised placements in schools or community programs. Most placements are in elementary schools to make the longest-lasting impact. The student tutors assist supervisors in developing activities.

Stonehill College (BA II)
Wednesday Academic Club for Kids
Grades served: E, M, HS   Schools served: 5   Year established: 1992
Location of schools served: UR, SU, RU Type of schools served: PUB, PRI

The Wednesday Academic Club for Kids was begun as a partnership of Stonehill College and five inner-city schools in the Brockton area. Stonehill education minors complete required prepracticum hours by tutoring students from these schools. The program, coordinated by college students, was the first effort of the Nehemiah Life Development Center, which organizers hope to develop into a comprehensive education facility providing courses focusing on topics from early childhood programs to adult literacy. The populations targeted by the center are dropouts and expelled students whom the founders hope to show something other than the streets.

Stonehill College (BA II)
Helping Each Other Reach Out
Grades served: M, HS   Schools served: 5   Year established: 1993
Location of schools served: UR, SU, RU   Type of schools served: PUB, PRI

This project involves Stonehill College and five schools. Designed for future teachers, it gives Stonehill students an opportunity to teach male juveniles, aged 11 to 17, who are in the Shelter Care Unit of the Old Colony YMCA awaiting their court appearances or transfer to another institution. The juvenile offenders are troubled youngsters who introduce the future educators to a social reality they cannot afford to ignore, facilitating the ability of both groups to communicate and learn from one another.

Stonehill College (BA II)
Brockton High School Access Center
Grades served: HS   Schools served: 2   Year established: 1987
Location of schools served: UR   Type of schools served: PUB, PRI

Stonehill, Bridgewater State, and Massasoit Community Colleges are engaged in a collaboration to assist in the retention of at-risk students through the Brockton High School Access Center. The center connects these students on site with appropriate agencies and institutions, including the Department of Employment, the YMCA, DSS, Public Welfare, Catholic Charities, Brockton Family Counseling, South Bay Mental Health, and Brockton District Court. Student volunteers from Stonehill majoring in secondary education mentor and tutor students as a prepracticum experience. The program is federally funded through the Brockton Area Private Industry Council.

MISSOURI

Webster University (MA I)
Student Literacy Corps

Grades served: E, M, HS | Schools served: NR | Year established: 1990
Location of schools served: UR | Type of schools served: PUB

Webster University Student Literacy Corps is a course (1-3 credits) through the university's Education Department. Students from all disciplines enroll. Participants receive literacy training during class meetings and agree to volunteer 60 hours within the community. Students serve in many different ways: in adult basic education and ESL classes; with children in an after-school program, as tutors for individual children, with adolescents as tutors for academic courses and parenting skills, and with families through a Literacy and Families (LAF) library at a homeless shelter and a family literacy program.

NEW MEXICO

New Mexico State University-Main Campus (RES I)
Hispanic Student Mentorship Program

Grades served: HS | Schools served: NR | Year established: NR
Location of schools served: NR | Type of schools served: NR

The Hispanic Student Mentorship Program identifies and recruits Hispanic high school students interested in international relations and provides faculty members to work closely with them to prepare them for graduate work in international relations. Students are selected by high school principals and NMSU faculty. The program's goals are to increase the participation of Hispanic students in the study of international relations and to prepare them for doctoral studies and a career in the field.

NEW YORK

City University of New York Herbert H. Lehman College (MA I)
After-School Tutoring Program

Grades served: E | Schools served: 10 | Year established: 1976
Location of schools served: UR | Type of schools served: PUB

The After-School Tutoring Program links Lehman College and ten area schools. It serves three purposes: to provide field sites for preservice elementary teachers; to provide tutoring and enrichment activities for neighborhood school children; and to provide workshops for parents who accompany their children. Students are brought to the college four afternoons a week by their parents and two mornings a week by their classroom teachers. Subject areas covered include reading, science, mathematics, social studies, art, and music. Lehman preteachers administer diagnostic tests, create IEPs for their students, and maintain records on students' progress.

Note: Each institution's Carnegie class is given in parentheses. **Key:** E=elementary school, HS=high school, M=middle school, NR=not reported, PRI=private, PUB=public, RU=rural, SU=suburban, UR=urban

College of New Rochelle (MA I)
Hispanic Society Mentoring

Grades served: HS   Schools served: 2   Year established: 1991
Location of schools served: SU   Type of schools served: PUB

The College of New Rochelle, through its Hispanic Society, links college student mentors with high school students who are of Hispanic heritage or are recent immigrants from Spanish-speaking countries. The mentors' goals are to assist students in adapting to the culture of the United States, to perfect their English, and to encourage students to aspire to higher education. The program currently includes 13 college students and 26 high school students. The Hispanic Society moderator and a guidance counselor from each participating high school coordinate the program.

College of New Rochelle (MA I)
New York State Mentoring

Grades served: E   Schools served: 1   Year established: 1993
Location of schools served: SU   Type of schools served: PUB

The College of New Rochelle participates in the New York State Mentoring Program founded by Matilda R. Cuomo. Mentors are students, staff, faculty, or administrators from the college who attempt to provide one-to-one support to elementary school students from a neighboring public school. The mentors meet with the students weekly in an effort to teach them how to develop a positive approach to life and to appreciate the value of education and work.

Rochester Institute of Technology (MA I)
Women in Science, Engineering, and Math Mentoring Program

Grades served: HS   Schools served: 6   Year established: 1993
Location of schools served: UR, SU   Type of schools served: PUB

This program links RIT, Pittsford Central Schools, and the New York State Education and Research Network. Network events and live introductory events include motivational speakers, problem-solving activities in science, tours of science facilities, and values auctions to clarify career interests and personal values. Most discussions take place via an Internet conferencing system. Mentors and students are involved in group discussions about science, math, career and lifestyle choices, and personal and ethical concerns with regard to scientific and technical careers.

Rochester Institute of Technology (MA I)
Teen Health Issues Network

Grades served: M, HS   Schools served: 7   Year established: 1993
Location of schools served: UR, SU   Type of schools served: PUB

The RIT Teen Health Issues Network links community and school cyberspace pioneers in addressing the health issues that challenge teens daily. RIT and the New York State Education and Research Network link school nurses, health teachers, guidance counselors, social workers, the AIDS Rochester staff, the University of Rochester Medical School (Department of Pediatrics), the RIT Allied Health staff, the County Health Department, local government, and other service agencies. Students and staffs are able to discuss issues. A distance learning network features topics of conflict resolution, drug and alcohol abuse, pregnancy and parenting, and permits access to data. Programs for students and professional development for teachers are included.

State University of New York at Albany (RES II)
Camp Liberty

Grades served: E

Schools served: NR

Year established: 1990

Location of schools served: UR

Type of schools served: PUB

Camp Liberty is a partnership of the university, several state agencies, and the New York State Public Schools designed to provide academic enrichment and to promote high self-esteem and academic aspirations in underserved urban youth who are at risk of leaving school before graduation. Participation in the summer Camp Liberty program enables students to continue enhancing skills that will contribute to their academic success. The children are given an opportunity to strengthen their reading and writing skills through creative writing assignments and group projects, enhance their analytical abilities by using computers, and develop problem-solving skills in the math manipulative lab.

OHIO

Kent State University-Tuscarawas Campus (AA)
Early English Composition Assessment Program (EECAP)

Grades served: HS

Schools served: 11

Year established: 1990

Location of schools served: UR, RU

Type of schools served: PUB, PRI

EECAP was designed by the Ohio Board of Regents to enhance the writing abilities of college-bound juniors, a cooperative arrangement in which colleges can be funded up to $30,000 per year for four years for working with school districts, which are expected to match the grants. The Tuscarawas Campus program worked with five county public schools, one Catholic school, and five independent systems, which assess all their students during their junior year. EECAP committee members score written essays, which are tallied by the program director. Committee members receive a stipend for attending a training workshop (2-3 days) and seven sessions during the year. Workshops on intervention strategies often include a presenter from the Ohio Writing Project. Outstanding writers receive Golden Pen awards at a recognition luncheon.

OREGON

Reed College (BA I)
Community Services Tutoring Program

Grades served: E, HS

Schools served: 5

Year established: 1990

Location of schools served: UR

Type of schools served: PUB

The Reed College Community Services Office coordinates tutors for students in four public schools and places tutors and mentors in several programs for at-risk youth. The college also places ESL tutors with immigrants through several programs, including some with Portland Community College. About 50 Reed students and staff spend two hours per week with students identified as needing special, one-on-one assistance. Tutors help with basic skills and homework and provide the attention that makes a big difference in a student's progress. Tutors themselves benefit from the opportunity to explore the profession of teaching, develop new relational skills, and meet new community members.

Note: Each institution's Carnegie class is given in parentheses. **Key:** E=elementary school, HS=high school, M=middle school, NR=not reported, PRI=private, PUB=public, RU=rural, SU=suburban, UR=urban

Reed College (BA I)
Take Charge

Grades served: M   Schools served: 14   Year established: 1992
Location of schools served: UR   Type of schools served: PUB

Take Charge urges students to take get on top of their individual educational experiences and involve family, school, and community resources. The program is coordinated by guidance counselors, Reed alumni, and representatives from the Reed College Admissions Office. Participants are selected in seventh or eighth grade; they are expected to complete algebra-level mathematics, one course in the natural sciences, and demonstrate a general understanding of computers before undertaking high school college preparatory courses. Reed guarantees admission to Take Charge scholars who graduate from high school and meet admissions requirements, offering them appropriate financial aid package.

PENNSYLVANIA

York College of Pennsylvania (BA II)
Adopt-a-School

Grades served: E   Schools served: 1   Year established: 1993
Location of schools served: UR   Type of schools served: PUB

Adopt-a-School, implemented by the National Interfraternity Conference, through a start-up grant from the W.K. Kellogg Foundation of Battle Creek, is available on 85 pilot campuses throughout the country. The program is designed to foster personal, one-to-one relationships between college students and elementary school children in an effort to improve the child's academic performance, enhance self-esteem, and increase attendance. The program's goals are to offer hands-on community service opportunities to college students and to develop a nationwide network of campuses involved in this program.

RHODE ISLAND

Brown University (RES I)
Pre-College Enrichment Program

Grades served: HS   Schools served: 5   Year established: 1993
Location of schools served: UR   Type of schools served: PUB

The Precollege Enrichment Program links Brown University and Providence public secondary schools. The program includes several important components that seek to demystify college, aiming to prepare students for the transition to college and to provide guidance to students and their families as they apply for admission and financial aid. Beginning in the second semester of grade 9, selected students participate in a Saturday morning program throughout their remaining high school years, working with undergraduate mentors and faculty to discover the university's resources, connect high school work with college expectations, and develop communication, group, and study skills.

TENNESSEE

Vanderbilt University (RES I)
PENCIL Foundation (Public Education: Nashville Citizens Involved in Leadership)

Grades served: HS   Schools served: 1   Year established: 1982
Location of schools served: NR   Type of schools served: PUB

The PENCIL Foundation, initiated by the Public Schools of Metropolitan Nashville, is an adopt-a-school program. The partnership between Vanderbilt University and Hume-Fogg Academic High School reflects the commitment of Vanderbilt's chancellor to improve elementary and secondary education. Vanderbilt students volunteer as mentors for Hume-Fogg students who need support in achieving their academic potential. Students who have completed advanced placement courses at Hume-Fogg in their junior year take courses at Vanderbilt tuition-free during their senior year. Additional services include faculty advisers on science projects, access to the university library and to special events, and donations to the school of surplus equipment. Hume-Fogg provides a student-teaching site for Vanderbilt students who are prospective teachers.

Pacific Lutheran University (MA I)
Center for Public Service

Grades served: E
Location of schools served: SU

Schools served: 1
Type of schools served: PUB

Year established: 1984

The center's After-School Enrichment Program is designed to provide individual attention and build self-esteem for at-risk first through third graders. The children, students at James Sales Elementary, spend two afternoons a week with their own big buddy, a PLU volunteer or work-study student. In addition to activities such as group games, snacks, and sharing, special events are planned throughout the semester — T-shirt painting, button making, videotaping, four chowdowns, and a visit from Santa Claus. Parents are encouraged to get to know their child's big buddy at the family dinner at the end of each semester.

University of Washington (RES I)
Early Scholars Outreach Program

Grades served: M
Location of schools served: UR, RU

Schools served: 9
Type of schools served: PUB

Year established: 1987

The Early Scholars Outreach Program is a partnership between the University of Washington's Office of Minority Affairs and nine Washington middle schools with large ethnic minority enrollments. It is designed to motivate students so that they see the connection between what is happening in their lives now and where that might lead them in the future. University of Washington role models are paid to tutor and mentor students at least four hours per week in grades 6, 7, and 8. Tutors highlight for students and their parents the importance of a daily commitment to academics and planning for college while in middle school.

Section Six
Career Exploration, Internships, or Apprenticeships

California School of Professional Psychology at Fresno (OTHER)
Teaching Psychology

Grades served: HS
Location of schools served: UR

Schools served: 6
Type of schools served: NR

Year established: 1988

The partnership between the California School of Professional Psychology and local schools enables psychology Ph.D. students to add a teaching component to their programs. Students enrolled in Teaching Psychology learn to design a course, use innovative techniques, promote discussion, improve lecturing, and evaluate outcomes. As a term project, students design a course and plan a related lecture, which is delivered to a high school psychology class. The instructional coordinator for the cooperating school provides the graduate students with instructors' names, and the graduate students arrange to give a lecture on their prepared topics to an appropriate class. Class response helps the graduate students to hone their skills and develop confidence.

Note: Each institution's Carnegie class is given in parentheses. **Key:** E=elementary school, HS=high school, M=middle school, NR=not reported, PRI=private, PUB=public, RU=rural, SU=suburban, UR=urban

<u>DISTRICT OF COLUMBIA</u>

George Washington University (RES II)
MIST (Minorities in Science & Technology)

Grades served: M, HS   Schools served: NR   Year established: 1991
Location of schools served: UR   Type of schools served: PUB

MIST sponsors an annual career fair for junior and senior high school students in the G.W. Marvin Center at George Washington University. The program and now involves about 1,000 students from grades 7-12. GWU contributes four staff members, one faculty member, and seven students, who each volunteer ten days of work during the year.

George Washington University (RES II)
Stars 2, 3, . . .

Grades served: M   Schools served: NR   Year established: NR
Location of schools served: UR   Type of schools served PUB

Stars 2, 3, . . . is a George Washington University program designed to keep junior high school students interested in careers in science and engineering and to encourage students to take more of the courses needed to pursue such careers. The program takes the form of one-day field trips for about 100 students from grades 7-9 each year. GWU contributes staff and faculty, training docents or others to carry out activities after the university field-tests them. The university also solicits new activities and field-tests each project, publicizes the program, hosts student groups, and conducts field trips.

George Washington University (RES II)
Science and Engineering Apprenticeship Program

Grades served: HS   Schools served: NR   Year established: 1987
Location of schools served: UR   Type of schools served: PUB

GWU's Science and Engineering Apprenticeship Program makes available to high school students paid apprenticeships with scientists or engineers from a U.S. Department of Defense lab in the D.C. area. The program provides information and experience to precollege students to try to influence them toward careers in science and engineering. Selections are based on grades, course work, standardized test scores, degree of personal interest, and teachers' recommendations. The eight-week summer program involves several hundred students, university faculty and staff, and at least two teaching assistants. The university provides publicity, recruits, and administers the program and follow-up activities.

George Washington University (RES II)
DC Stars

Grades served: M   Schools served: NR   Year established: NR
Location of schools served: UR   Type of schools served: PUB

DC Stars, cosponsored by the U.S. Department of Defense and GWU's School of Engineering and Applied Science, is designed to encourage academically talented junior high school students to take math and science courses in high school. A three-day career enhancement trip to an off-campus location involves 30 selected students from DC junior high schools. The university provides volunteer staff and administers the project, with support, on-site supervision, personnel, and facilities supplied as needed by the Department of Defense.

George Washington University (RES II)
Eastern High School Mentorship Program

Grades served: HS

Schools served: 1

Year established: 1980

Location of schools served: UR

Type of schools served: PUB

This program links Eastern High School and GWU's School of Medical and Health Sciences. Ten energetic health professionals at the university commit themselves to mentorship training and a minimum of 20 hours of contact annually with students in health careers from Eastern High School. Students are paired with mentors in their areas of interest wherever possible.

George Washington University (RES II)
Latino Youth Health Care Project

Grades served: M, HS

Schools served: NR

Year established: 1990

Location of schools served: UR

Type of schools served: PUB

George Washington University's Latino Youth Health Care Project supports the primary goal of the Kellogg Foundation in providing leadership and practical training to Latino youths, exposing them to a variety of health care professionals. During the spring and summer, health care workers at GWU's Medical Center give tours to provide these youths with an understanding of the health care environment. The program serves students from grades 7 to 9, with two university staff volunteering ten hours of work weekly.

George Washington University (RES II)
Conference on Career Opportunities in Public Service

Grades served: HS

Schools served: NR

Year established: 1989

Location of schools served: UR, SU

Type of schools served: PUB

GWU's Conference on Career Opportunities in Public Service is held every two or three years. It is designed to provide information about potential careers in public service to high school guidance counselors and high school students in the D.C. metropolitan area. Two faculty members and ten students volunteer a total of 150 hours to the program. The university hosts and coordinates the conference, sends out information, provides conference buddies for speakers, and solicits involvement by U.S. agencies, while non-GWU partners provide publicity, secure a main speaker, and provide job information.

FLORIDA

Valencia Community College (AA)
Nontraditional Careers Program

Grades served: HS

Schools served: 13

Year established: 1990

Location of schools served: NR

Type of schools served: PUB

Valencia Community College's Nontraditional Careers Program, a partnership with Orange County Public Schools, presents the Career Exploration Workshop, whose primary missions are to raise awareness of careers for ninth grade girls and to emphasize that high-paying jobs in the next decade will become more technical and require specialized postsecondary training. One hundred students participate in three hands-on activities exploring nontraditional careers for women. Guest speakers and presenters are women who are successful in nontraditional occupations. The workshop stresses the importance of math and science as keys to an unlimited future. School and college educators share an ongoing forum of communication.

Note: Each institution's Carnegie class is given in parentheses. **Key:** E=elementary school, HS=high school, M=middle school, NR=not reported, PRI=private, PUB=public, RU=rural, SU=suburban, UR=urban

GEORGIA

GEORGIA

Georgia Institute of Technology (RES I)
MITE (Minority Introduction to Engineering)

Grades served: HS

Location of schools served: NR

Schools served: NR

Type of schools served: NR

Year established: 1974

Georgia Tech's College of Engineering offers the MITE program to motivate rising senior minority students to consider careers in engineering. Two 1-week sessions of MITE are held each summer for approximately 140 participants from 14 states and Puerto Rico. Students are expected to pay for their transportation to and from the program, while the program provides six nights of dormitory lodging, all meals at campus dining facilities, transportation to field trip sites, and paid admission to group recreational events. Activities include film and slide experiments, visits to Tech's engineering schools, panel discussions with current engineering students at Tech, a minifair, and workshops.

Georgia Institute of Technology (RES I)
CASE (Career Awareness in Science and Engineering)

Grades served: M

Location of schools served: NR

Schools served: NR

Type of schools served: PUB

Year established: 1990

CASE is a summer program sponsored by Georgia Tech's College of Engineering with the assistance of undergraduate students. For one week, rising sixth and seventh grade students visit the Tech campus daily and learn about engineering and scientific principles and related careers. Through film and slide presentations, field trips to local industries, engineering-related experiments, tours of Tech's engineering schools, panel discussions with current engineering students at Tech, a career fair, and workshops with industrial representatives, students are encouraged to begin planning early in their secondary education for a career in engineering. Approximately 30 students participate each year.

HAWAII

University of Hawaii-Kapiolani Community College (AA)
RESHAPE

Grades served: HS

Location of schools served: UR

Schools served: 6

Type of schools served: PUB

Year established: 1985

RESHAPE is designed to improve the academic skills of prospective college students and increase their awareness about available programs before college enrollment. Kapiolani Community College provides orientation and testing to groups of tenth grade students who score within the middle stanines of the SAT. Five-hour sessions include information on the purpose, benefit, and relationship of college-level instruction to high school courses; promote a focus on math, English, and science requirements; brief students on various vocational training operations and preparation necessary to attend a four-year college; provide campus tours; and test for competency in English reading and math. Students and high school counselors receive follow-up letters with test results and recommendations for curricula reflecting career goals.

ILLINOIS

Loyola University of Chicago (DOC I)
Future Teachers

Grades served: HS   Schools served: 3   Year established: 1992
Location of schools served: UR   Type of schools served: PUB, PRI

The Future Teachers program is a partnership designed to recruit students, primarily from minority groups, into teaching in Chicago. The program includes 89 public and parochial high schools, eight Chicago universities, the City Colleges of Chicago, Community Youth Creative Learning Experience (CYCLE), the Chicago Urban League, the Golden Apple Foundation, the Chicago Board of Education, the Chicago Teachers Union, the Office of Catholic Education, the Illinois State Board of Education, and the U.S. Department of Education. The program involves more than 1,800 high school and college students in training, tutoring, and mentoring, and provides hands-on career exploration, teaching opportunities, exposure to college, and teacher preparation courses.

Southern Illinois University at Carbondale (RES II)
Careers in Aviation

Grades served: HS   Schools served: 1   Year established: 1992
Location of schools served: RU   Type of schools served: PUB

This partnership provides an opportunity for freshmen at Carbondale Community High School (East) to explore careers in the aviation industry. Presentations, demonstrations, and videotapes are used to show the wide variety of career options. A key feature of the partnership is to have the discussions led by current SIUC aviation students or recent SIUC aviation alums to facilitate communication between the discussion leaders and the high school freshmen. The partnership includes career days and/or tours of SIUC aviation facilities and aircraft.

University of Illinois at Urbana-Champaign (RES I)
Research Apprentice Program in Applied Sciences (RAP)

Grades served: HS   Schools served: 200   Year established: 1987
Location of schools served: UR, SU, RU   Type of schools served: PUB, PRI

RAP is a six-week enrichment program for selected junior and senior high school students (minorities and women) on UIUC's campus. Students serve as apprentices dealing with math, business, and science as they relate to food, agriculture, natural resources, and animal health. Apprentices work under the supervision of research scientists and perform appropriate tasks in research associated with the College of Agriculture and the College of Veterinary Medicine. In addition to the laboratory experience, participants are involved in career awareness activities, industry field trips, skill development, testing, and academic classes. At the end of the six weeks, participants are required to prepare and present a paper describing their summer laboratory projects.

Note: Each institution's Carnegie class is given in parentheses. **Key:** E=elementary school, HS=high school, M=middle school, NR=not reported, PRI=private, PUB=public, RU=rural, SU=suburban, UR=urban

INDIANA

Valparaiso University (MA I)
Da Vinci & Me: Exploring Engineering

Grades served: M

Schools served: 25

Year established: 1992

Location of schools served: UR, SU, RU

Type of schools served: PUB, PRI

The goal of Valparaiso University's Da Vinci & Me: Exploring Engineering is to instill an interest in science and engineering among students at a point in their academic programs where they can be positively influenced to select courses of study that will not prematurely exclude them from related study in college. This program targets minority and women students entering the seventh or eighth grade. Activities include hands-on laboratory experiments in civil, electrical, and mechanical engineering, computer use, and industrial field trips. Middle school mathematics and science teachers participate to learn about engineering and simultaneously enhance middle school science programs.

MAINE

Eastern Maine Technical College (AA)
MYAP (Maine Youth Apprenticeship Program)

Grades served: HS

Schools served: 27

Year established: 1993

Location of schools served: UR, RU

Type of schools served: NR

Maine Youth Apprenticeship Program is a statewide initiative with regional centers. EMT works with businesses and high schools to establish apprenticeships for students in their junior year of high school. Following two years of high school training, students enroll for a third year at EMT, resulting in a certificate of mastery that clearly identifies skills learned. Special academic schedules allow students to get needed prerequisites for college. Businesses fund the apprenticeships and provide trainers while students are is at the apprenticeship sites.

MASSACHUSETTS

Worcester State College (MA I)
Worcester Future Teachers Academy

Grades served: HS

Schools served: NR

Year established: 1992

Location of schools served: UR

Type of schools served: PUB

Worcester Future Teachers Academy is designed to attract minority high school students into teaching careers so that they will become role models for minority children and visible representatives for majority children.

Worcester State College (MA I)
Worcester Career Beginnings

Grades served: HS

Schools served: 3

Year established: 1990

Location of schools served: UR

Type of schools served: PUB

Worcester Career Beginnings is a partnership among the business community, Worcester Community College, local government, and local schools. The program involves workshops, tutoring, adult mentoring, summer employment, and school-based advising to help students develop the skills necessary to enroll and succeed in postsecondary education and subsequent employment. Students are given special training in civics/citizenship, speech, writing, computer science, study skills, critical thinking, cultural pluralism, and leadership skills.

MICHIGAN

University of Michigan-Dearborn (MA I)
Summer Internship Program

Grades served: HS   Schools served: 4   Year established: NR
Location of schools served: UR   Type of schools served: PUB

The School of Engineering Summer Internship Program involves a total of 15 students chosen following their junior year to work as paid assistants to engineering and computer science faculty in their technical research or other academic projects during a six-week period in July and August. Interns take part in engineering or computer science research, interacting with faculty sponsors. They are employed in areas related to their career interests and receive regular exposure to the university environment that encourages and values academic success. The program provides students with information about career options in engineering and computer science.

MINNESOTA

College of St. Catherine (MA II)
Explore Group

Grades served: HS   Schools served: NR   Year established: 1992
Location of schools served: NR   Type of schools served: NR

In conjunction with the Boy Scouts of America's Explore Program, the College of St. Catherine sponsors an Explore Group for Education. The intent of the program is to gather interested high school students and possibly college freshmen who have expressed an interest in careers in education to examine what is demanded in preparation for teaching and what the opportunities are for the profession. Regular semiweekly meetings prepare for matching students with professionals whom they will shadow for half a day each week for a month. Four college students, one or more college faculty members, and four or five K-12 teachers work with 30 students.

MISSOURI

Avila College (MA I)
PAVA (Performing and Visual Arts) Day

Grades served: HS   Schools served: 25   Year established: 1975
Location of schools served: UR, SU   Type of schools served: PUB, PRI

About 450 high school juniors and seniors participate in workshops as part of PAVA Day, which is sponsored each fall by the Art, Communication, English, Music, and Theater programs at Avila College. Workshops include video production, desktop publishing, photography, drawing, design, essay writing, musical performance, acting, and technical theater. Individual students' projects are evaluated as part of the workshops. Guest speakers from metropolitan Kansas City participate in the careers panel for each area as well. Avila faculty and students follow PAVA Day with high school presentations in stage combat, auditioning, drawing and painting, and design.

Note: Each institution's Carnegie class is given in parentheses. **Key:** E=elementary school, HS=high school, M=middle school, NR=not reported, PRI=private, PUB=public, RU=rural, SU=suburban, UR=urban

NEW JERSEY

Jersey City State College (MA I)
Adopt-a-School

Grades served: E, M	Schools served: 9	Year established: 1990
Location of schools served: UR	Type of schools served: PUB	

Adopt-a-School is a collaboration of the Hudson County Chamber of Commerce and Industry and Jersey City State College serving more than 2,000 students. The collaborative was initiated to offer field-based learning experiences to elementary school students. Three districts participate. More than 216 volunteer mentors from 49 firms meet monthly with their adopted sixth, seventh, and eighth graders. College and school faculty assisted by corporate mentors developed special modules for the three grade levels. Field trips and recreational activities complement the personal visits, and a newspaper disseminates information to follow up on mentors' training.

University of Medicine and Dentistry of New Jersey-New Jersey Medical School (MED)
Hispanic Center of Excellence Summer Youth Program

Grades served: HS	Schools served: NR	Year established: NR
Location of schools served: UR, SU, RU	Type of schools served: PUB, PRI	

The Hispanic Center of Excellence is a federally funded program designed to increase the number of Hispanic physicians nationally by offering high school, undergraduate, medical school, and faculty development programs. Skills development, awareness of the health care needs of the community, and development of role models are emphasized. The Summer Youth Program provides eight weeks of basic clinical exposure for motivated Hispanic students entering grades 10-12 who have expressed an interest in a medical career. Students chosen must be in good academic standing. Each student spends 30 to 32 hours on campus.

NEW MEXICO

New Mexico State University-Main Campus (RES I)
New Pathways

Grades served: HS	Schools served: 3	Year established: NR
Location of schools served: NR	Type of schools served: PUB	

New Pathways is designed to identify, orient, and provide exploratory career internships for high school students in occupations nontraditional to their gender. Three counselors, 40 teachers, and more than 1,600 high school students participate. The program's primary goals are to interest students in nontraditional occupations and assist them in exploring career opportunities. Plans are to continue this program for three years and to develop other career educational opportunities for students in the Las Cruces Public Schools.

NEW YORK

City University of New York Borough of Manhattan Community College (AA)
Executive Internship Program (EIP)

Grades served: HS	Schools served: NR	Year established: 1987
Location of schools served: UR	Type of schools served: PUB	

The Executive Internship Program invites professionals to share their time and knowledge with highly motivated and academically qualified high school students, including the handicapped. It is a department of City As School, a leader in alternative education. Since 1970 EIP has placed nearly 10,000 juniors and seniors with sponsors throughout New York City. The program involves experts in varied fields, from physicians to politicians, chefs to computer specialists, and buyers to broadcasters to bankers.

City University of New York Borough of Manhattan Community College (AA)
Women Making Strides

Grades served: HS

Schools served: 5

Year established: 1992

Location of schools served: NR

Type of schools served: PUB

Women Making Strides is a program for single parents offered in conjunction with the Liberty Partnership Program. The program targets 225 women enrolled in schools for pregnant women and parenting services, providing them with job-readiness skills, and introducing them to nontraditional careers and work experiences. Activities include a workshop on job readiness to be replicated in each school, career exploration workshops, paid internships, and job shadowing. The program also provides staff training covering such topics as trends in employment, training, educational requirements for employment, gender equity, and perception

City University of New York Kingsborough Community College (AA)
Sports, Fitness & Therapeutic Recreation

Grades served: HS

Schools served: 1

Year established: 1988

Location of schools served: UR

Type of schools served: PUB

This articulation program links Kingsborough Community College and a Brooklyn high school. It is primarily a transfer program that enables students who begin college study in high school to work toward a four-year degree in teaching or sports management. KCC offers courses in sports in American society (3 credits) and summer camp counseling (2 credits), taught in the high schools as part of their regular teaching schedule by high school health and physical education staff. The courses fit into one of two tracks: Sports and Fitness, or Community and Therapeutic Recreation. Students also receive high school credit.

City University of New York LaGuardia Community College (AA)
Experience-Based Career Education Program

Grades served: HS

Schools served: 1

Year established: 1991

Location of schools served: UR

Type of schools served: PUB

The Experience-Based Career Education Program is a partnership between Long Island City High School and LaGuardia Community College that targets third-year students with severe learning and educational handicaps by helping them to clarify career options, qualifications, personal values, and individual strengths and limitations, and to increase their employability and success in the workplace after graduation from high school. Realistic career goals, positive attitudes through improved self-reliance and self-image, effective interpersonal skills, reflective and analytical thinking, and socioeconomic survival skills are emphasized. The college provides curriculum support for faculty and structured, meaningful work sites for students. College staff monitor and supervise students' growth and development.

Clarkson University (DOC II)
Horizons

Grades served: M

Schools served: 60

Year established: 1987

Location of schools served: RU

Type of schools served: PUB

Horizons helps young women to understand that mathematics, science, and computer science will be important to future success. The program is aimed at junior high school women in an attempt to catch their interest before they plan high school curricula. In addition to instruction in these fields, students have opportunities to explore careers, understand personal development, and learn leadership skills. During evenings, students engage in team-building and social activities.

Note: Each institution's Carnegie class is given in parentheses. **Key:** E=elementary school, HS=high school, M=middle school, NR=not reported, PRI=private, PUB=public, RU=rural, SU=suburban, UR=urban

Clarkson University (DOC II)
Summer Research Program
Grades served: HS

Schools served: 12

Year established: 1985

Location of schools served: UR, SU, RU

Type of schools served: PUB, PRI

Clarkson University 's Summer Research Program provides an opportunity for high school students to spend several weeks during the summer conducting research in chemistry, biology, physics, math, computer science, and psychology under the direction of a university faculty member. They also participate in campus seminars in these fields, sometimes presenting at seminars themselves. This hands-on opportunity allows students to be involved in leading-edge research.

Cooper Union (ENGR)
Saturday Program
Grades served: HS

Schools served: 80

Year established: 1968

Location of schools served: UR

Type of schools served: PUB

The Saturday Program was initiated by Cooper Union undergraduates in a partnership with New York City high schools. Enrolling 150 students, the program offers studio courses in the arts and architecture, with instruction and materials provided without charge to the students. Students are exposed to varied careers through contact with professional artists. The program provides academic counseling to encourage students to seek higher education and provides inservice arts education, training, and innovative curriculum development for teachers.

Cornell University (RES I)
Cornell Youth and Work Program
Grades served: HS

Schools served: 6

Year established: 1990

Location of schools served: UR, SU, RU

Type of schools served: PUB

In collaboration with six school districts, the Broome-Tioga Board of Cooperative Educational Services (BOCES), and Broome Community College, the Cornell Youth and Work Program has designed and implemented a youth apprenticeship demonstration project that places juniors in work settings where they learn specified competencies over two to four years. Research and development are major purposes of the project, whose results helped to shape the School-to-Work Opportunities Act of 1993. Responsibility for directing the project has been turned over to a local organization to enable Cornell staff to emphasize research, development, dissemination, and training.

Cornell University (RES I)
Learning Web
Grades served: M, HS

Schools served: 6

Year established: 1972

Location of schools served: UR, SU, RU

Type of schools served: PUB, PRI

The Learning Web provides Tompkins County youth with hands-on experiences, including apprenticeships with mentors at work sites. Youth gain valuable job and life skills and are empowered through increased self-awareness and self-esteem to better make the transition to adult roles and responsibilities. The Learning Web operates several programs, including Youth Outreach, combining street outreach activities with intensive case management and paid apprenticeships for homeless teens; On Top, a summer apprenticeship program in the trades at Cornell University for minority and underrepresented youth; and Youth Scoops, the first youth-run Ben and Jerry's franchise store.

Hudson Valley Community College (AA)
Career Access Program

Grades served: HS | Schools served: 1 | Year established: 1992
Location of schools served: NR | Type of schools served: PUB

The partnership between Hudson Valley Community College and Shenendehowa Central School is part of the high school's Career Access Program, preparing students for technology in a continuum to structured postsecondary training. Targeted students are sophomores and juniors in the Construction Systems Technology and Automotive Systems Technology programs. Hudson Valley administers placement tests and coordinates a campus tour of the technology labs. Academic advisers from technology departments provide information about prerequisites and electives, test results, and recommendations for Course work. Curriculum reform is an early outcome of the program.

Rensselaer Polytechnic Institute (RES II)
Capital District Science and Technology Entry Program (STEP)

Grades served: M | Schools served: 7 | Year established: 1986
Location of schools served: UR, SU, RU | Type of schools served: PUB, PRI

The Capital District Science and Technology Entry Program is a consortium linking Rensselaer Polytechnic Institute, SUNY-Albany, Union College, and Schenectady County Community College to assist underrepresented minority or economically disadvantaged students in gaining access to health, health-related, scientific, and technical professions. The program provides tutoring; personal, academic, and career counseling; educational enrichment involving field trips and workshops; and employment in scientific and technical areas. Students in grades 7-12; qualified teachers of mathematics, science, problem-solving, writing, and reading teachers; and undergraduate and graduate student tutors work together to help participants improve knowledge, thinking, and learning skills.

State University of New York College at Oneonta (MA I)
SUNY's Best Academic Alliance

Grades served: HS | Schools served: 1 | Year established: 1990
Location of schools served: UR | Type of schools served: PUB

Under the auspices of the statewide SUNY's Best Academic Alliance, SUNY-Oneonta is linked with Edward R. Murrow High School in Brooklyn, in a partnership designed to build long-term relationships between rural colleges and urban high schools. The program provides early exposure to higher education for students and academic support for faculty. Activities include a college education course taught in the high school for preservice teachers, campus visits, faculty/student/parent workshops, and placement of student teachers. Research and evaluation are ongoing.

NORTH CAROLINA

Cleveland Community College (AA)
Career Day

Grades served: HS | Schools served: 6 | Year established: NR
Location of schools served: NR | Type of schools served: PUB, PRI

Cleveland Community College's Career Day is an annual day-long event designed to inform area students about career opportunities by giving them specific information about job choices from local and regional experts. Professionals share information about their jobs, the education that prepared them for their careers, salary ranges, and day-to-day, on-the-job duties. The college and local high schools jointly plan the program, which is held on the college campus, giving students an idea of what the college environment is like.

Note: Each institution's Carnegie class is given in parentheses. **Key:** E=elementary school, HS=high school, M=middle school, NR=not reported, PRI=private, PUB=public, RU=rural, SU=suburban, UR=urban

OHIO

Lourdes College (BA II)
Women in Science Day

Grades served: M, HS   Schools served: 45   Year established: 1987
Location of schools served: UR, SU, RU   Type of schools served: PUB, PRI

Lourdes College is host of the annual Regional Women in Science Day, designed to address the underrepresentation of women an science and the mechanism that leads to this imbalance. Junior high and senior high school women, grades 7-12, are invited to attend the program, which features women professionals who share their career choices, pay scales, educational needs, and the rewarding aspects of their careers. The college seeks to assist these young women in their choice of a science career by providing information and motivational models to help them in their decision making.

Ohio Northern University (BA II)
Jets Teams Competition

Grades served: HS   Schools served: NR   Year established: 1987
Location of schools served: UR, SU, RU   Type of schools served: PUB, PRI

This competition, sponsored by the College of Engineering, provides high school students from urban and rural areas a chance to explore the profession of engineering through a school competition. For the schools that qualify, a national competition follows regional competition. Each school may bring a varsity and a junior varsity team composed of no more than eight students. The competition is a group effort to solve realistic engineering problems. All students spend the day on campus, and receive T-shirts, lunch, and tours of the engineering facilities and the entire campus. The day ends with an awards ceremony.

OREGON

University of Oregon (RES II)
Career Information System Consortium

Grades served: M, HS   Schools served: NR   Year established: 1972
Location of schools served: UR, SU, RU   Type of schools served: PUB, PRI

Fifteen states are linked in the national Career Information System network, including the University of Oregon's consortium. The system is designed to help students discover and explore their options in education and employment. The system includes locally relevant information about occupations, job searches, entrepreneurship, vocational and academic programs of study, schools and colleges, and financial aid; user-oriented guides and microcomputer software for personal information and copies of output; a program of training and support for counselors and teachers; and a cooperative management and financing system that keeps quality high and costs low.

PENNSYLVANIA

University of Pennsylvania (RES I)
Adopt-a-School

Grades served: NR   Schools served: 1   Year established: 1989
Location of schools served: UR   Type of schools served: PUB

The University of Pennsylvania's Wharton School's Adopt-a-School program involves the university and the Business Education Department of the Murrell Dobbins Vocational Technical School. Wharton students act as volunteer mentors for the Dobbins students. The partnership plans workshops, review sessions, and counseling.

Medical University of South Carolina (MED)
Summer Undergraduate Research Awards Program (SURAP)

Grades served: NR   Schools served: NR   Year established: 1980
Location of schools served: UR, SU, RU   Type of schools served: PUB, PRI

The Summer Undergraduate Research Awards Program engages college students majoring in science or mathematics in investigative research. The university has been selected as a MARC (Minority Access to Research Careers) site, where selected students undertake research guided by mentors chosen for their scientific credentials and interest and experience in training. Program directors meet at least weekly with each student. Seminars, social events, formal lectures, and related literature engage students in interaction and encourage exchange of ideas and experience. Students deliver formal talks on their projects, often resulting in publication and involvement in further research.

Midlands Technical College (AA)
Adopt-a-School

Grades served: E   Schools served: 3   Year established: 1987
Location of schools served: SU, RU   Type of schools served: PUB

This Adopt-a-School partnership links Midlands Technical College and three elementary schools in programs designed to introduce fifth and sixth graders to career options and to experiential learning in mathematics and the sciences. College faculty collaborate with fifth and sixth grade teachers to develop, demonstrate, and maintain practical hands-on learning in math and science for a core group of 20 to 30 students, who spend two to three hours a month in a structured learning experience with college faculty on the campus.

Newberry College (BA II)
Higher Education Awareness Program (HEAP)

Grades served: M   Schools served: 4   Year established: 1993
Location of schools served: NR   Type of schools served: PUB

Newberry College's HEAP is designed to provide eighth graders with information about careers and the education required for them. The goal is to urge students to take the college preparatory curriculum and go on to further education beyond high school. A Tech-Prep 2+2 program enables them to follow a sequence of courses from junior- and senior-year programs in a vocational-technical area that is integrated into the academic courses in traditional disciplines.

Technical College of the Lowcountry (AA)
Career and Choices Exploration Program

Grades served: M, HS   Schools served: 11   Year established: 1988
Location of schools served: RU   Type of schools served: PUB

The Careers and Choices Exploration Program is designed specifically for high school and middle school students who are at risk of dropping out of school. The program provides a comprehensive curriculum to assist students in gaining career information, to identify career goals early in their academic programs, and to emphasize the value of education as relevant to those choices and to employability, thus decreasing the chance that they will drop out. The program is held one day a week, six periods a day, for seven weeks, with designated classes assigned by the schools to teach skills in self-awareness, problem solving, and career exploration.

Note: Each institution's Carnegie class is given in parentheses. **Key:** E=elementary school, HS=high school, M=middle school, NR=not reported, PRI=private, PUB=public, RU=rural, SU=suburban, UR=urban

University of South Carolina-Aiken (BA II)
Teacher Cadet Program
Grades served: HS

Schools served: 6

Year established: 1986

Location of schools served: SU, RU

Type of schools served: PUB

The Teacher Cadet Program is an introduction to the teaching profession. Designed to attract more African-American males and females into teaching careers, its main purpose is to encourage students who possess a high level of academic achievement and the personality traits found in good teachers to consider teaching as a career. Simulations and hands-on activities are designed to excite students about teaching. Students explore teaching careers and the education system through class discussions, observations and participation in public school classrooms, and interaction with successful administrators and teachers.

Wofford College (BA I)
Spartanburg County Partnership
Grades served: E, M, HS

Schools served: 7

Year established: 1980

Location of schools served: UR, SU, RU

Type of schools served: PUB, PRI

Working with schools in Spartanburg County, Wofford College offers a series of summer workshops designed to attract students to careers in scientific research and teaching. The program's specific goal is to increase the number of minorities and women pursuing scientific careers. Its three target areas are to increase research by students, improve scientific equipment and laboratories, and influence precollege students to consider scientific careers. Summer research projects are carried out by research teams consisting of Wofford professors and students and Spartanburg County high school students. Rising sixth-, seventh-, and eighth-grade students work with these teams by participating in two-week residential science programs on the campus.

TEXAS

University of Texas Health-Science Center at San Antonio (MED)
The Biomedical Program
Grades served: HS

Schools served: NR

Year established: NR

Location of schools served: UR

Type of schools served: PUB

The Biomedical Program, a four-year continuing education program, is designed for 20 new high school freshmen each year from the San Antonio Independent School District. Its goals are to enhance students' interest in a science or health profession, improve academic performance in the sciences, encourage students to pursue higher education, and assist in obtaining scholarships. It encourages students to finish high school, aspire to college or a specific career, and improve their specific skills or knowledge in the field.

UTAH

Weber State University (MA II)
Center for Science Education
Grades served: E, M, HS

Schools served: NR

Year established: 1984

Location of schools served: UR, SU, RU

Type of schools served: PUB, PRI

The Center for Science Education was founded to revitalize precollege science education by bringing the resources of working scientists to providing preservice and inservice teacher training, facilitating collaboration between science and education faculties at Weber State, and promoting partnerships with public and private schools. Typical past and present programs include Science Seminars for Superior Students, Utah State Science Olympiad, Science Information Hotline, Tours of the planetarium and natural history museum, Weber State/NASA Science Teacher Workshop, Weber State/NASA Space and Science Resource Materials Library, and the Space Education Data Resource Program. The programs bring together public school teachers and university science teachers.

VIRGINIA

Thomas Nelson Community College (AA)
Project FOCUS (Future Oriented Choices for Undecided Students)

Grades served: HS   Schools served: 2   Year established: 1988
Location of schools served: UR   Type of schools served: PUB

Project FOCUS is an educational partnership of Thomas Nelson Community College and Hampton City Schools designed to assist middle-ability high school students to make decisions about careers. High school guidance staff and English faculty assist the Project FOCUS counselor in administering the program. The primary goal of the partnership is to increase the college attendance rate of minority and low-income students. Project FOCUS students participate in field trips, panel discussions, career planning, and life skills workshops; they receive individual and career counseling.

WASHINGTON

Eastern Washington University (MA I)
School, College, and University Partnership Program (SCUP)

Grades served: M, HS   Schools served: 7   Year established: 1991
Location of schools served: RU   Type of schools served: PUB

The intent of this partnership, known locally as Project YES (Youth Engaged in Success), is to encourage low-income students to improve their academic skills and to prepare them for employment or postsecondary education. The provides a model of how small schools located in isolated rural communities can join with a regional university, area businesses, and agencies to effectively serve low-income, at-risk secondary school students, reducing dropout rates and improving their educational and employment prospects after graduation.

Western Washington University (MA I)
Program for the Advancement of Science Education

Grades served: HS   Schools served: 3   Year established: 1992
Location of schools served: NR   Type of schools served: PUB

The Program for the Advancement of Science Education at Western Washington University is designed to involve high school teachers and students as active participants in ongoing research conducted by university professors and students. The goal is to get high school students excited about the challenges associated with scientific research and to stimulate their interest in pursuing university studies and careers in the sciences. The program also serves to enhance communication between science teachers in different school districts, to provide teachers with opportunities to involve their students in joint scientific projects, and to strengthen the interaction between high school and university instruction.

□ □ □

Note: Each institution's Carnegie class is given in parentheses. **Key:** E=elementary school, HS=high school, M=middle school, NR=not reported, PRI=private, PUB=public, RU=rural, SU=suburban, UR=urban

Part Two
PROGRAMS AND SERVICES FOR EDUCATORS

Introduction

If the intent of nearly all school-college partnerships is to build structures that will improve students' learning, then partnerships that provide programs and services for educators are the foundation. An intriguing variety of programs have been carefully developed to directly address the needs of teachers and other educators. The exemplary programs in Part Two span the entire country; while many are local in origin, others have ties to regional or national networks and some have state legislative mandates. Quite often concerns about curriculum bring together researchers and classroom teachers to explore the best ways of linking theory and instruction.

Section One, "Professional Development and Inservice Training," includes programs and services targeted to the needs of experienced teachers. With the rapid changes occurring in many fields, particularly in science and technology, the quality of the education that students receive over the next two decades will depend, in large measure, on the continuing education of the current cadre of classroom teachers. Collaborative programs designed to meet these needs now include summer institutes, professional development seminars and workshops, regional conferences, and a variety of services customized to local sites. Many programs provide teachers with opportunities to strengthen and update their content expertise, share and demonstrate ideas, receive training in new learning technologies, discuss evaluation and assessment, and reflect on educational trends and the implications for curricular revision. For example, the Yale-New Haven Teachers Institute, established in 1978, serves to strengthen collegial ties between university and New Haven Public Schools faculty, providing an interschool and interdisciplinary forum for collaboration on new curricula. In 1990 the institute was recognized as a permanently established function of Yale University. Another example, the Center for Academic Interinstitutional Programs (CAIP) in the UCLA Graduate School of Education, provides talented faculty (K-community college) with the opportunity to share their teaching expertise while they increase their repertoire of teaching strategies and refine their understanding of content. Some who attend the institutes become teacher-consultants who present their ideas to colleagues at professional development workshops. CAIP seeks to improve students' preparation for postsecondary education by working with educators and influencing the curriculum at all levels, particularly in language arts, mathematics, science, history, and social sciences.

Section One also includes some important national models for faculty development and professional renewal, including programs based on the models or initiatives of the National Writing Project, the Academic Alliance Network, the National Geographic Society, the American Historical Association, and the American Physical Society. Many of the programs seek to build "communities of scholars," where school and college faculty come together to discuss common concerns, share significant research and instructional trends, and exchange teaching methods and curricular materials. The common denominator linking individuals from different sectors in a wide range of disciplines is a genuine concern for the improvement of the quality and continuity of students' learning that is based on a love of the content area. These programs focus on the need for the continuing revitalization of teachers as professionals and attempt to build an adult network from the nation's schools and colleges around many of the disciplines. Programs for teachers of writing and literature, foreign languages, history, science, and mathematics are flourishing. The Connecticut Writing Project, for example, is a collaboration of the University of Connecticut, 76 school districts, and interested regional agencies. Based at the university, it receives support from the Aetna Endowment and the National Writing Project. The project is designed to improve the teaching of writing in Connecticut by training teachers to teach other faculty, providing opportunities for inservice training in writing, and reflecting on classroom practice in light of current theory and practice. Follow-up programs are offered for teachers who attend summer institutes, and classroom research is encouraged. The program also provides opportunities for publishing the writing of K-12 students. A recognition night officially honors excellence in student writing.

Finally, Section One includes some examples of programs and services for school administrators. Principals, in particular, are critical to effecting change and innovation in the schools. Institutes, academies, centers, and projects have been designed to increase managerial effectiveness by improving leadership and problem-solving skills, budget management, resource acquisition and allocation, personnel evaluation, community support efforts, and administrative monitoring of instructional effectiveness. For example, Texas A&M University's Principals' Center, established in 1985, is nationally recognized for its leadership in supporting elementary and secondary school principals through preparation, assistance, and research. A Congress of Principals provides advice and leadership from the field, serving as a governing body that identifies emerging activities directed at instructional leadership, management skills, and self-renewal. The center also provides a clearinghouse for information, and provides connections to a nationwide network of such centers.

Section Two, "Recruitment and Retention, Preservice, Early Career Support, and Alternative Certification Programs," features partnerships concerned with attracting top talent into teaching by increasing the numbers of underrepresented groups, providing high-quality student-teaching experiences as components of undergraduate programs, and providing a variety of support services for beginning teachers. Programs preparing undergraduates for careers in teaching have traditionally necessitated close ties between teacher training institutions and local schools, as each group has a strong vested interest in the adequacy of such programs and makes a singular contribution to the training process.

Such preservice centers and programs also serve to better integrate theory and practice, improve mentoring and supervision in the field, facilitate resource sharing, and encourage the critical examination of all aspects of undergraduate education for future teachers. These programs provide many examples of creative retention strategies and ways to formalize mentoring relationships between beginning and experienced teachers. For example, the University of Wisconsin-Whitewater's Beginning Teacher Assistance Program has served teachers throughout southeastern Wisconsin since 1974, making it the longest continuously operating, university-based mentoring program for teachers in the United States. The collaborative nature of the program accounts for its success and longevity. The program unites personnel and resources of the university, small to medium school districts, and the Wisconsin Improvement Program in providing beginning teachers with a structured mentoring program to facilitate their transition from teacher education student to professional teacher.

Another example is Project PRIME (Programs to Recruit and Inspire Minorities into Education), which involves a coalition of partners that includes Morgan State University as the lead institution, the Baltimore City Public Schools, the Maryland MESA (Math, Engineering, and Science Achievement) program, and seven other area colleges and universities. These institutions are committed to implementing a plan that will dramatically increase the number of minority students in the Baltimore area who enroll in teacher education programs during the next five years. Successful implementation of Project PRIME will lay the groundwork for expansion of the initiative throughout Maryland and beyond.

Section Three, "Teacher Education Centers," features permanent resource centers and facilities created to provide for continuous learning and support from completion of college through retirement. These centers are often governed by boards, councils, or cabinets that include school and college faculty and administrators. Included are programs that attempt to attract the nation's best and brightest from a variety of fields to teaching careers. Several programs promote school-college faculty interaction through exchanges, continuing-education degree and certificate programs, and mechanisms to recognize and reward teaching excellence. Many of the centers described also facilitate the demonstration of model educational practices and important research findings. For example, the Fredonia-Hamburg Teacher Education Center in western New York, established in 1972, earned the 1985 Distinguished Program in Teacher Education Award from the National Association of Teacher Educators. The center is a cooperative venture between SUNY-College at Fredonia and the Hamburg Central School District. Seminars in curriculum and teaching strategy and three 11-week teaching internships make up this year-long, field-based, senior-level program. Seminars are conducted on site, so that theory and practice can be integrated throughout the program. Participants are assessed in five areas: concern for individuality, human relations, content skills and techniques, decision making, and philosophy.

A second example in this section is the Windham Professional Development Center, a collaboration of University of Connecticut faculty and students and the Windham Public School District. Its purpose is to promote change within schools and in teacher preparation. Participants share a vision of a revitalized urban school environment, led by properly prepared professionals. The center allows for supervised clinical experiences for prospective teachers. Participants are involved in several ongoing projects: peer tutoring, integrating the humanities curriculum, study skills development, educational mentoring, sibling tutoring, integrating reading/writing curricula, and integrating bilingual students into the mainstream.

Finally, Section Four, "Teaching Awards and New Faculty Roles," describes collaborative efforts to recognize and reward exemplary teaching, service, leadership, and curricular innovation. The University of Evansville, with support from the Bristol-Myers Squibb Company, and in conjunction with all public and private schools in Vanderburgh County, has established an Outstanding Educator Award; award-winning practicing teachers share experiences with college students and have inservice opportunities through the university. The Dean's Award for Excellence in Teaching is awarded annually by the SUNY-College at New Paltz's School of Education to outstanding teachers in New York's Mid-Hudson Valley region; teachers in each county are nominated by their superintendents, and a committee of faculty members at the college selects six to eight awardees.   □

Section One
Professional Development and Inservice Training

ALABAMA

University of North Alabama (MA I)
Center for Economic Education

Grades served: NR   Schools served: 127   Year established: 1993
Location of schools served: UR, SU, RU   Type of schools served: PUB, PRI

The Center for Economic Education promotes economic education for all students to prepare them for their own and the country's future. The program sets standards for economics education, trains teachers in workshops and courses designed to improve students' learning, develops curricula for a comprehensive K-12 program, produces guides and books containing proven strategies for teaching economics, and evaluates results, developing instruments for assessing students' performance. The purpose is to produce productive members of the workforce, responsible citizens, knowledgeable consumers, prudent investors, effective participants in the global economy, and competent decision makers.

University of South Alabama (MA I)
South Alabama Research's Inservice Center

Grades served: E, M, HS   Schools served: 200   Year established: 1984
Location of schools served: UR, SU, RU   Type of schools served: PUB

Staff development in Alabama is supported by this collaboration of higher education, local school districts, and the State Department of Education. Alabama's regional staff development centers, located in its 11 institutions of higher education, provide high-quality staff development and training for the state's 50,000 K-12 teachers and administrators. The centers combine the resources of higher education, K-12 education, and the State Department of Education to bring resources and training directly to the classroom. The $250,000 annual budget of the South Alabama Research and Inservice Center at the University of South Alabama is strongly leveraged through administrative and instructional technology.

ARIZONA

Glendale Community College (AA)
Glendale Region Educational Articulation Taskforce (GREAT)

Grades served: E, M, HS   Schools served: 24   Year established: 1991
Location of schools served: SU   Type of schools served: PUB

GREAT involves Arizona State University West, Glendale Community College, Glendale Union High School District, the city of Glendale, and Glendale Youth Center in a joint effort to use the resources of education, government, business, industry, and Glendale area community organizations to ensure that community members enter, reenter, and remain in school until their maximum learning goals are realized. Focus areas include mentoring and retention of students, family participation, literacy, tracking, middle colleges, technology exchange, alternative delivery systems, communication of educational opportunities, scholarship programs, and volunteerism.

Northern Arizona University (DOC I)
Sedona Professional Preparation Partnership Program

Grades served: NR
Location of schools served: RU

Schools served: 3
Type of schools served: PUB

Year established: 1991

The partnership between Sedona-Oak Creek Joint Unified School District and Northern Arizona University was initiated to bring classroom teachers, school administrators, and university professors and researchers together to learn from each other and to improve the educational process at all levels. Specifically, the program seeks to explore new patterns of organization for curricula, instruction, and schools; to explore new approaches to the preparation of professional educators; to bridge the gap between research and practice; to rethink roles, responsibilities, and relationships among educators in schools and universities; and to ensure that CEE programs are current with regard to best thinking, schooling practice, and educational research.

Northern Arizona University (DOC I)
EMPIRE (Exemplary Multicultural Practices in Rural Education) Partnership Project

Grades served: E, M, HS
Location of schools served: RU

Schools served: 8
Type of schools served: PUB

Year established: 1992

This school-university partnership centers on the work of eight rural schools in developing site-based projects that revolve around their own communities, own site-based definitions of exemplary practices and multicultural education, and responses to self-identified problems in their school communities. The eight schools in the project network include elementary schools with varying demographic profiles (including a boarding school on the Navajo Reservation and a community school on the Hopi Reservation), a middle school in a geographically isolated community, and a recently opened high school. The university supplies support and training in developing and sustaining a coalition to work with community-supported multicultural reform.

Northern Arizona University (DOC I)
Educational Personnel Training Program (USDOE, Title VII)

Grades served: E, M
Location of schools served: RU

Schools served: 40
Type of schools served: PUB

Year established: 1992

This training program, initiated under ESEA (Elementary and Secondary Education Act) Title VII, is an integrated plan to enhance the effectiveness of Arizona teachers in meeting the needs of their limited-English-proficient Native American students. For students, its goals are higher levels of academic achievement and English language proficiency; for teachers, increased ability to teach content, especially science and math, and language, by using instructionally and culturally appropriate strategies. Emphases are on using the students' home language in the classroom and with parents, assisting teachers in completing advanced degrees in ESL or bilingual endorsements, and strengthening beneficial alliances among the university, schools, and communities.

Phoenix College (AA)
Maricopa English Teachers' Network (METNET)

Grades served: HS
Location of schools served: UR

Schools served: 9
Type of schools served: NR

Year established: 1989

METNET is a partnership that provides an arena for dialogue among English instructors at Phoenix College, the Phoenix Union High School District, and other colleges and high schools in the area. Activities include regular monthly meetings, larger dialogue programs, student-to-student dialogues, and the distribution of the newsletter *The Coordinate Conjunction.*

Note: Each institution's Carnegie class is given in parentheses. **Key:** E=elementary school, HS=high school, M=middle school, NR=not reported, PRI=private, PUB=public, RU=rural, SU=suburban, UR=urban

ARKANSAS

Henderson State University (MA I)
Professional Development Alliance

Grades served: NR   Schools served: 4   Year established: 1992
Location of schools served: SU, RU   Type of schools served: PUB

This partnership of Henderson State University and four public school districts ensures that the university's teacher education program produces the best possible teachers. Collaborative efforts include recruitment and retention of minority teacher trainees, a first-year teacher program, and quality field experience for preservice teachers. HSU's School of Education faculty and administrators meet with their teacher interns, public school administrators, and cooperating teachers three times during the intern's professional semester (student teaching) to identify strengths and weaknesses of the program. Information gained is distributed to all participants and guides the restructuring of Henderson's program to meet the changing needs of education.

University of Arkansas-Main Campus (RES II)
Moore Center for Economic Education

Grades served: NR   Schools served: 19   Year established: 1979
Location of schools served: UR, SU, RU   Type of schools served: PUB, PRI

The Moore Center for Economic Education was established as an outreach program of the university's College of Business Administration to promote understanding of the American economic system. The Center provides instructional programs, develops instructional materials, conducts applied research, operates a lending library, and makes educational consultants available to schools and the community. It has provided programs for journalists, businesspeople, labor leaders, local government officials, and others. The center has national and state certification, and it has won five national awards for excellence in economics education.

CALIFORNIA

California State University-Fresno (MA I)
Professor in the Classroom

Grades served: E, M   Schools served: 30   Year established: 1990
Location of schools served: NR   Type of schools served: PUB

CSU-Fresno professors from all disciplines participate in this initiative. Approximately 40 professors spend a day in a K-8 classroom as volunteer substitutes so that teachers can attend a master teacher training program sponsored by the university's teacher education department. The arrangement saves the school districts the costs of paid substitutes, and teachers become more aware of the professors' commitment and understanding. Additionally, professors are able to talk about careers in higher education with the students, while teachers develop better skills and ideas to use in effectively mentoring/supervising student teachers.

California State University-Fresno (MA I)
Center for Collaboration for Children and Families

Grades served: E   Schools served: 3   Year established: 1993
Location of schools served: NR   Type of schools served: PUB

CSU-Fresno's Center for Collaboration for Children and Families includes tutoring, mentoring, and counseling programs, professional development initiatives, and instructional research, evaluation, and testing. It includes 35 faculty members representing 14 departments, three students, and 12 community/agency members, who arrange for informational speakers and meetings, participate in writing grants, and undertake research to benefit children and families, particularly those in underrepresented, minority, or at-risk populations.

California State University-Los Angeles (MA I)
Hands-On Physical Science
Grades served: E   Schools served: NR   Year established: 1990
Location of schools served: UR, SU   Type of schools served: PUB

The Hands-On Physical Science program links the university and elementary schools from various districts in Los Angeles County. It provides three weeks of intensive training for mentor teachers, who become science specialists, provide inservice training for other teachers, and implement a hands-on physical science program in their schools. The material, which is correlated with the California Science Framework, has been tested in elementary schools since 1990 and has won two state awards for excellence. Lesson plans and hands-on experiences provide practice in using process skills, models of teaching methods for divergent thinking, and a thorough understanding of the concepts involved.

California State University-Los Angeles (MA I)
The Constitution in Eighth Grade History
Grades served: M   Schools served: 15   Year established: 1985
Location of schools served: UR, SU, RU   Type of schools served: PUB, PRI

On an average of every second year, summer institutes train teachers in content and pedagogy to improve instruction of the U.S. Constitution in eighth grade history courses. Forty teachers from Los Angeles County study basic documents, hear lectures from major scholars, and prepare lesson plans based on the content. Participants continue after the institute to meet with the directors to discuss their experience in teaching the content. A book of lesson plans on the Constitution has been published, and a book on the Bill of Rights will be published soon.

California State University-San Bernardino (MA I)
Regional Network of California Foundation & Partnership Middle Schools
Grades served: M   Schools served: 162   Year established: 1987
Location of schools served: UR, SU, RU   Type of schools served: PUB

Participants in the network include San Bernardino, Riverside, Kern, and Mono County offices of education, the State Department of Middle Grade Support Services, and 162 junior high/middle schools in three regions. Established in a result of the state reform document *Caught in the Middle*, the program has twice been honored at CSU-SB for its outreach and support of middle school reform and restructuring. It has sponsored a statewide conference for middle-grade educators, provides assistance to schools changing from junior high to middle schools, consults with districts regarding scheduling and credentials, and provides other support services as needed.

California State University-San Bernardino (MA I)
Danforth School Board Training Partnership
Grades served: NR   Schools served: NR   Year established: NR
Location of schools served: NR   Type of schools served: PUB

The Danforth Foundation funds this annual training program for school board members. Training is designed to prepare school board members in leadership, communications, legal and fiscal matters, supervision, appropriate conduct, and the community's and parents' participation. Although emphasis is on preparing board candidates, incumbents are also welcome. Riverside and San Bernardino County offices of education and local school districts work together, while CSU-SB and the Danforth Foundation supply presenters and facilitators for the sessions, advertise meetings, and provide additional monetary support.

Note: Each institution's Carnegie class is given in parentheses. **Key:** E=elementary school, HS=high school, M=middle school, NR=not reported, PRI=private, PUB=public, RU=rural, SU=suburban, UR=urban

California State University-San Bernardino (MA I)
Bilingual Educators' Career Advancement (BECA)

Grades served: NR   Schools served: NR   Year established: NR
Location of schools served: NR   Type of schools served: PUB

Bilingual Educators' Career Advancement has five goals: to support bilingual teacher aides in the participating districts as they complete the BA in liberal studies and obtain teaching credentials for multiple subjects; to support emergency-credential bilingual teachers as they obtain a teaching credential; to support candidates for the MA in education, ESL option; to support candidates for the MA in education, bilingual/crosscultural option; and to support candidates in the bilingual/crosscultural master's degree program recently begun at CSU-SB and the Coachella Valley campus. In 1991-92, the program funded 69 scholars; in 1992-93, 59 received complete tuition reimbursement plus $633 per year in books, travel, and parking.

Occidental College (BA I)
TOPS (Teachers + Occidental = Partnership in Science)

Grades served: HS   Schools served: 20   Year established: 1991
Location of schools served: UR, SU   Type of schools served: PUB, PRI

TOPS seeks to increase interest in science as a career and to improve the self-image of science teachers. The program provides access to modern scientific equipment in the classroom. During a summer workshop, teachers become familiar with the equipment and develop lab write-ups and prelab activities for the classroom. The equipment, including gas chromatographs, spectrophotometers, computers, analytical balances, and microscale kits, is delivered to the school by the TOPS van for use by the students. Follow-up support includes seminars, summer research, and a second-year program where teachers develop new experiments with the TOPS equipment.

Occidental College (BA I)
Keck Foundation Curriculum Project

Grades served: M, HS   Schools served: 1   Year established: 1993
Location of schools served: NR   Type of schools served: PRI

This project (1994-97) is a continuation of a materials development and teacher enhancement project aimed at equipping secondary school mathematics teachers with innovative pedagogy using modern computer technology that they can apply to develop students' skills and interests. To further the development and dissemination of innovative teaching methods, a partnership between Occidental College and Polytechnic School is being formed with three essential components: residential workshops for secondary teachers, a planning session to revise courses, and the creation of animated sequences.

Orange Coast College (AA)
California Institute for Career Development

Grades served: E, M, HS   Schools served: NR   Year established: 1992
Location of schools served: UR, SU, RU   Type of schools served: PUB, PRI

The California Institute for Career Development was formed to develop and deliver career development inservice training to counseling service providers through enhanced technology communication resources. The goal is to support public and private service providers by giving them access to current career development information, methods, and strategies in the most expedient and cost-effective manner. Resources correspond with the National Career Development Guidelines and can be delivered using state-of-the-art technology. Service providers can include counselors and paraprofessionals of K-12 and postsecondary schools and any agencies or organizations striving to provide up-to-date career development services.

San Diego State University (DOC II)
San Diego Mathematics Enhancement Project

Grades served: E, M   Schools served: 12   Year established: 1991
Location of schools served: UR   Type of schools served: PUB

This project provides enhancement in mathematics for more than 200 teachers of underrepresented children. Participating teachers are drawn from grades 4-8 and from schools with large African-American and Latino enrollment. For 180 hours during one of four 2-year cycles, each teacher studies mathematics content; researches teaching and learning mathematics, and methodologies and curricular thrusts in mathematics; participates in an after-school mathematics laboratory program for children; and assists in implementing workshops designed to involve parents in their children's mathematics education.

Stanford University (RES I)
Stanford Educational Cooperative

Grades served: E, M, HS   Schools served: NR   Year established: 1986
Location of schools served: UR, SU, RU Type of schools served: PUB, PRI

The Stanford Educational Collaborative (formerly the Stanford/Schools Collaborative) supports an array of partnerships between Stanford University and school districts in the San Francisco Bay area. Its mission is to improve curriculum and instruction through research and professional development for educators in elementary/secondary schools and the university. A steering committee of school and university representatives guides the overall activities of the collaborative, which includes the Alliance for School-Based Change, the Professional Development Center, Service Learning 2000, the School Board Computer Bulletin Board (415-723-8190) teacher action research groups, research about collaboration, round tables and forums, and special conferences.

University of California-Davis (RES I)
Northern California Mathematics Project

Grades served: E, M, HS   Schools served: 229   Year established: 1982
Location of schools served: UR, SU, RU Type of schools served: PUB, PRI

Each year the Northern California Mathematics Project (NCMP) holds an invitational summer institute for 30 teachers (kindergarten through college) interested in leadership in improving the teaching of mathematics. The institute provides the opportunity to further develop the teachers' own math backgrounds and to present their ideas about mathematics reform to colleagues. The month-long institute is the first step, as participants become part of a growing regional network and continue to meet to work on specific projects and attend programs during the year and in ensuing summers. NCMP teachers provide workshops for colleagues, have developed professional organizations, and serve as mathematics leader-organizers in their districts and as project staff during the summer.

University of California-Davis (RES I)
Summer Agriscience Institute

Grades served: M, HS   Schools served: 150   Year established: 1988
Location of schools served: UR, SU, RU Type of schools served: PUB

The Summer Agriscience Institute is a partnership linking the university and California secondary school science and agriculture teachers in the integration of science and agriculture. Science teachers discover ways of using agricultural applications to make science more relevant to students, and agriculture teachers discover new ways of integrating science principles included in the California Science Framework. Students become more science literate and new community/school partnerships develop. Major activities include hands-on learning approaches, the use of Fast Plants and Bottle Biology as tools for teaching science, researchers working with teachers, teachers conducting research projects, and workshop presentations by participants to high school colleagues.

Note: Each institution's Carnegie class is given in parentheses. **Key:** E=elementary school, HS=high school, M=middle school, NR=not reported, PRI=private, PUB=public, RU=rural, SU=suburban, UR=urban

University of California-Irvine (RES I)
STEP (Student/Teacher Educational Partnership)

Grades served: E, M, HS   Schools served: 45   Year established: 1984
Location of schools served: UR   Type of schools served: PUB

STEP provides an organizational framework among four college campuses and the Santa Ana Unified School District for testing and adopting new methods of teaching, creating and implementing additional support services, and developing funding sources to improve the academic preparation of the district's 50,000 students for successful continuation into higher education. STEP tackles the problems of the entire district rather than those at selected schools or among selected groups of students. Professionally committed and unusually active educators share knowledge and experience in STEP's atmosphere of trust and respect.

University of California-Los Angeles (RES I)
Center for Academic Interinstitutional Programs (CAIP)

Grades served: E, M, HS   Schools served: 1000   Year established: 1980
Location of schools served: UR, SU   Type of schools served: PUB, PRI

The Center for Academic Interinstitutional Programs in UCLA's Graduate School of Education improves students' preparation for postsecondary education by working with educators and influencing curricula K-14. The center concentrates on language arts, mathematics, science, and history/social science, subjects required for university admission. Talented K-14 faculty are invited to attend institutes at UCLA to share their teaching expertise while they increase their repertoire of teaching strategies and refine their understanding of content. Some become teacher-consultants who present their ideas to colleagues at professional development workshops.

University of California-San Francisco (RES I)
Science and Health Education Partnership

Grades served: E, M, HS   Schools served: 121   Year established: 1987
Location of schools served: UR   Type of schools served: PUB

The Science and Health Education Partnership assists the San Francisco Unified School District in improving the quality of science education in the public schools and promoting healthy student behaviors. The partnership focuses on serving teachers, concentrating primarily on the life and health sciences. More than 300 active UC-SF volunteers interact with district teachers and K-12 students to make numerous UC-SF intellectual and physical resources available, bridging the gap between those who practice science and those who teach it.

University of Southern California (RES I)
USC Inter-Professional Initiative

Grades served: E, M, HS   Schools served: 2   Year established: 1991
Location of schools served: UR   Type of schools served: PUB

The USC Inter-Professional Initiative is a collaboration of USC' schools of Education, Social Work, Public Administration, Dentistry, and Medicine and the Department of Nursing to establish innovative training for new professionals. Interdisciplinary teams of interns provide comprehensive social services at five local inner-city sites: Excel Apartments, Family Resource Center, Foshay Middle School, Norwood Elementary School, and the Pediatric and Family Medical Center. The initiative also is involved in research in interdisciplinary education and training.

COLORADO

Adams State College (MA I)
Colorado Alliance for Science/Project Link-Up

Grades served: E, M   Schools served: 14   Year established: 1986
Location of schools served: RU   Type of schools served: PUB

Project Link-Up is a three-year program designed to improve science education in elementary and middle schools in the San Luis Valley of southcentral Colorado. The project has two main components. During a two-week summer workshop, participants (certified elementary and middle school teachers) carry out hands-on activities centered around a particular theme (e.g., environmental science, space science). The participants earn two hours of graduate credit and receive a modest stipend. During the academic year, participants meet four times to discuss science in the classroom, share hands-on activities with colleagues and students, and become reinvigorated.

Colorado School of Mines (DOC II)
Mobile Science Show

Grades served: E, M, HS   Schools served: NR   Year established: 1991
Location of schools served: UR, SU, RU   Type of schools served: PUB, PRI

The Mobile Science Show, which was started with a Presidential Award for Excellence in Science Teaching in 1990, was designed to reach K-12 teachers and students through presentations, summer workshops, and extensive follow-up activities. The Colorado School of Mines (CSM) provides logistical support and workshop facilities. The program has reached more than 3,000 teachers and approximately 7,000 students from all parts of the state. Each summer 50 teachers are brought to the campus for two weeks of intensive training in hands-on, experiential science/mathematics content and instruction. They are also given materials and supplies to take back to their schools and classrooms. These teachers then conduct workshops for teachers in their own districts, spreading the value of the program.

Mesa State College (BA I)
Mesa Math Mentorship Program

Grades served: E, M, HS   Schools served: NR   Year established: 1993
Location of schools served: UR   Type of schools served: PUB, PRI

The Mesa Math Mentorship Program (MMMP) is a partnership linking the Mesa State College Teacher Education Program's students, faculty, and administration with K-12 schools, teachers, parents, and communities throughout western Colorado. MMMP's primary mission involves ongoing mentorship support to expand its preservice, inservice, and retraining programs for mathematics and science teachers to increase their confidence, change their methods of approach, improve their performance, and decrease tendencies of students to avoid math and science. The MMMP laboratory includes a computer lab, a math/science community resource room, and hands-on training for participants.

Regis University (MA I)
Regis Institute of Chemical Education

Grades served: E, M, HS   Schools served: 75   Year established: 1990
Location of schools served: UR, SU, RU   Type of schools served: PUB, PRI

The Regis University Chemistry Department houses the Regis Institute of Chemical Education hands-on science programs. These programs offer science workshops for teachers during the summer and science camps for children that offer the teachers practical experience. Instructors from Regis follow up with visits to the schools and training with classroom kits. College and some high school students also assist in running the camps.

Note: Each institution's Carnegie class is given in parentheses. **Key:** E=elementary school, HS=high school, M=middle school, NR=not reported, PRI=private, PUB=public, RU=rural, SU=suburban, UR=urban

University of Colorado at Boulder (RES I)
Colorado Geographic Alliance
Grades served: E, M, HS

Schools served: NR

Year established: 1986

Location of schools served: UR, SU, RU

Type of schools served: PUB

The Colorado Geographic Alliance was established as part of the national network of state-based alliances supported by the National Geographic Society. COGA's membership consists of nearly 6,000 classroom teachers, administrators, professors, students, elected officials, and interested citizens dedicated to the proposition that promoting and improving geography education in Colorado schools will enhance the quality of education for all Colorado's citizens. COGA promotes education in disciplined geographic knowledge by teaching critical and reflective thinking about fundamental problems of human-environment relationships and the interdependence of peoples and places.

University of Colorado at Denver (DOC II)
Northern Colorado School Leadership Academy
Grades served: NR

Schools served: NR

Year established: NR

Location of schools served: NR

Type of schools served: PUB

The Northern Colorado School Leadership Academy is jointly sponsored by faculty in administration, supervision, and curriculum development at UCD and the Northern Colorado Board of Cooperative Educational Services (BOCES). The program is designed to provide graduates with a master's degree and a Type D certificate. Program planning, implementation, and review are managed by a steering committee of faculty, BOCES personnel, cooperating school district practitioners, and area business representatives, who cooperatively deliver instruction using a problem-based learning model. Problems encountered in the field drive the content of the program.

University of Colorado at Denver (DOC II)
Collaborative Network for School Quality Teaching and Research
Grades served: HS

Schools served: 2

Year established: NR

Location of schools served: NR

Type of schools served: PUB

This collaborative involves faculty members from two School of Education divisions (Curriculum and Pedagogy, and Administration) and at least two Denver-area public schools. The aims are to promote research on public school adoption of programs for the management of quality and, and to link this research directly with a six-credit, team-taught master's degree course focusing on management and curricular issues that arise when a school adopts total quality management. A research link has been established with Overland High School in the Cherry Creek Public School District, and discussions are under way with personnel in the Denver City Schools.

University of Northern Colorado (DOC I)
Greeley Strategic Planning Initiative
Grades served: NR

Schools served: 2

Year established: 1988

Location of schools served: NR

Type of schools served: PUB

This initiative involves professional and inservice training and faculty exchanges. With support from the National Science Foundation, the University of Northern Colorado and Weld County School District 6 participate in an ongoing staff development program to improve instruction in the sciences and to integrate the science curriculum with language arts. District 6 teachers are assigned annually to the university to work as teachers on special assignment; they affiliate with the Teacher Education Center in the College of Education. Other local teachers affiliate with the Mathematics and Science Teaching Center jointly operated by the colleges of Arts and Sciences and Education.

<u>CONNECTICUT</u>

Saint Joseph College (MA I)
Project Construct
Grades served: M   Schools served: 9   Year established: 1992
Location of schools served: NR   Type of schools served: PUB

Project Construct links Saint Joseph College and nine Hartford schools to provide professional development and inservice training for teachers of mathematics and science in the upper elementary and middle schools. The program uses teacher education centers, school-college faculty exchanges, and magnet schools to foster inquiry-based, hands-on activities, safety procedures, and gender and diversity equity. The aim is to provide a skilled teacher corps with training in these skills and in integrating science and mathematics, social studies, and the humanities. Requirements for teacher certification are met through the undergraduate program with a major in natural science or mathematics or through the Graduate Student Teacher Preparation Program for Science in the Middle Schools/Grades.

University of Connecticut (RES I)
Connecticut Academy for English, Geography and History
Grades served: E, M, HS   Schools served: NR   Year established: 1992
Location of schools served: UR, SU, RU   Type of schools served: PUB, PRI

The Connecticut Academy for English, Geography, and History, sponsored by the University of Connecticut, seeks to encourage multidisciplinary education. It organizes statewide conferences with keynote lectures by leading scholars and presentations of model lessons by master teachers. The academy has also hosted two summer institutes designed to further multidisciplinary education through seminars, lectures, model lessons, training in inservice presentation, and curriculum development.

University of Connecticut (RES I)
Hartford Professional Development Center
Grades served: E, M, HS   Schools served: 6   Year established: 1988
Location of schools served: UR   Type of schools served: PUB

The Hartford Professional Development Center (PDC) is a collaboration of the University of Connecticut and Hartford schools that is designed to enhance public education and prepare teachers. The PDC allows for varied clinical experiences in the preparation of teachers and other educational professionals. Collaborative research and reflection on current educational practice form the basis for the center. Developmental activities are under way in each of the six partnership schools. Each semester 80 students, nine faculty, and the dean work in these schools.

University of Connecticut (RES I)
Connecticut Writing Project
Grades served: E, M, HS   Schools served: NR   Year established: 1982
Location of schools served: UR, SU, RU   Type of schools served: PUB, PRI

The Connecticut Writing Project is a collaboration of the University of Connecticut, 76 school districts, and interested regional agencies. Based at the university, it is supported by the Aetna Endowment and the National Writing Project. The project is designed to improve the teaching of writing in Connecticut by training teachers to teach other faculty, providing opportunities for inservice training in writing, and reflecting on classroom practice in light of current theory and practice. Follow-up programs are offered for teachers who attend the summer institute, and classroom research is encouraged. The program also provides opportunities for publishing K-12 students' writing, and a recognition night.

Note: Each institution's Carnegie class is given in parentheses. **Key:** E=elementary school, HS=high school, M=middle school, NR=not reported, PRI=private, PUB=public, RU=rural, SU=suburban, UR=urban

Wesleyan University (BA I)
Project to Increase Mastery of Math and Science (PIMMS)

Grades served: M, HS

Schools served: 300

Year established: 1979

Location of schools served: UR, SU, RU

Type of schools served: PUB, PRI

PIMMS was started to acquaint selected teachers with new directions in mathematics and science curricula and to equip and inspire them to spearhead curriculum redevelopment in their own school districts and across the state. This means of dissemination (teachers trained to teach teachers) is an essential feature of the program. Institutes for physics and biology teachers are presented annually. The Technology Leadership Institute and Mathematics Technology Institute update teachers on various levels of technology. Programs for students include the Young Scholars Program and Multiply Your Options.

Western Connecticut State University (MA I)
Professional Practices Program

Grades served: E, M, HS

Schools served: 4

Year established: 1990

Location of schools served: UR

Type of schools served: PUB

The purposes of this program are to establish and maintain low-budget, highly efficient professional practice schools by placing elementary and secondary certification methods classes on site in K-12 schools, providing inservice training for participating classroom teachers on site, offering university professors opportunities to teach K-12 classes, and exposing education majors to team-teaching in culturally diverse urban schools. WCSU students develop curricular units for the K-12 classes and complete 15 semester hours of preteaching.

Yale University (RES I)
Yale-New Haven Teachers Institute

Grades served: NR

Schools served: 43

Year established: 1978

Location of schools served: UR

Type of schools served: PUB

The Yale-New Haven Teachers Institute was initiated as an educational partnership between Yale University and the New Haven Public Schools, designed to strengthen teaching and learning in the city and, by example, throughout the county. The Yale faculty and school teachers share a collegial relationship, and the institute provides an interschool and interdisciplinary forum for collaboration among teachers on new curricula. The institute addresses subjects identified by teachers, and participating teachers become Institute Fellows. Each Fellow prepares a curriculum unit to be taught the following year. In 1990 the institute was recognized as a permanently established function of the university, the first to be so recognized.

DELAWARE

University of Delaware (RES II)
Literacy Connections

Grades served: E, M

Schools served: 3

Year established: 1993

Location of schools served: NR

Type of schools served: PUB

Literacy Connections links University of Delaware literacy faculty with school districts across the state for the purpose of improving the teaching of reading and writing in grades K-8. Through year-long, district-level professional development seminars offered by trained teacher-leaders, teachers are helped to examine their teaching methods in light of current research and best practices. Teacher-leaders receive release time to mentor their colleagues. The program also produces a monthly newsletter and a conference, both designed to provide a forum for teachers to share concerns, problems, and successes.

University of Delaware (RES II)
Delmarva Power Energy Education Program

Grades served: E, M	Schools served: 30	Year established: 1989
Location of schools served: UR, SU, RU	Type of schools served: PUB, PRI	

Delmarva Power, the University of Delaware College of Education, and local schools have developed the Energy Education Program "BUZ." The activity-based unit, developed for grades 4-6, focuses on electrical circuits, safety, and conservation. Delmarva Power sponsored the development of the program by university personnel and provides materials and equipment to teachers trained to teach the unit. University personnel set up training courses for teachers. The unit has been adopted for use by several school districts and throughout the state.

DISTRICT OF COLUMBIA

Gallaudet University (MA I)
Pre-College Programs

Grades served: E, M, HS	Schools served: NR	Year established: NR
Location of schools served: NR	Type of schools served: NR	

The university's Pre-College Programs provide a model environment for education of the deaf in elementary and secondary schools through model schools on campus and curriculum dissemination and inservice training of teachers of the deaf for a national audience. Several regional centers regularly supply curriculum materials and inservice training in education of the deaf; a formal relationship between these centers and the university thereby fulfills part of Gallaudet's mission to enable deaf students everywhere to receive an appropriate education.

George Washington University (RES II)
Teachers Networking for Technology

Grades served: HS	Schools served: NR	Year established: NR
Location of schools served: UR, SU	Type of schools served: PUB	

Teachers Networking for Technology (TNT) is a program for high school math and science teachers designed to increase literacy in science, math, and technology. It encourages teachers to act as centers of influence for the Science and Engineering Apprentice Program (SEAP) high school student program and to strengthen the teaching of science in secondary schools. The program runs for eight Saturdays during the spring semester and for eight weeks in the summer. Twenty-five high school math teachers participate, and George Washington faculty are guest lecturers. George Washington offers a section of Engineering Management 298 (6 graduate credits) in an off-campus site during spring and summer.

Howard University (RES I)
Principals' Center

Grades served: NR	Schools served: NR	Year established: 1992
Location of schools served: UR	Type of schools served: PUB	

The Principals' Center recognizes that principals, as educational leaders, must be lifelong learners. The center allows school principals opportunities for professional growth and to build upon their knowledge, skills, and expertise to facilitate improved levels of performance in students. It supports the need for principals to share ideas addressing the challenges faced in today's schools.

Note: Each institution's Carnegie class is given in parentheses. **Key:** E=elementary school, HS=high school, M=middle school, NR=not reported, PRI=private, PUB=public, RU=rural, SU=suburban, UR=urban

FLORIDA

Chipola Junior College (AA)
Alternative Training Initiative
Grades served: E, M, HS   Schools served: 30   Year established: 1994
Location of schools served: UR, SU   Type of schools served: PUB

The Alternative Training Initiative is designed to address the critical shortages of teachers in programs for emotionally and mentally handicapped students, those with specific learning disabilities, and others with varying exceptional needs. The initiative seeks to ensure the availability of qualified teachers through the development, delivery, and evaluation of locally accessible training designed for teachers assigned out-of-field in the areas of these exceptional students. Chipola's program serves more than 30 area schools, helping teachers obtain the training needed to receive certification.

Florida International University (MA I)
FIU/Dade County Public Schools Joint Vocational Teacher Certification
Grades served: NR   Schools served: 119   Year established: 1978
Location of schools served: UR, SU   Type of schools served: PUB

The purpose of this program is to provide a coordinated program of teacher preparation that facilitates successful transition from business and industry to education for nondegree vocational teachers. The program integrates the efforts of local school leaders, supervisors, staff development personnel, and university faculty to provide more immediate teaching skills for new nondegree vocational teachers.

Florida State University (RES I)
Science for Life: Exploring Animal Models in Basic Research
Grades served: M, HS   Schools served: 1500   Year established: 1991
Location of schools served: UR, SU, RU   Type of schools served: PUB, PRI

This workshop for Florida middle and high school science teachers addresses the responsible use of animals, including basic research, care and treatment of laboratory animals, use of animals in the classroom, and the controversy surrounding the ethical use of animals. The project's goals are to increase scientific literacy by promoting public understanding of what basic research is, why it is necessary for progress in improving health, and why the responsible use of animals is necessary in basic as well as applied research. Resource materials include written materials, videos, and hands-on exercises for classroom use.

Nova University (DOC I)
University Liaison Project
Grades served: NR   Schools served: NR   Year established: 1991
Location of schools served: NR   Type of schools served: PUB

The University Liaison Project with the Broward County Schools is a wide-ranging effort to enhance the professional development and inservice training of teachers and administrators. Successful collaborations have included the Center for the Advancement of Teaching, providing teacher training in mathematics and science; a series of videotaped programs for training educators interacting with students of limited English proficiency; and the Preschool Family Resource Center, offering preschool classes and parenting instruction; and literacy programs for children.

University of West Florida (MA I)
Physics Alliance of Northwest Florida

Grades served: M, HS
Location of schools served: UR, SU

Schools served: 12
Type of schools served: PUB, PRI

Year established: 1991

The Physics Alliance of Northwest Florida is an association of physics teachers from 12 schools, one junior college, and the University of West Florida. Members meet at least once a month and discuss methods, strategies, and new experiments that can enhance enrollment in physics at the postsecondary level by initiating and sustaining students' interest. A major activity of the alliance is the annual Physics Olympics, in which 100 students from 12 schools compete for recognition, awards, and the championship through various scientific activities.

Valencia Community College (AA)
Evans High School Liaison Project

Grades served: HS
Location of schools served: NR

Schools served: 1
Type of schools served: PUB

Year established: 1991

The Evans High School Liaison Project links interdisciplinary courses and their teachers at the high school with the course and staff of the Interdisciplinary Studies Honors Program at Valencia Community College. Staff from Valencia provide guidance on curriculum planning, including integrating subject areas in topical or chronological formats, and provide inservice teacher training in the teaching of critical thinking, reading, and writing skills. High school students also tour the campus and sit in on college courses.

GEORGIA

Augusta College (MA I)
CSRA Math Collaborative

Grades served: NR
Location of schools served: UR, SU, RU

Schools served: 75
Type of schools served: PRI

Year established: 1992

The Central Savannah River Area (CSRA) Math Collaborative has a twofold mission: to lead mathematics education into the 21st century by fostering professional growth and communication among those who teach mathematics and those who use mathematics in job-related and consumer-related activities, and to unite the efforts of business, industry, civic groups, and educators with a vision of mathematics as a vitally important field and the learning of mathematics as an active, constructive process.

Bainbridge College (AA)
Bainbridge College/Bainbridge High School: Area Council of Teachers of English

Grades served: HS
Location of schools served: RU

Schools served: 8
Type of schools served: NR

Year established: 1987

The partnership between the Humanities Division of Bainbridge College and the English teachers of Bainbridge High School led to the formation of the Area Council of Teachers of English. The council coordinates the Humanities Essay Competition for high school seniors (complete with $300 scholarships), compiles an annual cultural calendar circulated in eight counties, and publishes *Southwest Georgia Stylus*.

Note: Each institution's Carnegie class is given in parentheses. **Key:** E=elementary school, HS=high school, M=middle school, NR=not reported, PRI=private, PUB=public, RU=rural, SU=suburban, UR=urban

Columbus College (MA I)
Columbus Regional Mathematics Collaborative

Grades served: E, M, HS
Location of schools served: UR, SU, RU
Schools served: 200
Type of schools served: PUB, PRI
Year established: 1989

The Columbus Regional Mathematics Collaborative serves K-12 mathematics teachers from school systems within a 65-mile radius of Columbus College. Professional development programs include frequently scheduled Birds of a Feather small-group networking opportunities, in-classroom support for teachers provided by staff of the collaborative, a resource center, and comprehensive summer institutes. Related programs are offered during the summer for preteen girls (Prep PRIME), rising ninth and tenth grade boys and girls (PRIME), and eleventh and twelfth grade mathematically talented students (Advanced Mathematics Seminar). The summer camps provide opportunities for the teachers to develop new teaching strategies.

Columbus College (MA I)
Muscogee County School District Leadership Academy

Grades served: NR
Location of schools served: NR
Schools served: 52
Type of schools served: PUB
Year established: 1994

The Leadership Academy is a training program for administrators and those qualified for administrative positions in the Muscogee County School District. Programs are designed to familiarize participants with current national and local issues and trends in administration, to acquaint them with the district's culture and its effect on administrative practice, to provide meaningful experiences at different local sites with experienced administrators, and to develop a network of supportive colleagues. The academy also offers a certification program for those with master's degrees who seek L-5 certification.

Georgia Institute of Technology (RES I)
Georgia Industrial Fellowships for Teachers (GIFT)

Grades served: M
Location of schools served: NR
Schools served: NR
Type of schools served: NR
Year established: NR

GIFT is a program designed to develop a cohort of Georgia teachers with experience in real-world applications of contemporary mathematics, science, and technology; Plans are to develop materials transferring these new experiences into classroom action plans, a long-term network of teachers with shared experiences, and a community of mathematics/science partners (corporate, university, local school system, and local community) dedicated to enhanced education in science and mathematics for Georgia students.

HAWAII

University of Hawaii at Manoa (RES I)
Philosophy in the Schools

Grades served: E, M, HS
Location of schools served: NR
Schools served: 35
Type of schools served: PUB
Year established: 1985

Philosophy in the Schools is a joint project of the university's Department of Philosophy and the State Department of Education. It seeks the transformation of public school classrooms from a model based on the transmission of information to a model based on a community of inquiry, and the establishment of philosophy as a recognized, essential component of the K-12 curriculum. Graduate students and faculty from the philosophy department work collaboratively in classrooms with teachers on a weekly basis, in monthly seminars, and summer workshops, assisting in the development of philosophical and social skills necessary to effect the transformation.

IDAHO

Idaho State University (DOC II)
League of Schools

Grades served: NR   Schools served: 76   Year established: 1982
Location of schools served: NR   Type of schools served: PUB

The League of Schools provides a vehicle by which participating school districts and the College of Education can mutually benefit from a collaborative arrangement for organizing staff improvement: assessing needs, prioritizing inservice training, identifying human and material resources, allocating financial resources, delivering staff improvement programs, and evaluating their effectiveness.

ILLINOIS

Loyola University of Chicago (DOC I)
Taft Institute Teaching Seminar

Grades served: E, M, HS   Schools served: NR   Year established: 1979
Location of schools served: UR, SU, RU   Type of schools served: PUB, PRI

Since 1979 Loyola University of Chicago has received an annual grant from the Robert A. Taft Institute of Government to conduct a two-week summer seminar for elementary and secondary school teachers on the functions of the U.S. government. The core component of the seminar emphasizes the institutions and processes of local, state, and national government. A component of minority studies focuses on special issues of teaching government and politics to minority populations. Guest lecturers include scholars and practitioners ranging from elected officials to lobbyists, media representatives, party officials, political consultants, judges, and curriculum specialists.

Northeastern Illinois University (MA I)
Cultural Linguistic Approach/Follow Through Project

Grades served: E   Schools served: 3   Year established: 1969
Location of schools served: UR   Type of schools served: PUB

The project, sponsored by Northeastern Illinois University, sustains and maintains the gains of children in Head Start and similar preschool programs. The program's instructional model uses the cultural strengths and culturally learned behaviors of certain ethnic groups as a springboard for further learning so as to include these children in the classroom mainstream. The project serves more than 400 Chicago public school children, 32 educators, and 200 parents each year.

Northeastern Illinois University (MA I)
Professional Development Program

Grades served: NR   Schools served: 10   Year established: 1989
Location of schools served: UR   Type of schools served: PUB

The Professional Development Program links the University with ten Chicago public schools in an effort to improve teaching and teacher education through the development of new roles and structures for educators and the restructuring of the systems in which they operate. Its aim is to create professional development schools (PDS). More than 450 teachers, 475 university students, and 86 university faculty have been involved in these efforts to combine continuing professional growth for experienced teachers, research opportunities for university faculty and teachers, and carefully structured field experiences for students of education.

Note: Each institution's Carnegie class is given in parentheses. **Key:** E=elementary school, HS=high school, M=middle school, NR=not reported, PRI=private, PUB=public, RU=rural, SU=suburban, UR=urban

School of the Art Institute of Chicago (ART)
Basic Art Support in the Curriculum (BASIC)
Grades served: E, M, HS   Schools served: NR   Year established: 1983
Location of schools served: UR, SU   Type of schools served: PUB, PRI

BASIC is a partnership of the School of the Art Institute of Chicago, an urban college of art, and Chicagoland elementary and secondary schools. The program's goals are to improve art instruction in public and private schools, to bring art instruction to a greater number of children in the Chicago metropolitan area, and to begin to identify students who wish to pursue art as a career through inservice training of art teachers.

University of Chicago (RES I)
Summer Seminars for Chicago Teachers
Grades served: HS   Schools served: NR   Year established: 1985
Location of schools served: UR, SU   Type of schools served: PUB, PRI

The university's Office of University-School Relations offers a series of eight intensive summer seminars for Chicago high school teachers in African history, African/American literature, the Bible in Western civilization, biology, earth science, ecology, mathematics, and recent American history. The program is designed to bring teachers up to date in their fields and to renew their intellectual interest in scholarly activity. Most meet for four weeks during June and July (mathematics meets for five weeks). Teachers receive three hours of Lane credit for successful completion of a seminar.

Western Illinois University (MA I)
CommTech Curriculum Integration Project
Grades served: E, M, HS   Schools served: 35   Year established: 1993
Location of schools served: UR   Type of schools served: PUB

The Western Illinois University College of Education received a Governor's Ameritech Edtech Grant to establish a program to train new and working educators in the classroom use of telecommunication-based teaching tools. In partnership with Springfield District 186 and the Springfield Urban League Head Start Program, College of Education faculty have access to demonstration and training sites for the integration of technology into classroom instruction. Compressed video communications technology between WIU and Springfield allows Springfield classrooms to receive instruction from WIU and interactive video teleconferencing among faculty at WIU and Springfield.

INDIANA

Valparaiso University (MA I)
Professional Development Coordinating Council
Grades served: E, M, HS   Schools served: NR   Year established: 1993
Location of schools served: UR, SU, RU   Type of schools served: PRI

The purpose of Valparaiso University's Professional Development Coordinating Council is to collaboratively design and initiate a coordinated, coherent process for professional development between K-12 schools and teacher education students to enhance the education of all children. The council includes practicing elementary, middle, and secondary school teachers from several school corporations, preservice teacher education students, and university teacher education faculty members. Members of the group include teachers from partner schools with students and faculty of diverse cultural, racial, and ethnic backgrounds.

IOWA

Coe College (BA I)
MAT (Master of Arts in Teaching)

Grades served: E, M, HS Schools served: 4 Year established: 1992
Location of schools served: UR Type of schools served: PUB

The MAT program at Coe College is a venture of the college and Cedar Rapids Community Schools, who jointly developed the program. Faculty are drawn from both institutions. Four public schools — one elementary school, one middle school, and a regular and an alternative high school — serve as learning sites. The guiding principles are active learning, participatory democracy, curriculum integration, collaboration, inquiry, reflection, and academic integrity. Teachers who participate in the program commit themselves to becoming educational leaders, influencing their school's improvement and collaborating in the process of educational renewal. They complete their study with an action project.

Iowa State University (RES I)
School Improvement Model

Grades served: E, M, HS Schools served: 35 Year established: 1979
Location of schools served: UR, SU, RU Type of schools served: PUB, PRI

The field-based School Improvement Model at Iowa State University involves a representative group of K-12 educators within a given school organization. Its primary mission is to make good schools even better. The three major activities center on curriculum renewal/criterion-referenced measures, systems development for performance evaluation of educational professionals, and staff development. Important elements within these activities include skill-building sessions for teachers and administrators, as well as research to help schools with systematic reform.

Teikyo Marycrest University (MA II)
TIP (Teacher Incentive Program)

Grades served: NR Schools served: NR Year established: 1987
Location of schools served: UR, SU, RU Type of schools served: PUB, PRI

The aim of the Teacher Incentive Program is to make graduate studies affordable for all certified teachers by offering graduate-level classes at less than half of regular tuition in all disciplines except computer science. TIP may be used for individual classes or for studies toward the master of arts in education degrees. Requirements for admission for TIP include a baccalaureate degree from a regionally accredited college or university and a valid teaching certificate.

University of Iowa (RES I)
Iowa Writing Project

Grades served: E, M, HS Schools served: NR Year established: 1978
Location of schools served: UR, SU, RU Type of schools served: PUB, PRI

The Iowa Writing Project works toward the improvement of K-12 teachers' instruction in writing and the extension of writing-across-the-curriculum programs in Iowa public schools. The project is a collaboration involving regional educational agencies, the Iowa Department of Education, local school districts, and the University of Iowa. Teachers first participate in Level I, a three-week summer institute. They then may choose to be involved in a seminar during the school year and/or a summer Level II workshop or a Workshop on Writing and Literature.

Note: Each institution's Carnegie class is given in parentheses. **Key:** E=elementary school, HS=high school, M=middle school, NR=not reported, PRI=private, PUB=public, RU=rural, SU=suburban, UR=urban

University of Northern Iowa (MA I)
Office of Student Field Experiences Network

Grades served: NR Schools served: 10 Year established: 1987
Location of schools served: NR Type of schools served: NR

This partnership involves the use of shared clinical supervisors hired jointly by the public schools and the University of Northern Iowa. These field-based practitioners assist the university in the supervision of the university's student teaching program. In addition to the field-based clinical supervision, several cadres of teaching associates were established in the ten geographic regions in Iowa. Their members serve as a network of field-based advisers, serving the university in a variety of other capacities: reviewing curriculum, working on field-based research about teaching and learning in collaboration with university professors, and piloting new programs and materials.

University of Northern Iowa (MA I)
Janesville Project

Grades served: E, M, HS Schools served: 1 Year established: 1992
Location of schools served: RU Type of schools served: PUB

The purpose of this partnership between the rural Janesville School District and the university's College of Education is to pursue cooperative strategies aimed at enhancing the educational programs of both partners. The partnership offers Janesville a creative alternative to closing or consolidating schools, with potential benefits to both agencies. Projects focus on comprehensive systemic change, including the institution of a pre-K program; alternative assessment, curricular integration, thematic instruction, and technology for grades K-6; conversion to middle schools; field-based professional/educational instruction for high school students; model classrooms for regional educators; and cohort groups for student teachers.

KANSAS

Emporia State University (MA I)
Jones Institute for Educational Excellence

Grades served: E, M, HS Schools served: 45 Year established: 1982
Location of schools served: UR, SU, RU Type of schools served: PUB, PRI

The Jones Institute for Educational Excellence is charged with providing services to the broader education community so as to impact the quality of instruction and the effectiveness of leadership in all areas of teaching and learning. Its primary mission is to serve school systems and practitioners in the field. The Institute serves as a dissemination center and repository for educational information; facilitates the extension of faculty expertise to school systems, community colleges, businesses, and corporations; assists with research and surveys; and conducts workshops, conferences, and training programs.

KENTUCKY

Madisonville Community College (AA)
Kennedy Center Performing Arts Centers and Schools: Partners in Education

Grades served: NR Schools served: 95 Year established: 1991
Location of schools served: SU, RU Type of schools served: PUB, PRI

Madisonville Community College's Fine Arts Center and the Badgett Regional Center for Educational Enhancement Consortium are members of this program of the John F. Kennedy Center for the Performing Arts. The partnership creates and develops arts programs to educate teachers on reaching the goals of the Kentucky Education Reform Act. The partnership provides opportunities for teachers to learn how to use the arts as a vehicle for teaching by participating in performance-based events, workshops, and a summer institute.

Murray State University (MA I)
West Kentucky Educational Cooperative

Grades served: E, M, HS   Schools served: 29   Year established: 1978
Location of schools served: SU, RU   Type of schools served: PUB

Murray State University, a charter member of the West Kentucky Educational Cooperative, is the site for the co-op's executive and clinical offices. The partnership includes a consortium for staff development, a subset of the larger group. Cooperative investments in technology, enhanced communication capabilities through development of an electronic mail system, joint efforts in training and in implementing reform, and partnerships providing internships and practicums for preservice students form the core of the university/school relationship. Using compressed video technology, schools share teachers and university faculty, and students serve as consultants, mentors, and tutors for participating schools in the co-op.

Pikeville College (BA II)
Pikeville College Math & Science Resource Center

Grades served: M, HS   Schools served: 10   Year established: 1989
Location of schools served: RU   Type of schools served: PUB

The Pikeville College Math & Science Resource Center is designed to upgrade, enhance, and expand the training of county physics, chemistry, and mathematics teachers and students as well as on-campus preservice teachers in those disciplines who will soon be employed in the area. The center's activities include workshops, special lectures for teachers and students, summer institutes, science fairs, a science information hotline, technical advice for teachers, and a training program for physical science and mathematics teachers to help alleviate the local shortage of teachers trained in these fields.

University of Louisville (DOC I)
Summer Institute for Teachers

Grades served: M, HS   Schools served: 150   Year established: 1986
Location of schools served: UR, SU, RU   Type of schools served: PUB, PRI

The Summer Institute for Teachers brings more than 120 school teachers each year to the campus of the University of Louisville's College of Arts and Sciences. The teachers participate in one-week institutes presented in collaboration with the Woodrow Wilson National Fellowship Foundation of Princeton, N.J. College faculty act as hosts for the sessions, which concentrate on new course content and new teaching methods in the fields of mathematics, science, and history. Follow-up sessions during the subsequent school year allow participants to share the effect that the institute has had in their classrooms.

Western Kentucky University (MA I)
Professional Development Center Network

Grades served: NR   Schools served: 185   Year established: 1976
Location of schools served: UR, RU   Type of schools served: PUB

The Professional Development Center Network is an educational consortium of 26 public school districts and the university's College of Education and Behavioral Sciences. The network, which spans an area of approximately 7,200 square miles, contains 185 schools, approximately 6,000 instructional staff, and 97,000 students. Funded with staff development funds allocated to each school district, the network's main focus is staff development and training for teachers and administrators, An annual needs assessment helps determine training needs. Feedback is gathered, summarized, and reported back on all training activities.

Note: Each institution's Carnegie class is given in parentheses. **Key:** E=elementary school, HS=high school, M=middle school, NR=not reported, PRI=private, PUB=public, RU=rural, SU=suburban, UR=urban

LOUISIANA

Louisiana Tech University (DOC II)
Project LIFE

Grades served: M   Schools served: 50   Year established: 1992
Location of schools served: UR, SU, RU   Type of schools served: PUB, PRI

Project LIFE is an exemplary systemic inservice initiative targeting life science teachers in the middle grades. Teachers receive training in science content and in the use of reform technologies to teach hands-on, minds-on science. The program components include a week-long inservice course for 32 participants, a month-long leadership training institute for teams of teachers, and extensive follow-up during the academic year that includes additional workshops and visits by a Project LIFE site coordinator. This project has served teachers in Louisiana, Texas, and Arkansas and is being extended to other states.

University of New Orleans (DOC II)
Portal School Project

Grades served: E, M   Schools served: 1   Year established: 1985
Location of schools served: UR   Type of schools served: PUB

The Portal School Project in Reading/Language Arts is a university/public school collaboration to strengthen teacher training and students' literacy in urban schools. The project's goals are to assist preservice teachers in developing a knowledge base for literacy instruction with at-risk students, to help preservice teachers to learn to think reflectively about their teaching and broader educational concerns, to assist inservice teachers to develop greater understanding of current literacy theories and instructional strategies, and to provide K-8 at-risk students with enhanced opportunities to develop positive self-images and increased literacy.

MAINE

University of Maine at Farmington (BA I)
Western Maine Partnership

Grades served: NR   Schools served: 18   Year established: 1991
Location of schools served: RU   Type of schools served: PUB

The Western Maine Partnership links the University of Maine at Farmington and 18 schools in the region to promote the renewal and growth of the schools, thereby ensuring an appropriate quality education for all children in western Maine. A variety of collaborative groups provide direction and support, keeping hierarchy and bureaucracy to a minimum. Significant funding from the Maine State Department of Education, Division of Special Education, is supplemented by membership fees.

MARYLAND

Carroll Community College (AA)
Institute for Drug and Alcohol Abuse Education

Grades served: NR   Schools served: 33   Year established: 1990
Location of schools served: RU   Type of schools served: PUB

The Institute for Drug and Alcohol Abuse Education is a partnership of Carroll Community College, Carroll County Public Schools, the Carroll County Health Department, and Junction, Inc., a nonprofit treatment program for addicts. It offers an intensive summer training program to prepare public school teachers, counselors, administrators, and community college personnel to identify, intervene, and prevent substance abuse in their schools. A comprehensive resource center is housed at the college, and a speakers bureau has been established to extend educational programs to the community. Materials developed include a model curriculum that has been distributed throughout the state and a local resource and reference guidebook.

Coppin State College (MA I)
Paraprofessional/Baltimore City Public Schools-Coppin State Collaborative

Grades served: E   Schools served: 185   Year established: 1991
Location of schools served: UR   Type of schools served: NR

Coppin State College, the Division of Compensatory Education, Curriculum, and Instruction, the Offices of Staff Development, Paras, and the Baltimore Teachers Union have formed a partnership to provide paras with training designed to support their needs and the requirements of the Chapter I program. The training is designed by Coppin State College instructors, paras, and other staff of the Baltimore City Public Schools and delivered by Coppin State College instructors and school staff. It includes an overview of child development, content, lesson planning, story telling, effective instructional practices, individualized reading, reinforcing activities, alternative strategies for skill development, learning styles, and personalized communication skills.

Towson State University (MA I)
Baltimore County Public Schools/Towson State University PreKindergarten Collaboration

Grades served: E   Schools served: 6   Year established: 1993
Location of schools served: UR   Type of schools served: PUB

This program is a collaboration allowing the College of Education to operate six prekindergarten classes in selected Baltimore County Public Schools. Among the project's many specific initiatives are monitoring the teachers hired by Towson State; staff development for prekindergarten teachers teaching in the selected schools; a parenting conference for prekindergarten parents; and a clinical setting for the university's preservice early childhood students.

University of Baltimore (MA I)
UB/Southwestern High School Partnership

Grades served: HS   Schools served: 1   Year established: 1986
Location of schools served: UR   Type of schools served: PUB

The partnership between the University of Baltimore and Southwestern Senior High School began as part of a citywide program involving the Community College of Baltimore and the Environmental Elements Corporation. The program focuses on staff development, including tuition waivers for graduate or undergraduate course work for teachers; sponsorship for a teacher, administrator, or librarian to attend the Taft Institute of Government offered by the university's Schaefer Center for Public Policy; and a university-conducted workshop on student discipline and crimes on school property. Students are invited to special events, mock trials, and other appropriate programs.

University of Maryland-College Park (RES I)
Center Alliance for Secondary School Teachers and Texts (CAST)

Grades served: HS   Schools served: 151   Year established: 1988
Location of schools served: UR, SU, RU   Type of schools served: PUB, PRI

The center provides programs for secondary school students and teachers from Maryland and Washington, D.C. Programs have included conferences and workshops; year-long institutes for the teaching of Shakespeare, world drama, and American literature; and drama festival days for high school students. Plans are to add a year-long lecture series for secondary school teachers and students in Howard, Prince George's, and Baltimore counties. Similar programs have been offered for other Maryland counties, including daylong workshops and conferences and a series of semester-long programs to introduce underachieving high school students to dramatic literature and performance.

Note: Each institution's Carnegie class is given in parentheses. **Key:** E=elementary school, HS=high school, M=middle school, NR=not reported, PRI=private, PUB=public, RU=rural, SU=suburban, UR=urban

University of Maryland-College Park (RES I)
Study Abroad: Multicultural Education in the Netherlands, Belgium & Germany

Grades served: NR   Schools served: 1,000   Year established: 1992
Location of schools served: UR, SU, RU   Type of schools served: PUB, PRI

Multicultural Education in the Netherlands, Belgium & and Germany was developed to enable Maryland teachers and university students to study and explore together multicultural education in a society other than the United States. The project is staffed by university and European faculty and funded by participating students and teachers. The study abroad program aims to improve staff development for Maryland schools, improve learning opportunities for university students, and assist in developing an international center for the College of Higher Education in Maastrict.

University of Maryland-College Park (RES I)
Joint Education Initiative

Grades served: E, M, HS   Schools served: 1000   Year established: 1992
Location of schools served: UR, SU, RU   Type of schools served: PUB, PRI

The Joint Education Initiative is a three-year workshop program to develop teachers' confidence and competence in accessing and using government-generated scientific data in teaching and learning. During the summer and the academic year, teachers of grades 6-12 work through and evaluate NOAH, NASA, and USGS data on specially developed CD-ROM discs. Scientists from these government agencies, university faculty, and industry personnel serve as mentors, providing ongoing technical assistance in the acquisition and instructional use of the hardware and software.

MASSACHUSETTS

Bridgewater State College (MA I)
Project SWIMS (Studying Whales Integrating Math and Science)

Grades served: M   Schools served: 50   Year established: 1991
Location of schools served: UR, SU, RU   Type of schools served: PUB, PRI

In this project, 180 teachers (60 per year) are engaged in a three-year summer and academic-year program involving the study of marine mammals and intended to expand their understanding of science and the application of mathematics and computers to answering scientific questions. The institute involves four phases: four presummer workshops; five summer research cruises; four postsummer workshop; and four half-day winter assessment sessions.

Harvard University (RES I)
American Council of Learned Societies (ACLS) Humanities Reform Project

Grades served: E, M, HS   Schools served: 11   Year established: 1992
Location of schools served: UR   Type of schools served: PUB

The ACLS Humanities Reform Project funds a collaboration of Harvard University, Brookline Public Schools, and Cambridge Public Schools. The project provides selected Cambridge and Brookline staff release time to attend a weekly humanities seminar at Harvard University, audit university classes, develop humanities curriculum using university resources, and bring their work to their colleagues for implementation.

Mount Holyoke College (BA I)
Partnership Advancing the Learning of Mathematics and Science (PALMS)
Grades served: E, M, HS   Schools served: 9   Year established: 1992
Location of schools served: UR, SU, RU   Type of schools served: PUB

PALMS is a self-sustaining program initiated by the Massachusetts Department of Education in conjunction with the National Science Foundation. The program is designed to improve the way mathematics and science are taught and learned in grades preK-12 learning centers in Massachusetts. The Department of Education supports partnerships among Mount Holyoke College, Holyoke Public Schools, Monsanto Company, the Springfield Science Museum, and Holyoke Adult Learning Opportunities to achieve these goals.

Salem State College (MA I)
Collaborative Project for Math and Science Education
Grades served: NR   Schools served: 20   Year established: 1985
Location of schools served: UR, SU, RU   Type of schools served: PUB, PRI

A cooperative venture among more than 1,000 individuals, the Collaborative Project for Mathematics and Science Education is housed in the college's Center for the New School, with representation from schools, colleges, businesses, and industries centered on the North Shore of Massachusetts. The project provides resources for inservice teachers and for students in several formats: inservice training in K-12 math and science with all-day and after-school workshops; communication networks through Internet and the Synergist; Project WISE, a career day for girls in grades 6-8 to attend workshops presented by women scientists and engineers; and an active video lending library.

Stonehill College (BA II)
Superintendents' Center for Leadership, Advocacy and Collaboration, Inc.
Grades served: E, M, HS   Schools served: 56   Year established: 1987
Location of schools served: UR, SU, RU   Type of schools served: PUB, PRI

The purpose of this collaboration between Stonehill College and 56 southeastern Massachusetts public and private schools are to develop and support the superintendents' capacity to play a more effective role in economic development and to promote greater collaboration between the educators and the community. It provides for professional development and inservice training, supports local compacts, and enables resource sharing among the partners.

Wheelock College (TEACH)
Cambridgeport Partnership
Grades served: E, M   Schools served: 3   Year established: 1992
Location of schools served: UR   Type of schools served: PUB

The Cambridgeport Partnership enhances professional development in community building, multicultural education, and leadership development. School and college faculty jointly developed planning and teaching models. At the King School, for example, a steering committee surveyed teachers and parents and reviewed achievement data to decide the focus of efforts. A Wheelock faculty member works with teachers and student teachers one day a week to develop a collaborative approach to curriculum design in the discipline identified for the year. Families are involved in supporting the students' learning.

Note: Each institution's Carnegie class is given in parentheses. **Key:** E=elementary school, HS=high school, M=middle school, NR=not reported, PRI=private, PUB=public, RU=rural, SU=suburban, UR=urban

MICHIGAN

Albion College (BA I)
Dramatics-In-Education Program

Grades served: E
Location of schools served: RU

Schools served: 4
Type of schools served: PUB

Year established: 1988

The Dramatics-In-Education program was initiated to introduce the use of dramatics in the public schools to encourage individual expression, foster self-esteem, and promote cooperative learning and communication among students, especially in the early grades. Twelve teachers from four elementary schools participate in a special course, Drama as a Teaching Tool, exploring the uses of drama in developing curricula, demonstrating drama's value and purpose, and suggesting ways to implement drama in their current teaching. Through the program, Theater-In-Education teams provide dramatic stimuli for learning at the elementary level. Teams prepare study guides, host teacher training, visit schools for special performances, and conduct curricular workshops.

Eastern Michigan University (MA I)
Collaborative School Improvement Program

Grades served: E, M, HS
Location of schools served: UR, SU, RU

Schools served: 25
Type of schools served: PUB

Year established: 1978

The Collaborative School Improvement Program has worked in conjunction with area public schools to improve education at the building and/or district level. Essential to the program's success is the teamwork between school staff and EMU faculty. Working with 16 different school districts in one year, the program enables school staff to set relevant goals for improvement and provides resources and support to meet the goals. Each participating school's improvement plan becomes a three-year project, chosen by and agreed to by at least 80% of the school's staff.

Ferris State University (MA II)
North Central Michigan Educational Partnership

Grades served: E, M, HS
Location of schools served: RU

Schools served: 30
Type of schools served: PUB

Year established: 1991

Founded by the university's College of Education, the North Central Michigan Educational Partnership brings together educational innovators at all levels with prominent business and civic leaders for three primary purposes: to facilitate school improvement, to expand opportunities for students, and to enhance the preparation of teachers. The partnership involves college faculty, staff, and students and local schools in six districts. Six specific initiatives are under way: a faculty/staff advisory council; a business and industry Excellence in Education task force; a tech-prep program; development and operation of a math, science, and technology center; the Explaining Today's Technology program; and an improved teacher preparation program.

Grand Valley State University (MA I)
Coalition for Excellence in Science and Math Education

Grades served: E, M, HS
Location of schools served: UR, SU, RU

Schools served: 45
Type of schools served: PUB, PRI

Year established: 1984

The Coalition for Excellence in Science and Math Education provides networks among government, businesses, and educators to improve science and mathematics education for K-12 students in west Michigan (Kent, Ottawa, and Muskegon counties) through publications, teacher alliances, science and mathematics competitions, inservice programs for faculty, and special events. The coalition is a cooperative venture of four colleges, two community colleges, and approximately 50 science- and mathematics-related industries. NSF and industry support provides teacher internships, outreach programs, and a monthly newsletter for more than 4,700 individuals.

Madonna University (MA I)
PSM³: Problem Solving With Mathematical Models and Manipulatives

Grades served: E

Schools served: 80

Year established: 1990

Location of schools served: UR, SU, RU

Type of schools served: PUB, PRI

This program is a partnership between Madonna University and elementary schools in the Detroit metropolitan area. The project provides a series of inservice workshops designed to strengthen K-6 teachers' (and parents') understanding of mathematical concepts through an activity-based, problem-solving approach to teaching. Parent orientation sessions, classroom visits, and an established administrative advisory council help to maintain ongoing support and communication.

Oakland University (MA I)
Oakland University Early Childhood Collaborative

Grades served: E

Schools served: 30

Year established: 1989

Location of schools served: UR, SU

Type of schools served: PUB

Oakland University's School of Education and Human Services has been engaged in a major program to improve educational opportunities for economically disadvantaged children from preschool through grade 3 and to strengthen the preparation of early childhood educators. Funded by a grant from W.K. Kellogg Foundation, the project is a collaboration of schools in Michigan urban centers. It conducts applied research and development focusing on the transition of children from preschool to elementary schools, children's early learning experiences in school, the appropriateness of instructional and curricular practices, and the professional development of teachers as leaders and advocates for children's learning development.

Oakland University (MA I)
K.B. White Professional Development School

Grades served: E

Schools served: 1

Year established: 1993

Location of schools served: UR

Type of schools served: PUB

The Katherine B. White Professional Development School is a partnership coordinated by an Oakland University faculty member and involving the Detroit Public Schools and six area universities: Eastern Michigan, University of Detroit-Mercy, Marygrove, Oakland, University of Michigan-Dearborn, and Wayne State University. The school focuses on developing an innovative early childhood program, a model site-based teacher education program, active parental and community involvement, school-based action research, a multicultural curriculum, higher order thinking skills, thematic instruction, and project-oriented learning.

Oakland University (MA I)
National Career Development Training Institute

Grades served: NR

Schools served: 3000

Year established: 1992

Location of schools served: UR, SU, RU

Type of schools served: PUB, PRI

The National Career Development Training Institute (at the University of South Carolina) is joined and supported by Oakland University's Continuum Center and Adult Career Counseling Center. The institute was initiated with congressional funding to train personnel in assisting students to understand themselves in the context of their career development, to be aware of the world of work, to understand the link between academic skills and work-related skills, and to make effective career decisions.

Note: Each institution's Carnegie class is given in parentheses. **Key:** E=elementary school, HS=high school, M=middle school, NR=not reported, PRI=private, PUB=public, RU=rural, SU=suburban, UR=urban

Spring Arbor College (BA II)
Learning Environments for the 21st Century
Grades served: E, M, HS   Schools served: 5   Year established: 1994
Location of schools served: SU, RU   Type of schools served: PUB, PRI

This project is a collaboration of higher education, business, and K-12 education. Its goal is to be a catalyst for change in education. Objectives are to create partnerships between educational and business communities that benefit both, and to create replicable prototype learning environments that will change the ways practicing K-12 teachers teach, preservice K-12 teachers are educated, and higher education faculty function. The project is designed to create technology centers that provide access to unlimited information that can be converted into useful knowledge by students, parents, educators, business people, and community members.

Wayne State University (RES I)
Institute for Enhancement of Mathematics Teaching
Grades served: HS   Schools served: 27   Year established: NR
Location of schools served: NR   Type of schools served: PUB

Wayne State faculty work with 24 selected high school mathematics teachers from a variety of school districts in the state to become master teachers, that is, heads of departments or resource people for their peers.

MINNESOTA

College of St. Catherine (MA II)
Mentorship Program
Grades served: NR   Schools served: NR   Year established: 1991
Location of schools served: NR   Type of schools served: PUB

The Catholic Education Center and the College of St. Catherine collaborate in preparing mentor (experienced) teachers to work with and support first-year teachers. The program consists of inservice for mentors and then joint meetings of mentors and their mentees that consider specific areas (classroom management, parent-teacher conferencing, and so on). In the first year of the program, mentors receive 1 graduate credit or 2.5 CEUs. In the second year, they receive 2.5 CEUs. Mentors are expected to attend each inservice session, to keep a journal, and to observe and be observed by their mentees.

MISSOURI

Maryville University (MA I)
Maryville/South High Collaborative
Grades served: M, HS   Schools served: 1   Year established: 1992
Location of schools served: SU   Type of schools served: PUB

The Maryville/South High Collaborative involves the university, the high school, and the Southwestern Bell Fund in an effort to rethink secondary teacher education along the lines of the Coalition of Essential Schools's Nine Essential Principles. The project involves South High teachers, Maryville teacher education faculty, and Maryville liberal arts faculty. The ultimate goals are strengthening the Coalition principles at South High and developing a site-based secondary teacher education program using those principles. The project is designed to promote systemic reform and to develop and implement performance standards for both high school students and teacher education graduates.

Rockhurst College (MA I)
Center for the Advancement of Reform in Education
Grades served: E, M, HS   Schools served: NR   Year established: 1992
Location of schools served: UR, SU, RU Type of schools served: PUB, PRI

The Center for the Advancement of Reform in Education is an extension of Rockhurst College's Education Department. Dedicated to furthering education that recognizes differences in learning styles (informed by research on hemispheric dominance in human intelligence) in grades K-12, the center works with an advisory board representing regional school systems to set national and regional agendas. Instruction in creating appropriate environments is available through an annual national conference, model teaching weeks, monthly discussion groups, inservice sessions with nationally known consultants, graduate courses, a resource library, and a regional newsletter.

University of Missouri-Kansas City (DOC I)
Metropolitan Area Schools Project
Grades served: NR   Schools served: NR   Year established: 1983
Location of schools served: UR, SU, RU Type of schools served: PUB, PRI

The Metropolitan Area Schools Project is a partnership linking the University of Missouri-Kansas City, the Metropolitan Community College system, and the 54 school districts in the Kansas City area. Program activities include quarterly inservice meetings for school superintendents; cooperative grant-writing projects; teacher councils that facilitate curricular reform and inservice training; the providing of university faculty and staff as consultants; training of high school faculty and staff to encourage and implement student academic support programs and to increase academic performance and student retention (e.g., supplemental instruction and video-based supplemental instruction); and other programs and services requested by the high school.

University of Missouri-St. Louis (DOC I)
Gateway Writing Project
Grades served: NR   Schools served: 10   Year established: 1978
Location of schools served: UR, SU, RU Type of schools served: PUB, PRI

The Gateway Writing Project, affiliated with the National Writing Project, links this urban state university, a historically Black teacher's college (Harris-Stowe State College), and the metropolitan area's school districts. GWP sponsors summer institutes for experienced teachers and inservice workshops led by teacher-consultant graduates of those institutes. Collaboration has led to classroom action-research teams; computer-equipped writing centers; publishing and curriculum development by teachers; and a few programs for children (e.g., a summer writing camp). The project has been especially involved in documenting and supporting good teaching in urban and culturally diverse settings.

Washington University (RES I)
Washington University/Soldan International Studies High School Collaborative
Grades served: HS   Schools served: 1   Year established: 1993
Location of schools served: UR   Type of schools served: PUB

The Washington University/Soldan High School collaborative links resources from WU with a newly established public magnet high school in St. Louis. Activities include four inservice workshops for teachers and seven forum programs for teachers and students presented by WU faculty; WU student mentors to help high school students prepare for math and science fairs; tutoring by WU students in French and Spanish; and visits by WU international students. Future collaboration will include tutoring in additional foreign languages, consultation on language instruction and use of the university's language lab, science enrichment, and activities in the arts and literature.

Note: Each institution's Carnegie class is given in parentheses. **Key:** E=elementary school, HS=high school, M=middle school, NR=not reported, PRI=private, PUB=public, RU=rural, SU=suburban, UR=urban

Montana College of Mineral Science and Technology (MA II)
Project Partners

Grades served: E, M, HS

Schools served: 100

Year established: 1980

Location of schools served: UR, RU

Type of schools served: PUB

Project Partners, Montana's prototype for industry-education partnerships, is supported by the mining industry, the Montana University system, K-12 education and the state government. Activities provide experiences that make science, mathematics, and technology relevant to rural Montanans. Programs include Teachers as Interns in Industry, Mineral Education Programs for Young Scholars, Environmental Partners: Educators and Industry, the Montana Science and Technology Education Center, and the Math/Science Resource Center, which lends equipment and materials to area science and mathematics teachers.

Montana State University (DOC II)
MSU/Bozeman Public School District Partnership

Grades served: NR

Schools served: 8

Year established: 1991

Location of schools served: RU

Type of schools served: PUB

This partnership was initiated to facilitate better working relationships between MSU's College of Education, Health, and Human Development and the Bozeman Public School District. The partnership focuses on MSU student practicums and related policies, jointly sponsored inservice activities, the district's early childhood education activities and policies, facilitation of individual partnerships between MSU teacher education faculty and school teachers, cooperation on research and evaluation projects, and joint faculty appointments.

Montana State University-Billings (MA I)
Professional Development Schools

Grades served: NR

Schools served: 7

Year established: 1991

Location of schools served: UR, SU, RU

Type of schools served: PUB, PRI

The Montana State University-Billings Professional Development Schools, a learning community of practitioners, university faculty, students, administrators, and preservice teachers, involves the university and seven area schools. The project is dedicated to the development of novice professionals, continued development of experienced professionals, and research and development of the teaching profession. School faculty and university representatives meet regularly to maintain effective communication among participants. University faculty assist the schools in achieving goals, and school faculty may serve as adjunct faculty at the university.

Creighton University (MA I)
Metro Area Teachers Institute (MATI)

Grades served: NR

Schools served: 25

Year established: 1988

Location of schools served: UR, SU

Type of schools served: PUB, PRI

The Metro Area Teachers Institute is an alliance between Creighton University and 25 secondary schools in greater Omaha. The goal of MATI is to help coordinate and expand secondary school faculty development and continuing education by centralizing related programs and pooling resources from participating school districts and Creighton. Participants in MATI seminars and workshops become Creighton University Fellows during the time they are enrolled, providing them with use of the university's libraries and other research facilities.

Sierra Nevada College (BA II)
EPA Grant

Grades served: E   Schools served: 100   Year established: 1992
Location of schools served: UR, SU, RU   Type of schools served: PUB

Sierra Nevada College works with the Washoe County Curriculum and Instruction Office under a grant funded by the Environmental Protection Agency to train elementary school teachers with no previous training in environmental science. The college presented a series of workshops to elementary school teachers at their schools and at the college to train them to teach environmental science in their classrooms.

Sierra Nevada College (BA II)
Eisenhower Grants In Math & Science

Grades served: NR   Schools served: 100   Year established: 1991
Location of schools served: UR, SU, RU   Type of schools served: PUB

Sierra Nevada College works with the Washoe County Gifted and Talented Office and the ESL Office to offer training in math and science to district teachers of gifted and talented and ESL students. College instructors present hands-on activities and emphasize project-based teaching and cooperative learning by having the teachers work together in groups. The project provides a booklet of ideas for lesson plans using these techniques to address the special needs of gifted and talented and ESL students.

NEW HAMPSHIRE

University of New Hampshire (DOC II)
Center for Educational Field Services (CEFS)

Grades served: NR   Schools served: 500   Year established: 1966
Location of schools served: UR, SU, RU   Type of schools served: PUB, PRI

The Center for Educational Field Services was begun to help New Hampshire schools improve the quality of public school education. The director serves as executive director of the New Hampshire School Boards Association and since 1976 has also served in that capacity for the School Administrators Association. CEFS staff plan and carry out more than 20 statewide workshops and two state conventions, for the 800 school board members and 63 superintendents. CEFS also offers consultant services and assistance in evaluating programs and facilities, assists in developing policy handbooks, and carries out research on state policy issues affecting the schools.

NEW JERSEY

Fairleigh Dickinson University (MA I)
Master of Arts in Science-Elementary Science Specialist Program

Grades served: NR   Schools served: NR   Year established: 1993
Location of schools served: UR, SU   Type of schools served: PUB, PRI

This program, offered by Fairleigh Dickinson University in conjunction with Plainfield and Jersey City School Districts, is a graduate interdisciplinary degree program specially designed to prepare elementary science specialists. The program also is made available to teachers from other nearby schools.

Note: Each institution's Carnegie class is given in parentheses. **Key:** E=elementary school, HS=high school, M=middle school, NR=not reported, PRI=private, PUB=public, RU=rural, SU=suburban, UR=urban

Montclair State College (MA I)
Project THISTLE (Thinking Skills in Teaching and Learning)

Grades served: E, M, HS   Schools served: NR   Year established: 1979
Location of schools served: NR   Type of schools served: PUB

Project THISTLE (Thinking Skills in Teaching and Learning) is a collaborative program developed by Montclair State College and the Newark Public Schools. Designed to assist classroom teachers to strengthen the critical thinking abilities of their students, the program defines aspects of basic skills as higher order thinking skills within content instruction and integrates curriculum and staff development.

Princeton University (RES I)
Institute for Secondary School Teachers

Grades served: M, HS   Schools served: 100   Year established: 1990
Location of schools served: UR, SU, RU   Type of schools served: PUB, PRI

Princeton University's summer Institute for Secondary School Teachers offers an intensive week-long program in molecular biology. It offers teachers from 100 high schools the opportunity to work with new methods widely used in molecular genetic research and to discuss, through a seminar, applications of the new genetics to the problems of disease and medicine. Participants develop curricula for their own classrooms; they communicate with one another and the Princeton faculty during the school year via an electronic bulletin board.

Princeton University (RES I)
History Institute for Secondary School Teachers

Grades served: M, HS   Schools served: 10   Year established: 1994
Location of schools served: UR, SU, RU   Type of schools served: PUB, PRI

Princeton's History Institute for Secondary School Teachers is sponsored by the university's History Department and Teacher Preparation Program. The two-week summer project involves university history professors, 20 public and private secondary school teachers, four undergraduates preparing to teach, and an administrator from the Teacher Preparation Program. The major goals are to provide teachers with hands-on training and experience in using and interpreting historical sources and to develop a corps of classroom teachers and Princeton Teacher Preparation undergraduates working cooperatively with the best research and materials available.

Ramapo College of New Jersey (BA II)
Project SPACE (Stars, Planets, Asteroids, Constellations for Educators)

Grades served: E   Schools served: NR   Year established: 1985
Location of schools served: UR, SU   Type of schools served: PUB, PRI

Project SPACE is a collaboration of Ramapo College and school districts in northern New Jersey and southern New York that focuses on the inclusion of astronomy in the elementary science curriculum. It is a field-based approach to educational change in which nonspecialist elementary teachers strengthen their knowledge of astronomy, subsequently becoming better equipped to implement the project's instructional materials in the classroom.

Rowan College of New Jersey (MA I)
Cooper's Poynt Professional Development Family School of Excellence

Grades served: E, M

Schools served: 1

Year established: 1991

Location of schools served: NR

Type of schools served: PUB

This collaboration of the Camden City Schools and Rowan College of New Jersey is based on the Holmes Group principles. The program establishes a K-8 professional development school, where teachers and college professors generate knowledge about education and put it into practice as a model for school reform and accountability. Stressing instructional methodology, action research, alternative assessment, and collaboration across the curriculum, the collaborative's major components are preservice teacher education, inservice programs, parental/community involvement, and collaborative research.

Rutgers, the State University of New Jersey-New Brunswick Campus (RES I)
MAPS (Mathematics Projects with Schools)

Grades served: E, M

Schools served: 20

Year established: 1984

Location of schools served: NR

Type of schools served: PUB, PRI

The model of teacher development offered by the Rutgers Mathematics Projects with Schools aims to create profound and lasting change in mathematics instruction by working intensively with teachers and administrators to establish programs in a number of elementary schools that are exemplary models of reform for the state and the nation. The foci of these programs include teachers' knowledge of science, mathematics, and technology; careful attention to children's thinking; and the knowledge, skills, and support necessary to effectively incorporate the ideas into classroom instruction.

Rutgers, the State University of New Jersey-New Brunswick Campus (RES I)
Rutgers Literacy Curriculum Network

Grades served: NR

Schools served: NR

Year established: 1990

Location of schools served: UR, SU

Type of schools served: PUB

The univrsity's Graduate School of Education has formed a network of 65 school districts interested in exploring literacy initiatives related to literature-based curricula, processes, and whole-language approaches to reading and writing, literacy across the curriculum, and assessment. The network facilitates the sharing of information among network personnel, administrators, and teachers throughout New Jersey. Monthly meetings allow participants to interact with nationally known speakers and educators whose work bears on these concerns. The network supports staff and curriculum development and the informed selection of materials. An annual fee of $500 per school district covers all participants at all events for the year.

Stevens Institute of Technology (DOC I)
Center for Improved Engineering and Science Education (CIESE)

Grades served: M, HS

Schools served: 160

Year established: 1988

Location of schools served: UR, SU, RU

Type of schools served: PUB, PRI

CIESE is a partnership of teachers, school administrators, and higher education. Its primary focus is to improve instruction and students' achievement by assisting middle and high school teachers to integrate computers in their classrooms. CIESE currently links Stevens Institute with 20 New Jersey school districts and six 2- and 4-year colleges that, in turn, have developed outreach programs for local schools. A series of teacher training videoconferences broadcast by the Satellite Educational Resources Consortium have enabled Stevens to work with teachers across the country. Tapes of twenty-one 90-minute videoconferences are available for teacher training.

Note: Each institution's Carnegie class is given in parentheses. **Key:** E=elementary school, HS=high school, M=middle school, NR=not reported, PRI=private, PUB=public, RU=rural, SU=suburban, UR=urban

William Paterson College (MA I)
Northern New Jersey Writing Consortium

Grades served: E, M, HS   Schools served: NR   Year established: 1984
Location of schools served: UR, SU, RU   Type of schools served: PUB, PRI

The Northern New Jersey Writing Consortium, modeled on the National Writing Project, is administered and housed at William Paterson College. The loose affiliation of schools and individuals from more than 22 local school districts trains teachers across the curriculum in the uses of process writing through inservice training and a summer writing institute. Monthly roundtable discussions bring school and college teachers together, and a cooperative publication, *Zero Draft*, is distributed twice yearly.

NEW MEXICO

New Mexico State University-Main Campus (RES I)
Systemic Initiative for Math and Science Education (SIMSE)

Grades served: M   Schools served: 3   Year established: NR
Location of schools served: NR   Type of schools served: PUB

SIMSE provides summer institutes for middle school math and science teachers to develop higher order reasoning and problem-solving skills in their students and to integrate math and science skills in their classrooms. The five-day institute involves the university's Department of Mathematics and Science faculty and teachers from three middle schools: Sierra and Zia (in Las Cruces) and Saracino (in Socorro). Innovative practices include hands-on math and science activities and the involvement of the communities in teaching and learning.

New Mexico State University-Main Campus (RES I)
Las Cruces Public Schools Bilingual Multicultural Teacher Education Institute

Grades served: NR   Schools served: NR   Year established: NR
Location of schools served: NR   Type of schools served: PUB

This two-week program offered in July and August is designed to train bilingual teachers for the Las Cruces Public Schools. The schools collaborated in planning the program, which is a workshop covering such topics as language acquisition, multicultural education, parents' involvement, and political implications of bilingual education. Donated services provide instruction in integrating technology in the classroom and mentorship of mathematics specialists.

University of New Mexico-Main Campus (RES I)
Albuquerque Public Schools-University of New Mexico Collaborative Programs

Grades served: NR   Schools served: 200   Year established: 1967
Location of schools served: UR, SU, RU   Type of schools served: PUB

Albuquerque Public Schools and the University of New Mexico participate in formal, contractual relationships designed to improve both preservice education at the university and inservice education in the schools. The exchange of services contract places fully certified university interns in public school classrooms at reduced salaries. The money saved through this device releases veteran teachers to work full time in teacher education in the university's preservice program and the district's inservice program. The program has produced a network of well-prepared instructional leaders and a greatly enhanced relationship between the districts and the university. It has received numerous awards for distinguished achievement.

NEW YORK

Bard College (BA I)
Institute for Writing & Thinking
Grades served: M, HS   Schools served: 200   Year established: 1982
Location of schools served: UR, SU, RU   Type of schools served: PUB, PRI

Bard College's Institute for Writing and Thinking is a professional development center for college and secondary teachers that offers workshops, conferences, and consulting nationally. In 1987, Bard College and six other colleges established the National Writing and Thinking Network to provide summer writing workshops for high school students. The institute collaborates with schools and teachers throughout the year in related projects; since 1982 it has served more than 25,000 teachers and several hundred schools.

Canisius College (MA I)
Western New York Writing Project
Grades served: E, M, HS   Schools served: 100   Year established: 1986
Location of schools served: UR, SU, RU   Type of schools served: PUB, PRI

The Western New York Writing Project (WNYWP) at Canisius is an affiliate of the National Writing Project. Its primary mission is to improve the teaching of writing in area K-16 schools by strengthening teachers' abilities during a five-week summer institute, Teachers Teaching Teachers. It offers intensive follow-up during the school year, including monthly workshops and miniconferences on teaching, a newsletter, and writers' workshops. WNYWP also provides intensive inservice training by teacher-consultants in area schools during the school year. WNYWP teacher-consultants work directly with area school children, sponsoring a Young Writers Conference, a Young Writers Anthology, and a Summer Writing Camp.

City University of New York Bernard M. Baruch College (MA I)
New York City Council on Economic Education at Baruch College
Grades served: HS   Schools served: 150   Year established: 1989
Location of schools served: UR   Type of schools served: PUB

This partnership links Baruch College with New York City High Schools. Its primary mission is to improve the quality of high school economics education. To accomplish this mission, the college has undertaken such projects as scholarships for a college economics course specifically designed for high school teachers, all-day topical economics seminars and workshops for students, all-day topical economics conferences on the teaching of high school economics, and on-site economics curriculum consultations.

City University of New York College of Staten Island (MA I)
Staten Island English Newsletter
Grades served: M, HS   Schools served: 8   Year established: 1985
Location of schools served: UR   Type of schools served: PUB

Staten Island English Newsletter is a collaboratively produced publication of teachers and professors from Brooklyn-Staten Island High Schools and the College of Staten Island. Original material by working teachers in both the secondary and postsecondary institutions encourages reform at the grassroots level. Articles showcase innovations within the system, reflecting the work of teachers on the editorial committee and their peers working together to refine and improve their own standards and skills. Teachers receive remuneration per session, and the college supports the cost of publication.

Note: Each institution's Carnegie class is given in parentheses. **Key:** E=elementary school, HS=high school, M=middle school, NR=not reported, PRI=private, PUB=public, RU=rural, SU=suburban, UR=urban

City University of New York Queens College (MA I)
Louis Armstrong Middle School, Queens College

Grades served: M
Location of schools served: UR

Schools served: 1
Type of schools served: PUB

Year established: 1979

Queens College and the New York City Board of Education are partners in this enterprise involving the exchange of personnel, resources, facilities, and ideas in an effort to develop a middle school that can serve as a model for other schools. Leaders include an on-site director and an intern supervisor. Professors work with the school faculty regularly, graduate interns spend three days a week at the school, student teachers work with Louis Armstrong faculty as clinical professors, and faculty and students collaborate on research projects.

College of New Rochelle (MA I)
Westchester Teacher Education Group

Grades served: NR
Location of schools served: UR, SU

Schools served: NR
Type of schools served: PUB, PRI

Year established: 1984

The Westchester Teacher Education Group (a program of the Westchester Education Coalition) offers various programs designed to bring together schools, colleges, and local businesses in Westchester County. The Wallace-Reader's Digest Westchester Fund sponsors a four-year school-college partnership designed to increase knowledge and skills in multicultural diversity, technology, mathematics/science education, and preparation of students for the workplace.

Cornell University (RES I)
Enhancement of High School Science Education: Equipment Lending Library

Grades served: HS
Location of schools served: UR, SU, RU

Schools served: 68
Type of schools served: PUB, PRI

Year established: 1990

The Enhancement of High School Science Education program is a collaboration of Cornell's Institute of Biology Teachers (CIBT) and area high schools. Selected high school biology teachers come to Cornell for three weeks during CIBT's summer program, where they work with Cornell faculty to develop laboratory modules for high school classrooms. Teachers are provided with computers to take back to their schools, which are their ongoing network with one another and with Cornell faculty. The program is supported by corporate sponsors.

Cornell University (RES I)
Latin American Studies Program

Grades served: E, M, HS
Location of schools served: RU

Schools served: NR
Type of schools served: PUB

Year established: NR

Cornell University's Latin American Studies Program (LASP) offers a wide variety of services to primary, secondary, and college teachers. LASP's outreach activities and materials include Latin American conferences, a biweekly film series, a video library, a speakers bureau, and "traveling suitcases" on Latin America. LASP also offers scholarships for teachers to participate in workshops on contemporary problems in Latin America, including ethnicity and conflict, economic reform, religion, and democratization. The program collaborates with area teachers to design educational materials, such as the interactive computer instructional program, "The Andean World."

Cornell University (RES I)
Institute on Science and the Environment for Teachers

Grades served: HS | Schools served: 15 | Year established: 1991
Location of schools served: UR, SU, RU | Type of schools served: PUB, PRI

The Institute on Science and the Environment for Teachers (ISET) is a project of Cornell University's Department of Education and the Center for the Environment. ISET brings teams of high school biology, chemistry, and earth science teachers to Ithaca to undertake an interdisciplinary study of watershed dynamics. Teams of teachers develop and implement school-specific curricular projects focusing on the study of a local problem involving water. In addition to training, the university provides teachers with equipment and supplies to analyze water in the field, remote sensing imagery, print materials, computer software, and support during the school year through visits to schools and communication over a computer bulletin board.

Long Island University-Brooklyn Campus (MA I)
School Psychology Program

Grades served: NR | Schools served: NR | Year established: 1984
Location of schools served: UR, SU | Type of schools served: PUB, PRI

The School Psychology Program is a master's degree program (60/61 credits) leading to provisional certification that trains students in human development and basic foundations of the discipline and in diagnosis and remediation of learning problems. It covers curriculum, educational assessment, intervention techniques, and professional issues. The program is offered on the Brooklyn and Westchester campuses, with enrollment in Brooklyn about 60% minority. A major revision in fall 1995 will emphasize skills and attitudes appropriate to working with diverse populations, professional communication, and increased labs and practice. Students work fulltime or halftime.

Onondaga Community College (AA)
Elementary Science Mentor Network

Grades served: E | Schools served: 38 | Year established: NR
Location of schools served: UR, SU, RU | Type of schools served: PUB, PRI

The Onondaga Community College's Elementary Science Mentor Network is a collaboration of the college and the Syracuse city public and private schools designed to improve the quality of elementary school science instruction. Thirty-nine educators and parents serve as mentors, assisting other teachers and parents to become mentors. Each participating elementary school appoints one teacher to serve as the building's science mentor, who attends inservice training, develops a school science program plan each year, and provides inservice training to teachers and parents in the home school. Training includes hands-on activities to improve problem solving and higher level thinking and experience in using science manipulatives.

State University of New York at Albany (RES II)
Institute for the Arts in Education

Grades served: E, M, HS | Schools served: 40 | Year established: 1983
Location of schools served: UR, SU, RU | Type of schools served: PUB, PRI

The Institute for the Arts in Education, a partnership of SUNY-Albany and more than 30 school districts, is designed to bring art-centered learning to children in elementary, middle, and high schools. Modeled on the Lincoln Center's arts-integration method, the institute provides participating schools a week-long intensive workshop on the arts in education for teachers; artist and teacher planning sessions to integrate artist residencies and performances into classroom studies; classroom residencies for writers, illustrators, and performing and visual artists; culturally varied performances and exhibitions; inservice programs; and a National Gallery of Art audiovisual materials loan program.

Note: Each institution's Carnegie class is given in parentheses. **Key:** E=elementary school, HS=high school, M=middle school, NR=not reported, PRI=private, PUB=public, RU=rural, SU=suburban, UR=urban

State University of New York at Albany (RES II)
Recombinant DNA Courses for High School Teachers/Students
Grades served: HS   Schools served: 100   Year established: 1987
Location of schools served: UR, SU, RU   Type of schools served: PUB, PRI

The Recombinant DNA Courses for High School Teachers/Students offered by SUNY-Albany make possible the training of 20 teachers per year for three years on how to introduce recombinant DNA laboratories into their classrooms. More than 80 teachers from 70 different high schools have been trained, and available funds will allow the training of 40 additional teachers. Teachers in the Albany area share sets of equipment, and the university oversees the distribution of equipment and purchases consumable supplies for area high schools that offer recombinant DNA laboratories.

State University of New York at Albany (RES II)
Capital Area School Development Association (CASDA)
Grades served: NR   Schools served: NR   Year established: 1949
Location of schools served: UR, SU, RU   Type of schools served: PUB, PRI

The Capital Area School Development Association is a study council affiliated with the university's School of Education. One of the oldest study councils in the United States, CASDA includes 115 school districts and private institutions from three large and several small cities, large and small urban and rural districts, and five BOCES. The council presents more than 130 professional development programs annually for all district personnel, publishes a quarterly newsletter and an annual statistical and financial study, and offers select seminars on important issues in education.

State University of New York at Albany (RES II)
Laboratory Research Opportunities
Grades served: E, M, HS   Schools served: 100   Year established: 1991
Location of schools served: UR, SU, RU   Type of schools served: PUB, PRI

Area school teachers who want to carry out scientific research can do so in the campus laboratories. The teachers selected are identified as teacher-fellows; they are funded partly by outside agencies, with supplemental funding from their Albany sponsors for expenses. The partnership offers teachers in the 12 area school districts an opportunity to pursue research questions; selections are made by the university sponsors.

State University of New York College at Cortland (MA I)
IBM/NYS Education Department Partnership
Grades served: E   Schools served: 1   Year established: 1990
Location of schools served: NR   Type of schools served: PUB

The IBM/NYS Education Department Partnership was initiated to show how technology can be used to improve achievement and how schools and classrooms should be organized to harness its power effectively. SUNY-Cortland and Remington Elementary School formed one of 12 partnerships under this program. An electronic network increases communication between the partners. Other benefits are training opportunities for college and public school instructors, development of new courses, and increased use of computers in the target schools, field trips, site visits, placement of preservice teachers in technologically rich environments, and inservice training.

State University of New York College at Cortland (MA I)
Center for Educational Exchange

Grades served: E, M, HS

Location of schools served: UR, SU, RU

Schools served: 100

Type of schools served: PUB, PRI

Year established: 1983

The SUNY-Cortland Center for Educational Exchange supports personal and professional exchanges among educators. Working within existing networks, the center provides preservice and inservice professional development for educators and coordinates programs for area public school students. Professional conferences for student teachers are held each semester, supported by Cortland faculty and local teachers and administrators. The center connects college faculty, departments, and others interested in collaborating with area schools and teachers, helps to plan informational meetings, institutes, and special courses, and collaborates in writing funding proposals. The advisory committee includes college faculty and administrators, area school representatives, and BOCES.

State University of New York College at Oswego (MA I)
Project SMART (Science/Mathematics Applied Resources for Teaching)

Grades served: E, M

Location of schools served: UR, SU, RU

Schools served: 32

Type of schools served: PUB, PRI

Year established: 1988

Project SMART is a partnership of schools, area industries, and SUNY-College at Oswego. It is designed to stimulate teachers' and students' interest in and understanding of science and mathematics as applied in the workplace. Teachers and college faculty work with businesses and industries to develop math and science units and kits. The industries involved make their plants available for field trips for children from area schools. Project SMART teachers and industry representatives offer staff development workshops for teachers. Research and dissemination are ongoing.

State University of New York College at Potsdam (MA I)
North Country School Study Council

Grades served: NR

Location of schools served: RU

Schools served: 46

Type of schools served: PUB

Year established: 1967

The North Country School Study Council links Potsdam College and the public schools in an effort to create the most cost-efficient mechanism for providing staff development. In return for a nominal membership fee, school district employees and board members are given an opportunity to attend one or more workshops addressing a broad range of educational issues. Recent topics, for example, have included special courses and programs related to job-training skills for school staff. Many programs are held on the Potsdam campus, others in the schools. The program has affected other aspects of school-college relationships, such as placement of student teachers and the annual speech tournament.

Syracuse University (RES II)
SUPER (Schools and University Partnership for Educational Responsibility)

Grades served: E, M, HS

Location of schools served: UR, SU, RU

Schools served: 38

Type of schools served: PUB, PRI

Year established: 1985

SUPER provides a continuum between elementary/secondary teachers and their Syracuse University counterparts whose aim is to build a collaborative environment among faculty within subject areas. Committees representing school and university equally are formed within subject areas and aided with administrative and funding support from the university and the schools; they plan symposia, workshops, and other events of interest open to all school and university faculty. Current committees operate in art, English, mathematics, modern languages, and social studies.

Note: Each institution's Carnegie class is given in parentheses. **Key:** E=elementary school, HS=high school, M=middle school, NR=not reported, PRI=private, PUB=public, RU=rural, SU=suburban, UR=urban

Union College (BA I)
Principles of Engineering Leadership Group

Grades served: HS   Schools served: 10   Year established: 1992
Location of schools served: UR, SU, RU   Type of schools served: PUB

The Capital District Area Principles of Engineering Leadership Group consists of a faculty member from Union College and about ten Principles of Engineering high school teachers from upper and central New York and Vermont. The Union College representative provides leadership for the group, which meets four or five times throughout the academic year. The group discusses such issues as electronic networking, teaching techniques, and educational materials related to Principles of Engineering course.

NORTH CAROLINA

Mars Hill College (BA I)
General Electric/Mars Hill College/3 School System Collaborative Effort

Grades served: M   Schools served: 8   Year established: 1992
Location of schools served: RU   Type of schools served: PUB

Projects LINC I and II (Learning Through Inquiry, Networking, and Collaboration) involve three county school systems, eight middle grade schools, and 16 teachers. LINC I provides middle school math and science teachers with opportunities to enhance skills specifically related to using computers as a teaching tool; a summer bridge program on the Mars Hill College campus for EdGE students is an outgrowth of the program. LINC II provides the same program for English and social studies teachers. The collaboration enables teachers in particular disciplines to work productively with at-risk students and to establish the notions of partnerships and collaborative learning.

University of North Carolina at Charlotte (MA I)
UNC Charlotte/Charlotte-Mecklenburg Schools Cooperative Program for Middle Grades Training

Grades served: M   Schools served: 17   Year established: 1993
Location of schools served: UR, SU, RU   Type of schools served: PUB

This program involves carefully planned course work designed to improve the quality of instruction in the school system's middle grades while addressing certification and professional advancement of middle school teachers, some of whom have come from elementary and high schools. A university faculty member coordinates the program with five university associates from the participating school system. The instructional team teaches the course work, which is specifically selected and individualized according to the needs of specific teachers and school, and provides mentoring and counseling.

University of North Carolina at Charlotte (MA I)
Project Supervisor: A Model Clinical Teaching Program

Grades served: NR   Schools served: NR   Year established: 1988
Location of schools served: SU, RU   Type of schools served: PUB

Project Supervisor is a collaboration of UNC-Charlotte and 13 regional public school systems. It is designed to prepare practicing master teachers from public school systems for roles as university supervisors of student teachers. The project's objectives are to expand and distribute opportunities for placement of student teachers to a variety of school systems served by UNC-Charlotte, to give recognition and renewed status to practicing public school teachers, to expand the opportunity for school systems, to have a major role in preparing teachers, and to maximize collaboration between the public schools and the university.

University of North Carolina at Greensboro (DOC I)
Piedmont Triad Horizons Education Consortium

Grades served: E, M, HS
Location of schools served: UR, SU, RU

Schools served: 184
Type of schools served: PUB

Year established: 1992

The Piedmont Triad Horizons Education Consortium is a collaboration of Piedmont Triad elementary through secondary schools, college and university officials, community college presidents, and business leaders, working together to invent ambitious educational reforms for the 21st century. The consortium provides professional development, collaborative endeavors in TQM, think-tank experiences, international school partnerships, and is establishing a model school in concert with the business community.

Wake Forest University (DOC II)
LIME (Logo-Integrated Mathematics Environment) Project

Grades served: M
Location of schools served: RU

Schools served: 8
Type of schools served: PUB, PRI

Year established: 1991

The LIME project was created to improve mathematics teaching and learning in grades 5-8 by integrating Logo computer programming activities into the curriculum. Twenty intermediate school teachers from rural Stokes County have participated in the project. Teachers were taught Logo programming in workshops during the school year and then attended a two-week summer program, where they constructed lesson plans that use Logo. After their plans were matched to the state's curriculum objectives, the teachers implemented the lessons with their students. The collection of lessons has been distributed to local schools and is under review for national distribution.

Wake Forest University (DOC II)
Writing to Learn Math and Science

Grades served: NR
Location of schools served: SU, RU

Schools served: 30
Type of schools served: PUB

Year established: 1988

Writing to Learn Math and Science focuses on developing strong conceptual math skills for elementary and middle school students. The program is based on the theory that writing helps students to deepen their understanding of math and science. Teachers use writing to help articulate how problems are solved. Seminars, workshops, and other inservice programs help teachers to integrate writing into their own repertoire of effective teaching strategies. The program is sponsored by the Western Triad Science and Mathematics Alliance.

Wake Forest University (DOC II)
Center for Research and Development in Law-Related Education

Grades served: NR
Location of schools served: UR, SU

Schools served: NR
Type of schools served: PUB, PRI

Year established: 1983

CRADLE is a national nonprofit organization affiliated with Wake Forest's School of Law. Funded by the U.S. Department of Education and private foundations, corporations, and individuals, CRADLE's mission is to support and challenge teachers who prepare students for effective citizenship through innovative strategies created by teachers for teachers. The center provides networking, mentors, institutes, and conferences.

Note: Each institution's Carnegie class is given in parentheses. **Key:** E=elementary school, HS=high school, M=middle school, NR=not reported, PRI=private, PUB=public, RU=rural, SU=suburban, UR=urban

Western Carolina University (MA I)
Administrator Academy

Grades served: NR   Schools served: 17   Year established: 1992
Location of schools served: SU, RU   Type of schools served: PUB

With funds from the North Carolina Department of Public Instruction, five academies for school administrators have been developed across the state. The program in the western-most region is aimed at providing opportunities for leadership and challenges for aspiring school administrators. Eight superintendents in western North Carolina nominated teachers in their districts to participate in the academy, a series of leadership experiences designed by a planning team composed of a university professor, department staff, and a principal. The result is a cohort of 14 highly respected teachers who learn how to become effective educational administrators.

NORTH DAKOTA

University of North Dakota-Main Campus (DOC II)
Lake Agassiz Professional Development School

Grades served: E   Schools served: 1   Year established: 1992
Location of schools served: SU   Type of schools served: PUB

Lake Agassiz Elementary School and Elementary Education faculty from the University of North Dakota collaborate in this program in support of preservice teachers, an internship program for beginning teachers, and the development of innovative interdisciplinary curricula with a strong focus on the arts. Portfolio assessment documents students' and teachers' progress. The program includes internships for specialist teachers, release of teachers to assume leadership roles, summer and ongoing curriculum workshops, a university and community resource bank, and parents' strong involvement in the curriculum fostered by the project. Documentation of the curriculum is available to other schools.

University of North Dakota-Main Campus (DOC II)
Walsh-Pembina Consortium

Grades served: NR   Schools served: 16   Year established: 1987
Location of schools served: RU   Type of schools served: PUB

The Walsh-Pembina Consortium involves 16 school districts, two special education units, a vocational center, and the University of North Dakota. A professor of educational administration at UND serves as the facilitator for activities and coordinates the consortium's collaborations. Activities include year-long comprehensive and coordinated inservice sessions for 400 teachers and administrators, development of an interactive television system to provide expanded course offerings in most of the schools, and pooling of grant funds (Drug-Free Schools and mathematics/science funds) to provide more comprehensive programs.

OHIO

Ashland University (MA I)
Ashland -Medina Graduate Studies Pilot

Grades served: NR   Schools served: NR   Year established: 1993
Location of schools served: SU   Type of schools served: PUB

This pilot program provides teachers with an opportunity to complete eight graduate credit hours of required courses toward a master's degree as they participate in restructuring of the district. The program's key goals and objectives and tasks of the required courses are aligned with goals, objectives, and tasks of the restructuring. Faculty are facilitators and resource specialists, tailoring the courses to the needs of teachers. The program recognizes the experiential value of teachers' professional responsibilities.

Ashland University (MA I)
Reading Recovery®

Grades served: E

Schools served: 51

Year established: 1986

Location of schools served: NR

Type of schools served: PUB

Reading Recovery® is an intervention program for first grade students who have been identified as at risk of failing to learn to read. The Ashland site currently offers teacher training and ongoing contact services to 20 school districts in northcentral Ohio. The site coordinator and teacher leaders emphasize specialized, one-to-one tutoring for at-risk first grade students, intensive ongoing inservice training for local teachers, consultative services for district personnel, and a systematic evaluation program of first graders' progress. The program, begun in New Zealand, is now disseminated through the National Diffusion Network and the North American Reading Recovery Council.

John Carroll University (BA I)
Institute for Educational Renewal

Grades served: E

Schools served: 6

Year established: 1991

Location of schools served: UR

Type of schools served: PUB, PRI

The Institute for Educational Renewal, cosponsored by John Carroll University and Ursuline College, is a staff development organization begun to improve the quality of school life for elementary-age children in the city of Cleveland. A team of consultants works with a school staff to design and implement a reform program, including graduate courses on site to update instruction and support of teachers in their classrooms 15 days each year. An outside evaluation has demonstrated that this project has a positive impact on teachers, students, curricula, and college classrooms where new teachers are educated.

Kent State University-Main Campus (RES II)
Assistant Principals Institute

Grades served: E, M, HS

Schools served: 24

Year established: 1987

Location of schools served: UR

Type of schools served: NR

The Assistant Principals Institute, which now includes all principals, is a year-long program of monthly workshops, seminars, and dialogue sessions to prepare assistant principals for their responsibilities. Kent State's Center for Educational Leadership Services participates with three other colleges serving Cleveland schools to translate each candidate's NASSP assessment profile into career paths and action plans. During the year's workshops and other activities, these colleges share presentations and visit candidates' buildings as part of an ongoing mentorship.

Kent State University-Main Campus (RES II)
Total Quality Instruction (TQI)

Grades served: E, M, HS

Schools served: 15

Year established: 1987

Location of schools served: UR

Type of schools served: NR

TQI (formerly Techniques of Responsive Intervention to Validate Effective Teaching) is a year-long staff development program involving teachers and principals in the collaborative analysis and improvement of classroom teaching. Developed by Kent State's Center for Educational Leadership, TQI has translated research on effective schools, teacher effectiveness, professional development, reform/restructuring, and total quality/outcome-based education into criteria for effective classroom teaching. These criteria are the bases for several modules included in training, planning, classroom management, instructional methods, climate, and student assessment. The four basic TQI processes are preobservation conferencing, script-taping, postobservation conferencing, and the collaborative development of an action plan.

Note: Each institution's Carnegie class is given in parentheses. **Key:** E=elementary school, HS=high school, M=middle school, NR=not reported, PRI=private, PUB=public, RU=rural, SU=suburban, UR=urban

Kent State University-Main Campus (RES II)
Mentor Training
Grades served: E, M, HS   Schools served: 200   Year established: 1991
Location of schools served: UR, SU, RU   Type of schools served: PUB, PRI

Through the Mentor Training workshops offered by Kent State's Center for Educational Leadership, veteran teachers are trained in how to assist and encourage new teachers. Among the topics covered are trust building, curriculum mapping and unit planning, classroom management and organization, instructional methods, classroom climate, and student assessment. Mentors are also prepared to conduct a variety of conferences and classroom observations to provide specific feedback for professional growth.

Kent State University-Stark Campus (AA)
Project Discovery
Grades served: M   Schools served: 15   Year established: 1992
Location of schools served: UR, SU, RU   Type of schools served: PUB

Project Discovery is part of a statewide systemic initiative designed to develop a shared vision for reform of science and mathematics education that involves business and industry, schools and universities, foundations and government. Its focus is on middle schools, providing training for teachers to improve their content expertise in science and mathematics, to provide model inquiry and problem-solving instruction, and to integrate mathematics and science and thereby enhance learning. Motivating girls and minority children to become interested in math and science and in related careers is particularly emphasized. Fifteen counties are involved in the program.

Sinclair Community College (AA)
Breakfast Forums
Grades served: M, HS   Schools served: 125   Year established: 1988
Location of schools served: UR, SU, RU   Type of schools served: PUB, PRI

Annual Sinclair Breakfast Forums offer separate programs for principals and counselors from a wide area of secondary schools, Dayton Public Schools counselors, and smaller, targeted groups such as African-American ministers and the Appalachian community. Each forum provides an opportunity to introduce and explain services and programs available at and through Sinclair, and to solicit information about new outreach programs the college should consider to better serve the targeted populations.

The Ohio State University-Main Campus (RES I)
Professional Development School (PDS) Network in Social Studies and Global Education
Grades served: E, M, HS   Schools served: 9   Year established: 1991
Location of schools served: UR, SU   Type of schools served: PUB

The Ohio State University's PDS Network in Social Studies and Global Education is a collaboration of social studies teachers in nine schools within six districts in central Ohio and faculty in the university's program in social studies and global education. The goals are to improve K-12 and college instruction in social studies and global education in a supportive learning community and to share the ideas with others through team-teaching methods courses, providing inservice education for colleagues, and presenting at professional meetings and conferences. Several articles and books have resulted from the network, and funding has provided honoraria for leaders.

The Ohio State University-Main Campus (RES I)
Reynoldsburg Professional Development Site

Grades served: NR   Schools served: 1   Year established: 1991
Location of schools served: SU   Type of schools served: PUB

The essential components of the Reynoldsburg Professional Development Site include school change and restructuring, empowerment of teachers, administrative leadership, teachers as decision makers, teachers as reflective practitioners, connections across disciplines, teachers as coaches, and students as active learners. Coupled with the Holmes principles that the site is to be a learning community, and working collaboratively with the university to provide professional development and opportunities for growth for preservice teachers, the Reynoldsburg Site adheres to Sizer's notion that no good school is exactly the same from one year to the next.

University of Akron, Main Campus (DOC I)
Magnet Schools Assistance Project-Akron Public Schools

Grades served: E, HS   Schools served: 8   Year established: 1993
Location of schools served: UR   Type of schools served: PUB

The University of Akron, through its College of Education, provides staff development for two Akron high schools and six elementary schools. The university is responsible for planning with the public schools administration and the schools for special developmental needs, identifying resources necessary for delivery of the services, and providing staff development.

OREGON

Lewis and Clark College (BA I)
Oregon Consortium for Quality Science and Math Education (OCQSME)

Grades served: E, M, HS   Schools served: 14   Year established: 1983
Location of schools served: UR, SU   Type of schools served: PUB, PRI

The Oregon Consortium for Quality Science and Math Education provides inservice training for elementary, middle, and secondary school teachers to update their math and science teaching, focusing on equity, innovation, and leadership. Participants meet throughout the year for presentations and training on a variety of science and math topics. The program culminates in a four-day workshop, where participants prepare new curricula to disseminate in their districts.

Portland State University (DOC II)
PSU Center for Science Education

Grades served: E, M, HS   Schools served: 150   Year established: 1985
Location of schools served: UR, SU, RU   Type of schools served: PUB, PRI

The missions of the center, which acts a liaison between the scientific and K-16 educational communities, are to provide science education leadership and to facilitate the enhancement of science education. The center's staff initiates and supports science education ventures inside and outside the university. Activities involve developing proposals, contracted programs, collaborative ventures, and research.

Note: Each institution's Carnegie class is given in parentheses. **Key:** E=elementary school, HS=high school, M=middle school, NR=not reported, PRI=private, PUB=public, RU=rural, SU=suburban, UR=urban

Reed College (BA I)
Partners in Science
Grades served: HS
Location of schools served: NR

Schools served: NR
Type of schools served: NR

Year established: NR

Providing high school science teachers with opportunities to work at the cutting edge of science is a primary goal of Partners in Science awards, enabling them to bring inquiry-based methodologies into the classroom. Teachers and academic scientists collaborate to advance science, growing professionally in the process. All partners develop a broader understanding of the link between high school and college education.

University of Oregon (RES II)
Oregon Writing Project
Grades served: E, M, HS
Location of schools served: UR, SU, RU

Schools served: 130
Type of schools served: PUB, PRI

Year established: 1978

The Oregon Writing Project at the University of Oregon collaborates with agencies, schools, and private Oregon foundations to provide continuing professional education for teachers throughout the state to improve the writing and literacy of their students. Programs include summer workshops on campus following the National Writing Project model, inservice work during the school year, and conferences for demonstrating effective strategies for teaching writing and fostering teacher leadership in educational change. Some scholarships, from foundation grants, are awarded to teachers from small schools and rural areas who could not otherwise participate.

PENNSYLVANIA

California University of Pennsylvania (MA I)
Teacher Enhancement Center
Grades served: E, M, HS
Location of schools served: SU, RU

Schools served: 135
Type of schools served: PUB

Year established: 1985

The Teacher Enhancement Center is designed to offer programs beneficial for teachers by upgrading teaching skills; updating knowledge in particular fields, such as English, math, science, social studies, and technology; and providing opportunities for personal contact between and among professionals through visits to schools, industrial sites, and businesses, attendance at conventions, and participation in workshops and seminars. All K-12 teachers in the school districts of Washington, Fayette, Greene, Westmoreland, and Allegheny counties of southwestern Pennsylvania are included in this effort to enhance participants' self-image and professional pride.

California University of Pennsylvania (MA I)
Alliance of California University and Western Pennsylvania English Teachers (ACUWPET)
Grades served: NR
Location of schools served: UR, SU, RU

Schools served: 100
Type of schools served: PUB, PRI

Year established: 1991

The Alliance of California University and Western Pennsylvania English Teachers is a professional education organization involving 400 teachers from 100 schools to foster professional development and dialogue among school and college English faculty in southwestern Pennsylvania. ACUWPET holds a conference each fall, with presentations geared to the interests of English and language arts teachers at all grade levels. The *ACUWPET Journal* is published three times a year to inform the membership of new ideas and practices in the teaching of English. University English faculty unite with area school teachers to improve curricula and teacher education.

Clarion University of Pennsylvania (MA I)
Center for Economic Education

Grades served: E, M, HS
Location of schools served: UR, RU

Schools served: NR
Type of schools served: PUB, PRI

Year established: 1977

The Clarion Center for Economic Education is affiliated with the Pennsylvania Council for Economic Education and the National Council for Economic Education, which provides materials, training, and financial support for the center's programs. The center's responsibilities include sponsoring, cosponsoring, and conducting inservice teacher training in economics, and providing consultation to local schools, individuals, and organizations engaged in curricular development. The center also works with community and school groups to implement activities in economic education for adults.

Delaware Valley College (BA II)
Pine Run Elementary School/Delaware Valley College Collaborative

Grades served: E
Location of schools served: SU

Schools served: 1
Type of schools served: PUB

Year established: 1990

This collaborative is designed to strengthen the teaching of mathematics and science in elementary schools. College faculty and elementary school instructors work together to develop in-depth units presenting high-interest, hands-on scientific instruction that increases knowledge, students' interest in science, and student awareness of careers in science. Faculty exchanges and shared materials benefit participants and promote a sense of community commitment to science education.

Franklin & Marshall College (BA I)
Commonwealth Partnership

Grades served: E, M, HS
Location of schools served: UR, SU, RU

Schools served: 200
Type of schools served: PUB, PRI

Year established: 1983

The Commonwealth Partnership conducts collaborative, discipline-based programs by joining precollege and college faculty in common study for the benefit of their students. Since 1985 the partnership has conducted 16 such programs — 11 in the humanities and five in biology — more than 450 precollege teachers in the Mid-Atlantic as Commonwealth Teaching Fellows and reaching more than 5,000 additional teachers through outreach activities. The newest program is designed to engage K-12 teacher teams in the interdisciplinary study of math and science and development of fully articulated, problem-based curriculum projects.

Juniata College (BA I)
Science Outreach Program

Grades served: M, HS
Location of schools served: RU

Schools served: 45
Type of schools served: PUB, PRI

Year established: 1985

Juniata College's Science Outreach Program is designed to improve science education in 45 Pennsylvania high schools. Two vans, equipped by Juniata with more than $100,000 worth of state-of-the-art science equipment and driven by high school science teachers, visit schools to work with local teachers in setting up experiments and developing curricula. A spring science fair awards equipment and plaques to the winning schools, and each summer teachers attend any of several two-week workshops involving the latest technologies, curricula, and experiments. Teachers may also spend the summer in research with college faculty. Consultation and support from college faculty are available year-round.

Note: Each institution's Carnegie class is given in parentheses. **Key:** E=elementary school, HS=high school, M=middle school, NR=not reported, PRI=private, PUB=public, RU=rural, SU=suburban, UR=urban

Pennsylvania State University-Beaver Campus (AA)
Communication Skills Consortium

Grades served: HS   Schools served: 17   Year established: 1984
Location of schools served: NR   Type of schools served: PUB, PRI

This consortium links the university's English Department with the English faculty of Beaver County public and parochial schools to strengthen instruction and promote systemic change in the teaching of English and communication skills. A consortium core committee of 12 representatives of the local districts and interested members of Penn State's Beaver Campus English faculty plan activities. An advisory board includes representatives of government, media, academe, and industry. Changes in teaching styles, formats, and evaluation of composition have resulted from the consortium's efforts.

Pennsylvania State University-Main Campus (RES I)
Center for Total Quality Schools

Grades served: E, M, HS   Schools served: 27   Year established: 1992
Location of schools served: RU   Type of schools served: NR

The Center for Total Quality Schools (CTQS) at Penn State University is the first university-based project devoted exclusively to providing K-12 teachers and administrators with the training, support, and research base necessary to implement total quality management (TQM). School district teams meet monthly for an intensive and sustained program designed to train the trainers in TQM. Having completed the initial training, the teams return to their respective organizations to begin implementing TQM in their operations. CTQS provides advice and support during implementation. Districts may elect to serve as research sites for doctoral dissertations on TQM in education.

Temple University (RES I)
Temple-LEAP (Law, Education, and Participation)

Grades served: E, M, HS   Schools served: 300   Year established: 1974
Location of schools served: UR, SU, RU   Type of schools served: PUB, PRI

Temple-LEAP is designed to teach nonlawyers about the law and citizenship. The program is the Pennsylvania branch of a national network that promotes law-related and civic education. Temple-LEAP began working in the Philadelphia area in 1974 and across Pennsylvania in 1985, extending today beyond the state. With a focus on conflict resolution and delinquency prevention, the program delivers a message of involvement and empowerment to elementary and secondary schools throughout the state. It also offers training for educators and a source of informational classroom materials and related research.

University of Pennsylvania (RES I)
Center for School Study Councils

Grades served: NR   Schools served: 350   Year established: 1943
Location of schools served: UR, SU, RU   Type of schools served: PUB

The Center for School Study Councils links the university with 55 school districts in ongoing professional development activities, using superintendents as the entry point. Its mission is for superintendents to learn, speak out, and act on important issues. Activities include workshops and seminars that enable superintendents and educators in their districts to develop and share their knowledge and expertise. The center issues position papers to create a context for identifying and resolving problems. It also provides a platform for collaboration to improve education improvement and help schools and school districts create a context for systemic reform.

Wilkes University (MA I)
Project LEARN (Local Educational Action Resource Network)

Grades served: NR

Location of schools served: NR

Schools served: 76

Type of schools served: PUB, PRI

Year established: 1989

Project LEARN links 22 basic and higher education institutions, local businesses and industries, and community service organizations in Luzerne and Wyoming counties. LEARN has organized three regional conferences and several focused conferences, which are planned and implemented by teams of K-16 teachers. Each major conference has brought more than 4,000 people together to improve student learning through new approaches in teaching and educational leadership. Following each conference, participants work together to implement ideas presented at the conference. Project LEARN has received national recognition as an effective collaboration.

PUERTO RICO

Catholic University of Puerto Rico (MA I)
Adopted Schools

Grades served: E, M, HS

Location of schools served: UR, RU

Schools served: 10

Type of schools served: PUB, PRI

Year established: 1990

This partnership offers teachers professional development, curricular and instructional development, inservice training, and instruction in innovative uses of learning/teaching styles and models. The university's sports and library facilities are available for teachers and students of the adopted schools, and the university sponsors science fairs and math and language olympiads.

University of Puerto Rico Humacao University College (BA II)
Workshops on Problem Solving Based on the NCTM Standards

Grades served: E, M

Location of schools served: UR, SU

Schools served: 70

Type of schools served: PUB, PRI

Year established: 1986

The main objective of Humacao University College's Workshops on Problem Solving Based on NCTM (National Council of Teachers of Mathematics) Standards is to retrain elementary and intermediate school teachers in mathematics problem-solving skills. Participants solve and propose problems to be solved by students. Problems reflecting NCTM's standards and techniques guide the project; they will be collected and built into a well-organized bank. Workshops involve active participation, didactic discussions modeling different techniques, and use of manipulative objects and calculators.

RHODE ISLAND

Brown University (RES I)
Institute for Secondary Education

Grades served: M, HS

Location of schools served: UR, SU, RU

Schools served: NR

Type of schools served: PUB, PRI

Year established: 1984

The Institute for Secondary Education, a partnership of Brown University and schools in Rhode Island and southeastern Massachusetts, brings together university faculty and secondary and middle school teachers in conversations about teaching and learning to provide pedagogical, intellectual, and institutional collaboration. Programs combine intensive study of the latest developments in subject areas and their application to the classroom. Providing teachers with research and laboratory experiences to enhance their own academic expertise is emphasized. Many programs are interdisciplinary and intercultural. The institute supports teachers and administrators who are attempting to restructure curricula and pedagogy or design programs reflecting high expectations for all students.

Note: Each institution's Carnegie class is given in parentheses. **Key:** E=elementary school, HS=high school, M=middle school, NR=not reported, PRI=private, PUB=public, RU=rural, SU=suburban, UR=urban

SOUTH CAROLINA

Furman University (BA I)
Center of Excellence in Foreign Language Instruction
Grades served: E   Schools served: 3   Year established: 1990
Location of schools served: SU, RU   Type of schools served: PUB

Funded largely by the South Carolina Commission on Higher Education, the Center for Excellence in Foreign Language Instruction (CEFLI) works to improve the quality of foreign language teaching in South Carolina by providing opportunities for inservice professional development and increasing awareness of the importance of foreign languages in elementary schools (FLES). CEFLI has developed numerous courses in methods and content for French, Spanish, and German teachers, provided professional development grants for inservice teachers, and been instrumental in establishing three FLES pilot programs.

Lander University (MA II)
Greenwood Area Consortium
Grades served: E, M, HS   Schools served: 10   Year established: 1983
Location of schools served: NR   Type of schools served: PUB

The Greenwood Area Consortium is composed of Lander University and school districts in Abbeville, Edgefield, Greenwood, Laurens, McCormick, Newberry, and Saluda counties. Through the Staff Development Network, the consortium makes possible increased school-college cooperation focusing on academic training and preservice and inservice teachers and applied research activities, including a 2+2 tech-prep program, regional articulation agreements, and the development of curricular materials and evaluations.

Midlands Technical College (AA)
Counselors' Conference
Grades served: M, HS   Schools served: NR   Year established: 1984
Location of schools served: UR, SU, RU   Type of schools served: PUB

The Counselors' Conference is an annual event jointly planned, sponsored, and funded by Midlands Technical College and the South Carolina State Department of Education. It provides professional development and collaboration for counseling personnel from middle schools, high schools, two- and four-year colleges, and local community agencies. Themes and topics focus on specific issues requiring special attention and joint efforts by these constituencies, such as cultural pluralism, legal and ethical issues in education, facilitating the success of at-risk student populations, and preparing youth for careers and college.

Spartanburg Technical College (BA II)
Math TRANSIT (Technology Reform and Network Specialist Inservice Training)
Grades served: NR   Schools served: 5   Year established: 1994
Location of schools served: SU, RU   Type of schools served: PUB

The major goals of Math TRANSIT are to establish regional sites that will train classroom mathematics teachers as technology specialists, to foster regional efforts nationwide at those TRANSIT sites throughout the United States, to train at least 180 technology specialists to give technology-based inservice training to classroom mathematics teachers, and to produce six exemplary modules. Regional site leaders and technology specialists will use the modules to conduct workshops, while classroom teachers will use them to give technology-based mathematics lessons.

Technical College of the Lowcountry (AA I)
Lowcountry HUB

Grades served: NR

Location of schools served: SU, RU

Schools served: 5

Type of schools served: PUB

Year established: 1993

Lowcountry HUB is one of 13 NSF-funded centers that support the South Carolina State Systematic Initiative for the development and dissemination of mathematics and science education materials and services to teachers and students. Members of the HUB are the public school districts of Beaufort, Colleton, Hampton, and Jasper counties, Technical College of the Lowcountry, University of South Carolina-Beaufort, and University of South Carolina-Salkehatchie. The HUB's major functions are to conduct Teacher Leadership Institutes, to develop or acquire educational materials, and to support the implementation of the state curriculum frameworks in mathematics and science.

University of South Carolina-Columbia (RES II)
Educators In Industry

Grades served: NR

Location of schools served: NR

Schools served: 270

Type of schools served: PUB, PRI

Year established: 1982

Educators in Industry is a program offered to 25 teachers, counselors, and administrators of public and private schools once a year. Course content is applied and practical, offering hands-on experience for participants, who investigate fields of work into which their students will eventually move. Each year the content is new, updated, or revised to fit current employment trends, allowing participants to experience the types of work being studied. The course provides participants with the opportunity to link the concepts of their teaching with the world of work and to use the concepts they have learned in teaching, counseling, and administration.

University of South Carolina-Columbia (RES II)
Professional Development Schools

Grades served: E, M, HS

Location of schools served: UR, SU, RU

Schools served: 11

Type of schools served: PUB

Year established: 1990

Professional Development Schools Network is a collaboration of preK-12 schools and the university designed to facilitate the simultaneous renewal of both entities to ensure that all students become successful lifelong learners. The program's shared governance is committed to the continuous improvement of curricula and instructional practice and supportive of collaborative inquiry and innovation. Other components include the identification of new roles for school and university personnel, development of a climate appreciative and respectful of diversity, and recognition of the clinical experience as a vital element in development of professional educators. The 11 schools served include all socioeconomic and grade levels.

University of South Carolina-Salkehatchie (AA)
Teachers' Aides Program

Grades served: NR

Location of schools served: RU

Schools served: 76

Type of schools served: PUB

Year established: 1989

This program provides tuition-free courses to noncertified employees of school districts that are members of the Salkehatchie Consortium. Courses have been offered at five locations in lower South Carolina. The program's goal is to combat high teacher turnover rates in area school districts by assisting school employees with roots in the area to complete courses toward teacher certification.

Note: Each institution's Carnegie class is given in parentheses. **Key:** E=elementary school, HS=high school, M=middle school, NR=not reported, PRI=private, PUB=public, RU=rural, SU=suburban, UR=urban

Winthrop University (MA I)
Project PRISM

Grades served: E

Schools served: 37

Year established: 1991

Location of schools served: SU, RU

Type of schools served: PUB

Project PRISM, a grant through the Dwight D. Eisenhower Mathematics and Science Education Act, is a partnership of Winthrop University and local businesses, community groups, and the school districts in the Winthrop Olde English Consortium. Its purpose is to provide innovative inservice training for K-6 math and science teachers. During their training, teachers continue to teach in beacon schools, which serve as models for science and math instruction. The mission of the lead teachers is to become change agents, sharing their newly acquired educational methods with students and other teachers. During 1992-93, the project prepared 54 pairs of public school math and science teachers, and nine administrators.

TENNESSEE

Carson-Newman College (BA II)
Foxfire Teacher Outreach: East Tennessee Teachers Network (ETTN)

Grades served: E, M, HS

Schools served: 125

Year established: 1989

Location of schools served: UR, SU, RU

Type of schools served: PUB, PRI

Carson-Newman College and Foxfire Teacher Outreach offer a tuition-free three-hour graduate course, The Foxfire Approach to Teaching, to K-12 teachers in east Tennessee. The course is designed to help teachers create active, collaborative, learner-centered classrooms that connect with their communities, produce real work, and stress academic integrity; ETTN provides ongoing training and support for the course. Network teachers have opportunities to have classroom projects funded, visit Foxfire classrooms, share teaching ideas, serve as instructors for the Foxfire course, and participate in the leadership and governance of the network.

University of Memphis (DOC I)
Professional Development Schools

Grades served: E, M, HS

Schools served: 10

Year established: 1991

Location of schools served: UR, RU

Type of schools served: PUB, PRI

Recent restructuring at the university resulted in improved teacher education programs and more collaborative activities for preK-12 classes through ten professional development schools. Expanded roles for teachers include in-school research, writing, presenting of professional papers, grant writing, serving as gatekeepers of the profession, and active participation as university decision makers. Expanded roles for university faculty include team-teaching with their preK-12 peers, collaborative research in the schools, providing staff development in schools, serving as permanent members of the school improvement team, and daily interaction with children and teachers in schools.

University of Tennessee at Martin (MA I)
21st Century Partner Schools

Grades served: NR

Schools served: 4

Year established: 1990

Location of schools served: SU

Type of schools served: NR

21st Century Partner Schools is a contractual agreement between a school system and the university's Center of Excellence for Science and Mathematics Education. Through these contracts, which include equipment purchases and professional development activities, the center works with individual teachers to improve the teaching of science and mathematics. These teachers and their classrooms then become models for other teachers in the region. During the one- to three-year partnership, research is conducted on student attitudes and achievement.

TEXAS

East Texas State University (DOC I)
Northeast Texas Center For Professional Development & Technology
Grades served: E, M

Location of schools served: NR

Schools served: 22

Type of schools served: PUB

Year established: 1991

The Northeast Texas Center for Professional Development and Technology is a collaborative of East Texas State University, 22 public schools in four districts, and Texas Instruments. Goals include restructuring education for teachers and administrators as field-based programs within professional development schools; integrating effective teaching and technology; and aligning teacher development and graduate education. About 130 university students and 13 faculty were involved in 1993-94. Plans are to transform all preservice programs, involving 400-500 teacher-candidates per year, into experientially based programs in which students complete 30 to 36 hours of course work in field settings.

Howard Payne University (BA II)
Big Country Center for Professional Development and Technology
Grades served: NR

Location of schools served: UR

Schools served: 7

Type of schools served: PUB, PRI

Year established: 1992

The Big Country Center for Professional Development and Technology is a partnership of four universities (Abilene Christian, Hardin-Simmons, Howard Payne, and McMurry) and three school districts of 2,000 to 19,000 students. A state service center and the education committees of two chambers of commerce are included in the center. The center's purposes are to simultaneously change teacher education and public school teaching methodology by cooperatively designing teacher education courses and field experiences through an infusion of more than $500,000 in technology, to encourage schools to use innovative practices, and to provide extensive staff development.

Kilgore College (AA)
Oil and Gas Institute for School Teachers
Grades served: M, HS

Location of schools served: RU

Schools served: 50

Type of schools served: PUB, PRI

Year established: 1988

The Oil and Gas Institute is a 12-day graduate-level interdisciplinary course that examines a spectrum of environmental issues. Offered by the University of Texas at Tyler, classes meet at Kilgore College, with field trips to a water treatment plant, a high-tech municipal incinerator, a water analysis company, and other similar facilities in east Texas. The course is designed to broaden middle and high school teachers' understanding of environmental problems, government regulations, the technologies involved, and the complexity of international environmental issues.

Rice University (RES II)
Center for Education
Grades served: NR

Location of schools served: UR

Schools served: 152

Type of schools served: PUB, PRI

Year established: 1988

The Center for Education at Rice University brings together the resources of the university and the broader community to work on long-term, structural problems in schools: reducing teachers' isolation from the forefront of knowledge in their fields, reorganizing schools to make students more involved in learning, and rethinking ways to evaluate learning. A founding grant from the Brown Foundation enables the center to expand the Department of Education's mission beyond training new teachers to create structures that support the ongoing learning of teachers already in the classroom and bring the resources of the university, corporations, and charitable foundations to bear on school improvement.

Note: Each institution's Carnegie class is given in parentheses. **Key:** E=elementary school, HS=high school, M=middle school, NR=not reported, PRI=private, PUB=public, RU=rural, SU=suburban, UR=urban

Texas A&M University (RES I)
Principals' Center
Grades served: NR   Schools served: 300   Year established: 1985
Location of schools served: UR, SU, RU   Type of schools served: PUB, PRI

Texas A&M University's Principals' Center is nationally recognized for its leadership in supporting elementary and secondary school principals through preparation, assistance, and research. A Congress of Principals provides advice and leadership from the field, serving as a governing body that identifies emerging problems and concerns of Texas principals. The center's activities include sponsoring professional staff development directed toward instructional leadership, management skills, and self-renewal for principals; providing a clearinghouse for information for Texas principals; participating in a nationwide network of centers for principals; assessing and developing principals' job skills; and developing materials and means of disseminating preservice and inservice training.

University of Houston-Clear Lake (MA I)
University of Houston-Clear Lake Teacher Center
Grades served: E, M, HS   Schools served: 22   Year established: 1975
Location of schools served: UR, SU, RU   Type of schools served: PUB

The University of Houston-Clear Lake Teacher Center is a state-mandated body whose overall goal is the successful preparation of K-12 teachers through the collaboration of its membership: individual school districts, the University, professional organizations, and the community. Among its objectives are to study needs and recommend changes for the education program; to review and approve programs; to provide inservice training; and to participate cooperatively in setting guidelines for all field experiences.

University of Texas at Arlington (DOC I)
CREST (Collaborative Redesign of Education Systems in Texas)
Grades served: NR   Schools served: 4   Year established: 1993
Location of schools served: NR   Type of schools served: PUB

CREST is a field-based teacher education program sponsored by the Texas Education Agency and collaboratively developed by the University of Texas at Arlington, the Arlington Independent School District, and other education and business representatives. First-semester university students (interns) and second-semester students (residents) at each Center for Professional Development and Technology (CPDT) site are assigned to an instructional leadership team made up of two to four classroom teachers with whom they spend Monday through Friday learning about decision making, classroom management and discipline, and instructional strategies. Demonstration of specific outcomes determines competency and certification.

University of Texas-Pan American (MA I)
UTPA and Hidalgo County School Districts Teaming Initiative Partnership
Grades served: NR   Schools served: NR   Year established: 1994
Location of schools served: NR   Type of schools served: PUB

This partnership links UTPA's School of Education and four school districts. Its primary mission is to work with school districts to design and deliver a site-based master's program allowing teachers to develop a philosophy and knowledge base of developmentally appropriate strategies to meet the specific needs of students. School district specialists in reading, with options for professional certification in ESL, bilingual education, and early childhood education are created from the teachers selected to participate. These specialists in turn aid in further professional development on their campuses.

<u>UTAH</u>

Brigham Young University (RES II)
BYU/Public School Partnership

Grades served: E, M, HS   Schools served: 43+   Year established: 1984
Location of schools served: SU, RU   Type of schools served: PUB

The BYU/Public School Partnership is the oldest continually functioning partnership in the National Network for Educational Renewal. BYU's College of Education and five surrounding school districts participate as six equal partners, sharing governance, resources, and responsibilities. Forty-three elementary schools and a number of secondary schools are involved in special projects. The partnership's primary mission is to improve teaching and learning by merging theory and practice through preservice and inservice education, curriculum development, and research/inquiry.

University of Utah (RES I)
Utah Education Consortium

Grades served: NR   Schools served: NR   Year established: 1990
Location of schools served: UR, SU   Type of schools served: PUB

This consortium designed to pursue educational research, develop preservice and inservice professional development programs, create support networks for members, recruit individuals from underrepresented minority groups into education, provide technological support for instruction, and support the development and examination of educational policy. It is governed by an executive committee of district superintendents, associate superintendents, an associate superintendent and coordinator from the Utah State Office of Education, the dean and associate deans of the university's Graduate School of Education, and department chairs from the college.

Weber State University (MA II)
Teacher Academy

Grades served: E, M, HS   Schools served: NR   Year established: 1989
Location of schools served: UR, SU, RU   Type of schools served: PUB, PRI

The Teacher Academy, created to devise ways to improve the quality of teaching, reward outstanding teachers, reinforce partnerships in the educational system, and stimulate teachers' professional growth, was an outgrowth of Project 30, a national network of 30 colleges and universities that pursued similar goals with the support of the Carnegie Corporation. School districts select their best teachers in particular subject areas to participate as academy fellows, creating a five-year cycle that rotates through social studies, science and healthy lifestyles, arts and humanities, English, and mathematics.

Weber State University (MA II)
Ogden Area History Teaching Alliance

Grades served: NR   Schools served: NR   Year established: 1985
Location of schools served: UR, SU, RU   Type of schools served: PUB, PRI

The Ogden Area History Teaching Alliance is one of the oldest and most successful programs for history teachers in the country. The alliance brings together university and school teachers into a network designed to foster mutual professional development and awareness of current affairs. Twenty school teachers are admitted annually to attend a June workshop, while many more teachers are invited to attend monthly meetings. Workshop instructors are teachers from all levels. Monthly evening meetings feature presentations by professors, teachers, and visiting national and international figures. Participating teachers have an opportunity to earn higher education and recertification credit.

Note: Each institution's Carnegie class is given in parentheses. **Key:** E=elementary school, HS=high school, M=middle school, NR=not reported, PRI=private, PUB=public, RU=rural, SU=suburban, UR=urban

VERMONT

Middlebury College (BA I)
Vermont Elementary Science Project

Grades served: E, M   Schools served: 27   Year established: 1990
Location of schools served: RU   Type of schools served: PUB

The Vermont Elementary Science Project offers inservice training in physics for teams of K-6 teachers and administrators from 27 schools in Vermont's Champlain Valley. The project, funded by an NSF grant, has developed a model of sustained support that is effecting a permanent change in how and how much science (physics in particular) is taught and learned in the early grades.

Saint Michael's College (MA I)
Vermont Rivers Teacher Enhancement Project

Grades served: M, HS   Schools served: 15   Year established: 1990
Location of schools served: UR, SU, RU   Type of schools served: PUB, PRI

This project provides an intensive three-week inservice, residential summer institute for middle-level and ninth and tenth grade teachers. The project's focus is on activity-based aquatic ecology as a vehicle for developing and teaching integrative mathematics, science, and technology to teachers and students. Telecomputing links partner schools to one another and to the campus for sharing data. The interpretation of data generated by collection points along each river and subsequent analysis is emphasized.

Trinity College (BA II)
Summer Math/Science Teacher Institute

Grades served: E, M   Schools served: 5   Year established: 1991
Location of schools served: NR   Type of schools served: PUB

This partnership links Trinity College with local elementary and middle schools. It includes a graduate course for teachers, followed by a one-week Discovery Camp for K-6 children. Having taken the graduate course, teachers then work in pairs with small groups of children during the camp to conduct inquiry-based activities in a variety of topics — e.g., motion, structures, habitats, and so on. College faculty from the Education and Science/Mathematics Departments participate as resource consultants, observers, and learners in a relationship that continues throughout the academic year.

VIRGINIA

Clinch Valley College at the University of Virginia (BA II)
Southwest Virginia Public Education Consortium

Grades served: E, M, HS   Schools served: NR   Year established: 1992
Location of schools served: RU   Type of schools served: PUB

This consortium, located at Clinch Valley College, is a legislated partnership of 11 school districts and eight colleges. Its purpose is to improve the public school districts throughout this rural region by working toward common goals and sharing resources and expertise. The major vehicles for this improvement are professional development, technology, pilot projects in the latest pedagogies and systems, leadership training, and community support programs. The consortium benchmarks effective practices of other programs, primarily in Northern Virginia, through the Virginia Economic Bridge Initiative. Funding agencies are state, federal, and private.

Marymount University (MA I)
Mathematics and Science Workshops for Washington D.C. Public School Teachers
Grades served: M

Schools served: 15

Year established: 1991

Location of schools served: UR

Type of schools served: PUB

This project brings middle school teachers and students from inner-city schools to the college campus for intensive study focusing on improvement of teaching and learning in mathematics and science in the sixth, seventh, and eighth grades. College professors use the Teaching Integrated Mathematics and Sciences (TIMS) program materials developed at the University of Illinois at Chicago to strengthen the mathematics and science knowledge of the teachers while modeling classroom behaviors and strategies for working with the students.

University of Virginia (RES I)
Virginia School-University Partnership
Grades served: HS

Schools served: 8

Year established: 1985

Location of schools served: UR, SU, RU

Type of schools served: PUB

The Virginia School-University Partnership links the University of Virginia with eight school divisions in central Virginia. Its mission is to facilitate systemic improvement of educational practices across member institutions. By combining resources and expertise of the member divisions, attention can be given to change that individual members could not bring to bear on their own. Activities include inservice education for central office administrators, principals' forums on current issues in education, staff development projects in areas such as working with at-risk students, and an annual conference for high school students.

University of Virginia (RES I)
Center for the Liberal Arts
Grades served: E, M, HS

Schools served: NR

Year established: 1984

Location of schools served: UR, SU, RU

Type of schools served: PUB, PRI

The mission of the Center for the Liberal Arts is to make the most talented faculty members of the University of Virginia, and other institutions, available to the schools of Virginia for instruction, consultation, and debate. Its goal is to assist teachers in mastering the subjects they teach and to join teachers and professors, schools, and the university in a lifetime learning network. With grant support, the center offers a range of inservice programs including summer seminars and residential institutes, lecture/discussion courses, weekend workshops and colloquia, and summer fellowships.

WASHINGTON

Eastern Washington University (MA I)
Project High Need
Grades served: E

Schools served: 6

Year established: 1992

Location of schools served: NR

Type of schools served: PUB

The overall goal of this project is to assess the outcomes of Project High Need for meeting the academic, class deportment, and social needs of children identified as having serious emotional disorders (SEDs) and those at risk of developing such disorders. The primary population under study is elementary school children with SEDs and those at risk for school failure at six target schools. Repeated measurement of outcomes will be made according to the outcomes and implementation measures established at the beginning of the project. The project aims to collect common subject-characteristic data to probe demographic and other variables that might predict the degree of change obtained through the Project High Need treatment package.

Note: Each institution's Carnegie class is given in parentheses. **Key:** E=elementary school, HS=high school, M=middle school, NR=not reported, PRI=private, PUB=public, RU=rural, SU=suburban, UR=urban

WEST VIRGINIA

Concord College (BA II)
West Virginia Geographic Alliance
Grades served: E, M, HS   Schools served: 75   Year established: 1991
Location of schools served: UR, SU, RU   Type of schools served: PUB, PRI

The West Virginia Geographic Alliance is supported by the Governor's Office, working with the West Virginia State Board of Education and the National Geographic Society in a program designed to revitalize the study of geography and in the nation's classrooms, to contribute to better classroom teaching of geography through education and empowerment of teachers, to improve materials (for example, by integrating geography with other subjects) and educational technologies, to support nationwide educational reform by developing world standards of what students should know, and to measure progress through new assessment tools, such as the 1994 National Assessment of Educational Progress proposal.

Marshall University (MA I)
Southwestern Consortium for Excellence in Science, Mathematics, and Technology
Grades served: E, M, HS   Schools served: 162   Year established: 1992
Location of schools served: NR   Type of schools served: PUB, PRI

Marshall University has initiated a partnership with several area agencies and businesses to retrain and assist teachers in the implementation of new mathematics, science, and technology curricula, and to enhance teacher training and business-community involvement. The program's partners include Regional Education Service Agency II, six county school systems, Inco Alloys International, NASA, Wheeling Jesuit College, Huntington Museum of Art, the Huntington Chamber of Commerce, and the VA Hospital.

West Virginia University (RES I)
Professional Development Schools
Grades served: E, HS   Schools served: 5   Year established: 1989
Location of schools served: SU, RU   Type of schools served: PUB

The Benedum Project, funded by grants from the Claude Worthington Benedum Foundation, is a collaborative reform effort in West Virginia. More than 400 participants from public schools and West Virginia University have worked together to completely redesign WVU's teacher education program and to establish professional development schools, where faculties engage in shared decision making that involves teachers in schoolwide planning.

WISCONSIN

Edgewood College (MA I)
Yahara Watershed Education Network
Grades served: E, M, HS   Schools served: 15   Year established: 1991
Location of schools served: UR, SU, RU   Type of schools served: PUB, PRI

The Yahara Watershed Education Network, sponsored by Edgewood College in collaboration with the University of Wisconsin-Madison and various other agencies and organizations, supports the development of a regional network of teachers and students participating in long-term study of local watersheds. The goal is to enhance the effectiveness of science and interdisciplinary education by combining student inquiry-based and teachers-as-researchers approaches, by providing inservice professional development for K-12 teachers, and by promoting new links among students, teachers, researchers, educational outreach specialists, and public policy makers.

Saint Norbert College (BA II)
Assistive Technology Project

Grades served: E, M, HS   Schools served: NR   Year established: 1991
Location of schools served: UR   Type of schools served: PUB

The Assistive Technology Project is a partnership of St. Norbert College and the Milwaukee Public Schools that provides on-site training for staff in Milwaukee in the areas of computer graphics and assistive computer technology. Because nearly one of eight children in the public schools today has exceptional educational needs, it has become increasingly important for educators at all levels to learn how to adapt curriculum and to integrate the latest in assistive computer technology to adequately meet the educational needs of all children.

University of Wisconsin-Eau Claire (MA I)
Cray Academy

Grades served: E, M, HS   Schools served: 100   Year established: 1988
Location of schools served: UR, SU, RU Type of schools served: PUB, PRI

Cray Academy is a two-week summer series of workshops involving more than 1,100 educators annually. It is intended to improve K-12 education in mathematics, science, and technology and to encourage the integration of these subjects by demonstrating their relationship to the world outside education. The academy is an effective regional business partnership with education to improve teaching and learning in schools.

University of Wisconsin-Eau Claire (MA I)
Microcomputer and Technology Fair

Grades served: NR   Schools served: 100   Year established: 1980
Location of schools served: UR, SU, RU Type of schools served: PUB, PRI

The Microcomputer and Technology Fair is a two-and-one-half-day annual event typically attended by more than 700 participants. It is intended to help educators explore new uses of technology in educational settings by offering workshops by practitioners on the cutting edge of technological applications. A large array of exhibits allows attendees to view the latest in hardware and software technology. A preview laboratory allows participants to practice using hardware and software applications.

University of Wisconsin-Oshkosh (MA I)
School Based Peer Mediation

Grades served: E, M, HS   Schools served: 20   Year established: 1991
Location of schools served: UR, SU, RU Type of schools served: PUB

The Center for Career Development at the University of Wisconsin-Oshkosh, in cooperation with the Winnebago Conflict Resolution Center, offers training in mediation to elementary through high school students and staff. The emphasis is on conflict management at the local level, and most training takes place at the local school. Other services provided include ongoing assistance with existing programs, development of new programs to combat violence, and a forum for educators to exchange information about their programs.

Note: Each institution's Carnegie class is given in parentheses. **Key:** E=elementary school, HS=high school, M=middle school, NR=not reported, PRI=private, PUB=public, RU=rural, SU=suburban, UR=urban

University of Wisconsin-Parkside (MA II)
Regional Staff Development Center
Grades served: NR

Schools served: 24

Year established: 1985

Location of schools served: UR, SU, RU

Type of schools served: PUB

The Regional Staff Development Center is a dynamic cooperative of educators in Kenosha and Racine counties who believe that professional development is essential for school reform. The center was the initial project of the Educators' Consortium for Excellence of southeastern Wisconsin, a collaboration of faculty, administrators, teacher unions, and school boards in the two-county area. The center provides regional networking of resources, linking organizations and projects dedicated to ensuring students' academic success: alliances and networks, breakfast seminars for administrators, the Educators' Hall of Fame, Elementary Science Fellows, interdistrict projects, school board inservice training, special regional workshops and seminars.

University of Wisconsin-River Falls (MA I)
St. Croix Valley Association of Teacher Educators (SCVATE)
Grades served: E, M, HS

Schools served: 25

Year established: 1965

Location of schools served: UR, SU, RU

Type of schools served: PUB, PRI

The SCVATE, sponsored by the university's College of Education, is open to all persons interested in education. Membership includes university faculty and students, K-12 teachers and administrators, school board members, and parents. Monthly meetings focus on topics of mutual interest, such as strategic planning in teacher education, the knowledge base for the teacher education program, student teaching, and beginning teacher assistance programs. Other programs have shared international educators and coordinated opportunities in international education. Many UW-RF collaborative activities with area schools have been outcomes of SCVATE meetings.

University of Wisconsin-Stevens Point (MA I)
CO-STAR (Collaboration: Starting Teachers Achieving Results)
Grades served: E, M, HS

Schools served: 25

Year established: 1989

Location of schools served: RU

Type of schools served: PUB

CO-STAR is a program for beginning teachers sponsored by the university and several school districts. The jointly planned year-long professional development program provides local mentors and three credits to new teachers.

Section Two
Recruitment and Retention, Preservice, Early Career Support, and Alternative Certification Programs

ALABAMA

Samford University (MA I)
Hoover Elementary School Program

Grades served: E   Schools served: NR   Year established: NR
Location of schools served: NR   Type of schools served: PUB

The Hoover Elementary School Program is a cooperative effort of the Hoover City School System and the university's Department of Teacher Education. Six 1-week summer sessions are offered during June and July; classes are held from 9:00 AM to 1:00 PM daily, and day care is available. Enrichment and reinforcement classes are offered in science, reading, math, social studies, and the art. Master teachers and Samford University student tutors teach and assist the children in such activities as magic, cartooning, map making, science experiments, extended reading, math games, and first aid.

Troy State University at Dothan (MA I)
Learning Coalitions/Professional Development Schools

Grades served: E   Schools served: 7   Year established: 1993
Location of schools served: UR, SU, RU   Type of schools served: PUB

Troy State University at Dothan and local school systems have formed a learning coalition/professional development relationship to provide faculty and students the opportunity to collaborate on effective teaching models and processes. The program prepares undergraduate students to be reflective, informed decision makers as they enter the profession.

ARIZONA

Arizona State University (RES I)
Teacher Residency Project

Grades served: E   Schools served: 5   Year established: 1987
Location of schools served: NR   Type of schools served: PUB

The Arizona State University/Maricopa County Teacher Residency Project links the university's College of Education, five local Maricopa County school districts, and the Arizona State Department of Education in a partnership designed to provide instructional support and guidance for resident teachers. It does so by training mentors selected by school administrators as highly competent, experienced nurturing teachers. Mentors provide the resident teachers support and encouragement, share instructional resources, observe, and coach. Mentors are trained in a workshop in preparation for working with the residents for at least one year as they progress through student teaching to becoming instructional leaders in their own classrooms.

Note: Each institution's Carnegie class is given in parentheses. **Key:** E=elementary school, HS=high school, M=middle school, NR=not reported, PRI=private, PUB=public, RU=rural, SU=suburban, UR=urban

Northern Arizona University (DOC I)
Ford Foundation Navajo Nation Teacher Training Program
Grades served: E   Schools served: 23   Year established: 1993
Location of schools served: RU   Type of schools served: PUB

The Ford Foundation/Navajo Nation Teacher Training Program is a partnership of the Ford Foundation, the Navajo Nation, and the Center for Excellence in Education at Northern Arizona University. Its purpose is to train Navajo elementary education teachers for service in Navajo schools. Classes are offered at four sites on the Navajo Reservation.

Northern Arizona University (DOC I)
DeWitt-Wallace/NAU Peace Corps Fellows Program
Grades served: NR   Schools served: 11   Year established: 1992
Location of schools served: SU, RU   Type of schools served: PUB

The DeWitt-Wallace/NAU Peace Corps Fellows Program is a partnership of Northern Arizona University, the DeWitt-Wallace Foundation, the Peace Corps, and eleven schools. The purpose of the partnership is to prepare returned volunteers for service as teachers. The Fellows complete classes at NAU over three summers. A special arrangement with the Arizona Department of Education permits the Fellows to work in schools on Indian Reservations for two years.

ARKANSAS

University of Arkansas at Pine Bluff (BA II)
Arkansas Coalition for Diversity in Education
Grades served: HS   Schools served: 20   Year established: 1988
Location of schools served: NR   Type of schools served: PUB, PRI

The mission of the Arkansas Coalition for Diversity in Education is to expand the pool of minority teachers in the public schools of Arkansas through vigorous recruitment, to foster viable programs to retain minority persons in teacher education programs, and to ensure equitable employment for minorities. This mission is realized through three main goals: to coordinate efforts to increase the pool of minority teachers, to develop short-term strategies, and to advocate programs and policies to enhance the quality of teaching by ensuring diversity in the profession.

CALIFORNIA

California State University-Dominguez Hills (MA I)
Aide-to-Teacher Program (ATT)
Grades served: E   Schools served: NR   Year established: 1987
Location of schools served: UR   Type of schools served: PUB

The Aide-to-Teacher Program recruits culturally diverse and bilingual paraprofessional classroom aides from eight local school districts. The program is designed to provide paraprofessionals with the financial, academic, and personal support they need to continue part-time employment as classroom aides while completing their undergraduate degree and receiving elementary teaching credentials. It has gradually expanded over the past seven years and currently accepts about 25 classroom aides from eight Los Angeles school districts each year.

California State University-Fresno (MA I)
Parent Power Project

Grades served: E, M, HS   Schools served: 175   Year established: 1985
Location of schools served: UR, SU, RU   Type of schools served: PUB, PRI

Recipient of the 1992 Christa McAuliffe award, the Parent Power Project was begun to provide pre- and inservice teachers with an opportunity to work directly with families whose K-12 children have learning difficulties. Students interview parents and the child's teacher; model teaching strategies while gradually turning over the tutoring to the families; review records; lead the children's self-esteem and parents support groups; and prepare resource notebooks, progress reports, and a summary. After field research, students design activities to involve parents for their own (or future) sites. Former students remain actively involved in spin-off projects, related master's theses, and professional presentations.

California State University-Fresno (MA I)
Teacher In Preparation (TIP) Internship Program

Grades served: E, M, HS   Schools served: 35   Year established: 1992
Location of schools served: UR, RU   Type of schools served: PUB

This program is sponsored by the university's School of Education and Human Development in partnership with numerous school districts in central California. Its primary mission is to offer qualified individuals an alternative to obtaining a California teaching credential. During the year-long program, teacher interns attend special summer sessions and regular semester evening courses while working in one of the partnership school districts. Interns earn a modest salary; they are supervised and mentored by university faculty and cooperating school teachers at the site.

California State University-San Bernardino (MA I)
Learning Handicapped Intern Program

Grades served: NR   Schools served: NR   Year established: NR
Location of schools served: NR   Type of schools served: NR

The Learning Handicapped Intern Program is a collaboration of CSU-SB and the school districts. A total of 24 interns will complete all the requirements for a learning-handicapped credential and most requirements for a master's degree in education, special education option. Interns are employed as full-time special education teachers during the two-year program cycle. The university and district personnel provide ongoing guidance, support, and supervision. Additionally, the university coordinator, supervisors, and district personnel collaborate on selecting interns and in monitoring their progress and retention.

California State University-San Bernardino (MA I)
Collaborative Learning Network: Project Genesis

Grades served: NR   Schools served: NR   Year established: 1993
Location of schools served: NR   Type of schools served: NR

Project Genesis is an innovative teacher education project collaboratively developed by university faculty, school district personnel, principals, and teachers to provide a consistent, supportive program for university students during their preservice year and their first two years of teaching. During the first year, teaching/learning theory, methodology, and management course work are combined with teaching practice; at the end of that year, university students receive a California preliminary teaching credential. During the second and third years, project students who are hired continue to receive support from team members and attend inservice and staff development programs. At the end of the second year, students earn a California clear credential; at the end of the third, a master's degree in elementary education.

Note: Each institution's Carnegie class is given in parentheses. **Key:** E=elementary school, HS=high school, M=middle school, NR=not reported, PRI=private, PUB=public, RU=rural, SU=suburban, UR=urban

Humboldt State University (MA I)
Project MOST (Minority Opportunities for Successful Teaching)

Grades served: HS	Schools served: NR	Year established: 1989
Location of schools served: RU	Type of schools served: PUB, PRI	

Project MOST seeks to recruit and retain minority persons in the teaching profession. MOST is an intersegmental effort by Humboldt State University, College of the Redwoods, and the Humboldt County Office of Education. Services provided include career awareness, exploration, mapping, training, and assistance in placement. Recruitment reaches high school students, teacher aides, and community college and university students. MOST has specialized counselors and offers stipends for students. Efforts to retain students extend beyond preservice training to professional development.

Saint Mary's College of California (MA I)
Beginning Teacher Support and Assessment Program

Grades served: E, M, HS	Schools served: NR	Year established: 1992
Location of schools served: UR, SU, RU	Type of schools served: PUB, PRI	

This program is a partnership involving Saint Mary's College School of Education, the Alameda County Office of Education, the Contra Costa County Office of Education, and 11 school districts. It is designed to connect students' achievements with systematic professional development of teachers, both preservice and inservice. Portfolios and classroom observations are used to provide valid and authentic measures of teachers' performance. The program has developed a format and process for a learner-centered decision model, consistent with its Framework of Knowledge, Skills, and Abilities.

University of California-Riverside (RES II)
Project TEAMS (Teacher Excellence and Authorization in Math and Science)

Grades served: M	Schools served: 1072	Year established: 1991
Location of schools served: UR, SU, RU	Type of schools served: PUB, PRI	

Project TEAMS is a special program that serves as a model for improving the teaching of mathematics and science in the middle grades, providing a direct vehicle to credential teachers to teach these subjects at that level. It provides an in-depth study of mathematics and science content that is thoroughly integrated with innovative teaching strategies for crossover teachers and those who need to be retrained to obtain supplementary authorization to teach mathematics in science at the middle grades. The project makes a concentrated effort to recruit minority teachers and teachers of underrepresented students.

COLORADO

University of Colorado at Denver (DOC II)
Collaborative Special Education Teacher Training (C-SETT)

Grades served: M	Schools served: 1	Year established: NR
Location of schools served: NR	Type of schools served: PUB	

C-SETT is a collaboration involving Adams School District #14 and UCD. The program provides financial support for graduate students who wish to become special education teachers, focusing on preparing persons from a variety of linguistic and ethnic backgrounds. Their training emphasizes skills needed to work with special education students in inclusive classrooms. C-SETT interns complete field practice in a middle school in Adams #14 under the collaborative guidance of grade-level teams of teachers who provide supervision, support, and feedback. The U.S. Department of Education funds the project.

University of Colorado at Denver (DOC II)
Stanley British Primary School Alternative Teacher Certification Program

Grades served: E

Location of schools served: UR

Schools served: 3

Type of schools served: PUB

Year established: 1992

Faculty from UCD's School of Education and other instructors provide seminars for prospective teacher interns at Stanley British Primary School (SBPS) in Denver. Interns spend a year in classrooms at SBPS, with on-the-job mentoring by master teachers. Since fall 1992, SBPS has taken a leadership role in assisting the Denver Public Schools to implement a British primary model at Crofton-Ebert Elementary School and in certain classrooms at Steele Elementary School. Starting in 1994, interns have the option of taking additional courses to receive a master's degree in early childhood education or curriculum and instruction.

University of Colorado at Denver (DOC II)
Urban Partnership

Grades served: E, M, HS

Location of schools served: UR

Schools served: NR

Type of schools served: PUB

Year established: NR

The purpose of this project, funded by the U.S. Department of Education, is to provide financial support for graduate students from diverse cultural and linguistic backgrounds who are preparing to be special education teachers. The project brings together personnel from Adams #14 School District, the Denver Public Schools, and two divisions of the university's school of education (Special Education and School Psychology; and Language, Literacy, and Culture). In addition to the advising and course work UCD faculty provide, interns engage in full-time guided teaching in the public schools, led by mentor teachers who provide extensive supervision and feedback.

CONNECTICUT

Saint Joseph College (MA I)
Compensatory Education Internships

Grades served: E

Location of schools served: SU

Schools served: 10

Type of schools served: PUB

Year established: 1986

This partnership links Saint Joseph College and ten West Hartford schools in a program serving underrepresented, at-risk, and minority populations. Twenty-four graduate interns are selected annually for a year of graduate training that combines theory and research with applied classroom experience and compensatory education. These 24 interns provide educational services to approximately 500 students annually, with results that show significant outcomes in state tests of eighth grade students in writing and reading. Interns must be certified elementary or special education teachers or be eligible for certification before admission to the program.

DISTRICT OF COLUMBIA

Howard University (RES I)
Project Pipeline for Science and Mathematics Teachers

Grades served: HS

Location of schools served: NR

Schools served: NR

Type of schools served: NR

Year established: 1990

Project Pipeline is a collaboration to increase the number of underrepresented minority teachers of mathematics and science in California public schools, colleges, and universities by helping high school and college students, recent college graduates, and early retirees from science or mathematics fields to gain teaching credentials. Besides Howard University, North Carolina A&T, Atlanta University, Tuskegee University, and the University of Arkansas are involved in the project. Howard University's program is funded by a grant from the California Postsecondary Education Commission to the Center Unified School District and National University.

Note: Each institution's Carnegie class is given in parentheses. **Key:** E=elementary school, HS=high school, M=middle school, NR=not reported, PRI=private, PUB=public, RU=rural, SU=suburban, UR=urban

FLORIDA

Flagler College (BA II)
Workstudy Program with the Florida School for the Deaf and the Blind

Grades served: E, M, HS   Schools served: 1   Year established: 1987
Location of schools served: NR   Type of schools served: PUB

Flagler College provides a work-study program for interested students at the Florida School for the Deaf and the Blind (FSDB), which is fewer than two miles from the Flagler campus. The two schools share funding for the program equally. Flagler students who plan to teach or work with persons who are hearing-impaired, visually impaired, or who experience other exceptionalities have the opportunity to add a practical dimension to their classroom studies, while FSDB students receive the benefits of having Flagler students on their campus to tutor, direct recreational activities, chaperon travel and field trips, and do peer counseling.

GEORGIA

Augusta College (MA I)
Minority Recruitment in Teacher Education

Grades served: HS   Schools served: 1   Year established: 1993
Location of schools served: UR   Type of schools served: PUB

The goal of this project is to increase the number of high school minority students entering teacher education programs. A collaboration of Augusta College and Lucy Laney High School, the program provides mentoring, tutoring, career awareness, and career counseling services for students in grades 9-12 who are interested in teaching. Graduate students supervise the establishment and continuation of teacher education-based organizations in the high school

Georgia College (MA I)
Project PEACH (Partners in Education of All Children)

Grades served: E   Schools served: 5   Year established: 1988
Location of schools served: RU   Type of schools served: PUB

Project PEACH is a partnership of Georgia College and the Baldwin County Board of Education. An adaptation of Missouri's Parents as Teachers program, its missions are to teach parents about child growth and development and to train preservice teachers to work effectively with parents. Home educators accompanied by preservice teachers regularly visit homes with parents and children to model effective parenting skills for both parents and preservice teachers. Other activities include parent panels for student teachers, parent workshops, and parent support groups.

HAWAII

University of Hawaii at Manoa (RES I)
Hawaii School University Partnership

Grades served: NR   Schools served: 9   Year established: 1986
Location of schools served: UR   Type of schools served: PUB

This partnership links the Hawaii State Department of Education, the Kamehameha Schools, and the University of Hawaii at Manoa. Part of the National Network for Educational Renewal, the program's agenda focuses on simultaneous renewal of schools and education of educators. The partnership is committed to addressing the major problems of school-age youth in Hawaii, giving special attention to the education of the disadvantaged, who may include at-risk and/or minority students. The partnership includes preservice teacher education and principal training programs jointly developed by the participating institutions and implemented through partnerships with public schools.

<u>ILLINOIS</u>

Loyola University of Chicago (DOC I)
Teachers for Chicago
Grades served: E, M, HS   Schools served: 40   Year established: 1991
Location of schools served: UR   Type of schools served: PUB

Teachers for Chicago is a collaborative project of Chicago-area universities and colleges, the Chicago Teachers Union, and the Chicago Public Schools to bring people looking to change careers into the public schools. The program pays tuition for a master's degree at a participating university to persons who possess a bachelor's degree and have previous work experience who wish to teach in the Chicago Public Schools. After a summer of preparation, these students serve as interns in a public school, where they are assisted by a mentor. Graduate courses are scheduled to support the work the interns perform in the schools.

Northeastern Illinois University (MA I)
Preparing Bilingual Teacher Aides as Special Educators: A Field-Based Project
Grades served: E   Schools served: 15   Year established: 1993
Location of schools served: UR   Type of schools served: PUB

Preparing Bilingual Teacher Aides as Special Educators is a field-based program at Northeastern Illinois University to address the critical shortage of bilingual personnel in special education. Students enrolled in the program are employed as teacher aides in Chicago area schools and use their work sites to complete field-based assignments as part of the course work for the special education undergraduate major. Each student works cooperatively at the site with a mentor teacher, who keeps in close contact with university supervisors. The U.S. Department of Education funds the project.

Northeastern Illinois University (MA I)
RAISE (Russian/American Initiative to Strengthen Education)
Grades served: NR   Schools served: 2   Year established: 1992
Location of schools served: NR   Type of schools served: NR

RAISE is an umbrella organization created by Northeastern Illinois University to support collaboration between Russian and U.S. educational institutions to improve educational practices. Currently, a formal partnership exists between the Urals State Pedagogical University and the Sverdlosk Engineering Pedagogical University in Ekaterinburg, Russia, and Northeastern Illinois University. The partnership, in cooperation with the Russian Ministry of Education, held two conferences in April 1994 to assist other institutions of higher education to develop similar partnerships linking Russian and U.S. educators. The partnership is designed to restructure education in a wide range of disciplines.

Northeastern Illinois University (MA I)
Teachers for Chicago
Grades served: E, M, HS   Schools served: 3   Year established: 1982
Location of schools served: UR   Type of schools served: PUB

The Chicago Public Schools, the Chicago Teachers Union, the Council of the Chicago Area Deans of Education, and the Golden Apple Foundation for Excellence in Teaching have designed Teachers for Chicago to enable college graduates to meet Illinois certification standards and earn their master's degree while developing their teaching skills in Chicago classrooms. Candidates complete the internship, residency, and course work required within two school years and three summers. Northeastern interns, under supervision of mentor teachers, are in charge of their own classrooms at Dusable High School, Wirth Elementary School, and Senn Academy.

Note: Each institution's Carnegie class is given in parentheses. **Key:** E=elementary school, HS=high school, M=middle school, NR=not reported, PRI=private, PUB=public, RU=rural, SU=suburban, UR=urban

KANSAS

Wichita State University (DOC II)
Peace Corps Fellow/USA Program

Grades served: NR

Schools served: NR

Year established: 1992

Location of schools served: UR

Type of schools served: NR

The university's College of Education, in cooperation with the Peace Corps, offers a special, postbaccalaureate certification for returned Peace Corps volunteers. The program offers ten to 15 qualified persons employment as full-time teachers.

KENTUCKY

Madisonville Community College (AA)
ED 201 Total Immersion Program

Grades served: E, M

Schools served: 2

Year established: 1992

Location of schools served: NR

Type of schools served: PUB

The ED 201 Total Immersion Program links sophomore teacher education students with a public elementary or middle school. The mission is twofold: to provide teacher education students an opportunity to practice what they have learned, gain classroom experience, and explore teaching as a career by assisting in a regular classroom for an hour and a half each week; and to provide classroom teachers with an assistant one morning each week. Experienced classroom teachers gain access to new methods and materials, and education students gain a wealth of knowledge from experienced teachers while receiving hands-on training in a real classroom.

University of Kentucky (RES I)
Teacher Opportunity Program

Grades served: E

Schools served: 1

Year established: 1993

Location of schools served: UR

Type of schools served: PUB

The Teacher Opportunity Program is a one-year alternative certification, postbaccalaureate program designed to recruit underrepresented minority candidates into the teaching profession. The program was developed to meet the pressing need for minority teachers and it is limited to candidates seeking certification to teach grades K-4. This collaborative program is sponsored jointly by the university and the Fayette County Schools, with financial support provided by the Kentucky Department of Education and BellSouth Foundation. The school district has made a commitment to hire successful candidates for the year following program completion.

MARYLAND

Morgan State University (MA I)
Project PRIME (Programs to Recruit and Inspire Minorities into Education)

Grades served: E, M, HS

Schools served: 50

Year established: 1992

Location of schools served: UR, SU

Type of schools served: PUB

Project PRIME involves a coalition of partners that includes Morgan State as the lead institution as well as the Baltimore City Public Schools, the Maryland MESA Program, and several colleges and universities (Johns Hopkins University, Loyola College of Maryland, Coppin State College, Towson State University, the College of Notre Dame in Maryland, Baltimore City Community College, and Dundalk Community College). These institutions are committed to implementing a five-year plan that will dramatically increase the number of minority students in the Baltimore area who enroll in teacher education programs. Successful implementation of Project PRIME will lay the groundwork for expansion of the initiative throughout Maryland and beyond.

MASSACHUSETTS

University of Massachusetts at Amherst (RES I)
MESTEP (Math/English/Science/Technology Project)

Grades served: M, HS

Schools served: 9

Year established: 1983

Location of schools served: UR, SU

Type of schools served: PUB

MESTEP was initiated in cooperation with selected corporate partners to recruit, select, prepare, place, support and retain recent college graduates who are interested in beginning careers in teaching. After preliminary training, participants complete two paid internships: one at a public school and one at a corporate site. This 15-month secondary certification program is approved by the Massachusetts Department of Education; it leads to a master's in education.

Wheelock College (TEACH)
Wheelock-Boston-Walker School Partnership

Grades served: E, M

Schools served: 3

Year established: 1993

Location of schools served: UR, SU

Type of schools served: PUB, PRI

Wheelock and its three school partners represent a range of integration efforts for students with special needs. The Mason School integrates children with mild to moderate special needs; Walker is a substantially separate setting that educates and treats children with severe behavioral and learning needs. Each school has hired Wheelock master's degree students as full-time coteachers. Mentor teachers, principals, and college-based faculty share teacher preparation. Collaborators coteach Wheelock College classes in addition to working in their schools. College course work is designed to use experience in teaching and curriculum practice to generate and investigate theory and research, reversing the common approach.

MINNESOTA

University of Minnesota-Morris (BA I)
Teacher Education

Grades served: E, M, HS

Schools served: 20

Year established: 1960

Location of schools served: NR

Type of schools served: PUB

This program uses personalized instruction and opportunities for student teaching inside and outside the United States to prepare teachers for effective instruction of diverse populations of learners. Prospective teachers are prepared to demonstrate knowledge of themselves, learners, and the human environment; skill in all aspects of teaching and dispositions associated with effective teaching; self-assessment in relation to learners and learning; and leadership when confronting educational issues.

Winona State University (MA I)
WSU/ISD 535 Graduate Induction Program

Grades served: E

Schools served: 1

Year established: 1986

Location of schools served: RU

Type of schools served: PUB

The Graduate Induction Program is a K-12/university partnership between Winona State University and the Rochester (MN) Public School District. The program's major goals include providing support for 18 first-year teachers, enhancing the clinical supervision of student teachers through the use of veteran teachers, and providing veteran teachers with opportunities for professional growth. Each graduate fellow assumes full responsibility for an elementary classroom. The program gives them credit for one year of teaching experience. Over a 15-month period, they receive a $11,000 fellowship and tuition waivers for credits leading to a master of science in education degree.

Note: Each institution's Carnegie class is given in parentheses. **Key:** E=elementary school, HS=high school, M=middle school, NR=not reported, PRI=private, PUB=public, RU=rural, SU=suburban, UR=urban

MISSOURI

Central Missouri State University (MA I)
Graduated Entry

Grades served: E, M, HS   Schools served: 6   Year established: 1987
Location of schools served: NR   Type of schools served: PUB

Graduated Entry is the primary feature of the elementary education program that the university's Curriculum and Instruction Department redesigned in 1985-86 and is expanding to K-12 teacher preparation. Graduated Entry is designed to foster students' early contact with the realities of a teaching career, encouraging a sound decision to continue toward becoming a teacher. It also builds the observation, instructional, and reflection/problem-solving skills of elementary teaching candidates to a high level of competence in incremental, field-based steps. The redesigned program also includes a foreign language requirement and upgraded classroom applications of technology.

Northeast Missouri State University (MA I)
Summer School

Grades served: M   Schools served: 1   Year established: 1992
Location of schools served: RU   Type of schools served: PUB

This partnership enables academically at-risk middle school students to earn a grade promotion and develop a renewed interest in their own education by successfully completing summer school. While each class section has a teacher-of-record (a combination of middle school faculty and university graduate students), the students provide the major share of instruction as part of their preteaching internship requirement. Instructors benefit from postteaching debriefing sessions.

University of Missouri-Columbia (RES I)
Minority Intern Program

Grades served: E, M, HS   Schools served: 25   Year established: 1989
Location of schools served: SU   Type of schools served: PUB

The Minority Intern Program seeks to develop a professional staff reflecting the racial diversity of the community and to attract and retain high-quality teachers and administrators. It is designed to foster and maintain minority students' interest in a teaching career by providing college students with opportunities to observe and work with professional educators in and out of the classroom. Program participants work with teachers, educational specialists, and administrators. Interns observe and practice student management strategies, interpersonal relationship skills, student assessment techniques, and effective teaching strategies. Interns may work with parents and the schools' business partnership program.

NEVADA

University of Nevada-Las Vegas (MA I)
Cultural Diversity Bridge to Academic Success

Grades served: E   Schools served: 40   Year established: 1991
Location of schools served: UR   Type of schools served: PUB

This program, aimed at providing more minority teachers for Southern Nevada schools, was selected by the Association of Teacher Educators as the winner of the 1993 Distinguished Program in Teacher Education Award. A major part of the program is a cooperative effort through which qualified school district employees interested in becoming elementary and special education teachers study toward education degrees at UNLV. The participating employees, who include teacher aides and secretaries, come from culturally diverse backgrounds. Business donations cover the costs of tuition and books.

New Mexico State University-Main Campus (RES I)
Dove Learning Center

Grades served: NR   Schools served: NR   Year established: NR
Location of schools served: NR   Type of schools served: NR

Four preschool programs operate under the College of Education's Dove Learning Center. The Dona Ana Head Start Program operates two 3½-hour sessions (mornings and afternoons four days a week). Tresco Outreach and Training Services is a service to families with children under 3 years of age who are at biological, medical, or environmental risk. The NMSU Preschool includes a child-centered enrichment program for children aged 3½-5 years, and the Preschool for the Gifted targets selected children aged 3-4 years. All provide for research and professional training in model programs.

New Mexico State University-Main Campus (RES I)
New/Beginning Teacher Program (Agriculture Education)

Grades served: NR   Schools served: NR   Year established: NR
Location of schools served: NR   Type of schools served: NR

This annual program is designed to assist new teachers to become successful in their profession. The program usually involves beginning teachers at three to seven schools. Some 30 to 40 teachers are selected and come to the university's campus for seminars on how to start the new year, basic curriculum, mid-year evaluation and replanning, closing out the school year, preparing a five-year plan, and summer activities planning. Funding is provided by an annual vocational education grant from the state.

Adelphi University (DOC I)
Bellmore-Merrick School District-Adelphi University Partnership

Grades served: M, HS   Schools served: 6   Year established: 1991
Location of schools served: SU   Type of schools served: PUB

The mission of this partnership is to provide an innovative preservice teacher training site for university student teachers and graduate interns. A graduate internship program places highly qualified graduate students for one year on a team of teachers and interns who work with at-risk students. The program is overseen by one full-time Adelphi faculty member and a clinical adjunct faculty member, formerly a principal in the district.

Long Island University-Brooklyn Campus (MA I)
Special Education-Partnership for Training

Grades served: NR   Schools served: NR   Year established: 1988
Location of schools served: UR   Type of schools served: PUB

Partnership for Training is a federally funded program linking the university and the New York Board of Education. Its goals are to provide training at reduced tuition for newly assigned, provisionally certified special education teachers as they work toward full certification, to improve retention rates for teachers, and to respond to the critical need for bilingual special education teachers. The program, offering four selected graduate courses in special education, holds regular after-school peer group meetings led by the master teacher to provide support for the first year of teaching.

Note: Each institution's Carnegie class is given in parentheses. **Key:** E=elementary school, HS=high school, M=middle school, NR=not reported, PRI=private, PUB=public, RU=rural, SU=suburban, UR=urban

Nazareth College of Rochester (MA I)
Teacher Opportunity Corps (TOC)

Grades served: NR   Schools served: 2   Year established: 1987
Location of schools served: UR   Type of schools served: PUB

The Teacher Opportunity Corps is designed to train minority entry-level graduate students from racial and ethnic groups historically underrepresented in teaching with the skills, attitudes, and behaviors essential for survival in New York state schools serving a high concentration of at-risk students. Upon successful completion of the program, TOC students receive a master of science in education, with provisional certification in their chosen subject areas.

State University of New York at Buffalo (RES I)
BRIET (Buffalo Research Institute on Education for Teaching)

Grades served: E, M, HS   Schools served: 2   Year established: 1988
Location of schools served: UR, SU   Type of schools served: PUB

BRIET reflects the commitment of the university's Graduate School of Education to educational reform and the enhancement of teacher education, teaching, and learning. It is a collegium of faculty and students from the university and area schools who join research with teacher education program development to better understand and improve elementary and secondary schooling. Field teams composed of prospective and experienced teachers and university faculty work together. Clinical faculty — outstanding teachers from the Buffalo and Williamsville schools — coteach methods courses, participate in collaborative research, and contribute to the BRIET teacher education program design.

State University of New York College at Brockport (MA I)
Teacher Opportunity Corps (TOC)

Grades served: E, M   Schools served: 2   Year established: 1987
Location of schools served: UR   Type of schools served: PUB

This partnership links SUNY-Brockport and the Rochester City School District. Its primary focus is the recruitment and retention of historically underrepresented groups in teacher education. The partnership also includes an articulation agreement with Monroe Community College, through which its students receive the same services as the university's students. Through mentoring, tutoring, and a specialized curriculum, TOC participants work with predominantly at-risk youth in elementary and middle schools. The program provides financial assistance, tutoring, and counseling to participants, and mentoring during the first year of teaching.

State University of New York College at Cortland (MA I)
Elementary Reading Clinic

Grades served: E   Schools served: NR   Year established: NR
Location of schools served: SU, RU   Type of schools served: PUB, PRI

The Elementary Reading Clinic at SUNY-Cortland is run in conjunction with a graduate course, Practicum in Reading. Teachers from the elementary schools in Cortland County recommend young children for the fall, spring, or summer clinics and provide supporting information on recommended students. Graduate students tutor under the supervision of college faculty. The experience enables students (mainly teachers) to qualify for certification as reading specialists and to improve their skills of assessment and instruction. Approximately 45 tutors and 45 children participate in the summer clinics; the fall and spring clinics serve approximately 20 students and 20 tutors.

State University of New York College at Potsdam (MA I)
Akwesasne Potsdam College Teacher Education Partnership

Grades served: E, M, HS Schools served: 7 Year established: 1993
Location of schools served: RU Type of schools served: PUB

This partnership links seven schools on the Mohawk Reservation and two northern New York rural towns with SUNY-College at Potsdam's School of Education. College students gain preteaching field experience in K-9 science methods, math, reading, and language arts. Classroom teachers and college faculty assist students in designing interdisciplinary instructional units that integrate methods with local communities' knowledge and culture. Students deliver units in the final weeks of the semester, classroom teachers retain the kits, and teachers' evaluations are added to the students' portfolios.

NORTH CAROLINA

Appalachian State University (MA I)
Appalachian State University/Public School Partnership

Grades served: E, M, HS Schools served: 85 Year established: 1987
Location of schools served: RU Type of schools served: PUB

This partnership has as its mission the development of a strong cooperative program by and among its members. Members work closely as equals to make improvements in educational areas of mutual concern, paying attention to the preparation of teachers and to continuous professional development. The programs involves 35,000 students in seven partnership schools and 2,000 teacher education majors at Appalachian State.

East Carolina University (MA I)
Model Clinical Teaching Program

Grades served: E, M, HS Schools served: 6 Year established: 1988
Location of schools served: SU, RU Type of schools served: NR

The Model Clinical Teaching Program is a collaboratively conceptualized, implemented, and evaluated program for the professional development of inservice and preservice teachers. It was developed by the East Carolina University's School of Education and the Pitt County Public Schools. The program provides an extended clinical experience with reflective action that allows these teachers to integrate theory and practice and to be better decision makers about complex issues of teaching and learning. The participants share the belief that preparation of preservice teachers in a year-long clinical setting with mentors to guide their observations, discussions, practice, and reflections ensures optimal professional growth.

University of North Carolina at Charlotte (MA I)
Project REACH (Reaching Every At-Risk Child)

Grades served: E, M Schools served: 5 Year established: 1989
Location of schools served: NR Type of schools served: PUB

Project REACH is an alternative student teaching experience in year-round schools for specially selected postbaccalaureate students. These student teachers begin part time in the classroom in March, continue with full time throughout the summer, and end their assignment in August. In addition to fulfilling all regular student teaching requirements, REACH student teachers receive additional preparation in instructional and management strategies for working with at-risk students and other learners with special needs in a regular classroom.

Note: Each institution's Carnegie class is given in parentheses. **Key:** E=elementary school, HS=high school, M=middle school, NR=not reported, PRI=private, PUB=public, RU=rural, SU=suburban, UR=urban

NORTH DAKOTA

University of North Dakota-Main Campus (DOC II)
UND/North Dakota School for the Blind

Grades served: E, M, HS

Location of schools served: NR

Schools served: NR

Type of schools served: PUB

Year established: 1973

The alliance between the University of North Dakota and the North Dakota School for the Blind aims to improve service to all visually impaired persons in North Dakota, and to provide preservice training for prospective vision consultants and inservice training for vision teachers throughout the state. Vision teachers throughout the state and faculty at UND jointly teach course work for preservice teachers and share equipment and materials. Preservice students at UND complete internships throughout the school year with students who come to NDSB for training. UND faculty provide cost-free inservice assistance to NDSB personnel in exchange for their resources.

OHIO

Bowling Green State University (DOC I)
BGSU Cooperative Schools Instrumental Music Project

Grades served: E, M

Location of schools served: UR, SU

Schools served: 2

Type of schools served: PRI

Year established: 1979

The Cooperative Schools Instrumental Music Project addresses concerns about perceived weakness in postsecondary methods courses, the absence of realistic early field experiences for preservice teachers, and the limited opportunities for faculty to work with school-age students. Students in the cooperating schools in grades 5-8 receive group instruction two to three times each week and participate in performances. The program progresses through an instructional cycle that begins in the theory classroom, moves to practice in the schools, and returns for university classroom evaluation. The school gains comprehensive, competency-based instruction by preservice music teachers, who in turn benefit from the field experience.

Malone College (BA II)
Child Development Associate (CDA) Credentialing Program

Grades served: Preschool

Location of schools served: UR, SU

Schools served: 20

Type of schools served: PUB, PRI

Year established: 1992

Malone College collaborates with Head Start and other early childhood programs to provide child development associate staff training. College personnel instruct and guide teachers enrolled with the National Council for Recognition of Early Childhood Professionals through fieldwork, course work, and final evaluation. Participants are observed in their work settings during the first phase, instructed in classroom settings during the second phase, and guided through a series of exercises that demonstrate their competency in working with young children and their families in the third phase.

University of Akron, Main Campus (DOC I)
University-Urban School Collaboration

Grades served: HS

Location of schools served: UR

Schools served: 2

Type of schools served: PUB

Year established: 1984

The University of Akron and the Akron Public Schools have created a teacher education partnership stemming from the Kenmore Project in which English teachers from the high school mentor teacher education students. This expanded partnership includes Kenmore and Firestone high schools and involves both math and English. College students serve as interns in the high schools and tutor students in math and English. Selected interns receive the School-University Student Teaching Award and student teaching positions at the schools. The most successful are later considered for employment in the district. The project has been proclaimed an NCTE Center of Excellence.

University of Akron, Main Campus (DOC I)
Adapted Physical Education Lab

Grades served: E, M, HS   Schools served: 4   Year established: 1992
Location of schools served: UR   Type of schools served: PUB

The Adapted Physical Education Lab is part of the undergraduate adapted class that meets on Friday mornings. The lab is set up to provide University of Akron students majoring in physical education an opportunity to get hands-on experience in working with children with disabilities. Each semester 20 children with disabilities from the Akron Public Schools come to campus so physical education students can work with them in the gymnasium and the natatorium. Each student is responsible for one child's Individualized Education Plan in both settings.

University of Akron, Main Campus (DOC I)
Professional Development Schools

Grades served: E, M, HS   Schools served: 2   Year established: 1991
Location of schools served: SU, RU   Type of schools served: PUB

Collaborative agreements between the University of Akron and the Medina City Schools allow the use of outstanding special educators employed by Medina City Schools as models and mentors for students in special education teacher preparation programs in multihandicaps and severe behavior handicaps.

OKLAHOMA

Oklahoma State University (RES II)
Educational Alliance

Grades served: E, M, HS   Schools served: NR   Year established: 1990
Location of schools served: RU   Type of schools served: PUB

The primary mission of the Educational Alliance between Oklahoma State University, Frontier Public Schools, and the Otoe-Missouria Tribe is to provide preservice teachers with early and sustained clinical experience in a culturally diverse public school setting. The alliance also enhances communication links among the school district, the Native American community, and the university community; extends tribe-specific cultural understanding among faculty and staff of the university and school district; provides inservice training for Frontier teachers; and introduces Frontier students to postsecondary programs and support services.

University of Oklahoma-Norman Campus (RES I)
Responsive Leaders for All Children

Grades served: NR   Schools served: NR   Year established: 1992
Location of schools served: UR, SU, RU   Type of schools served: PUB

This partnership of the Danforth Foundation and the university focuses on better meeting the needs of all children and improving the preparation of professionals who work with children in schools, social work, law enforcement, and the judicial system. Efforts in the first year included developing a state-level model to ensure success by examining beliefs related to collaboration, a vision statement, barriers to collaboration, and solutions to those barriers. The partnership now focuses on six diverse school districts, with the final goal of helping the districts better use available resources to meet the needs of children and their families.

OREGON

Portland State University (DOC II)
Portland Teachers' Program

Grades served: M, HS   Schools served: 7   Year established: 1990
Location of schools served: UR   Type of schools served: PUB

The Portland Teachers' Program is a partnership of the Portland Public Schools, Portland Community College, and the university to recruit, prepare, and retain historically underrepresented groups into the teaching profession. The program provides upper-division, postbaccalaureate, and graduate course work required for a bachelor's degree and teaching credential; it includes classroom work and field placements in public and community educational settings. Specialized advising, priority registration, required meetings and seminars, support services, and peer networking systems are integral parts of the program.

PENNSYLVANIA

Elizabethtown College (BA II)
Supporting Urban Student and Teacher Learning

Grades served: E   Schools served: 1   Year established: 1992
Location of schools served: UR   Type of schools served: PUB

Supporting Urban Student and Teacher Learning is a partnership linking college education and social work students with K-6 students, teachers, and families at a multiracial public school. Its aims are to better understand and serve the needs of children and families who are experiencing difficulty with schooling, to build a multicultural professional development site for preservice and inservice teachers, and to collaborate with other professionals, agencies, and community resources in support of families and children at risk for school failure. School administrators, teachers, parents, and college faculty are also collaborating in the reform, renewal, and restructuring of the school.

Indiana University of Pennsylvania (DOC I)
Pittsburgh Collaborative

Grades served: HS   Schools served: NR   Year established: 1988
Location of schools served: UR   Type of schools served: PUB

The Pittsburgh Collaborative is a partnership linking Indiana University of Pennsylvania, Duquesne University, and the University of Pittsburgh with the Pittsburgh Public Schools. Its primary mission is to develop innovative practices for the education of teachers who will work in urban multicultural schools. The program provides special training for university supervisors and cooperating teachers (all called clinical instructors), special student teacher seminars, and a community involvement program.

Slippery Rock University of Pennsylvania (MA I)
Partnership in a Laboratory School for Exceptional Children

Grades served: NR   Schools served: 1   Year established: 1993
Location of schools served: NR   Type of schools served: PUB

In 1965 the Slippery Rock Lab School for Exceptional Children was established as part of the teacher education training program at Slippery Rock University. Since then the school has provided educational programming for exceptional children whose needs could not be met in a regular classroom. Beginning in September 1993, Midwestern Intermediate Unit IV assumed operation of the school as a campus laboratory school; it works with the Special Education Department to place teacher trainees in the school. Its location on the Slippery Rock campus allows the lab school to capitalize on the resources available at the university.

SOUTH CAROLINA

Winthrop University (MA I)
South Carolina Center for Teacher Recruitment

Grades served: M, HS   Schools served: 200   Year established: 1985
Location of schools served: UR, SU, RU Type of schools served: PUB

The South Carolina Center for Teacher Recruitment is a collaboration of the state's universities, public schools, businesses, education agencies, and the legislature to provide leadership in identifying, attracting, placing, and retaining well-qualified teachers for South Carolina. The center's major initiatives include the Teacher Cadet and ProTeam Programs, nationally recognized precollegiate recruitment programs for high school and middle school students, respectively; the State Teacher Forum; College HelpLine; the Teacher Job Bank; summer recruitment institutes; and the Teacher/Professor-in-Residence Program.

TEXAS

Lamar University-Beaumont (MA I)
Spindletop Center for Excellence in Teaching Technology

Grades served: E, M, HS   Schools served: 7   Year established: 1993
Location of schools served: UR   Type of schools served: PUB

SCETT is a collaboration ensuring quality education for the diverse population of Texas children by training teachers in a state-of-the-art, interdisciplinary, field-based program. The collaboration includes Lamar University-Beaumont, the Port Arthur and Beaumont independent school districts, the Region V Educational Service Center, DuPont, and Southwestern Bell. Preservice teachers study for two semesters in local professional partnership schools, where they learn to integrate theory and practice. The program emphasizes the integration of technology into the curriculum; an extensive program of staff development for teachers, administrators, and university faculty; and initiatives to build and nurture strong school-family ties.

Southwest Texas State University (MA I)
SWT Center for Professional Development and Technology

Grades served: NR   Schools served: 4   Year established: 1992
Location of schools served: NR   Type of schools served: PUB

This school-university-community partnership focuses on restructuring teacher preparation in central Texas. Each site is equipped with state-of-the-art technology fully integrated into the educational program for children and the teacher preparation program. University professors and public school educators jointly plan and deliver teacher preparation programs. These efforts have established five fully interactive classrooms that make distance learning easily achieved.

University of Houston-Clear Lake (MA I)
BAER[2] (Bay Area Education Recruitment and Retention)

Grades served: HS   Schools served: 3   Year established: 1993
Location of schools served: SU   Type of schools served: PUB

BAER[2], a collaboration of Goose Creek Consolidated Independent School District, Lee College, and the University of Houston-Clear Lake, aims to bring students into a teaching career and into the Baytown area public schools. The three institutions work together to provide a step-by-step training program for future teachers in the Baytown area. The program's services include special advising, scholarships, and employment opportunities. Many graduates of the program will seek employment in Baytown area schools.

Note: Each institution's Carnegie class is given in parentheses. **Key:** E=elementary school, HS=high school, M=middle school, NR=not reported, PRI=private, PUB=public, RU=rural, SU=suburban, UR=urban

UTAH

Weber State University (MA II)
Educational Technology Initiative
Grades served: E, M, HS   Schools served: 20   Year established: 1990
Location of schools served: UR, SU, RU   Type of schools served: PUB

Weber State University's Educational Technology Initiative was established with funding from the Utah Legislature to encourage businesses and the public sector's support of the effective use of technology to improve education in Utah's public schools. In addition to its focus on preservice teacher education, the initiative also works directly with nearby public schools by providing inservice workshops, establishing partnerships with particular schools to strengthen student teaching through telecommunications, and consulting with schools to improve curricular practices with regard to technology, teacher-university faculty exchanges, software development, and development of a database of exemplary practices.

VIRGINIA

Virginia Commonwealth University (RES I)
Project BEST (Basic Educational Skills and Training)
Grades served: M   Schools served: 1   Year established: 1989
Location of schools served: UR   Type of schools served: PUB

Project BEST is a collaboration between the university's School of Education and the Richmond Public Schools designed to encourage retention of minority college students and at-risk students in middle school. The program's principal components include a three-tiered mentorship program in which VCU faculty mentor VCU students and the college students mentor middle school students; a tutorial program in which the college students tutor/mentor middle school students; workshops for both student populations to enhance academic and affective skills; and a program in which college students participate at local community events with faculty and their middle school mentees.

Virginia Polytechnic Institute and State University (RES I)
Tomorrow's Teachers Program (TTP)
Grades served: HS   Schools served: 7   Year established: 1988
Location of schools served: NR   Type of schools served: PUB

TTP is a collaboration among the school division, the business community, and the university designed to recruit and retain minority students for careers in teaching. It offers extensive precollegiate recruiting for high school students who participate in the program, beginning in grade 10, and emphasizes comprehensive collegiate retention for students when they matriculate. Students who qualify for TTP could be eligible for a full scholarship, which includes tuition, room and board, books, and supplies.

WASHINGTON

Evergreen State College (BA II)
Applied Professional Preparation of Leaders in Education (APPLE)
Grades served: E, M, HS   Schools served: 2   Year established: 1991
Location of schools served: SU   Type of schools served: PUB

The APPLE program, developed by the North Thurston School District and supported in part by a grant to Evergreen's Master in Teaching Program, is a limited partnership designed, developed, and implemented by school district faculty. Its primary long-term goal is to improve ethnic diversity among the teaching staff in the North Thurston School District. Students enroll in a course that includes a field internship designed to inform them about teaching as a career and to develop their skills of communication, organization, and leadership. Evergreen faculty serve as invited guest speakers in the course, and students are invited to a college seminar with their graduate student colleagues.

WISCONSIN

Alverno College (BA II)
DeWitt Wallace-Reader's Digest New Pathways to Teaching Careers

Grades served: NR

Location of schools served: NR

Schools served: NR

Type of schools served: PUB

Year established: 1993

This program allows Alverno College and the University of Wisconsin-Milwaukee to work with the Milwaukee Public Schools in a four-year effort to assist 50 students to qualify for teaching licenses. The program targets minority candidates who are emergency-licensed teachers or are educational assistants, providing them with scholarship assistance and academic support. By making the Milwaukee Public Schools a cocampus, the program involves principals and colleagues of the Pathways scholars in building a supportive environment at the local school level.

University of Wisconsin-Whitewater (MA I)
Beginning Teacher Assistance Program

Grades served: NR

Location of schools served: UR, SU, RU

Schools served: 25

Type of schools served: PUB, PRI

Year established: 1974

This program is the longest continuously operating, university-based mentoring program for teachers in the United States. It unites personnel and resources of the university, small to medium school districts, and the Wisconsin Improvement Program in providing beginning teachers with a structured mentoring program aimed at facilitating their transition from teacher education student to professional teacher. Mentors receive basic and advanced training, and mentors and beginning teachers attend monthly meetings at the university.

Section Three
Teacher Education Centers

ARKANSAS

John Brown University (BA II)
JBU/Siloam Springs Professional Development Schools

Grades served: E, M, High School

Location of schools served: NR

Schools served: 5

Type of schools served: PUB

Year established: 1991

This partnership uses the resources of the university, the school district, and the total community in a comprehensive program designed to bring about simultaneous restructuring of teacher education programs and the K-12 school system. The K-12 professional development schools involve instructional teams composed of university students, university faculty, public school teachers, and parents; a community Adopt-a-School program; a community education program; and a Student and Family Resource Center.

Note: Each institution's Carnegie class is given in parentheses. **Key:** E=elementary school, HS=high school, M=middle school, NR=not reported, PRI=private, PUB=public, RU=rural, SU=suburban, UR=urban

CALIFORNIA

San Diego State University (DOC II)
Model Education Center

Grades served: NR   Schools served: 2   Year established: 1984
Location of schools served: UR   Type of schools served: PUB

This partnership of San Diego State University and Cajon Valley Union School District was formed to develop a field-based training center where the partners' educational expertise could be joined to reform schools. It resulted after a year of planning for change that carefully addressed each partner's educational needs. The program works in three-year cycles. Teams share the responsibility of meeting the collaboration's goals: a model of planned change and evaluation of products and process.

University of Southern California (RES I)
Center to Advance Precollege Science Education

Grades served: E   Schools served: 32   Year established: 1990
Location of schools served: UR   Type of schools served: PUB

USC's Center to Advance Precollege Science Education operates two projects, whose aims are teacher training and school reform: PRAXIS, funded by the National Science Foundation, and the California Science Project, funded by the state of California. The two projects work with 32 inner-city elementary schools to achieve whole-school change in science education by working with teams of teachers and the principal from each school over three years. The teams attend summer and winter training institutes in life, physical, and earth sciences, leadership, and technology. Transdisciplinary teacher cadres of scientists, secondary and elementary science teachers, and curriculum specialists train participants.

CONNECTICUT

University of Connecticut (RES I)
Windham Professional Development Center

Grades served: E, M, High School   Schools served: 5   Year established: 1990
Location of schools served: UR   Type of schools served: PUB

The Windham Professional Development Center is a collaboration of University of Connecticut faculty and students and Windham schools. Its purpose is to promote change within schools and in teacher preparation. Participants share a vision of a revitalized urban school environment, led by properly prepared professionals. The center allows for supervised clinical experiences for prospective teachers. Participants are involved in several ongoing projects: peer tutoring, integrating the humanities curriculum, developing study skills, educational mentoring, sibling tutoring, integrating reading/writing curriculum, writing workshops, and integrating bilingual students into the mainstream.

DISTRICT OF COLUMBIA

Georgetown University (RES I)
Summer Institute on International Relations

Grades served: M, HS   Schools served: 60   Year established: 1992
Location of schools served: UR, SU, RU   Type of schools served: PUB, PRI

Georgetown University's School of Foreign Service, in partnership with the World Affairs Council of Washington, D.C., sponsors an annual Summer Institute on International Relations to acquaint secondary school teachers from the metropolitan Washington area with current trends and critical issues in international affairs. Discussions with experts in the fields and presentations by expert speakers from a variety of backgrounds— academic, government, private industry, the press, nonprofit organizations, the United Nations, medical institutions, foreign embassies — provide a broad base for exploring curricular change. Interactive learning, simulations, role playing, and case studies engage participants.

ILLINOIS

Southern Illinois University at Carbondale (RES II)
Aviation Technology Program

Grades served: E, M
Schools served: NR
Year established: 1988

Location of schools served: UR, SU, RU
Type of schools served: PUB, PRI

The Aviation Technology Program, in cooperation with the Rotor and Wing Association, the Aerospace Education Committee of Southern Illinois, and other agencies, has formulated a number of initiatives designed to promote aviation education. The primary focus has been on the integration of aviation and space topics into grade schools and middle schools, aimed at both students and teachers. Additional emphasis is on aviation career orientation.

INDIANA

Indiana State University (DOC II)
Professional Development Schools Program

Grades served: E, M, HS
Schools served: 10
Year established: 1992

Location of schools served: NR
Type of schools served: PUB

This program is a partnership linking Indiana State University with four area school districts involving five elementary, one middle, and four high schools. The thrusts of this partnership are to improve the way public school and university personnel work together to facilitate higher levels of learning by all children and those who teach them, to promote a better school environment for preparing teachers and other educational professionals, and to create a more supportive site for renewal of and inquiry by experienced teachers, administrators, school service personnel, and university faculty.

KANSAS

Butler County Community College (AA)
Center for Teaching Excellence

Grades served: E, M, HS
Schools served: NR
Year established: NR

Location of schools served: RU
Type of schools served: PUB

Butler County Community College's Center for Teaching Excellence is a resource for both BCCC faculty and teachers of the nine unified school districts in the county. Through a grant from Texaco Foundation, the center provides BCCC faculty with professional development opportunities, funding for special projects, the latest in instructional equipment, and a library of resources devoted to teaching. Butler County school teachers are eligible for monetary awards from Texaco that recognize innovative K-12 classroom projects. The center also sponsors the Master Teacher Seminar for area secondary school teachers and offers a variety of learning opportunities to K-12 staff.

Note: Each institution's Carnegie class is given in parentheses. **Key:** E=elementary school, HS=high school, M=middle school, NR=not reported, PRI=private, PUB=public, RU=rural, SU=suburban, UR=urban

MARYLAND

University of Maryland-College Park (RES I)
Mid-Atlantic Region Japan-in-the-Schools (MARJiS) Program

Grades served: E, M, HS   Schools served: 500   Year established: 1985
Location of schools served: UR, SU, RU   Type of schools served: PUB, PRI

This program is a regional partnership linking the International Center for the Study of Education Policy and Human Values, and the Department of Education Policy, Planning, and Administration at the University of Maryland-College Park. It maintains a resource center that lends books, curricula, multimedia sets, videos, and other resources on intercultural education and Japan-related instruction; provides inservice education for faculty, policy leaders, and administrators; produces a monthly instructional newsletter and other publications; provides consultant services; and prepares educators to lead Japan-related curricular and intercultural exchanges.

MINNESOTA

Mankato State University (MA I)
Laboratory District Teacher Education

Grades served: NR   Schools served: NR   Year established: 1988
Location of schools served: UR, SU, RU   Type of schools served: PUB

The Laboratory District Teacher Education Center at Mankato State University is a consortium involving the university and 15 public school districts. The center's purpose is to develop partnerships that bridge the gap between theory and practice, ensure a successful transition from preservice to inservice for teachers, and provide continuing enrichment opportunities for practitioners at all levels. Partnerships within the center include an induction/mentoring program; fifth-year graduate internship; a global education program; a multicultural and gender fair; a disability awareness program; classroom evaluation and action research; leadership development and mathematics programs; and a professional practicum. The center also maintains formal and informal links with many professional education groups.

MISSOURI

University of Missouri-Kansas City (DOC I)
Teacher Education

Grades served: NR   Schools served: NR   Year established: 1991
Location of schools served: UR, SU   Type of schools served: PUB

This partnership envisions a jointly developed, funded, and implemented program for the development of excellence in teaching. Its primary purpose is to ensure that area schools are staffed by intelligent, knowledgeable, skilled, and committed teachers. In addition, the university and the school district have increased opportunities to cost-effectively share materials and people through joint appointments of instructors. As a result of the collaboration, preservice teachers, experienced public school teachers, and university faculty have increased opportunities for educational research and instructional improvement.

MONTANA

Western Montana College (BA II)
Butte/Western Partnership

Grades served: NR   Schools served: 2   Year established: 1992
Location of schools served: NR   Type of schools served: PUB

The Butte/Western Partnership was formed to improve teacher education. Teachers from the schools help to design and deliver the teacher education program at the college. Important components of the program are delivered in the school district in the form of exploratory and professional field experiences and student teaching. Groups of teachers plan field experiences for cohort groups of student teachers.

<u>NEW YORK</u>

State University of New York College at Fredonia (MA I)
Fredonia-Hamburg Teacher Education Center

Grades served: NR
Location of schools served: SU, RU

Schools served: 6
Type of schools served: PUB

Year established: 1972

The Fredonia-Hamburg Teacher Education Center, a winner of the 1985 Distinguished Program in Teacher Education Award from the National Association of Teacher Educators, is a cooperative venture between SUNY-College at Fredonia and the Hamburg Central School District. Seminars in curriculum and teaching strategies and three 11-week teaching internships make up this year-long, field-based, senior-level program. Seminars are conducted on site, so that theory and practice can be integrated throughout the program. Participants are assessed in five competency areas: concern for individuality, human relations, content skills and techniques, decision making, and philosophy.

Syracuse University (RES II)
Physics-Teacher Workshops

Grades served: HS
Location of schools served: UR, SU, RU

Schools served: 20
Type of schools served: PUB, PRI

Year established: 1991

Physics Teacher Workshops are a cooperative endeavor of central New York high school physics teachers and Syracuse University's Physics Department. Workshops are held on Saturday mornings (about six per year) and attended by 15 to 20 teachers from as many schools. The purpose of the program is to improve the teaching of physics in the high schools. Participants exchange ideas for presenting concepts in the classroom and the laboratory. An educational equipment library, housed at the university, makes equipment available to share through interinstitutional loan.

Syracuse University (RES II)
Professional Development School

Grades served: E, M, HS
Location of schools served: UR, SU, RU

Schools served: 20
Type of schools served: PUB

Year established: 1989

This professional development school links preservice and inservice teacher education. It provides opportunities for participants to study and engage in experiences that add to their professional knowledge, skills, and values. Using cadres and academies of students, teachers, and administrators at the elementary and secondary levels, the school organizes those committed to excellence in teaching and teacher education so that they can achieve their goals.

<u>SOUTH CAROLINA</u>

Midlands Technical College (AA)
South Carolina Hall of Science and Technology

Grades served: E, M, HS
Location of schools served: UR, SU, RU

Schools served: NR
Type of schools served: PUB, PRI

Year established: 1993

In this project, the South Carolina Science Council (the professional organization for public school science teachers), the South Carolina State Museum, and Midlands Technical College fund and plan collaborative events. One such event was the induction ceremony of astronaut Charles Bolden into the Hall, located on the Midlands campus. Five hundred middle school students and teachers were invited to the ceremony and to regularly participate in workshops designed for them by college faculty in math, science, and computer-aided design and manufacturing.

Note: Each institution's Carnegie class is given in parentheses. **Key:** E=elementary school, HS=high school, M=middle school, NR=not reported, PRI=private, PUB=public, RU=rural, SU=suburban, UR=urban

Winthrop University (MA I)
Winthrop University/Public School Partnership

Grades served: E, M

Location of schools served: SU, RU

Schools served: 6

Type of schools served: PUB

Year established: 1993

This partnership was established to focus efforts on the simultaneous renewal of teacher education and public education. Four elementary and two middle schools work with the university on new models for inservice and preservice, curricula, and research and evaluation. The pilot program is affiliated with the National Network for Educational Renewal through its relationship with the South Carolina Center for the Advancement of Teaching and School Leadership. During 1994-95, the partnership received funds from the state Commission on Higher Education targeted for professional development schools to explore ways of integrating university faculty into the schools.

TEXAS

Baylor University (DOC II)
Baylor University-Waco ISD Collaborative

Grades served: E, M

Location of schools served: NR

Schools served: 1

Type of schools served: PUB

Year established: 1993

This collaboration of Baylor University and the Waco Independent School District was formed to facilitate systemic change in teacher education. The collaborative is reviewing all aspects of teacher education: organization and delivery of field-based experiences, support systems for new teachers, mentor training for supervising teachers, and the necessity for continuous collaboration between school districts and university teacher education programs. All members of the collaborative are committed to preparing future teachers with the skills they need to meet the challenges of contemporary classrooms and to provide a child-centered learning environment that reflects best educational practice.

Texas Woman's University (DOC I)
College of Education and Human Ecology C⁵ Program

Grades served: E, M, HS

Location of schools served: NR

Schools served: NR

Type of schools served: PUB

Year established: 1992

The C^5 Program embodies the power of *collaboration* among its members, predefined teacher *competencies,* outcome-driven *curriculum,* infusion of *computers* and technology into teaching and learning, and *commitment* to excellence and quality. A partnership of five local school districts and a state regional education service center, the program was designed in part to affect students' achievement by restructuring undergraduate teacher education and creating developmentally oriented enhancement and renewal for career teachers. State-of-the-art teaching and measurable student outcomes are intrinsic parts of the program.

UTAH

Weber State University (MA II)
Center for Social Science Education

Grades served: E, M, HS

Location of schools served: UR, SU, RU

Schools served: 230

Type of schools served: PUB, PRI

Year established: 1991

The Center for Social Science Education is a partnership designed to promote and coordinate social science education in the schools. It links the university's Social and Behavioral Sciences College, departments of Geography and Economics, and College of Education, public and private school teachers, the business community, and the community at large in conducting preservice and inservice courses, workshops, and seminars; participating in the master's of education program; and assisting in coordinating and promoting involvement in the Ogden Area History Teaching Alliance and the Utah Geographic Alliance. The center has organized an international outreach program involving Weber State's international students as a teaching resource for local educators.

Weber State University (MA II)
Utah Geographic Alliance
Grades served: HS
Schools served: NR
Year established: 1987
Location of schools served: UR, SU, RU
Type of schools served: PUB

The Utah Geographic Alliance fosters professional development for teachers, curricular improvement in schools, and public awareness of geographic issues. Members include teacher from throughout Utah. Weber State and Utah State University provide staff support, while school teachers provide much of the leadership for specific programs through a steering committee and individual assignments. Activities include the annual Geography Awareness Conference, a regional Geography Awareness Week, an annual Geography Olympiad for secondary students, the national Geography Bee, and summer institutes. Participating schools have access to curricular resources and receive a newsletter.

Saint Norbert College (BA II)
Menominee/Oneida Teacher Preparation Program
Grades served: E, M, HS
Schools served: 5
Year established: 1987
Location of schools served: RU
Type of schools served: PUB, PRI

This partnership links Saint Norbert College, the Menominee and Oneida Tribal Schools, and the Menominee Indian School District. Menominee and Oneida tribal members enroll in a four-year teacher certification program designed to increase the pool of competent and fully qualified Native American teachers who are licensed to teach grades preK-12.

University of Wisconsin-Oshkosh (MA I)
Educational Service Center
Grades served: E, M, HS
Schools served: NR
Year established: 1977
Location of schools served: UR, SU, RU
Type of schools served: PUB, PRI

The Educational Service Center provides diagnosis and remediation for learners at all levels to enhance the quality of teacher education programs and service to the community. Its goals are to provide experiences in diagnosis, teaching, and remediation for undergraduate and graduate teacher education students; resources for diagnosis and remediation; a setting for research in the learning and testing of teaching and supervisory models in teacher education programs; and a community service by meeting the instructional needs of all preK-12 learners.

Note: Each institution's Carnegie class is given in parentheses. **Key:** E=elementary school, HS=high school, M=middle school, NR=not reported, PRI=private, PUB=public, RU=rural, SU=suburban, UR=urban

Section Four
Teaching Awards and New Faculty Roles

CALIFORNIA

Sonoma State University (MA I)
Jack London Award for Educational Excellence
Grades served: E, M, HS   Schools served: NR   Year established: 1988
Location of schools served: NR   Type of schools served: PUB

The Jack London Award for Educational Excellence is given annually to an innovative program that has made an exemplary contribution to education in a K-12 public school in Sonoma County. Sonoma State University faculty and business, community, and educational leaders serve as judges for the award, providing on-site evaluation of programs and gaining insight into public schools. Criteria for the award include direct relationships between program goals and methods, measurable student outcomes, a program's adaptability to other schools, novel and creative approaches, and teacher responsibility, commitment, and empowerment.

University of Redlands (MA I)
University of Redlands/Franklin Elementary School Partnership
Grades served: E   Schools served: 1   Year established: 1988
Location of schools served: SU   Type of schools served: PUB

The major purpose of this partnership is to improve the educational opportunities for at-risk elementary students at Franklin and to provide increased opportunities for field work for University of Redlands teacher candidates. The program includes a teacher center and focuses on support for professional development and resources for preservice and experienced teachers.

COLORADO

University of Northern Colorado (DOC I)
Partnership for Professional Renewal of Master Teachers
Grades served: E, M, HS   Schools served: 10   Year established: 1988
Location of schools served: UR, SU, RU   Type of schools served: PUB, PRI

Through the collaborative efforts of the University of Northern Colorado's Teacher Induction Partnership and local school districts, this program enables master teachers to assume faculty status, teach methods classes, and supervise student teachers. The university provides a graduate intern to participating school districts in exchange for a master teacher. The link between the theoretical expertise of educators at the university and the practical expertise of master K-12 teachers enhances teaching and learning at both levels.

Southern Illinois University at Carbondale (RES II)
Southern Illinois School-College Collaboration Committee

Grades served: HS

Schools served: 9

Year established: NR

Location of schools served: RU

Type of schools served: PUB

With support from high school and university administrators, the Southern Illinois School-College Collaboration Committee was formed to address the needs of English departments in the area. The committee consists of representatives from English departments in nine area high schools and Southern Illinois University. Its primary mission is to provide opportunities for interaction among teachers and students. Activities include a speakers bureau, which brings graduate students into the public schools, and meetings twice a semester to exchange lesson plans or read students' essays. Future plans include yearly workshops and a newsletter.

INDIANA

University of Evansville (MA I)
Outstanding Educator Award

Grades served: E, M, HS

Schools served: 60

Year established: 1993

Location of schools served: UR, SU

Type of schools served: PUB, PRI

The Outstanding Educator Award is a cooperative effort to recognize outstanding teachers for their contributions of service, instruction, curricula, and leadership. The effort links the University of Evansville, all private and public schools in Vanderburgh County, and Bristol-Myers Squibb Company. In addition, award-winning practicing teachers share experiences with college students and have inservice opportunities through the university.

KANSAS

Saint Mary College (BA II)
River Valley English Alliance

Grades served: M, HS

Schools served: 40

Year established: 1990

Location of schools served: UR, SU, RU

Type of schools served: PUB, PRI

The River Valley English Alliance is a fluid group of middle school through university English teachers who meet five times a year at a luncheon/workshop to exchange ideas, materials, and structural resources common to the teaching of English. Member schools take turns hosting the group of two dozen or fewer. Typical programs have featured methods of teaching literature, learning centers, writing-across-the-curriculum, portfolio assessment, and computer-assisted instruction.

MARYLAND

Johns Hopkins University (RES I)
Baltimore School and Family Connections Project

Grades served: E, M, HS

Schools served: 26

Year established: 1987

Location of schools served: UR, SU, RU

Type of schools served: PUB

This project links Johns Hopkins University and the schools in a set of projects to design, implement, evaluate, and disseminate methods of family-school-community collaboration. Projects include a variety of parent involvement activities in elementary, middle, and high schools, work with parental roles in homework for language arts and science-health in two middle schools, activities with parent volunteers in social studies and art in two middle schools, and support of the Mayor's Grants for family-school partnerships in ten schools.

Note: Each institution's Carnegie class is given in parentheses. **Key:** E=elementary school, HS=high school, M=middle school, NR=not reported, PRI=private, PUB=public, RU=rural, SU=suburban, UR=urban

Madonna University (MA I)
Integrating the Humanities and Teacher Preparation
Grades served: E, M, HS   Schools served: 3   Year established: 1994
Location of schools served: SU   Type of schools served: PUB, PRI

Integrating the Humanities and Teacher Education links Madonna University with Livonia and Plymouth-Canton Public Schools in an NEH-funded project designed to promote dialogue about the significant role of the humanities in teacher education and cooperation among general education faculty in the humanities, master teachers from surrounding K-12 school districts, and professional education faculty. The two-year project teams four university faculty members per year with master teachers in the schools to learn about one another's pedagogical demands and to share their content expertise. One component of the grant is a Humanities Professors in the Schools program.

City University of New York LaGuardia Community College (AA)
Mathematics Adjunct Program
Grades served: NR   Schools served: 3   Year established: 1992
Location of schools served: UR   Type of schools served: PUB

The Mathematics Adjunct Program recognizes and seeks to harness the excellence and expertise of secondary school teachers in Queens. To do so, the department has set aside adjunct faculty positions, selecting teachers to serve for two 12-week semesters. In addition to their regular instructional responsibilities, adjuncts attend department meetings and work closely with faculty mentors, who in turn make themselves available to attend meetings and mathematics programs in each adjunct's school, with the intent to develop mutually useful projects and activities.

City University of New York Queens College (MA I)
Project SCOPE (School-College Operation in Physical Education)
Grades served: NR   Schools served: 7   Year established: 1980
Location of schools served: UR   Type of schools served: PUB, PRI

Project SCOPE is a partnership linking college personnel and school practitioners from schools in the New York City area. The project targets the separate domains of school curricula, staff development, and teacher education (preservice and inservice), integrating them to effect systemic change and improvement. Participants have produced more than 25 collaborative works, engaged in new professional roles, and conducted action-research studies to effect change. The project, one of the oldest in the nation, is one of the few that takes a comprehensive, holistic approach to improving and reforming education.

State University of New York College at New Paltz (MA I)
Dean's Award for Excellence in Teaching
Grades served: NR   Schools served: 45   Year established: 1983
Location of schools served: UR, RU   Type of schools served: PUB

The Dean's Award for Excellence in Teaching is awarded annually by the School of Education at SUNY-College at New Paltz to teachers in the Mid-Hudson Valley. Teachers in each county are nominated by their superintendents, and a committee of faculty members at the college select six to eight teachers.

NORTH CAROLINA

Western Carolina University (MA I)
Model Clinical Teaching Program

Grades served: E, M, HS   Schools served: 10   Year established: 1988
Location of schools served: RU   Type of schools served: PUB

The Model Clinical Teaching Program at Western Carolina University focuses on this collaboration with public schools in the region to improve teacher education. Education majors receive support from public school teachers during early field experiences and during student teaching. Clinical faculty from public schools and the university team-teach selected methods courses. The program is part of a statewide network that has 11 other programs in universities throughout North Carolina.

OHIO

Ashland University (MA I)
Teacher Team Leader Program

Grades served: NR   Schools served: 1   Year established: 1991
Location of schools served: NR   Type of schools served: PUB

The Teacher Team Leader Program is a collaboration of Ashland University and Wellington Exempted Village Schools. Each year a Wellington Schools teacher, who has been trained to be a team leader is selected to spend one full year working with faculty and students at Ashland University and teachers in Wellington Schools. Teacher-leaders teach college-level courses on the university campus, supervise student teachers, and assist and coach Wellington teachers for the improvement of instruction.

PENNSYLVANIA

Susquehanna University (BA II)
Susquehanna University/Liberty Valley Project

Grades served: E   Schools served: 1   Year established: 1991
Location of schools served: RU   Type of schools served: PUB

This partnership links the university and one elementary school in the Danville School District. University faculty, administrators, and students; school district teachers and administrators; and student teachers design, carry out, and evaluate the student teaching experience. Practicum master teachers provide seminars on current trends and practices. Students are teamed in the school (four to six per site), and the university supervisor is in residence one day each week during student teaching. The university is adapting this model for use with two additional school districts.

□ □ □

Note: Each institution's Carnegie class is given in parentheses. **Key:** E=elementary school, HS=high school, M=middle school, NR=not reported, PRI=private, PUB=public, RU=rural, SU=suburban, UR=urban

Part Three
ARTICULATION, DEVELOPMENT, AND EVALUATION OF CURRICULUM AND INSTRUCTION

Introduction

A natural arena for cooperation between schools and colleges is the development and evaluation of courses, even entire curriculum, for the purpose of improving students' achievement. School and college faculty are combining their talents to figure out what students need to know and how best to teach them. Together, they are working to design learning materials, including advanced computer software, to integrate more fully powerful learning technologies into instruction. The programs and agreements featured in Section One, "Curriculum and Instructional Materials Development," include those created for major curricular revision and for better articulating instruction in various content areas as students move from school to college. Inservice training for teachers is often a key component of these cooperative arrangements. For example, Webster University's For the Love of Mathematics project links university faculty and school district curriculum specialists from 14 elementary schools in producing videos focusing on theory, strategies, and materials for developing students' enthusiasm for math. Teachers also receive on-site consultation and seminar-based support throughout the school year.

In another program, more than 200 schools collaborate with the Colorado School of Mines in the Denver Earth Science Project. A partnership of corporations, federal agencies, school districts, and other universities has developed a series of educational modules addressing topics in earth science. The modules, prepared by teams composed of experienced earth science teachers and practicing scientists, deal with critical issues facing society. Each module incorporates input from teachers and industrial and government partners to ensure technical accuracy and relevance to current situations.

Section Two, "Instructional Research, Evaluation, and Testing," presents programs whose primary focus is educational research and evaluation in critical areas such as teacher education and staff development, curricular design, student assessment, the process and content of instruction, parenting skills, the special needs of certain at-risk populations, and the relationship of schools to their communities. Through such collaborations, schools, colleges, and universities pool their talent and resources to create research agendas, set priorities, disseminate results, and improve communication among institutions at all levels. For example, for the past 20 years, Mississippi State University and 25 regional urban, suburban, and rural school districts have supported the Program for Research and Evaluation in Public Schools (PREPS). With support from grants, contracts, and membership fees, PREPS focuses exclusively on longitudinal research and evaluation projects identified by member districts. In a similar arrangement, the University of Wisconsin-Eau Claire entered into a formal partnership with area school districts in 1988 to provide systematic K-12 program evaluation as part of the university's educational outreach. Funding for the partnership comes from a statewide organization, the Wisconsin School Evaluation Consortium, whose member districts pay an annual fee to the consortium. An evaluation consultant from the university provides consulting and inservice training for teachers in northwest Wisconsin.

A rapidly growing category of collaborative programs, thanks in part to funding from the Perkins Act, is represented through the examples in Section Three, "Tech-Prep 2+2 and Coordinated Vocational-Technical Programs." This section describes how such programs are intended to carefully articulate the sequence of instruction for students in grades 11-14 — that is, during the final two years of high school and two years of technical or community college. Such programs can shorten the time required to earn an associate's degree, reduce duplication of instruction or the need for remediation, and make better use of scarce community educational resources. Inherent in such partnerships is a close working relationship among school faculty, college faculty, and the business community regarding curriculum development and assessment of students' learning. Many of the cooperative models in this section feature the option for high school students to earn college credits for completing approved course sequences. In addition to improved curricular articulation, other benefits of these programs include resource-sharing agreements, counseling and career awareness services, student scholarships, and special incentives and services for underrepresented and disadvantaged students. CUNY-Bronx's Tech Prep Program, for example, is a partnership involving CUNY-Bronx, CUNY-Lehman, the New York City public and vocational high schools, the Bronx Educational Opportunity Center, and the Superintendent's Office of Occupational Education. The program seeks to develop a seamless, nonduplicative, four-year (grades 11-14) course of study leading to associate degrees in allied health, nursing, or health records. Mathematics, sciences, communications, and health technologies are emphasized. Another tech-prep consortium links Western Nebraska Community College with eight area secondary schools to offer students a curriculum that blends academic and vocational subjects, preparing students for technical and collegiate degrees to meet the goals of Work Force 2000. The consortium also provides inservice training in applied and integrated academics, financial support in purchasing curriculum materials and equipment, career assessment, articulation of curriculum among secondary and postsecondary instructors and the business community, and a summer internship program for teachers in the private sector.   □

Section One
Curriculum and Instructional Materials Development

CALIFORNIA

University of California-Davis (RES I)
College Preparatory Mathematics: Change From Within
Grades served: M, HS   Schools served: 457   Year established: 1989
Location of schools served: UR, SU, RU   Type of schools served: PUB, PRI

The College Preparatory Mathematics program was originally a partnership involving two mathematicians from two local universities and a group of 30 secondary math teachers, half from three school districts and half teacher-leaders involved in the Northern California Mathematics Project. Their purpose was to create, pilot, and revise curricula and teaching methods used in traditional algebra and geometry courses. Through presentations at conferences and inservice workshops given by teachers who became involved in the program, it has become a statewide effort; its focus is now on developing alternative approaches to assessment, including classroom research.

University of Redlands (MA I)
Implementing "It's Elementary!" Through Collaborative Arrangements
Grades served: E   Schools served: 4   Year established: 1993
Location of schools served: UR, SU   Type of schools served: PUB

Elementary educators accept in theory the goals and themes in the California Department of Education's "It's Elementary!" reform document, but the practical application of these ideas in the classroom is often difficult. One way to increase classroom application is to provide support and opportunities for collaboration to all participants involved in elementary education: preservice teachers, inservice teachers, and support personnel. This project brings student teachers, master teachers, school administrators, and college faculty together to increase their knowledge of the recommendations in the document and to provide the necessary support to implement them.

Note: Each institution's Carnegie class is given in parentheses. **Key:** E=elementary school, HS=high school, M=middle school, NR=not reported, PRI=private, PUB=public, RU=rural, SU=suburban, UR=urban

COLORADO

Colorado School of Mines (DOC II)
Denver Earth Science Project

Grades served: E, M, HS   Schools served: 200   Year established: 1989
Location of schools served: UR, SU, RU   Type of schools served: PUB, PRI

The Denver Earth Science Project is a K-12 curriculum development effort coordinated by the Colorado School of Mines. A partnership of corporations, federal agencies, school districts, and other universities is developing a series of educational modules addressing topics in earth science. The modules, prepared by teams composed of experienced earth science teachers and practicing scientists, deal with critical issues facing society. Teachers design and write the materials, with input from industrial and government partners to ensure technical accuracy and relevance to current situations.

DELAWARE

University of Delaware (RES II)
Project 21

Grades served: E, M, HS   Schools served: 17   Year established: 1991
Location of schools served: UR, SU, RU   Type of schools served: PUB

The university's Project 21, funded by the National Science Foundation, is part of the state's New Directions reform initiative. Focusing specifically on math and science teaching, the project has three goals: to develop models of new, effective teaching, learning, and assessment practices in science and mathematics based on the needs of particular schools; to develop teachers who can effectively implement these practices; and to incorporate the practices into every classroom in every school, bringing math and science alive for every child.

University of Delaware (RES II)
Delaware Teacher Enhancement Project (DTEP)

Grades served: M   Schools served: 3   Year established: 1992
Location of schools served: NR   Type of schools served: PUB

The goals of the Delaware Teacher Enhancement Project include increasing mathematical power in middle school teachers and helping to develop curricula based on the content standards recommended by the National Council of Teachers of Mathematics. DTEP features partnerships between project staff and middle school teachers, development of local teachers' and administrators' leadership, enhancement of school/community environments supporting instructional change, and promotion of such concepts as teacher-as-learner, teacher-as-researcher, context-driven teaching, interdisciplinary approaches to mathematics teaching, and technologically rich learning environments.

FLORIDA

University of South Florida–St. Petersburg (RES II)
Rawlings Elementary School Developmental Writing Program

Grades served: E   Schools served: 1   Year established: 1992
Location of schools served: UR, SU   Type of schools served: PUB

The University of South Florida-St. Petersburg and Pinellas County Schools are engaged in a partnership and professional outreach program at Marjorie Kinnan Rawlings Elementary, an innovative developmental writing school. The Poynter Institute for Media Studies also supports the program. A university faculty member on site works with teachers and university interns and supports curriculum development. The intensive on-site training for teachers improves their skill in teaching writing and helping students use writing to learn. Rawlings has adopted an inclusion model for special education.

Manchester College (BA II)
Environmental Education-Through Koinonia Environmental Center of Manchester College

Grades served: E, M, HS   Schools served: 13   Year established: 1985
Location of schools served: SU, RU   Type of schools served: PUB

This project has involved Whitko Community School Corporation and Manchester College in an effort to integrate environmental lessons across all disciplines. The program was developed by math, English, art, social studies, and science teachers. Plans for tech-prep and curriculum development workshops for biology teachers in seven regional tech-prep consortium high schools are under way.

University of Maine at Farmington (BA I)
Institute on the Common Core of Learning

Grades served: E, M, HS   Schools served: 2   Year established: 1992
Location of schools served: RU   Type of schools served: PUB

The Institute on the Common Core of Learning, a three-year partnership funded by Champion International Paper Company, involves two school districts in Maine and the University of Maine at Farmington. The partnership examines the effect that the Maine Common Core of Learning will have on curricula, assessment, teaching, and learning at the two districts and the university. The project has networked with other school districts engaged in systematic reform and shared project results at a statewide conference in June 1995.

Bridgewater State College (MA I)
High Schools/High Skills

Grades served: E, M, HS   Schools served: 6   Year established: 1993
Location of schools served: SU   Type of schools served: PUB

High Schools/High Skills trains and educates southeastern Massachusetts youth and adults in state-of-the-art technologies that will provide new career and educational opportunities for the region and enhance plans for regional economic development. Technology centers will be established in K-12 schools, area colleges, and collaboratives throughout the region. The goal is to establish a regional framework of tech centers for disseminating information and services, linking educational organizations, businesses, employment boards, and technology manufacturers.

Worcester Polytechnic Institute (DOC II)
WPI School-College Collaborative

Grades served: E, M, HS   Schools served: 70   Year established: 1988
Location of schools served: UR, SU   Type of schools served: PUB, PRI

The WPI School-College Collaborative involves WPI, a private university; the Massachusetts Academy for Mathematics and Science, a public high school on the WPI campus; and participating regional public and private K-12 schools. Its goals are to improve math and science education through WPI students' and teachers' conducting experiments in curriculum reform, and to promote discussions about pedagogy among K-16 teachers. Both goals are supported by the academy, which in turn provides opportunities for inservice training and outreach to communities lacking technologically based education.

Note: Each institution's Carnegie class is given in parentheses. **Key:** E=elementary school, HS=high school, M=middle school, NR=not reported, PRI=private, PUB=public, RU=rural, SU=suburban, UR=urban

St. Louis Community College at Meramec (AA)
Landmarks

Grades served: M, HS	Schools served: 15	Year established: 1985
Location of schools served: UR, SU, RU	Type of schools served: PUB, PRI	

Landmarks creates a learning community of art, social studies, humanities, and writing teachers to improve teaching and learning. Participants design a collaborative research project to document local aspects of a shared annual theme. Students research primary documents, do interviews, and observe as a class team. Classes then design, write, and edit collaborative articles to submit to a juried annual book showcasing students' work, where their teachers also report goals, processes, and results related to the question pursued. The program also includes a one-week seminar, periodic team meetings of teachers, support for improving students' academic motivation and their skills of research, critical thinking, writing, and presentation across the curriculum.

University of Missouri-Columbia (RES I)
Instructional Materials Laboratory

Grades served: E, M, HS	Schools served: NR	Year established: 1969
Location of schools served: UR, SU, RU	Type of schools served: PUB	

The nationally recognized Instructional Materials Laboratory (IML) involves faculty, leadership of the Vocational and Adult Education section of the Department of Elementary and Secondary Education, and the laboratory's staff in cooperatively developing instructional materials. IML is distinctive among curriculum development labs around the country in that it uses input from faculty in the pedagogical development effort and teacher and industry advisory committees to ensure that the materials are appropriate.

Webster University (MA I)
For the Love of Mathematics

Grades served: E	Schools served: 14	Year established: 1993
Location of schools served: SU	Type of schools served: PUB	

For the Love of Mathematics is a collaboration of Webster University and the Webster Groves School District. University professors and school district curriculum specialists jointly produce videos aimed at developing the love of mathematics among teachers and their pupils. The project focuses on the theory, strategies, and materials for developing students' enthusiasm in math and tools for identifying students' concepts and attitudes about mathematics. Teachers receive on-site consultation and seminar-based support throughout the school year.

New Mexico State University-Main Campus (RES I)
TV Earth

Grades served: M	Schools served: 100	Year established: 1992
Location of schools served: UR, SU, RU	Type of schools served: PUB	

TV Earth was created to provide videotapes to middle schools across New Mexico to teach environmental concepts. Interactive video programs are being developed. The program's sponsors plan to move to an interactive video format and to expand it beyond the 100 New Mexico middle schools currently involved.

NEW YORK

Mohawk Valley Community College (AA)
Science of Toys

Grades served: E, M, HS   Schools served: 26   Year established: 1989
Location of schools served: UR, SU, RU   Type of schools served: PUB, PRI

Science of Toys is a presentation/demonstration of how science is involved in making and using many of the toys children of all ages, nursery through high school, play with. Its purpose is to interest children in science and technology at an early age and eventually to motivate them to consider study and careers in the fields.

State University of New York College at Cortland (MA I)
Cortland Curriculum Confab

Grades served: E, M, HS   Schools served: NR   Year established: 1990
Location of schools served: UR, SU, RU   Type of schools served: PUB

The Cortland Curriculum Confab is a group of local school administrators interested in issues involving curriculum. The coordinator of the educational administration program at Cortland and the director of curriculum for Homer Central Schools share responsibility for the program. Approximately 12 people from surrounding schools and the college meet monthly to address concerns in an informal, focused atmosphere. Topics include implementation of the Compact for Learning, planning for special education, teacher preparation, and staff development.

NORTH CAROLINA

University of North Carolina at Charlotte (MA I)
Mathematics and Science Education Center

Grades served: M, HS   Schools served: 423   Year established: 1983
Location of schools served: UR, SU, RU   Type of schools served: PUB, PRI

A major focus of the Mathematics and Science Education Center is to foster and establish partnerships among K-12 schools, community colleges, state and local agencies, and businesses and industries to address local, state, and national concerns in mathematics and science. The Knight Foundation Mathematics Pathways Project, for example, is a joint effort of the university, Central Piedmont Community College, and the Charlotte-Mecklenburg School System to improve instruction and learning in prealgebra and algebra. The program seeks to support faculty development of an integrated, articulated mathematics curriculum, and specific programs for minority and female students.

Wake Forest University (DOC II)
LEGACY (Linking Educators and the Gifted With Attorneys for Civics: Yes!)

Grades served: NR   Schools served: NR   Year established: 1992
Location of schools served: UR, SU, RU   Type of schools served: PUB, PRI

LEGACY consists of an annual teacher institute where teachers from all 50 states review and develop civics curricula for gifted and talented students. The Center for Research and Development in Law-Related Education (CRADLE), a national, nonprofit organization affiliated with Wake Forest's School of Law, also teams those teachers with volunteer attorneys in cooperation with Phi Alpha Delta Public Service Center in Washington, D.C.

Note: Each institution's Carnegie class is given in parentheses. **Key:** E=elementary school, HS=high school, M=middle school, NR=not reported, PRI=private, PUB=public, RU=rural, SU=suburban, UR=urban

OHIO

The Ohio State University-Main Campus (RES I)
ESEP (Earth Systems Education Program)

Grades served: E, M, HS	Schools served: NR	Year established: 1990
Location of schools served: UR, SU, RU	Type of schools served: PUB	

ESEP is a regional school-university program designed to restructure the K-12 science education program, and provide a cooperative classroom environment. Schools from ten Central Ohio school systems have been actively involved in the program, supported by several federal and state agencies and the Ohio State University. ESEP provides teacher enhancement and curriculum development programs cooperatively planned and staffed by elementary, middle, and high school teachers and university science education and science faculty.

OKLAHOMA

Oklahoma State University (RES II)
Early Placement Evaluation in Mathematics

Grades served: M, HS	Schools served: 140	Year established: 1987
Location of schools served: UR, SU, RU	Type of schools served: PUB, PRI	

This program, a cooperative project of higher education and the schools of Oklahoma, supports teachers' effort to motivate students by linking school and college mathematics and by providing individual evaluations of preparation in mathematics for college. Modeled on projects in Ohio (EMPT) and California (MDTP), mathematics articulation is supported through diagnostic and early placement testing for grades 7-12. Approximately 140 schools and 25,000 students participate annually.

PENNSYLVANIA

Lebanon Valley College (BA II)
Science Education Partnership

Grades served: E, M	Schools served: NR	Year established: 1993
Location of schools served: NR	Type of schools served: PUB, PRI	

This partnership focuses on teacher and curriculum development for grades 4-8 in 14 school districts in a five-county area. It offers summer workshops, inservice training, an equipment and experiment lending library, and a communications network to all the schools.

Temple University (RES I)
Temple University-School District of Philadelphia Exemplary Schools Project

Grades served: E, M, HS	Schools served: 3	Year established: 1986
Location of schools served: UR	Type of schools served: PUB	

This project is designed to demonstrate the feasibility and effectiveness of implementing and institutionalizing the improvement of instruction and learning in urban neighborhood schools through the shared responsibility of school, home, and the community. Drawing together the resources and expertise of Temple University, the School District of Philadelphia, community social service agencies, and local businesses, the project demonstrates community-based efforts to build effective urban schools. The overall goal is to develop and demonstrate model instruction and service delivery systems to improve learning.

SOUTH CAROLINA

University of South Carolina-Columbia (RES II)
SC Comprehensive School Health Education Coalition

Grades served: E, M, HS	Schools served: NR	Year established: 1992
Location of schools served: UR, SU, RU	Type of schools served: PUB	

The South Carolina Division of the American Cancer Society serves as the institutional home for this coalition, whose members include institutions of higher education, community health and PTA organizations, state agencies, school districts, and health- and education-related professional organizations. The purpose of the coalition is to promote the development of effective school health education programs that include quality instruction and a supportive, healthful school environment for K-12 student in South Carolina. The coalition includes committees on resources, advocacy, curriculum, and higher education.

TEXAS

Northeast Texas Community College (AA)
Quality Work Force Planning

Grades served: E, M, HS	Schools served: 50	Year established: 1988
Location of schools served: UR, SU, RU	Type of schools served: PUB, PRI	

Quality Work Force Planning is a partnership established among employers, educators, and trainers to develop a skilled and educated workforce. With growing international competition and the impact of advances in technology, northeast Texas employers realize they must incorporate more sophisticated equipment and processes in their operations. Students receive tutoring, mentoring and counseling toward postsecondary education and careers and coordinated tech-prep and vocational-technical opportunities. Inservice support and training are available for teachers in the cooperating schools.

University of Texas Health Science Center at San Antonio (MED)
MESS (Modules for the Exploration of Science in Schools)

Grades served: E, M, HS	Schools served: NR	Year established: NR
Location of schools served: NR	Type of schools served: NR	

The Department of Microbiology, in partnership with UT-San Antonio's Alliance for Education, conducts a summer demonstration project for primary and secondary school teachers (including math, biology, physics, music, and art specialists) to create a library of reusable, innovative modules for the exploration of science and biotechnology. Other programs established by the department include MISS (Microbiology Instruction for Secondary Schools), MET (Microbiology for Elementary Teachers), and MIMS (Microbiology Instruction for Middle Schools). The program aims to improve teachers' and staff members' education and enhance the schools' academic, health, and social environments.

Note: Each institution's Carnegie class is given in parentheses. **Key:** E=elementary school, HS=high school, M=middle school, NR=not reported, PRI=private, PUB=public, RU=rural, SU=suburban, UR=urban

Christopher Newport University (BA II)
Stars Project

Grades served: HS	Schools served: 11	Year established: 1993
Location of schools served: UR	Type of schools served: PUB	

Christopher Newport University, Thomas Nelson Community College, and the Newport News, Hampton, and York County public schools are cooperating on a series of five interrelated reforms for grades 9-14. The reforms treat teachers and students as researchers, and provide a seamless curriculum in science, mathematics, and computer science from grade 9 through introductory college. The project serves a region whose population is 31% minority and is the dominant center for high-tech development in Virginia outside of Washington, D.C.

Section Two

Instructional Research, Evaluation, and Testing

CALIFORNIA

Stanford University (RES I)
Stanford Educational Cooperative

Grades served: E, M, HS	Schools served: NR	Year established: 1986
Location of schools served: UR, SU, RU	Type of schools served: PUB, PRI	

The Stanford Educational Collaborative (formerly the Stanford/Schools Collaborative) supports an array of partnerships between Stanford University and school districts in the San Francisco Bay area. Its mission is to improve curricula and instruction through research and professional development for educators in elementary/secondary schools and the university. A steering committee of school and university representatives guides the overall activities of the collaborative, which includes the Alliance for School-Based Change, the Professional Development Center, Service Learning 2000, the school board computer bulletin board, teacher action research groups, research about collaboration, round tables and forums, and special conferences.

University of California-Davis (RES I)
CRESS (Cooperative Research and Extension Services for Schools) Center

Grades served: E, M, HS	Schools served: 2500	Year established: 1988
Location of schools served: UR, SU, RU	Type of schools served: PUB, PRI	

The CRESS Center is an effort by the University of California-Davis to strengthen its research contributions toward the improvement of elementary and secondary education. Administered through the Division of Education, the center employs extension specialists, who serve as intermediaries between university researchers and school practitioners. The center also manages long-term research and development relationships with several schools in the greater Sacramento area. Faculty and staff from the Davis campus and colleagues from participating schools meet to cooperatively design and conduct projects in educational research, curriculum development, and professional development for teachers and administrators.

University of California-Riverside (RES II)
California Educational Research Cooperative (CERC)
Grades served: NR   Schools served: NR   Year established: 1988
Location of schools served: UR, SU, RU   Type of schools served: PUB

CERC is a partnership of county offices of education, local school districts, and the university's School of Education, which pools fiscal and personnel resources to support improved educational planning and decision making. It serves as a research and development center for cooperating members, combining the professional experience and practical wisdom of practicing professionals with the theoretical interests and research talents of faculty in UCR's School of Education. CERC's Research Planning Council provides a cooperative forum for systematic study of and joint action addressing pressing problems facing public school leaders.

University of California-Santa Barbara (RES I)
UCSB/Schools/SBCC Partnership
Grades served: E, M, HS   Schools served: 102   Year established: 1987
Location of schools served: UR, SU, RU   Type of schools served: PUB

The UCSB/Schools/SBCC (Santa Barbara City College) Partnership was formed to create an intellectual forum for addressing issues confronting K-12 education, focusing on issues related to diversity, and to improve the local schools' communication with and access to the resources of the university's Graduate School of Education. Past activities of the partnership have included a yearly leadership institute and a quarterly speaker series for area administrators, school board members, and others. Current efforts include monthly meetings conducted by the county superintendent's office and faculty involvement in school-based research.

COLORADO

University of Colorado at Denver (DOC II)
Colorado Literacy Project
Grades served: E   Schools served: NR   Year established: NR
Location of schools served: NR   Type of schools served: PUB

A team of ten UCD researchers, in cooperation with the Denver Public Schools, is investigating the development of literacy skills of students from minority backgrounds. The study involves approximately 1,200 fourth- and fifth-grade students in 40 classrooms in schools with high enrollments of minority students from low-income neighborhoods. The purpose of the research is to describe classrooms that successfully develop proficiency in reading and writing. The research team has collected a wide variety of data (observations, interviews, student writing samples, attitude surveys, open-ended reading tests) to study the relationships between types of instruction and student outcomes.

INDIANA

Purdue University-Main Campus (RES I)
High School Testing Program-School of Science
Grades served: M, HS   Schools served: 210   Year established: 1984
Location of schools served: UR, RU   Type of schools served: PUB, PRI

This program provides students and teachers with a critical assessment of their achievements. Teachers may administer any of five exams (Algebra I, Algebra II, Trigonometry, Calculus I, Calculus II) at any time; results are supplied in approximately ten days. Each school is provided with individual results for each student, data analysis on questions, and information on how their students and their school compare with other students and schools in the state.

Note: Each institution's Carnegie class is given in parentheses. **Key:** E=elementary school, HS=high school, M=middle school, NR=not reported, PRI=private, PUB=public, RU=rural, SU=suburban, UR=urban

Morehead State University (MA I)
Eastern Kentucky Regional KERA Alliance Action Research Project

Grades served: M	Schools served: 2	Year established: 1993
Location of schools served: NR	Type of schools served: PUB	

The central objective of Morehead State University's and Pikeville Elementary School's participation in the KERA (Kentucky Education Reform Act of 1990) Alliance is to investigate exemplary organizational and curricular models to determine a long-range plan for implementation of KERA initiatives in Pikeville in the intermediate grades. KERA requires schools to increase their attendance rates; reduce dropout rates; reduce physical and mental barriers to learning; and increase students' successful transition to postsecondary education or employment. With the help of MSU faculty, the school team invites a teacher/consultant to share his or her experience in implementation of a plan responding to KERA in an attempt to reach consensus on a long-term plan for Pikeville.

University of Louisville (DOC I)
Center for Collaborative Advancement of the Teaching Profession

Grades served: NR	Schools served: 100	Year established: 1987
Location of schools served: NR	Type of schools served: PUB	

The Center for Collaborative Advancement of the Teaching Profession was established in the School of Education by the Kentucky Council on Higher Education. The center develops, implements, and studies collaborative efforts to improve teaching. More than 20 projects are affiliated with the center, including redesign of the university's teacher education programs, establishment of professional development schools, a college/school/business partnership for joint governance of two schools, and programs to recruit minority teachers.

Johns Hopkins University (RES I)
Model Middle Schools

Grades served: M	Schools served: 4	Year established: 1989
Location of schools served: UR	Type of schools served: PUB	

The Johns Hopkins Model Middle Schools project works with several Baltimore City Public Schools to design, institute, and evaluate new practices to increase students' motivation, attachment to school, and learning. Recent innovations include a new cooperative-education-based curriculum in reading and writing (Student Team Reading), advanced use of interdisciplinary teacher teams, advisory curricula, and methods for providing extra academic help to students who need it.

Johns Hopkins University (RES I)
Beginning School Study

Grades served: E, M, HS	Schools served: NR	Year established: 1982
Location of schools served: UR	Type of schools served: PUB	

The Johns Hopkins Beginning School Study is a longitudinal research project that has followed a random sample of about 800 students who began first grade in Baltimore in 1982 to the present. Its purpose is to shed light on the cognitive, socioemotional, and general educational development of normal youngsters, both African-American and white, from all socioeconomic levels.

University of Maryland-College Park (RES I)
Drug Use Survey in Prince George's County Public Schools

Grades served: E, M, HS
Schools served: 200
Year established: 1989
Location of schools served: NR
Type of schools served: PUB

This survey is a collaboration of the university and the Prince George's County school system. The first drug survey, of approximately 2,800 students (grades 4- 6), was conducted during spring 1989. The results were used to select sites for after-school programs. A second survey is designed to accrue annual information about the nature, extent, and natural history of drug involvement in preadolescents and adolescents. Additional surveys will examine factors contributing to identified links between involvement with drugs and gender, neighborhood, exposure to violence, status as a latchkey child, and influence of peers.

MICHIGAN

Wayne State University (RES I)
University Public School

Grades served: M
Schools served: 1
Year established: 1991
Location of schools served: NR
Type of schools served: PUB

University Public School is a Michigan coeducational, public middle school operated by Wayne State University. The school emphasizes educational innovation and change, with the overall goal to create a school that will prepare students for high school and beyond in an innovative, creative, and competency-based atmosphere that will allow teaching professionals to work as a highly motivated team. All students in grades 6-8 living in the city of Detroit are eligible to attend. Students are selected by random lottery.

MINNESOTA

Mayo Foundation-Mayo Graduate School (HLTH)
Rochester Area Math/Science Partnership

Grades served: E, M, HS
Schools served: 8
Year established: 1991
Location of schools served: SU, RU
Type of schools served: PUB, PRI

The Rochester Area Math/Science Partnership was formed to improve the participation and achievement in math, science, and technology of all K-12 students in the Rochester area. The Mayo Foundation-Mayo Graduate School and IBM have joined with Rochester Public Schools and the Zumbro Education District to support targeted projects. A long-term project also has been developed to incorporate world-class standards for the way math and science are taught in area schools.

University of Minnesota-Twin Cities (RES I)
Center for Applied Research and Educational Improvement

Grades served: E, M, HS
Schools served: 30
Year established: 1987
Location of schools served: UR, SU, RU
Type of schools served: PUB, PRI

The Center for Applied Research and Educational Improvement (CAREI) is a collaboration of the University of Minnesota's College of Education and 30 school districts. CAREI attempts to foster long-term links between university faculty and Minnesota schools, to nurture collaborative research that develops and applies theory while addressing important issues confronting schools, and to provide ways for schools to draw upon relevant research. The center sponsors seminars in curriculum content, organizes collaborative research, conducts evaluation research, provides a range of publications and services, and is developing capabilities for disseminating information via the Internet.

Note: Each institution's Carnegie class is given in parentheses. **Key:** E=elementary school, HS=high school, M=middle school, NR=not reported, PRI=private, PUB=public, RU=rural, SU=suburban, UR=urban

MISSISSIPPI

Mississippi State University (RES II)
Program for Research and Evaluation in Public Schools, Inc. (PREPS)
Grades served: E, M, HS
Location of schools served: UR, SU, RU

Schools served: 25
Type of schools served: PUB

Year established: 1976

PREPS is a private, nonprofit corporation and a program of the Bureau of Educational Research and Evaluation at Mississippi State University. Its resources, from membership fees, grants, and contracts, are devoted exclusively to research and evaluation designated by member districts. Research and evaluation are longitudinal, running from three to seven years. Mississippi school districts become members because of their interest in various research projects.

NEW HAMPSHIRE

Dartmouth College (DOC II)
Collaborative Learning
Grades served: E, M, HS
Location of schools served: SU, RU

Schools served: 5
Type of schools served: PUB

Year established: 1981

Collaborative Learning is a partnership of educators at Dartmouth College and the Dresden School District that was the first interstate school compact in the United States. Combining research and practice, Dartmouth and Dresden faculty and local businesses develop teaching methods for improving thinking and problem solving and create and evaluate curricular modules and teaching methods to enhance collaborative learning for students in all grades. Faculty teach in on another's classrooms, take sabbaticals in each other's schools, conduct research in each other's classrooms, and serve on one another's committees, and their students participate in one another's classes.

NEW YORK

Cornell University (RES I)
Mathematics Education Research Collaboration
Grades served: E, M, HS
Location of schools served: SU, RU

Schools served: 5
Type of schools served: PUB

Year established: 1986

The Mathematics Education Research Collaboration works closely with local schools to implement new curricula and to examine their impact on students' learning. At the elementary level, projects have focused on the early introduction to multiplication, division, and ratios through applied problem solving and model building. Projects during summer programs for middle and high schools have concentrated on the use of contextual problems, multi representational software and transformations to introduce functions to students through summer programs. An all-year program with the Alternative Community School in Ithaca integrates physics and trigonometry. A new project introducing algebra through the use of technology design projects has been proposed for middle schools.

OHIO

Malone College (BA II)
Consultants for Even Start Family Literacy Programs
Grades served: E
Location of schools served: RU

Schools served: NR
Type of schools served: PUB

Year established: 1992

The purpose of this partnership between Malone College and the Even Start Family Literacy Program of Wayne County is to determine the extent to which the program has been successful. Consultants compare objectives and outcomes for the family literacy center and then recommend changes in the curriculum, instruction, and program delivery.

VIRGINIA

College of William and Mary (DOC I)
Tidewater Area School/University Research Consortium
Grades served: E, M, HS   Schools served: 15   Year established: 1993
Location of schools served: UR, SU, RU   Type of schools served: PUB

This consortium links the college and the public schools in an effort to motivate and guide systemic reform. The consortium investigates questions of interest to the schools regarding appropriate policy and successful educational practice. It facilitates collaborative research between the college and local school divisions to improve students' learning, providing a context for ongoing dialogue about high-priority educational needs in Virginia schools.

WISCONSIN

University of Wisconsin-Eau Claire (MA I)
Wisconsin Consortium for School Improvement
Grades served: E, M, HS   Schools served: NR   Year established: 1988
Location of schools served: UR, SU, RU   Type of schools served: PUB, PRI

This partnership provides systematic K-12 program evaluation as part of the university's educational outreach. Funding for the partnership comes from a statewide organization, the Wisconsin School Evaluation Consortium (SEC), whose member districts pay an annual fee to the consortium. An evaluation consultant from the university provides consulting and inservice training for teachers in approximately 55 school districts in northwest Wisconsin. Teachers, guided by the consultant, conduct the evaluation studies so they can improve their programs.

Section Three
Tech-Prep 2+2 and Coordinated Vocational-Technical Programs

ALABAMA

Chattahoochee Valley State Community College (AA)
Tech-Prep Articulation
Grades served: HS   Schools served: 2   Year established: 1992
Location of schools served: UR, RU   Type of schools served: PUB

This articulation agreement is designed to establish a procedure to grant credit at CVSCC for competencies mastered in designated programs at Central High School and Russell County High School. Criteria were developed to maintain the integrity of the articulated courses. School and college faculty jointly participate in inservice training, program enhancement, and development.

ARIZONA

Cochise College (AA)
2+2 Program

Grades served: HS

Schools served: 4

Year established: 1992

Location of schools served: RU

Type of schools served: NR

This program is a formal curricular agreement between Cochise College and county high schools involving selected business and office education courses. If the faculty at a participating high school and college faculty agree that the student competency level for a particular course is identical at both the high school and college levels, the student may elect to transfer high school credit to the college for that course. The course then appears on the student's college transcripts upon the student's enrollment at the college.

Glendale Community College (AA)
Tech Prep

Grades served: HS

Schools served: 16

Year established: 1991

Location of schools served: SU

Type of schools served: PUB

This 2+2 tech-prep program includes drafting, business, child and family studies, and automotives. The main goal of the project is to develop an articulated curriculum that reflects the needs of business and industry. The college seeks funding for equipment that is relevant to current industry practices and for continued coordination of the program.

Pima County Community College District (AA)
Pima County Tech Prep Consortium

Grades served: HS

Schools served: 20

Year established: 1982

Location of schools served: UR

Type of schools served: PUB

The Pima County Tech Prep Consortium includes 20 high schools in seven school districts cooperating to produce sequenced, four-year curricula in advanced technology, office support, and automotive technology. With support from employers, the programs begin in the junior year of high school and end in an associate's degree.

ARKANSAS

Mississippi County Community College (AA)
Tech Prep 2+2 Program

Grades served: HS

Schools served: 4

Year established: 1991

Location of schools served: NR

Type of schools served: PUB

This program links the last two years of high school with the first two years of postsecondary training. It emphasizes associate's degree programs in business management, computer information systems, and office technology. Students select and enter a structured program of study in either college prep or tech-prep, with the opportunity to switch programs through grade 11. The partnership's schools, Osceola and Rivercrest High Schools, Cotton Boll Technical Institute, and Mississippi County Community College, have worked together to plan the project, focusing on computer applications, applied academics, hands-on applications, workplace readiness, and career/occupational readiness.

North Arkansas Community Technical College (AA)
North Arkansas Tech Prep Consortium
Grades served: HS   Schools served: 21   Year established: 1991
Location of schools served: NR   Type of schools served: PUB

The North Arkansas Tech Prep Consortium links the college and 21 area secondary schools. The mission of model school Jasper High School's Educational Reform Team is to ensure that all high school graduates complete a career action plan and obtain the skills necessary to be successful in their chosen careers, personal lives, and as lifelong learners. Major areas of focus include improving school structure to facilitate change and integrative activities; developing articulated 2+2 programs in business technologies, faculty-based career advising, implementing career action plans; and coordinating secondary-postsecondary evaluation, monitoring, and tracking systems.

CALIFORNIA

Bakersfield College (AA)
Kern/Southern Tulare Tech Prep Consortium
Grades served: HS   Schools served: 46   Year established: 1992
Location of schools served: UR, SU, RU   Type of schools served: PUB

The Kern/Southern Tulare Tech Prep Consortium, led by Bakersfield College, is composed of four community colleges, ten high school/unified districts, 46 high schools and Regional Occupational Centers, California State University-Bakersfield, California Employment Development, Employer's Training Resource, and private businesses and industries. Its emphasis is on developing tech-prep associate's degree majors for grades 11-14. The consortium provides teacher training, curriculum materials, some funding for equipment, information for students and parents, consultation, and support.

College of San Mateo (AA)
Tech Prep
Grades served: HS   Schools served: 10   Year established: 1993
Location of schools served: SU   Type of schools served: PUB

The consortium between the college and the San Mateo Union High School District and other high schools in San Mateo County is designed to articulate college courses in the community college, having identified courses in high school that will allow students to receive advanced placement and/or credit at the community college. Currently, programs in computer assisted drafting and business occupations have been articulated. The consortium also provides inservice training for instructors and curriculum alignment between the high school and community college.

Santa Barbara City College (AA)
Santa Barbara Articulation Council
Grades served: M, HS   Schools served: 6   Year established: 1986
Location of schools served: UR, SU   Type of schools served: PUB, PRI

This articulation council links Santa Barbara High School, Santa Barbara City College, the Carpinteria Unified School District, and the Santa Barbara County Schools. The council implements and supports programs to enable students to move from high school to college without losing time or resources. The program includes 2+2 arrangements that provide for transfer of credit or advanced standing in postsecondary institutions. Underrepresented junior high students receive options and opportunities for higher education, with follow-up surveys and college tours. Bilingual representatives keep Hispanic families informed of options, encouraging family involvement in students' planning.

COLORADO

Community College of Denver (AA)
TECH-PREP Project

Grades served: HS

Schools served: 2

Year established: 1991

Location of schools served: SU

Type of schools served: PUB

The primary mission of this partnership between the Denver Public Schools and the College of Denver is to offer the middle 50% of the high school population an opportunity to enroll in a 2+2+2 business/marketing and industrial technology program. It allows students to increase their competence in mathematics and communication, knowledge of technology, to experience success, and develop persistence.

Mesa State College (BA I)
Unified Technical Education Center (UTEC)

Grades served: HS

Schools served: 5

Year established: 1989

Location of schools served: SU, RU

Type of schools served: PUB

The Unified Technical Education Center is a joint venture of Mesa State College and Mesa County Valley School District No. 51 dedicated to lifelong learning and individualized vocational-technical education for school-age youth through adult. During the partnership's first phase, UTEC established a site in an industrial park; it plans to construct a campus capable of training individuals for business and industry, strongly tied to local economic. UTEC allows a continuum of study from high school to postsecondary certificates and degrees and joint use of funding.

CONNECTICUT

Naugatuck Valley Community-Technical College (AA)
Tech Prep (2+2) Program

Grades served: HS

Schools served: 30

Year established: 1992

Location of schools served: UR, SU

Type of schools served: PUB

This program serves approximately 1,000 students in 30 schools in 22 school districts. High school students must meet the same standards required of their community college peers, with proficiency tests administered to validate outcomes. The program offers students an opportunity to study accounting, auto technology, business, computers, computer drafting, early childhood education, hospitality, office administration, and technical drafting; it also offers inservice training for high school faculty, administrators, and guidance staff and programs for parents and students.

FLORIDA

Central Florida Community College (AA)
Mid-Florida Tech Prep Consortium

Grades served: HS

Schools served: 13

Year established: 1992

Location of schools served: UR, SU

Type of schools served: PUB

This consortium is a cooperative educational program that includes Central Florida Community College, the Citrus County school board, the Marion County School System, and the school board of Levy County. Its purpose is to develop a strong 4+2 tech-prep program by establishing comprehensive links between the college and member school districts, enabling students to prepare for high-wage technical occupations in business and office systems, health, engineering, and environmental technologies. The consortium emphasizes and implements applied course work in math, communications, and science. Students master skills required for more advanced courses and/or postsecondary educational programs, or for employment requiring technical skills in these fields.

Daytona Beach Community College (AA)
Volusia/Flagler Tech-Prep Consortium, Program of Applied Academics and Technical Studies

Grades served: HS   Schools served: 8   Year established: 1992
Location of schools served: NR   Type of schools served: PUB

The Program of Applied Academics and Technical Studies is a 2+2 tech-prep program involving Daytona Beach Community College, Volusia County Schools, and Flagler County Schools. It supports career counseling and goal setting in elementary and middle schools; academic courses to support the program; enhanced articulation models in technology, business, and health; dual-enrollment college credit courses during high school; and strategies to improve the technical competence of teachers and counselors involved in the program.

Polk Community College (AA)
Polk County Tech Prep Consortium

Grades served: HS   Schools served: 14   Year established: 1992
Location of schools served: UR, SU, RU   Type of schools served: PUB

This consortium develops and implements coherent, sequential programs of vocational and academic study leading to an associate degree in public service technology, business technology, and industrial technology. These programs of vocational and academic study combine four years of high school with two years of postsecondary education in an articulated sequence of courses emphasizing a strong academic core of applied mathematics, science communication, and computer science, with new and upgraded vocational secondary courses.

Seminole Community College (AA)
Tech Prep Consortium

Grades served: HS   Schools served: 6   Year established: 1991
Location of schools served: NR   Type of schools served: PUB

All six high schools participating in this consortium teach Applied Math I and II and have fully equipped Principals of Technology labs. The college has 77 articulation agreements in 24 articulation areas. Tech-prep seniors visit the campus every May to visit labs, learn about financial aid, and talk with counselors about course requirements and scheduling. In June, 100 sophomore girls are invited to the campus for a one-week program on nontraditional careers. Some students receive credit through academic appraisal of portfolios or year-end institutional exams administered by professionals.

GEORGIA

Brunswick College (AA)
Southeast Coastal Georgia Tech Prep Program

Grades served: M, HS   Schools served: 4   Year established: 1992
Location of schools served: RU   Type of schools served: PUB

This partnership of Brunswick College and feeder public schools emphasizes design and implementation of a seamless 2+2 occupational education curriculum in business, metals technology, and drafting. Major emphasis in the secondary schools is on implementing technology-based academic subjects, upgrading occupational subjects, and conducting activities designed to achieve public understanding and support of the program. In collaboration with the public schools and local business and industry leaders, college faculty are modifying the curriculum and programs to ensure articulation and introduction of advanced technologies.

Note: Each institution's Carnegie class is given in parentheses. **Key:** E=elementary school, HS=high school, M=middle school, NR=not reported, PRI=private, PUB=public, RU=rural, SU=suburban, UR=urban

Darton College (AA)
DoleecoTech Prep Consortium

Grades served: HS   Schools served: 6   Year established: 1991
Location of schools served: UR, RU   Type of schools served: PUB

Darton College, in partnership with two local public school systems and a local technical institute, has established a tech-prep program linking secondary and postsecondary courses of study. Planned sequencing of courses combines intensive technical preparation emphasizing critical thinking skills and the application of problem-solving techniques to real-world situations; coordinates academic and technical secondary and postsecondary instruction; uses business and industry input to create a climate encouraging all students to prepare for the technical workforce; and ensures articulation among educational and business groups to establish relationships among policies and procedures, programs and people.

ILLINOIS

Kaskaskia College (AA)
Tech Prep/Regional Delivery System

Grades served: HS   Schools served: NR   Year established: NR
Location of schools served: NR   Type of schools served: PUB

The Marion/Clinton/Washington Counties and Bond/Fayette/Effingham Counties Regional Delivery System has as its primary purpose the coordination of vocational courses offered at the high schools within the counties served with the requirements at Kaskaskia College. Certain programs have been specifically articulated with the college so that college credit may be earned through high school course work and proficiency exams taken at the college.

McHenry County College (AA)
Basic Nurse Assistant

Grades served: HS   Schools served: 3   Year established: 1989
Location of schools served: NR   Type of schools served: PUB

McHenry County College offers the Basic Nurse Assistant program for high school students. Upon completion, students receive high school and college credit plus certification to work as nurse assistants. The program serves students interested in health care careers and those seeking certification for employment. Plans were to serve five county high schools by fall 1994.

Moraine Valley Community College (AA)
Moraine Area Career System

Grades served: HS   Schools served: 11   Year established: 1987
Location of schools served: SU   Type of schools served: PUB

The Moraine Area Career System is a consortium of six high school districts and Moraine Valley Community College. The consortium, representing 25 suburban communities of southwestern Chicago, responds to the challenge of reforming education and works to develop an educational path integrating preparation for postsecondary course work with rigorous technical education so students possess the knowledge and skills demanded by modern business and industry.

Rock Valley College (AA)
Youth Apprenticeship

Grades served: HS

Location of schools served: NR

Schools served: 4

Type of schools served: PUB

Year established: 1992

A coalition of six manufacturing firms, four area high schools, the U.S. Department of Labor, and Rock Valley College developed the Youth Apprenticeship program in response to manufacturers' needs for well-trained employees. The program, modeled after the German apprenticeship system, gives students a chance to gain meaningful training that can be applied toward a high school diploma, credit for an apprenticeship, associate's credit, and a gratifying career.

IOWA

Iowa Lakes Community College (AA)
Secondary Automotive Tech Program

Grades served: HS

Location of schools served: RU

Schools served: 5

Type of schools served: PUB, PRI

Year established: 1973

The Secondary Automotive Tech Program links Iowa Lakes Community College with secondary school districts. Its primary mission is to make available vocational-technical courses to school districts that do not offer or offer only a limited number of courses in such occupations. These jointly sponsored programs also give the smaller school district more curricular offerings, helping them to meet state requirements for secondary schools.

Iowa Lakes Community College (AA)
Secondary Health Occupation Program

Grades served: HS

Location of schools served: NR

Schools served: 3

Type of schools served: PUB, PRI

Year established: 1973

This jointly sponsored program links Iowa Lakes Community College with secondary schools. Its primary mission is to make available vocational-technical courses to school districts that do not offer or offer a limited number of courses in such occupations. These jointly sponsored programs also give the smaller school districts more curricular offerings, helping them to meet state requirements for secondary schools.

Kirkwood Community College (AA)
Kirkwood Partnerships–High School Health Program

Grades served: HS

Location of schools served: UR, SU, RU

Schools served: NR

Type of schools served: PUB

Year established: 1987

High School Health Program links Kirkwood Community College and secondary schools in the area, making a quality introductory health careers program accessible to high school juniors and seniors. Kirkwood administers class content, and students from participating schools meet at a central location for the class. Students explore health careers, learn basic anatomy and physiology, and exit with an employable skill. Upon completion, students are eligible to take the 75-hour nurse aide exam, and those who enter a Kirkwood health science program can articulate up to 7.5 credits.

Kirkwood Community College (AA)
Kirkwood Partnerships–Articulation Agreements
Grades served: HS   Schools served: 90   Year established: 1988
Location of schools served: UR, SU, RU   Type of schools served: PUB, PRI

Kirkwood developed articulation agreements with more than 90 area school districts that allow high school students to earn advanced placement in vocational programs at Kirkwood for competencies developed while in high school. The program strengthens relations between school and college faculty and smooths the transition to college for students.

Kirkwood Community College (AA)
Kirkwood Partnerships–Jointly Administered High School Vocational Programs
Grades served: HS   Schools served: 22   Year established: 1988
Location of schools served: UR, SU, RU   Type of schools served: PUB, PRI

Students from 22 area schools cooperate with Kirkwood in education programs in health careers, auto collision repair, welding, and small engine repair. The competency-based programs are articulated with Kirkwood's vocational programs. Health careers programs are scheduled in local hospitals and care centers to develop students' job skills as nurse aides and give high school students advanced placement at Kirkwood in postsecondary health science programs.

Marshalltown Community College (AA)
MCC-MHS Nurse Training Program
Grades served: HS   Schools served: 1   Year established: 1992
Location of schools served: UR   Type of schools served: NR

This program is a partnership between a large community high school and a regional community college. Faculties in the two institutions developed a two-year sequence of high school courses that articulate into the college's nursing programs. A goal of the project is to help students learn about the health occupations as they choose a career.

KANSAS

Cowley County Community College (AA)
South Central Kansas Tech Prep Associate Degree Consortium
Grades served: M, HS   Schools served: 14   Year established: 1991
Location of schools served: UR, SU, RU   Type of schools served: PUB

This consortium unites Cowley County Community College, area vocational technical schools, and 14 school districts, plus area businesses and industries. The partnership's program meets the academic and technical demands of today's job market by establishing uniform course content and program standards linking secondary and postsecondary facilities and curricula into a progressive learning sequence. Students are prepared for employment after completing the associate degree, certificate, or apprenticeship program, or they can transfer into a baccalaureate program.

Neosho County Community College (AA)
Tech Prep Program
Grades served: HS   Schools served: 4   Year established: 1993
Location of schools served: RU   Type of schools served: NR

Neosho County Community College now has articulation agreements with four high schools in automotive technology: auto body and automotive tech, and engineering technology. The foundation for the programs is the high schools' Principles of Technology program. The competency-based college program meets national certification standards in the occupational area and SCANS (Secretary's Commission on Achieving Necessary Skills). Students receive three credit hours per semester that may be applied toward an associate of applied science degree. The overall program emphasizes lifelong learning to prepare students for the challenges of the workplace.

LOUISIANA

Southeastern Louisiana University (MA I)
Tangipahoa Tech Prep Partnership

Grades served: HS	Schools served: 9	Year established: 1991
Location of schools served: RU	Type of schools served: PUB	

The Tangipahoa Tech Prep Partnership is a resource and facilitator for any individual or group working to ensure a successful transition for youth from school to work or to postsecondary education. It provides structure for collaborative work among high schools, the technical institute, and Southeastern Louisiana University. The concept of 2+2+2 is a coordinated sequence of academic and technical courses starting in 11th grade and ending with a associate's or baccalaureate degree in a technical field from the university. The partnership includes leaders from public schools, the area's technical institute, state government, business, industry, organized labor, and the university.

MAINE

Eastern Maine Technical College (AA)
Tech Prep Program

Grades served: HS	Schools served: 27	Year established: 1992
Location of schools served: UR, RU	Type of schools served: NR	

This program follows the national model for tech-prep activities. The college is implementing applied courses through collaborative efforts with high schools and offers inservice programs for teachers, administrators, and guidance counselors. Articulation committees meet to discuss curricular content and to set the track from high school to technical college.

MARYLAND

Hagerstown Junior College (AA)
Tech-Prep Consortium

Grades served: HS	Schools served: 8	Year established: 1975
Location of schools served: SU, RU	Type of schools served: NR	

Washington County's Tech-Prep Consortium is a multifaceted student and program development agency. Members include the Washington County Board of Education (seven comprehensive high schools), Hagerstown Business College, and Hagerstown Junior College. Eight program areas are fully articulated, and work is under way to articulate three others. The programs are based on federal standards for job skills and SCANS (Secretary's Commission on Achieving Necessary Skills). Activities include instructional integration, faculty development, and designing of school-to-work transition experiences. Specific interaction links this effort to similar ones at Coastal Community College (Jacksonville, NC) and Richland Community College (Dallas, TX).

Note: Each institution's Carnegie class is given in parentheses. **Key:** E=elementary school, HS=high school, M=middle school, NR=not reported, PRI=private, PUB=public, RU=rural, SU=suburban, UR=urban

MASSACHUSETTS

Bristol Community College (AA)
Tech Prep Consortium

Grades served: HS

Schools served: 18

Year established: 1986

Location of schools served: UR, SU

Type of schools served: PUB

Bristol Community College's Tech Prep Consortium is a collaboration of the community college and 18 secondary schools. Participating high schools implement academic core courses that ensure a logical progression to community college and eventually to the workplace. Under a series of articulated agreements, the consortium supports collaborative curriculum development, inservice training for teachers, college credit for competencies learned in high school, early access to college courses, student recruitment activities, and student counseling services.

MICHIGAN

Charles S. Mott Community College (AA)
Project Cadmaster

Grades served: M, HS

Schools served: 2

Year established: 1990

Location of schools served: NR

Type of schools served: PUB

Project Cadmaster focuses on computer-aided drafting and design. A partnership of Lakeville and Millington Community Schools, Mott Community College, and local businesses, the project encourages systemic educational improvement through the cooperation of its partners and the articulation of a seamless educational pathway from middle school through community college and beyond. Essential elements include career exploration beginning in middle school, goal setting, and developing of individualized educational development plans.

Charles S. Mott Community College (AA)
Office Information Systems Programs

Grades served: HS

Schools served: 7

Year established: 1992

Location of schools served: UR

Type of schools served: NR

This associate's degree program offers high school students in seven Flint/Genesee County high schools who enter the college's 62-credit Office Information Systems program the opportunity to earn 10-12 college credits. The purpose of the articulation agreement is to encourage high school students to further their education by giving credit for high school work of the same content as college courses leading to the associate's degree.

Gogebic Community College (AA)
Secretarial, Auto, Building Trades, Computer-Aided Design, Commercial Art

Grades served: HS

Schools served: 9

Year established: 1972

Location of schools served: RU

Type of schools served: PUB

Gogebic Community College and the Gogebic-Ontonagon Intermediate School District have articulated occupational programs in secretarial, auto, building trades, computer-aided design, and commercial art fields, resulting in advanced placement at the college. The arrangement has been a model for other tech-prep programs in the area.

Kalamazoo Valley Community College (AA)
Health Occupations Program

Grades served: HS

Schools served: 13

Year established: 1985

Location of schools served: UR, SU, RU

Type of schools served: PUB

The Health Occupations Program is a one- or two-year high school curriculum shared by all the school districts in Kalamazoo County. A collaboration involving the schools, the Intermediate School District, the community college, and several health care delivery agencies, including hospitals, it is one of several occupational cluster tracts within a larger tech-prep program. Students enrolled in the Health Occupations Program earn high school and college credits while gaining occupational skills and increasing their employability through a variety of on-the-job experiences in health care. Courses meet in one of the participating hospitals.

Muskegon Community College (AA)
Tech-Prep

Grades served: HS

Schools served: 14+

Year established: 1989

Location of schools served: UR, SU

Type of schools served: PUB, PRI

This program enhances applied academics in more than 14 high schools in partnership with Muskegon Community College. The project is intended to assist high schools in developing viable career paths for students interested in pursuing postsecondary education oriented toward a career. Staff development for high school instructors has been conducted in applied mathematics, principles of technology, applied communications, and applied biochemistry. The Muskegon Economic Growth Alliance, connecting city business, industry, and health organizations with education, is also involved.

MINNESOTA

North Hennepin Community College (AA)
Tech-Prep Consortium

Grades served: HS

Schools served: 13

Year established: 1991

Location of schools served: SU

Type of schools served: NR

This consortium links 13 school districts, Hennepin Technical College, Normandale Community College, and North Hennepin Community College. Its missions are to develop and implement an effective system of career awareness, exploration, and assessment for all students and to develop a curriculum that will provide students with a seamless, articulated secondary/postsecondary education in five occupational clusters.

Rochester Community College (AA)
Rochester Area Tech Prep Consortium

Grades served: M, HS

Schools served: 7

Year established: 1990

Location of schools served: RU

Type of schools served: PUB

This consortium involves the Rochester Public Schools, Minnesota Riverland Technical College, and Rochester Community College. It seeks to increase career awareness, establish articulation agreements between local high schools and Minnesota Riverland Technical College and Rochester Community College, and emphasize math, science, technical, and communication skills for all students, integrating these concepts in a hands-on, applied environment. The consortium's goal is to prepare students for successful transition from high school to community colleges, technical colleges, or work.

Note: Each institution's Carnegie class is given in parentheses. **Key:** E=elementary school, HS=high school, M=middle school, NR=not reported, PRI=private, PUB=public, RU=rural, SU=suburban, UR=urban

MISSISSIPPI

Copiah-Lincoln Community College (AA)
Tech Prep

Grades served: M, HS

Schools served: 36

Year established: 1991

Location of schools served: UR, SU, RU

Type of schools served: PUB

This partnership links the community college and secondary schools, leading to a two-year degree or certificate. It provides a sequential series of integrated academic and vocational courses, starting in junior high school, that will increase students' understanding of career opportunities. Other components include applied academic course work for students and training for teachers to connect concepts with real-life experiences; career guidance for students and training for counselors; and partnerships between education and business and industry.

MISSOURI

St. Charles County Community College (AA)
Mid Rivers Tech Prep Consortium

Grades served: HS

Schools served: 15

Year established: 1988

Location of schools served: NR

Type of schools served: PUB, PRI

St. Charles County Community College started a partnership linking its business programs in accounting, business management and marketing, office management, and computer science with the business programs at the high schools and the vocational-technical school in St. Charles County. With the approval of the Mid Rivers Tech Prep Consortium in 1992, the community college joined other schools in St. Charles, Pike, and Lincoln Counties. By December 1994, all high schools and vocational-technical schools in all three counties had articulation agreements in place with the college that met their individual situations. The next step will be to include parochial schools.

NEBRASKA

Western Nebraska Community College (AA)
Western Nebraska Tech Prep

Grades served: HS

Schools served: 8

Year established: 1992

Location of schools served: NR

Type of schools served: PUB

This consortium is a partnership linking the college and secondary schools in the area. It offers students a meaningful sequence of courses and opportunities that blend academic and vocational subjects. The tech-prep curriculum prepares students for technical and collegiate degrees to meet the goals of Work Force 2000. The consortium provides inservice training in applied and integrated academics, financial support in purchasing curriculum materials and equipment, career assessment, articulation of curriculum among secondary and postsecondary instructors and businesses and industries, and a summer internship program with businesses and industries for teachers.

NEW JERSEY

Atlantic Community College (AA)
Tech Prep 2+2

Grades served: HS

Schools served: 9

Year established: 1991

Location of schools served: NR

Type of schools served: PUB

Atlantic Community College's Tech Prep 2+2 program is part of the South Jersey Regional Health Tech Prep Consortium's articulation arrangements with area vocational schools. Students at the vocational schools who complete certain allied health curricula at specified competency levels are granted credit for specific college courses when they are admitted to one of the college's allied health degree programs.

Camden County College (AA)
Curriculum Articulation Agreements
Grades served: HS

Location of schools served: NR

Schools served: 19

Type of schools served: PUB

Year established: 1988

Camden County College and 19 local high schools have executed more than forty 2+2 articulation agreements since 1988 in six academic and technology disciplines: computer-integrated manufacturing, CAD/CAM, office systems technology, automotive technology, business and marketing, and early childhood education. The partnership enhances the high school curriculum, smoothing the transition between high school and college and eliminating the need for remediation during the college freshman year.

Cumberland County College (AA)
Two Plus Two Tech Prep
Grades served: HS

Location of schools served: RU

Schools served: 9

Type of schools served: PUB

Year established: 1989

This 2+2 program provides secondary school students with an opportunity to earn college credits and start preparing for a career in a technical field requiring trained workers. Students enroll in the program by taking an articulated high school course. Credit is granted on the teacher's certification that students have demonstrated mastery of predetermined competencies for the appropriate college course. Equivalency credits may be used only to fulfill requirements of the degree program specified in the articulation agreement. Transcripts specify the college course title and credit hours. No tuition is charged for courses for which the student receives advanced placement credit.

Mercer County Community College (AA)
Automotive Technology AAS Degree
Grades served: HS

Location of schools served: NR

Schools served: 1

Type of schools served: PUB

Year established: 1983

This collaboration of Mercer County Community College and Mercer County Vocational/Technical School offers qualified high school graduates and students who have met equivalent requirements an opportunity to enroll in an apprenticeship program sponsored by area Chrysler dealers. Students receive a combination of on-the-job automotive training and classroom instruction, leading to an associate's degree after completion of 61 credits.

Warren County Community College (AA)
Transitions
Grades served: HS

Location of schools served: NR

Schools served: 6

Type of schools served: PUB, PRI

Year established: 1989

Transitions is a collaboration of Warren County Community College and the county's secondary schools. The program enables high school students to acquire a maximum of 15 "T" credits for courses specifically identified in the AAS degree program in business management. The objective of the program is to encourage high school students to consider pursuing a college education by providing a clearly articulated educational sequence that begins in high school and leads to the AAS degree.

Note: Each institution's Carnegie class is given in parentheses. **Key:** E=elementary school, HS=high school, M=middle school, NR=not reported, PRI=private, PUB=public, RU=rural, SU=suburban, UR=urban

NEW YORK

Broome Community College (AA)
Tech Prep

Grades served: HS   Schools served: 8   Year established: 1992
Location of schools served: UR, SU, RU   Type of schools served: PUB

This partnership between Broome Community College's Greater Broome Tech Prep and eight area high schools is an articulated program of at least two years of high school and two years of postsecondary preparation. Its common core of math, science, communications, and technology is designed to produce well-trained workers and/or associate's degree graduates. It is a serious attempt to restructure education for the 70% of the population who do not need a bachelor's degree.

City University of New York Bronx Community College (AA)
Tech Prep Program

Grades served: HS   Schools served: 5   Year established: 1992
Location of schools served: UR   Type of schools served: PUB

The Bronx Tech Prep Program is a partnership involving CUNY-Bronx Community College; CUNY-Lehman College; the New York City Public Schools' Division of High Schools, Jane Addams Vocational High School, the Superintendent's Office of Occupational Education; and the Bronx Educational Opportunity Center. The college's Tech Prep Office administers the program, which offers a nonduplicative, four-year (grades 11-14) course of study leading to associate's degrees in allied health or nursing sciences from Bronx Community College or two-year certificates in health records from Lehman College. Mathematics, sciences, communications, and health technologies are emphasized. Students are encouraged to explore several career options in allied health fields.

Corning Community College (AA)
TAM (Technology Awareness Module)

Grades served: M, HS   Schools served: 6   Year established: 1992
Location of schools served: NR   Type of schools served: PUB

Corning Community College, in partnership with four area high schools and two BOCES facilities, is developing a 2+2 program in manufacturing technology. As part of the effort and in cooperation with two regional industries, the college purchased a Technology Awareness Module (TAM) designed by RPI and built by Hudson Valley Community College — a mobile unit with a PC with AutoCad software, printer, robot, and milling machine. The TAM is rotated among participating high schools to introduce computer-integrated manufacturing to students to make them aware of educational requirements and career opportunities in this occupation.

Fashion Institute of Technology (ART)
FIT Tech-Prep Consortium

Grades served: HS   Schools served: 3   Year established: 1992
Location of schools served: UR   Type of schools served: PUB

The FIT Tech-Prep Consortium links the institute with High School of the Fashion Industries and Murray Bergtraum High School to provide a seamless four-year (grades 11-14) course of study in the disciplines represented by the major areas of study in FIT's Business and Technology Division. Particular curricular focus is directed toward the AAS degree in textile development and marketing, manufacturing management, and fashion buying and merchandising. In addition to academic preparation, the consortium offers computerized career guidance, a Saturday program, and a summer employment program for students.

Genesee Community College (AA)
Genesee Region Tech Prep Consortium
Grades served: M, HS   Schools served: 9   Year established: 1991
Location of schools served: RU   Type of schools served: PUB

This consortium links Genesee Community College and nine secondary institutions in a 2+2, planned, sequential career preparation program combining the last two years of high school and two years of college, leading to an associate's degree. Curricula in advanced business, technology, and allied health fields are supported by a practical approach to mathematics and science. The program also provides career awareness for students, starting in the seventh grade, to assist them in making appropriate academic and vocational choices. Open lines of communication between the college and the secondary schools benefit students and teachers in the cooperating institutions.

Jamestown Community College (AA)
Tech Prep
Grades served: HS   Schools served: 14   Year established: 1989
Location of schools served: RU   Type of schools served: PUB

College faculty visit area high schools annually to explain the tech-prep program to math classes and to encourage students to continue their studies in mathematics, science, and communications. Tech-prep students are invited to campus events, and they receive a waiver of Engineering Drawing I upon entrance to the college. High school teachers are provided with seminars in CAD and digital electronics and may borrow computers with a 3-D CAD package installed or digital electronic trainers for students' use.

State University of New York College of Agriculture and Technology at Cobleskill (AA)
Agri-Tech Prep
Grades served: HS   Schools served: 15   Year established: 1991
Location of schools served: UR, SU, RU Type of schools served: PUB

Agri-Tech Prep prepares students for careers in the food and agriculture industry, a field that boasts approximately three job openings for each agriculture graduate. A seamless curriculum moves students from high school to college, combining the junior and senior high school program and the program in agriculture and technology at SUNY's two-year colleges, culminating in an associate's degree. Students who complete the program's high school curriculum are guaranteed admission to one of the participating two-year SUNY colleges, which could award advanced credit based on the student's portfolio.

State University of New York College of Technology at Farmingdale (AA)
SUNY-Farmingdale's Liberty Partnerships Program
Grades served: M, HS   Schools served: 10   Year established: 1989
Location of schools served: SU   Type of schools served: PUB

The Liberty Partnerships Program was initiated at SUNY-Farmingdale in collaboration with several area school districts, and community service and business organizations to proactively assist at-risk students in grades 7-12 to complete high school and advance to postsecondary education. Related support for students includes academic tutoring, student advocacy, college or career preparation, personal and family counseling, mentoring, cultural/athletic enrichment, and field trips. Professional development programs serve faculty and staff who work with students. Community-based organizations offer counseling, home visits, referrals/intervention, rap programs, and workshops for parents, students, and teachers.

Note: Each institution's Carnegie class is given in parentheses. **Key:** E=elementary school, HS=high school, M=middle school, NR=not reported, PRI=private, PUB=public, RU=rural, SU=suburban, UR=urban

NORTH CAROLINA

Brunswick Community College (AA)
Tech Prep and Coordinated Vocational-Tech Programs
Grades served: HS   Schools served: 3   Year established: 1991
Location of schools served: RU   Type of schools served: PUB

Brunswick Community College and the Brunswick Public Schools have entered a partnership agreement that allows qualified high school students to enroll in challenging freshman courses during their senior year of high school. Courses range from electronics engineering technology to automotive technology and cosmetology. The program offers recertification courses for public school teachers and a forum for communication between educators from the community college and the public schools.

Carteret Community College (AA)
Tech-Prep Associate Degree
Grades served: HS   Schools served: 3   Year established: 1989
Location of schools served: NR   Type of schools served: PUB

This partnership links the Carteret County Public Schools to community colleges in eastern North Carolina. Its mission is to reach the middle majority of high school students in general studies and to educate this population so that they are ready to advance directly to a community college. If they pass proficiency tests, students receive advanced placement and college credit for certain courses taken while in high school. Part of the program is faculty and staff development at the community college and the high schools, training high school counselors, and systematic collection of data to determine the program's success.

Cleveland Community College (AA)
Tech Prep
Grades served: M, HS   Schools served: 8   Year established: 1990
Location of schools served: RU   Type of schools served: PUB

This state-award-winning tech-prep program is a 4+2 collaboration serving students in grades 8-14. Combining the resources and commitments of three public school systems and one community college, it has the support of businesses and industries in Cleveland County, evident in leadership, service on advisory committees, donations toward scholarships, training, resource sharing, and tours.

James Sprunt Community College (AA)
Tech-Prep Program
Grades served: HS   Schools served: 4   Year established: 1974
Location of schools served: RU   Type of schools served: PUB

This articulation program in was approved by the State Board of Education as a joint effort of James Sprunt Community College and the Duplin County Public Schools, which jointly developed the program with advice and support from business and industry. Curricula cover automotive mechanics, business education, and mechanical drafting.

Richmond Community College (AA)
Tech Prep

Grades served: M, HS   Schools served: 5   Year established: 1986
Location of schools served: RU   Type of schools served: PUB

This 4+2 program is designed to meet the need for more students with at least an associate's degree as they enter the American workplace. With a blend of academic and vocational-technical competencies, it focuses on technical careers for the middle majority of students who do not enroll in a four-year postsecondary program. The program is a partnership of the secondary and postsecondary schools, businesses, community leaders, parents, and students.

OHIO

Jefferson Technical College (AA)
Jefferson County Tech Prep Consortium

Grades served: HS   Schools served: 9   Year established: 1989
Location of schools served: UR, RU   Type of schools served: PUB, PRI

This consortium involves all the school districts of Jefferson County, the Joint Vocational School, Jefferson Technical College, and the Franciscan University of Steubenville. It plans to develop a program in manufacturing engineering technology based on the state model and reflecting the needs of local and regional businesses and industries. The consortium plans to create new educational options and opportunities, implement an individual career plan for each high school student, develop and expand partnerships, develop instructional committees for staff development, and increase students' academic, employability, and occupational competencies.

Terra State Community College (AA)
Workforce Development Council

Grades served: HS   Schools served: 33   Year established: 1989
Location of schools served: UR, RU   Type of schools served: PUB

The Workforce Development Council is a curriculum development partnership of Terra State Community College, Bowling Green State University-Firelands, secondary schools, businesses, labor, government, and industries in a six-county region. Its primary mission is to encourage a competent workforce and its the first project is an industrial technician (IT) tech-prep associate's degree that begins in high school. The council recently completed curricular design using the Tech Prep Competency Profile (TCP), in which the partners created a comprehensive competency profile for the IT degree.

University of Akron, Main Campus (DOC I)
Mechanical Engineering Technology

Grades served: HS   Schools served: 1   Year established: 1993
Location of schools served: UR   Type of schools served: NR

The tech-prep program at East High School in Akron teaches students about polymer technology in an effort to prepare and encourage their entry into the polymer industry and/or their enrollment in computer and technology college in a technology program. The school serves primarily the African-American community.

Note: Each institution's Carnegie class is given in parentheses. **Key:** E=elementary school, HS=high school, M=middle school, NR=not reported, PRI=private, PUB=public, RU=rural, SU=suburban, UR=urban

OKLAHOMA

Tulsa Junior College (AA)
Planning for High School and Beyond

Grades served: M, HS | Schools served: 1 | Year established: 1978
Location of schools served: UR | Type of schools served: PUB

Since the Cooperative Articulation Project between Tulsa Junior College and Tulsa Area Vocational Technical School began, more than 30 programs have been articulated between the two institutions, and new programs are selected each year covering business, computer science, engineering/technology, health professions, occupational education, and others. This project has been important in conveying information to students about options and benefits available through vocational education and career planning.

OREGON

Mt. Hood Community College (AA)
Mt. Hood Regional Cooperative Consortium

Grades served: HS | Schools served: 7 | Year established: 1986
Location of schools served: SU | Type of schools served: PUB

This consortium incorporates Mt. Hood Community College, its seven district high schools, and the education service district. It has implemented 78 written articulation agreements in 16 professional-technical areas. In 1991 the American Association of Community Colleges designated MHCC as one of the top three community colleges in the nation for tech-prep associate's degree education. In 1992 the U.S. Department of Education selected it as one of nine organizations to serve two years as national tech-prep demonstration centers to disseminate and evaluate tech-prep activities.

Portland Community College (AA)
PAVTEC Education Consortium

Grades served: HS | Schools served: 27 | Year established: 1984
Location of schools served: UR, SU, RU | Type of schools served: PUB

Portland Community College, 12 local school districts, and private sector partners make up the PAVTEC Education Consortium, which encompasses 15,000 square miles and 850,000 residents. The tech-prep curriculum offers preparation in 20 occupational areas, targeting arts and communications, health occupations, human resource systems, industry engineering, business and management, and natural resources. Career information and a talent assessment program are available for all students. Guides about 2+2 tech-prep, articulation procedures, and marketing materials have been provided to students, teachers, and counselors. PAVTEC also has expertise in working with local school districts via the minigrants process.

PENNSYLVANIA

California University of Pennsylvania (MA I)
Mon Valley-Southpointe Tech Prep Consortium

Grades served: M, HS | Schools served: 33 | Year established: 1991
Location of schools served: RU | Type of schools served: PUB

The university is the coordinating agency for the Mon Valley-Southpointe Tech Prep Consortium. The project's goals include the articulation of a 4+2 competency-based curriculum between secondary and postsecondary institutions; professional inservice training for teachers, faculty, and staff; business-educational partnerships; extensive marketing/promotional campaigns; and coordinated career exploration/enhancement for guidance counselors, parents, and students. Its long-term goal is educational reform affecting secondary and postsecondary institutions and businesses and industries resulting in an associate's degree or discipline-related job placement for the students.

Harrisburg Area Community College (AA)
Vocational-Technical Partnerships
Grades served: HS   Schools served: 5   Year established: 1986
Location of schools served: UR, SU, RU   Type of schools served: PUB

Harrisburg Area Community College works with area vocational-technical schools to provide advanced standing and college credit in selected vocational programs. Faculty at the community college and vocational-technical schools work together on course content so that students get information early about careers and the academic preparation necessary.

Pennsylvania State University-DuBois Campus (AA)
Tech Prep For Tomorrow
Grades served: HS   Schools served: 5   Year established: 1991
Location of schools served: RU   Type of schools served: PUB

This program currently involves five local secondary schools. Its primary objective is to provide direction and purpose to secondary school students who have no goals or motives. Penn State-Dubois offers vocational courses in three engineering technologies, health-related fields, wildlife technologies, and business administration. After successfully completing two years of postsecondary education, the student earns an associate's degree.

SOUTH CAROLINA

Aiken Technical College (AA)
Aiken County Consortium on Preparation for the Technologies
Grades served: M, HS   Schools served: 8   Year established: 1991
Location of schools served: UR, SU, RU   Type of schools served: PUB

This consortium links the Aiken County School District and Aiken Technical College to provide a coordinated program of study for students interested in pursuing careers in technology. The consortium employs a tech-prep coordinator and a secretary who coordinate staff development, curricular reform, relationships with area businesses and industries, and student enrichment. It also works with the University of South Carolina-Aiken, enabling tech-prep students who wish to continue their education toward a baccalaureate degree to do so within the community.

Spartanburg Technical College (AA)
Area Vocational-Technical Center in Engineering Technologies
Grades served: HS   Schools served: 5   Year established: 1983
Location of schools served: NR   Type of schools served: PUB

The Joint Metalworking Advisory Committee, with representatives from Spartanburg Technical College, five area vocational-technical centers, and industry, has been active for a number of years in developing curricula and providing college-level course work for rising seniors. The group has been expanded recently to develop a youth apprenticeship program. Instructors and industry representatives are working together to develop agreements regarding competencies, curriculum design, evaluation standards and methods, advisory materials for students, and work arrangements.

Note: Each institution's Carnegie class is given in parentheses. **Key:** E=elementary school, HS=high school, M=middle school, NR=not reported, PRI=private, PUB=public, RU=rural, SU=suburban, UR=urban

TEXAS

North Harris Montgomery Community College District (AA)
NHCC/SISD Automotive Technology Program
Grades served: HS   Schools served: 2   Year established: 1986
Location of schools served: SU   Type of schools served: PUB

This partnership of North Harris College and the Spring Independent School District links specific secondary and postsecondary technical programs. Its primary mission is to offer qualified high school seniors the opportunity to enroll in automotive, air conditioning, and welding courses and qualified juniors the opportunity to enroll in automotive technology courses. Students successfully completing course requirements receive both high school and college credit.

North Harris Montgomery Community College District (AA)
Tech Prep
Grades served: HS   Schools served: NR   Year established: NR
Location of schools served: NR   Type of schools served: PUB

Kingwood College, a part of the North Harris Montgomery Community College District, and local high schools are involved in one of the first state-approved tech-prep programs in Texas. Humble Independent School District graduates can continue at the college, earning an associate's degree in medical office specialist, legal secretary, and desktop publishing programs. A miniconsortium of the New Caney, Splendora, Cleveland, and Huggman Independent School Districts plans similar programs. Students in high school sections of marketing education courses can continue at the college, earning an associate's degree in travel and tourism, with advanced skills in convention and meeting planning and System One (Continental Airline's on-line reservation system).

Texas State Technical College-Sweetwater (AA)
West Central Texas Tech Prep Consortium
Grades served: M, HS   Schools served: NR   Year established: 1992
Location of schools served: RU   Type of schools served: PUB

This consortium is a broad-based group of educators and industry representatives whose goal is to restructure technical education and secondary over a large geographic area. Innovative approaches in piloting basic technology courses through cooperative agreements and articulation have resulted in the enrollment of more than 3,000 high school students in secondary technical education courses. Faculty development, resource sharing, and curriculum development have been major components of the initiative, which encompasses 37 independent school districts, five community/technical colleges, and several regional universities.

WASHINGTON

South Seattle Community College (AA)
Tech Prep Consortium
Grades served: HS   Schools served: 14   Year established: 1990
Location of schools served: UR   Type of schools served: PUB

This consortium links ten high schools, three alternative high schools, three community colleges, and a vocational institute whose borders coincide with the city of Seattle. In the diverse student body of the Seattle Public Schools, more than 77 languages and dialects are spoken within a K-12 enrollment of 44,500. Articulation agreements are updated annually in applied math, communications, principles of technology, business computing, manufacturing technology, computer-assisted drafting, and other traditional professional technical programs. Business and industry representatives act as advisers and steering committee members, and assist in curriculum review and placement of interns in jobs.

□ □ □

Part Four
RESTRUCTURING

Introduction

This part features examples of partnerships whose focus is restructuring our educational system. Such partnerships link many types of institutions and agencies — state education departments, education associations, colleges and universities, school districts covering a wide geographic area — and their activities and goals often are multifaceted, covering broad-based curricular reform, career counseling, programs for at-risk and disadvantaged students, and interagency agreements. Several of the programs featured have developed comprehensive articulation agreements specifically to facilitate communication, promote the sharing of resources, and provide a forum for long-range educational planning.

Many of the partnerships in Section One, "Citywide or Regional Compacts," have as their primary goal the systemic reform of educational institutions and services. Such collaborative efforts are often locally controlled and jointly administered, stress regular assessment and reporting, critically examine reward structures, and offer a variety of support services for teachers, administrators, and staff. The Coalition of Essential Schools for the Los Angeles region, for example, works with the University of Southern California, the Los Angeles County Office of Education, and the California Center for School Restructuring. The center provides ongoing technical assistance to Essential School members, focusing on student outcomes, curriculum, pedagogy and assessment, school governance, decision-making processes, development of school plans, school culture, assessment of organizational effectiveness, communication systems, progressional growth, school structures, and the relationship of the school to the district. It also provides opportunities for exploring and planning schools.

The College of Education at Florida State University and the Leon County Public School System have collaborated to implement a portion of Blueprint 2000, the state's effort toward comprehensive educational reform. A faculty member from the College of Education serves on a school advisory council (a site-based management team made up of teachers, parents, and community members) at one of the local schools. Fifty-five faculty members serve 41 schools. The faculty members, while serving as resource persons for the school advisory councils, also garner information from the meetings to enhance their own teaching and research.

A third example is the University of Georgia's Program for School Improvement (PSI). Established in 1988, the program is dedicated to improving public education by promoting the school as a professional workplace: a place where shared governance and action research are used to plan and implement improved instruction. Based on PSI's initial collaboration, the League of Professional Schools, PSI facilitates school/university networks, grounded in the belief that schools should be driven by internal decisions and the schools' own criteria for success; that is, instructional decisions should be made through a full democratic process that includes all teachers and administrators, with carefully solicited input from students, parents, and community members.

Section Two, "Coordinating Agencies, Regional Articulation Councils and Agreements, and Joint Governance," features some interesting examples of partnerships that serve as coordinating agencies to promote the sharing of resources and to improve articulation of programs and services. The Boston Higher Education Partnership, for example, is a consortium of 25 Boston-area colleges and universities working with the Boston Public Schools. It includes public and independent, two- and four-year institutions. It began in 1975 with court-ordered desegregation and has grown to a multimillion-dollar enterprise involved with all aspects of school restructuring, curricular reform, professional development, and student services and support. Since 1983 its members have provided more than $50 million in student scholarships, more than $27 million in pro bono contributions, and nearly $25 million in external grants to the Boston Public Schools.

Another example is the New England Network of Academic Alliances in Foreign Languages and Literatures. Established in 1990, the alliances are made up of foreign language professionals from elementary, secondary, and postsecondary schools who meet regularly to share knowledge and experience in an effort to provide high-quality professional development for participating faculty. The network is currently working with the College Board and ACTFL in a three-year FIPSE-funded project to develop articulated learning outcomes and matching classroom-based assessments for foreign language instruction in grades 7-14.

The final section, "New Achievement Standards and Assessment Mechanisms," features programs such as

Kent State University's Early Assessment for Exceptional Potential. The project uses computer-aided technology to develop a model for identifying young gifted and talented minority and/or economically disadvantaged students. Teams of primary classroom teachers, administrators, and College of Education faculty have determined behavioral attributes of exceptional potential observed during demonstration teaching in primary science and social studies lessons. Computer-assisted training tapes for inservice teacher training have been developed, and portfolio assessment focusing on 18 primary identifiers is used to determine individual student's strengths.

Finally, Clayton State College, working with six school systems, has developed and implemented an outcome-focused, assessment-based, student-centered teacher education program. The Middle Level Teacher Education program, leading to a BA degree, is the first of its type; it has a strong liberal arts foundation in mathematics, science, social science, and language arts. All education courses have been developed and are taught by school-based education experts. This new initiative has a precollegiate component of Future Educators of America in chapters in all middle and high schools, with a cadet teacher option available in the high schools. Plans are to work with the school systems, continuing professional support for graduates through their first year of teaching.   □

Section One
Citywide or Regional Compacts

ALABAMA

University of Alabama at Birmingham (RES I)
The Birmingham Compact

Grades served: E, M, HS	Schools served: 78	Year established: 1994
Location of schools served: UR	Type of schools served: PUB	

The Birmingham Compact is a collaboration of the Birmingham Public Schools, Jefferson State Community College, Lawson State Community College, the University of Alabama at Birmingham, and other key community leaders to increase the number of urban youth who persist to postsecondary graduation or certification. Its current three-year plan focuses on collaborative strategies for eliminating barriers to K-16 students' success. The compact 's objectives are related primarily to parental involvement, school organization and management, curriculum and instruction, and college and career counseling.

ARKANSAS

University of Central Arkansas (MA I)
Center for Academic Excellence

Grades served: E, M, HS	Schools served: NR	Year established: 1984
Location of schools served: UR, SU, RU	Type of schools served: PUB	

The Center for Academic Excellence is the service, outreach, and research unit of the University of Central Arkansas's College of Education. Established with the mission of improving public education in Arkansas by cooperating and sharing University resources, the Center has provided services to approximately 125 school districts desiring external technical assistance in addressing locally identified needs. The faculty of the College of Education serve as consultants and furnish leadership in planning, designing, and implementing the improvements. A major component in the delivery of service is to promote and model educational collaboration. All of the center's services are available at no cost upon written request from school administrators.

Note: Each institution's Carnegie class is given in parentheses. **Key:** E=elementary school, HS=high school, M=middle school, NR=not reported, PRI=private, PUB=public, RU=rural, SU=suburban, UR=urban

CALIFORNIA

California Institute of Technology (RES I)
Caltech Precollege Science Initiative

Grades served: E, M, HS   Schools served: 27   Year established: 1986
Location of schools served: NR   Type of schools served: PUB

The Caltech Precollege Science Initiative is an effort to promote collaboration between scientists and educators in improving K-12 science education. A major effort has been a partnership with the Pasadena Schools that has successfully implemented a hands-on, inquiry-based science curriculum in all 500 K-6 classrooms and resulted in inquiry-based curricula for middle schools and high schools. Additionally, a collaborative with the Claremont Graduate School has developed an inquiry-based undergraduate science course for preservice teachers. Cooperation with NASA's Jet Propulsion Laboratory produces computer simulations that enhance the K-6 curriculum.

University of Southern California (RES I)
Coalition of Essential Schools

Grades served: NR   Schools served: 45   Year established: 1988
Location of schools served: UR, SU   Type of schools served: PUB

The Coalition of Essential Schools for the Los Angeles region works with the University of Southern California, the Los Angeles County Office of Education, and the California Center for School Restructuring. The center provides ongoing technical assistance to Essential School members, focusing on student outcomes, curriculum, pedagogy and assessment, school governance, decision-making processes, development of school plans, school culture, assessment of organizational effectiveness, communication systems, professional growth, school structures, and the relationship of the school to the district. It also provides opportunities for exploring and planning schools.

COLORADO

University of Northern Colorado (DOC I)
Project SPAN (Standards and Performance Based Academic Networking)

Grades served: E, M, HS   Schools served: NR   Year established: 1992
Location of schools served: SU, RU   Type of schools served: PUB

Faculty members from five UNC departments (chemistry, mathematics, Spanish, history, and speech communication) and their counterparts from Weld County School District No. 6 and the UNC Laboratory School formed a K-16 leadership team whose missions were to write graduation standards for each academic major, define performance indicators for the standards, develop challenging performance tasks to benchmark students' progress, and design scoring formats for the tasks. During the project's second and third years, K-16 faculty will evaluate students' success in meeting graduation standards, determine students' strengths and weaknesses, and design changes in curricula and assessments.

University of Southern Colorado (BA II)
Educational Alliance of Pueblo

Grades served: E, M, HS   Schools served: 34   Year established: 1991
Location of schools served: UR, SU   Type of schools served: NR

The Educational Alliance of Pueblo is a contractual agreement between the University of Southern Colorado and Pueblo School District No. 60. The alliance combines resources from both institutions with the goals of improving educational delivery from kindergarten through the university and better using taxpayers' dollars. The alliance's scope spans several disciplines and affects all 34 district schools and the university. Its successes include consolidating the management of facilities, faculty exchanges, and collaborating on a seamless K-16 curriculum. Seventeen partnerships sponsored by the alliance have generated more than $5 million dollars in grants.

FLORIDA

Florida State University (RES I)
FSU College of Education/Leon County Schools Collaboration

Grades served: E, M, HS   Schools served: 41   Year established: 1993
Location of schools served: UR, SU, RU   Type of schools served: PUB

The FSU College of Education and the Leon County Public School System have collaborated to implement a portion of Blueprint 2000, the state's comprehensive educational reform effort. A faculty member from the College of Education serves on a school advisory council (a site-based management team of teachers, parents, and community members) at one of the local schools. Fifty-five faculty members serve 41 schools. The faculty members, while serving as resource persons for the advisory councils, also garner information from the meetings to enhance their own teaching and research.

GEORGIA

Kennesaw State College (MA II)
Cobb Education Consortium

Grades served: E, M, HS   Schools served: 120   Year established: 1990
Location of schools served: NR   Type of schools served: NR

The Cobb Education Consortium is a partnership linking all K-12 systems, technical institutes, and senior colleges in Cobb County and serving the surrounding area. It is pledged to combine resources, energies, and talents to address common areas of concern in moving public education in Cobb from its current level of excellence to the superior levels that will be needed to prepare students for responsible leadership in the 21st century. The consortium's vision is to build a community culture supporting a seamless web of learning for life, with excellence as the minimum requirement.

University of Georgia (RES I)
Program for School Improvement

Grades served: NR   Schools served: 75   Year established: 1988
Location of schools served: NR   Type of schools served: PUB

The University of Georgia's Program for School Improvement (PSI) is dedicated to improving public education by promoting the school as a professional workplace: a place where shared governance and action research are used to plan and implement improvement in instruction. Based on PSI's initial collaboration, the League of Professional Schools, PSI facilitates school/university networks, grounded in the belief that schools should be driven by internal decisions and the school's own criteria for success; that is, instructional decisions should be made through a full democratic process that includes all teachers and administrators, with carefully solicited input from students, parents, and the community.

ILLINOIS

Northeastern Illinois University (MA I)
CUBE (Coalition of Universities and Businesses for Education)

Grades served: NR   Schools served: 22   Year established: 1991
Location of schools served: UR, SU   Type of schools served: PUB

CUBE was initially a three-year project involving 22 universities. Each university assembled a team that included the university president, the vice president for academic affairs, the dean of education, the dean of arts and sciences, a business leader, and the superintendent of a local school district. Each team planned improvements in education and reported on progress during three annual national conferences. Themes of the conferences included advances in technology, total quality management in education, and ways to make change happen. The project is continuing at NIU.

Note: Each institution's Carnegie class is given in parentheses. **Key:** E=elementary school, HS=high school, M=middle school, NR=not reported, PRI=private, PUB=public, RU=rural, SU=suburban, UR=urban

KENTUCKY

Northern Kentucky University (MA I)
Northern Kentucky Cooperative for Educational Services
Grades served: E, M, HS   Schools served: NR   Year established: 1986
Location of schools served: UR, SU, RU   Type of schools served: PUB

The Northern Kentucky Cooperative for Educational Services (NKCES) was formed by 17 school districts and the university to provide services to school districts that can be more effectively and efficiently provided by an organization with a large student base (K-12 enrollment of NKCES member schools is 60,000). Services for special education students and inservice programs for faculty and administrators have been the major projects of the cooperative to date.

MICHIGAN

Madonna University (MA I)
Livonia Education Television Consortium (LETC)
Grades served: E, M, HS   Schools served: 4   Year established: 1983
Location of schools served: SU   Type of schools served: PUB, PRI

This consortium links Madonna College, Livonia public schools, Livonia non-public schools, the Clarenceville School District, and Schoolcraft Community College. A franchise agreement between MetroVision Cable Television and the city of Livonia provides two access channels for education and funding to set up television production facilities at the sites. The two colleges supply college-level telecourses and programming for secondary and elementary students. Internships for college students are provided, and programs are planned involving students and families as participants, with students working as part of the production team.

NEW YORK

City University of New York Bronx Community College (AA)
Bronx Educational Alliance
Grades served: E   Schools served: 2   Year established: 1992
Location of schools served: UR   Type of schools served: PUB

The Bronx Educational Alliance is a partnership of the Office of the Borough President, Community School Districts 7-12, the Bronx High School, Superintendent's Office, health care and social service agencies, Bronx Community College, Hostos Community College, and Lehman College. It links borough educational institutions with business, government, and community-based organizations to ensure that students are academically prepared for the transitions between levels of schooling and for entrance to and graduation from two- and four-year colleges. Educational/job training and mentoring are available for administrators, teachers, students, and parents.

State University of New York College at Purchase (BA II)
SUNY Purchase/Westchester School Partnership
Grades served: E, M, HS   Schools served: 160   Year established: 1984
Location of schools served: SU   Type of schools served: NR

This partnership of SUNY-College at Purchase, 26 Westchester County School Districts, and the Westchester Boards of Cooperative Educational Services is designed to coordinate its efforts with those of business and community agencies to develop programs enhancing instruction and to identify effective approaches to significant educational problems. The partnership has established the Teacher Center at Purchase College, the Northeast Regional Center for Science and Mathematics Education, the Westchester Center for Economic Education, the Foreign Language Program (an offshoot of which is the Multicultural Program), the Great Potential Program for At-Risk Youth, and the Young Scholars at Purchase Program.

NORTH DAKOTA

Valley City State University (BA II)
Curriculum Leadership Institute-North Dakota
Grades served: E, M, HS   Schools served: 66   Year established: 1993
Location of schools served: RU   Type of schools served: PUB

This project assists 66 rural schools involved in 12 educational consortia to coordinate a comprehensive, systemic approach to the improvement of K-12 education and curriculum development. The assistance includes two years of training for curriculum coordinators from the consortia at a central location, and on-site technical assistance between training sessions. The focus is on assisting educational cooperatives to develop the local capacity to lead and sustain meaningful school improvements.

OREGON

Chemeketa Community College (AA)
Partnership Programs
Grades served: HS   Schools served: 26   Year established: 1980
Location of schools served: NR   Type of schools served: PUB, PRI

Chemeketa Community College provides alternative high school education, GED preparation, dropout recovery programs, advanced placement programs, and leadership in 2+2 and tech prep activities within its district through facility sharing, articulation, and special programs.

Clatsop Community College (AA)
North Coast Educational Consortium
Grades served: M, HS   Schools served: 8   Year established: 1991
Location of schools served: RU   Type of schools served: PUB

This partnership includes Clatsop Community College, six rural K-12 school districts, and one education service district. The primary purposes of the consortium are to improve K-14 students' academic success and to implement regionally Oregon's Educational Reform Act. The consortium's activities include coordinated teacher inservice/staff development programs; curriculum development; 2+2 tech prep associate's degrees in integrated technologies and office systems technology; Early Collegiate Opportunity classes for high school seniors; Trio Grants (Talent Search, Upward Bound, and Student Support Services); coordinated cooperation education; and selection as one of six pilot sites statewide to implement the Act.

Portland State University (DOC II)
PEN (Portland Education Network)
Grades served: M, HS   Schools served: 50   Year established: 1991
Location of schools served: UR   Type of schools served: PUB

This partnership of PSU, schools, government and community agencies, and business and industry works to increase the access to education of students and potential students in the Portland metropolitan area and helps to ensure their success.

Note: Each institution's Carnegie class is given in parentheses. **Key:** E=elementary school, HS=high school, M=middle school, NR=not reported, PRI=private, PUB=public, RU=rural, SU=suburban, UR=urban

PENNSYLVANIA

East Stroudsburg University of Pennsylvania (MA I)
Partners in Education

Grades served: M, HS   Schools served: NR   Year established: 1985
Location of schools served: RU   Type of schools served: PUB, PRI

Partners in Education links East Stroudsburg University and four school systems (East Stroudsburg, Stroudsburg, Pleasant Valley, and Pocono Mountain) in its immediate region. The superintendents of the four districts, the director of Intermediate Unit 20, the director of the Monroe County Vocational-Technical School, the principal of Notre Dame High School, and the dean of the School of Professional Studies plan cooperative programs. Among them are Project Challenge for gifted high schools students; Special Day for Special Kids for special education students; teacher inservice programs; and PA-LEAD, an inservice program for administrators on diversity, parent-school relationships, and instructional technology.

Indiana University of Pennsylvania (DOC I)
Partnerships in Education

Grades served: HS   Schools served: NR   Year established: 1983
Location of schools served: NR   Type of schools served: PUB

Indiana University of Pennsylvania has instituted more than 40 projects involving links with the public schools. The Mentorship Project, for example, links IUP faculty in mathematics, biology, physics, chemistry, and computer programming as mentors for high-ability Armstrong and Diana County high school students in grades 9-12. The University School helps to mainstream children enrolled in special education; its faculty consists of public school certified teachers and university professors, and it has access to IUP's School of Education and the departments of Special Education and Speech and Language. The university also provides inservice training and workshops for the schools.

Temple University (RES I)
The Learning City Program

Grades served: E   Schools served: 3   Year established: 1993
Location of schools served: UR   Type of schools served: PUB

The Learning City Program is designed to radically improve students' learning, especially students in major cities, through coordinating, using, and expanding existing resources. Learning City communities integrate services within neighborhoods by linking schools within a particular community with all other learning environments, including the home, libraries, museums, churches, postsecondary education institutions, business establishments, and workplaces. Expected outcomes include restructuring school organizations to implement advances in effective schooling; developing a plan for developing instructional leadership; and forging collaboratives among multiagency services to ensure a lifelong commitment to learning by children, families, and the community.

University of Pennsylvania (RES I)
West Philadelphia Improvement Corps (WEPIC)

Grades served: E, M, HS   Schools served: 13   Year established: 1985
Location of schools served: UR   Type of schools served: PUB

WEPIC is a school-based revitalization project in which the University of Pennsylvania is a permanent partner. WEPIC's goal is to produce comprehensive community schools that serve the entire community. It operates 13 public schools and involves more than 2,000 children and adults in cultural, recreational, job training, and community service activities during the school day, after school, and on weekends. Programs during the school day emphasize the integration of service-learning with academics and job readiness. Other partners include the West Philadelphia Partnership of hospitals, unions, and churches.

RHODE ISLAND

Brown University (RES I)
Coalition of Essential Schools

Grades served: E, M, HS

Schools served: 693

Year established: 1984

Location of schools served: UR, SU, RU

Type of schools served: PUB, PRI

The Coalition of Essential Schools (CES) works to redesign U.S. high schools to ensure better learning and achievement for students. CES includes nearly 700 schools in 38 states, serving more than 600,000 students. Nine Common Principles advocating active, personalized, and demonstrated learning guide the Coalition and its member schools. The staff of CES is based at Brown, where its work focuses on professional development, research, and collaboration with other organizations to promote a climate receptive to changes in schools.

TEXAS

North Harris Montgomery Community College District (AA)
Montgomery College Partnerships

Grades served: HS

Schools served: NR

Year established: NR

Location of schools served: NR

Type of schools served: PUB

Among the community partnerships created by the college are arrangements that include adoption of a 12-point cooperative framework between NHMCCD trustees and the Conroe Independent School District school board; the college president's participation in long-range planning committees of Conroe and Willis ISDs; the sharing of facilities at Conroe High School for evening college courses; joint planning for technology compatibility between Conroe ISD and the college; special educational initiatives to encourage minority students to go on to postsecondary education (specifically, night classes); student support, including entry placement testing on site at local high schools in partnership with counseling staff; and planning for dual-credit course work.

Texas Tech University (RES II)
Professional Development School Collaborative

Grades served: E, M, HS

Schools served: 28

Year established: 1990

Location of schools served: UR, SU, RU

Type of schools served: PUB

This partnership links 11 colleges and universities in west Texas. Its primary mission reflects that of the Holmes Group: to invent an institutional coalition that brings together universities, colleges of education, education service centers, and public schools to improve the profession of teaching and learning opportunities for students. In carrying out this mission, members of the collaborative conduct research, plan and hold training conferences, and mutually engage in continuous program renewal K-graduate school.

Note: Each institution's Carnegie class is given in parentheses. **Key:** E=elementary school, HS=high school, M=middle school, NR=not reported, PRI=private, PUB=public, RU=rural, SU=suburban, UR=urban

University of Texas at El Paso (MA I)
El Paso Collaborative for Academic Excellence

Grades served: E, M, HS   Schools served: 135   Year established: 1991
Location of schools served: UR   Type of schools served: PUB, PRI

The El Paso Collaborative for Academic Excellence involves local university, community college, school district, community, business, and civic leaders in a broad effort to improve teaching and learning and to ensure academic success for all young people in El Paso. Specific initiatives of the El Paso Collaborative include institutes for teachers, principals, and parents to assist them in assessing the strengths and limitations of their education programs, to set high academic standards for all students, and to design and implement a school improvement plan; efforts to engage parents meaningfully in school improvement; and work with the university, especially in the Colleges of Education and Science, to ensure greater academic success among university students and to restructure teacher preparation into a clinical, professional development program.

Section Two
Coordinating Agencies, Regional Articulation Councils and Agreements, and Joint Governance

ARIZONA

Cochise College (AA)
Cochise College-Douglas Unified School District Joint Venture

Grades served: E, M, HS   Schools served: 2   Year established: 1993
Location of schools served: NR   Type of schools served: PUB

This joint venture is a collaboration of neighboring educational institutions to solve common educational problems and provide a more comprehensive, higher level of educational services to the community. It is based on a formal intergovernmental agreement that provides funding for a liaison position, joint sponsorship of a community-based ABE/GED/ESL program, an alternative high school, elementary pupil tutoring by college students, advanced science courses, and the development of externally funded joint projects, such as summer science camps and parent education.

Northern Arizona University (DOC I)
Arizona Small and Rural School Association

Grades served: NR   Schools served: 100   Year established: 1990
Location of schools served: UR, SU, RU   Type of schools served: PUB

This partnership provides a forum for discussion of issues, problems, and opportunities for small and/or rural schools in Arizona. An annual congress, held at the university, includes workshops for teachers, administrators, and board members and culminates in a town hall meeting focusing on an issue related to small schools and/or rural education. A quarterly newsletter provides a forum for members to share creative approaches to education. Members are informed of legislative and state board regulations that could affect them in providing educational services to their communities.

California Academic Partnership Program (U)
CAPP

Grades served: M, HS	Schools served: 200	Year established: 1984
Location of schools served: UR, SU, RU	Type of schools served: PUB	

CAPP is an effort to improve the readiness and motivation of middle and high school students from groups underrepresented in California higher education so they can enter and succeed in college. CAPP supports establishing academic partnerships between secondary schools and community colleges, public or private baccalaureate degree-granting institutions, and business enterprises aimed at transforming relationships between educational institutions to directly benefit students; improving curricula in subject areas required for admission to college; strengthening teachers' capacities to enable all students to learn; enhancing the ability of students to benefit from these changes; and bettering partners' understanding of these students' educational needs.

Intersegmental Coordinating Council (U)
ICC

Grades served: NR	Schools served: NR	Year established: 1987
Location of schools served: UR, SU, RU	Type of schools served: PUB, PRI	

The California Education Round Table, a group composed of the leaders of the five educational segments and the California Postsecondary Education Commission, established the ICC to ensure that individuals from all groups, ethnicities, and socioeconomic backgrounds have full opportunities for quality education. The ICC oversees and coordinates intersegmental programs and activities undertaken by the five educational segments. It includes faculty, students, and policymakers capable of fulfilling commitments made by the constituent institutions, and it works with other institutions to ensure that intersegmental activities are consistent with priorities established by the Round Table through the ICC in consultation with those most directly involved.

Boston Higher Education Partnership (U)
Boston Higher Education Partnership

Grades served: E, M, HS	Schools served: 123	Year established: 1975
Location of schools served: UR	Type of schools served: PUB	

The Boston Higher Education Partnership is a consortium of 25 Boston-area colleges and universities working with the Boston Public Schools. It includes public and independent, two- and four-year institutions. It has grown to a multimillion-dollar enterprise involved with all aspects of school restructuring, curricular reform, professional development, and student services and support. Since 1983 its members have provided more than $50 million in student scholarships, more than $27 million in pro bono contributions, and nearly $25 million in external grants to the Boston Public Schools.

Boston University (RES I)
Boston University/Chelsea Partnership

Grades served: E, M, HS	Schools served: 10	Year established: 1988
Location of schools served: UR	Type of schools served: PUB	

The Boston University/Chelsea Partnership is a comprehensive effort to reform the public schools of Chelsea to provide a national model for urban school reform. Under a ten-year contract, Boston University accepted responsibility for the entire public school system of Chelsea, a small, densely populated city north of Boston. The partnership has emphasized early childhood education, teacher training, health care, and curricular reform.

Five Colleges Inc. (U)
Five College/Public School Partnership

Grades served: E, M, HS	Schools served: 43	Year established: 1984
Location of schools served: UR, SU, RU	Type of schools served: PUB, PRI	

This partnership is dedicated to exploring a variety of collaborative models that can support and strengthen the professional development of school and college faculty as they work together. During the academic year, the partnership sponsors conferences and seminars for high school faculty in a variety of subject areas (in 1992-93 nearly 1,000 individuals participated in 67 events). During the summer, the partnership sponsors institutes and task forces. A clearinghouse for information and technical assistance, the partnership publishes a bimonthly newsletter *(Partnership Calendar)* with a regular circulation of 4,000 school and 1,000 college educators.

New England Network of Academic Alliances (U)
New England Network of Academic Alliances in Foreign Languages and Literatures

Grades served: M, HS	Schools served: 250	Year established: 1990
Location of schools served: UR, SU, RU	Type of schools served: PUB, PRI	

The New England Network of Academic Alliances in Foreign Languages and Literatures comprises 28 alliances in the six-state New England region. The alliances are made up of foreign language professionals from elementary, secondary, and postsecondary schools who meet regularly to share knowledge and experience in an effort to provide high-quality professional development for participating faculty. The network is currently working with the College Board and ACTFL in a three-year FIPSE-funded project to develop articulated learning outcomes and matching classroom-based assessments for foreign language instruction in grades 7-14.

Woods Hole Oceanographic Institution (U)
Woods Hole Science and Technology Education Partnership (WHSTEP)

Grades served: E, M, HS	Schools served: 16	Year established: 1989
Location of schools served: SU, RU	Type of schools served: PUB, PRI	

WHSTEP is a partnership of schools, scientific institutions, businesses, and community resources. Its purpose is to support, promote, and expand science and technology education and science literacy in the participating communities.

NEVADA

Truckee Meadows Community College (AA)
Joint Occupational Council

Grades served: HS

Schools served: 8

Year established: 1986

Location of schools served: UR

Type of schools served: PUB

This council was formed to advise both the school district and the community college regarding occupational programs. It oversees technical skills committees for program areas; provides input on community needs and training; supports legislation supporting occupational programs; oversees grants; reviews articulation agreements developed for program areas; assists the district and college with special services, such as work experience sites for students and internships; provides support for existing school/industry program partnerships; and makes program recommendations to the top administration at the college and in the district.

NEW YORK

Western New York Consortium of Higher Education (U)
King Urban Life Center

Grades served: E

Schools served: 2

Year established: 1990

Location of schools served: UR

Type of schools served: PUB

The King Urban Life Center is a national prototype program in which the higher education community of western New York, in partnership with leaders of Buffalo's East Side, is developing a community center and early childhood school devoted to serving the needs of children and families. The center will provide comprehensive services to support families, making the care and education of children from birth to eight years of age the focal point of its work. It is founded on the idea that providing for and educating children must involve, support, and care for the entire family.

OHIO

The Ohio State University-Main Campus (RES I)
Project Learn: Closing the Gap

Grades served: E, M, HS

Schools served: NR

Year established: 1992

Location of schools served: UR, SU, RU

Type of schools served: PUB

This partnership focuses on learning strengths, curricular reform, instructional strategies, and action research. Data about learning and teachers' styles provide a framework for teachers, administrators, parents, college professors, and children to collaborate as they work to close the learning gaps in education. Excellence, lifelong learning, and increased achievement for everyone are major goals, attained through informed relationships between teaching and learning styles.

OKLAHOMA

Eastern Oklahoma State College (AA)
Tri-County Association of Public Schools

Grades served: NR

Schools served: 35

Year established: 1988

Location of schools served: RU

Type of schools served: PUB

The Tri-County Association of Public Schools helps public school officials to promote education issues to area legislators and to share common problems and find unified answers for local school districts. Thirty-five schools make up the association, providing a working partnership between common education, vocational-technical education, and higher education. Participants recognize that all sectors make up public education and must form a cohesive planning group to effectively serve the needs of the public. To achieve this primary goal, the association meets quarterly at EOSC.

Note: Each institution's Carnegie class is given in parentheses. **Key:** E=elementary school, HS=high school, M=middle school, NR=not reported, PRI=private, PUB=public, RU=rural, SU=suburban, UR=urban

SOUTH CAROLINA

Orangeburg-Calhoun Technical College (AA)
Articulation Agreements

Grades served: HS   Schools served: 9   Year established: 1992
Location of schools served: RU   Type of schools served: NR

The Orangeburg-Calhoun Technical College articulation agreements with area high schools include competencies for numerous courses agreed upon by both secondary and postsecondary faculty. Tech Prep sponsored the program, with leadership provided by the college.

University of South Carolina-Columbia (RES II)
South Carolina Health Education Partnership

Grades served: E   Schools served: NR   Year established: 1992
Location of schools served: UR, SU, RU   Type of schools served: PUB

The purpose of this partnership is to strengthen the implementation of comprehensive elementary school health education in South Carolina. The project mobilizes resources of higher education, community health organizations and PTAs, state agencies, school districts, and schools to improve health education in elementary schools. Regional partnerships assess training and other school needs, and implement and evaluate plans to address them. The result is increased networking among health education faculty in institutions around the state and cooperative efforts to improve the preparation of preservice health teachers statewide.

TEXAS

Hispanic Association of Colleges and Universities (U)
Hispanic Student Success Program (HASP)

Grades served: E, M, HS   Schools served: 52   Year established: 1988
Location of schools served: NR   Type of schools served: PUB, PRI

HASP is a partnership linking the Hispanic Association of Colleges and Universities with six public school districts, three community colleges, and four 4-year colleges/universities. Its primary mission is to increase the rate at which Hispanic students graduate from high school, enroll in college, and graduate from college. HASP's specific initiatives include enrichment centers, leadership development clubs, academic year enrichment activities, EXCEL (a summer program), and joint admissions agreements and other mechanics, including a transfer center, to help community college students transfer to senior institutions. Outstanding teachers receive Class Act Awards.

Section Three
New Achievement Standards and Assessment Mechanisms

COLORADO

Colorado School of Mines (DOC II)
Statewide Systemic Initiative

Grades served: E, M, HS   Schools served: 12   Year established: 1993
Location of schools served: NR   Type of schools served: PUB

Colorado School of Mines and Jefferson County School District R-1 represent one of 12 partnerships in Colorado's Statewide Systemic Initiative funded by the National Science Foundation. The goals are to increase the achievement, participation, and interest of all students in mathematics and science through standards-based assessment, curriculum, instruction, teacher preparation, and professional development. The partnership links national, state, and local resources to provide technical support for implementation of systemic change.

University of Colorado at Denver (DOC II)
Columbia Area Writing Project

Grades served: E, M, HS   Schools served: 1   Year established: NR
Location of schools served: NR   Type of schools served: PUB

This cooperative project between the University of Colorado at Denver and the Columbine Area Accountability Committee of the Jefferson County Public Schools seeks to improve the quality of students' writing. The Columbine area comprises five elementary schools. The goal of the Accountability Committee is to articulate all aspects (both in assessment and instruction) of the new district proficiency in developing effective communicators. A committee representing the participating schools is working with UCD faculty to design a set of procedures that can be used to assess students' development in becoming effective communicators at grades 3, 5, 7, 9, and 11, and better link assessment and instruction to meet students' individual needs.

DISTRICT OF COLUMBIA

Gallaudet University (MA I)
Annual Survey of Hearing-Impaired Children and Youth

Grades served: NR   Schools served: 8500   Year established: 1968
Location of schools served: UR, SU, RU   Type of schools served: PUB, PRI

Gallaudet's Center for Assessment and Demographic Studies has contacted special education programs serving hearing-impaired children in its annual survey of deaf and hard-of-hearing children and youth. The purpose of this national survey is to collect demographic, audiological, and educational data on these children to improve their educational opportunities. Major projects associated with the annual survey include the development of norms for hearing-impaired children on the Stanford Achievement Test and numerous special studies, which resulted in two books: *Deaf Children in America* and *Deaf Students and the School-to-Work Transition*.

Note: Each institution's Carnegie class is given in parentheses. **Key:** E=elementary school, HS=high school, M=middle school, NR=not reported, PRI=private, PUB=public, RU=rural, SU=suburban, UR=urban

FLORIDA

University of South Florida (RES II)
Centennial Elementary Professional Development School

Grades served: E   Schools served: 1   Year established: 1991
Location of schools served: SU, RU   Type of schools served: PUB

Centennial Elementary Professional Development School (PDS) is a partnership of the University of South Florida-Tampa and Pasco County Schools. The purpose of the PDS is the preparation of teachers and administrators, the continuing staff development of its experienced professionals, and the research and development of programs that lead to superior educational outcomes for students. Centennial Elementary operates the school using a continuous progress model. Children are in primary or intermediate houses and spend three years working with the same team of teachers. A USF faculty member works on site with teachers and university interns.

GEORGIA

Clayton State College (BUS)
Middle Level Teacher Education (B.A. Degree)

Grades served: M, HS   Schools served: 136   Year established: 1991
Location of schools served: UR, SU   Type of schools served: PUB

Clayton State College, working with six school systems, has developed and implemented an outcome-focused, assessment-based, student-centered teacher education program. The degree, awarded has a strong liberal arts foundation in mathematics, science, social science, and language arts. All education courses have been developed and are taught by school-based education experts. This new initiative has a precollegiate component of Future Educators of America in chapters in all middle and high schools, with a cadet teacher option available in the high schools. Plans are to work with the school systems, continuing professional support for graduates through their first year of teaching.

MAINE

University of Southern Maine (MA I)
Southern Maine Partnership

Grades served: E, M, HS   Schools served: 184   Year established: 1987
Location of schools served: UR, SU, RU   Type of schools served: PUB, PRI

The Southern Maine Partnership assists in developing and maintaining learner-centered schools through teacher development and school restructuring. An ongoing systematic approach involves individual teachers working in classrooms and whole school staffs working within their districts and communities. The partnership links the University of Southern Maine, the Maine College of Art, 26 school districts and three private schools in southern Maine in offering regional conversations, workshops and seminars, and an annual assessment conference.

OHIO

Kent State University-Main Campus (RES II)
Early Assessment for Exceptional Potential

Grades served: E   Schools served: 12   Year established: 1990
Location of schools served: UR, SU   Type of schools served: PUB

Kent State University's Early Assessment for Exceptional Potential project uses computer-aided technology to develop a model for identifying young gifted and talented minority and/or economically disadvantaged students. Teams of primary classroom teachers, administrators, and College of Education faculty have determined behavioral attributes of exceptional potential observed during demonstration teaching in primary science and social studies lessons. Computer-assisted training tapes for inservice teacher training have been developed, and portfolio assessment focusing on 18 primary identifiers is used to determine individual students' strengths.

Alverno College (BA II)
Assessing Learning

Grades served: M, HS

Schools served: 9

Year established: 1993

Location of schools served: UR

Type of schools served: PUB

Alverno College's Assessing Learning Project is a partnership with the Milwaukee Public Schools. The project involves teams of teachers in a two-week summer institute, followed by a year of follow-up assistance in their schools. It seeks to develop a team of teachers at each middle and high school who are knowledgeable about performance assessment and capable of working with students and other members of the staff to strengthen the district's emphasis on the development of strong communications skills in young people. The project involves a five- year plan to work with teams of teachers from all of the district's middle and high schools.

□ □ □

Part Five
LEARNING TECHNOLOGIES AND NEW ALLIANCES

Introduction

This fifth part is divided into four sections: "Innovative Uses of Learning/Communication Technologies," "School-College-Business Partnerships," "Resource-Sharing Agreements," and "Magnet Schools." While such a grouping of partnerships might appear to be eclectic at first glance, a common, fundamental principle underlies the programs. All of the partnerships have fashioned a whole greater than the sum of their respective parts by the careful and creative sharing of resources, whether by offering less-common foreign languages such as Chinese and Russian to multiple schools via interactive video communications, or by combining school, college, and local business resources to promote science education, or by bringing institutions as diverse as museums and medical schools together with schools and colleges to form magnet schools.

Section One, "Innovative Uses of Learning/Communication Technologies," provides 19 examples of partnerships using the Internet, instructional television, fiber-optic networks, and other technologies to link schools and colleges. For example, Kent State University uses the Internet to reduce professional isolation of teachers in school-based deaf-education programs. With the assistance of Georgia Institute of Technology faculty, Norcross High School uses Internet access to promote communication in French between pen pals in France and the United States. Western Illinois University's Science Alive Scientific Literacy Program brings a series of interactive, televised staff development sessions to K-12 science teachers via the university's Satellite Education Network.

Section Two, "School-College-Business Partnerships," often focuses on strengthening the curriculum, as typified by the University of Delaware's Science Alliance, which brings corporations like Dupont and Hercules together with public and private schools throughout the state to promote the teaching of mathematics, science, and technology. Businesses also contribute valuable equipment to partnerships, as evidenced by Louisiana Tech's Mobile Automated Learning Laboratory, donated by Entergy Corporation and Louisiana Power and Light. This 28-foot motorcoach, equipped with computers and interactive video stations, serves the needs of undereducated adult workers at 14 sites. Such partnerships also build bridges between practicing teachers and other professionals. Lesley College's Creating Lasting Links program, for example, links elementary school teachers with scientists in one of 70 businesses for a two-week "partnering experience."

Section Three, "Resource-Sharing Agreements," describes a group of programs that imaginatively share an array of services and facilities. Adopt-a-school partnerships, such as the one among Augusta College, Lucy Craft Laney High School, and Joseph Lamar Elementary School, involve tutoring arrangements, cooperative staff development programs, courtesy admission to college events, library access, and free continuing education. Canisius College's Laboratory Equipment Assistance Program distributes, on a rotating basis, equipment donated by local chemical industries to more than 50 area high school science departments. This partnership also involves workshops, seminars, site visits to industries, and internships for teachers to keep them abreast of new scientific and technological developments.

Section Four, "Magnet Schools," describes a small but important group of partnerships focused on special schools with distinctive academic missions, such as the University of Southern California's Science Museum School Collaborative, offered in partnership with the Los Angeles Unified School District and the California Museum of Science and Industry, which emphasizes science, mathematics, and technology. USC is also involved in a partnership with Francisco Bravo Medical Magnet High School that focuses on biomedical science education. Alternatively, the Miami Connection, a partnership between Miami University-Hamilton Campus and Fairfied High School, is aimed at students who have been dismissed from the regular high school program. Offered at the Hamilton campus, the program combines morning academic sessions and afternoon work-study jobs. □

Section One
Innovative Uses of Learning/Communication Technologies

GEORGIA

Georgia College (MA I)
Georgia College Educator's Network (GCEduNET)

Grades served: E, M, HS   Schools served: 3,600   Year established: 1988
Location of schools served: UR, SU, RU   Type of schools served: PUB, PRI

GCEduNET links the University System of Georgia and the K-12 education community in Georgia. Its primary mission is to act as an electronic brokerage house bringing education information providers and consumers together under one electronic roof. Currently the system has more than 9,000 members and is growing at the rate of 200 new members per month. The network requires no membership fees or connect time charges, and telephone costs to users are eliminated through the use of dial-up facilities provided by the university system's data network, PeachNet, and by INWATS service.

Georgia Institute of Technology (RES I)
Internet Access Pilot Project for High School

Grades served: HS   Schools served: 1   Year established: NR
Location of schools served: NR   Type of schools served: NR

Norcross High School and Open Campus share a facility at Norcross, Georgia. A computer network has been installed in the school, and the media center provides some computer access to students. When the media center's dial-in phone lines for accessing computer bulletin boards proved insufficient, a pilot project was set up, with some Georgia Tech faculty donating personal time to teach interested faculty about the Internet and to help get access into the school through the PeachNet dial-in lines. Students use this access to reach pen pals in France and to communicate daily in French. Information from the Internet news and library searches has been downloaded to the local media center.

ILLINOIS

Southern Illinois University at Carbondale (RES II)
Southern Illinois Instructional Technology Association

Grades served: E, M, HS   Schools served: 245   Year established: 1961
Location of schools served: RU   Type of schools served: PUB, PRI

The Southern Illinois Instructional Technology Association (SIITA), a division of SIUC Broadcasting Service and WSIU/WUSI-TV, is a partnership of area preK-12 schools and Southern Illinois University at Carbondale. Its primary mission is to offer more than 120 instructional programs for 4,000 teachers and 56,000 students in public, private, and parochial schools. SIUC Broadcasting provides other services as well, including staff development and distance learning activities for preschool, K-12, and adult learners. National projects include the Public Broadcasting System's Ready to Learn and Mathline services, GED on TV, and the National Teacher Training Institute in Math, Science, and Technology.

Note: Each institution's Carnegie class is given in parentheses. **Key:** E=elementary school, HS=high school, M=middle school, NR=not reported, PRI=private, PUB=public, RU=rural, SU=suburban, UR=urban

Western Illinois University (MA I)
Science Alive Scientific Literacy Program

Grades served: E, M, HS   Schools served: NR   Year established: 1993
Location of schools served: UR, SU, RU   Type of schools served: PUB, PRI

Science Alive from the Satellite Education Network at Western Illinois University is a series of ten 30-minute interactive television programs of staff development training resources for K-12 science teachers. The purpose of the ten programs is to present teachers with practical examples and suggestions of how to teach scientific principles and concepts addressing goals for biology and the physical sciences identified by the Illinois State Board of Education. Participating teachers receive a set of printed materials with detailed lesson plans supporting the visual content in each TV segment.

IOWA

Iowa Lakes Community College (AA)
Galaxy Schools Program

Grades served: M, HS   Schools served: 19   Year established: 1992
Location of schools served: NR   Type of schools served: PUB, PRI

The Galaxy Schools Program among Iowa Lakes Community College, the Lakeland Area Education Agency, secondary schools, and high school students promotes interdisciplinary education. Students conduct research and exchange hypotheses electronically with other area schools through PSINET and share their findings over the Iowa Communication Network with other students. The project provides students and high school faculty members the opportunity to develop problem-solving strategies. It also provides inservice training for high school instructors, a continuing forum for communication between instructors and students, a research setting, and an evaluation process.

Kirkwood Community College (AA)
Kirkwood Partnerships–Kirkwood Telecommunications Partnership

Grades served: HS   Schools served: 20   Year established: 1983
Location of schools served: UR, RU   Type of schools served: PUB, PRI

Kirkwood leads a secondary school network of 15 area high schools to share high school and college credit courses via the college's live, interactive television system. Kirkwood is the fiscal and coordinating agency to deliver high school courses in Russian, technical math, environmental science, and career development. High school students can also earn college credit in calculus, psychology, sociology, and history through the system. The Grant Wood Area Education Agency, an intermediate agency serving local K-12 school districts, uses the Kirkwood Telecommunications System to deliver a major program of teacher inservice education to teachers in a seven-county area.

MARYLAND

University of Maryland-College Park (RES I)
ICONS (International Communication and Negotiation Simulations)

Grades served: HS   Schools served: 110   Year established: 1986
Location of schools served: UR, SU, RU   Type of schools served: PUB, PRI

ICONS is a computer-assisted simulation of international relations in which groups of students at schools around the world role-play as decision makers of various countries. The students negotiate solutions to real-world issues using a computer network to exchange messages and conduct live, on-line conferences. Issues include the global environment, trade, arms control, human rights, economic development, and world health. In addition to the University of Maryland, regional centers have been started to tailor the simulations to meet the needs and interests of various geographic areas.

MINNESOTA

St. Cloud State University (MA I)
Rural/Urban Link

Grades served: HS   Schools served: NR   Year established: 1993
Location of schools served: UR, RU   Type of schools served: PUB

Rural/Urban Link is a program using two-way television to link rural and urban high school classes to explore issues of regional stereotyping and lead to better understanding of stereotyping, particularly the more volatile forms harmful to our society. Urban sites are high school classes in Minneapolis, and rural sites are drawn from approximately 30 high schools connected to regional television networks in central Minnesota. Coordinators attempt to match subject and grade levels as closely as possible. Most links provide sufficient lead time of two class sessions, generally one week apart, and follow-up is encouraged.

MISSOURI

Harris-Stowe State College (TEACH)
Harris-Stowe State College-Waring Academy of Basic Instruction Partnership

Grades served: E   Schools served: 1   Year established: 1989
Location of schools served: UR   Type of schools served: PUB

The partnership between Harris-Stowe State College and Waring Academy of Basic Instruction involves a relationship between a historically black college with emphasis in teacher education and a basic skills magnet elementary school in the St. Louis Public Schools. Emphasis is on providing inservice support for the Waring faculty and enhancing their students' experiences through interaction with Harris-Stowe faculty and students. All Waring students use computers at the college, and Waring faculty develop computer-based materials and class projects with the assistance of college faculty. Harris-Stowe students gain preservice experience by working with Waring students in a classroom lab setting or individually.

NEW YORK

Rochester Institute of Technology (MA I)
Rochester Area Interactive Telecommunications Network

Grades served: HS   Schools served: 5   Year established: 1991
Location of schools served: UR, SU   Type of schools served: PUB

The Rochester Area Interactive Telecommunications Network is a partnership involving the Rochester Telephone Corporation, Rochester Institute of Technology, NYSERNet, Monroe Board of Cooperative Educational Services (BOCES), SUNY-Brockport, Brighton High Schools, and four area school districts. This fiber optic network enables full-motion two-way audio and video between RIT and the four districts, and high-speed Internet connections. Several RIT courses are offered for credit. Special events and electronic field trips have included an AIDS awareness panel, an imaging workshop for science and math teachers, and a diversity series exploring issues of prejudice. Programs are followed by on-line Internet discussions.

Note: Each institution's Carnegie class is given in parentheses. **Key:** E=elementary school, HS=high school, M=middle school, NR=not reported, PRI=private, PUB=public, RU=rural, SU=suburban, UR=urban

NORTH CAROLINA

Wake Forest University (DOC II)
LREnet (Law-Related Education Network)

Grades served: NR

Schools served: NR

Year established: 1991

Location of schools served: UR, SU, RU

Type of schools served: PUB, PRI

LREnet is an electronic bulletin board for education in citizenship and a special service in the field of law-related education. Teachers can download lesson plans, documents, and Supreme Court case summaries directly to their own computers via LREnet. They can also communicate with other teachers in the network and participate in regular conferences on specific topics of current interest. LREnet is sponsored by CRADLE (the Center for Research and Development in Law-Related Education, a national nonprofit organization affiliated with Wake Forest's School of Law).

OHIO

Case Western Reserve University (RES I)
Cleveland FreeNet (Academy One)

Grades served: E, M, HS

Schools served: 168

Year established: 1991

Location of schools served: UR, SU, RU

Type of schools served: PUB, PRI

Case Western Reserve University provides its networked bulletin board and electronic mail service, Cleveland FreeNet, free to the local community (through dial-in and direct access to the Internet); to the state (through direct access to the Internet using the state network, OARnet); and worldwide to members of the Internet. More than 40,000 active users aged 5-80 use the service. Nearly 35,000 users log in weekly.

Kent State University-Ashtabula Campus (AA)
Ashtabula County Interactive Television Network

Grades served: HS

Schools served: 9

Year established: 1990

Location of schools served: NR

Type of schools served: PUB

This network links the county's eight public high schools, the joint vocational school, and Kent State's Ashtabula campus in a fiber-optic network. It resulted from a partnership including the Civic Development Corporation, a county capital-funds provider, educational institutions, the Ohio State Legislature, and four telephone companies. In operation since the Fall 1991 semester, the network's primary purpose is to enable public high school students to take courses that would not otherwise be available to them because their schools are too small.

Kent State University-Main Campus (RES II)
Deaf Education Professional Development Network

Grades served: E, M, HS

Schools served: 12

Year established: 1991

Location of schools served: UR, SU, RU

Type of schools served: PUB

The Deaf Education Professional Development Network at Kent State University is designed to use telecommunications in an effort to reduce professional isolation and increase collaboration between school-based deaf education programs and Kent State University. The network shares curriculum development and, working with 14 local systems, develops instructional technology practicums and field experiences. Internet-based, the program serves students and instructors.

<u>TENNESSEE</u>

Chattanooga State Technical Community College (AA)
Distance Learning Program

Grades served: E, M, HS   Schools served: 5   Year established: NR
Location of schools served: NR   Type of schools served: NR

Chattanooga State's Distance Learning Program provides access to college for persons constrained from attending a site by distance, time, or personal commitments. It serves a seven-county region in Tennessee and three or four counties each in Georgia and Alabama. The program provides classes by live interactive television at two rural high schools and at Southeast Tennessee State Regional Correctional Center. The program also enrolls corrections officers at two other prisons, and offers broadcast courses and video-based correspondence courses. In fall 1994, three 1-year certificate courses were added via the Electronic University Network through America On-Line. The program is also joining in the development of a statewide network using compressed video delivery and is the Internet K-12 instruction access for Chattanooga State's service region.

<u>TEXAS</u>

University of Texas Health Science Center at San Antonio (MED)
Texas Math and Science Hotline

Grades served: E, M, HS   Schools served: NR   Year established: NR
Location of schools served: UR, SU, RU   Type of schools served: PUB, PRI

The Texas Society of Biomedical Research has established a toll-free telephone system for students, teachers, and Texas residents with questions in science and mathematics. The service provides Texans with up-to-date answers within 48 hours from a network of resources at the state's colleges, universities, and government agencies. Its purpose is to enhance the academic, health, and social environment of the schools, improving math and science skills and knowledge and education for teachers and staff education.

<u>UTAH</u>

Weber State University (MA II)
WEMATH

Grades served: E, M, HS   Schools served: 83   Year established: 1986
Location of schools served: UR, SU, RU   Type of schools served: PUB

The Northern Utah Mathematics Network (WEMATH) was inspired as a low-cost way to bring the computer into the classroom as an improvement over the chalkboard. Through the network, teachers learn to program their own original ideas into software accessible from any modem-equipped classroom in the region. Weber State provides central training facilities and staff, aided by major grants from AT&T, the National Science Foundation, the U.S. Department of Education, U.S. West, and software vendors. The participating school districts supply computers, modems to connect classrooms to the network, and other forms of support. In 1987, the U.S. Department of Education recognized WEMATH as an exemplary project.

Note: Each institution's Carnegie class is given in parentheses. **Key:** E=elementary school, HS=high school, M=middle school, NR=not reported, PRI=private, PUB=public, RU=rural, SU=suburban, UR=urban

WISCONSIN

University of Wisconsin Centers (AA)
Distance Learning

Grades served: E, M, HS	Schools served: 5	Year established: 1992
Location of schools served: SU, RU	Type of schools served: PUB	

The University of Wisconsin Center in Rock County offers a diverse continuing education outreach program grounded in the campus's liberal studies mission. Classes in the arts, sciences, and humanities serve the general adult population and K-12 teachers to help meet requirements for license renewal. Workshops in science and math help K-12 teachers keep abreast of changes in their fields. High school students are offered postsecondary courses via distance learning and an off-campus summer program in the prevention of alcohol and other drug abuse. Younger students participate in College for Kids, a nine-day summer academic and arts program. The Continuing Education Office sponsors a lecture and discussion series at a community environmental education center and college credit courses at business sites.

University of Wisconsin-Whitewater (MA I)
Ameritech-Whitewater Curriculum Integration Project

Grades served: E, M, HS	Schools served: NR	Year established: 1993
Location of schools served: UR, RU	Type of schools served: PUB, PRI	

This project is designed to use telecommunications technologies to develop a thematic approach to the K-12 curriculum. Twenty-four teachers from eight school districts spend a year working with university faculty to develop a multidisciplinary approach to classroom instruction. Teachers are linked through the Internet and a local electronic bulletin board to share multimedia curricular materials designed to teach a range of thematically integrated subjects, including art, mathematics, science, geography, English, and reading.

___

Section Two
School-College-Business Partnerships

CALIFORNIA

Woodbury University (MA II)
Verdugo Intensive Partnership

Grades served: HS	Schools served: 1	Year established: 1991
Location of schools served: SU	Type of schools served: PUB	

The Verdugo Intensive Partnership links Woodbury University and Verdugo Hills High School in a program designed to provide greater access to higher education for underrepresented students (African-American, Hispanic, and those with limited English proficiency) by strengthening the high school mathematics program through changes implemented in algebra I and II and geometry. Mathematics is taught in terms of its value and practical application in the workplace, in other disciplines, and in postsecondary pursuits. Parents' and students' participation is nurtured through increased communication among the high school, postsecondary institutions, the business partner, and the home.

COLORADO

Colorado School of Mines (DOC II)
Tri-Partnership to Benefit Math and Science Education

Grades served: E, M, HS   Schools served: 22   Year established: 1993
Location of schools served: UR, SU   Type of schools served: PUB

Adams County School District 50, Colorado School of Mines, and Electronic Data Systems (EDS) have entered into an educational three-way partnership. The collaboration is designed to strengthen curricular offerings, particularly in mathematics, science, and engineering, and to provide opportunities in training and staff development for all three entities.

DELAWARE

University of Delaware (RES II)
Science Alliance

Grades served: E, M, HS   Schools served: 100   Year established: 1988
Location of schools served: UR, SU   Type of schools served: PUB, PRI

The University of Delaware, in conjunction with Delaware Technical and Community College, Delaware State University, the Dupont Company, Hercules, Zeneca, other industries, public and private schools, and concerned citizens, works to enhance precollege science education in Delaware. The alliance currently emphasizes science, math, and technology at all levels. Projects include the Teacher/Volunteer Partnership Project, the Science, Math, and Technology Resource Center, career awareness programs, excellence in science teaching awards, and summer employment in industry for teachers.

GEORGIA

Berry College (MA I)
Educators-In-Industry

Grades served: NR   Schools served: 30   Year established: 1981
Location of schools served: UR, SU   Type of schools served: PUB, PRI

Educators-In-Industry provides teachers with an opportunity to learn about the perspectives and needs of businesses and industries and to translate this knowledge into classroom/school practices that integrate career education programming for students within the school and the classroom. The program is designed to provide information and experience in the U.S. economic system and to help teachers become more effective in their efforts to prepare children with the skills, attitudes, and work habits necessary to be successful in that system. The program also provides business and industry with the opportunity to influence education to train a more prepared and motivated workforce.

Georgia Institute of Technology (RES I)
Southeastern Consortium for Minorities in Engineering (SECME)

Grades served: NR   Schools served: 339   Year established: NR
Location of schools served: NR   Type of schools served: NR

This consortium is an organization of the engineering colleges of 31 southern universities from nine states and the District of Columbia and 65 corporations. SECME built a synergistic organization that, through the involvement of teachers, communities, school systems, university leaders, and industry representatives, provides minority students better academic preparation and a broader field of career opportunities.

Note: Each institution's Carnegie class is given in parentheses. **Key:** E=elementary school, HS=high school, M=middle school, NR=not reported, PRI=private, PUB=public, RU=rural, SU=suburban, UR=urban

INDIANA

Butler University (MA I)
Partners in Education

Grades served: M   Schools served: 1   Year established: 1993
Location of schools served: NR   Type of schools served: PUB

The mission of Butler University's Partners in Education program is to bring together business and education to better prepare Indianapolis Public School students for work and rewarding lives. The program's objectives are to provide learning experiences for the students of Harshman Middle School and the clinical students of Butler University's College of Education in a prestudent teaching practicum.

LOUISIANA

Louisiana State University in Shreveport (MA I)
Shreveport Urban Community Service Consortium

Grades served: M, HS   Schools served: 23   Year established: 1993
Location of schools served: UR   Type of schools served: PUB

Louisiana State University in Shreveport, Southern University, Bossier Parish Community College, Regional Technical Institute, the city of Shreveport, the Chamber of Commerce, and the Caddo Parish School System in Shreveport have established a workforce preparation program to upgrade education and training of urban residents for employment in the 21st century. The program includes a mobile learning lab, middle school remediation, high school career activities, internships, planning, and research.

Louisiana Tech University (DOC II)
Mobile Automated Learning Laboratory (MALL)

Grades served: HS   Schools served: 14   Year established: 1991
Location of schools served: NR   Type of schools served: NR

The MALL is a cooperative effort of business/industry and education. Donated by Entergy Corporation and Louisiana Power and Light, the MALL is staffed and jointly managed by Louisiana Tech University and Grambling State University. It is designed to provide a better-educated workforce by meeting the needs of undereducated adults. The 28-foot motorcoach, equipped with computer and interactive video stations, travels more than 2,000 miles per month to 14 sites, serving 600 students aged 16 to 72, of whom 60 recently completed their GED. The program has received two national awards for excellence in education.

MAINE

Bates College (BA I)
Bates College/Lewiston Junior High School Adopt-A-School Program

Grades served: M   Schools served: 1   Year established: 1992
Location of schools served: UR   Type of schools served: PUB

This partnership links Bates college and Lewiston Junior High School through a communitywide adopt-a-school business/education program. It is one of several collaborations in the area. Others include participation in a community task force studying readiness for school, a summer institute for teachers, a secondary education certification program for Bates students with a tutoring/classroom component in area schools, a mentoring program in science for middle-school girls, and a program offering high school students the opportunity to enroll in courses at Bates.

<u>MASSACHUSETTS</u>

Harvard University (RES I)
Cambridge Partnership for Public Education
Grades served: E, M, HS   Schools served: 14   Year established: 1986
Location of schools served: UR   Type of schools served: PUB

This partnership links higher education, business and industry, community leaders, teachers, and parents in an effort to improve Cambridge Public Schools. CPPE is dedicated to improving the quality of education in Cambridge by channeling university and corporate resources to the public schools. Harvard's participation includes establishing priorities for effecting improvements in such areas as teacher fellowships and professional development, and technical assistance.

Lesley College (MA I)
Creating Lasting Links
Grades served: E   Schools served: 9   Year established: 1992
Location of schools served: UR   Type of schools served: PUB

Creating Lasting Links is a four-year project funded by the National Science Foundation that links elementary school teachers and scientists. Based at Lesley College, the project selects up to three teachers for a two-week partnership in each of several businesses. The scientists then collaborate on classroom activities during the following school year. Partners also attend bimonthly meetings to tour other businesses and share their experiences. By 1995, the program involved 140 teachers and 70 businesses.

Smith College (BA I)
Secondary Math and Science Outreach Program
Grades served: HS   Schools served: 50   Year established: 1990
Location of schools served: UR, SU, RU   Type of schools served: PUB, PRI

This program is designed to encourage young women to continue their studies in math and science. It includes three components: the Current Students/Future Scientists and Engineers Workshop, which helps math and science teachers and counselors develop and implement appropriate projects within their own schools; TRI-ON, a day of science at Smith College, which invites female high school students to participate in hands-on labs in math and science; and teaching internships, which expose college women majoring in math and science to the rewards and excitement of classroom teaching.

Springfield College (MA I)
Springfield College/DeBerry School Partnership
Grades served: E   Schools served: 1   Year established: 1993
Location of schools served: UR   Type of schools served: PUB

This partnership provides college students with an opportunity to provide physical education, tutoring, and assistance in producing a school newspaper to children of urban families. DeBerry School is a K-5 elementary school with a high percentage of children from low-income and minority families, particularly Latino and African-American. The volunteering college students represent a variety of majors, and they provide programming and support that could not otherwise be possible. Some funding is provided by the Nellie Mae Fund for Education.

Note: Each institution's Carnegie class is given in parentheses. **Key:** E=elementary school, HS=high school, M=middle school, NR=not reported, PRI=private, PUB=public, RU=rural, SU=suburban, UR=urban

Charles S. Mott Community College (AA)
Project Design
Grades served: M, HS   Schools served: 21   Year established: 1993
Location of schools served: NR   Type of schools served: PUB

Project Design is a partnership between educational institutions and industry to provide career-specific skills to students interested in design/engineering. It combines a strong career awareness component with educational reform from middle school through community college and four-year institution. Important components include the use of applied academics, enhanced drafting/design and related technology programs, articulation between educational levels, cooperative work experiences, 2+2 college agreements, and industrial involvement in curricular development. It combines the expertise of school and industry to develop educational experiences to meet students' and industry's needs.

Siena Heights College (BA II)
Payback for Education
Grades served: M   Schools served: 12   Year established: 1991
Location of schools served: SU, RU   Type of schools served: PUB, PRI

The purpose of this program is to expose students to the world of work as they begin to design their high school curriculum. The program is a joint venture of two private liberal arts colleges, a community college, the local school systems, and the local business community. Payback for Education hosts an annual daylong conference that brings 150 eighth grade students to a college campus for a career-planning workshop, followed by half-day visits (in small groups) to 25 work sites. A profound side effect of the program has been the forging of stronger relationships between the educational community and local employers.

Rochester Community College (AA)
Manufacturing Electronics Youth Apprenticeship
Grades served: HS   Schools served: 8   Year established: 1993
Location of schools served: RU   Type of schools served: PUB

This partnership involves IBM, Rochester Community College, Minnesota Riverland Technical College, and area high schools. Its primary mission is to offer qualified high school students the opportunity to enroll in a challenging technical/vocational program, beginning in the ninth grade. The apprenticeship program expands applied academic courses through staff training, links academic course work to employment, develops students' skills to meet or surpass world standards in manufacturing electronics, establishes school-based and work-based youth apprenticeship coordinators, and conducts evaluation and competency-based assessment.

Rockhurst College (MA I)
Science Alliance
Grades served: NR   Schools served: NR   Year established: 1990
Location of schools served: UR, SU, RU   Type of schools served: PUB, PRI

Rockhurst is the facilitator for this alliance of science and mathematics educators and business and community leaders dedicated to broad-scale and long-term improvement in science and math education. The goals of the alliance are the sharing of resources, increased coordination of programs, and better distribution of information. Rockhurst facilitates the activities of the constituent groups while initiating programs to meet area science needs with the approval of the alliance. Activities include the publication of an environmental resource directory, summer interactive science workshops and camp, a Meet-the-Mentor program, and excellence in teaching awards for science and math teachers.

NEBRASKA

Metropolitan Community College (AA)
Omaha Job Clearinghouse

Grades served: M, HS   Schools served: 7   Year established: 1990
Location of schools served: UR   Type of schools served: PUB

The Omaha Job Clearinghouse targets educationally disadvantaged and non-college-bound students in grades 7-12. It incorporates multiple strategies and activities to improve the transition into work and/or postsecondary education for disadvantaged and non-college-bound students. The program begins with career awareness for junior high students and culminates in work experiences for students entering their senior year and job placement with and/or incentives for entering postsecondary education upon graduation. It targets teachers and counselors in the schools, parents, members of the business community, and community services.

Nebraska Wesleyan University (BA I)
Ventures in Partnership (VIP)

Grades served: E   Schools served: 1   Year established: 1987
Location of schools served: NR   Type of schools served: PUB

Ventures in Partnerships fosters cooperation and understanding between the schools in Lincoln and area businesses and organizations. Through VIP, a school and business or a school and community organization can form a mutually beneficial partnership to help each other achieve identified goals.

Western Nebraska Community College (AA)
Adopt-a-School

Grades served: E   Schools served: 15   Year established: 1989
Location of schools served: NR   Type of schools served: PUB

This project is a branch of the local Chamber of Commerce. Its purpose is to link businesses and industries with local schools to provide opportunities for learning. Western Nebraska Community College, for example, was linked with Northfield Elementary for the 1993-94 school year. The primary objective was to provide elementary students the opportunity to understand what it means for a community to be served by a community college. The major activities of the project are faculty guest speakers, writing experiences with the college newspaper, and theater and sports activities.

NEW JERSEY

Middlesex County College (AA)
Central Region Competitive Events Miniconference

Grades served: HS   Schools served: 20   Year established: 1970
Location of schools served: UR, SU Type of schools served: NR

Middlesex County College works with the Central Region Marketing Education Coordinators Association and the Central Region (NJ) DECA to plan and operate the Central Region Competitive Events Miniconference. The conference enables students to demonstrate competence in events related to marketing, to develop interpersonal skills necessary for related careers, and to develop a good understanding of the relationship between classroom studies and business and industrial practice. Funds are raised by the DECA clubs, and representatives from business and industry volunteer their time and act as judges for competitive events.

Note: Each institution's Carnegie class is given in parentheses. **Key:** E=elementary school, HS=high school, M=middle school, NR=not reported, PRI=private, PUB=public, RU=rural, SU=suburban, UR=urban

NEW YORK

City University of New York LaGuardia Community College (AA)
Career Exploration Project

Grades served: HS   Schools served: 2   Year established: 1993
Location of schools served: UR   Type of schools served: PUB

The Career Exploration Project links LaGuardia Community College, Bryant and Newtown High Schools, and such major corporations and government agencies as the Nippon Bank, the Department of Consumer Affairs, and Eastman Kodak in a program designed by high school and college faculty. Miniseminars, career exploration workshops, site visits to corporate workplaces, and day-long symposia are designed primarily for ninth and tenth grade students for whom few career exploration experiences are available. At Bryant High School, efforts are directed toward students in the mathematics enrichment and research classes; at Newtown High School, toward students with limited English proficiency who are entering its Business Institute.

State University of New York at Albany (RES II)
Capital Area Science Advisory Council

Grades served: NR   Schools served: 100   Year established: 1993
Location of schools served: UR, SU, RU   Type of schools served: PUB, PRI

The Capital Area Science Advisory Council comprises 35 members representing superintendents and teachers from inner-city schools, rural schools, and elementary to high schools; at least one representative from every institution of higher education in the region; and representatives from Lockheed-Martin, GE, Albany Medical College, and the Wadsworth Labs. Four working committees have been formed in mentoring, motivation, current resources, and research. Beyond the desire to support and encourage science education, an important goal of the council is to solve administrative problems connected with science research in the high schools.

NORTH CAROLINA

Haywood Community College (AA)
Haywood County Public/Private Educational Compact

Grades served: HS   Schools served: 1   Year established: 1989
Location of schools served: NR   Type of schools served: PUB

The Haywood County Public/Private Educational Compact is designed to bring the resources of public education, community colleges and four-year institutions, businesses, industries, community agents, parents, local government, and the community at large to work together on behalf of students at risk. Efforts focus on successful training, study, and employment in business, computer science, engineering/technology, health sciences, and occupational therapy in an effort to raise the percentage of students who complete high school and go on to successful postsecondary study or employment.

North Carolina Central University (MA I)
Central Carolina Consortium

Grades served: E, M, HS   Schools served: 249   Year established: 1993
Location of schools served: UR, SU, RU   Type of schools served: PUB, PRI

The primary mission of the Central Carolina Consortium is to improve educational practices and enhance economic development in central North Carolina, providing momentum for restructuring public education to meet the requirements of the 21st century. A collaboration of business and education, it is headquartered in the Chancellor's Office in Durham, where it serves as a broker of services to members. The membership comprises seven colleges and universities, five community colleges, 12 school systems, and 28 business partners.

University of North Carolina at Greensboro (DOC I)
Invitational Education and Next Century Schools

Grades served: M   Schools served: 2   Year established: 1989
Location of schools served: NR   Type of schools served: PUB

The Department of Counselor Education in the School of Education, in cooperation with Cumberland County Schools, subcontracted with RJR Nabisco Next Century Schools Project to address the concerns of two large Cumberland County junior high schools.

Wake Forest University (DOC II)
Western Triad Science and Mathematics Alliance

Grades served: E, M, HS   Schools served: 153   Year established: 1992
Location of schools served: UR, SU, RU   Type of schools served: PUB

The Western Triad Science and Mathematics Alliance, a regional partnership of the North Carolina Science and Mathematics Alliance, was established to systematically transform science and mathematics education. The partnership, linking business and industry, the universities and community colleges, schools, parents, and communities, plans and implements relevant and effective reforms. The alliance's three goals are to transform science and mathematics instruction into inquiry-based, problem-solving exploration; to develop and sustain enhanced access and participation for minorities and women in science and mathematics; and to support excellence in science and mathematics teaching and learning.

OHIO

Kent State University-Main Campus (RES II)
Cooperative Alliance for Gifted Education

Grades served: E, M, HS   Schools served: 5   Year established: 1991
Location of schools served: UR   Type of schools served: PUB

The Cooperative Alliance for Gifted Education addresses a national need for development of high-quality educational programs for tomorrow's technology-based communities. Its primary purpose is to reform educational practices through the use of technology to enhance the intellectual development of all children. The Center for School Improvement of the Cleveland Public Schools, IBM-EduQuest Corporation, and Kent State University's College of Education are the three major partners, but representatives from community agencies, teachers, museums, and libraries also participate. Cooperative Alliance serves 24 teachers and 1,600 urban students in grades 1-12 in the Cleveland Public Schools.

PENNSYLVANIA

Thiel College (BA II)
Mercer County School/Business Partnership

Grades served: HS   Schools served: 15   Year established: 1992
Location of schools served: UR, SU, RU   Type of schools served: PUB, PRI

The Mercer County School/Business Partnership is a cooperative effort of area businesses, high schools, and colleges in Mercer County, and surrounding areas. It was formed to provide a vehicle for communication between businesses and schools, and to help develop area students into qualified employees for Mercer County businesses. The partnership also encourages county students to gather experiences that will help them obtain professional positions. Ideally, the program will enable more local graduates to remain in Mercer County following graduation.

Note: Each institution's Carnegie class is given in parentheses. **Key:** E=elementary school, HS=high school, M=middle school, NR=not reported, PRI=private, PUB=public, RU=rural, SU=suburban, UR=urban

<u>SOUTH CAROLINA</u>

Greenville Technical College (AA)
General Manufacturing Certification Program
Grades served: NR   Schools served: 4   Year established: 1988
Location of schools served: UR, SU, RU   Type of schools served: PUB, PRI

Cryovac, a division of W.R. Grace and Company, and Greenville Technical College collaborated in developing the General Manufacturing Certification Program, because qualified workers were unavailable for Cryovac's manufacturing plant in Simpsonville. Based on a job task analysis, preliminary tests were prepared for reading, math, and mechanical aptitude. Program applicants must successfully complete the assessment before they may register for five courses that they must successfully complete. After completing the courses, applicants are guaranteed a job interview and have the potential to ascend to the highest level of operator.

Tri-County Technical College (AA)
Anderson County Business and Education Partnership
Grades served: E, M, HS   Schools served: 47   Year established: 1987
Location of schools served: NR   Type of schools served: PUB

This partnership provides an opportunity for a business to work directly with a school to enrich the learning of public school students through access to the many resources in the company. The program also enhances the business by improving students' understanding of the business world, giving employees access to school facilities and programs, and increasing opportunity to collaborate to improve the education system. The partnership emphasizes the improvement of educational performance through incentives, management assistance, volunteer support, and special projects.

University of South Carolina-Aiken (BA II)
Partner Schools
Grades served: E, M   Schools served: 4   Year established: 1993
Location of schools served: SU, RU   Type of schools served: PUB

Through the Center for School Leadership, a statewide and state-sponsored initiative for school reform, USC-Aiken has established partnerships with four schools. The purpose of the partnerships is to initiate and foster school reform through the collaboration of higher education, the schools, and businesses. The focus is on the development of teachers as leaders who are able to implement changes that will best serve the instructional needs of children.

<u>TEXAS</u>

University of Texas at Tyler (MA I)
Quality Work Force Planning Committee
Grades served: M, HS   Schools served: 80   Year established: 1989
Location of schools served: SU   Type of schools served: PUB

The planning committee is a 50-member board of business/industry representatives and leaders in secondary and two-year postsecondary colleges. The committee provides data and a service delivery plan to improve programs in accordance with requirements of the regional workforce. The efforts have resulted in changes to programs and processes in the region and have created ongoing links between business/industry and the schools.

<u>VIRGINIA</u>

James Madison University (MA I)
Valley of Virginia Partnership for Education
Grades served: E, M, HS   Schools served: 23   Year established: 1991
Location of schools served: UR, SU, RU   Type of schools served: PUB, PRI

This partnership is a joint effort of the business and education communities of the Shenandoah Valley of Virginia that seeks to maximize the educational investments of participating communities through partnerships, resource sharing, coordination of activities, joint projects, and communication. The partnership serves as a regional resource center and coordinating group to encourage and support partnerships among K-12 education, higher education, adult education, and business/industry to seek to improve the quality, accessibility, educational access, and work force preparation for all persons in the greater Shenandoah Valley.

<u>WISCONSIN</u>

University of Wisconsin-Oshkosh (MA I)
Partnerships for School Improvement
Grades served: E, M, HS   Schools served: NR   Year established: 1993
Location of schools served: SU   Type of schools served: PUB, PRI

The Partnership for School Improvement is designed to develop a systematic approach based on the seven forms of intelligence, to establish a common vision for education and a set of community values, to develop specific quality training to enhance change, to define the leadership structure for educational change, and to develop a plan to upgrade and finance technology needs in the schools. The program serves the Oshkosh community, area businesses, K-12 schools, the University of Wisconsin, Oshkosh, Fox Valley Technical College, and elected officials. The council consists of representatives from the cooperating groups.

Section Three
Resource-Sharing Agreements

<u>GEORGIA</u>

Augusta College (MA I)
Augusta College Adopt-a-School Programs
Grades served: E, HS   Schools served: 2   Year established: 1983
Location of schools served: NR   Type of schools served: PUB

The Augusta College Adopt-a-School Program is a partnership structured in a way that provides for the sharing of staff, programs, and other resources between the college and Lucy Craft Laney High School and Joseph Lamar Elementary School. Sharing takes the form of tutoring, honor recognition, staff development, free passes to campus events, library use, free continuing education, and campus visits.

Note: Each institution's Carnegie class is given in parentheses. **Key:** E=elementary school, HS=high school, M=middle school, NR=not reported, PRI=private, PUB=public, RU=rural, SU=suburban, UR=urban

IOWA

Kirkwood Community College (AA)
Kirkwood Partnerships–Wilson Elementary School Partnership

Grades served: E   Schools served: 1   Year established: 1991
Location of schools served: NR   Type of schools served: PUB

This resource-sharing partnership involves a neighborhood school near the Kirkwood campus. During the partnership's initial year, Kirkwood faculty and students assisted Wilson Elementary in designing a landscape plan for the school grounds, producing a videotape orienting new students, developing an Earth Day program, and preparing a tour program for Wilson students at the new Kirkwood floriculture/horticulture facility. Wilson faculty and staff allowed Kirkwood access to the school's computer lab for adult literacy classes. Wilson also welcomes Kirkwood students in education careers to study the school's holistic scoring program for writing instruction.

Teikyo Marycrest University (MA II)
Quad-LINC (Quad City Libraries IN Cooperation)

Grades served: E, M, HS   Schools served: NR   Year established: 1972
Location of schools served: UR, SU, RU   Type of schools served: PUB, PRI

Quad-LINC is a group of 23 public, academic, school, and corporate libraries that share an automated library system enabling users to locate materials at area libraries in eastern Iowa and western Illinois. Users may borrow the items directly or have them delivered to their local library through an interlibrary loan service.

NEW JERSEY

Fairleigh Dickinson University (MA I)
Adopt-A-School Program

Grades served: HS   Schools served: 6   Year established: 1986
Location of schools served: UR   Type of schools served: PUB

This adopt-a-school program joins Fairleigh Dickinson University and nearby high schools in Hackensack, North Arlington, Morris, Englewood, North Bergen, Paterson, and Plainfield in an effort to recruit and retain minority students. Activities for the high school students and their parents and teachers include special lectures and exhibits, a celebration of Black History Month, and Minority Athletes Networking (MAN). Teachers participate in lectures on campus, and university faculty and staff visit the schools for informational and advisory meetings.

NEW YORK

Canisius College (MA I)
Laboratory Equipment Assistance Program (LEAP)

Grades served: HS   Schools served: 50   Year established: 1988
Location of schools served: UR, SU, RU   Type of schools served: PUB, PRI

The Laboratory Equipment Assistance Program is a collaborative linking Canisius College and 50 high school science departments and chemical industries in western New York. Through LEAP, the college purchases and maintains laboratory equipment with industry funds. The equipment is then distributed on a rotating basis to high schools for use in regularly scheduled laboratories. Summer workshops, monthly seminars, industry visits, and work internships are all part of the program, which serves to educate high school teachers about scientific developments in industrial chemistry.

PENNSYLVANIA

Edinboro University of Pennsylvania (MA I)
Institute for Curriculum, Instruction, and Collaboration

Grades served: E, M, HS	Schools served: NR	Year established: 1992
Location of schools served: UR, SU, RU	Type of schools served: PUB, PRI	

Edinboro University's Institute for Curriculum, Instruction, and Collaboration is one of four institutes making up the Center for Excellence in Teaching. Among its goals are to build a repository of materials on collaborative teaching between education and business; to promote the development and refinement of effective instruction; to investigate new university/public school partnerships; to expand classroom research at all educational levels; to develop inservice programs and workshops for public and nonpublic school and university faculty; and to strengthen lines of communication among university academic units, student support services, and the Northwest Tri-County Intermediate Unit 5.

Mansfield University of Pennsylvania (MA I)
Access PA

Grades served: M, HS	Schools served: 1100	Year established: 1987
Location of schools served: UR, SU, RU	Type of schools served: PUB, PRI	

Access PA is a statewide program enabling school students to access library materials owned by other institutions through a CD-ROM catalog. The project includes more than 1,300 members. Mansfield University is one of three academic institutions that loans books, and videos to any of the participating schools.

TENNESSEE

Carson-Newman College (BA II)
Family Resource Center

Grades served: E, M	Schools served: 1	Year established: 1993
Location of schools served: NR	Type of schools served: PUB	

The Family Resource Center is a partnership linking Rush Strong School, the Jefferson County Chamber of Commerce, the Jefferson County Health Department and Department of Human Services, Carson-Newman College, and numerous other county and regional agencies. Its primary mission is to serve as the link through which preventive and intervening services are more readily available to at-risk families, enabling them to develop the protective, nurturing, and stable home environments that lead to positive educational experiences for each child.

TEXAS

Texas Lutheran College (BA II)
Facilities Sharing

Grades served: HS	Schools served: 1	Year established: 1985
Location of schools served: NR	Type of schools served: PUB	

This program allows Sequin High School and Texas Lutheran College to share facilities. The college maintains an extensive biology field station at nearby Lake McQueeney and holds classes at that site. High school classes are encouraged to frequent the site and use the facilities provided. The high school recently developed extensive media studies equipment for radio and television. Selected college students are involved in internships at the high school to obtain hands-on experience in broadcast media, receiving college credit upon successful completion of the prescribed program.

Note: Each institution's Carnegie class is given in parentheses. **Key:** E=elementary school, HS=high school, M=middle school, NR=not reported, PRI=private, PUB=public, RU=rural, SU=suburban, UR=urban

Tyler Junior College (AA)
Forest Trail Library Consortium

Grades served: E, M, HS   Schools served: 31   Year established: 1988
Location of schools served: SU, RU Type of schools served: PUB, PRI

The Forest Trail Library Consortium is an agent for cooperation, fundraising, and sharing of collections among its members, including libraries of public and private schools, colleges, universities, hospitals, and foundations as well as public libraries in central east Texas. The consortium's broad goal is to provide more information, knowledge, culture, and research to more people, more of the time, for less cost. Activities include sharing collections and resources through electronic networks, reciprocal borrowing, and a shared database.

VIRGINIA

Ferrum College (BA II)
Ferrum College/Franklin County High School

Grades served: HS   Schools served: 2   Year established: NR
Location of schools served: NR Type of schools served: PUB, PRI

The Ferrum College/Franklin County High School partnership is a collaborative designed to deliver quality education. The college provides access to equipment, library resources, field trips, special programs, guest lectures, and concerts. College faculty prepare questions for and judge the Academic Excellence League; serve as advisers and judges in science fairs; and hold workshops for teachers on computer use, techniques of pedagogy, and curriculum design. The high school provides the opportunity for teacher education students to observe and to serve as teacher aids, tutors, interns, and student teachers. Students and faculty assist in campus music programs and share athletic fields and equipment.

Section Four
Magnet Schools

CALIFORNIA

University of Southern California (RES I)
U.S.C./Bravo Science Partnership

Grades served: M, HS   Schools served: 2   Year established: 1990
Location of schools served: NR Type of schools served: PUB

This partnership links the USC's Medical School with Francisco Bravo Medical Magnet High School, with the overall goal of enhancing biomedical science education. The university provides stipends for teachers and students to work in research laboratories at the medical school. The partnership provides workshops for teachers, computer interactive learning methods, tutoring in the areas of science and math, and science, health, and career fairs. It also sponsors a bridge program for ninth grade students, providing training in study skills and organizing workshops for parents.

University of Southern California (RES I)
Science Museum School Collaborative
Grades served: E   Schools served: 1   Year established: NR
Location of schools served: NR   Type of schools served: PUB

This partnership between the University of Southern California, the Los Angeles Unified School District, and the California Museum of Science and Industry has been established to design and build a science museum elementary school for grades K-5. This neighborhood school will serve students with a new curriculum emphasizing science, math, and technology, integrated social services, and dissemination of the program through a science education resource center. The partners view the school as family-oriented museum outreach, an opportunity for professional practice, and a model of what science, math, and technology education can become.

MARYLAND

Towson State University (MA I)
Parkville Magnet High School
Grades served: HS   Schools served: 1   Year established: 1993
Location of schools served: NR   Type of schools served: NR

Towson State University's College of Natural and Mathematical Sciences, through the Center for Mathematics and Sciences Education, initiated this partnership with the Parkville Center for Mathematics, Science, and Computer Science at Parkville High School. The partnership is partially supported by local funding. Its mission is to provide the high school's students and faculty access to specialized university facilities and courses, a bridge to local industry and business, access to additional resources, and a mechanism for collaboration to develop innovative programs in mathematics and science.

MICHIGAN

Wayne State University (RES I)
Golightly Elementary School
Grades served: E   Schools served: 1   Year established: 1960
Location of schools served: UR   Type of schools served: PUB

Golightly Elementary Schools is an alternative school in the Detroit Public School System with research and curricular ties to Wayne State University's College of Education.

NEW YORK

City University of New York Herbert H. Lehman College (MA I)
Macy Medical Sciences Honors Programs at DeWitt Clinton High School
Grades served: HS   Schools served: 1   Year established: 1984
Location of schools served: UR   Type of schools served: PUB

This house program within the school increases the postsecondary and career options of its minority students through a rigorous and challenging curriculum. The program features professional development, smaller class sizes, expanded counseling services, longer school days, yearly assessments using the PSAT and SAT, summer research internships, and college courses as early as the students' junior year. All of the students graduate in four years and almost all attend college, most with full scholarships to prestigious institutions. Students score higher than average on standardized tests.

Note: Each institution's Carnegie class is given in parentheses. **Key:** E=elementary school, HS=high school, M=middle school, NR=not reported, PRI=private, PUB=public, RU=rural, SU=suburban, UR=urban

D'Youville College (MA II)
The D'Youville/da Vinci High School Partnership

Grades served: HS
Location of schools served: UR

Schools served: 1
Type of schools served: PUB

Year established: 1987

This partnership provides space on the college campus for the high school, allowing qualified high school students to take beginning college courses. The partnership provides college faculty, at the request of the high school staff, to supplement and enrich high school courses in the sciences, social sciences, and humanities. It offers tutoring, mentoring, and SAT preparation to virtually all high school students.

OHIO

Miami University-Hamilton Campus (AA)
Miami Connection

Grades served: HS
Location of schools served: UR

Schools served: 1
Type of schools served: PUB

Year established: 1990

The Miami Connection is an alternative school program offered on Miami's Hamilton campus for students who have been dismissed from the regular program at Fairfield High School. Students attend classes five mornings a week and have work-study jobs in the afternoon. A high school faculty of four teach traditional academic subjects. The university makes four classrooms available, plus one office for the director and staff. To resolve any conflict between the Fairfield students and university students, the school district conducts sensitivity sessions.

VIRGINIA

Danville Community College (AA)
Regional Governor's School

Grades served: HS
Location of schools served: SU, RU

Schools served: 16
Type of schools served: PUB

Year established: 1993

The Southside Virginia Regional Governor's School for Global Economics and Technology meets half-days on six campuses of five different colleges, including Danville Community College. The school's mission is to educate selected students in global economics and technology to serve as catalysts for expanded educational opportunities for high school students throughout southside Virginia. Approximately 200 juniors and seniors from the high schools of the 12 participating school divisions are enrolled, with more than 50 located on the Danville campus. Other host colleges are Southside Virginia Community College, Longwood College, St. Paul's College, and Averett College.

□ □ □

INDEX TO PARTNERSHIPS ABSTRACTED IN PARTS 1-5

(arranged by *partnership* name)

Note: For an index by *college/university* name of those partnerships abstracted in Parts 1-5, see the National Directory beginning on page 317.

Note: For an index by *college/university* name of those partnerships abstracted in Parts 1-5, see the National Directory beginning on page 317.

Note: For an index by *college/university* name of those partnerships abstracted in Parts 1-5, see the National Directory beginning on page 317.

□ □ □

Note: For an index by *college/university* name of those partnerships abstracted in Parts 1-5, see the National Directory beginning on page 317.

NATIONAL DIRECTORY OF SCHOOL-COLLEGE PARTNERSHIPS

(arranged by *college/university* name)

A

Abilene Christian University
Big Country Center for Professional Development and Technology
Colleen Durrington
Chair, Department of Education, ACU Station, Box 8228, Abilene, TX 79699-8228
(915) 674-2112
Ref: 31382.003537
PF: Professional Development, Inservice

Adams State College
Adams State College and San Luis Valley Public School Districts
J. Milford Clark
Dean, School of Education and Behavioral Science, Alamosa, CO 81102
(719) 589-7936
jclark@cc4.adams.edu
Ref: 20301.001345
PF: Resource Sharing

▶ Adams State College   [154]
Colorado Alliance for Science/Project Link-Up
Martin Jones
Professor of Chemistry, Alamosa, CO 81102
(719) 589-7256
mjones@cc4.adams.edu
Ref: 20300.001345
PF: Professional Development, Inservice

Adelphi University
Adelphi University–District 26 Partnership
Alan R. Sadounik
Assoc. Professor and Chair, 120 Harvey Hall, Garden City, NY 11530
(516) 877-4067
Ref: 30215.002666
PF: Recruit, Preservice, Certification

▶ Adelphi University   [216]
Bellmore-Merrick School District-Adelphi University Partnership
Alan R. Sadovnak
Assoc. Professor and Chair, 120 Harvey Hall, Garden City, NY 11530
(516) 877-4067
Ref: 30214.002666
PF: Recruit, Preservice, Certification

Adelphi University
School-University Partnership Providing Opportunities for Real Teaching in Physical Education (SUPPORT PE)
Gary T. Barrette
Coordinator, Teacher Preparation- PE, Department of Physical Education, Woodruff Hall, Garden City, NY 11530
(516) 877-4271
Ref: 30216.002666
PF: Professional Development, Inservice

▶ Aiken Technical College   [266]
Aiken County Consortium on Preparation for the Technologies
Mary Gene Ryan
Dean, Academic Support Division, P.O. Drawer 696, Aiken, SC 29802-0696
(803) 593-9231
Ref: 30823.010056
PF: Tech-Prep/2+2

Aiken Technical College
Career Center Articulation
Richard J. Smith
Dean, P.O. Box 696, Aiken, SC 29802
(803) 593-9231
Ref: 30822.010056
PF: Tech-Prep/2+2

▶ Albany State College   [28]
Albany State College/Southside Middle School/Professional Development School
Charles Love
Asst. Professor of Education, 2209-c Champagne Lane, Albany, GA 31707
(912) 430-4722
Ref: 30623.001544
PF: Minority, At-Risk

▶ Albertus Magnus College   [23]
AM Bassetters Go to College
Kathleen A. Reilly
Director of Continuing Education, 700 Prospect Street, New Haven, CT 06511
(203) 773-8585
Ref: 31793.001374
PF: Minority, At-Risk

▶ Albion College   [171]
Dramatics-in-Education Program
Tom Oosting
Professor of Theatre, Adrian, MI 49224
(517) 629-0346
toosting@albion.bitnet
Ref: 20403.002235
PF: Professional Development, Inservice

Albright College
Adopt-A-School
Sarel P. Fuchs
Chair, Education Department, P.O. Box 15234, Reading, PA 19612-5234
(610) 921-7790
Ref: 30463.003229
PF: Professional Development, Inservice

Albright College
Consultation Task Forces for Science Instruction and Strategic Planning
James Pitts
Academic Dean, P.O. Box 15234, Reading, PA 19612-5234
(610) 921-2381
Ref: 30462.003229
PF: Resource Sharing

Key: "▶" denotes those partnerships abstracted in Parts 1-5; the corresponding page numbers are given in brackets. "PF:" denotes the partnership's "primary focus." "Ref:" denotes the partnership's assigned reference number in the National School-College Partnership Database (see Appendix B).

Albuquerque T-VI A Community College
Associate Degree Prep Program
Ruth S. Tangman
Assoc. Vice President for Instruction, 525 Buena
    Vista Drive SE, Albuquerque, NM 87106
(505) 224-4231
Ref: 31467.004742
PF: Tech-Prep/2+2

Allan Hancock College
Central Coast Articulation Group
Marjorie Carson
Dean, Academic Affairs, 800 S. College, Santa
    Maria, CA 93454-6399
(805) 922-6966
Ref: 20444.001111
PF: Tech-Prep/2+2

Allentown College of Saint Francis de Sales
Allentown College High School Scholars Program
Karen Doyle Walton
Vice-President for Academic Affairs, 2755 Station
    Avenue, Center Valley, PA 18034
(215) 282-1100
kdwalton@pooch1.allencol.edu
Ref: 30447.003986
PF: College Courses for Students

Allentown College of Saint Francis de Sales
Allentown College Mathematics and Science
    Workshops
Karen Doyle Walton
Vice-President for Academic Affairs, 2755 Station
    Avenue, Center Valley, PA 18034
(215) 282-1100
kdwalton@pooch1.allencol.edu
Ref: 30446.003986
PF: Professional Development, Inservice

Alverno College
Alverno College-Forest Home Partnership
Kathryn Henn-Reinke
Assoc. Professor, P.O. Box 343922, Milwaukee,
    WI 53234-3922
(414) 382-6387
Ref: 31075.003832
PF: Professional Development, Inservice

▶ **Alverno College**   [284]
Assessing Learning
Julie Stoffels
Assoc. Professor, P.O. Box 343922, Milwaukee,
    WI 53234-3922
(414) 382-6414
Ref: 31078.003832
PF: New Achievement, Assessment Standards

Alverno College
The College Connection
Glenn Kraft
Asst. Professor, P.O. Box 343922, Milwaukee, WI
    53234-3922
(414) 382-6290
Ref: 31076.003832
PF: Professional Development, Inservice

▶ **Alverno College**   [224]
DeWitt Wallace-Reader's Digest New Pathways to
    Teaching Careers
Virginia Schuldenburg
Asst. Professor, P.O. Box 343922, Milwaukee, WI
    53234-3922
(414) 382-6215
Ref: 31077.003832
PF: Recruit, Preservice, Certification

American Physical Society
Physics Alliances — A Program for
    School-College Collaboratives
Brian Schwartz
One Physics Ellipse, College Park, MD 20740
Ref: 21264.U00006
PF: Umbrella Programs

▶ **American River College**   [69]
American River College/Grant Union/San Juan
    Unified/Center Unified Articulation Council
Stephen M. Epler
Vice President, 4700 College Oak Avenue,
    Sacramento, CA 95841
(916) 484-8411
Ref: 21173.009552
PF: College Courses for Students

▶ **The American University**   [70]
High School/College Internship Program
    (HI/SCIP)
David Owens
Director, Office of Multicultural Affairs, 4400
    Massachusetts Avenue NW, Butler 404,
    Washington, DC 20016
(202) 885-3633
Ref: 20693.001434
PF: College Courses for Students

▶ **Anderson University**   [94]
Health, Safety, and Physical Education for
    Elementary Grades
Rebecca Hull
Chair, Physical Education, Health Science
    Department, 1100 E. Fifth Street, Anderson, IN
    46012-3462
(317) 641-4484
Ref: 30943.001785
PF: Enrichment, Gifted

Angelina College
High School/College Concurrent Enrollment
    Program
Patricia McKenzie
Dean, Instruction and Admissions, P.O. Box 1768,
    Lufkin, TX 75901
(409) 639-1301
Ref: 20104.006661
PF: College Courses for Students

Anoka-Ramsey Community College
Concurrent Enrollment
Al Baas
Assoc. Dean, Cambridge, MN 55008
(612) 689-1536
Ref: 20827.002332
PF: College Courses for Students

▶ **Appalachian State University**   [218]
Appalachian State University/Public School
    Partnership
Elizabeth W. Long
Director, Reich College of Education, Boone, NC
    28608
(704) 262-6108
longw@appstate.edu
Ref: 20260.002906
PF: Recruit, Preservice, Certification

Aquinas College
Midwest Regional Teaching and Learning Center
Katy Lux
Assoc. Professor, 1607 Robinson Road, Grand
    Rapids, MI 49506
(616) 459-8281
Ref: 31633.002239
PF: Recruit, Preservice, Certification

Arizona State University
Bureau of Educational Research and Service
Margaret Mangini
Director, College of Education, Tempe, AZ
    85287-2611
(602) 965-3538
Ref: 20381.001081
PF: Curriculum Development

▶ **Arizona State University**   [206]
Teacher Residency Project
Gary Anderson
Director, College of Education, Tempe, AZ
    85287-0311
(602) 965-6378
Ref: 20307.001081
PF: Recruit, Preservice, Certification

▶ **Art Academy of Cincinnati**   [105]
High School Workshop Program
Anthony Batchelor
Professor and Chair, Foundations Department,
   1125 St. Gregory Street, Cincinnati, OH 45202
(513) 721-5205
Ref: 21213.003011
PF: Enrichment, Gifted

Ashland University
Aesthetic Awareness Workshops
Kay Raplenovich
Arts Outreach Coordinator, 210 A/H, Ashland, OH
   44805
(419) 289-5133
Ref: 30911.003012
PF: Professional Development, Inservice

Ashland University
Economic Education
Joe Latona
Asst. Director, Gill Center, Ashland, OH 44805
(419) 289-5730
Ref: 30910.003012
PF: Teacher Education Centers

▶ **Ashland University**   [187]
Ashland-Medina Graduate Studies Pilot
Philip A. Griswold
Assoc. Professor, Bixler Hall, Ashland, OH 44805
(419) 289-5334
au22@class.org
Ref: 30914.003012
PF: Professional Development, Inservice

▶ **Ashland University**   [188]
Reading Recovery®
James R. Schnug,
Site Coordinator, 205 Bixler Hall, Ashland, OH
   44085
(419) 289-5359
Ref: 30913.003012
PF: Professional Development, Inservice

Ashland University
Small School Network
Ronald Walker
Professor of Education, 307 Bixler Hall, Ashland,
   OH 44805
(419) 289-5257
Ref: 30909.003012
PF: Professional Development, Inservice

▶ **Ashland University**   [234]
Teacher Team Leader Program
Ronald Walker
Professor of Education, 307 Bixler Hall, Ashland,
   OH 44805
(419) 289-5257
Ref: 30912.003012
PF: Shared Faculty

▶ **Atlantic Community College**   [259]
Tech Prep 2+2
Pat Conn
Assoc. Professor, Business/CIS Department,
   5100 Black Horse Pike, Mays Landing, NJ
   08330
(609) 343-4976
Ref: 30113.002596
PF: Tech-Prep/2+2

Auburn University
Auburn City Schools/Auburn University College of
   Education Professional Development System
Anita Hardin
Director, Truman Pierce Institute, 1228 Haley
   Center, Auburn, AL 36849-5228
(205) 844-4488
hardia1@mail.auburn.edu
Ref: 30682.008310
PF: Professional Development, Inservice

▶ **Augusta College**   [300]
Augusta College Adopt-a-School Programs
Roscoe Williams
Assoc. Dean of Students, 2500 Walton Way,
   Augusta, GA 30904
(706) 737-1411
Ref: 21134.001552
PF: Resource Sharing

Augusta College
Certificate of Academic Achievement
Patti Peabody
Admissions Recruiter, Office of Admissions, 2500
   Walton Way, Augusta, GA 30904-2200
(706) 737-1632
ppeabody@admin.ac.edu
Ref: 30605.001552

▶ **Augusta College**   [92]
Augusta College's Coca-Cola Young Writers
   Contest
Lillie B. Johnson
Acting Chair, Languages and Literature
   Department, Augusta, GA 30904-2200
(706) 737-1500
ljohnson@admin.ac.edu.
Ref: 30606.001552
PF: Enrichment, Gifted

▶ **Augusta College**   [160]
CSRA Math Collaborative
Edward Pettit
Chair, Math and Computer Science Department,
   Augusta, GA 30904-2200
(706) 737-1672
crychly@admin.ac.edu
Ref: 30608.001552
PF: Professional Development, Inservice

▶ **Augusta College**   [92]
CSRA Science and Engineering Fair
Tom Crute
Asst. Professor of Chemistry, 2500 Walton Way,
   Augusta, GA 30910
(706) 737-1541
Ref: 30612.001552
PF: Enrichment, Gifted

Augusta College
History Day
Edward J. Cashin
Chair, History Department, Augusta, GA 30910
(706) 737-1709
Ref: 30611.001552
PF: Enrichment, Gifted

▶ **Augusta College**   [73]
Joint Enrollment
Joe Bobrowskas
Admissions Representative, 2500 Walton Way,
   Augusta, GA 30904-2210
(706) 737-1632
jbobrows@admin.ac.edu
Ref: 30609.001552
PF: College Courses for Students

Key: "▶" denotes those partnerships abstracted in Parts 1-5; the corresponding page numbers are given in brackets. "PF:" denotes the partnership's "primary focus." "Ref:" denotes the partnership's assigned reference number in the National School-College Partnership Database (see Appendix B).

▶ **Augusta College** [121]
Augusta College Literacy in Action/Metro Adult
  Literacy Council
Paulette Harris
Acting Dean, 2500 Walton Way, Augusta, GA
  30904
(706) 737-1499
Ref: 30602.001552
PF: Tutoring, Counseling

Augusta College
Math Contest
Carol Rychly
Asst. Professor, Math and Computer Science
  Department, Augusta, GA 30904-2200
(706) 737-1672
crychly@admin.ac.edu
Ref: 30607.001552
PF: Enrichment, Gifted

Augusta College
Mini-Workshops in Chemistry, Physics, and
  Biology for Public Schools
Gary G. Stroebel
Assoc. Professor, Chemistry and Physics
  Department, Augusta, GA 30910
(706) 737-1541
Ref: 30610.001552
PF: Minority, At-Risk

▶ **Augusta College** [211]
Minority Recruitment in Teacher Education
Barbara Blackwell
Coordinator of Education Leadership, 2500
  Walton Way, Augusta, GA 30904
(706) 737-1496
Ref: 30603.001552
PF: Recruit, Preservice, Certification

Augusta College
Summer Scholars
Karlise C. Terrell
Minority Recruiter, 2500 Walton Way, Office of
  Admissions, Augusta, GA 30904
(706) 737-1632
Ref: 30604.001552
PF: Minority, At-Risk
PF: Enrichment, Gifted

▶ **Austin Community College** [76]
11th and 12th Grade Enrollment Program
Roger Boughton
Dean of Instruction, 1600 8th Avenue NW, Austin,
  MN 55912
(507) 433-0516
Ref: 20071.002335
PF: College Courses for Students

Avila College
Avila-AWIS Young Women's Math and Science
  Challenge
Larry Sullivan
Chair, Natural Science and Mathematics
  Department, 11901 Wornall Road, Kansas City,
  MO 64145
(816) 942-8400
Ref: 31235.002449
PF: Enrichment, Gifted

Avila College
College Financial Aid Application Workshops
Cindy Butler
Director of Financial Aid, 11901 Wornall Road,
  Kansas City, MO 64145
(816) 942-8400
Ref: 31238.002449
PF: Retention, Continuing Education

Avila College
Healthy Children Program
Susan Hildebrand, R.N.
Chairperson, Department of Nursing, 11901
  Wornall Road, Kansas City, MO 64145
(816) 942-8400
Ref: 31234.002449
PF: Student Health, Welfare

▶ **Avila College** [42]
PASS (Project Avila – Stay in School)
Nancy Wormington
Service Learning Coordinator, 11901 Wornall
  Road, Kansas City, MO 64145
(816) 942-8400 x2370
Ref: 31232.002449
PF: Minority, At-Risk

▶ **Avila College** [136]
PAVA (Performing and Visual Arts) Day
Daniel Paul Larson
Chair, Department of Humanities, 11901 Wornall
  Road, Kansas City, MO 64145
(816) 942-8400
Ref: 31233.002449
PF: Career, Internships, Apprenticeships

Avila College
School/Community Partnership
Marie Joan Harris, C.S.J.
Vice President and Dean of Academic Affairs,
  11901 Wornall Road, Kansas City, MO 64145
(816) 942-8400
Ref: 31236.002449
PF: Professional Development, Inservice

Avila College
TEXT–Teaching EXcellence Teams
Kathleen Miller
Field Coordinator, 11901 Wornall Road, Kansas
  City, MO 64145
(816) 942-8400 x2420
Ref: 31237.002449
PF: Recruit, Preservice, Certification

B

▶ **Bainbridge College** [160]
Bainbridge College/Bainbridge High School: Area
  Council of Teachers of English (ACE)
Mariella Hartsfield
Chairman, Humanities Division, Highway 84 East,
  Bainbridge, GA 31717
(912) 248-2560
mhartsfi@catfish.bbc.peachnet.edu
Ref: 30627.011074
PF: Professional Development, Inservice

Bainbridge College
Bainbridge College Regional Secondary &
  Elementary Science Fairs
Nancy Goodyear
Professor of Biology, Bainbridge, GA 31717
(912) 248-2560
ngoodyea@catfish.bbc.peachnet.edu
Ref: 30629.011074
PF: Enrichment, Gifted

Bainbridge College
International Night/Foreign Language Fair
Stan Webb
Professor of English and French, Highway 84
  East, Bainbridge, GA 31717
(912) 248-2560
swebb@catfish.bbc.peachnet.edu
Ref: 30628.011074
PF: Professional Development, Inservice

▶ **Bainbridge College** [29]
Mentor Program
Karen B. Hill
Director of Admissions and Records, Bainbridge,
  GA 31717
(912) 248-2504
Ref: 30624.011074
PF: Minority, At-Risk

Bainbridge College
Postsecondary Options (Statewide Program)
Karen B. Hill
Director of Admissions and Records, Bainbridge,
   GA 31717
(912) 248-2504
Ref: 30625.011074
PF: College Courses for Students

Bainbridge College
Social Science Fair
Raymond L. Chambers
Professor and Chairman, Division of Sciences,
   Bainbridge, GA 31717-0953
(912) 248-2560
rchamber@catfish.bbc.peachnet.edu
Ref: 30626.011074
PF: Professional Development, Inservice

Bainbridge College
Tech Prep
Robert U. Coker
Chairman, Division of Technical Studies, Highway
   84 East, Bainbridge, GA 31717
(912) 248-2530
rcoker@catfish.bbc.peachnet.edu
Ref: 30630.011074
PF: Tech-Prep/2+2

Baker College of Muskegon
Data Processing Vocational Consortium
Bob Hogan
Vice President, 141 Hartford, Muskegon, MI
   43022
(616) 726-4904
Ref: 20035.002296
PF: Career, Internships, Apprenticeships

▣ **Bakersfield College**   [250]
Kern/Southern Tulare Tech Prep Consortium
Charles R. Carlson
Dean for Planning, 1801 Panorama Boulevard,
   Bakersfield, CA 93305
(805) 395-4539
Ref: 31647.001118
PF: Tech-Prep/2+2

Ball State University
Burris Laboratory School
Philip L. Borders
Superintendent, University Schools, Wagoner
   Halls, Muncie, IN 47306
(317) 285-7455
Ref: 30977.001786
PF: Teacher Education Centers

▣ **Ball State University**   [95]
Indiana Academy for Science, Mathematics, and
   Humanities
Philip L. Borders
Superintendent, University Schools, Wagoner
   Halls, Muncie, IN 47306
(317) 285-7455
Ref: 30978.001786
PF: Enrichment, Gifted

Baltimore City Community College
Project Success
McCarroll Nole
Area Director for State and Federal Programs,
   2901 Liberty Heights Avenue, Baltimore, MD
   21215
(410) 333-7414
Ref: 30546.002061
PF: Minority, At-Risk

▣ **Bard College**   [180]
Institute for Writing & Thinking
Paul Connolly
Director, Annandale-on-Hudson, NY 12504
(914) 758-7431
connolly@levy.bard.edu
Ref: 30240.002671
PF: Professional Development, Inservice

▣ **Barry University**   [71]
Barry Early Credit Program
Eileen McDonough
Director, 11300 N.E. 2nd Avenue, Miami Shores,
   FL 33161
(305) 899-3480
Ref: 20948.001466
PF: College Courses for Students

Barry University
Summer Scholars Program
Eileen McDonough
Dean and Director, 11300 N.E. 2nd Avenue,
   Miami Shores, FL 33161
(305) 899-3480
Ref: 30649.001466
PF: College Courses for Students

▣ **Bates College**   [293]
Bates College/Lewiston Junior High School
   Adopt-A-School Program
Rebecca Swanson Conrad
Assistant to the President, 214 Lane Hall,
   Lewiston, ME 04240
(207) 786-6102
rconrad@bates.edu
Ref: 30059.002036
PF: School-College-Business Partnerships

▣ **Baylor University**   [229]
Baylor University-Waco ISD Collaborative
Betty Conaway
Director of Professional Development Schools,
   P.O. Box 97314, Waco, TX 76798-7314
(817) 755-3113
betty_conaway@education.baylor.edu
Ref: 31331.003545
PF: Teacher Education Centers

Beaver College
Beaver-Leeds Visitation
Angela C. Senior
Coordinator, Multicultural Affairs, 450 S. Easton
   Road, Glenside, PA 19038
(215) 572-4088
Ref: 30448.003235
PF: Minority, At-Risk

Beaver College
Beaver/Martin Luther King High School Senior
   Scholars
William D. Biggs
Dean, Continuing Education, Glenside, PA 19038
(215) 572-2921
Ref: 20786.003235
PF: Minority, At-Risk

Beaver College
Guaranteed Investments for Tomorrow's Scholars
   (G.I.F.T.S.)
Angela C. Senior
Coordinator of Multicultural Affairs, 450 S. Easton
   Road, Glenside, PA 19038
(215) 572-4088
Ref: 30449.003235
PF: Tutoring, Counseling

Belhaven College
Project Beacon
Stephen D. Livesay
Director of Secondary Education, 1500 Peachtree
    Street, Jackson, MS 39202
(601) 968-5974
Ref: 30702.002397
PF: Recruit, Preservice, Certification

▶ **Bellarmine College**   [75]
ACCP (Advanced College Credit Program)
Muzaffar Ali
Director, Department of Mathematics and CIS,
    2001 Newburg Road, Louisville, KY 40205
(502) 452-8410
Ref: 20117.001954
PF: College Courses for Students

Belmont Abbey College
Project Outreach
Aidan O. Dunleavy
Chair of Education, Belmont, NC 28012
(704) 825-6838
Ref: 30732.002910
PF: Minority, At-Risk

Beloit College
Beloit College Partnership
Thomas F. Warren
Professor and Chair, Department of Education,
    700 College Street, Beloit, WI 53511-5595
(608) 363-2336
warrent@beloit.edu
Ref: 31079.003835
PF: College Courses for Students

Bergen Community College
Bergen ITV (Interactive Television)
Joseph H. Moskowitz
Dean, Business Administration and Technology,
    400 Paramus Road, Paramus, NJ 07652
(201) 447-7184
Ref: 30344.04736
PF: Technology Application

▶ **Berry College**   [93]
Berry College Mathematics League
Robert Cantanzano
Professor of Mathematics Education, Box 5014,
    Mount Berry, GA 30149
(404) 232-5374 x2377
Ref: 20720.001554
PF: Enrichment, Gifted

Berry College
Economics America Schools Program
Ouida W. Dickey
Director, Center for Economic Education, Box
    5031, Mount Berry, GA 30149-5031
(706) 236-2229
Ref: 30598.001554
PF: Curriculum Development

▶ **Berry College**   [292]
Educators-In-Industry
Gerald D. Jennings
Professor of Psychology, Mount Berry, GA 30149
(706) 236-2202
Ref: 30600.001554
PF: School-College-Business Partnerships

▶ **Berry College**   [121]
Student Literacy Corps
Jacqueline Anglin
Director of Research and Sponsored Programs,
    Box 206, Mount Berry, GA 30149-0206
(706) 236-2270
Ref: 30599.001554
PF: Tutoring, Counseling

Bethany College
College Stategies and Early Intervention Program
Gary R. Forney
Vice-President and Dean of Admissions, Bethany,
    WV 26032
(304) 829-7611
Ref: 30596.003808
PF: Minority, At-Risk

▶ **Binghamton University**   [46]
Binghamton Liberty Partnership Project
Jerry Rhodes
Project Director, P.O. Box 6000, LNG 326,
    Binghamton, NY 13902-6000
(607) 777-2468
Ref: 30291.002862
PF: Minority, At-Risk

▶ **Binghamton University**   [46]
Home and School Partnerships
Allison Alden
Director, P.O. Box 6000, Science III, Room 215,
    Binghamton, NY 13902-6000
(607) 777-4604
Ref: 21030.002836
PF: Minority, At-Risk

▶ **Binghamton University**   [46]
More Math for More Females Project
Kathryn H. Fisher
Project Coordinator, LNG272-CRSEE, P.O. Box
    6000, Binghamton, NY 13902-6000
(607) 777-6044
Ref: 20183.002862
PF: Minority, At-Risk

Blinn College
Brazos Valley Tech Prep
Rick Hernandez
Director, 301 Post Office, Bryan, TX 77801-2142
(409) 822-6109
Ref: 31344.003549
PF: Tech-Prep/2+2

Bloomfield College
The Link Community School Youth Mentoring
    Program
Irene Rosenzweig
Director, Mentoring Programs, 12 Austin Place,
    Bloomfield, NJ 07003
(201) 748-9000
Ref: 30083.002597
PF: Minority, At-Risk

**Bloomsburg University of
Pennsylvania**
Bloomsburg University/Danville School District
    Partnership
Ann L. Lee
Asst. Dean, School of Education, 3102
    McCormick Center for Human Services,
    Bloomsburg, PA 17815
(717) 389-4073
Ref: 30430.003315
PF: Teacher Education Centers

Bluefield State College
BSC-Mercer County Schools Partnership &
    Academic Alliance
Tom Blevins
Director of Teacher Education, 219 Rock Street,
    Bluefield, WV 24701
(304) 327-4059
tblevins@bscvar.wvnet.edu
Ref: 30588.003809
PF: Professional Development, Inservice

Bluffton College
BC/SAFY Tutoring Program
Jean Roth Hawk
Professor of Education, 280 W. College Avenue,
    Bluffton, OH 45817
(419) 358-3329
Ref: 30940.003016
PF: Minority, At-Risk

Bluffton College
English/Communication Festival
Wesley Richard
Director, 280 W. College Avenue, Bluffton, OH
    45817
(419) 358-3298
Ref: 30939.003016
PF: Enrichment, Gifted

Bluffton College
The Lion and the Lamb Peace Arts Center
Diane Neal
Asst. Professor of Art, 280 W. College Avenue,
    Bluffton, OH 45817
(419) 358-3328
Ref: 30941.003016
PF: Enrichment, Gifted

Bluffton College
Scholastic Art and Writing Awards
Jaye Bumbaugh
Professor of Art, 280 W. College Avenue, Bluffton,
    OH 45817
(419) 358-3263
Ref: 30942.003016
PF: Enrichment, Gifted

▶ **Boston Higher E ducation
Partnership**   [278]
Boston Higher Education Partnership
Robert I. Sperber
Executive Director, Boston University, 147 Bay
    State Road, Boston, MA 02215
(617) 353-9166
Ref: 30033.U00004
PF: Umbrella Programs

▶ **Boston University**   [279]
Boston University/Chelsea Partnership
Douglas A. Sears
Chairman, Boston University/Chelsea
    Management Team, 147 Bay State Road,
    Boston, MA 02215
(617) 353-5950
Ref: 30034.002130
PF: Joint Governance

▶ **Bowling Green State University**   [219]
BGSU Cooperative Schools Instrumental Music
    Project
P. Thomas Tallarico
Professor, Department of Music Education,
    Bowling Green, OH 43403
(419) 372-8549
Ref: 20820.003018
PF: Recruit, Preservice, Certification

▶ **Bowling Green State University**   [55]
Music Plus
Victor Ellsworth
Chair, Department of Music Education, College of
    Musical Arts, Bowling Green, OH 43403
(419) 372-8852
Ref: 20006.003018
PF: Minority, At-Risk

Bradley University
Project Opportunity: An Inst. to Promote Science,
    Math, and Health Career Preparation for
    Minority High School Students in Central Illinois
Angela M. Roberson
Assoc. Director of Enrollment Management,
    Swords Hall, Peoria, IL 61625
(309) 677-1000
Ref: 20039.001641
PF: Minority, At-Risk

Brescia College
Western Kentucky Math-Science Alliance
Bob Cinnamond
Chairman, Math-Science Department, 707
    Fredereia Street, Owensboro, KY 42301
(502) 686-4279
Ref: 20338.001958
PF: Professional Development, Inservice

Bridgewater State College
Center for Global Education
Reed Stewart
Co-Director, Office of Earth Sciences and
    Geography, Bridgewater, MA 02325
(508) 697-1390
Ref: 30038.002183
PF: Curriculum Development

Bridgewater State College
Curriculum Leadership Center
Charles Robinson
Coordinator, Bridgewater, MA 02325
(508) 697-1347
Ref: 20142.002183
PF: Professional Development, Inservice

▶ **Bridgewater State College**   [238]
High Schools/High Skills
Ann Lydecker
Dean, School of Education, Burnell Campus
    School, Bridgewater, MA 02325
(508) 697-1347
alydecker@fred.bsc.mass.edu
Ref: 30035.002183
PF: Curriculum Development

Bridgewater State College
Partnerships Advancing the Learning of
    Mathematics and Science (PALMS)
Ann Lydecker
Dean, School of Education, Burnell Campus
    School, Bridgewater, MA 02325
(508) 697-1347
alydecker@fred.bsc.mass.edu
Ref: 30036.002183
PF: Professional Development, Inservice

▶ **Bridgewater State College**   [169]
Project SWIMS (Studying Whales Integrating
    Math and Science)
John Jahoda
Principal Investigator, Department of Biological
    Sciences, Conant Science Building,
    Bridgewater, MA 02325
(508) 697-1358
Ref: 30039.002183
PF: Professional Development, Inservice

Bridgewater State College
Center for Global Education
Reed Stewart
Co-Director, Office of Earth Sciences and
    Geography, Bridgewater, MA 02325
(508) 697-1390
Ref: 30038.002183
PF: Curriculum Development

▶ **Brigham Young University**   [200]
BYU/Public School Partnership
Robert Patterson
Dean, College of Education, 343 McKay Building,
    Provo, UT 84602
(801) 378-3695
patterson@yvax.byu.edu
Ref: 20354.003670
PF: Professional Development, Inservice

▶ **Bristol Community College**   [257]
Tech Prep Consortium
Frank Llamas
Tech Prep Coordinator, 777 Elsbree Street,
    C-203, Fall River, MA 02720
(508) 678-2811 x2339
Ref: 21100.002176
PF: Tech-Prep/2+2

▶ **Broome Community College** [261]
Tech Prep
Penny Corino
Consortium Director, P.O. Box 1017, Binghamton, NY 13902
(607) 778-5415
Ref: 30290.002862
PF: Tech-Prep/2+2

▶ **Brown University** [276]
Coalition of Essential Schools (CES)
Don Ernst
Director, CES Development, Communications, and Policy, Box 1969, Providence, RI 02912
(401) 863-3384
Ref: 30052.003401
PF: City/Regional Compacts

▶ **Brown University** [194]
Institute for Secondary Education
Sharon Lloyd Clark
Director, 21 Manning Walk, Box 1938, Providence, RI 02912
(401) 863-1486
Ref: 21047.003401
PF: Professional Development, Inservice

▶ **Brown University** [59]
MEDAC Program
James H. Wyche
Assoc. Provost, Box 1963, Providence, RI 02912-1963
(401) 863-1474
jwyche@brownvm.brown.edu
Ref: 30136.003401
PF: Minority, At-Risk

▶ **Brown University** [129]
Pre-College Enrichment Program (PCEP)
Heather Woodcock
Assoc. Director of Admission, Admission Office, Box 1876, Providence, RI 02912
(401) 863-7930
heather.woodcock@brown.edu
Ref: 30051.003401
PF: Tutoring, Counseling

Brunswick College
Academic Alliances in Mathematics, English, Foreign Language
Watson L. Holloway
Chair, Division of General Studies, Brunswick, GA 31523
(912) 264-7233
holloway@s1500.bc.peachnet.edu
Ref: 30617.001558
PF: Professional Development, Inservice

▶ **Brunswick College** [252]
Southeast Coastal Georgia Tech Prep Program
Morgan L. Stapleton
Vice-President for Academic Affairs, 3700 Atlanta Avenue, Brunswick, GA 31520-3644
(912) 264-7203
Ref: 30616.001558
PF: Tech-Prep/2+2

▶ **Brunswick Community College** [263]
Tech Prep and Coordinated Vocational-Tech Programs
Johnnie Simpson
Vice President for Instruction, P.O. Box 30, Suppey, NC 28462
(910) 754-6900
Ref: 30749.021707
PF: Tech-Prep/2+2

Bunker Hill Community College
BHCC/Edwards Middle School Collaboration
Robert G. Ross
Asst. Vice President for Academic Affairs, 250 Rutherford Avenue, Boston, MA 02129
(617) 241-8600
Ref: 30023.011210
PF: Resource Sharing

▶ **Bunker Hill Community College** [114]
BHCC/Fenway Middle College High School
C. Scully Stikes
President, 250 Rutherford Avenue, Boston, MA 02129
(617) 241-8600
Ref: 30022.011210
PF: Middle/Early Colleges

Bunker Hill Community College
Boston Higher Education Partnership
Robert G. Ross
Asst. Vice President for Academic Affairs, 250 Rutherford Avenue, Boston, MA 02129
(612) 241-8600
Ref: 31716.011210
PF: Enrichment, Gifted

▶ **Bunker Hill Community College** [39]
Community Compact For Student Success
Robert G. Ross
Asst. Vice President for Academic Affairs, 250 Rutherford Avenue, Boston, MA 02129
(617) 241-8600
Ref: 30024.011210
PF: Minority, At-Risk

Bunker Hill Community College
Compact for College Success
Robert G. Ross
Asst. Vice President, 250 Rutherford Avenue, Boston, MA 02118
(617) 241-8600
Ref: 30017.011210
PF: Minority, At-Risk

Bunker Hill Community College
Greater Boston Urban Education Collaborative
Robert G. Ross
Asst. Vice President for Academic Affairs, 250 Rutherford Avenue, Boston, MA 02129
(617) 241-8600
Ref: 30025.011210
PF: City/Regional Compacts

Bunker Hill Community College
Kids to College
Judy Benson
Admissions Recruiter, 250 New Rutherford Avenue, Boston, MA 02129
(617) 241-8600
Ref: 30021.011210
PF: Minority, At-Risk

Bunker Hill Community College
Shooting for the Start
Shirley Cassara
Professor, Behavioral Sciences, 250 New Rutherford Avenue, Boston, MA 02129
(617) 241-8600
Ref: 30020.011210
PF: Minority, At-Risk

Bunker Hill Community College
Tech Prep/Metro Boston
Janet Sorter
Asst. Dean, Academic Affairs, 250 Rutherford Avenue, Boston, MA 02129
(617) 241-8600
Ref: 30019.011210
PF: Tech-Prep/2+2

▶ **Bunker Hill Community College** [125]
Tutoring for Literacy
Ted Carlson
Professor, Mathematics/Tutoring Department, 250 New Rutherford Avenue, Boston, MA 02129
(617) 241-8600
Ref: 30018.011210
PF: Tutoring, Counseling

Butler County Community College
Butler 2000
Tom Erwin
Division Chair, Instructional Support Services, 901
    S. Haverhill Road, El Dorado, KS 67042
(316) 322-3133
Ref: 31252.001906
PF: Minority, At-Risk

▶ **Butler County Community College**   [226]
Center for Teaching Excellence
J. Carney
Coordinator, 901 S. Haverhill Road, El Dorado,
    KS 67042
(316) 322-3136
Ref: 31253.001906
PF: Teacher Education Centers

Butler County Community College
Southwest Seminar Honors Program
Don Kole
Director, 901 S. Haverhill Road, El Dorado, KS
    67042
(316) 322-3175
Ref: 31251.001906
PF: Enrichment, Gifted

▶ **Butler University**   [293]
Partners in Education
Roger Boop
Acting Dean, College of Education, 4600 Sunset
    Avenue, Indianapolis, IN 46208
(317) 283-9752
boop@butler.edu
Ref: 30961.001788
PF: School-College-Business Partnerships

C

Cabrini College
Student Literacy Corps
Sharon Schwarze
Professor of Philosophy, Radnor, PA 19087
(610) 971-8333
Ref: 31844.003241
PF: Minority, At-Risk

Caldwell College
CNN-Caldwell College-Caldwell Schools-Newark
    Schools
Joseph Simplicio
Asst. Professor, 9 Ryerson Avenue, Caldwell, NJ
    07006
(201) 228-4424
Ref: 30082.002598
PF: Minority, At-Risk

▶ **California Academic Partnership
Program**   [278]
CAPP (California Academic Partnership Program)
Frank W. Young
Director, Office of the Chancellor, California State
    University, 400 Golden Shore, Suite 132, Long
    Beach, CA 90802-4275
(310) 985-2608
frank_young@qm.calstate.edu
Ref: 21208.U00008
PF: Umbrella Programs

▶ **California Institute of Technology**   [271]
Caltech Precollege Science Initiative
Jerome Pine
Professor of Biophysics, Box 56-48, Pasadena,
    CA 91125
(818) 395-6677
Ref: 31509.001131
PF: City/Regional Compacts

▶ **California Institute of Technology**   [13]
The W.M. Keck Foundation High School Outreach
    Program at Caltech
David L. Goodstein
Vice Provost, Box 104-31, Pasadena, CA 91125
(818) 395-6365
david_goodstein@starbase1.caltech.edu
Ref: 31508.001131
PF: Minority, At-Risk

▶ **California School of Professional
Psychology at Fresno**   [130]
Teaching Psychology
Lelia Veaco
Assoc. Professor, 1350 M Street, Fresno, CA
    93721
(209) 486-0432
Ref: 20998.011881
PF: Career, Internships, Apprenticeships

**California State Polytechnic University–
Pomona**
Young Scholar Program
Georgia Todd
Program Coordinator, Distance Learning Center,
    3801 W. Temple Avenue, Pomona, CA 91768
(909) 869-4560
gctodd@csupomona.edu
Ref: 21083.001144
PF: Minority, At-Risk

California State University–Bakersfield
M.E.S.A. (Math, Engineering, Science
    Achievement)
Sergio A. Guerra
Director, 9001 Stockdale Highway, Bakersfield,
    CA 93311
(805) 664-2431
Ref: 20730.007993
PF: Minority, At-Risk

▶ **California State University–Dominguez
Hills**   [207]
Aide-to-Teacher Program (ATT)
Mimi Frank
Coordinator, Liberal Studies, School of Education,
    Carson, CA 90747
(310) 516-3832
Ref: 31504.001141
PF: Recruit, Preservice, Certification

California State University–Dominguez Hills
California History/Social Science Project
Priscilla Porter
Codirector, School of Education, Carson, CA
    90747
(310) 516-4216
Ref: 31505.001141
PF: Professional Development, Inservice

▶ **California State University–Fresno**   [13]
California Mini-Corps Enhancement
Jacques Bennigan
Chair, School of Education and Human
    Development, Fresno, CA 93740
(204) 278-0250/0360
jackb@zimmer.calstate.edu
Ref: 31529.001147
PF: Minority, At-Risk

▣ **California State University–Fresno** [149]
Center for Collaboration for Children and Families
Doris O. Smith
Director, School of Education and Human
    Development, 5005 N. Maple, Fresno, CA
    93740-0202
(209) 278-0267
Ref: 31829.001147
PF: Professional Development, Inservice

▣ **California State University–Fresno** [117]
Elementary Teacher Cadet Program
Berta Gonzalez
Director, International and Special Projects,
    School of Education and Human Development,
    5005 N. Maple, Fresno, CA 93740-0001
(209) 278-0209
Ref: 31827.001147
PF: Tutoring, Counseling

▣ **California State University–Fresno** [208]
Parent Power Project
Deanna Evans-Schilling
Project Director, School of Education and Human
    Development, Fresno, CA 93740
(209) 278-0291
Ref: 31828.001147
PF: Recruit, Preservice, Certification

▣ **California State University–Fresno** [149]
Professor in the Classroom
Joan Henderson Sparks
Asst. Professor, Fresno, CA 93740
(209) 278-0306
Ref: 31832.001147
PF: Professional Development, Inservice

California State University–Fresno
Surcoll
Susan Harris
Assoc. Professor, 5005 N. Maple, Fresno, CA
    93740-0002
(209) 278-0356
Ref: 31831.001147
PF: Instructional Research

▣ **California State University–Fresno** [208]
Teacher In Preparation (TIP) Internship Program
Berta Gonzalez
Director of Teacher Internships, School of
    Education and Human Development, 5005 N.
    Maple, Fresno, CA 93740-0001
(209) 278-0209
Ref: 31830.001147
PF: Recruit, Preservice, Certification

▣ **California State University–Hayward** [13]
College Readiness Program
Lori Knight
Coordinator, 25800 Carlos Bee Boulevard,
    Hayward, CA 94542
(510) 881-3983
Ref: 20021.001138
PF: Minority, At-Risk

California State University–Hayward
CSUH-New Haven Partnership Program
Phil Duren
Professor, Department of Teacher Education,
    Hayward, CA 94542
(510) 881-3010
Ref: 31541.001138
PF: Recruit, Preservice, Certification

California State University–Hayward
High School Outreach Program
Roberto Rivera
Assoc. Director, Student Affirmative Action,
    Hayward, CA 94542
(510) 881-3982
Ref: 20020.001138
PF: Minority, At-Risk

California State University–Hayward
Individual, Family, Community Counseling
Jack A. Guthrie
Professor, 309 AE Building, Hayward, CA 94542
(510) 881-7429
Ref: 31542.001138
PF: Recruit, Preservice, Certification

California State University–Long Beach
County of Los Angeles Social Work Internships
Julie A. O'Donnell
Director of Research, 1250 Bellflower Boulevard,
    Long Beach, CA 90840-0902
(310) 985-5041
Ref: 31645.001139
PF: Minority, At-Risk

California State University–Long Beach
Fordham University Network Collaboration
Julie A. O'Donnell
Director of Research, 1250 Bellflower Boulevard,
    Long Beach, CA 90840-0902
(310) 985-5041
Ref: 31646.001139
PF: Recruit, Preservice, Certification

▣ **California State University–Long
Beach** [14]
Long Beach Access Program
Roger Bauer
Program Director, 1250 Bellflower Boulevard,
    Long Beach, CA 90840
(310) 985-8640
Ref: 31506.001139
PF: Minority, At-Risk

California State University–Long Beach
Perceptual Skills in Drawing
Betty Edwards
Professor of Art, Art Department, Long Beach, CA
    90840
(310) 985-7905
hglicksm@csulb.edu
Ref: 31644.001139
PF: Minority, At-Risk

California State University–Los Angeles
Accelerated College Enrollment Program (ACE)
George Bachmann
Assoc. Director of Admissions and University
    Outreach, 5151 State University Drive, Los
    Angeles, CA 90032
(213) 343-3131
Ref: 31479.001140
PF: College Courses for Students

California State University–Los Angeles
Accelerated Schools Project: Los Angeles Center
J. Sabrina Mims
Project Director, 5151 State University Drive, Los
    Angeles, CA 90032-8142
(213) 343-4362
Ref: 31478.001140
PF: Minority, At-Risk

California State University–Los Angeles
Art Education
Dawn Marie Patterson
Dean, Office of Continuing Education, 5151 State
    University Drive, Los Angeles, CA 90032-8619
(213) 343-4907
dpatter@atss.calstatela.edu
Ref: 31483.001140
PF: Professional Development, Inservice

California State University–Los Angeles
Bilingual Education
Dawn Marie Patterson
Dean, Office of Continuing Education, 5151 State
    University Drive, Los Angeles, CA 90032-8619
(213) 343-4907
dpatter@atss.calstatela.edu
Ref: 31485.001140
PF: Professional Development, Inservice

▣ **California State University–Los Angeles** [69]
College Credit Program
William A. Taylor
Assoc. Vice President for Academic Affairs-Planning and Resources, 5151 State University Drive, Los Angeles, CA 90032-8251
(213) 343-3810
wtaylor@oasis.calstatela.edu
Ref: 31488.001140
PF: College Courses for Students

California State University–Los Angeles
Conference: Implementing the Hughes Bill Regulations
Dawn Marie Patterson
Dean, Office of Continuing Education, 5151 State University Drive, Los Angeles, CA 90032-8619
(213) 343-4907
dpatter@atss.calstatela.edu
Ref: 31484.001140
PF: Professional Development, Inservice

▣ **California State University–Los Angeles** [150]
The Constitution in Eighth Grade History
Donald O. Dewey
Dean, Natural and Social Sciences, Los Angeles, CA 90032
(213) 343-2000
ddewey@csula.bitnet
Ref: 31490.001140
PF: Professional Development, Inservice

California State University–Los Angeles
CSLA/LAU SD Cooperative Admin. Service Credential & Master's Program
R. Carol Sweeney
Division Chair, 5151 State University Drive, Los Angeles, CA 90032
(213) 343-4250
Ref: 31493.001140
PF: Professional Development, Inservice

California State University–Los Angeles
CSLA/Marshall Fundamental School Partnership
William A. Taylor
Assoc. Vice President for Academic Affairs-Planning and Resources, 5151 State University Drive, Los Angeles, CA 90032-8251
(213) 343-3810
wtaylor@oasis.calstatela.edu
Ref: 31487.001140
PF: Minority, At-Risk

California State University–Los Angeles
CSLA, USC Medical School, Francisco Bravo and King-Drew Med. Magnet High Schools Collaboration
Rosemarie Marshall
Professor, Department of Biology/Microbiology, 5151 State University Drive, Los Angeles, CA 90032
(213) 343-2035
Ref: 31494.001140
PF: Minority, At-Risk

▣ **California State University–Los Angeles** [150]
Hands-On Physical Science
Dawn Marie Patterson
Dean, Office of Continuing Education, 5151 State University Drive, Los Angeles, CA 90032-8619
(213) 343-4907
dpatter@calstatela.edu
Ref: 31491.001140
PF: Professional Development, Inservice

California State University–Los Angeles
Head Start State Pre-School Program
Dawn Marie Patterson
Dean, Office of Continuing Education, 5151 State University Drive, Los Angeles, CA 90032-8619
(213) 343-4907
dpatter@atss.calstatela.edu
Ref: 31486.001140
PF: Professional Development, Inservice

▣ **California State University–Los Angeles** [14]
Improving School and Community Services to Children and Families in the Inner City
Andrea Zetlin
Professor of Education, School of Education, 5151 State University Drive, Los Angeles, CA 90032
(213) 343-4410
Ref: 31639.001140
PF: Minority, At-Risk

California State University–Los Angeles
Mathematics Education for Secondary Teachers
Dawn Marie Patterson
Dean, Office of Continuing Education, 5151 State University Drive, Los Angeles, CA 90032-8619
(213) 343-4907
dpatter@atss.calstatela.edu
Ref: 31482.001140
PF: Professional Development, Inservice

California State University–Los Angeles
Mathematics, Engineering, Science Achievement (MESA)
Elizabeth Erickson
Director, School of Engineering and Technology, 5151 State University Drive, Los Angeles, CA 90032
(213) 343-2490
Ref: 31492.001140
PF: Minority, At-Risk

California State University–Los Angeles
Pre-Accelerated College Enrollment Program (PACE)
George Bachmann
Assoc. Director of Admissions and University Outreach, 5151 State University Drive, Los Angeles, CA 90032
(213) 343-3131
Ref: 31479.001140
PF: Enrichment, Gifted

California State University–Los Angeles
Understanding and Teaching the Gifted Child
Dawn Marie Patterson
Dean, Office of Continuing Education, 5151 State University Drive, Los Angeles, CA 90032-8619
(213) 343-4907
dpatter@atss.calstatela.edu
Ref: 31481.001140
PF: Professional Development, Inservice

California State University–Los Angeles
University Preparatory Program
William A. Taylor
Assoc. Vice President for Academic Affairs-Planning and Resources, 5151 State University Drive Los Angeles, CA 90032-8251
(213) 343-3810
wtaylor@oasis.calstatela.edu
Ref: 31489.001140
PF: Minority, At-Risk

California State University–Northridge
Access to Algebra
Warren Furumoto
Vice President for Academic Affairs, 18111 Nordhoff Street, Northridge, CA 91330
(818) 885-2354
Ref: 31507.001153
PF: Professional Development, Inservice

▶ **California State University–San Bernardino** [151]
Bilingual Educators' Career Advancement (BECA)
Lynne Diaz-Rico
School of Education, 5500 University Parkway,
　San Bernardino, CA 92407
(909) 880-5600
Ref: 31762.001142
PF: Professional Development, Inservice

California State University–San Bernardino
California Transition Center
Louise Fulton
School of Education, 5500 University Parkway,
　San Bernardino, CA 92407
(909) 880-5600
Ref: 31763.001142
PF: Minority, At-Risk

California State University–San Bernardino
The Center for Research on Integrative Learning
　and Teaching
Renate Caine
School of Education, 5500 University Parkway,
　San Bernardino, CA 92407
(909) 880-5600
Ref: 31764.001142
PF: Curriculum Development

California State University–San Bernardino
Christopher Columbus Consortium
Susan Cooper
School of Education, 5500 University Parkway,
　San Bernardino, CA 92407
(909) 880-5600
Ref: 31765.001142
PF: Curriculum Development

California State University–San Bernardino
Coachella Valley Curriculum Change Project
Barbara Flores
School of Education, 5500 University Parkway,
　San Bernardino, CA 92407
(909) 880-5600
Ref: 31766.001142
PF: Curriculum Development

▶ **California State University–San Bernardino** [208]
Collaborative Learning Network: Project Genesis
Kathy Weed
School of Education, 5500 University Parkway,
　San Bernardino, CA 92407
(909) 880-5600
Ref: 31767.001142
PF: Recruit, Preservice, Certification

▶ **California State University–San Bernardino** [14]
Community Service in Tutoring At-Risk
　Adolescents (Student Literacy Corps Project)
Sherry Howie
School of Education, 5500 University Parkway,
　San Bernardino, CA 92407
(909) 880-5600
Ref: 31768.001142
PF: Minority, At-Risk

▶ **California State University–San Bernardino** [150]
Danforth School Board Training Partnership
Billie Blair
School of Education, 5500 University Parkway,
　San Bernardino, CA 92407
Ref: 31769.001142
PF: Professional Development, Inservice

California State University–San Bernardino
Environmental Education Resource Center
Darlene Stoner
5500 University Parkway, San Bernardino, CA
　92407
(909) 880-5600
Ref: 31770.001142
PF: Professional Development, Inservice

California State University–San Bernardino
Hillside-University Demonstration School
Ellen Kronowitz
School of Education, 5500 University Parkway,
　San Bernardino, CA 92407
(909) 880-5600
Ref: 31771.001142
PF: Recruit, Preservice, Certification

California State University–San Bernardino
Inland Area History-Social Science Project
Al Wolf
5500 University Parkway, San Bernardino, CA
　92407
(909) 880-5600
Ref: 31772.001142
PF: Professional Development, Inservice

California State University–San Bernardino
Integrating the Learning Community Model into
　Teacher Education
Francisco Hidalgo
School of Education, 5500 University Parkway,
　San Bernardino, CA 92407
(909) 880-5600
Ref: 31773.001142
PF: Recruit, Preservice, Certification

▶ **California State University–San Bernardino** [208]
Learning Handicapped Intern Program
Marjorie McCabe
School of Education, 5500 University Parkway,
　San Bernardino, CA 92407
(909) 880-5600
Ref: 31774.001142
PF: Recruit, Preservice, Certification

California State University–San Bernardino
Moreno Valley/Val Verde Principals' Project
Billie Blair
School of Education, 5500 University Parkway,
　San Bernardino, CA 92407
(909) 880-5600
Ref: 31775.001142
PF: Professional Development, Inservice

California State University–San Bernardino
Pacific High School/CSUSB Partnership
Jean Ramage
School of Education, 5500 University Parkway,
　San Bernardino, CA 92407
(909) 880-5600
Ref: 31776.001142
PF: Retention, Continuing Education

▶ **California State University–San Bernardino** [14]
Reading Recovery™
Stan Swartz
School of Education, 5500 University Parkway,
　San Bernardino, CA 92407
(909) 880-5600
Ref: 31777.001142
PF: Minority, At-Risk

▶ **California State University–San Bernardino** [150]
Regional Network of California Foundation &
　Partnership Middle Schools
Irvin Howard
School of Education, 5500 University Parkway,
　San Bernardino, CA 92407
(909) 880-5600
Ref: 31778.001142
PF: Professional Development, Inservice

California State University–San Bernardino
RIMSCAP
Joe Gray
School of Education, 5500 University Parkway,
　San Bernardino, CA 92407
(909) 880-5600
Ref: 31779.001142
PF: Professional Development, Inservice

California State University–San Bernardino   [191]
Rural Innovations in Special Education (Project RISE)
Louise Fulton
5500 University Parkway, San Bernardino, CA 92407
(909) 880-5600
Ref: 31780.001142
PF: Recruit, Preservice, Certification

California State University–San Bernardino
Science Education and Equity
Esteban Diaz
School of Education, 5500 University Parkway, San Bernardino, CA 92407
(909) 880-5600
Ref: 31781.001142
PF: Professional Development, Inservice

California State University–San Bernardino
Science Teaching Development Project
Bonnie Brunkhorst
School of Education, 5500 University Parkway, San Bernardino, CA 92407
(909) 880-5600
Ref: 31782.001142
PF: Instructional Research

California State University–San Bernardino
Teacher Diversity
Juan Gutierrez
School of Education, 5500 University Parkway, San Bernardino, CA 92407
(909) 880-5600
Ref: 31783.001142
PF: Recruit, Preservice, Certification

California State University–San Bernardino
Upland Unified School District: B1/B2 Partnership
Jean Ramage
School of Education, 5500 University Parkway, San Bernardino, CA 92407
(909) 880-5600
Ref: 31784.001142
PF: Enrichment, Gifted

California State University–Stanislaus
Single Subject (Secondary) Credential Program
Jane Dickman
Assoc. Professor, 801 St. Monta Vista, Turlack, CA 95382
(209) 667-3367
Ref: 21043.001157
PF: Teacher Education Centers

▶ **California University of Pennsylvania**   [191]
Alliance of California University and Western Pennsylvania English Teachers (ACUWPET)
Bill Hendricks
Assoc. Professor, English Department, California, PA 15419
(412) 938-4218
Ref: 30398.003316
PF: Professional Development, Inservice

California University of Pennsylvania
Environmental Education
Thomas C. Moon
Professor, Biology Department, California, PA 15419
(412) 938-4200
Ref: 30397.003316
PF: Professional Development, Inservice

▶ **California University of Pennsylvania**   [191]
Teacher Enhancement Center
John B. Fardo
Director, 208 Old Main, California, PA 15419
(412) 938-5956
Ref: 21248.003316
PF: Professional Development, Inservice

▶ **California University of Pennsylvania**   [265]
Mon Valley-Southpointe Tech Prep Consortium
Harry M. Langley
Assoc. Dean, College of Science and Technology, 250 University Avenue, California, PA 15419
(412) 938-4169
Ref: 30396.003316
PF: Tech-Prep/2+2

California University of Pennsylvania
Youth Apprenticeship
Harry M. Langley
Assoc. Dean, College of Science and Technology, 250 University Avenue, California, PA 15419
(412) 938-4169
Ref: 30395.003316
PF: Tech-Prep/2+2

California Western School of Law
California Western School of Law-Roosevelt Junior High School's Partnership Program
Ellen Dannin
Professor, 225 Cedar Street, San Diego, CA 92116
(619) 525-1449
cwslfac@cerf.net
Ref: 31517.013106
PF: Minority, At-Risk

▶ **Camden County College**   [260]
Curriculum Articulation Agreements
Edward T. McDonnell
Dean, Community Education, P.O. Box 200, Blackwood, NJ 08012
(609) 227-7200
Ref: 30111.006865
PF: Tech-Prep/2+2

Camden County College
Dual Credit
Edward T. McDonnell
Dean, Community Education, P.O. Box 200, Blackwood, NJ 08012
(609) 227-7200
Ref: 30110.006865
PF: College Courses for Students

Camden County College
Faculty Development Institute
Edward T. McDonnell
Dean, Community Education, P.O. Box 200, Blackwood, NJ 08012
(609) 227-7200
Ref: 30112.006865
PF: Professional Development, Inservice

Camden County College
Tech Prep
Edward T. McDonnell
Dean, Community Education, P.O. Box 200, Blackwood, NJ 08012
(609) 227-72000
Ref: 31807.006865
PF: Tech-Prep/2+2

Canisius College
Communicating with Computers
Barry Berlin
Assoc. Professor of Communication Studies, Buffalo, NY 14208
(716) 888-2116
Ref: 30293.002681
PF: Technology Application

Canisius College
From Monomers to Magic
Frank J. Dinan
Professor, Chemistry Department, 2001 Main
    Street, Buffalo, NY 14208
(716) 888-2399
dinan@canisius.bitnet
Ref: 30294.002681
PF: Enrichment, Gifted

▶ **Canisius College**   [301]
Laboratory Equipment Assistance Program
    (LEAP)
Joseph F. Bieron
Professor of Chemistry, 2001 Main Street, Buffalo,
    NY 14208
(716) 888-2357
Ref: 21249.002681
PF: Resource Sharing

Canisius College
Western New York Physical Education
    Consortium
James Sylvis
Chair, Department of Physical Education, Buffalo,
    NY 14208
(716) 888-2953
Ref: 30295.002681
PF: Professional Development, Inservice

▶ **Canisius College**   [180]
Western New York Writing Project
David A. Lauerman
Director, Buffalo, NY 14208
(716) 888-2659
Ref: 30296.002681
PF: Professional Development, Inservice

▶ **Cape Fear Community College**   [54]
Alliance for Achievement
Alice Marie Mumaw
Vice President for Instruction and Student
    Development, 411 N. Front Street, Wilmington,
    NC 28401
(910) 251-5125
Ref: 30748.005320
PF: Minority, At-Risk

Carleton College
Summer Academic Enrichment Program for
    Multicultural Seventh and Eighth Graders
Bruce A. King
Advisor to the President on Multicultural Affairs, 1
    N. College Street, Northfield, MN 55057
(507) 663-4014
bking@carleton.edu
Ref: 20750.002340
PF: Minority, At-Risk

▶ **Carroll Community College**   [167]
Institute For Drug and Alcohol Abuse Education
Deborah Wright
Project Director, 1601 Washington Road,
    Westminster, MD 21157
(410) 876-9610
Ref: 30535.666396
PF: Professional Development, Inservice

Carson-Newman College
Excel
B. F. Bull
Assoc. Professor, Box 71925, Jefferson City, TN
    37760
(615) 471-3319
Ref: 30690.003481
PF: College Courses for Students

▶ **Carson-Newman College**   [302]
Family Resource Center
Peggy Hypes
Chair, Graduate Studies Department, Box 31782,
    Jefferson City, TN 37760
(615) 471-3309
Ref: 30694.003481
PF: Resource Sharing

▶ **Carson-Newman College**   [197]
Foxfire Teacher Outreach: East Tennessee
    Teachers Network (ETTN)
Sharon T. Teets
Foxfire Coordinator, CN 71952, Jefferson City, TN
    37760
(615) 471-3461
Ref: 30692.003481
PF: Professional Development, Inservice

Carson-Newman College
Health Education Fair
Cynthia Huff
Asst. Professor of Nursing, Box 71903, Jefferson
    City, TN 37760
(615) 471-3429
Ref: 30693.003481
PF: Enrichment, Gifted

Carson-Newman College
High School Programming Contest
Rebekah Tidwell
Asst. Professor, Box 1973, Jefferson City, TN
    37760
(615) 471-3321
71533.372@compuserve.com
Ref: 30691.003481
PF: Enrichment, Gifted

Carteret Community College
Computer Collaborative
Paul R. Stokes
Chairman, Business Technical Division, 3505
    Arendell Street, Moorehead City, NC 28557
(919) 247-3097
Ref: 20713.008081
PF: College Courses for Students

▶ **Carteret Community College**   [263]
Tech-Prep Associate Degree
Dan Krautheim
Dean of the College, 3505 Arendell Street,
    Moorehead City, NC 28557
(919) 247-3058
Ref: 30751.008081
PF: Tech-Prep/2+2

▶ **Case Western Reserve University**   [55]
Case Early Exposure to Engineering for Minority
    Students (CE³MS)
Margaret E. Boulding
Asst. Dean, 10900 Euclid Avenue, Baker Building
    116, Cleveland, OH 44106-7029
(216) 368-2904
Ref: 20078.003024
PF: Minority, At-Risk

Case Western Reserve University
Case Pro-Engineering Program (C-PEP)
Margaret E. Boulding
Asst. Dean, 10900 Euclid Avenue, Baker Building
    116, Cleveland, OH 44106-7029
(216) 368-2904
meb7@po.cwru.edu
Ref: 20118.003024
PF: Minority, At-Risk

▶ **Case Western Reserve University**   [289]
Cleveland FreeNet (Academy One)
H. Wendell Klingensmith
Asst. Vice President of Information Sources,
    10900 Euclid Avenue, Cleveland, OH
    44106-7072
(216) 368-2982
hwk@po.cwru.edu
Ref: 20884.003024
PF: Technology Application

Case Western Reserve University
Cleveland Health Education Program
Susan Wentz, M.D.
Program Director, CWRU Urban AHEC, School of
    Medicine, 10900 Euclid Avenue, Cleveland, OH
    44106
(216) 368-5493
Ref: 30858.003024
PF: Recruit, Preservice, Certification

▶ **Case Western Reserve University** [106]
LTV Steel Science & Technology Institute
Margaret E. Boulding
Asst. Dean, 10900 Euclid Avenue, Baker Building
116, Cleveland, OH 44106
(216) 368-2904
Ref: 30859.003024
PF: Enrichment, Gifted

▶ **Case Western Reserve University** [56]
Minority Engineers Industrial Opportunity Program
Margaret E. Boulding
Asst. Director, 10900 Euclid Avenue, Baker
Building 116, Cleveland, OH 44106-7029
(216) 368-2904
meb7@po.cwru.edu
Ref: 20079.003024
PF: Minority, At-Risk

▶ **Case Western Reserve University** [81]
Pre-College Scholars Program
Margaret Robinson
Assoc. Dean, Office of Collegiate Affairs, 10900
Euclid Avenue, Cleveland, OH 44106
(216) 368-2928
Ref: 30857.003024
PF: College Courses for Students

▶ **Case Western Reserve University** [56]
Upward Bound: Special Program for
Preprofessional Students in the Health
Sciences (SPPSHS)
Carrie A. R. Reeves
Director, 10900 Euclid Avenue, Cleveland, OH
44106-7045
(216) 368-3750
Ref: 20110.003024
PF: Minority, At-Risk

▶ **Casper College** [86]
BOCES (Board of Cooperative Educational
Services)
F.E. Skip Gillum
Vice President of Academic Affairs, 125 College
Drive, Casper, WY 82601
(307) 268-2540
Ref: 31431.003928
PF: College Courses for Students

Catholic University of Puerto Rico
Adopt-One-School
Jaime Ortiz Vega
Dean, #482 S. Post Street, Mayaguez, PR 00680
(809) 834-5151
Ref: 30335.003936
PF: Career, Internships, Apprenticeships

▶ **Catholic University of Puerto Rico** [194]
Adopted Schools
Haydee Piris
Vice President, Special Programs and
Accreditation, Postal Station 6, Ponce, PR
00732
(809) 841-2000 x284
Ref: 30338.003936
PF: Professional Development, Inservice

Catholic University of Puerto Rico
The Reform of Elementary Preservice Teacher
Education in Science and Mathematics
Carmen L. Pereles
Director, College of Sciences, General Science
Department, Ponce, PR 00732
(809) 841-2000 x287
Ref: 30336.003936
PF: Recruit, Preservice, Certification

Catholic University of Puerto Rico
Summer Camp for 7th and 10th Graders, and
Saturday Academy for Junior and High School
Students
Carmen L. Velazquez
Director, College of Sciences, Chemistry
Department, Station 6, Ponce, PR 00732
(809) 841-2000 x284
Ref: 30337.003936
PF: Enrichment, Gifted

▶ **Cayuga County Community College** [78]
Cayuga Secondary Linkage
Keith Batman
Assoc. Academic Dean, and Director of
Continuing Education, 197 Franklin Street,
Auburn, NY 13021
(315) 255-1743
Ref: 30243.002861
PF: College Courses for Students

Cayuga County Community College
Gifted & Talented Mini Courses
Keith Batman
Assoc. Academic Dean and Director of Continuing
Education, 197 Franklin Street, Auburn, NY
13021
(315) 255-1743
Ref: 30244.002861
PF: Enrichment, Gifted

▶ **Cayuga County Community College** [46]
Nontraditional Careers for Women: Role Models &
Networking
Gayle Scroggs
Project Director, Auburn, NY 13021
(315) 255-1743
Ref: 30242.002861
PF: Minority, At-Risk

Cedarville College
Clinical/Field Programs
Merlin Ager
Chairman, Department of Education, Box 601,
Cedarville, OH 45314
(513) 766-2211
Ref: 21004.003025
PF: Recruit, Preservice, Certification

Centenary College
Northwest Partnering
Joyce Huth Munro
Chair, Education Division, 400 Jefferson Street,
Hackettstown, NJ 07840
(908) 852-1400
Ref: 30142.007729
PF: Technology Application

Central Carolina Technical College
Career Peers
Rose Raynak
Recruitment Coordinator, 506 N. Guignard Drive,
Sumter, SC 29150
(803) 778-6697
Ref: 31710.003995
PF: Tutoring, Counseling

Central Carolina Technical College
Higher Education Awareness Program
Rose Raynak
Recruitment Coordinator, 506 N. Guignard Drive,
Sumter, SC 29150
(803) 778-6697
Ref: 31708.003995
PF: Career, Internships, Apprenticeships

Central Carolina Technical College
Office Systems Presentations Program
Rose Raynak
Recruitment Coordinator, 506 N. Guignard Drive,
Sumter, SC 29150
(803) 778-6697
Ref: 31706.003995
PF: Career, Internships, Apprenticeships

Central Carolina Technical College
Starbound
Rose Raynak
Recruitment Coordinator, 506 N. Guignard Drive,
    Sumter, SC 29150
(803) 778-6697
Ref: 31709.003995
PF: College Courses for Students

Central Carolina Technical College
Tech Prep
Rose Raynak
Recruitment Coordinator, 506 N. Guignard Drive,
    Sumter, SC 29150
(803) 778-6697
Ref: 31707.003995
PF: Tech-Prep/2+2

Central Community College-Platte Campus
Central Nebraska Educational Articulation
    Consortium
Roger Augspurger
Interim Campus President, Box 1027, Columbus,
    NE 68602-1027
(402) 562-1211
Ref: 20080.020995
PF: College Courses for Students

▶ **Central Florida Community College**   [71]
Legacies From Our Past: Florida Archaeology
Ira Holmes
Dean, Humanities and Social Science, P.O. Box
    1388, Ocala, FL 34478
(904) 854-2322
Ref: 30665.001471
PF: College Courses for Students

▶ **Central Florida Community College**   [251]
Mid-Florida Tech Prep Consortium
J. Michael Horan
Director, P.O. Box 1388, Ocala, FL 34478-1388
(904) 237-2111
horanm@firnvx.firn.edu
Ref: 30666.001471
PF: Tech-Prep/2+2

Central Maine Technical College
Central Maine Tech/Prep Consortium
Diane Dostie
Tech/Prep Director, 1250 Turner Street, Auburn,
    ME 04210
(207) 784-2385
Ref: 30058.005276
PF: Tech-Prep/2+2

▶ **Central Missouri State University**   [215]
Graduated Entry
John R. Zelazek
Assoc. Professor, 302-F Lovinger Hall,
    Warrensburg, MO 64093
(814) 543-4235
Ref: 21019.002454
PF: Recruit, Preservice, Certification

▶ **Central Missouri State University**   [99]
Young Author's Conference
Kathryn Carr
Director of the Reading Center, Warrensburg, MO
    64093
(816) 543-8725
kcarr@cmsuvmb.cmsu.edu
Ref: 20748.002454
PF: Enrichment, Gifted

▶ **Central Piedmont Community
College**   [55]
Even Start Families Learning Together for
    Success
Cynthia Johnston
Department Head, ABE/GED, P.O. Box 35009,
    Charlotte, NC 28235
(704) 342-6716
Ref: 30744.002915
PF: Minority, At-Risk

Central Piedmont Community College
Tech Prep
Thomas C. Leitzel
Dean of Business, Health and Technologies, P.O.
    Box 35009, Charlotte, NC 28235
(704) 342-6909
Ref: 30745.002915
PF: Tech-Prep/2+2

Central State University
Adopted School Program
Cheryl D. Marcus
Program Coordinator, Urban Literacy Center,
    Wilberforce, OH 45384
(513) 376-6390
Ref: 20532.003026
PF: Minority, At-Risk

Central Virginia Community College
Dual Enrollment
L. Thomas Barber
Dean of Instruction, 3506 Wards Road,
    Lynchburg, VA 24502
(804) 386-4523
Ref: 30583.004988
PF: College Courses for Students

Central Virginia Community College
Tech Prep Region 2000 Educational Consortium
Richard B. Carter, Sr.
Tech Prep Coordinator, 3506 Wards Road,
    Lynchburg, VA 24502
(804) 386-4511
Ref: 30582.004988
PF: Tech-Prep/2+2

Central Washington University
Central Washington University/Superintendent of
    Public Instruction
F. Ross Byrd
Chair, Business Education and Administration
    Management, Ellensburg, WA 98926
(509) 963-2611
Ref: 20351.003771
PF: Recruit, Preservice, Certification

Centre College
Learning Is Fun Together (LIFT)
Ann Young
Director of Volunteer Programs, 600 W. Walnut,
    Danville, KY 40422
(606) 238-5480
Ref: 30839.001961
PF: Minority, At-Risk

▶ **Centre College**   [35]
M²SE (Minorities in Math, Science & Engineering)
John C. Ward
Dean of the College, 600 W. Walnut Street,
    Danville, KY 40422
(606) 238-5225
Ref: 31750.001961
PF: Minority, At-Risk

Centre College
Summer Science Camp
Chris Barton
Asst. Professor of Biology, 600 W. Walnut,
    Danville, KY 40422
(606) 238-5322
Ref: 30837.001961
PF: Enrichment, Gifted

Centre College
Summer Science Workshops for High School
    Teachers
Chris Barton
Asst. Professor of Biology, 600 W. Walnut,
    Danville, KY 40422
(606) 238-5322
Ref: 30838.001961
PF: Teacher Education Centers

Chabot College
Regional Health Occupations Resource Center
Barbara Hockett
Project Coordinator, 25555 Hesperian Boulevard,
   Hayward, CA 94545
(510) 786-9677
Ref: 31824.001162
PF: Minority, At-Risk

Charles County Community College
The Southern Maryland Early Intervention,
   College Preparation Program
Robert R. St. Pierre
Director, Student Development, P.O. Box 910,
   Mitchell Road, La Plata, MD 20646
(301) 934-2251
Ref: 30508.002064
PF: Minority, At-Risk

Charles County Community College
Talent Search Program
Edith Patterson
Director, La Plata, MD 20646
(301) 934-2251
Ref: 30509.002064
PF: Minority, At-Risk

Charles S. Mott Community College
Dental Assisting Program Articulation Agreement
Darlene Boersema
Coordinator, 1401 E. Court Street, Flint, MI 48503
(810) 762-0493
Ref: 31020.002261
PF: Tech-Prep/2+2

Charles S. Mott Community College
Genesee Area Skill Center
Mamie Howard
Dean, School of Health Science and Vocational
   Education, 1401 E. Court Street, Flint, MI
   48503
(313)762-0317
Ref: 31024.002261
PF: College Courses for Students

Charles S. Mott Community College
Interpreter Training Program (Providing Student
   Interns)
Linda Lee Massoud
Coordinator, 1401 E. Court Street, Flint, MI
   48503-2383
(810) 762-0272
Ref: 31021.002261
PF: Resource Sharing

▶ **Charles S. Mott Community College**   [257]
Office Information Systems Programs
Marilee Knapp
Co-Op Coordinator, 1401 E. Court Street, Flint, MI
   48503
(313) 232-7601
Ref: 31019.002261
PF: Tech-Prep/2+2

▶ **Charles S. Mott Community College**   [40]
One and One and All Together Project
Dan Hodgins
Coordinator, Child Development, 1401 E. Court
   Street, Flint, MI 48503
(313) 762-0489
Ref: 31025.002261
PF: Minority, At-Risk

▶ **Charles S. Mott Community College**   [257]
Project Cadmaster
Thomas D. Crampton
Assoc. Professor, 1401 E. Court Street, Flint, MI
   48503
(810) 762-0506
Ref: 31023.002261
PF: Tech-Prep/2+2

▶ **Charles S. Mott Community College**   [295]
Project Design
Thomas D. Crampton
Assoc. Professor, 1401 E. Court Street, Flint, MI
   48503
(810) 762-0506
Ref: 31022.002261
PF: School-College-Business Partnerships

Charleston Southern University
Trident Business-Education Partnership
Rick Brewer
Assistant to the President, P.O. Box 118087,
   Charleston, SC 29423
(803) 863-7503
Ref: 20908.003419
PF: Minority, At-Risk

▶ **Chattahoochee Valley State Community
College**   [248]
Tech-Prep Articulation
Sam Morton
Chair, Business Department, 2602 College Drive,
   Phenix City, AL 36867
(205) 291-4954
Ref: 30683.012182
PF: Tech-Prep/2+2

▶ **Chattanooga State Technical Community
College**   [290]
Distance Learning Program
Sue Hyatt
4501 Amnicola Highway, Chattanooga, TN 37406
(615) 697-4408
Ref: 31718.003998
PF: Technology Application

**Chattanooga State Technical Community
   College**
Joint Enrollment
Kathy Loftis
4501 Amnicola Highway, Chattanooga, TN 37406
(615) 697-4427
Ref: 31717.003998
PF: College Courses for Students

▶ **Chemeketa Community College**   [274]
Partnership Programs
Richard Levine
Vice President, Academic Services, P.O. Box
   14007, Salem, OR 97309
(503) 399-5144
Ref: 31577.003218
PF: City/Regional Compacts

Chesterfield-Marlboro Technical College
Senior Success
Sandra H. Barbour
Vice-President for Instruction, Drawer 1007,
   Cheraw, SC 29520
(803) 537-5286
Ref: 30803.007602
PF: College Courses for Students

▶ **Chipola Junior College**   [159]
Alternative Training Initiative
Gloria Peacock
Coordinator, Continuing Education, 3094 Indian
   Circle, Marianna, FL 32446
(904) 526-2761
Ref: 31712.001472
PF: Professional Development, Inservice

▶ **Chipola Junior College**   [91]
Chipola Regional Science & Engineering Fair
Paul Huang
Director, 3094 Indian Circle, Marianna, FL
   32446-2053
(904) 526-2761
Ref: 30639.001472
PF: Enrichment, Gifted

Chipola Junior College
Dual Enrollment
Earl Carroll
Academic Dean, 3094 Indian Circle, Marianna, FL
   32446
(904) 526-2761
Ref: 31743.001472
PF: College Courses for Students

▶ **Christopher Newport University**   [111]
Annual High School Theatre Festival
Jay Paul
Chair, English Department, 50 Shoe Lane,
   Newport News, VA 23606
(804) 594-7072
Ref: 20101.003706
PF: Enrichment, Gifted

Christopher Newport University
Mathews High School/CNU Scholars Program
Keith F. McLoughland
Dean of Admissions, Newport News, VA
   23606-2998
(804) 594-7015
Ref: 20099.003706
PF: Enrichment, Gifted

Christopher Newport University
Project EXCEL: Focused on Physics
Randall Caton
Department of Physics, 50 Shoe Lane, Newport
   News, VA 23606
(804) 594-7188
rcatm@pcs.cnu.edu
Ref: 30574.003706
PF: Minority, At-Risk

▶ **Christopher Newport University**   [243]
Stars Project
Edward Weiss
Professor of Biology, 50 Shoe Lane, Newport
   News, VA 23606
(804) 594-7100
eweiss@powhatan.cc.cnu.edu
Ref: 30573.003706
PF: Curriculum Development

▶ **Christopher Newport University**   [111]
Summer Institute for the Arts
Rita C. Hubbard
Chair, Arts and Communication, Newport News,
   VA 23606-2988
(804) 594-7073
Ref: 21147.003706
PF: Enrichment, Gifted

The Citadel, The Military College of South Carolina
Project Challenge
Stephenie Hewett
Department of Education, Charleston, SC 29409
(803) 953-5097
Ref: 30792.003423
PF: Minority, At-Risk

Citrus College
Tech Prep
Kim Holland
Tech Prep Coordinator, 1000 W. Foothill,
   Glendora, CA 91741
(818) 914-8503
Ref: 31515.001166
PF: Tech-Prep/2+2

▶ **City University of New York–Bernard M. Baruch College**   [78]
Academy of Finance
David Wilson
Acting Director of Administration, SBPA, 17
   Lexington Avenue, Box 303, New York, NY
   10010
(212) 447-3295
Ref: 30154.004766
PF: College Courses for Students

▶ **City University of New York–Bernard M. Baruch College**   [180]
New York City Council on Economic Education at
   Baruch College
Terrence F. Martell
Professor of Finance, 17 Lexington Avenue, Box
   405, New York, NY 10010
(212) 447-3395
Ref: 30153.004766
PF: Professional Development, Inservice

▶ **City University of New York–Borough of Manhattan Community College**   [78]
Distance Learning Project
Sandra Rumayor
Director, Partnerships and Collaboratives, 199
   Chambers Street, New York, NY 10007
(212) 346-8527
Ref: 30146.002691
PF: College Courses for Students

City University of New York–Borough of Manhattan Community College
Liberty Partnerships Program
Sandra Rumayor
Director, Partnerships and Collaboratives, 199
   Chambers Street, New York, NY 10007
(212) 346-8527
Ref: 30147.002691
PF: Minority, At-Risk

▶ **City University of New York–Borough of Manhattan Community College**   [137]
Executive Internship Program (EIP)
Sandra Rumayor
Director, Partnerships and Collaboratives, 199
   Chambers Street, New York, NY 10007
(212) 346-8527
Ref: 30149.002691
PF: Career, Internships, Apprenticeships

City University of New York–Borough of Manhattan Community College
High School Articulation Program
Sandra Rumayor
Director, Partnerships and Collaboratives, 199
   Chambers Street, New York, NY 10007
(212) 346-8527
Ref: 30150.002691
PF: Minority, At-Risk

▶ **City University of New York–Borough of Manhattan Community College**   [47]
Sex Equity Math/Science Project
Sandra Rumayor
Director, Partnerships and Collaboratives, 199
   Chambers Street, New York, NY 10007
(212) 346-8527
Ref: 30148.002691
PF: Minority, At-Risk

City University of New York–Borough of Manhattan Community College
Success Bridge Program
Sandra Rumayor
Director, Partnerships and Collaboratives, 199
   Chambers Street, New York, NY 10007
(212) 346-8527
Ref: 30152.002691
PF: College Courses for Students

▶ **City University of New York–Borough of Manhattan Community College**   [138]
Women Making Strides
Sandra Rumayor
Director, Partnerships and Collaboratives, 199
   Chambers Street, New York, NY 10007
(212) 346-8527
Ref: 30151.002691
PF: Career, Internships, Apprenticeships

▶ **City University of New York–Bronx Community College**   [273]
Bronx Educational Alliance
Michael C. Gillespie
Director, W. 181st Street and University Avenue,
   GH-317, Bronx, NY 10453
(718) 220-6079
Ref: 30166.002692
PF: City/Regional Compacts

City University of New York–Bronx Community College
Family College
Winifred Washington
Project Director, W. 181st Street and University Avenue, Bronx, NY 10453
(718) 220-6450
Ref: 30168.002692
PF: Retention, Continuing Education

▶ **City University of New York–Bronx Community College**   [261]
Tech Prep Program
Rudean Leinaeng
Professor, W. 181st Street and University Avenue, Bronx, NY 10453
(718) 220-6159
Ref: 30167.002692
PF: Tech-Prep/2+2

▶ **City University of New York–Bronx Community College**   [115]
University Heights High School
Mitchell Wenzell
W. 181st Street and University Avenue, Bronx, NY 10453
(718) 220-6397
Ref: 20573.002692
PF: Middle/Early Colleges

▶ **City University of New York–College of Staten Island**   [47]
The Liberty Partnership Program
Debi Rose
Director, 2800 Victory Boulevard, Building 1A, Room 206, Staten Island, NY 10314
(718) 982-2343
Ref: 30159.002698
PF: Minority, At-Risk

City University of New York–College of Staten Island
Mathematics Collaborative Program
Michael Sormani
Coordinator, 2800 Victory Boulevard, Building 1S, Room 209, Staten Island, NY 10314
(718) 982-3615
Ref: 30161.002698
PF: Tutoring, Counseling

▶ **City University of New York–College of Staten Island**   [102]
Mathematics/Computer Science Olympics
Carolyn A. Fazzolari
Assoc. Dean of Faculty for Freshman Programs, 2800 Victory Boulevard, Building 25, Room 212, Staten Island, NY 10314
(718) 982-2350
Ref: 30164.002698
PF: Enrichment, Gifted

City University of New York–College of Staten Island
Science & Technology Entry Program
Mary Ann Langelle
Project Director, 2800 Victory Boulevard, 1L-117, Staten Island, NY 10314
(718) 982-3963
Ref: 30160.002698
PF: Minority, At-Risk

▶ **City University of New York–College of Staten Island**   [102]
Science Olympics
Carolyn A. Fazzolari
Assoc. Dean of Faculty for Freshman Programs, 2800 Victory Boulevard, South Administration Building, Room 207, Staten Island, NY 10314
(718) 982-2350
Ref: 30163.002698
PF: Enrichment, Gifted

▶ **City University of New York–College of Staten Island**   [180]
Staten Island English Newsletter
William Bernardt
Assoc. Professor of English, 2800 Victory Boulevard, Building 25, Room 212, Staten Island, NY 10314
(718) 982-3671
Ref: 30162.002698
PF: Professional Development, Inservice

▶ **City University of New York–Herbert H. Lehman College**   [126]
After-School Tutoring Program
Shirley Gilwit
Program Coordinator, 250 Bedford Park Boulevard W, Bronx, NY 10468
(718) 960-8167
Ref: 30176.007022
PF: Tutoring, Counseling

▶ **City University of New York–Herbert H. Lehman College**   [48]
Hughes Biological Science Program
Thomas Jensen
Program Director, 250 Bedford Park Boulevard W, Bronx, NY 10468
(718) 960-8569
Ref: 30170.007022
PF: Minority, At-Risk

▶ **City University of New York–Herbert H. Lehman College**   [304]
Macy Medical Sciences Honors Programs at DeWitt Clinton High School
Thomas K. Minter
Dean of Professional Studies, 250 Bedford Park Boulevard W, Bronx, NY 10468
(718) 960-8401
tkmlc@cunyvm
Ref: 30178.007022
PF: Magnet Schools

▶ **City University of New York–Herbert H. Lehman College**   [102]
MASTER (Mathematics and Science Through Excellence and Research)
Anne L. Rothstein
Assoc. Provost, 250 Bedford Park Boulevard W, Bronx, NY 10468
(718) 960-8569
alrlc@cunyvm
Ref: 30177.007022
PF: Enrichment, Gifted

City University of New York–Herbert H. Lehman College
New York City Mathematics Project
Ray Durney
Director, Institute for Literacy Studies, 250 Bedford Park Boulevard W, Bronx, NY 10468-1589
(718) 960-8758
Ref: 30180.007022
PF: Professional Development, Inservice

City University of New York–Herbert H. Lehman College
New York City Writing Project
Elaine Avidon
Director, Institute for Literacy Studies, 250 Bedford Park Boulevard W, Bronx, NY 10468-1589
(718) 960-8758
Ref: 30181.007022
PF: Professional Development, Inservice

City University of New York–Herbert H.
Lehman College
Northwest Bronx Educational Park
Judith Guskin
Director, 250 Bedford Park Boulevard W, Bronx,
NY 10468
(718) 960-8330
Ref: 30173.007022
PF: City/Regional Compacts

City University of New York–Herbert H.
Lehman College
Phoenix 1000
Pedro L. Baez
Project Director, 250 Bedford Park Boulevard W,
Bronx, NY 10468
(718) 960-8966
baez@lcvax.lehman.cuny.edu
Ref: 30169.007022
PF: Minority, At-Risk

▶ City University of New York–Herbert H.
Lehman College   [47]
PRISMMS (Program to Increase Student Mastery
in Mathematics & Science)
Pamela Floyd
Program Coordinator Carman B-29, 250 Bedford
Park Boulevard W, Bronx, NY 10468
(718) 960-8569
Ref: 30171.007022
PF: Minority, At-Risk

▶ City University of New York–Herbert H.
Lehman College   [47]
STEP (Science and Technology Entry Program)
Margaret Watkins
Project Coordinator, 250 Bedford Park Boulevard
W, Bronx, NY 10468
(718) 960-8569
Ref: 30174.007022
PF: Minority, At-Risk

City University of New York–Herbert H.
Lehman College
Walton High School/Lehman College
Pre-Teaching Academy
Anne L. Rothstein
Assoc. Provost, 250 Bedford Park Boulevard W,
Bronx, NY 10468
(718) 960-8569
alrlc@cunyvm
Ref: 30172.007022
PF: Magnet Schools

▶ City University of New York–Herbert H.
Lehman College   [115]
Walton/Lehman Bridge to College
David Fletcher
Program Coordinator, 250 Bedford Park,
Boulevard W, Bronx, NY 10468
(718) 960-8569
alrlc@cunyvm
Ref: 30179.007022
PF: Middle/Early Colleges

City University of New York–Herbert H.
Lehman College
Writing Teachers Consortium
Richard Sterling
Director, Institute for Literacy Studies, 250
Bedford Park Boulevard W, Bronx, NY 10468
(718) 960-8758
rfsl@cunyvm.cuny.edu
Ref: 30183.007022
PF: Professional Development, Inservice

City University of New York–Hostos
Community College
The Bronx Educational Alliance
Cory Schwarzschild
Project Coordinator, 500 Grand Concourse, Room
B447, Bronx, NY 10451
(718) 518-6722
Ref: 30165.008611
PF: Minority, At-Risk

City University of New York–Hunter College
American Social History Project High School
Collaboration
Bret Eynon
Educational Director, 695 Park Avenue, New
York, NY 10021
(212) 772-4129
Ref: 30197.002689
PF: Professional Development, Inservice

▶ City University of New York–John Jay
College of Criminal Justice   [78]
ASCENT (Advanced Standing for College
Entrance) Program
Sylvia Lopez
Admissions Counselor, 445 W. 59th Street, New
York, NY 10019
(212) 237-8897
Ref: 31760.002693
PF: College Courses for Students

City University of New York–John Jay College
of Criminal Justice
In-Service Mathematics Training For Elementary
School Teachers
Sydney Samuel
Chairman, Math Department, 445 W. 59th Street,
New York, NY 10019
(212) 237-8923
Ref: 31757.002693
PF: Professional Development, Inservice

City University of New York–John Jay College
of Criminal Justice
Liberty Partnership Program
Gregory Bryant
Director, 445 W. 59th Street, Room 1533 North,
New York, NY 10019
(212) 237-8054/55
Ref: 30155.002693
PF: Minority, At-Risk

▶ City University of New York–Kingsborough
Community College   [79]
College Now Program
Stuart Suss
Director, 2001 Oriental Boulevard, Brooklyn, NY
11235
(718) 368-5170
Ref: 21095.002694
PF: College Courses for Students

▶ City University of New York–Kingsborough
Community College   [138]
Sports, Fitness & Therapeutic Recreation
Richard A. Kaye
Professor, 2201 Oriental Boulevard, Brooklyn, NY
11235
(718) 368-5831/5696
Ref: 20662.002694
PF: Career, Internships, Apprenticeships

▶ City University of New York–LaGuardia
Community College   [115]
American Social History Project/Middle College
High School Consortium National Project
Roberta S. Matthews
Assoc. Dean for Academic Affairs, 31-10
Thomson Avenue, Long Island City, NY 11101
(718) 482-5404
Ref: 30201.010051
PF: Middle/Early Colleges

▶ **City University of New York–LaGuardia Community College** [297]
Career Exploration Project
Arlene M. Kahn
Director, 31-10 Thomson Avenue, M-418, Long Island City, NY 11101
(718) 482-5418
Ref: 30204.010051
PF: School-College-Business Partnerships

City University of New York–LaGuardia Community College
College Connection
Arlene M. Kahn
Director, School/College Collaboration, 31-10 Thomson Avenue, M-418, Long Island City, NY 11101
(718) 482-5418
Ref: 30195.010051
PF: College Courses for Students

City University of New York–LaGuardia Community College
College for Children/Programs for Teens
Hiawatha Baron
Program Director, 31-10 Thomson Avenue, M-141, Long Island City, NY 11101
(718) 482-5323
Ref: 30205.010051
PF: Enrichment, Gifted

City University of New York–LaGuardia Community College
College Now!
Arlene M. Kahn
Director, 31-10 Thomson Avenue, M-418, Long Island City, NY 11101
(718) 482-5418
Ref: 30196.010051
PF: College Courses for Students

▶ **City University of New York–LaGuardia Community College** [138]
Experience-Based Career Education Program
Dean Dorrie E. Williams
Program Director, 31-10 Thomson Avenue, Long Island City, NY 11101
(718) 482-5210
Ref: 30194.010051
PF: Career, Internships, Apprenticeships

▶ **City University of New York–LaGuardia Community College** [115]
International High School
Janet Lieberman
Special Assistant to the President, 31-10 Thomson Avenue, Long Island City, NY 11101
(718) 482-5049
Ref: 21185.010051
PF: Middle/Early Colleges

▶ **City University of New York–LaGuardia Community College** [233]
Mathematics Adjunct Program
Jorge Perez
Chairperson, Mathematics Department, 31-10 Thomson Avenue, Long Island City, NY 11101
(718) 482-5711
Ref: 30200.010051
PF: New Faculty Roles

▶ **City University of New York–LaGuardia Community College** [116]
Middle College High School
Janet Lieberman
Special Assistant to the President, 31-10 Thomson Avenue, Long Island City, NY 11101
(718) 482-5049
Ref: 21103.010051
PF: Middle/Early Colleges

▶ **City University of New York–LaGuardia Community College** [48]
Northeast Consortium
Ted Tyler
Coordinator, 31-10 Thomson Avenue, Long Island City, NY 11101
(718) 482-5347
Ref: 30203.010051
PF: Minority, At-Risk

City University of New York–LaGuardia Community College
Queens Urban Educational Partnership
Hazel M. Carter
Project Director, 31-10 Thomson Avenue, Long Island City, NY 11101
(718) 482-5049
Ref: 30206.010051
PF: Minority, At-Risk

City University of New York–LaGuardia Community College
Teacher Sabbatical Program
Richard Lieberman
Director, LaGuardia and Wagner Archives, 31-10 Thomson Avenue, Long Island City, NY 11101
(718) 482-5065
Ref: 30198.010051
PF: Professional Development, Inservice

City University of New York–Queens College
College Preparatory Programs/Townsend Harris Project
Ron Scapp
Director, 65-30 Kissena Boulevard, Flushing, NY 11367
(718) 997-3175
Ref: 21115.002690
PF: College Courses for Students

▶ **City University of New York–Queens College** [181]
Louis Armstrong Middle School, Queens College
Paul Longo
Assoc. Dean, 65-30 Kissena Boulevard, Flushing, NY 11367
(718) 997-5505
Ref: 21158.002690
PF: Professional Development, Inservice

▶ **City University of New York–Queens College** [233]
Project SCOPE (School-College Operation in Physical Education)
Linda A. Catelli
Director, 65-30 Kissena Boulevard, Flushing, NY 11367
(718) 520-7213
Ref: 30211.002690
PF: New Faculty Roles

▶ **Clackamas Community College** [57]
Vocational Options Program
Rene Rathburn
Asst. Dean, 19600 S. Molallo, Oregon City, OR 97045
(503) 657-6958
Ref: 20728.004878
PF: Minority, At-Risk

▶ **Clarion University of Pennsylvania**   [192]
Center for Economic Education
William N. Ross
Director, 337 Still Hall, Clarion, PA 16214
(814) 226-2627
Ref: 30406.009235
PF: Professional Development, Inservice

Clarion University of Pennsylvania
Clarion County Partnership
John S. Shropshire
Dean, Enrollment Management and Academic
   Records, Clarion, PA 16214
(814) 226-2306
Ref: 30407.009235
PF: Minority, At-Risk

Clarion University of Pennsylvania
Penn Rivers Writing Project
Charles R. Duke
Director, 101 Stevens Hall, Clarion, PA 16214
(814) 226-2146
Ref: 30408.009235
PF: Professional Development, Inservice

Clarion University of Pennsylvania
Program of Scholastic Enrichment
Rhonda J. McMillen
Project Director, Center for Educational
   Leadership, G66 Carlson, Clarion, PA 16214
(814) 226-2072
Ref: 30409.009235
PF: Minority, At-Risk

Clark College
Articulation Agreements, Tech Prep Coordinated
   Programs
Nancy A. Johnson
Tech Prep/Workforce Training Coordinator, 1800
   E. McLoughlin Boulevard, Vancouver, WA
   98663
(206) 699-0228
Ref: 31595.003773
PF: Tech-Prep/2+2

Clark College
Running Start
Nancy A. Johnson
Tech Prep/Workforce Training Coordinator, 1800
   E. McLoughlin Boulevard, Vancouver, WA
   98663
(206) 699-0228
Ref: 31594.003773
PF: College Courses for Students

Clarke College
Clarke-St. Anthony Partnership
Jan Stoffel
Director of Public Relations, 1550 Clarke Drive,
   Dubuque, IA 52001
(319) 588-6318
Ref: 31056.001852
PF: Professional Development, Inservice

Clarke College
Dubuque Community Schools Business
   Partnerships
Jan Stoffell
Director of Public Relations, 1550 Clarke Drive,
   Dubuque, IA 52001
(319) 588-6318
jstoffe@keller.clarke.edu
Ref: 31055.001852
PF: Professional Development, Inservice

▶ **Clarkson University**   [116]
The Clarkson School's Bridging Year Program
Gary F. Kelly
Headmaster, The Clarkson School, Box 5650,
   Potsdam, NY 13699-5650
(315) 268-4434
Ref: 21105.002699
PF: Middle/Early Colleges

▶ **Clarkson University**   [103]
High School of Excellence
Gary F. Kelly
Headmaster, The Clarkson School, Box 5650,
   Potsdam, NY 13699-5650
(315) 268-4434
Ref: 30285.002699
PF: Enrichment, Gifted

▶ **Clarkson University**   [138]
Horizons
Patricia Prashaw
Program Coordinator, Continuing Education, Box
   5570, Potsdam, NY 13699-5570
(315) 268-6647
Ref: 30286.002699
PF: Career, Internships, Apprenticeships

Clarkson University
Project Challenge
Gary F. Kelly
Headmaster, The Clarkson School, Box 5650,
   Potsdam, NY 13699-5650
(315) 268-4434
Ref: 30287.002699
PF: Enrichment, Gifted

Clarkson University
SCOPES
Richard Watkins
Director, Box 5650, Potsdam, NY 13699-5650
(315) 268-4425
Ref: 30284.002699
PF: Career, Internships, Apprenticeships

▶ **Clarkson University**   [139]
Summer Research Program
James Peploski
Asst. Professor, Chemistry Department, Box
   5810, Potsdam, NY 13699-5810
(315) 268-3813
Ref: 20147.002699
PF: Career, Internships, Apprenticeships

▶ **Clatsop Community College**   [274]
North Coast Educational Consortium
David W. Phillips
Vice President, Instructional Programs/Student
   Services, 1653 Jennie, Astoria, OR 97103
(503) 325-0910
Ref: 31569.003189
PF: City/Regional Compacts

▶ **Clayton State College**   [283]
Middle Level Teacher Education (B.A. Degree)
Janet L. Towslee
Director of Teacher Education, 5900 N. Lee
   Street, Morrow, GA 30260-0285
(404) 961-3578
towslee@gg.csc.peachnet.edu
Ref: 30601.008976
PF: New Achievement, Assessment Standards

Cleveland Community College
Auto Body
Gene C. Cox
Dean, Vocation Engineering Technology, 137 S.
   Post Road, Shelby, NC 28150
(704) 484-4000
Ref: 30739.008082
PF: College Courses for Students

▶ **Cleveland Community College**   [140]
Career Day
Caroline Moore
Admissions Counselor, 137 S. Post Road, Shelby,
   NC 28150
(704) 484-4073
Ref: 30736.008082
PF: Career, Internships, Apprenticeships

▶ **Cleveland Community College**   [55]
Inservice Program for Underrepresented Students
    in the Middle Schools and High Schools of
    Cleveland County
Ronald Wright
Dean, Arts, Sciences, and Public Services, 137 S.
    Post Road, Shelby, NC 28150
(704) 484-4093
Ref: 30735.008082
PF: Minority, At-Risk

Cleveland Community College
Quiz Bowl
Caroline Moore
Admissions Counselor, 137 S. Post Road, Shelby,
    NC 28150
(704) 484-4073
Ref: 30737.008082
PF: Enrichment, Gifted

▶ **Cleveland Community College**   [263]
Tech Prep
Beth Cartwright
Vice President, Academic Programs, 137 S. Post
    Road, Shelby, NC 28150
(704) 484-4019
Ref: 30738.008082
PF: Tech-Prep/2+2

▶ **Cleveland Institute of Art**   [106]
Summer Scholars Program
William M. Jean
Director of Continuing Education, 11141 E. Bend,
    Cleveland, OH 44106
(216) 421-7460
Ref: 20059.003982
PF: Enrichment, Gifted

Cleveland State University
Greater Cleveland Educational Development
    Center
Linda Freeman
Director, Euclid Avenue at E. 24th Street, Rhodes
    Tower 901, Cleveland, OH 44115
(216) 523-7107
Ref: 20401.003032
PF: Professional Development, Inservice

Cleveland State University
Urban/Suburban Consortium
Robert H. MacNaughton
Chair and Professor, College of Education,
    Cleveland, OH 44115
(216) 523-7128
Ref: 21054.003032
PF: Recruit, Preservice, Certification

▶ **Clinch Valley College at the University of
    Virginia**   [201]
Southwest Virginia Public Education Consortium
Marsha Quenberry
Executive Director, Wise, VA 24293
(703) 328-0319
Ref: 30578.003747
PF: Professional Development, Inservice

▶ **Clovis Community College**   [77]
Eastern Plains Instructional Television
    Cooperative
Kathy Cogdill
School Relations Coordinator, 417 Schepps
    Boulevard, Clovis, NM 88102
(505) 769-4084
Ref: 31468.004743
PF: College Courses for Students

▶ **Cochise College**   [249]
2 + 2 Program
Claudia LaClair
Chair, Information Management Division, 901 N.
    Colombo, Sierra Vista, AZ 85635
(602) 458-7110
Ref: 31450.001072
PF: Tech-Prep/2+2

▶ **Cochise College**   [277]
Cochise College-Douglas Unified School District
    Joint Venture
David M. Pettes
Dean of Instruction, Douglas, AZ 85635
(602) 364-0212
Ref: 31447.001072
PF: Joint Governance

Cochise College
Cochise County Tech Prep Consortium
Bill Morrison
Director, Occupational Education, 901 N.
    Colombo, Sierra Vista, AZ 85635
(602) 458-7110
Ref: 31449.001072
PF: Tech-Prep/2+2

▶ **Cochise College**   [69]
Honors-Dual Credit Program
Beth Roberts
Dean of Instruction-Sierra Vista Campus, 901 N.
    Colombo, Sierra Vista, AZ 85635
(602) 459-9742
Ref: 31448.001072
PF: College Courses for Students

Coe College
FRIENDS Program and Coe/Johnson Partnership
Roger Johanson
Assoc. Professor of Teacher Education and Chair,
    Education Department, 1220 First Avenue NE,
    Cedar Rapids, IA 52402
(319) 399-8510
Ref: 31059.001854
PF: Tutoring, Counseling

▶ **Coe College**   [164]
(MAT) Master of Arts in Teaching
Roger Johanson
Assoc. Professor of Teacher Education and Chair,
    Education Department, 1220 First Avenue NE,
    Cedar Rapids, IA 52402
(319) 399-8575
Ref: 31058.001854
PF: Professional Development, Inservice

Colby Community College
Senior Transition Program
Joe Mildrexler
Dean of Community Services, 1255 S. Range,
    Colby, KS 67701
(913) 462-3984
Ref: 31257.001911
PF: College Courses for Students

College of the Canyons
Career Incentive Fund Grant
Joan Waller
Director, Child Development Programs, 26455 N.
    Rockwell Canyon Road, Valencia, CA 91355
(805) 252-7284
Ref: 31511.008903
PF: Recruit, Preservice, Certification

College of the Canyons
Extended Opportunity Programs and Services
    (EOPS)/Migrant Education Program
Stuart Ferdman
Coordinator, 26455 N. Rockwell Canyon Road,
    Valencia, CA 91355
(805) 259-7800
Ref: 31510.008903
PF: Minority, At-Risk

College of the Canyons
Tech-Prep
Helen C. Lusk
Asst. Dean of Professional Programs, 26455 N.
    Rockwell Canyon Road, Valencia, CA 91355
(805) 259-7800 x368
Ref: 31512.008903
PF: Tech-Prep/2+2

Key: "▶" denotes those partnerships abstracted in Parts 1-5; the corresponding page numbers are given in brackets. "PF:" denotes the partnership's "primary focus." "Ref:" denotes the partnership's assigned reference number in the National School-College Partnership Database (see Appendix B).

▶ **College of Charleston** [59]
Project SEARCH (Selection, Enrichment and
   Acceleration of Rural Children)
Julie Swanson
Asst. Director, School of Education, 66 George
   Street, Charleston, SC 29424
(803) 953-5106
Ref: 30794.003428
PF: Minority, At-Risk

▶ **College of Charleston** [59]
South Carolina Accelerated Schools Project
Christine Finnan
Director, School of Education, Charleston, SC
   29424
(803) 953-4826
Ref: 30793.003428
PF: Minority, At-Risk

College of Lake County
Project Succeed
Oneida Henry
Coordinator, 19351 Washington Street,
   Grayslake, IL 60030
(708) 223-6601
Ref: 31842.007694
PF: Minority, At-Risk

College of Marin
College of Marin/Novato Unified Partnership
Dona Boatright
Vice President for Academic Affairs, Kentfield, CA
   94904
(415) 485-9505
Ref: 31547.006993
PF: Tech-Prep/2+2

College of Marin
College of Marin/San Rafael City Schools
   Articulation
Dona Boatright
Vice President for Academic Affairs, Kentfield, CA
   94904
(415) 485-9505
Ref: 31545.006993
PF: Tech-Prep/2+2

College of Marin
College of Marin/Tamalpais Union High School
   District Area Council
Dona Boatright
Vice President for Academic Affairs, Kentfield, CA
   94904
(415) 485-9505
Ref: 31546.006993
PF: Tech-Prep/2+2

▶ **College of New Rochelle** [48]
BIZKIDS
Russel R. Taylor
Director, Taylor Institute, New Rochelle, NY
   10805
(914) 654-5403
Ref: 30190.002704
PF: Minority, At-Risk

College of New Rochelle
Bridge to Secondary Schools
Sr. Barbara Calamari, O.S.U.
Director, Secondary School Relations, 29 Castle
   Place, New Rochelle, NY 10805
(914) 654-5487
Ref: 30185.002704
PF: Minority, At-Risk

College of New Rochelle
ChemSource/Small-Scale Institutes
Mary Virginia Orna
Professor, Chemistry Department, New Rochelle,
   NY 10805-2308
(914) 654-5302
Ref: 30189.002704
PF: Professional Development, Inservice

▶ **College of New Rochelle** [48]
CNR Sisters
Diane Quandt
Asst. Professor, New Rochelle, NY 10805
(914) 654-5579
Ref: 30192.002704
PF: Minority, At-Risk

College of New Rochelle
College Enhancement
Sr. Barbara Calamari, O.S.U.
Director, Secondary School Relations, 29 Castle
   Place, New Rochelle, NY 10805
(914) 654-5487
Ref: 30187.002704
PF: College Courses for Students

▶ **College of New Rochelle** [127]
Hispanic Society Mentoring
Yolanda T. De Mola, S.C.
Assistant to the VPAA-Special Projects, College
   Center 304, New Rochelle, NY 10805
(914) 654-5296
Ref: 30188.002704
PF: Tutoring, Counseling

College of New Rochelle
Leadership and Diversity Training
Karenann Carty
Director, Campus Activities, 29 Castle Place, New
   Rochelle, NY 10805
(914) 654-5400
Ref: 30186.002704
PF: Enrichment, Gifted

▶ **College of New Rochelle** [127]
New York State Mentoring
Sr. Barbara Calamari, O.S.U.
Director, Secondary School Relations, 29 Castle
   Place, New Rochelle, NY 10805
(914) 654-5487
Ref: 30191.002704
PF: Tutoring, Counseling

▶ **College of New Rochelle** [181]
Westchester Teacher Education Group
Mildred Haipt
Professor, Education Department, 29 Castle
   Place, New Rochelle, NY 10805
(914) 654-5578
Ref: 30184.002704
PF: Professional Development, Inservice

College of Notre Dame of Maryland
Lovely Lexington Terrace Tutoring Program
Sr. Kathleen Jager, S.S.N.D.
Director, Campus Ministry, 4701 N. Charles
   Street, Baltimore, MD 21210
(410) 532-5565
Ref: 30545.002065
PF: Minority, At-Risk

College of the Redwoods
North Coast Articulation Council
Maren Rose
Special Populations/Tech Prep. Coordinator, 7351
   Tompkins Hill Road, Eureka, CA 95501
(707) 445-6962
Ref: 31561.001185
PF: Tech-Prep/2+2

College of St. Catherine
Consortium of Catholic Schools for the Future
   (CCSF)
Linda Distad
St. Paul, MN 55105
(612) 690-6798
Ref: 31691.002342
PF: Technology Application

College of St. Catherine
Creative Drama Workshops
Sr. Peggy O'Connell
St. Paul, MN 55105
(612) 690-6614
Ref: 31692.002342
PF: Enrichment, Gifted

▷ **College of St. Catherine**   [136]
Explore Group
Angela Schreiber, C.S.J.
St. Paul, MN 55105
(612) 690-6945
Ref: 31694.002342
PF: Career, Internships, Apprenticeships

College of St. Catherine
Institute for Grade 6-12 Educators
Carol Tauer
St. Paul, MN 55105
(612) 690-6660
Ref: 31696.002342
PF: Curriculum Development

▷ **College of St. Catherine**   [173]
Mentorship Program
Angela Schreiber, C.S.J.
St. Paul, MN 55105
(612) 690-6945
Ref: 31695.002342
PF: Professional Development, Inservice

College of St. Catherine
One World, Many Faces
Angela Schreiber, C.S.J.
St. Paul, MN 55105
(612) 690-6945
Ref: 31693.002342
PF: Tutoring, Counseling

▷ **College of San Mateo**   [250]
Tech Prep
Lora Todesco
Dean, Business, 1700 W. Hillsdale Boulevard,
    San Mateo, CA 94402
(415) 574-6494
Ref: 31540.001181
PF: Tech-Prep/2+2

▷ **College of William and Mary** [248]
Tidewater Area School/University Research
    Consortium
James Stronge
School of Education, Jones 224, Williamsburg, VA
    23187-8795
(804) 221-2339
Ref: 30571.003705
PF: Instructional Research

▷ **Colorado School of Mines**   [237]
Denver Earth Science Project
Marsha Barber
Director, Office of Continuing Education, Golden,
    CO 80401
(303) 273-3494
mbarber@flint.mines.colorado.edu
Ref: 31423.001348
PF: Curriculum Development

▷ **Colorado School of Mines**   [154]
Mobile Science Show
Sue Anne Berger
Program Director, Golden, CO 80401
(303) 273-3830
Ref: 31420.001348
PF: Professional Development, Inservice

▷ **Colorado School of Mines** [282]
Statewide Systemic Initiative
John U. Trefny
Professor and Head, Department of Physics,
    Golden, CO 80401
(303) 273-3833
jtrefny@iola.mines.colorado.edu
Ref: 31421.001348
PF: New Achievement, Assessment Standards

▷ **Colorado School of Mines**   [292]
Tri-Partnership to Benefit Math and Science
    Education
John U. Trefny
Professor and Head, Department of Physics,
    Golden, CO 80401
(303) 272-3833
jtrefny@iola.mines.colorado.edu
Ref: 31422.001348
PF: School-College-Business Partnerships

▷ **Columbia College**   [99]
Partners-In-Education
Faye Burchard
Dean of Students, 1001 Rogers Street, Columbia,
    MO 65216
(314) 875-7401
fcburchard@ccishp.ccis.edu
Ref: 20628.002456
PF: Enrichment, Gifted

▷ **Columbus College**   [29]
Bridges Pre-College Program
Roderick C. Jungbauer
Coordinator, Tower Center, 4225 University
    Avenue, Columbus, GA 31907-5645
(706) 568-2330
Ref: 30631.001561
PF: Minority, At-Risk

▷ **Columbus College**   [161]
Columbus Regional Mathematics Collaborative
Helen P. Purks
Assoc. Director for Mathematics Education,
    Center for Excellence in Mathematics and
    Science Education, Columbus, GA 31907-5645
(706) 568-2480
Ref: 30632.001561
PF: Professional Development, Inservice

Columbus College
High School Joint Enrollment Program/PSO (Post
    Secondary Options)
Patty L. Ross
Director of Admissions, Columbus, GA 31907
(706) 568-2035
Ref: 30633.001561
PF: College Courses for Students

▷ **Columbus College**   [161]
Muscogee County School District Leadership
    Academy
Rochelle P. Ripple
Asst. Professor of Education, Department of
    Educational Technology, Administration and
    Foundations, Columbus, GA 31907-5645
(706) 568-2250
Ref: 31790.001561
PF: Professional Development, Inservice

Columbus State Community College
Central Ohio Tech Prep Consortium
Deborah Coleman
Coordinator, Columbus, OH 43216
(614) 227-5455
Ref: 30852.006867
PF: Tech-Prep/2+2

Community College of Allegheny County North Campus
Project STEP
Daniel E. Batenburg
Asst. Dean, Career Programs, 5800 Grand Avenue, Neville Technical Center, Pittsburgh, PA 15225
(412) 269-4944
Ref: 30394.008809
PF: College Courses for Students

Community College of Denver
Career Education Dual Enrollment
Bruce C. Perryman
Dean, Business and Governmental Studies, P.O. Box 173363, Campus Box 900, Denver, CO 80217-3363
(303) 556-2485
bruce@mash.colorado.edu
Ref: 31394.009542
PF: College Courses for Students

▶ **Community College of Denver**   [22]
Denver Education Network
Ben Cordova
Executive Director, Campus Box 614, P.O. Box 173363, Denver, CO 80217-3363
(303) 556-3786
Ref: 31397.009542
PF: Minority, At-Risk

▶ **Community College of Denver**   [22]
Hispanic Entrepreneurship Program (HEP)
Andres Salazar
Coordinator, P.O. Box 173363, Campus Box 900, Denver, CO 80217-3363
(303) 556-4690
bruce@mash.colorado.edu
Ref: 31395.009542
PF: Minority, At-Risk

▶ **Community College of Denver**   [23]
Mentoring Girls for Careers in Science & Technology
Dianne K. Halleck
Dean, Science and Technology, Campus Box 800, P.O. Box 173363, Denver, CO 80217-3363
(303) 556-2460
dianne@mash.colorado.edu
Ref: 31392.009542
PF: Minority, At-Risk

▶ **Community College of Denver**   [251]
TECH-PREP Project
Bruce C. Perryman
Dean, Business and Governmental Studies, P.O. Box 173363, Campus Box 900, Denver, CO 80217-3363
(303) 556-2485
Ref: 31396.009542
PF: Tech-Prep/2+2

▶ **Community College of Denver**   [22]
Youth Fair Chance
Levi Crespin
Dean, TEC-West, 2420 W. 26th Avenue, Denver, CO 80211
(303) 477-5864
Ref: 31393.009542
PF: Minority, At-Risk

Community College of Rhode Island
Tech Prep Associate Degree Program
Judy Marmaras
Tech Prep Director, 400 East Avenue, Warwick, RI 02886
(401) 825-2143
Ref: 20508.003408
PF: Tech-Prep/2+2

▶ **Concord College**   [203]
West Virginia Geographic Alliance
Joe Manzo
Professor of Geography, Box 68, Athens, WV 24712
(304) 384-5208
Ref: 31745.003810
PF: Professional Development, Inservice

Concordia University
Promise Plus
Shirley K. Morganthaler
Professor of Early Childhood Education, 7400 Augusta, River Forest, IL 60305
(708) 209-3076
Ref: 31154.001666
PF: Professional Development, Inservice

▶ **Connecticut College**   [24]
High School Students Advancement Program
Arthur Ferrari
Director, 270 Mohegan Avenue, Box 5467, New London, CT 06320
(203) 439-2297
Ref: 30079.001379
PF: Minority, At-Risk

▶ **Cooper Union**   [139]
Saturday Program
Marina Gutierrez
Director, 41 Cooper Square, New York, NY 10003
(212) 353-4108
Ref: 20817.002710
PF: Career, Internships, Apprenticeships

▶ **Copiah-Lincoln Community College**   [259]
Tech Prep
Shirley A. Knapp
Tech Prep Coordinator, P.O. Box 649, Wesson, MS 39191
(601) 643-8386
Ref: 30701.002402
PF: Tech-Prep/2+2

Copiah-Lincoln Community College
Upward Bound
Barbara Webb
Director, P.O. Box 649, Wesson, MS 39191
(601) 643-8407
Ref: 31758.002402
PF: Minority, At-Risk

▶ **Coppin State College**   [168]
Paraprofessional/Baltimore City Schools-Coppin State Collaborative
Herman Howard
Dean, Division of Education, 2500 W. North Avenue, Baltimore, MD 21216
(410) 383-5530
Ref: 31727.002068
PF: Professional Development, Inservice

Cornell University
American Indian Program Outreach
Barbara Abrams
Director, 300 Caldwell Hall, Ithaca, NY 14853
(607) 255-8402
ba2@cornell.edu
Ref: 30318.002711
PF: Minority, At-Risk

Cornell University
Cornell Institute for Biology Teachers
Rita Calvo
Assoc. Director for Outreach, 301 Biotechnology Building, Ithaca, NY 14853
(607) 254-4796
rita_calvo@qmrelay.mail.cornell.edu
Ref: 30331.002711
PF: Professional Development, Inservice

▶ **Cornell University**   [49]
Cornell ON-TOP (Opportunities in Non-Traditional
    Occupation Programs)
Bruce Bush
Supervisor, Tech. Shops, Humphreys Service
    Building, Ithaca, NY 14853
(607) 255-6618
bruce_bush@qmrelay.mail.cornell.edu
Ref: 30326.002711
PF: Minority, At-Risk

Cornell University
Cornell/Schools Math Resource Program
Avery Solomon
Senior Lecturer, 406 White Hall, Ithaca, NY 14853
(607) 255-3894
Ref: 30319.002711
PF: Professional Development, Inservice

▶ **Cornell University**   [79]
Cornell University Summer College
Abby H. Eller
Director, B20 Day Hall, Ithaca, NY 14853
(607) 255-6203
abby_eller@cornell.edu
Ref: 30322.002711
PF: College Courses for Students

▶ **Cornell University**   [139]
Cornell Youth and Work Program
Stephen Hamilton
Director, G62C MVR Hall, Ithaca, NY 14853-4401
(607) 255-8394
steveh@msmail.human.cornell.edu
Ref: 30323.002711
PF: Career, Internships, Apprenticeships

Cornell University
Early Identification Project
Mary A. DeSouza
Asst. Director, Office of Equal Opportunity, 234
    Day Hall, Ithaca, NY 14853
(607) 255-3976
Ref: 30324.002711
PF: Minority, At-Risk

▶ **Cornell University**   [181]
Enhancement of High School Science Education:
    Equipment Lending Library
Margaret Arion
Executive Director, 130 Biotech Building, Ithaca,
    NY 14853
(607) 255-3374
Margaret_Arion@QMRelay.Mail.Cornell.edu
Ref: 30329.002711
PF: Professional Development, Inservice

▶ **Cornell University**   [49]
Expanding Your Horizons in Math, Science and
    Engineering
Mary Sansalone
Assoc. Director and Professor, Civil and
    Environmental Engineering, 313 Hollister Hall,
    Ithaca, NY 14853
(607) 255-2348
Ref: 30328.002711
PF: Minority, At-Risk

▶ **Cornell University**   [49]
Exploring Careers in Information Technologies
Mary A. DeSouza
Asst. Director, Office of Equal Opportunity, 234
    Day Hall, Ithaca, NY 14853
(607) 255-3976
Ref: 30327.002711
PF: Minority, At-Risk

▶ **Cornell University**   [103]
Graduate Student Outreach Project
Cindy Kramer
Coordinator, Public Service Center, 14 East
    Avenue, Ithaca, NY 14853
(607) 255-0255
Ref: 30333.002711
PF: Enrichment, Gifted

▶ **Cornell University**   [103]
H.F. Johnson Museum of Art Education
    Department
Linda Price
Coordinator of School and Children's Programs,
    H.F. Johnson Museum, Ithaca, NY 14853
(607) 255-6464
Ref: 30317.002711
PF: Enrichment, Gifted

▶ **Cornell University**   [182]
Institute on Science and the Environment for
    Teachers
William S. Carlsen
Assoc. Professor, Science Education, Kennedy
    Hall, Ithaca, NY 14853
(607) 255-9257
wsc2@cornell.edu
Ref: 30332.002711
PF: Professional Development, Inservice

▶ **Cornell University**   [181]
Latin American Studies Program
Mary Jo Dudley
Assoc. Director, 190 Vris Hall, Ithaca, NY 14853
(607) 255-3345
mjd9@cornell.edu
Ref: 30330.002711
PF: Professional Development, Inservice

▶ **Cornell University**   [139]
Learning Web
Mary Ann Lapinski
Coordinator, 117 Anabel Taylor Hall, Ithaca, NY
    14853
(607) 255-5026
Ref: 30321.002711
PF: Career, Internships, Apprenticeships

▶ **Cornell University**   [247]
Mathematics Education Research Collaboration
Jere Confrey
Assoc. Professor, Department of Education, 422
    Kennedy Hall, Ithaca, NY 14853
(607) 255-1255
jc56@cornell.edu
Ref: 30320.002711
PF: Instructional Research

Cornell University
National Science and Technology Week
Tina Snead
Director, Corporate Research Outreach and
    Research Communication, Office of the VP-
    Research, 314 Day Hall, Ithaca, NY 14853
(607) 255-1532
ewis@cornell.edu
Ref: 30334.002711
PF: Career, Internships, Apprenticeships

Cornell University
School Outreach, Public Service Center
Cindy Kramer
Coordinator, 14 East Avenue, Ithaca, NY 14853
(607) 255-0255
ck31@cornell.edu
Ref: 21122.002711
PF: Minority, At-Risk

Cornell University
The Science and Mathematics Saturday Academy
Mary A. DeSouza
Asst. Director, Office of Equal Opportunity, 234
    Day Hall, Ithaca, NY 14853
(607) 255-3976
Ref: 30325.002711
PF: Minority, At-Risk

Key: "▶" denotes those partnerships abstracted in Parts 1-5; the corresponding page numbers are given in brackets. "PF:" denotes the partnership's "primary focus." "Ref:" denotes the partnership's assigned reference number in the National School-College Partnership Database (see Appendix B).

▶ **Cornell University** [49]
Sidney High School Partnership
Bruce Ganem
Professor and Chairman, Department of
Chemistry, 122 Baker Laboratory, Ithaca, NY
14853
(607) 255-4175
Ref: 31791.002711
PF: Minority, At-Risk

Corning Community College
Accelerated College Education (ACE)
David N. Biviano
Director, Admissions, 1 Academic Drive, Corning,
NY 14830
(607) 962-9221
Ref: 30314.002863
PF: College Courses for Students

Corning Community College
High School Class Presentation/Career and
Transfer Services
Karen Record
Career Counselor, 1 Academic Drive, Corning, NY
14830
(607) 962-9228
Ref: 30316.002863
PF: Career, Internships, Apprenticeships

Corning Community College
Law Day
Gregory Dalton
1 Academic Drive, Corning, NY 14830
(607) 962-9424
Ref: 30315.002863
PF: Career, Internships, Apprenticeships

Corning Community College
Math Career Day
Patrick Keeler
Professor, Math Department, 1 Academic Drive,
Corning, NY 14830
(607) 962-9377
keeler@sccvc.corning-cc.edu
Ref: 30313.002863
PF: Career, Internships, Apprenticeships

▶ **Corning Community College** [261]
TAM (Technology Awareness Module)
Dr, George Gifford
Chairman, M/P/T Division, Corning, NY 14830
(607) 962-9243
Ref: 30312.002863
PF: Tech-Prep/2+2

Cowley County Community College
Advanced Placement Program
Conrad Jimison
Assoc. Dean, Continuing Education, 125 S.
Second, Arkansas City, KS 67005
(316) 442-0430
Ref: 31249.001902
PF: College Courses for Students

▶ **Cowley County Community College** [255]
South Central Kansas Tech Prep Associate
Degree Consortium
Ben L. Cleveland
Coordinator, 125 S. Second, Arkansas City, KS
67005
(316) 442-5311
Ref: 31250.001902
PF: Tech-Prep/2+2

▶ **Creighton University** [175]
Metro Area Teachers Institute (MATI)
Kathryn A. Thomas
Assoc. Vice President for Academic Affairs, 24th
at California Street, Omaha, NE 68178
(402) 280-2130
kthomas@creighton.edu
Ref: 20299.002542
PF: Professional Development, Inservice

Cuesta College
The Bridge Program
Bill Snider
Professor of Management, P.O. Box 8106, San
Luis Obispo, CA 93401
(805) 546-3272
Ref: 31532.001192
PF: Minority, At-Risk

Culver-Stockton College
Summer-Fest
C. Thomas Wiltshire
Interim Dean of the College, One College Hill,
Canton, MO 63435
(314) 288-5221
Ref: 31224.002460
PF: Enrichment, Gifted

Cumberland County College
Dual Credit Program
Leslie McDuffie
Director of Articulation/Tech Prep, P.O. Box 517,
Vineland, NJ 08360
(609) 691-8600
Ref: 20471.002601
PF: College Courses for Students

▶ **Cumberland County College** [260]
Two Plus Two Tech Prep
Leslie McDuffie
Director of Articulation/Tech Prep, P.O. Box 517,
Vineland, NJ 08360
(609) 691-8600
Ref: 20470.002601
PF: Tech-Prep/2+2

D

Dabney S. Lancaster Community College
Dual Enrollment
Gary Keener
Director of Continuing Education, Box 1000,
Clifton Forge, VA 24422
(703) 862-4246
Ref: 30579.004996
PF: College Courses for Students

Dabney S. Lancaster Community College
Educational Talent Search
Anita Clayton
Project Director, P.O. Box 1000, Clifton Forge, VA
24422
(703) 862-4246
Ref: 30580.004996
PF: Minority, At-Risk

Dabney S. Lancaster Community College
Tech Prep in Electronics Tech. and Mechanical
Design
Gary Keener
Director of Continuing Education, P.O. Box 1000,
Clifton Forge, VA 24422
(703) 862-4246
Ref: 30581.004996
PF: Tech-Prep/2+2

Daemen College
Liberty Partnership Program
Traci Howard
Director, 4380 Main Street, Amherst, NY 14226
(716) 839-8275
Ref: 30297.002808
PF: Minority, At-Risk

Danville Community College
Better Information Project: Pre-College
Awareness Program
Edward T. White
Chair, Business Division, 1008 S. Main Street,
Danville, VA 24541
(804) 797-8474
dcwhite@vccswest
Ref: 30584.003758
PF: Minority, At-Risk

Danville Community College
Dual Enrollment
Ed Polhamus
Chair, Division of Arts and Sciences, 1008 S.
    Main Street, Danville, VA 24541
(804) 797-8402
dcpolhe@vccswest
Ref: 30586.003758
PF: College Courses for Students

▶ **Danville Community College**   [305]
Regional Governor's School
Ed Polhamus
Chair, Division of Arts and Sciences, 1008 S.
    Main Street, Danville, VA 24541
(804) 797-8402
dcpolhe@vccswest
Ref: 30585.003758
PF: Magnet Schools

Danville Community College
Tech Prep
Boyd E. Motley
Division Chair, 1008 S. Main Street, Danville, VA
    24541
(804) 797-8440
dcmotlb@vccswest
Ref: 30587.003758
PF: Tech-Prep/2+2

▶ **Dartmouth College**   [247]
Collaborative Learning
G. Christian Jernstedt
Professor, Psychology Department, Hanover, NH
    03755
(603) 646-2778
g.christian.jernstedt@dartmouth.edu
Ref: 30054.002573
PF: Instructional Research

Dartmouth College
School Leadership Project
Faith Dunne
Director, Hanover, NH 03755
(603) 646-3448
Ref: 30137.002573
PF: Professional Development, Inservice

▶ **Darton College**   [29]
Adventures in Science
Michael Stoy
Chair, Science/Mathematics, 2400 Gillionvelle
    Road, Albany, GA 31707-3098
(912) 430-6830
Ref: 30622.001543
PF: Minority, At-Risk

▶ **Darton College**   [253]
DoleecoTech Prep Consortium
Elizabeth Ragsdale
Coordinator, 2400 Gllionville Road, Albany, GA
    31707
(912) 430-6870
Ref: 30620.001543
PF: Tech-Prep/2+2

Darton College
Early County Tech Prep Consortium
Elizabeth Ragsdale
Coordinator, 2400 Gillionville Road ,Albany, GA
    31707
(912) 430-6870
Ref: 30621.001543
PF: Tech-Prep/2+2

Darton College
Partners in Excellence-Lee County School
    System
Elizabeth Ragsdale
Coordinator, 2400 Gillionville Road, Albany, GA
    31707
(912) 430-6870
Ref: 30619.001543
PF: Minority, At-Risk

Darton College
Partners in Excellence-Martin Luther King, Jr.,
    Middle School
Elizabeth Ragsdale
Coordinator, 2400 Gillionville Road, Albany, GA
    31707
(912) 430-6870
Ref: 30618.001543
PF: Minority, At-Risk

Davenport College of Business
Creston High School-Davenport Connection
Elmer Vruggink
Dean, 415 E. Fulton, Grand Rapids, MI 49504
(616) 451-3511
Ref: 31034.002249
PF: College Courses for Students

Davidson College
Independence High School-Teacher Education
    Program Partnership
Grace Mitchell
Chairperson, Department of Education, Davidson,
    NC 28036
(704) 892-2130
Ref: 31732.002918
PF: Recruit, Preservice, Certification

Davidson College
Teachers Education Program at Davidson
    College-Lincoln County Schools Partnership
Grace Mitchell
Chairperson, Department of Education, Davidson,
    NC 28036
(704) 892-2130
Ref: 30733.002918
PF: Recruit, Preservice, Certification

▶ **Daytona Beach Community College**   [252]
Volusia/Flagler Tech-Prep Consortium, Program
    of Applied Academics and Technical Studies
Howard Turner
Dean of Technologies, P.O. Box 2811, Daytona
    Beach, FL 32120
(904) 254-4437
Ref: 30635.001475
PF: Tech-Prep/2+2

▶ **De Anza College**   [15]
Middle College Program
Steven L. Sellitti
Dean, Special Education/Programs, 21250
    Stevens Creek Boulevard, Cupertino, CA 95014
(408) 864-8923
Ref: 20618.004480
PF: Minority, At-Risk

Del Mar College
Coastal Bend Tech Prep Consortium
Lee W. Sloan
Consortium Director, 101 Baldwin, Room 206 W.
    Administration, Corpus Christi, TX 78404
(512) 886-1787
lwsloan@tenet.edu
Ref: 31361.003563
PF: Tech-Prep/2+2

Del Mar College
College Bound
Linda Herndon-Evans
Asst. Director of Admissions, Corpus Christi, TX
    78404
(512) 886-1248
Ref: 31362.003563
PF: Technology Application

▶ **Delaware Technical and Community College-Southern Campus** [70]
Academic Challenge Program
Sharon Adams
Instructor/Instructional Coordinator, Georgetown, DE 19947
(302) 855-1600
Ref: 30471.007053
PF: College Courses for Students

Delaware Technical and Community College-Terry Campus
Delaware Consortium on Technical Preparation Programs
H. Earl Roberts
Acting Dean, Instruction Department, 1832 N. DuPont Parkway, Dover, DE 19901
(302) 739-5421
00969@calvin.dtcc.edu
Ref: 20424.011727
PF: Tech-Prep/2+2

▶ **Delaware Valley College** [192]
Pine Run Elementary School/Delaware Valley College Collaborative
Dominic A. Montileone
Assoc. Dean, 700 E. Butler Avenue, Doylestown, PA 18901-2697
(215) 345-1500
Ref: 30445.003253
PF: Professional Development, Inservice

Delgado Community College
Tech Prep
Anthony L. Molina
Dean of Technology, 615 City Park Avenue, New Orleans, LA 70119
(504) 483-1846
Ref: 20482.004626
PF: Tech-Prep/2+2

▶ **Dominican College of San Rafael** [15]
Communities in Schools
Katherine Henderson
Vice President for Academic Affairs, 50 Acacia Avenue, San Rafael, CA 94901
(415) 485-3291
Ref: 31648.001196
PF: Minority, At-Risk

Drury College
Adopt-A-School
Daniel R. Beach
Director of Teacher Education, 900 N. Benton, Springfield, MO 65802
(417) 873-7271
Ref: 20562.002461
PF: Enrichment, Gifted

Duquesne University
The School District/University Collaborative
Derek Whordley
Dean, School of Education, Pittsburgh, PA 15282
(412) 396-6093
Ref: 20158.003258
PF: Recruit, Preservice, Certification

D'Youville College
D'Youville College-Porter Academy School #3 Partnership
Robert A. Di Sibio
Chairman, Division of Education and Social Work, 320 Porter Avenue, Buffalo, NY 14201
(716) 881-7629
Ref: 20990.002712
PF: Minority, At-Risk

▶ **D'Youville College** [305]
The D'Youville/da Vinci High School Partnership
David Kelly
Chair, Division of Liberal Arts, Buffalo, NY 14201
(716) 881-3200
Ref: 20991.002712
PF: Magnet Schools

E

▶ **East Carolina University** [218]
Model Clinical Teaching Program (MCTP)
Betty G. Beacham
Director, Speight Building ECU, Greenville, NC 27834
(919) 757-4357
edbeacham@ecuvm.cis.ecu.edu
Ref: 30728.002923
PF: Recruit, Preservice, Certification

East Central Community College
Tech Prep
Maudean Sanders
Tech Prep Coordinator, Box 129, Decatur, MS 39327
(601) 635-2111
Ref: 30704.002404
PF: Tech-Prep/2+2

East Stroudsburg University of Pennsylvania
402 School/ESU Partnership
Michael Davis
Dean, School of Professional Studies, East Stroudsburg, PA 18301
(717) 424-3211
Ref: 30434.003320
PF: Teacher Education Centers

▶ **East Stroudsburg University of Pennsylvania** [275]
Partners in Education
Michael Davis
Dean, School of Professional Studies, East Stroudsburg, PA 18301
(717) 427-3377
Ref: 20774.003320
PF: City/Regional Compacts

East Stroudsburg University of Pennsylvania
Tutoring At Risk Students
Cummings A. Piatt
Assoc. Professor, East Stroudsburg, PA 18301
(717) 424-3363
Ref: 30435.003320
PF: Minority, At-Risk

East Texas State University
The Mayo Center for Rural/Small Schools
Gwen Schroth
Asst. Professor, Department of Education Administration, Commerce, TX 75429-3011
(903) 886-5179
Ref: 31315.003565
PF: Resource Sharing

▶ **East Texas State University** [198]
Northeast Texas Center For Professional Development & Technology
Elton G. Stetson
Project Director, Box 3035, Commerce, TX 75429
(903) 886-5559
Ref: 31314.003565
PF: Professional Development, Inservice

▶ **Eastern Maine Technical College** [135]
MYAP (Maine Youth Apprenticeship Program)
Joyce B. Hedlund
Vice President, EMTC, 354 Hogan Road, Bangor, ME 04401
(207) 941-4600
Ref: 31812.005277
PF: Career, Internships, Apprenticeships

▶ **Eastern Maine Technical College** [256]
Tech Prep Program
Joyce B. Hedlund
Vice President, EMTC, 354 Hogan Road, Bangor, ME 04401
(207) 941-4600
Ref: 31811.005277
PF: Tech-Prep/2+2

▶ **Eastern Michigan University**   [171]
Collaborative School Improvement Program
Donna M. Schmitt
Assoc. Dean, College of Education, 129 Boone
   Hall, Ypsilanti, MI 48197
(313) 487-3134
Ref: 20367.002259
PF: Professional Development, Inservice

▶ **Eastern Oklahoma State College**   [280]
Tri-County Association of Public Schools
Bill Hill
President, 1301 W. Main, Wilburton, OK 74578
(918) 465-2361
Ref: 31286.003155
PF: Joint Governance

Eastern Shore Community College
Tech Prep Consortium
Linda Gayle
Coordinator, 29300 Lankford Highway, Melfa, VA
   23417
(804) 7878-9447
Ref: 30572.003748
PF: Tech-Prep/2+2

Eastern Washington University
EWU-Hutton Elementary School Project
Benjamin W. Brucker
Professor, Department of Education, MS-90,
   Cheney, WA 99004
(509) 359-2243
Ref: 31604.003775
PF: Recruit, Preservice, Certification

Eastern Washington University
Field Placement/Portfolio Program
Marsha Grace
Asst. Professor, Department of Education, MS-90,
   Cheney, WA 99004
(509) 359-7045
mgrace@ewu.edu
Ref: 31602.003775
PF: Recruit, Preservice, Certification

▶ **Eastern Washington University**   [111]
International Field Study (IFS)
John E. Vickrey
Director, MS-11, L.A. Hall, Cheney, WA 99004
(509) 458-6275
Ref: 31598.003775
PF: Enrichment, Gifted

▶ **Eastern Washington University**   [202]
Project High Need
Ron Nelson
Asst. Professor, Department of Applied
   Psychology, Cheney, WA 99004
(509) 359-2815
rnelson@eagle.ewu.edu
Ref: 31600.003775
PF: Professional Development, Inservice

▶ **Eastern Washington University**   [144]
School, College, and University Partnership
   Program (SCUP)
Valerie Appleton
Director, MS-92, Cheney, WA 99004
(509) 359-6662
Ref: 31601.003775
PF: Career, Internships, Apprenticeships

Eastern Washington University
Spokane Area Language Teachers Association
Sally Winkle
Chair, Department of Modern Languages,
   Cheney, WA 99004
(509) 359-2860
Ref: 31603.003775
PF: Professional Development, Inservice

Eastern Washington University
Teacher Intern Clinic (Elementary)
Steve Spacek
Coordinator, Professional Laboratory Experience,
   310-B Williamson Hall, Cheney, WA 99004
(509) 359-7027
Ref: 31605.003775
PF: Recruit, Preservice, Certification

Eastern Washington University
Teacher Intern Clinic Program
Jackson J. Martin
Professor of Education, 315 Williamson Hall,
   Cheney, WA 99004
(509) 359-6095
Ref: 31606.003775
PF: Teacher Education Centers

Eastern Washington University
Washington Geographic Alliance
Daniel E. Turbeville
Asst. Professor, Geography, Cheney, WA 99004
(509) 359-2270
Ref: 31599.003775
PF: Professional Development, Inservice

▶ **Edgewood College**   [203]
Yahara Watershed Education Network
James Lorman
Professor of Biology, 855 Woodrow Street,
   Madison, WI 53711
(608) 257-4861
lorman@edgewood.edu
Ref: 31081.003848
PF: Professional Development, Inservice

Edinboro University of Pennsylvania
Adopt-A-School
Marilyn Sheerer
Chair, Department of Elementary Education,
   Butterfield Hall, Edinboro, PA 16444
(814) 732-2750
msheerer@vax.edinboro.edu
Ref: 30412.003321
PF: Minority, At-Risk

▶ **Edinboro University of
   Pennsylvania**   [302]
Institute for Curriculum, Instruction, and
   Collaboration
Kenneth Adams
Chairman, 309 Butterfield Hall, Edinboro, PA
   16444
(814) 732-2292
adams@vax.edinboro.edu
Ref: 30413.003321
PF: Resource Sharing

▶ **Edinboro University of
   Pennsylvania**   [57]
Partnership for Academic Progress
Richard E. Arnold
Asst. Dean of Education, 325 Butterfield Hall,
   Edinboro, PA 16444
(814) 732-2872
arnold@vax.edinboro.edu
Ref: 30414.003321
PF: Minority, At-Risk

Edinboro University of Pennsylvania
Project Enhance
Richard E. Arnold
Asst. Dean of Education, 325 Butterfield Hall,
   Edinboro, PA 16444
(814) 732-2872
arnold@vax.edinboro.edu
Ref: 30411.003321
PF: Enrichment, Gifted

Edinboro University of Pennsylvania
Project ERIE
James R. Flynn
Chairperson, Department of Educational Services, 322 Butterfield Hall, Edinboro, PA 16444
(814) 732-2830
Ref: 20838.003321
PF: Minority, At-Risk

Edinboro University of Pennsylvania
Rural Education Access Program: On Track
Shirley Stennis-Williams
Director, Counseling and Human Development Department, 11 Compton Hall, Edinboro, PA 16444
(814) 732-2546
sstenniswill@vax.edinboro.edu
Ref: 30410.003321
PF: Retention, Continuing Education

Edison State Community College
Tech Prep
Karen Grady Sharp
Coordinator, Piqua, OH 45356
(513) 778-8600
Ref: 30919.012270
PF: Tech-Prep/2+2

The Education Resources Institute (TERI)
Higher Education Information Center
Ann Coles
Executive Director, 330 Stuart Street #500, Boston, MA 02116
(617) 426-0681 x235
Ref: 31813.U00002
PF: Umbrella Programs

El Centro College
El Centro Middle College High
Wright L. Lassiter, Jr.
President, Main and Lamar Streets, Dallas, TX 75202
(214) 746-2011
Ref: 20800.004453
PF: Middle/Early Colleges

Elizabeth City State University
Educational Talent Search Program
Cheryl J. Lewis
Director, 1704 Weeksville Road, Elizabeth City, NC 27909
(919) 335-3656
Ref: 30731.002926
PF: Minority, At-Risk

Elizabeth City State University
Upward Bound
Maxine Baskerville
Director, 1704 Weeksville Road, Campus Box 785, Elizabeth City, NC 27909
(919) 335-3369
Ref: 30730.002926
PF: Minority, At-Risk

▶ **Elizabethtown College** [221]
Supporting Urban Student and Teacher Learning
Jill S. Bartoli
Assoc. Professor, Education Department, Elizabethtown, PA 17022-2298
(717) 361-1379
Ref: 30425.003262
PF: Recruit, Preservice, Certification

▶ **Ellsworth Community College** [74]
Postsecondary Enrollment Act
David A. Felland
Dean of Instruction, Iowa Falls, IA 50126
(515) 648-4611
Ref: 31826.001862
PF: College Courses for Students

▶ **Emporia State University** [165]
Jones Institute for Educational Excellence
Leo W. Pauls
Executive Director, Campus Box 4036, Emporia, KS 66801
(316) 341-5372
Ref: 31248.001927
PF: Professional Development, Inservice

Erie Community College
High School Articulation Agreements
Robert Slawinowski
Asst. Academic Dean for Technologies, 6205 Main Street, Williamsville, NY 14221-7095
(716) 632-0414
Ref: 20494.002865
PF: Minority, At-Risk

▶ **Essex County College** [44]
Newark Educational Partnership
John H. Seabrook
Special Assistant to the President, Newark, NJ 07102
(201) 877-1867
Ref: 30088.007107
PF: Minority, At-Risk

Essex County College
Talent Search
Betty Foster
Director of Special Programs, 303 University Avenue, Newark, NJ 07102
(201) 877-3196
Ref: 20941.007107
PF: Minority, At-Risk

Essex County College
Upward Bound
Betty Foster
Director of Special Programs, 303 University Avenue, Newark, NJ 07102
(201) 877-3196
Ref: 20940.007107
PF: Minority, At-Risk

Evangel College
Partners in Education
Becky Huechteman
Asst. Professor of Education, 1111 N. Glenstone, Springfield, MO 65802
(417) 865-2815
Ref: 20557.002463
PF: Minority, At-Risk

▶ **Evergreen State College** [223]
Applied Professional Preparation of Leaders in Education (APPLE)
Elizabeth Diffendal
Coordinator, Pew Charitable Trusts Grant, TESC, L2102, Olympia, WA 98505
(206) 866-6000 x6028
Ref: 31652.008155
PF: Recruit, Preservice, Certification

Evergreen State College
Upward Bound
Denny Hurtado
Director, Olympia, WA 98505
(206) 866-6000
Ref: 31653.008155
PF: Minority, At-Risk

F

▶ **Fairfield University** [24]
GTE Math/Focus Program
Beverly L. Kahn
Asst. Dean, College of Arts and Sciences,
    Fairfield, CT 06430
(203) 254-4000 x2246
bkahn@fair1.fairfield.edu
Ref: 30081.001385
PF: Minority, At-Risk

▶ **Fairleigh Dickinson University** [301]
Adopt-A-School Program
Kenneth T. Vehrkens
Dean and Assoc. Vice President, Lifelong
    Learning, 150 Kotte Place, Hackensack, NJ
    07601
(201) 692-2671
Ref: 30101.008770
PF: Resource Sharing

Fairleigh Dickinson University
Bergen Brain Busters
Kenneth T. Vehrkens
Dean and Assoc. Vice President, Lifelong
    Learning, 150 Kotte Place, Hackensack, NJ
    07601
(201) 692-2671
Ref: 30096.008770
PF: Enrichment, Gifted

Fairleigh Dickinson University
Bergen County Consortium for Teachers of the
    Gifted
Kenneth T. Vehrkens
Dean and Assoc. Vice President, Lifelong
    Learning, 150 Kotte Place, Hackensack, NJ
    07601
(201) 692-2671
Ref: 30097.008770
PF: Enrichment, Gifted

Fairleigh Dickinson University
Football Giants Outreach Program
Kenneth T. Vehrkens
Dean and Assoc. Vice President, Lifelong
    Learning, 150 Kotte Place, Hackensack, NJ
    07601
(201) 692-2671
Ref: 30100.008770
PF: Resource Sharing

▶ **Fairleigh Dickinson University** [176]
Master of Arts in Science-Elementary Science
    Specialist Program
Malcolm Sturchio
Professor, Chemistry Department, TO5C,
    Teaneck, NJ 07666
(201) 692-2606
Ref: 30104.008770
PF: Professional Development, Inservice

▶ **Fairleigh Dickinson University** [114]
Middle College
Kenneth T. Vehrkens
Dean and Assoc. Vice President, Lifelong
    Learning, 150 Kotte Place, Hackensack, NJ
    07601
(201) 692-2671
Ref: 30102.008770
PF: Middle/Early Colleges

Fairleigh Dickinson University
North Jersey Invitational Debate Tournament
Kenneth T. Vehrkens
Dean and Assoc. Vice President, Lifelong
    Learning, 150 Kotte Place, Hackensack, NJ
    07601
(201) 692-2671
Ref: 30099.008770
PF: Enrichment, Gifted

Fairleigh Dickinson University
Rogate Academic Interest Lectures
Kenneth T. Vehrkens
Dean and Assoc. Vice President, Lifelong
    Learning, 150 Kotte Place, Hackensack, NJ
    07601
(201) 692-2671
Ref: 30098.008770
PF: Enrichment, Gifted

▶ **Fashion Institute of Technology** [261]
FIT Tech-Prep Consortium
Judith Parkas
Program Coordinator, 27th Street at 7th Avenue,
    New York, NY 10001
(212) 760-7605
Ref: 30144.002866
PF: Tech-Prep/2+2

▶ **Fashion Institute of Technology** [50]
High School Partnership Program for Design Arts
    Students
Cynthia Wellins
Grants Officer, 27th Street at 7th Avenue, New
    York, NY 10001
(212) 760-7652
wellinsc@snyfitva.bitnet
Ref: 30145.002866
PF: Minority, At-Risk

Faulkner University
Educational Talent Search
Ward Webster
Director, 5345 Atlanta Highway, Montgomery, AL
    36109
(205) 260-6270
Ref: 30680.001003
PF: Tutoring, Counseling

Felician College
Tech Prep 2 + 2
Beate A. Schiwek
Vice President and Dean, Academic Affairs, 262
    S. Main Street, Lodi, NJ 07644
(201) 778-1190
Ref: 30103.002610
PF: Tech-Prep/2+2

▶ **Ferris State University** [171]
North Central Michigan Educational Partnership
Scott D. Whitener
Dean, College of Education, 1349 Cramer Circle,
    602 Bishop Hall, Big Rapids, MI 49307
(616) 592-3648
Ref: 31032.002260
PF: Professional Development, Inservice

▶ **Ferrum College** [303]
Ferrum College/Franklin County High School
Joseph L. Carter
Dean of the College, Ferrum, VA 24088
(703) 365-4206
Ref: 20256.003711
PF: Resource Sharing

Finger Lakes Community College
Tech Prep
Patricia Pietropaolo
Project Director, Canandaigua, NY 14424
(716) 394-3500
Ref: 30299.007532
PF: Tech-Prep/2+2

▶ **Five Colleges Inc.** [279]
Five College/Public School Partnership
Mary Alice B. Wilson
Coordinator, P.O. Box 740, Amherst, MA 01004
(413) 256-8316
mwilson@titan.ucs.umass.edu
Ref: 21048.U00001
PF: Umbrella Programs

▶ **Flagler College** [211]
Workstudy Program With the Florida School for
the Deaf and the Blind
Reuben Sitton
Director of Financial Aid, P.O. Box 1027, St.
Augustine, FL 32085-1027
(904) 829-6481
Ref: 31748.007893
PF: Recruit, Preservice, Certification

Florence-Darlington Technical College
Articulation Agreements
Rick L. Garrett
Dean, Technological Studies, P.O. Box 100548,
Florence, SC 29501
(803) 661-8161
Ref: 30797.003990
PF: Regional Articulation

Florence-Darlington Technical College
College-High School Partnership (Access &
Equity)
Perry T. Kirven
Director of Admissions, P.O. Box 100548,
Florence, SC 29501
(803) 661-8153
Ref: 30802.003990
PF: Minority, At-Risk

Florence-Darlington Technical College
Education Talent Search Program
Pamela Blake Grant
Program Director, P.O. Box 100548, Florence, SC
29501-0548
(803) 661-8025
Ref: 30801.003990
PF: Minority, At-Risk

Florence-Darlington Technical College
Preparation for the Technologies (Tech Prep)
Shirley Corbett
Coordinator, P.O. Box 100548, Florence, SC
29501
(803) 661-8014
Ref: 30799.003990
PF: Tech-Prep/2+2

Florence-Darlington Technical College
Sex Equity
Kathy Holland
Program Director, P.O. Box 100548, Florence, SC
29501-0548
(803) 661-8115
Ref: 30798.003990
PF: Minority, At-Risk

Florence-Darlington Technical College
Upward Bound
Shirley A. March
Counselor, P.O. Box 100548, Florence, SC 29501
(803) 661-8070
Ref: 30800.003990
PF: Minority, At-Risk

Florida Atlantic University
A World in Motion
Sharon M. Schlossberg
Director of Pre-Collegiate Programs, Boca Raton,
FL 33431
(407) 367-2680
Ref: 31734.001481
PF: Enrichment, Gifted

Florida Atlantic University
Adopt-A-School
Sharon M. Schlossberg
Director of Pre-Collegiate Programs, Boca Raton,
FL 33431
(407) 367-2680
Ref: 31735.001481
PF: Tutoring, Counseling

▶ **Florida Atlantic University** [27]
Expanding Horizons
Sharon M. Schlossberg
Director of Pre-Collegiate Programs, Boca Raton,
FL 33431
(407) 367-2680
Ref: 31740.001481
PF: Minority, At-Risk

▶ **Florida Atlantic University** [71]
FAU-Ely Partnership
Sharon M. Schlossberg
Director of Pre-Collegiate Programs, Boca Raton,
FL 33431
(407) 367-2680
Ref: 20923.001481
PF: College Courses for Students

Florida Atlantic University
IBM/FAU Executive Mentorship Program
Sharon M. Schlossberg
Director of Pre-Collegiate Programs, Boca Raton,
FL 33431
(407) 367-2680
Ref: 31739.001481
PF: Tutoring, Counseling

Florida Atlantic University
Olympiad
Sharon M. Schlossberg
Director of Pre-Collegiate Programs, Boca Raton,
FL 33431
(407) 367-2680
Ref: 31741.001481
PF: Enrichment, Gifted

Florida Atlantic University
(SECME) Southeastern Consortium for Minorities
in Engineering
Sharon M. Schlossberg
Director of Pre-Collegiate Programs, Boca Raton,
FL 33431
(407) 367-2680
Ref: 20951.001481
PF: Minority, At-Risk

▶ **Florida Atlantic University** [91]
TC-94 The Technology Connection
Sharon M. Schlossberg
Director of Pre-Collegiate Programs, Boca Raton,
FL 33431
(407) 367-2680
Ref: 31737.001481
PF: Enrichment, Gifted

▶ **Florida Atlantic University** [27]
WISE Speakers' Bureau
Sharon M. Schlossberg
Director of Pre-Collegiate Programs, Boca Raton,
FL 33431
(407) 367-2680
Ref: 31738.001481
PF: Minority, At-Risk

Florida International University
College Reach-Out
Newton Moore
Coordinator, Pre-College Programs, GC-216,
University Park, Miami, FL 33199
(305) 348-2436
Ref: 30652.009635
PF: Minority, At-Risk

▶ **Florida International University**   [159]
FIU/Dade County Public Schools Joint Vocational
   Teacher Certification
Dominic A. Mohamed
Assoc. Professor, Vocational and Technical
   Education, Miami, FL 33199
(305) 348-3388
Ref: 31628.009635
PF: Professional Development, Inservice

▶ **Florida International University**   [120]
Intergenerational Law Advocacy Program
John F. Stack, Jr.
Acting Director, Institute for Public Policy and
   Citizenship Studies, University Park, Miami, FL
   33199
(305) 348-2977
stackj@servax.fiu.edu
Ref: 30650.009635
PF: Tutoring, Counseling

▶ **Florida International University**   [27]
PIP (Partners In Progress)
Newton Moore
Coordinator, Pre-College Programs, GC-216,
   University Park, Miami, FL 33199
(305) 348-2436
Ref: 30651.009635
PF: Minority, At-Risk

Florida State University
Capitol Regional Science and Engineering Fair
Ellen Granger
Director, Office of Science Teaching Activities,
   Department of Biological Sciences,
   Tallahassee, FL 32306-2043
(904) 644-6747
granger@bio.fsu
Ref: 20738.001489
PF: Enrichment, Gifted

Florida State University
CASE-A Mentor Program
April Pinton
Field Coordinator/Director, 115 Stone Building,
   Tallahassee, FL 32306
(904) 386-5100
Ref: 20242.001489
PF: Recruit, Preservice, Certification

Florida State University
Family/School/Community Partnership Program
Frances K. Kochan
University School Director, Box 3025,
   Tallahassee, FL 32306-3025
(904) 644-3086
Ref: 20617.001489
PF: Student Health, Welfare

Florida State University
Florida State University School/Full Service
   School Partnership Program
Dot Inman-Crews
Program Administrator, Box S-3025, Tallahassee,
   FL 32306
(904) 644-6118
Ref: 31626.001489
PF: Minority, At-Risk

▶ **Florida State University**   [272]
FSU College of Education/Leon County Schools
   Collaboration
Jack Miller
Dean, College of Education, 236 Stone Building,
   Tallahassee, FL 32306
(904) 644-6885
Ref: 30636.001489
PF: City/Regional Compacts

Florida State University
Physical Education Teacher Exchange Program
Dwayne J. Johnson
Chair, Department of Physical Education, 106
   Tully Gym, Tallahassee, FL 32306-3045
(904) 644-7907
Ref: 30637.001489
PF: Recruit, Preservice, Certification

Florida State University
Project TEAMS
Robert Reiser
Principal Investigator, Department of Education
   Research, Tallahassee, FL 32306
(904) 644-4592
Ref: 30638.001489
PF: Curriculum Development

▶ **Florida State University**   [92]
Saturday-at-the-Sea
Ellen Granger
Director, Office of Science Teaching Activities,
   Department of Biological Sciences,
   Tallahassee, FL 32306-0643
(904) 644-6747
granger@bio.fsu
Ref: 20740.001489
PF: Enrichment, Gifted

▶ **Florida State University**   [159]
Science for Life: Exploring Animal Models in Basic
   Research
Ellen Granger
Director, Office of Science Teaching Activities,
   Department of Biological Sciences,
   Tallahassee, FL 32306-2043
(904) 644-6747
Ref: 30660.001489
PF: Professional Development, Inservice

▶ **Florida State University**   [91]
Young Scholars Program
Ellen Granger
Director, Office of Science Teaching Activities,
   Department of Biological Sciences, 227
   Conradi Building, Tallahassee, FL 32306-2043
(904) 644-6747
granger@bio.fsu
Ref: 20737.001489
PF: Enrichment, Gifted

▶ **Foothill College**   [87]
Foothill College Summer Children's Program
Nancy Clark
Children's Program Coordinator, 12345 El Monte
   Road, Los Altos Hills, CA 94022
(415) 949-7023
Ref: 31539.001199
PF: Enrichment, Gifted

▶ **Foothill College**   [70]
Foothill Summer Youth College
Janice Carr
Program Coordinator, 12345 El Monte Road, Los
   Altos Hills, CA 94022
(415) 949-7613
Ref: 31538.001199
PF: College Courses for Students

Foothill College
Instructional Support Center
Art Turmelle
Coordinator, 12345 El Monte Road, Los Altos
   Hills, CA 94022
(415) 949-7614
Ref: 20632.001199
PF: College Courses for Students

▶ **Foothill College**   [113]
Middle College
Marilyn McDonald
Dean of Instructional Services and Libraries,
   12345 El Monte Road, Los Altos Hills, CA
   94022
(415) 949-7721
mcdonald@admin.fhda
Ref: 31537.001199
PF: Middle/Early Colleges

Fordham University
Visiting High School Students Program
Robert O'Brien
Asst. Dean, The College at Lincoln Center, 113
   W. 60th Street, New York, NY 10023
(212) 636-6242
Ref: 30345.002722
PF: College Courses for Students

▶ **Fordham University**   [50]
Science and Technology Entry Program (STEP)
Michael A. Molina
Director, Collins Hall, Room 303, Bronx, NY
   10458
(718) 817-3265
Ref: 20905.002722
PF: Minority, At-Risk

Forsyth Technical Community College
Forsyth Technical Community College Satellite
   Counseling Program
Susan Quick Phelps
Dean, Student Development Services, 2100 Silas
   Creek Parkway, Winston-Salem, NC 27103
(910) 723-0371
Ref: 20706.005317
PF: Tutoring, Counseling

Franklin College of Indiana
Running Start
Julianne Butler
Assoc. Director, 501 E. Monroe Street, Franklin,
   IN 46131
(317) 738-8064
Ref: 20775.001798
PF: College Courses for Students

▶ **Franklin & Marshall College**   [192]
Commonwealth Partnership
Ellen R. Trout
Director, P.O. Box 3003, Lancaster, PA 17604
(717) 291-4303
Ref: 21276.003265
PF: Professional Development, Inservice

Franklin Pierce College
Jaffrey-Rindge/Franklin Pierce College
   Partnership
Robert Condon
Vice President and Dean, Enrollment Services,
   Rindge, NH 03461
(603) 899-4050
Ref: 30343.002575
PF: College Courses for Students

Front Range Community College
North Central Tech-Prep Consortium
Nina Harris
Tech-Prep Coordinator, 3645 W. 112th Avenue,
   Westminster, CO 80030
(303) 466-8811
Ref: 31386.007933
PF: Tech-Prep/2+2

▶ **Front Range Community College**   [117]
Partners for Success
Eddie Lopez
Coordinator of Recruitment, 3645 W. 112th
   Avenue, Westminster, CO 80030
(303) 466-8811 x230
Ref: 31387.007933
PF: Tutoring, Counseling

▶ **Front Range Community College**   [118]
Student Literacy Corps
Pearl C. Crespin
Director, 3645 W. 112th Avenue, Westminster,
   CO 80030
(303) 466-8811
Ref: 31385.007933
PF: Tutoring, Counseling

Frostburg State University
Frostburg State University/Garrett County
   Professional Development Center
Norman W. Nightingale
Coordinator of Field Experiences, Office of Field
   Experiences, Frostburg, MD 21532
(301) 689-4217
Ref: 30566.002072
PF: Teacher Education Centers

Fulton-Montgomery Community College
Math Tech Prep
Robert Kusek
Dean of Career Education, Johnstown, NY 12095
(518) 762-4651
Ref: 30225.002687
PF: Tech-Prep/2+2

▶ **Furman University**   [195]
Center of Excellence in Foreign Language
   Instruction
A. L. Prince
Professor of Modern Languages, Greenville, SC
   29613
(803) 294-3180
Ref: 30806.003434
PF: Professional Development, Inservice

Furman University
Upstate Schools Consortium
Herbert B. Tyler
Professor, Greenville, SC 29613
(803) 294-3086
Ref: 20261.003434
PF: Professional Development, Inservice

G

▶ **Gallaudet University**   [282]
Annual Survey of Hearing-Impaired Children and
   Youth
Arthur N. Schildroth
Senior Research Associate, Center for
   Assessment and Demographic Studies, 800
   Florida Avenue NE, Washington, DC 20002
(202) 651-5575
cads_schigdr@gallua.bitnet
Ref: 21036.001433
PF: New Achievement, Assessment Standards

▶ **Gallaudet University**   [158]
Pre-College Programs
David S. Martin
Dean, School of Education, Washington, DC
   20002
(202) 651-5000
dsmartin@gallua.bitnet
Ref: 21178.001443
PF: Professional Development, Inservice

Gallaudet University
Summer Science Program
Richard W. Meisegeier
Director, Honors Program, 800 Florida Avenue
    NE, Washington, DC 20002
(202) 651-5550
rwmeisegeier@gallua.bitnet
Ref: 20685.001443
PF: Minority, At-Risk

▶ **Gallaudet University**   [26]
Young Scholars Program
Richard W. Meisegeier
Director, Honors Program, 800 Florida Avenue
    NE, Washington, DC 20002
(202) 651-5550
rwmeisegeier@gallua.bitnet
Ref: 21275.001443
PF: Minority, At-Risk

Garden City Community College
School-College Partnerships
Emerson Stewart
Asst. Dean of Instruction, 801 Campus Drive,
    Garden City, KS 67846
(316) 276-9532
Ref: 20459.001919
PF: Tech-Prep/2+2

▶ **Genesee Community College**   [79]
Genesee Community College Enrichment
    Program
John Murray
Assoc. Dean of Curriculum and Instruction, One
    College Road, Batavia, NY 14020
(716) 343-0055
Ref: 20670.006782
PF: College Courses for Students

▶ **Genesee Community College**   [262]
Genesee Region Tech Prep Consortium
Linnea LoPresti
Director, One College Road, Batavia, NY 14020
(716) 343-0055
Ref: 30292.006782
PF: Tech-Prep/2+2

▶ **George Mason University**   [66]
Early Identification Program
Hortensia B. Cadenas
Director, Fairfax, VA 22030-4444
(703) 993-3120
Ref: 20096.003749
PF: Minority, At-Risk

▶ **George Washington University**   [71]
Anacostia High School College Bound Program
Rebecca Jackson
Gelman Library, Washington, DC 20052
(202) 994-6049
Ref: 30472.001444
PF: College Courses for Students

George Washington University
Anacostia Public Service Academy
Kathryn Newcomer
School of Business and Public Management,
    Department of Public Administration,
    Washington, DC 20052
(202) 994-6295
Ref: 30473.001444
PF: Career, Internships, Apprenticeships

▶ **George Washington University**   [90]
ARTS (Artistic Reinforcement for Talented
    Students)
Melvin Brock
Multicultural Student Services Center,
    Washington, DC 20052
(202) 994-7010
Ref: 30474.001444
PF: Enrichment, Gifted

George Washington University
Beta Alpha Psi School Visit
Keith Smith
School of Business and Public Management,
    Department of Accountancy, Washington, DC
    20052
(202) 994-7461
Ref: 30475.001444
PF: Career, Internships, Apprenticeships

▶ **George Washington University**   [26]
BOOKS Project
Deborah Menkart
Human Services Department, Washington, DC
    20052
(202) 676-5257
Ref: 30476.001444
PF: Minority, At-Risk

▶ **George Washington University**   [132]
Conference on Career Opportunities in Public
    Service
Kathryn Newcomer
School of Business and Public Management,
    Department of Public Administration,
    Washington, DC 20052
(202) 994-6295
Ref: 30506.001444
PF: Career, Internships, Apprenticeships

▶ **George Washington University**   [131]
DC Stars
Marilyn Krupsaw
School of Engineering and Applied Science,
    Washington, DC 20052
(202) 994-2234
Ref: 30477.001444
PF: Career, Internships, Apprenticeships

▶ **George Washington University**   [119]
DC Works
Valerie Epps
Multicultural Student Services Center,
    Washington, DC 20052
(202) 994-7010
Ref: 30496.001444
PF: Tutoring, Counseling

▶ **George Washington University**   [132]
Eastern High School Mentorship Program
Leroy Charles
School of Medical and Health Sciences,
    Washington, DC 20052
(202) 994-8452
Ref: 30478.001444
PF: Career, Internships, Apprenticeships

▶ **George Washington University**   [120]
Elementary School Partnership
NROTC Unit, Washington, DC 20052
(202) 994-5880
Ref: 30479.001444
PF: Tutoring, Counseling

George Washington University
High School College Internship Program
    (HI/SCIP)
Valerie Epps
Multicultural Student Services Center,
    Washington, DC 20052
(202) 994-7010
Ref: 20862.001444
PF: College Courses for Students

▶ **George Washington University**   [119]
Independent Living Program
Robert Cannaday
Multicultural Student Services Center,
    Washington, DC 20052
(202) 994-7010
Ref: 30480.001444
PF: Tutoring, Counseling

George Washington University
Kramer Anacostia Planning Project (KAPP)
Margaret O'Bryon
Washington, DC 20052
(202) 676-4454
Ref: 30481.001444
PF: Career, Internships, Apprenticeships

▶ **George Washington University**   [132]
Latino Youth Health Care Project
Leroy Charles
George Washington Medical Center, Washington,
    DC 20052
(202) 994-8452
Ref: 30482.001444
PF: Career, Internships, Apprenticeships

George Washington University
Lincoln Junior High School
Denice Cora-Bramble, M.D.
School of Medical and Health Sciences,
    Washington, DC 20052
(202) 917-2991
Ref: 30483.001444
PF: Minority, At-Risk

George Washington University
MacFarland Junior High School
Leroy Charles
School of Health and Medical Sciences,
    Washington, DC 20052
(202) 994-8452
Ref: 30484.001444
PF: Minority, At-Risk

George Washington University
Minority High School Student Research
    Apprentice Program
Astra Bain-Dowell
School of Medicine and Health Sciences,
    Washington, DC 20052
(202) 994-2995
Ref: 30497.001444
PF: College Courses for Students

▶ **George Washington University**   [131]
MIST (Minorities in Science & Technology)
Marilyn Krupsaw
Washington, DC 20052
(202) 994-2234
Ref: 31759.001444
PF: Career, Internships, Apprenticeships

George Washington University
Neighbors
Peter Konwerski
Washington, DC 20052
(202) 994-6555
Ref: 30485.001444
PF: Minority, At-Risk

George Washington University
NJROTC Annual Meet
NJROTC Unit, Washington, DC 20052
(202) 994-5880
Ref: 30486.001444
PF: Enrichment, Gifted

George Washington University
Pro-Am D.C. Summer Classic
Julius Green
George Washington Health Plan, Washington, DC
    20052
(202) 973-7665
Ref: 30498.001444
PF: Tutoring, Counseling

George Washington University
Program Three/Two
Valerie Epps
Multicultural Student Services Center,
    Washington, DC 20052
(202) 994-7010
Ref: 30499.001444
PF: Tutoring, Counseling

George Washington University
Project Outreach Educational Program
Peter Konwerski
Office of Community Service, Washington, DC
    20052
(202) 994-6555
Ref: 30487.001444
PF: Minority, At-Risk

George Washington University
Saturday Seminars on Engineering & Applied
    Sciences
Peter Keiller
School of Engineering and Applied Sciences,
    Washington, DC 20052
(202) 994-7447
Ref: 30488.001444
PF: Tutoring, Counseling

George Washington University
School Without Walls (SWW)
B.J. Moreland
Washington, DC 20052
(202) 994-6370
Ref: 30489.001444
PF: College Courses for Students

▶ **George Washington University**   [131]
Science and Engineering Apprenticeship Program
Marilyn Krupsaw
School of Engineering and Applied Science,
    Washington, DC 20052
(202) 994-2234
Ref: 30500.001444
PF: Career, Internships, Apprenticeships

George Washington University
Science and Engineering Initiative for Young
    Minority Women
Dianne Martin
School of Engineering and Applied Science,
    Washington, DC 20052
(202) 994-8238
Ref: 30490.001444
PF: Minority, At-Risk

▶ **George Washington University**   [119]
Slowe Elementary Mentoring Program
Valerie Epps
Multicultural Student Services Center,
    Washington, DC 20052
(202) 994-7010
Ref: 30491.001444
PF: Tutoring, Counseling

▶ **George Washington University**   [131]
STARS 2,3, ..
Marilyn Krupsaw
School of Engineering and Applied Science,
    Washington, DC 20052
(202) 994-2234
Ref: 30492.001444
PF: Career, Internships, Apprenticeships

George Washington University
Street Law Program
Eric Sirulmik
National Law Center, Washington, DC 20052
(202) 994-7463
Ref: 30493.001444
PF: Tutoring, Counseling

George Washington University
Summer Athletic Campus
Mary Jo Warner
Charles E. Smith Center, Department of Athletics
  and Recreation, Washington, DC 20052
(202) 994-6650
Ref: 30501.001444
PF: Enrichment, Gifted

▶ **George Washington University**   [90]
Summer Scholar Program
B.J. Moreland
Washington, DC 20052
(202) 994-6370
Ref: 30502.001444
PF: Enrichment, Gifted

▶ **George Washington University**   [119]
Super Leaders (SL)
John Williams
School of Medicine and Health Sciences,
  Washington, DC 20052
(202) 994-3506
Ref: 30494.001444
PF: Tutoring, Counseling

▶ **George Washington University**   [158]
Teachers Networking for Technology
Marilyn Krupsaw
School of Engineering and Applied Science,
  Washington, DC 20052
(202) 994-2234
Ref: 30504.001444
PF: Professional Development, Inservice

George Washington University
Theater Workshop for High School Students
Alan Wade
Department of Theater and Dance, Washington,
  DC 20052
(202) 994-3661
Ref: 30503.001444
PF: Enrichment, Gifted

George Washington University
Twenty-First Century Scholars
Sammy Robinson
Admissions Office, Washington, DC 20052
(202) 994-6040
Ref: 30495.001444
PF: Minority, At-Risk

George Washington University
Washington Urban League Summer Youth
  Program
Leroy Charles
Washington, DC 20052
(202) 994-8452
Ref: 30505.001444
PF: Career, Internships, Apprenticeships

▶ **Georgetown University**   [225]
Summer Institute on International Relations
Sandy McMahon
Project Researcher, 37th and O Streets NW, 801
  ICC, Washington, DC 20057
(202) 687-5113
Ref: 30507.001445
PF: Teacher Education Centers

▶ **Georgia College**   [286]
Georgia College Educator's Network
  (GCEduNET)
Frank Lowney
Director, Regional Teacher Education Center, Box
  034, Milledgeville, GA 31032
(912) 453-5260
flowney@mail.gac.peachnet.edu
Ref: 20149.001602
PF: Technology Application

▶ **Georgia College**   [211]
Project PEACH (Partners in Education of All
  Children)
Kathryn Powell
Project Director, 103 Kilpatrick Building,
  Milledgeville, GA 31061
(912) 453-5498
kpowell@mail.gac.peachnet.edu
Ref: 21032.001602
PF: Recruit, Preservice, Certification

▶ **Georgia Institute of Technology**   [133]
CASE (Career Awareness in Science and
  Engineering)
Lytia R. Howard
College of Engineering, Atlanta, GA 30332
(404) 894-2000
Ref: 31677.001569
PF: Career, Internships, Apprenticeships

▶ **Georgia Institute of Technology**   [93]
CHIPS
Lytia R. Howard
College of Engineering, Atlanta, GA 30332
(404) 894-2000
Ref: 31675.001569
PF: Enrichment, Gifted

Georgia Institute of Technology
Computer Network Design in a City School
  System
Ron Hutchins
Network Services, Atlanta, GA 30332
(404) 894-2000
Ref: 31681.001569
PF: Technology Application

Georgia Institute of Technology
Cobb County Educational Initiative
Martha Willis
Atlanta, GA 30332
(404) 897-2000
Ref: 31655.001569
PF: Enrichment, Gifted

Georgia Institute of Technology
Elementary Science Project
Lynn Fountain
CEISMC, Atlanta, GA 30332
(404) 894-2000
Ref: 31662.001569
PF: Professional Development, Inservice

Georgia Institute of Technology
Environmental Issues and Children
David Jacobs
GTRI/ESTL, Atlanta, GA 30332
(404) 894-2000
Ref: 31672.001569
PF: Enrichment, Gifted

Georgia Institute of Technology
Freshman Engineering Workshop (FEW)
Lytia R. Howard
College of Engineering, Atlanta, GA 30332
(404) 894-2000
Ref: 31676.001569
PF: Career, Internships, Apprenticeships

Georgia Institute of Technology
Futurescape
Charlotte Jacobs-Blecha
GTRI/CSITL/ERB, Atlanta, GA 30332-0800
(404) 894-8970
Ref: 31656.001569
PF: Minority, At-Risk

Georgia Institute of Technology
Garrett Middle School Science Fair
Tim M. Strike
GTRI/ESML, Atlanta, GA 30332
(404) 894-2000
Ref: 31660.001569
PF: Enrichment, Gifted

Key: "▶" denotes those partnerships abstracted in Parts 1-5; the corresponding page numbers are given in brackets. "PF:" denotes the partnership's "primary focus." "Ref:" denotes the partnership's assigned reference number in the National School-College Partnership Database (see Appendix B).

Georgia Institute of Technology
Georgia Class Connect
Kim Kappel
Atlanta, GA 30332
(404) 894-2000
Ref: 31669.001569
PF: Professional Development, Inservice

▶ **Georgia Institute of Technology** [161]
Georgia Industrial Fellowships for Teachers
   (GIFT)
Joanna Hornig Fox
College of Sciences, Atlanta, GA 30332-0365
(404) 894-2000
Ref: 31668.001569
PF: Professional Development, Inservice

Georgia Institute of Technology
Huntsville Adopt-a-School Program-General
   Computer Assistance
Richard P. Stanley
GTRI-HRL, P.O. Box 9162, Huntsville, AL 35812
(404) 894-2000
Ref: 31680.001569
PF: Professional Development, Inservice

▶ **Georgia Institute of Technology** [286]
Internet Access Pilot Project for High School
Ron Hutchins
Network Services, Atlanta, GA 30332
(404) 894-2000
Ref: 31661.001569
PF: Technology Application

Georgia Institute of Technology
Joint Enrollment Program for High School
   Students
Thomas G. Tornabene
Academic Advisor, College of Sciences, Atlanta,
   GA 30332
(404) 894-2000
Ref: 31654.001569
PF: College Courses for Students

▶ **Georgia Institute of Technology** [93]
Junior Toastmasters
Rosita Jackson
Student Services Center, Atlanta, GA 30332
(404) 894-2550
Ref: 31670.001569
PF: Enrichment, Gifted

▶ **Georgia Institute of Technology** [122]
Meet-the-Mentor Day
Lynn Fountain
Staff Sponsor, CEISMC, Atlanta, GA 30332
(404) 894-2000
Ref: 31664.001569
PF: Tutoring, Counseling

▶ **Georgia Institute of Technology** [133]
MITE (Minority Introduction to Engineering)
Lytia R. Howard
College of Engineering, Atlanta, GA 30332
(404) 894-2000
Ref: 31674.001569
PF: Career, Internships, Apprenticeships

Georgia Institute of Technology
Odyssey of the Mind
Spencer Rugaber
College of Computing, Atlanta, GA 30332
(404) 894-2000
Ref: 31678.001569
PF: Enrichment, Gifted

Georgia Institute of Technology
Partners in Interactive Education (PIE)
Sally Hammock
Atlanta, GA 30332
(404) 894-2000
Ref: 31667.001569
PF: Tutoring, Counseling

▶ **Georgia Institute of Technology** [29]
Playing and Inventing
Walter Rodriguez
Civil Engineering, Atlanta, GA 30332-0355
(404) 894-2390
Ref: 31679.001569
PF: Minority, At-Risk

Georgia Institute of Technology
PREP, Pre-College Engineering Program
Lytia R. Howard
College of Engineering, Atlanta, GA 30332
(404) 894-2000
Ref: 31673.001569
PF: Career, Internships, Apprenticeships

▶ **Georgia Institute of Technology** [93]
Regional Science Olympiad
Milton Stombler
Atlanta, GA 30332
(404) 894-2000
Ref: 31665.001569
PF: Enrichment, Gifted

▶ **Georgia Institute of Technology** [292]
Southeastern Consortium for Minorities in
   Engineering (SECME)
R. Guy Vickers
Executive Director, SECME, Atlanta, GA 30332
(404) 894-2000
Ref: 31671.001569
PF: School-College-Business Partnerships

Georgia Institute of Technology
Summer Institute for Teachers
Myrna Goldberg
Center for Education and Sciences, Mathematics
   and Computing, Atlanta, GA 30332-0282
(404) 894-8994
Ref: 31659.001569
PF: Professional Development, Inservice

Georgia Institute of Technology
Summerscape
Myrna Goldberg
Center for Education and Sciences, Mathematics
   and Computing, Atlanta, GA 30332-0282
(404) 894-8994
Ref: 31658.001569
PF: Enrichment, Gifted

Georgia Institute of Technology
Tech Summer Academy
Myrna Goldberg
Center for Education and Sciences, Mathematics
   and Computing, Atlanta, GA 30332-0282
(404) 894-8994
Ref: 31657.001569
PF: Enrichment, Gifted

▶ **Georgia Institute of Technology** [121]
Techwood Tutorial Project (TTP)
Sally Hammock
Student Center Program Director, Atlanta, GA
   30332
(404) 894-2000
Ref: 31666.001569
PF: Tutoring, Counseling

Georgian Court College
The Whiz Kid Alliance
Linda F. Capuano
Director, Student Support Services, 900
   Lakewood Avenue, Lakewood, NJ 08701
(908) 363-4292
Ref: 30119.002608
PF: Minority, At-Risk

Gettysburg College
Project for Informed Choice
Neil W. Beach
Asst. Provost, Gettysburg, PA 17325
(717) 337-6823
Ref: 20577.003268
PF: Retention, Continuing Education

▶ **Glendale Community College**   [147]
Glendale Region Educational Articulation
    Taskforce (GREAT)
Alberto Sanchez
Dean, Educational Services, 6000 W. Olive
    Avenue, Glendale, AZ 85302
(602) 435-3012
Ref: 31445.001076
PF: Professional Development, Inservice

▶ **Glendale Community College**   [249]
Tech Prep
Nik Zatezalo
Tech Prep Coordinator, 6000 W. Olive Avenue,
    Glendale, AZ 85302
(602)435-3074
Ref: 31446.001076
PF: Tech-Prep/2+2

▶ **Gogebic Community College**   [257]
Secretarial, Auto, Building Trades, Computer-
    Aided Design, Commercial Art
Dale Johnson
Dean of Instruction, E4946 Jackson Road,
    Ironwood, MI 49938
(906) 932-4231
Ref: 31036.002264
PF: Tech-Prep/2+2

Gordon College
Northeast Massachusetts Middle Grades
    Regional Alliance
Janis D. Flint-Ferguson
Asst. Professor, Education/English Department,
    255 Grapevine Road, Wenham, MA 01984
(508) 927-2300
Ref: 30015.002153
PF: Professional Development, Inservice

▶ **Goucher College**   [36]
Science Mentoring to Achieve Rewarding
    Transition (SMART)
Hubert M. Zachary
Coordinator, 1021 Dulaney Valley Road,
    Baltimore, MD 21204
(410) 337-6521
Ref: 30544.002073
PF: Minority, At-Risk

▶ **Grand Valley State University**   [171]
Coalition for Excellence in Science and Math
    Education
David Tanis
Executive Director, 103 Loutit Hall, Allendale, MI
    49401
(616) 895-2238
tanisd@gvsu.edu
Ref: 20365.002268
PF: Professional Development, Inservice

Grayson County College
Senior Express
David Petrash
Vice President for Admissions/Records, 6101
    Grayson Drive, Denison, TX 75020
(903) 463-8650
Ref: 31761.003570
PF: College Courses for Students

Greenfield Community College
The Math Connection
Karen Green
Director, 1 College Drive, Green field, MA 01301
(413) 774-3131 x334
Ref: 30007.002169
PF: Minority, At-Risk

▶ **Greenville Technical College**   [299]
General Manufacturing Certification Program
F. M. Rogers
Director, Career Advancement Center, P.O. Box
    5616, Greenville, SC 29606-5616
(803) 250-8204
rogersfmr@a7.gvltec.edu
Ref: 20707.003991
PF: School-College-Business Partnerships

Grinnell College
Des Moines I Have a Dream Program
James C. Work
Executive Director, P.O. Box 805, Grinnell, IA
    50112
(515) 269-3178
work@admin.grin.edu
Ref: 20046.001868
PF: Minority, At-Risk

Guilford College
Chemsense-Science Enrichment
David F. Macinnes, Jr.
Chemistry Department, Greensboro, NC 27410
(910) 316-2262
macinnes@rascal.guilford.edu
Ref: 30723.002931
PF: Enrichment, Gifted

Guilford Technical Community College
Advanced Placement
Howard Hicks
Assistant to the Vice President, P.O. Box 309,
    Jamestown, NC 27282
(910) 454-1126
Ref: 30720.004838
PF: College Courses for Students

Guilford Technical Community College
Concurrent/Dual Enrollment
Howard Hicks
Assistant to the Vice President, P.O. Box 309,
    Jamestown, NC 27282
(910) 454-1126
Ref: 30722.004838
PF: College Courses for Students

Guilford Technical Community College
Tech Prep
Guy Loftin
Dean, Tech Prep, P.O. Box 309, Jamestown, NC
    27282
(910) 334-4822
Ref: 30721.004838
PF: Tech-Prep/2+2

Gwynedd-Mercy College
Health Careers Opportunity Program
Sr. Maureen B. McCann, R.S.M.
Director, Gwynedd Valley, PA 19437
(215) 641-5562
Ref: 30458.003270
PF: Minority, At-Risk

H

▶ **Hagerstown Junior College**   [256]
Tech-Prep Consortium
Michael H. Parsons
Dean of Instruction, 751 Robinwood Drive,
    Hagerstown, MD 21740
(301) 790-2800
Ref: 20780.002074
PF: Tech-Prep/2+2

Halifax Community College
Roanoke Valley Tech Prep Consortium
Evelyn Lewis
Director, Resource Development Planning, P.O.
   Box 809, Weldon, NC 27890
(919) 536-7289
Ref: 30729.007986
PF: Tech-Prep/2+2

Hampden-Sydney College
Enrichment Program
Florence C. Watson
Registrar, Hampden-Sydney, VA 23943
(804) 223-6203
Ref: 30576.003713
PF: College Courses for Students

▶ **Hampshire College**   [97]
Hampshire College Summer Studies in
   Mathematics
David C. Kelly
Director, Box NS, Amherst, MA 01002-5001
(413) 582-5375
dkelly@hamp.hampshire.edu
Ref: 30005.004661
PF: Enrichment, Gifted

▶ **Hardin-Simmons University**   [198, see
Howard Payne University]
Big Country Center for Professional Development
   and Technology
Peter Gilman
Dean, School of Education, Drawer E, Abilene, TX
   79698
(915) 670-1347
Ref: 31381.003571
PF: Teacher Education Centers

▶ **Harford Community College**   [75]
ELI Project (Extended Learning Initiative)
Norman E. Tracy
Director, Special Programs, 401 Thomas Run
   Road, Bel Air, MD 21015
(410) 836-4343
Ref: 30530.002075
PF: College Courses for Students

Harford Community College
JTPA Vocational Skills Training Programs
Sharon Dellinger
Coordinator, 401 Thomas Run Road, Bel Air, MD
   21015
(410) 836-4171
Ref: 30534.002075
PF: Minority, At-Risk

▶ **Harford Community College**   [123]
Project PASS/Partnership for Learning
Linda Parker
Admissions Specialist, Multicultural Affairs, 401
   Thomas Run Road, Bel Air, MD 21015
(410) 836-4423
Ref: 30532.002075
PF: Tutoring, Counseling

Harford Community College
Science Enhancement for Northern Chesapeake
   Elementary School Teachers
Floyd M. Grimm
Professor of Biology, Bel Air, MD 21015
(410) 836-4372
Ref: 30533.002075
PF: Professional Development, Inservice

Harford Community College
Tech Prep
Carl Henderson
Coordinator, 401 Thomas Run Road, Bel Air, MD
   21015
(410) 836-4300
Ref: 30531.002075
PF: Tech-Prep/2+2

▶ **Harris-Stowe State College**   [288]
Harris-Stowe State College-Waring Academy of
   Basic Instruction Partnership
Patricia Nichols
Vice President, Academic and Student Services,
   3026 Laclede Avenue, St. Louis, MO 63103
(314) 340-3611
Ref: 31206.002466
PF: Technology Application

▶ **Harrisburg Area Community College**   [266]
Vocational-Technical Partnerships
Ronald Young
Asst. Dean, Academic Affairs, Mathematics,
   Engineering and Technology, One HACC Drive,
   Harrisburg, PA 17110
(717) 780-2503
Ref: 30426.003273
PF: Tech-Prep/2+2

▶ **Harvard University**   [169]
American Council of Learned Societies (ACLS)
   Humanities Reform Project
Vito Perrone
Professor of Education, Graduate School of
   Education, Longfellow Hall, Cambridge, MA
   02138
(617) 495-7748
Ref: 30026.002155
PF: Professional Development, Inservice

▶ **Harvard University**   [294]
Cambridge Partnership for Public Education
Mary Ann Jarvis
Assoc. Director, Community Relations, 2 Garden
   Street, Cambridge, MA 02138
(617) 495-4955
Ref: 30135.002155
PF: School-College-Business Partnerships

▶ **Harvey Mudd College**   [15]
Mathematics, Engineering, Science Achievement
Linda Dell'Osso
Director, Claremont, CA 91711
(909) 621-8240
Ref: 20019.001171
PF: Minority, At-Risk

Hastings College
Early College Program
Dwayne S. Strasheim
Dean of the College, Hastings, NE 68902-0269
(402) 461-7360
Ref: 20068.002548
PF: College Courses for Students

▶ **Hawaii Pacific University**   [73]
Collegiate Advanced Placement Program (CAP)
Nancy L. Ellis
Vice-President, Student Support Services, 1164
   Bishop Street, Honolulu, HI 96813
(808) 544-0287
Ref: 31568.007279
PF: College Courses for Students

▶ **Haywood Community College**   [297]
Haywood County Public/Private Educational
   Compact
Walter Plexico
Dean of Instruction, Clyde, NC 28721
(704) 627-4611
Ref: 20589.008083
PF: School-College-Business Partnerships

Hazard Community College
Destination Graduation
Lisa Helf
Learning Center Coordinator, One Community
   College Drive, Hazard, KY 41701
(606) 436-5721
Ref: 20114.006962
PF: Minority, At-Risk

▶ **Henderson State University**   [149]
Professional Development Alliance
Johnnie Roebuck
Assoc. Professor, Box 7751, Arkadelphia, AR
    71923
(501) 246-5511 x3016
roebuck@holly.hsu.edu
Ref: 31637.001098
PF: Professional Development, Inservice

Herkimer County Community College
Tech Prep
Henry Testa
Chairman, Business Division, 100 Reservoir
    Road, Herkimer, NY 13350
(315) 866-0300
Ref: 30256.004788
PF: Tech-Prep/2+2

Herkimer County Community College
Tech Prep Program
Antonette Cleveland
Dean of Academic Affairs, Herkimer, NY 13350
(315) 866-0300
Ref: 31615.004788
PF: College Courses for Students

Hinds Community College
Pearl/Rankin Vo-Tech
James Pettigrew
Director, 3805 Highway 80 East, Pearl, MS 39208
(601) 936-5535
Ref: 30703.002407
PF: Tech-Prep/2+2

▶ **Hispanic Association of Colleges and
Universities**   [281]
Hispanic Student Success Program (HASP)
Pam Hill
Transfer Center Director and Counselor, Palo Alto
    Community College, 1400 W. Villaret, San
    Antonio, TX 78224
(210) 921-5270
Ref: 31882.U00008
PF: Umbrella Programs

Holy Names College
East Bay Foreign Language Project
Sr. Miriam Daniel Fahey
Principal Investigator, 3500 Mountain Boulevard,
    Oakland, CA 94619
(510) 436-1144
Ref: 31543.001183
PF: Professional Development, Inservice

▶ **Holy Names College**   [15]
Holy Names-Oakland High School Upward Bound
Barbara Essig
Director of Upward Bound, 3500 Mountain
    Boulevard, Oakland, CA 94619
(510) 208-3416
Ref: 31544.001183
PF: Minority, At-Risk

Hood College
FOCUS, Friends of Children-Caring,
    Understanding and Sharing
Ellen Gorfinkel
Asst. Professor, Frederick, MD 21701
(301) 696-3466
Ref: 30567.002076
PF: School-College-Business Partnerships

▶ **Hope College**   [98]
Program for the Academically Talented at Hope
    (PATH)
Marty Swank
Program Director, Education Department, P.O.
    Box 9000, Holland, MI 49422-9000
(616) 394-7742
swank@hope.cit.hope.edu
Ref: 20771.002273
PF: Enrichment, Gifted

Horry-Georgetown Technical College
PACE (Program for Accelerated College
    Enrollment)
Drew Matonak
Dean of Students, P.O. Box 1966, Conway, SC
    29526
(803) 347-3186
Ref: 30804.004925
PF: College Courses for Students

Horry-Georgetown Technical College
Tech Prep
Drew Matonak
Dean of Students, P.O. Box 1966, Conway, SC
    29526
(803) 347-3186
Ref: 30805.004925
PF: Tech-Prep/2+2

▶ **Howard Payne University**   [198]
Big Country Center for Professional Development
    and Technology
Oscar T. Jarvis
Dean, School of Education, HPU Box 822,
    Brownwood, TX 76801
(915) 643-7814
Ref: 31332.003575
PF: Professional Development, Inservice

▶ **Howard University**   [120]
J.C. Nalle Elementary School Partnership in
    Education
Aaron B. Stills
School of Education, Washington, DC 20059
(202) 806-7522
Ref: 31839.001448
PF: Tutoring, Counseling

▶ **Howard University**   [90]
Mathematics/Science Initiative Program
Joseph E. Bell
Director, School of Education, Washington, DC
    20059
(202) 806-5702
Ref: 31838.001448
PF: Enrichment, Gifted

▶ **Howard University**   [158]
Principals' Center (PIE Program)
Sam Woodard
School of Education, Washington, DC 20059
(202) 806-7340
Ref: 31837.001448
PF: Professional Development, Inservice

▶ **Howard University** [210]
Project Pipeline for Science and Mathematics
   Teachers
Eric Williams
School of Education, Washington, DC 20059
(202) 806-7354
Ref: 31836.001448
PF: Recruit, Preservice, Certification

Howard University
Spingarn Senior High Academy of Justice and
   Security
James E. Newby
School of Education, Washington, DC 20059
(202) 806-7540
Ref: 31835.001448
PF: Career, Internships, Apprenticeships

▶ **Howard University** [120]
Student to Student Substance Abuse Prevention
   Project
Esther E. Berry
School of Education, Washington, DC 20059
(202) 806-7343
Ref: 31834.001448
PF: Tutoring, Counseling

Howard University
Tri-School Learning Academy (PIE Program)
Riner Cash
Assoc. Dean, School of Education, Washington,
   DC 20059
(202) 806-7522
Ref: 31833.001448
PF: Minority, At-Risk

▶ **Howard University** [91]
Tubman 6th Graders Study/Poets Theater 208
Nancy Arnez
School of Education, Washington, DC 20059
(202) 806-7342
Ref: 31841.001448
PF: Enrichment, Gifted

▶ **Howard University** [26]
Upward Bound
Joseph E. Bell
Director, School of Education, Washington, DC
   20059
(202) 806-5702
Ref: 31840.001448
PF: Minority, At-Risk

▶ **Hudson Valley Community College** [140]
Career Access Program
Kathleen Quirk
Director of Testing, 80 Vandenburgh Avenue,
   Troy, NY 12180
(518) 270-7255
Ref: 30364.002868
PF: Career, Internships, Apprenticeships

Hudson Valley Community College
The College Students of the Future Program
Richard E. Bennett III
Asst. Director, Continuing Education, 80
   Vandenburgh Avenue, Troy, NY 12180
(518) 270-7338
Ref: 30366.002868
PF: Tutoring, Counseling

Hudson Valley Community College
Early Alert Program
Kathleen Quirk
Director of Testing, 80 Vandenburgh Avenue,
   Troy, NY 12180
(518) 270-7255
Ref: 30367.002868
PF: Minority, At-Risk

▶ **Hudson Valley Community College** [103]
Summer Technology Enrichment Program (STEP)
Chris Helwig
Asst. Director/Continuing Education, Troy, NY
   12180
(518) 270-7338
Ref: 30365.002868
PF: Enrichment, Gifted

Hudson Valley Community College
Using a College Library, Program for High School
   Students
Susan Griswold Blandy
Asst. Librarian, Troy, NY 12180
(518) 270-7319
blandsus@office.hvcc.edu
Ref: 20131.002868
PF: Enrichment, Gifted

▶ **Humboldt State University** [209]
Project MOST (Minority Opportunities for
   Successful Teaching)
Sheila Anne Webb
Director, 218 Harry Griffith Hall, Arcata, CA 95521
(707) 826-5872
Ref: 31563.001149
PF: Recruit, Preservice, Certification

▶ **Humboldt State University** [16]
Project PARITY (Promoting Academic Retention
   for Indian Tribal Youth)
Sheila Anne Webb
Director, 218 Harry Griffith Hall, Arcata, CA 95521
(707) 826-5872
Ref: 31562.001149
PF: Minority, At-Risk

I

▶ **Idaho State University** [162]
League of Schools
Angela Luckey
Coordinator, Box 8059, Pocatello, ID 83209
(208) 236-3203
Ref: 21063.001620
PF: Professional Development, Inservice

Idaho State University
Upper Snake River/Magic Valley Staff
   Development Consortium
E.E. (Gene) Davis
Director, Bureau of Education Research and
   Services, Campus Box 8059, Pocatella, ID
   83209
(208) 236-2481
Ref: 31432.001620
PF: City/Regional Compacts

**Illinois Eastern Community Colleges- System
   Office**
Articulation Agreement
Rita Ladner
Program Director, College Support Services, 233
   E. Chestnut Street, Olney, IL 62450
(618) 393-2982
Ref: 20045.009155
PF: Tech-Prep/2+2

Illinois Wesleyan University
Minority Teacher Recruitment Project
Diana P. McCauley
Chair, Education Department, Bloomington, IL
   61702
(309) 556-3504
Ref: 31194.001696
PF: Recruit, Preservice, Certification

▶ **Indiana State University**   [226]
Professional Development Schools Program
Robert O. Williams
Director, School of Education, Terre Haute, IN
    47809
(812) 237-2862
Ref: 30984.009563
PF: Teacher Education Centers

▶ **Indiana University at Bloomington**   [74]
Advance College Project (ACP)
Leslie J. Coyne
Director, Maxwell 154, Bloomington, IN 47405
(812) 855-5048
lcoyne@ucs.indiana.edu
Ref: 21094.001809
PF: College Courses for Students

Indiana University Kokomo
Destination: Education IUK
Emita B. Hill
Chancellor, 2300 S. Washington Street, Kokomo,
    IN 46904
(317) 453-2000
Ref: 30972.001814
PF: Minority, At-Risk

▶ **Indiana University of Pennsylvania**   [275]
Partnerships in Education
John Butzow
Dean, College of Education, 104 Stouffer Hall,
    Indiana, PA 15705
(412) 357-2480
jwbutzow@grove.iup.edu
Ref: 21232.008810
PF: City/Regional Compacts

▶ **Indiana University of Pennsylvania**   [221]
Pittsburgh Collaborative
John Butzow
Dean, College of Education, 104 Stouffer Hall,
    Indiana, PA 15705
(412) 357-2480
jwbutzow@grove.iup.edu
Ref: 30400.008810
PF: Recruit, Preservice, Certification

▶ **Indiana University Purdue University at
Fort Wayne**   [33]
Future Academic Scholar's Track (FAST)
Bettye J. Poignard
Program Administrator, 2101 E. Coliseum
    Boulevard, Fort Wayne, IN 46805-1499
(219) 481-6605
Ref: 20085.001812
PF: Minority, At-Risk

**Indiana University Purdue University at
Indianapolis**
Center for Economic Education
Debra Kaseman
Department of Economics, CA-516, 425 N.
    University Boulevard, Indianapolis, IN
    46202-5140
(317) 274-4756
Ref: 30950.001813
PF: Professional Development, Inservice

**Indiana University Purdue University at
Indianapolis**
Children's Dental Health Fair
Susan Crum
Director, Publications, 1121 W. Michigan, Room
    104, Indianapolis, IN 46202-5186
(317) 274-8135
Ref: 30960.001813
PF: Student Health, Welfare

**Indiana University Purdue University at
Indianapolis**
Community Health Nursing Projects
Lorraine Smith
Asst. Professor of Nursing, 1111 W. Middle Drive,
    Room 467, Indianapolis, IN 46202-5107
(317) 274-8742
Ref: 30947.001813
PF: Enrichment, Gifted

**Indiana University Purdue University at
Indianapolis**
Correspondence Program (School of Liberal Arts)
Mary Sauer
Lecturer in English, IUPUI Writing Center, CA-
    506, 425 N. University Boulevard, Indianapolis,
    IN 46202-5140
(317) 274-0091
Ref: 30949.001813
PF: Enrichment, Gifted

**Indiana University Purdue University at
Indianapolis**
Educators of Tomorrow
Denise Newsome
902 W. New York Street, Indianapolis, IN
    46202-5155
(317) 274-0649
Ref: 30956.001813
PF: Minority, At-Risk

**Indiana University Purdue University at
Indianapolis**
Good Friends
Claudia Richardson
Secretary, Alumni Association, 850 W. Michigan
    Street, Suite 200, Indianapolis, IN 46202-5198
(317) 274-5060
Ref: 30954.001813
PF: Tutoring, Counseling

**Indiana University Purdue University at
Indianapolis**
Herron Saturday School
Lance Baber
Assoc. Professor of Art Education and Herron
    School of Art, 111 E. 16th Street, Indianapolis,
    IN 46202-2401
(317) 920-2450
Ref: 30957.001813
PF: Enrichment, Gifted

**Indiana University Purdue University at
Indianapolis**
Interdenominational Churches for Educational
    Excellence
Regina Turner
Campus Interrelations, Office of the Vice
    Chancellor for Undergraduate Education, 355
    N. Lansing Street, AO-112, Indianapolis, IN
    46202-2896
(317) 274-8990
Ref: 30944.001813
PF: Tutoring, Counseling

**Indiana University Purdue University at
Indianapolis**
Investigate the Unseen Medical Professions With
    Inspector Path
Linda Marler
Assoc. Professor of Medical Technology, Room
    409, Fesler Hall, Indianapolis, IN 46202
(317) 274-1269
Ref: 30952.001813
PF: Enrichment, Gifted

**Indiana University Purdue University at
Indianapolis**
IUPUI Moving Company Dance Performance &
    Workshop
Mary Maitland Kimball
901 W. New York Street, Room 255, Indianapolis,
    IN 46202-5193
(317) 274-0611
Ref: 30946.001813
PF: Enrichment, Gifted

Indiana University Purdue University at Indianapolis
Mentoring Corps
Tonya Conour
Director, Peer Support Center, 902 W. New York Street, Indianapolis, IN 46202-5155
(317) 274-2369
Ref: 30959.001813
PF: Minority, At-Risk

Indiana University Purdue University at Indianapolis
Metro Mentors
Robert Lovell
Basketball Coach-Men, Office of Intercollegiate Athletics, 901 W. New York Street, Indianapolis, IN 46202-5193
(317) 274-0622
Ref: 30955.001813
PF: Tutoring, Counseling

Indiana University Purdue University at Indianapolis
Minority Engineering Advancement Program (MEAP)
James Patton
Asst. Professor of Architectural Technology, 799 W. Michigan, ET-1211, Indianapolis, IN 46202-5160
(317) 274-0809
Ref: 30958.001813
PF: Minority, At-Risk

▶ **Indiana University Purdue University at Indianapolis**   [122]
Obesity in Children: Effectiveness of a School-Based Program
Karyl Rickard
Professor of Nutrition and Dietetics, Riley Hospital, Room 1010, Indianapolis, IN 46202
(317) 274-9924
Ref: 30953.001813
PF: Tutoring, Counseling

Indiana University Purdue University at Indianapolis
Scientist Apprentice Program
Gordon Fricke
Assoc. Professor of Chemistry, 402 N. Blackford Street, LD-3222D, Indianapolis, IN 46202
(317) 274-0633
Ref: 30945.001813
PF: Enrichment, Gifted

Indiana University Purdue University at Indianapolis
SPAN
Annette Cwikla
Senior Administrative Secretary, Honors Program, 902 W. New York Street, ES-2126, Indianapolis, IN 46202-5155
(317) 274-2660
Ref: 30951.001813
PF: College Courses for Students

Indiana Vocational Technical College-Central Indiana
Ivy Tech Prep Program
Kenneth E. King
Tech Prep Coordinator, P.O. Box 1763, Indianapolis, IN 46206-1763
(317) 921-4582
Ref: 30973.009917
PF: Tech-Prep/2+2

Indiana Vocational Technical College-Kokomo
Dual-Credit Classes at High Schools
Sharon Lowry
Director of Instruction and Student Affairs, 1815 E. Morgan Street, Kokoma, IN 46901
(317) 459-0561
Ref: 31802.010041
PF: College Courses for Students

▶ **Indiana Vocational Technical College-Southcentral**   [33]
Region 14 Vocational Education Planning-Communications Group
Jack W. Womack
Manager, Special Projects, 8204 Highway 311, Sellersburg, IN 47172
(812) 246-3301
Ref: 30976.010109
PF: Minority, At-Risk

Inter American University of Puerto Rico-Ponce Regional Campus
Inter American University Sponsorship Project
Margarita Casselman
Dean, Academic Affairs, Carretera #1 Bo. Sabanetas, Mercedita, Ponce, PR 00715
(809) 840-9090
Ref: 30001.005029
PF: Professional Development, Inservice

▶ **Intersegmental Coordinating Council (ICC)**   [278]
ICC
John M. Smart
Senior Consultant, 621 J Street, Sacramento, CA 95814
(916) 324-8593
Ref: 31821.U00007
PF: Umbrella Programs

Iowa Lakes Community College
College for Kids
Trudy Kattner
Assoc. Dean, P.O. Box 680, Algona, IA 50511
(515) 295-9455
Ref: 31039.001864
PF: Enrichment, Gifted

▶ **Iowa Lakes Community College**   [34]
Educational Talent Search
Julie Carlson
Director, 3200 College Drive, Emmetsburg, IA 50536
(712) 852-2246
Ref: 31044.001864
PF: Minority, At-Risk

▶ **Iowa Lakes Community College**   [287]
Galaxy Schools Program
Charles Ullom
Executive Vice President, 19 S. 7th, Estherville, IA 51334
(712) 362-2601
Ref: 31053.001864
PF: Technology Application

Iowa Lakes Community College
Iowa Conservation Corps
Ken Brase
Director, 300 S. 18th, Estherville, IA 51334
(712) 362-2604
Ref: 31051.001864
PF: Minority, At-Risk

Iowa Lakes Community College
Iowa Distance Education Alliance-Star Schools
Gary Feddern
Instructor of Television Center, 300 S. 18th, Estherville, IA 51334
(712) 362-2604
Ref: 31052.001864
PF: Technology Application

Iowa Lakes Community College
Post Secondary Options
Ronald F. Della Croce
Coordinator of Secondary Programs, 3200 College Drive, Emmetsburg, IA 50536
(712) 852-3554
Ref: 31043.001864
PF: College Courses for Students

Iowa Lakes Community College
Upward Bound
Julie Carlson
Director, 3200 College Drive, Emmetsburg, IA 50536
(712) 852-2246
Ref: 31041.001864
PF: Minority, At-Risk

▶ **Iowa Lakes Community College**   [254]
Secondary Automotive Tech Program
Ronald F. Della Croce
Coordinator, 3200 College Drive, Emmetsburg, IA
    50536
(712) 852-3554
Ref: 31045.001864
PF: Tech-Prep/2+2

▶ **Iowa Lakes Community College**   [254]
Secondary Health Occupation Program
Ronald F. Della Croce
Coordinator of Secondary Programs, 3200
    College Drive, Emmetsburg, IA 50536
(712) 852-3554
Ref: 31042.001864
PF: Tech-Prep/2+2

Iowa Lakes Community College
Student Support Services or SAVE (Secondary
    Alternative Vocational Ed)
Ann Petersen
Special Needs Director, 3200 College Drive,
    Emmetsburg, IA 50536
(712) 852-3554
Ref: 31634.001864
PF: Minority, At-Risk

▶ **Iowa Lakes Community College**   [34]
Success Alternatives High School
Sally Bohmer
Lead Instructor, 300 S. 18th Street, Estherville, IA
    51334
(712) 362-2604
Ref: 31054.001864
PF: Minority, At-Risk

Iowa Lakes Community College
Tech Prep 2+2/Associate Degree Training
Judy Thomas
Coordinator, 3200 College Drive, Emmetsburg, IA
    50536
(712) 852-3554
Ref: 31040.001864
PF: Tech-Prep/2+2

▶ **Iowa State University**   [164]
School Improvement Model
Richard P. Manatt
Director, N239 Lagomarcino Hall, Ames, IA 50011
(515) 294-5521
Ref: 20359.001869
PF: Professional Development, Inservice

▶ **Iowa State University**   [34]
Science Bound
Jackie Manatt
Program Manager, 218 O & L Building, Ames, IA
    50011
(515) 294-4985
Ref: 20837.001869
PF: Minority, At-Risk

▶ **Ithaca College**   [50]
Access to College Education (ACE)
William A. Scoomes
Director, Center for Teacher Education, 368 NSB,
    Ithaca, NY 14850
(607) 274-1488
arockey@oa.ithaca.edu
Ref: 20690.002739
PF: Minority, At-Risk

Ithaca College
Cooperative Swim Program
Sarah M. Rich
Assoc. Professor, 35 Hill Center, Ithaca, NY
    14850
(607) 274-3407
rich@ithaca.edu
Ref: 20688.002739
PF: Minority, At-Risk

Ithaca College
Ithaca College Summer Institute for Secondary
    Science Teachers
Peter Seligmann
Professor, Physics Department, 264 New Science
    Building, Ithaca, NY 14850
(607) 274-3966
Ref: 20372.002739
PF: Professional Development, Inservice

▶ **Ithaca College**   [50]
Special Children's Center Swim/Gym Program
Sarah Rich
Assoc. Professor, 35 Hill Center, Ithaca, NY
    14850
(607) 274-3407
rich@ithaca.edu
Ref: 30199.002739
PF: Minority, At-Risk

Ithaca College
Speech-Language Enhancement Program
Marie Sanford
Clinical Faculty, Department of Speech-Language
    Pathology, Ithaca, NY 14850
(607) 274-3248
sanford@ithaca.bitnet
Ref: 20686.002739
PF: Minority, At-Risk

J

▶ **J. Sargeant Reynolds Comm. College**   [67]
Urban Community College Transfer Opportunities
    Program
Betsey Woolf
Coordinator, P.O. Box C-32040, Richmond, VA
    23261-2040
(804) 786-6815
Ref: 20777.003759
PF: Minority, At-Risk

▶ **James Madison University**   [300]
Valley of Virginia Partnership for Education
John B. Noftsinger, Jr.
Executive Director, Paul Street House,
    Harrisonburg, VA 22807
(703) 568-7088
Ref: 30570.003721
PF: School-College-Business Partnerships

▶ **James Sprunt Community College**   [263]
Tech-Prep Program
Donald L. Reichard
President, P.O. Box 398, Kenansville, NC 28349
(910) 296-2414
Ref: 20479.007687
PF: Tech-Prep/2+2

▶ **Jamestown Community College**   [262]
Tech Prep
Charles Rondeau
Chairman, Division of Applied Science and
    Mathematics, 525 Falconer Street, Jamestown,
    NY 14701
(716) 665-5220
Ref: 30311.002869
PF: Tech-Prep/2+2

Jarvis Christian College
Institute for Innovative Pedagogy
Florine J. White
Asst. Professor, School of Education, P.O. Drawer
    G, Hawkins, TX 75765
(903) 769-5814
Ref: 31321.003637
PF: Teacher Education Centers

Jarvis Christian College
Upward Bound
Mary Berry
Director, TRIO Program, P.O. Drawer G, Hawkins,
    TX 75765
(903) 769-5727
Ref: 31322.003637
PF: Minority, At-Risk

Jefferson College
Students in Transition
Dan Steadman
Vice President, Academic Affairs, 1000 Viking
    Drive, Hillsboro, MO 63050
(314) 789-3951
Ref: 31205.007102
PF: College Courses for Students

Jefferson Community College
The Career Institute
Neil Thompson
Coffeen Street, Watertown, NY 13601
(315) 786-2354
Ref: 31804.002870
PF: Minority, At-Risk

Jefferson Community College
CLS (College Learning Skills) 104
Richard Young
Coffeen Street, Watertown, NY 13601
(315) 786-2228
Ref: 30265.002870
PF: College Courses for Students

Jefferson Community College
Junior Visitation Day
Rosanne N. Weir
Director of Admissions, Coffeen Street,
    Watertown, NY 13601
(315) 786-2408
Ref: 30266.002870
PF: Retention, Continuing Education

Jefferson Community College
Project Tilt
Neil Thompson
Coffeen Street, Watertown, NY 13601
(315) 786-2354
Ref: 31805.002870
PF: Professional Development, Inservice

▶ **Jefferson Technical College**   [264]
Jefferson County Tech Prep Consortium
Louis F. Lamatrice
Director, Steubenville, OH 43952
(614)264-5591
Ref: 20036.007275
PF: Tech-Prep/2+2

▶ **Jersey City State College**   [137]
Adopt-a-School
Maria Cobarrubias
Executive Director, HC4CC, 2039 Kennedy
    Boulevard, Jersey City, NJ 07305
(201) 200-2349
Ref: 30092.002613
PF: Career, Internships, Apprenticeships

Jersey City State College
College Bound
F. Louise Diaz
Director, 2039 Kennedy Boulevard, Jersey City,
    NJ 07305
(201) 200-2347
Ref: 20938.002613
PF: Minority, At-Risk

▶ **Jersey City State College**   [45]
Linkages
Maria Cobarrubias
Executive Director, HC4CC, 2039 Kennedy
    Boulevard, Jersey City, NJ 07305
(201) 200-2349
Ref: 30094.002613
PF: Minority, At-Risk

Jersey City State College
Youth Apprenticeship Program
Maria Cobarrubias
Executive Director, HC4CC, 2039 Kennedy
    Boulevard, Jersey City, NJ 07305
(201) 200-2349
Ref: 30093.002613
PF: Tutoring, Counseling

▶ **John Brown University**   [224]
JBU/Siloam Springs-Professional Development
    Schools
Roger G. Iddings
Chair, Division of Teacher Education, Siloam
    Springs, AR 72761
(501) 524-7147
Ref: 31279.001100
PF: Teacher Education Centers

▶ **John Carroll University**   [188]
Institute for Educational Renewal
Aileen Kassen
Director, University Heights, OH 44118
(216) 397-3073
Ref: 30860.003050
PF: Professional Development, Inservice

John Carroll University
School-Based M.Ed. Program
Kathy Roskos
Chairperson, 20700 N. Park Boulevard, University
    Heights, OH 44118
(216) 397-4331
Ref: 30861.003050
PF: Recruit, Preservice, Certification

▶ **Johns Hopkins University**   [232]
Baltimore School and Family Connections Project
Joyce L. Epstein
Co-Director, Center on Families, Communities,
    Schools, and Childhood Learning, 3505 N.
    Charles Street, Baltimore, MD 21218
(410) 516-0370
Ref: 30549.002077
PF: New Faculty Roles

▶ **Johns Hopkins University**   [245]
Beginning School Study
Karl Alexander
Professor, Department of Sociology, Baltimore,
    MD 21218
(410) 516-7627
Ref: 30550.002077
PF: Instructional Research

▶ **Johns Hopkins University**   [95]
Center for Talented Youth (CTY)
William G. Durden
Director, 3400 N. Charles Street, Baltimore, MD
    21218
(410) 516-0337
Ref: 21126.002077
PF: Enrichment, Gifted

▶ **Johns Hopkins University**   [37]
Center for Technology in Education
Jacqueline Nunn
Director, 181 N. Bend Road, Baltimore, MD 21229
(410) 646-3000
Ref: 30555.002077
PF: Minority, At-Risk

▶ **Johns Hopkins University** [95]
CTY/Community School District 22 Project
Luciano Corazza
Director of Academic Programs, CTY-JHU 3400,
 N. Charles Street, Baltimore, MD 21218
(410) 516-0182
corazza@jhuvm.hcf.jhu.edu
Ref: 30548.002077
PF: Enrichment, Gifted

▶ **Johns Hopkins University** [36]
Hopkins/Dunbar Health Professions Program
Warren C. Hayman
Program Coordinator, 105 Whitehead Hall,
 Baltimore, MD 21218
(410) 516-8273
Ref: 21086.002077
PF: Minority, At-Risk

▶ **Johns Hopkins University** [124]
JHU Tutorial Project
Weslie F. Wornom
Director, Office of Volunteer Services, 3400 N.
 Charles Street, Levering Hall, Baltimore, MD
 21218
(410) 516-7673
Ref: 30556.002077
PF: Tutoring, Counseling

▶ **Johns Hopkins University** [37]
Maryland's Tomorrow Program
Marion Pines
Senior Fellow, Institute for Policy Studies, Shriver
 Hall, Baltimore, MD 21218
(410) 516-7169
Ref: 30558.002077
PF: Minority, At-Risk

Johns Hopkins University
Masters Program in Math/Science Elementary
 Education
Toni Ungaretti
Chair, Teacher Development and Leadership, 105
 Whitehead Hall, Baltimore, MD 21218
(410) 516-8273
Ref: 30552.002077
PF: Professional Development, Inservice

▶ **Johns Hopkins University** [245]
Model Middle Schools
James McPartland
Co-Director, Center for Social Organization of
 Schools, 3505 N. Charles Street, Baltimore, MD
 21218
(410) 516-0370
Ref: 30551.002077
PF: Instructional Research

▶ **Johns Hopkins University** [37]
The Peabody Preparatory/Baltimore City Schools
 Partnership Program
Fran G. Zarubick
Dean, 21 E. Mount Vernon Place, Baltimore, MD
 21202
(410) 659-8125
Ref: 30547.002077
PF: Minority, At-Risk

Johns Hopkins University
Professional Development School-Johns Hopkins
 University/Howard County Schools
Ralph Fessler
Director and Professor, Division of Education, 101
 Whitehead Hall, Baltimore, MD 21218
(410) 516-8273
Ref: 30554.002077
PF: Teacher Education Centers

▶ **Johns Hopkins University**
Teach Baltimore [37]
Matthew Boulay
Director, Volunteer Services, Levering Hall,
 Baltimore, MD 21218
(410) 516-4777
Ref: 30553.005077
PF: Minority, At-Risk

Johns Hopkins University
Transition to Work
Gloria M. Lane
Asst. Professor, 100 Whitehead Hall, Baltimore,
 MD 21218
(410) 516-8273
Ref: 30557.002077
PF: Professional Development, Inservice

▶ **Johnson County Community College** [74]
College Now
James M. Williams
Asst. Dean, Communications Division, 12345
 College Boulevard, Overland Park, KS
 66210-1299
(913) 469-8500 x3450
Ref: 21093.008244
PF: College Courses for Students

Juniata College
New Visions/Voyages
Fay Glosenger
Professor, School of Education, Box 947,
 Huntingdon, PA 16652
(814) 643-4310
Ref: 30417.003279
PF: Enrichment, Gifted

▶ **Juniata College** [192]
Science Outreach Program
Donald J. Mitchell
Director, Department of Chemistry, Huntingdon,
 PA 16652
(814) 643-4310
mitchell@juncol.juniata.edu
Ref: 20157.003279
PF: Professional Development, Inservice

K

Kalamazoo Valley Community College
Education for Employment
Richard F. Roder
Dean Business and Technical Studies, 6767 W. O
 Avenue, Kalamazoo, MI 49007
(616) 372-5219
Ref: 31026.006949
PF: Tech-Prep/2+2

▶ **Kalamazoo Valley Community
College** [258]
Health Occupations Program
Chuck Philip
Dean of Health and Sciences, 6767 W. O Avenue,
 Kalamazoo, MI 49009
(616) 372-5208
philip01@vax.kvcc.edu
Ref: 31029.006949
PF: Tech-Prep/2+2

▷ **Kalamazoo Valley Community College** [41]
Kalamazoo Academic Partnership
Willis Cain
Director of Special Programs, 6767 W. O Avenue, Kalamazoo, MI 49007
(616) 372-5402
Ref: 31027.006949
PF: Minority, At-Risk

▷ **Kalamazoo Valley Community College** [40]
Project Success–Eighth Grade Academic Summer Camp
Jacqueline Cantrell
Director, 6767 W. O Avenue, Kalamazoo, MI 49009
(616) 372-5349
Ref: 31028.006949
PF: Minority, At-Risk

Kankakee Community College
Kankakee Community College Course Program
Rick Manuel
Vice President for Student Services, P.O. Box 888, River Road, Kankakee, IL 60901
(815) 933-0225
Ref: 20916.007690
PF: College Courses for Students

Kankakee Community College
Kankakee Community College-Prevention Efforts
Rick Manuel
Vice President for Student Services, P.O. Box 888, River Road, Kankakee, IL 60901
(815) 933-0225
Ref: 31786.007690
PF: Minority, At-Risk

Kankakee Community College
Kankakee Community College-Transfer Center
Rick Manuel
Vice President for Student Services, P.O. Box 888, River Road, Kankakee, IL 60901
(815) 933-0225
Ref: 31787.007690
PF: Tutoring, Counseling

Kankakee Community College
Upward Bound
Richard Braun
Director, P.O. Box 888, River Road, Kankakee, IL 60901
(815) 933-0281
Ref: 31785.007690
PF: Minority, At-Risk

▷ **Kaskaskia College** [253]
Tech Prep/Regional Delivery System
George Hinton
Assoc. Dean, 27210 College Road, Centralia, IL 62801
(618) 532-1981
Ref: 31198.001701
PF: Tech-Prep/2+2

Kean College of New Jersey
Project Adelante
Ana Maria Schuhmann
Dean, School of Education, Morris Avenue, Union, NJ 07083
(908) 527-2136
Ref: 20910.002622
PF: Minority, At-Risk

Kennebec Valley Technical College
Tech Prep Articulation Agreement
Fairfield, ME 04937
(207) 453-5000
Ref: 31609.009826
PF: Tech-Prep/2+2

▷ **Kennesaw State College** [272]
Cobb Education Consortium
M. L. Anderegg
Executive Director, P.O. Box 444, Education Building, Room 103, Marietta, GA 30061
(404) 423-6482
mandereg@kscmail.kennesaw.edu
Ref: 30597.001577
PF: City/Regional Compacts

Kennesaw State College
Kennesaw State College History-Political Science Teaching Alliance
Helen S. Ridley
Professor of Political Science, P.O. Box 444, Marietta, GA 30061
(404) 423-6251
hridley@kscmail.kennesaw.edu
Ref: 21270.001577
PF: Professional Development, Inservice

▷ **Kent State University–Ashtabula Campus** [289]
Ashtabula County Interactive Television Network
John Mahan
Dean, 3325 W. 13th Street, Ashtabula, OH 44004
(216) 964-4211
Ref: 30856.003052
PF: Technology Application

Kent State University–Main Campus
Academic STARS
Gloria McCullough
Director, 204 MSC, Kent, OH 44242
(216) 672-3102
Ref: 30865.003051
PF: College Courses for Students

Kent State University–Main Campus
Akron Public Schools Project
Sonya Blixt
Director, BRTS, 507 White Hall, Kent, OH 44242
(216) 672-7918
Ref: 30866.003051
PF: Minority, At-Risk

▷ **Kent State University–Main Campus** [188]
Assistant Principals Institute
Judith March
Director, Center for Educational Leadership Services, 418 White Hall, Kent, OH 44242
(216) 672-2280
Ref: 30870.003051
PF: Professional Development, Inservice

▷ **Kent State University–Main Campus** [298]
Cooperative Alliance for Gifted Education
Beverly D. Shakles
Co-Principal Investigator, Teaching Leadership and Curriculum Studies, Kent, OH 44242
(216) 672-2580
Ref: 30863.003051
PF: School-College-Business Partnerships

▷ **Kent State University–Main Campus** [289]
Deaf Education Professional Development Network
Harold A. Johnson
Assoc. Professor, 507 White Hall, Kent, OH 44242
(216) 672-7918
Ref: 31751.003051
PF: Technology Application

▷ **Kent State University–Main Campus** [283]
Early Assessment for Exceptional Potential
Beverly D. Shaklee
Assoc. Professor, Teaching, Leadership and Curriculum Studies, Kent, OH 44242
(216) 672-2580
bshaklee@kentvm.kent.edu
Ref: 30867.003051
PF: New Achievement, Assessment Standards

Kent State University–Main Campus
Field Research Laboratory in Partnership Studies
Lyle Barton
Asst. Dean, 507 White Hall, Kent, OH 44242
(216) 672-7918
Ref: 30864.003051
PF: Instructional Research

▶ **Kent State University–Main Campus**   [189]
Mentor Training
Judith March
Director, Center for Educational Leadership
    Services, 418 White Hall, Kent, OH 44242
(216) 672-2280
Ref: 30868.003051
PF: Professional Development, Inservice

Kent State University–Main Campus
Peer Review
Judith March
Director, Center for Educational Leadership
    Services, 418 White Hall, Kent, OH 44242
(216) 672-2280
Ref: 30871.003051
PF: Professional Development, Inservice

▶ **Kent State University–Main Campus**   [188]
Total Quality Instruction (TQI)
Judith March
Director, Center for Educational Leadership
    Services, 418 White Hall, Kent, OH 44242
(216) 672-2280
Ref: 30869.003051
PF: Professional Development, Inservice

Kent State University–Stark Campus
Early English Composition Assessment Program
    (EECAP)
Tenney C. Hammond
Instructor in English, 6000 Frank Avenue NW,
    Canton, OH 44720
(216) 499-9600
Ref: 30907.003054
PF: Professional Development, Inservice

Kent State University–Stark Campus
The Education Enhancement Partnership, Inc.
Jack McWhorter
Asst. Professor of Art, 6000 Frank Avenue NW,
    Canton, OH 44720
(216) 499-9600
Ref: 30905.003054
PF: Professional Development, Inservice

▶ **Kent State University–Stark Campus**   [189]
Project Discovery
Myra West
Assoc. Professor of Physics, 6000 Frank Road
    NW, Canton, OH 44720
(216) 499-9600
Ref: 30906.003054
PF: Professional Development, Inservice

▶ **Kent State University–Tuscarawas
Campus**   [128]
Early English Composition Assessment Program
    (EECAP)
Dan Fuller
Program Director, New Philadelphia, OH 44663
(216) 339-3391
Ref: 30898.003062
PF: Tutoring, Counseling

Kent State University–Tuscarawas Campus
Tech Prep
Harold Shade
Project Director, 330 University Drive NE, New
    Philadelphia, OH 44663
(216) 339-33991
Ref: 30899.003062
PF: Tech-Prep/2+2

Kentucky State University
Frankfort/Franklin County Community Education
Debbie C. Tillett
Assoc. Director, Room 310, Academic Services
    Building, Frankfort, KY 40601
(502) 227-6634
Ref: 31632.001968
PF: City/Regional Compacts

▶ **Kenyon College**   [56]
Kenyon Summer Seminars
Peter Rutkoff
Director, Education Outreach, History
    Department, Gambier, OH 43022
(614) 427-5316
rutkoff@kenyon.edu
Ref: 30851.003065
PF: Minority, At-Risk

▶ **Kenyon College**   [81]
School-College Articulation Program (SCAP)
Peter Rutkoff
Director of Education Outreach, Department of
    History, Gambier, OH 43022
(614) 427-4178
rutkoff@kenyon.edu
Ref: 20031.003065
PF: College Courses for Students

Keuka College
Realistic Reading Preparation
Sally C. Wedge
Division Chair, Keuka Park, NY 14478
(315) 536-5277
Ref: 30388.002744
PF: Curriculum Development

Kilgore College
Dual Credit
Charly B. Florio
Administrative Dean, 1100 Broadway, Kilgore, TX
    75662
(903) 983-8102
Ref: 31317.003580
PF: College Courses for Students

▶ **Kilgore College**   [198]
Oil or Gas Institute for School Teachers
Charly B. Florio
Administrative Dean, 1100 Broadway, Kilgore, TX
    75662
(903) 983-8102
Ref: 31318.003580
PF: Professional Development, Inservice

▶ **King College**   [83]
Howard Hughes Medical Institute High School
    Science Scholars Program
Charles Owens
Professor and Chairman of Biology, 1350 King
    College Road, Bristol, TN 37620
(615) 652-4805
Ref: 30687.003496
PF: College Courses for Students

King College
King Scholar Summer Academy
Gregory Jordan
Dean of Faculty, 1350 King College Road, Bristol,
    TN 37620
(615) 652-4736
Ref: 30688.003496
PF: Enrichment, Gifted

▶ **Kirkwood Community College**   [255]
Kirkwood Partnerships–Articulation Agreements
David R. Bunting
Dean, Off-Campus Instruction, 912 18th Avenue
    SW, Cedar Rapids, IA 52404
(319) 366-0142
Ref: 31060.004076
PF: Tech-Prep/2+2

▶ **Kirkwood Community College** [254]
Kirkwood Partnerships–High School Health
  Program
Susan Willig
Department Assistant, Health Sciences
  Department, P.O. Box 2068, Cedar Rapids, IA
  52406
(319) 398-5566
Ref: 20461.004076
PF: Tech-Prep/2+2

▶ **Kirkwood Community College** [255]
Kirkwood Partnerships–Jointly Administered High
  School Vocational Programs
David R. Bunting
Off-Campus Instruction, 912 18th Avenue SW,
  Cedar Rapids, IA 52404
(319) 366-0142
Ref: 31803.004076
PF: Tech-Prep/2+2

▶ **Kirkwood Community College** [287]
Kirkwood Partnerships–Telecommunications
  Partnership
David R. Bunting
Dean, Off-Campus Instruction, 912 18th Avenue
  SW, Cedar Rapids, IA 52404
(319) 366-0142
Ref: 31062.004076
PF: Technology Application

Kirkwood Community College
Kirkwood Partnerships–VITAL
Chuck Hinz
Director, Developmental Education, P.O. Box
  2068, Cedar Rapids, IA 52406
(319) 398-5624
Ref: 31063.004076
PF: Minority, At-Risk

▶ **Kirkwood Community College** [301]
Kirkwood Partnerships–Wilson Elementary School
  Partnership
David R. Bunting
Dean, Off-Campus Instruction, 912 18th Avenue
  SW, Cedar Rapids, IA 52404
(319) 366-0142
Ref: 31061.004076
PF: Resource Sharing

L

Lackawanna Junior College
Dual Credit Program
Joseph G. Morelli
President, 901 Prospect Avenue, Scranton, PA
  18505
(717) 961-7850
Ref: 30444.003283
PF: College Courses for Students

Lake City Community College
Tech Prep Program
Victor A. Pattison
Coordinator, Route 3, Box 7, Lake City, FL 32055
(904) 752-1822
Ref: 30634.001501
PF: Tech-Prep/2+2

▶ **Lake Michigan College** [41]
Winner Within Program
Leonard Seawood
Director of Multicultural Affairs, 2755 E. Napier
  Avenue, Benton Harbor, MI 49022
(616) 927-8100 x5206
Ref: 20060.002277
PF: Minority, At-Risk

▶ **Lake-Sumter Community College** [92]
Children's Theatre Series
Jared S. Graber
Assoc. Dean, Arts and Sciences, 9501 U.S.
  Highway 441, Leesburg, FL 34788
(904) 365-3582
Ref: 30668.001502
PF: Enrichment, Gifted

Lake-Sumter Community College
College Night
Denise Joiner
9501 U.S. Highway 441, Leesburg, FL 34788
(904) 787-3747
Ref: 30671.001502
PF: Career, Internships, Apprenticeships

Lake-Sumter Community College
Counselor Articulation
Jane Miller
Manager, Enrollment Services, 9501 U.S.
  Highway 441, Leesburg, FL 34788
(904) 365-3571
Ref: 30672.001502
PF: Professional Development, Inservice

▶ **Lake-Sumter Community College** [72]
Dual Enrollment Program
Jared S. Graber
Assoc. Dean, Arts and Sciences, 9501 U.S.
  Highway 441, Leesburg, FL 34788
(904) 365-3582
Ref: 30667.001502
PF: College Courses for Students

▶ **Lake-Sumter Community College** [27]
Nursing Department and Lake County Adult
  Education
Susan Pennacchia
Nursing Program Director, 9501 U.S. Highway
  441, Leesburg, FL 34788
(904) 365-3519
Ref: 30669.001502
PF: Minority, At-Risk

Lake-Sumter Community College
Volunteer Services
Melissa Stephan
Student Activities Coordinator, 9501 U.S. Highway
  441, Leesburg, FL 34788
(904) 365-3543
Ref: 31729.001502
PF: Enrichment, Gifted

Lake-Sumter Community College
Youth Leadership
Melissa Stephan
Student Activities Coordinator, 9501 U.S. Highway
  441, Leesburg, FL 34788
(904) 787-3747
Ref: 30670.001502
PF: Enrichment, Gifted

Lamar University–Beaumont
Lamar Early Access Program
Ed McCaskill
Program Director, P.O. Box 10034, Beaumont, TX
  77710
(409) 880-8214
Ref: 20934.003581
PF: College Courses for Students

▶ **Lamar University–Beaumont** [222]
Spindletop Center for Excellence in Teaching
  Technology
Paula Allison Nichols
Director, P.O. Box 10034, Beaumont, TX 77710
(409) 880-1847
Ref: 31343.003581
PF: Recruit, Preservice, Certification

▶ **Lander University**   [195]
Greenwood Area Consortium
Sheila B. Marino
Acting Dean, School of Education, 320 Stanley
   Avenue, Greenwood, SC 29649
(803) 229-8225
Ref: 30811.003435
PF: Professional Development, Inservice

Lander University
S.C. Scholastic Art Awards Competition
Roxanna Albury
Asst. Professor of Art, Greenwood, SC 29649
(803) 229-8323
Ref: 31723.003435
PF: Enrichment, Gifted

▶ **Lander University**   [60]
Summer Smart Program
Lafayette Harrison
Director, Box 6142, Greenwood, SC 29649
(803) 229-8814
Ref: 31689.003435
PF: Minority, At-Risk

Lander University
Ware Shoals High School Students Program
Leonard Lundquist
Interim Vice President, Academic Affairs,
   Greenwood, SC 29649-2099
(803) 229-8320
Ref: 31823.003435
PF: College Courses for Students

Lawson State Community College
The Adopt-A-School Partnership Program
Charles McFarland
Acting Book Store Manager, 3060 Wilson Road
   SW, Birmingham, AL 35221
(205) 929-6310
Ref: 30673.001059
PF: Tutoring, Counseling

Lebanon Valley College
Lebanon Valley Educational Partnership
Dan McKinley
Coordinator, Annville, PA 17003
(717) 867-6249
mckinley@admin.lvc.edu
Ref: 30423.003288
PF: Minority, At-Risk

▶ **Lebanon Valley College**   [241]
Science Education Partnership
Mary McLeod
Coordinator, Annville, PA 17003
(717) 867-6175
Ref: 30424.003288
PF: Curriculum Development

Lehigh Carbon Community College
Tech Prep: The Gateway Program
Patricia A. Gardner
Director, 4525 Education Park Drive,
   Schnecksville, PA 18078
(610) 799-1120
Ref: 30433.006810
PF: Tech-Prep/2+2

Lenoir-Rhyne College
Computer Enrichment Program
Mark Dewalt
Assoc. Professor of Education, Box 4797,
   Hickory, NC 28603
(704) 328-7143
mark_d@mike.lrc.edu
Ref: 30752.002941
PF: Enrichment, Gifted

▶ **Lesley College**   [294]
Creating Lasting Links
Nancy Roberts
Project Director, 29 Everett Street, Cambridge,
   MA 02138-2790
(617) 349-8419
roberts@mitvma.mit.edu
Ref: 30027.002160
PF: School-College-Business Partnerships

Lewis University
Teacher Education Program
James C. Moses
Chairperson, Education Department, Route 53,
   Romeoville, IL 60441
(815) 838-0500
Ref: 31155.001708
PF: Recruit, Preservice, Certification

▶ **Lewis and Clark College**   [190]
Oregon Consortium for Quality Science and Math
   Education (OCQSME)
Phil Brady
Visiting Assoc. Professor of Education, Teacher
   Education, 0615 S.W. Palatine Mill Road,
   Portland, OR 97219-9953
(503) 769-7756
brady@lclark.edu
Ref: 31575.003197
PF: Professional Development, Inservice

Lewis and Clark College
The Partners in Education Mentoring Program
Dale Holloway
Coordinator, Student Support Services, Portland,
   OR 97219
(503) 768-7175
holloway@lclark.edu
Ref: 31576.003197
PF: Minority, At-Risk

Lewis-Clark State College
Project 2000
Eileen M. Wright
Chair, Division of Education, 500 8th Avenue,
   Lewiston, ID 83501
(208) 799-2260
Ref: 31638.001621
PF: Professional Development, Inservice

Limestone College
Limestone Mentoring Program
Joe Pitts
Asst. Professor of Education, 1115 College Drive,
   Gaffney, SC 29340
(803) 489-7151
Ref: 30791.003436
PF: Tutoring, Counseling

Limestone College
Youth Opportunities Unlimited (YOU)
Archie Fowler
Director, 1115 College Drive, Gaffney, SC 29340
(803) 488-4530
Ref: 30790.003436
PF: Minority, At-Risk

Linfield College
Site-Based Secondary Methods Block
Fred Ross
Chairperson, Education Department, McMinnville,
    OR 97128
(503) 434-2202
fross@calvin.linfield.edu
Ref: 31570.003198
PF: Recruit, Preservice, Certification

Livingstone College [80]
Mathematics and Science Intervention Program
Yen-Wan Hung
Chair, Department of Life and Physical Sciences,
    701 W. Monroe Street, Salisbury, NC 28144
(704) 638-5618
Ref: 30734.002942
PF: Minority, At-Risk

▶ **Long Island University–Brooklyn
Campus** [79]
Bridge Programs
Connie Yu
Coordinator, One University Plaza, c/o Honors
    Program, Brooklyn, NY 11201
(718) 488-1049
Ref: 20899.004779
PF: College Courses for Students

Long Island University–Brooklyn Campus
Intensive Teacher Institute TESOL and Bilingual
    Education
Gurprit S. Bains
Coordinator, One University Plaza, Brooklyn, NY
    11201
(718) 488-1103
Ref: 30207.004779
PF: Recruit, Preservice, Certification

▶ **Long Island University–Brooklyn
Campus** [182]
School Psychology Program
Nelda Cajigas-Segredo
Assoc. Professor, One University Plaza, M-207,
    Brooklyn, NY 11201
(718) 488-1385
Ref: 31618.004779
PF: Professional Development, Inservice

▶ **Long Island University–Brooklyn
Campus** [216]
Special Education-Partnership for Training
Edith B. Wolf
Director, One University Plaza, Brooklyn, NY
    11201
(718) 488-1044
Ref: 30210.004779
PF: Recruit, Preservice, Certification

Long Island University–C.W. Post Campus
FAST–Freshman Academic Study for Talented
    High School Seniors
Donald K. Frank
Director, History Department, Brookville, NY
    11548
(516) 299-2407
Ref: 20957.002754
PF: College Courses for Students

▶ **Long Island University–C.W. Post
Campus** [80]
SCALE (Secondary Collegiate Articulated
    Learning Experience)
Charles W. Silkie
Director, Contract/Continuing Education Program,
    Brookville, NY 11548
(516) 299-2211
scale@vax86.liunet.edu
Ref: 21096.002754
PF: College Courses for Students

▶ **Long Island University–Southampton
Campus** [80]
Accelerated College Entry (ACE)
Pat Dzintarnieks
Director, Off-Campus and Contract Programs,
    Southampton, NY 11968
(516) 287-8315
Ref: 30224.002755
PF: College Courses for Students

Longview Community College
Independent Study Program
Sue Borg
Asst. Coordinator, 500 S.W. Longview Road,
    Lee's Summit, MO 64081
(816) 672-2030
Ref: 20749.009140
PF: Minority, At-Risk

▶ **Longview Community College** [114]
PACE (Program for Adult College Education)
Sarah Hopkins
Director, 500 S.W. Longview Road, Lee's Summit,
    MO 64081
(816) 672-2218
Ref: 31228.009140
PF: Middle/Early Colleges

Longview Community College
Project ABLE (Academic Bridges to Learning
    Effectiveness)
Mary Ellen Jenison
Coordinator, 500 S.W. Longview Road, Lee's
    Summit, MO 64081-2105
(816) 672-2366
Ref: 31229.009140
PF: Minority, At-Risk

Longwood College
Longwood Talented and Gifted Program
Nancy A. Andrews
Professor, HPER, Lancer Hall, Farmville, VA
    23901
(804) 395-2541
nandrews@lwcmi.lwc.edu
Ref: 20859.003719
PF: Professional Development, Inservice

Loras College
The Dubuque Partnership
Donna Loewen
Director of Continuing Education, 1450 Alta Vista
    Street, Dubuque, IA 52004-0178
(319) 588-7139
Ref: 31057.001873
PF: Tutoring, Counseling

Lord Fairfax Community College
Lord Fairfax Community College Tech Prep
    Consortium
Diane Melby
Project Coordinator, P.O. Box 47, Middletown, VA
    22645
(703) 869-1120
Ref: 30569.008659
PF: Tech-Prep/2+2

Louisiana State University and A & M College
Louisiana State Youth Opportunities Unlimited
Suzan N. Gaston
Project Director, 236 Peabody Hall, Baton Rouge,
    LA 70803
(504) 388-1751
Ref: 20770.002010
PF: Minority, At-Risk

▶ **Louisiana State University at
Alexandria** [35]
STARS (Summer Tutorial for At-Risk Students)
Walter Connell
Director, Highway 8100 South, Alexandra, LA
    71302
(318) 473-6434
Ref: 20835.002011
PF: Minority, At-Risk

▶ **Louisiana State University in
Shreveport** [293]
Shreveport Urban Community Service Consortium
Will Mitchell
Assoc. Vice Chancellor, One University Place,
    Shreveport, LA 71115
(318) 797-5167
shwill@lsuvm.bitnet
Ref: 31268.002013
PF: School-College-Business Partnerships

Louisiana Tech University
Health and Physical Education: Drugs and Sport
John Paul Muczko
Asst. Professor, P.O. Box 3176, Tech Station,
    Ruston, LA 71272-0001
(318) 257-4432
Ref: 31274.002008
PF: Minority, At-Risk

Louisiana Tech University
LaSIP Inservice Program in Mathematics
Carolyn Talton
Director, Laboratory Experiences, P.O. Box 3163,
    T.S., Ruston, LA 71272
(318) 257-2794
Ref: 31269.002008
PF: Professional Development, Inservice

Louisiana Tech University
Louisiana Tech Summer Youth Program
Nancy Alexander
Project Director, P.O. Box 3161, Ruston, LA
    71272
(318) 257-3446
Ref: 31272.002008
PF: Minority, At-Risk

▶ **Louisiana Tech University** [293]
Mobile Automated Learning Laboratory (MALL)
Sam V. Dauzat
Area Coordinator, Teacher Education, Ruston, LA
    71272
(318) 257-4609
Ref: 31721.002008
PF: School-College-Business Partnerships

Louisiana Tech University
NSF Middle Grades Math/Science Project
Carolyn Talton
Director, Laboratory Experiences, P.O. Box 3163,
    T.S., Ruston, LA 71272
(318) 257-2794
Ref: 31270.002008
PF: Professional Development, Inservice

▶ **Louisiana Tech University** [167]
Project LIFE
David Radford
Asst. Professor, Department of Teacher
    Education, Ruston, LA 71272
(318) 257-2676
Ref: 31271.002008
PF: Professional Development, Inservice

▶ **Louisiana Tech University** [123]
Student Literacy Corps
Sam V. Dauzat
Area Coordinator, Teacher Education, Ruston, LA
    71272
(318) 257-4609
Ref: 31273.002008
PF: Tutoring, Counseling

Lourdes College
Collaborative Natural Science Learning Center
    Program
Sr. Rosine Sobczak, O.S.F.
Coordinator, Natural and Mathematical Sciences,
    6832 Convent Boulevard, Sylvania, OH 43560
(419) 885-3211 x306
Ref: 20564.003069
PF: Enrichment, Gifted

Lourdes College
Lourdes College and CCMT Connection
Sr. Maria Goretti Sodd, O.S.F.
Director of Continuing Education, Sylvania, OH
    43560
(419) 885-3211
Ref: 30854.003069
PF: Minority, At-Risk

▶ **Lourdes College** [141]
Women in Science Day
Dolores Kurek
Assoc. Professor, 6832 Convent Boulevard,
    Sylvania, OH 43560
(419) 885-3211
Ref: 20056.003069
PF: Career, Internships, Apprenticeships

▶ **Loyola University of Chicago** [30]
The Access 2000 Chicago Partnership
Eric Hamilton
Director, 6525 N. Sheridan Road, Chicago, IL
    60626
(312) 508-3582
Ref: 31183.001710
PF: Minority, At-Risk

Loyola University of Chicago
Alliance for Community Education (AED)
Diane Schiller
Assoc. Professor of Education, 6525 N. Sheridan
    Road, Chicago, IL 60626
(312) 508-8383
Ref: 31189.001710
PF: Minority, At-Risk

Loyola University of Chicago
College Development
Sheryl Washington
Asst. Director, Undergraduate Admissions, 820 N.
    Michigan Avenue, Chicago, IL 60611
(312) 915-6500
Ref: 31160.001710
PF: Minority, At-Risk

▶ **Loyola University of Chicago** [73]
College Option Program (COP)
Bren Ortega Murphy
Dean, CAS College Programs, 6525 N. Sheridan
    Road, Chicago, IL 60626
(312) 508-3523
Ref: 31184.001710
PF: College Courses for Students

▶ **Loyola University of Chicago** [134]
Future Teachers
Anna Lowe
Asst. Dean for Teacher Education, 6525 N.
    Sheridan Road, Chicago, IL 60626
(312) 508-8100
Ref: 31185.001710
PF: Career, Internships, Apprenticeships

Loyola University of Chicago
Learning Enrichment for Academic Progress
Sheryl Washington
Asst. Director of Undergraduate Admissions, 820
    N. Michigan Avenue, Chicago, IL 60611
(312) 915-6500
Ref: 31158.001710
PF: Minority, At-Risk

Loyola University of Chicago
Link Unlimited
Sheryl Washington
Asst. Director of Undergraduate Admissions, 820
    N. Michigan Avenue, Chicago, IL 60611
(312) 915-7085
Ref: 31159.001710
PF: Minority, At-Risk

▶ **Loyola University of Chicago** [122]
Loyola Clemente Partners Program
Angeles L. Eames
Dean, Multicultural Affairs, 6525 N. Sheridan
    Road, Chicago, IL 60626
(312) 508-3334
aeames@orion.it.luc.edu
Ref: 31187.001710
PF: Tutoring, Counseling

Loyola University of Chicago
New Principal Support Program
Max Bailez
Chair, Professor of Leadership and Education
Policy Studies, 820 N. Michigan Avenue,
Chicago, IL 60611
(312) 915-6004
Ref: 31157.001710
PF: Professional Development, Inservice

▶ **Loyola University of Chicago** [30]
Project Enrichment
Angeles L. Eames
Dean, Multicultural Affairs, 6525 N. Sheridan
Road, Chicago, IL 60626
(312) 508-3334
aeames@orion.it.luc.edu
Ref: 31186.001710
PF: Minority, At-Risk

Loyola University of Chicago
Smart Teams
Eric Hamilton
Director, Access 2000, 6525 N. Sheridan Road,
Chicago, IL 60626
(312) 508-3582
Ref: 31182.001710
PF: Minority, At-Risk

▶ **Loyola University of Chicago** [162]
Taft Institute Teaching Seminar
Alan R. Gitelson
Professor, Department of Political Science,
Chicago, IL 60626
(312) 508-3065
agitels@luccpua.it.luc.edu
Ref: 20355.001710
PF: Professional Development, Inservice

▶ **Loyola University of Chicago** [212]
Teachers for Chicago
Mary Wojnicki
Director of Clinical Experiences, 6525 N. Sheridan
Road, Chicago, IL 60626
(312) 508-8282
Ref: 31188.001710
PF: Recruit, Preservice, Certification

Luther College
Clinical Schools Approach to Teacher Education
Edgar V. Epperly
Professor of Education, Koren 103, Decorah, IA
52101
(319) 387-1540
Ref: 20177.001874
PF: Teacher Education Centers

Lynchburg College
Accelerated Learning Project
Ed Dolloway
Dean, School of Education, Lynchburg, VA 24501
(804) 522-8381
Ref: 31623.003720
PF: Minority, At-Risk

Lyon College
Liberal Arts Teacher Education Program
George C. Stone
The Roundtree Caldwell Bryan Distinguished
Professor, Lyon Building, Batesville, AR 72501
(501) 698-4373
Ref: 31752.001088
PF: Teacher Education Centers

M

Macon College
Adopt-a-School Program
Claudia T. Pecor
Chair, 100 College Station Drive, Macon, GA
31297
(912) 471-2812
Ref: 30613.007728
PF: Tutoring, Counseling

Macon College
Early Intervention Program-Project Yes
Claudia T. Pecor
Coordinator, 100 College Station Drive, Macon,
GA 31297
(912) 471-2812
Ref: 30614.007728
PF: Minority, At-Risk

▶ **Macon College** [94]
Reading and Writing Across the Curriculum at
Southwest High School
Robert T. Trammell
Vice-President for Academic Affairs, 100 College
Station Drive, Macon, GA 31210
(912) 471-2730
Ref: 30615.007728
PF: Enrichment, Gifted

Madison Area Technical College
MATC Tech Prep/School-to-Work Consortium
Catherine Chew
Director, 211 N. Carroll Street, Madison, WI
53703
(608) 259-2909
Ref: 31080.004007
PF: Tech-Prep/2+2

▶ **Madisonville Community College** [165]
Kennedy Center Performing Arts Centers and
Schools: Partners in Education
Barbie Hunt
Director, Fine Arts Center, 2000 College Drive,
Madisonville, KY 42431
(502) 821-2250
Ref: 30850.009010
PF: Professional Development, Inservice

Madisonville Community College
Tech Prep With Madisonville North Hopkins High
School
Judith K. Moore
Professor, 2000 College Drive, Madisonville, KY
42431
(502) 821-2250
Ref: 30849.009010
PF: Tech-Prep/2+2

▶ **Madisonville Community College** [213]
ED 201 Total Immersion Program
Susan Edington
Professor, Teacher Education, Madisonville, KY
42431
(502) 821-2250
Ref: 30848.009010
PF: Recruit, Preservice, Certification

Madonna University
Barrios De Michigan
Sr. Mary Martinez
Director, Office of Multicultural Affairs, 36600
Schoolcraft Road, Livonia, MI 48150
(313) 591-5170
Ref: 30994.002282
PF: Enrichment, Gifted

▶ **Madonna University** [233]
Integrating the Humanities and Teacher
Preparation
Richard Sax
Assoc. Professor, 36600 Schoolcraft Road,
Livonia, MI 48150
(313) 591-5077
Ref: 30997.002282
PF: Faculty Exchanges

▶ **Madonna University** [273]
Livonia Education Television Consortium (LETC)
Patricia A. Derry
Director of Media Services, 36600 Schoolcraft
Road, Livonia, MI 48150
(313) 591-5118
Ref: 20587.002282
PF: City/Regional Compacts

Madonna University
Madonna/Livonia Public Schools Co-Op
    Agreement
Sr. Mary Lydia
Library Director, 36600 Schoolcraft Road, Livonia,
    MI 48150
(313) 591-5015
Ref: 30996.002282
PF: Resource Sharing

Madonna University
Partnership With Ladywood High School
Earnest I. Nolan
Dean, College of Arts and Humanities, Livonia, MI
    48150
(313) 591-5084
Ref: 30998.002282
PF: College Courses for Students

▶ **Madonna University** [172]
PSM³: Problem Solving With Mathematical
    Models and Manipulatives
Miriam Long
Asst. Professor, 36600 Schoolcraft Road, Livonia,
    MI 48150
(313) 591-5104
Ref: 30995.002282
PF: Professional Development, Inservice

Madonna University
Summer Institute
Sr. Nancy Marie
Vice President for Student Life, 36600 Schoolcraft
    Road, Livonia, MI 48150-1173
(313) 591-5060
Ref: 30999.002282
PF: Enrichment, Gifted

Madonna University
The Tutoring Team
Sr. Mary Martinez
Director of Multicultural Affairs, 36600 Schoolcraft
    Road, Livonia, MI 48150
(313) 591-5170
Ref: 30993.002282
PF: Tutoring, Counseling

▶ **Malone College** [219]
Child Development Associate (CDA) Credentialing
    Program
Jerri Helmreich
Instructor, 515 25th Street NW, Canton, OH
    44709
(216) 471-8264
Ref: 30904.003072
PF: Recruit, Preservice, Certification

▶ **Malone College** [247]
Consultants for Even Start Family Literacy
    Programs
Patricia Long
Professor of Education, 515 25th Street NW,
    Canton, OH 44709
(216) 471-8222
Ref: 30902.003072
PF: Instructional Research

Malone College
Explorers: Extension of Boy & Girl Scouts of
    America
Maxine Burgett
Asst. Professor of Education, 515 25th Street NW,
    Canton, OH 44709
(216) 471-8301
Ref: 30903.003072
PF: Career, Internships, Apprenticeships

Malone College
Free Enterprise
Daniel J. Hoskins
Chair, 515 25th Street NW, Canton, OH 44709
(216) 471-8190
Ref: 30900.003072
PF: Enrichment, Gifted

Malone College
Prescriptive Tutoring Lab
Donna L. Brandon
Asst. Professor of Education, 515 25th Street NW,
    Canton, OH 44709
(216) 471-8332
Ref: 30901.003072
PF: Recruit, Preservice, Certification

Malone College
Teacher Advisory Committee Inservice
Martha J. B. Cook
Chair, Department of Education, 515 25th Street
    NW, Canton, OH 44709
(216) 471-8220
Ref: 31756.003072
PF: Recruit, Preservice, Certification

Manchester College
Adapted Physical Education
Kim A. Duchane
Asst. Professor, Department of Heath and
    Physical Education, Box 135, Physical
    Education and Recreation Center, North
    Manchester, IN 46962
(219) 982-5382
Ref: 30975.001820
PF: Professional Development, Inservice

▶ **Manchester College** [238]
Environmental Education-Through Koinonia
    Environmental Center of Manchester College
Barbara Ehrhardt
Director, Box 36, North Manchester, IN 46962
(219) 982-5010
bjehrhardt@manchester.edu
Ref: 30974.001820
PF: Curriculum Development

▶ **Manhattan College** [51]
Project CHAMP (Children Having Additional Motor
    Power)
William Merriman
Project Director, School of Education and Human
    Services, 4513 Manhattan College Parkway,
    Bronx, NY 10471
(718) 920-0355
Ref: 20877.002758
PF: Minority, At-Risk

▶ **Mankato State University** [227]
Laboratory District Teacher Education
Harold D. Burch
Director, Laboratory District Teacher Center, P.O.
    Box 8400, MSU 52, Mankato, MN 56002-8400
(507) 389-1217
Ref: 20364.002360
PF: Teacher Education Centers

▶ **Mansfield University of
Pennsylvania** [302]
Access PA
Larry L. Nesbit
Director of Library Sciences and Instructional
    Resources, Main Library, Mansfield, PA 16933
(717) 662-4672
lnesbit@vmhostl.mnsfld.edu
Ref: 30419.003324
PF: Resource Sharing

Mansfield University of Pennsylvania
Parents as Education Partners Program (PEPP)
Betty L. Mack
Coordinator, 119 Doane Center, Mansfield, PA
    16933
(717) 662-4241
Ref: 30418.003324
PF: Retention, Continuing Education

Marian College of Fond Du Lac
High School/College Dual Credit Program
Michael J. Puglisi
Asst. Dean of Academic Affairs, 45 S. National
    Avenue, Fond Du Lac, WI 54935
(414) 923-7621
Ref: 31118.003861
PF: College Courses for Students

Marian College of Fond Du Lac
Multicultural Teacher Initiatives Project
Leslie L. Youngsteadt
Project Coordinator, 45 S. National Avenue, Fond
    Du Lac, WI 54935
(414) 923-7600
Ref: 20776.003861
PF: Minority, At-Risk

▶ **Marian College of Fond Du Lac** [85]
Post Secondary Enrollment Options Program
    (PSEO)
Michael J. Puglisi
Asst. Dean of Academic Affairs, 45 S. National
    Avenue, Fond Du Lac, WI 54935
(414) 923-7621
Ref: 31119.003861
PF: College Courses for Students

▶ **Mars Hill College** [185]
General Electric/Mars Hill College/3 School
    System Collaborative Effort
Richard Hoffman
Assistant to the President, Box 490, Mars Hill, NC
    28754
(704) 689-1142
Ref: 30758.002944
PF: Professional Development, Inservice

Marshall University
Automotive Technology Program
F. David Wilkin
Dean, Community and Technical College,
    Huntington, WV 25755
(304) 696-3008
Ref: 30594.003815
PF: Tech-Prep/2+2

Marshall University
Eagles' Nest
Stan Maynard
Professor, College of Education, 205 Northcott
    Hall, Huntington, WV 25755-2480
(304) 696-2890
Ref: 30592.003815
PF: Minority, At-Risk

Marshall University
Electronics Technology Program
F. David Wilkin
Dean, Community and Technical College,
    Huntington, WV 25755
(304) 696-3008
Ref: 20492.003815
PF: Resource Sharing

▶ **Marshall University** [67]
External Diploma Program
Stan Maynard
Professor, College of Education, 205 Northcott
    Hall, Huntington, WV 25755-2480
(304) 696-2890
Ref: 30593.003815
PF: Minority, At-Risk

▶ **Marshall University** [67]
Parent Involvement Program
Stan Maynard
Professor, College of Education, 205 Northcott
    Hall, Huntington, WV 25755-2480
(304) 696-2890
Ref: 30590.003815
PF: Minority, At-Risk

▶ **Marshall University** [203]
Southwestern Consortium for Excellence in
    Science, Mathematics, and Technology
Stan Maynard
Professor, College of Education, 205 Northcott
    Hall, Huntington, WV 25755-2480
(304) 696-2890
Ref: 30591.003815
PF: Professional Development, Inservice

▶ **Marshalltown Community College** [255]
MCC-MHS Nurse Training Program
Gerald J. McCright
Dean, 3700 S. Center Street, Marshall Town, IA
    50158
(515) 753-7876
Ref: 31037.001875
PF: Tech-Prep/2+2

▶ **Mary Baldwin College** [84]
Program for the Exceptionally Gifted (PEG)
Allison J. Young
Assoc. Director for Program Advancement,
    Staunton, VA 24401
(703) 887-7039
Ref: 21240.003723
PF: College Courses for Students

Mary Washington College
James Farmer Scholars Program
Venitta C. McCall
Program Director, Fredericksburg, VA 22401
(703) 899-4663
Ref: 20937.003746
PF: Minority, At-Risk

Marymount College [202]
Academic Alliances in Foreign Languages and
    Literatures
Ellen S. Silber
National Project Director, Tarrytown, NY 10591
(914) 332-4917
Ref: 20251.002768
PF: Professional Development, Inservice

▶ **Marymount University** [202]
Mathematics and Science Workshops for
    Washington DC Public School Teachers
Larry Padberg
Vice President for Enrollment Management,
    Arlington, VA 22207
(703) 284-3810
Ref: 30568.003724
PF: Professional Development, Inservice

Marymount Manhattan College
Options/DDE Program
Peter H. Baker
Chairperson, Math and Science Department, 221
    E. 71st Street, New York, NY 10021
(212) 517-0522
Ref: 30157.002769
PF: Minority, At-Risk

Marymount Manhattan College
Settlement College/Readiness Program/Step
    Program
Peter H. Baker
Chairperson, Math and Science Department, 221
    E. 71st Street, New York, NY 10021
(212) 517-0522
Ref: 30158.002769
PF: Minority, At-Risk

Maryville College
Erskine Tutorial Program
James A. Porter
Co-Coordinator, P.O. Box 2213, Maryville, TN
    37801
(615) 981-8407
Ref: 30695.003505
PF: Tutoring, Counseling

▶ **Maryville University**   [173]
Maryville/South High Collaborative
Mary Ellen Finch
Dean, School of Education, 13550 Conway Road,
    Gander Hall, St. Louis, MO 63141
(314) 576-9466
Ref: 31221.002482
PF: Professional Development, Inservice

Maryville University
Maryville/Wilkinson Early Childhood Professional
    Development School
Dolores Longley
PDS Coordinator, 13550 Conway Road, Gander
    Hall, St. Louis, MO 63141
(314) 576-9486
Ref: 31220.002482
PF: Professional Development, Inservice

Marywood College
Pathways
Ann O'Neill
Program Coordinator, School of Continuing
    Education, Scranton, PA 18509
(717) 348-6237
Ref: 30436.003296
PF: College Courses for Students

Marywood College
Science Teacher Enhancement Project
Lois K. Draina
Project Coordinator, 2300 Adams Avenue,
    Scranton, PA 18509
(717) 348-6289
Ref: 30437.003296
PF: Professional Development, Inservice

Mater Dei College
College Courses to High School Students
Marie E. Truax
Director of Continuing Education, R.R. #2, Box
    #45, Ogdensburg, NY 13669
(315) 393-5930
Ref: 30271.002771
PF: College Courses for Students

▶ **Mayo Foundation-Mayo Graduate
School**   [246]
Rochester Area Math/Science Partnership
Cathy Chellgren
Registrar, Mayo Graduate School, 200 First Street
    SW, 5 Siebens Building, Mayo Clinic,
    Rochester, MN 55905
(507) 284-3163
Ref: 31822.666719
PF: Instructional Research

McHenry County College
Adult Education & Literacy
Doug Van Nostran
Assoc. Dean, 8900 U.S. Highway 14, Crystal
    Lake, IL 60012-2796
(815) 455-8764
Ref: 31148.007691
PF: Minority, At-Risk

▶ **McHenry County College**   [253]
Basic Nurse Assistant
Joan Witte
Coordinator, 8900 U.S. Highway 14, Crystal Lake,
    IL 60012
(815) 455-8742
Ref: 31147.007691
PF: Tech-Prep/2+2

McHenry County College
Early Childhood Education
Susan Maifield
Program Coordinator/Instructor, 8900 U.S.
    Highway 14, Crystal Lake, IL 60012
(815) 455-8679
Ref: 31146.007691
PF: College Courses for Students

Medaille College
Inner City Academy
Tom Rookey
Dean, 18 Aggasiz Circle, Buffalo, NY 14214
(716) 884-3281
Ref: 31616.002777
PF: Minority, At-Risk

▶ **Medical University of South
Carolina**   [108]
Summer Research Program
Hester Young
Coordinator, College of Graduate Studies,
    Charleston, SC 29425
(803) 792-9620
Ref: 30795.003438
PF: Enrichment, Gifted

▶ **Medical University of South
Carolina**   [142]
Summer Undergraduate Research Awards
    Program (SURAP)
Henry Martin
Director, Department of Physiology, 171 Ashley
    Avenue, Charleston, SC 29425
(803) 792-2540
Ref: 30796.003438
PF: Career, Internships, Apprenticeships

▶ **Meharry Medical College**   [62]
P.M. Scientists Program
Frederick Hamilton
Assoc. Project Director, Division of Biomedical
    Sciences, 1005 D.B. Todd Boulevard, Nashville,
    TN 37208
(615) 327-6508
hamilt95@ccvax.mmc.edu
Ref: 30685.003506
PF: Minority, At-Risk

▶ **Meharry Medical College**   [63]
Saturday Scientists Program
Frederick Hamilton
Assoc. Project Director, Division of Biomedical
    Sciences, 1005 D.B. Todd Boulevard, Nashville,
    TN 37203
(615) 327-6508
hamilt95@ccvax.mmc.edu
Ref: 30684.003506
PF: Minority, At-Risk

▶ **Meharry Medical College**   [63]
Science Motivation Program (SMP)
Frederick Hamilton
Assoc. Project Director, Division of Biomedical
    Sciences, 1005 D.B. Todd Boulevard, Nashville,
    TN 37208
(615) 327-6508
hamilt95@ccvax.mmc.edu
Ref: 20950.003506
PF: Minority, At-Risk

▶ **Meharry Medical College**   [62]
Summer Biomedical Sciences Program (SBSP)
John E. Wilson
Asst. Dean, School of Graduate Studies and
    Research, 1005 D.B. Todd Boulevard,
    Nashville, TN 37208
(615) 327-6533
Ref: 30686.003506
PF: Minority, At-Risk

Merced College
Merced Tech Prep Consortium
Anne Newins
Tech Prep Project Director, 3600 M Street,
    Merced, CA 95348
(209) 384-6112
Ref: 31559.001237
PF: Tech-Prep/2+2

▶ **Mercer County Community College** [260]
Automotive Technology AAS Degree
Albert Magson
Chairperson, Division of Tech/Comp/Math, P.O.
  Box B, Trenton, NJ 08690
(609) 586-4800 x755
Ref: 30087.004740
PF: Tech-Prep/2+2

Mercer County Community College
Heating/Refrigeration/Air Conditioning Technology
Albert Magson
Chairperson, Division of Tech/Comp/Math, P.O.
  Box B, Trenton, NJ 08690
(609) 586-4800 x755
Ref: 30086.004740
PF: Tech-Prep/2+2

Mercy College
Mercy College High School Articulation Program
Paula Kelly
Asst. Dean, Academic Administration, 555
  Broadway, Dobbs Ferry, NY 10522
(914) 674-7223
Ref: 20918.002772
PF: College Courses for Students

Mesa State College
Connect: Colorado Statewide Systemic Initiative
Norma J. Smith
Director, Mesa TEP and MMMP, P.O. Box 2647,
  Grand Junction, CO 81502
(303) 248-1787
smith@banner1.mesa.colorado.edu
Ref: 31429.001358
PF: New Achievement, Assessment Standards

▶ **Mesa State College** [154]
Mesa Math Mentorship Program
Norma J. Smith
Director, Mesa TEP and MMMP, P.O. Box 2647,
  Grand Junction, CO 81502
(303) 248-1787
smith@banner1.mesa.colorado.edu
Ref: 31430.001358
PF: Professional Development, Inservice

Mesa State College
Pre-Collegiate Development Program (PCDP)
Sherri L. Pea
Asst. Vice President for Student Life, Grand
  Junction, CO 81506
(303) 248-1608
Ref: 31427.001358
PF: Minority, At-Risk

▶ **Mesa State College** [251]
Unified Technical Education Center (UTEC)
Jack P. Smith
Asst. Vocational Director, 508 Blicamann Avenue,
  Grand Junction, CO 81505
(303) 248-1999
Ref: 31428.001358
PF: Tech-Prep/2+2

▶ **Metropolitan Community College** [296]
Omaha Job Clearinghouse
Randy Schmnailzl
Director, Enrollment Management, P.O. Box 3777,
  Omaha, NE 68103-0777
(402) 449-8418
Ref: 31260.012586
PF: School-College-Business Partnerships

▶ **Metropolitan Community College** [44]
Project FREE (Family Reading Encourages
  Education)
Peggy Swanson
Coordinator, P.O. Box 3777, Omaha, NE
  68103-0777
(402) 449-8312
Ref: 31259.012586
PF: Minority, At-Risk

Metropolitan Community College
Tech Prep
Nadine Possehl
Tech Prep Coordinator, P.O. Box 3777, Omaha,
  NE 68103-0777
(402) 499-0242
Ref: 31258.012586
PF: Tech-Prep/2+2

▶ **Miami University–Hamilton Campus** [305]
Miami Connection
Robert Baer
Asst. Executive Director, 1601 Peck Boulevard,
  Hamilton, OH 45011
(513) 863-8833
bdbaer@mosler.ham.muohio.edu
Ref: 30917.003079
PF: Magnet Schools

Middlebury College
Area High School Academic Enrichment
John D. Emerson
Vice President for Student Affairs, Middlebury, VT
  05753
(802) 388-3711 x5393
Ref: 30065.003691
PF: College Courses for Students

▶ **Middlebury College** [66]
Dewitt Clinton High School/Middlebury College
Leroy Nesbitt, Jr.
Special Assistant to the President, Old Chapel,
  Middlebury, VT 05753
(802) 388-3711
Ref: 30064.003691
PF: Minority, At-Risk

▶ **Middlebury College** [201]
Vermont Elementary Science Project
Robert Prigo
Professor of Physics, Department of Physics,
  Middlebury, VT 05753
(802) 388-3711 x5425
prigo@middlebury.edu
Ref: 30066.003691
PF: Professional Development, Inservice

Middlesex Community College
School/College Collaborative
Frank M. Falcetta
Dean, Economic and Community Development,
  Springs Road, Bedford, MA 01730
(617) 280-3534
Ref: 20909.009936
PF: Minority, At-Risk

Middlesex County College
A Partnership for Business Education
Robert Fishco
Dean, Division of Business Technologies, 155 Mill
  Road, Edison, NJ 08818
(908) 906-2502
Ref: 30132.002615
PF: Career, Internships, Apprenticeships

▶ **Middlesex County College** [296]
Central Region Competitive Events
  Miniconference
Robert Fishco
Dean, Division of Business Technologies, 155 Mill
  Road, Edison, NJ 08818
(908) 906-2502
Ref: 30125.002615
PF: School-College-Business Partnerships

Middlesex County College
Eisenhower Projects-Teacher In-Service
Darlene S. Yoseloff
Coordinator, Office of School Relations, 155 Mill
  Road, Edison, NJ 08818
(908) 906-2554
Ref: 30121.002615
PF: Professional Development, Inservice

Middlesex County College
Gateway
Joseph L. Cardone
Division of Continuing Education, 155 Mill Road,
    Edison, NJ 08818
(908) 906-2509
Ref: 30124.002615
PF: Enrichment, Gifted

Middlesex County College
High School Participation Program
Barbara Greene
Director, Continuing Studies, 155 Mill Road,
    Edison, NJ 08818
(908) 906-2509
Ref: 30123.002615
PF: College Courses for Students

Middlesex County College
High School Writing Conference/Contest
Santi Buscemi
Chair, Department of English, 155 Mill Road,
    Edison, NJ 08818
(908) 906-2591
Ref: 30120.002615
PF: Enrichment, Gifted

Middlesex County College
John E. McGowan Continuing Education Day
D. Michelle Goffe
Dean, Student Services, 155 Mill Road, Edison,
    NJ 08818
(908) 906-2514
Ref: 30133.002615
PF: Tutoring, Counseling

Middlesex County College
Middlesex County Job Opportunity and Career
    Exploration Fair
Darlene S. Yoseloff
Coordinator, Office of School Relations, 155 Mill
    Road, Edison, NJ 08818
(908) 906-2554
Ref: 30127.002615
PF: Career, Internships, Apprenticeships

Middlesex County College
Middlesex County Science Fair
Alan Sherman
Director, Edison, NJ 08818
(908) 548-6000
Ref: 30131.002615
PF: Enrichment, Gifted

Middlesex County College
Middlesex Tech Prep Initiative
Darlene S. Yoseloff
Coordinator, Office of School Relations, 155 Mill
    Road, Edison, NJ 08818
(908) 906-2554
Ref: 30122.002615
PF: Tech-Prep/2+2

Middlesex County College
PACE: Personal Awareness & Career Exploration
Krystal Gill
Coordinator, 317 George Street, New Brunswick,
    NJ 08901
(908) 249-6207
Ref: 30130.002615
PF: Minority, At-Risk

Middlesex County College
Showcase of Achievement
Darlene S. Yoseloff
Coordinator, Office of School Relations, 155 Mill
    Road, Edison, NJ 08818
(908) 906-2554
Ref: 30129.002615
PF: Enrichment, Gifted

Middlesex County College
Summer in the Technologies
Tory Payne
Director, Grant Funded Projects, 155 Mill Road,
    Edison, NJ 08818
(908) 906-2556
Ref: 30126.002615
PF: Minority, At-Risk

▶ **Middlesex County College**   [100]
Vanguard: A Symposium for Future Leaders
Darlene S. Yoseloff
Coordinator, Office of School Relations, 155 Mill
    Road, Edison, NJ 08818
(908) 906-2554
Ref: 30128.002615
PF: Enrichment, Gifted

▶ **Midlands Technical College**   [142]
Adopt-a-School
Peggy McClure
Instructor in Science, P.O. Box 2408, Columbia,
    SC 29202
(803) 822-3356
Ref: 30772.003993
PF: Career, Internships, Apprenticeships

Midlands Technical College
Cities-in-Schools
Stan Frick
Chair, Department of Developmental Studies,
    P.O. Box 2408, Columbia, SC 29202
(803) 738-7794
Ref: 30763.003993
PF: Minority, At-Risk

▶ **Midlands Technical College**   [195]
Counselors' Conference
Sandi Oliver
Assoc. Vice President for Student Development,
    P.O. Box 2408, Columbia, SC 29202
(803) 738-7699
olivers%mtc1@citadel.edu
Ref: 30766.003993
PF: Professional Development, Inservice

Midlands Technical College
Educators in Industry
Sandi Oliver
Assoc. Vice President for Student Development,
    P.O. Box 2408, Columbia, SC 29202
(803) 738-7699
olivers%mtc1@citadel.edu
Ref: 30764.003993
PF: Professional Development, Inservice

▶ **Midlands Technical College**   [228]
South Carolina Hall of Science and Technology
Tom Reeves
Chair, Department of Science, P.O. Box 2408,
    Columbia, SC 29202
(803) 822-3554
Ref: 30771.003993
PF: Enrichment, Gifted

▶ **Midlands Technical College**   [60]
JTPA School-to-College Articulation Agreement
Ron Dooley
Director, Special Programs, P.O. Box 2408,
    Columbia, SC 29210
(803) 822-3506
Ref: 30768.003993
PF: Minority, At-Risk

Midlands Technical College
Math HUB (MIMS-Midlands Improving
    Mathematics and Science)
Lisa LaBorde
Instructor in Mathematics, P.O. Box 2408,
    Columbia, SC 29202
(803) 822-3352
Ref: 30767.003993
PF: Professional Development, Inservice

Midlands Technical College
Midlands Mathematics Meet
John Long
Instructor in Mathematics, P.O. Box 2408,
    Columbia, SC 29202
(803) 738-7677
Ref: 30762.003993
PF: Enrichment, Gifted

Midlands Technical College
Pre-Dental Assisting Program
Martha Hanks
Program Director, P.O. Box 2408, Columbia, SC
    29202
(803) 822-3451
Ref: 30770.003993
PF: Resource Sharing

Midlands Technical College
Tech Prep
Mary B. Robertson
Assoc. Vice President for Education, P.O. Box
    2408, Columbia, SC 29202
(803) 738-7606
robertsonm%mtc1@citadel.edu
Ref: 30765.003993
PF: Tech-Prep/2+2

Midlands Technical College
W A Perry Sealant Clinic-Dental Hygiene Program
Martha Hanks
Program Director, P.O. Box 2408, Columbia, SC
    29202
(803) 822-3451
Ref: 30770.003993
PF: Resource Sharing

Millersville University of Pennsylvania
Lancaster Partnership Program
Minor W. Redmond, Jr.
Director, P.O. Box 1002, Millersville, PA
    17551-0302
(717) 871-2027
Ref: 30429.003325
PF: Minority, At-Risk

▶ **Minneapolis Community College** [42]
Minneapolis Pathways
Hugh Yamamoto
1501 Hennepin Avenue, Minneapolis, MN 55403
(612) 341-7000
Ref: 31121.002362
PF: Minority, At-Risk

▶ **Mississippi County Community
College** [249]
Tech Prep 2+2 Program
Ann Declerk
Project Director, P.O. Box 1109, Blytheville, AR
    72316
(501) 762-1020
Ref: 31276.012860
PF: Tech-Prep/2+2

Mississippi Gulf Coast Community College
Alliance for Achievement
Marie Davis-Hein
Developmental Studies, Perkinston Campus,
    Perkinston, MS 39573
(601) 928-6221
Ref: 31703.008763
PF: Minority, At-Risk

Mississippi Gulf Coast Community College
Dual Enrollment
Patricia Hollowly
Student Services, Jefferson Davis Campus,
    Gulfport, MS 39573
(601) 896-3355 x500
Ref: 31702.008763
PF: College Courses for Students

Mississippi Gulf Coast Community College
Perk Plus Summer Program-JTPA
Marie Davis-Hein
Developmental Studies Program, Perkinston
    Campus, Perkinston, MS 39573
(601) 928-6221
Ref: 31704.008763
PF: Minority, At-Risk

Mississippi Gulf Coast Community College
Quickstart Plus
Diane Roberts
Recruiter, Learning Resource Center, Perkinston
    Campus, Perkinston, MS 39573
(601) 928-6268
Ref: 31705.008763
PF: Minority, At-Risk

▶ **Mississippi State University** [247]
Program for Research and Evaluation in Public
    Schools, Inc. (PREPS)
Hugh I. Peck
Executive Director, P.O. Box 5365, MS 39762
(601) 325-3720
preps@ra.msstate.edu
Ref: 21040.002423
PF: Instructional Research

Missouri Southern State College
Business Education Partnership
Earle F. Doman
Director of Counseling Services, 3950 E. Newman
    Road, Joplin, MO 64801-1595
(417) 625-9595
Ref: 31242.002488
PF: School-College-Business Partnerships

Missouri Southern State College
Dual Credit Program
Ray Malzahn
Interim Vice President for Academic Affairs, 3950
    E. Newman Road, Joplin, MO 64801-1595
(417) 625-9394
Ref: 31241.002488
PF: College Courses for Students

Missouri Southern State College
Hammons Enhancement/Scholarship Program
Kelly E. Binns
Counseling Service Assistant, 3950 E. Newman
    Road, Joplin, MO 64801-1595
(417) 625-9363
Ref: 31240.002488
PF: Minority, At-Risk

Mohawk Valley Community College
Bridge Program
L.C. Robinson
Director of Counseling, 1101 Sherman Drive,
    Utica, NY 13501
(315) 792-5325
Ref: 30258.002871
PF: College Courses for Students

Mohawk Valley Community College
College Now
Satya Tandon
Coordinator, 1101 Sherman Drive, Utica, NY
    13501
(315) 792-5447
Ref: 30259.002871
PF: College Courses for Students

Mohawk Valley Community College
MATE
Marie Czarnecki
Assoc. Professor, 1101 Sherman Drive, Utica, NY
    13501
(315) 792-5540
Ref: 20426.002871
PF: Professional Development, Inservice

Mohawk Valley Community College
Modern Manufacturing Institute
Linda M. Spink
Vice President for Instruction, 1101 Sherman
    Drive, Utica, NY 13501
(315) 792-5301
lspink@sunymvcc
Ref: 30257.002871
PF: Tech-Prep/2+2

Mohawk Valley Community College
Mohawk Valley Review
Jim Laditka
Assoc. Professor, 1101 Sherman Drive, Utica, NY
    13501
(315) 792-5617
Ref: 30261.002871
PF: Enrichment, Gifted

Mohawk Valley Community College
Partnership Task Force
Maryanne DiMeo
Chairman, 1101 Sherman Drive, Utica, NY 13501
(315) 792-5314
Ref: 30262.002871
PF: Tech-Prep/2+2

▶ **Mohawk Valley Community College**   [240]
Science of Toys
Celia Domser
Professor, 1101 Sherman Drive, Utica, NY 13501
(315) 792-5633
Ref: 30260.002871
PF: Curriculum Development

Monroe Community College
Liberty Partnerships
Carol Adams
Dean, Developmental Education, 1000 E.
    Henrietta Road, Rochester, NY 14623
(716) 292-2341
Ref: 30304.002872
PF: Minority, At-Risk

Monroe Community College
Minority High School Apprenticeship Program
Quintin Bullock
Director, Center for Urban Educational Studies,
    1000 E. Henrietta Road, Rochester, NY 14623
(716) 292-2000
Ref: 30303.002872
PF: Career, Internships, Apprenticeships

Monroe Community College
Monroe County Tech Prep Consortium
Nelson Ronsvalle
Director, Tech Prep, 228 E. Main Street,
    Rochester, NY 14604
(716) 262-1668
nronsvalle@eckert.acadcomp.monroecc.edu
Ref: 30306.002872
PF: Tech-Prep/2+2

Monroe Community College
Portfolio Partnership Project
Nelson Ronsvalle
Director, Tech Prep, 228 E. Main Street,
    Rochester, NY 14604
(716) 262-1668
nronsvalle@eckert.acadcomp.monroecc.edu
Ref: 30305.002872
PF: School-College-Business Partnerships

Monroe Community College
Scholars Working in Scientific Excellence
    (SWISE)
Quintin Bullock
Director, Center for Urban Educational Studies,
    1000 E. Henrietta Road, Rochester, NY 14623
(716) 292-2000 x5148
Ref: 30302.002872
PF: Enrichment, Gifted

Monroe Community College
Science & Technology Entry Program (STEP)
Quintin Bullock
Director, Center for Urban Educational Studies,
    1000 E. Henrietta Road, Rochester, NY 14623
(716) 292-2000 x5148
Ref: 30307.002872
PF: Minority, At-Risk

▶ **Montana College of Mineral Science and
Technology**   [175]
Project Partners
Nina A. Klein
Mont. Tech, 1300 W. Park Street, Butte, MT
    59701
(406) 496-4289
nklein@mtvms2.mtech.edu
Ref: 31143.002531
PF: Professional Development, Inservice

▶ **Montana State University–Billings**   [175]
Professional Development Schools
Ernest Rose
Assoc. Dean, 1500 N. 30th Street, Billings, MT
    59101
(406) 657-2336
ed_rose@vino.emcmt.edu
Ref: 31142.002530
PF: Professional Development, Inservice

▶ **Montana State University–Bozeman**   [175]
MSU/Bozeman Public School District Partnership
Randy Hitz
Dean, College of Education, Bozeman, MT 59717
(406) 994-4133
addrh@msu.oscs.montana.educ
Ref: 31144.002532
PF: Professional Development, Inservice

Montclair State College
Clinical Schools Network
Charles P. Mitchel
Executive Director, Upper Montclair, NJ 07043
(201) 655-7641
Ref: 30084.002617
PF: Teacher Education Centers

▶ **Montclair State College**   [177]
Project THISTLE (Thinking Skills in Teaching and
    Learning)
Wendy Oxman
Director, Upper Montclair, NJ 07043
(201) 655-5184
Ref: 20332.002617
PF: Professional Development, Inservice

Monterey Institute of International Studies
Science in Spanish
Ruth Larimer
Assoc. Dean, 425 Van Buren Street, Monterey,
    CA 93940
(408) 647-4185
Ref: 31530.001241
PF: Enrichment, Gifted

▶ **Monterey Peninsula College**   [16]
Upward Bound
Mary Ann Hamann
TRIO Director, 980 Fremont Street, Monterey, CA
    93940
(408) 646-4246
Ref: 31531.001242
PF: Minority, At-Risk

Key: "▶" denotes those partnerships abstracted in Parts 1-5; the corresponding page numbers are given in brackets. "PF:" denotes the partnership's "primary focus." "Ref:" denotes the partnership's assigned reference number in the National School-College Partnership Database (see Appendix B).

Montgomery College– Rockville Campus
Gifted & Talented/Honors Program
Sandra Sonner
Program Director, Office of Continuing Education,
    51 Mannakee Street, Rockville, MD 20850
(301) 251-7913
Ref: 31620.002082
PF: Enrichment, Gifted

Montgomery College–Rockville Campus
Kids' College
Sandra Sonnor
Program Director, Office of Continuing Education,
    51 Mannakee Street, Rockville, MD 20850
(301) 251-7913
Ref: 31621.002082
PF: Minority, At-Risk

▶ **Montgomery College–Rockville Campus**   [96]
Summer Student Writing Institute
Sandra Sonner
Program Director, Office of Continuing Education,
    51 Mannakee Street, Rockville, MD 20850
(301) 251-7913
Ref: 31622.002082
PF: Enrichment, Gifted

Moore College of Art and Design
Adopted School Program
Hilda Schoenwetter
Director, Art Certification and Young Artists'
    Program, 20th and Parkway, Philadelphia, PA
    19103
(215) 568-4515 x1128
Ref: 30450.003300
PF: Minority, At-Risk

▶ **Moraine Valley Community College**   [253]
Moraine Area Career System
Richard C. Hinckley
Dean of Business/Industrial Technology, 10900 S.
    88th Avenue, Palos Hills, IL 60465
(708) 974-5733
Ref: 20646.007692
PF: Tech-Prep/2+2

Moravian College
Moravian College/Freedom High School Theatre
    Company
Jack Ramsey
Professor, Drama Department, 1200 Main Street,
    Bethlehem, PA 18018
(610) 861-1489
Ref: 30432.003301
PF: Curriculum Development

▶ **Morehead State University**   [245]
Eastern Kentucky Regional KERA Alliance Action
    Research Project
Timothy E. Miller
Director, Kentucky Teacher Intern Program,
    Ginger Hall 801, Morehead, KY 40351
(606) 783-5159
Ref: 30836.001976
PF: Instructional Research

▶ **Morgan State University**   [213]
Project PRIME (Programs to Recruit and Inspire
    Minorities into Education)
Brenda P. Haynes
Director, Cold Spring Lane and Hillen Road,
    Jenkins Building 421, Baltimore, MD 21239
(410) 319-3780
Ref: 30564.002083
PF: Recruit, Preservice, Certification

Morningside College
Morningside/Longfellow Partnership
Jerry Israel
President, 1501 Morningside Avenue, Sioux City,
    IA 51102
(712) 274-5100
Ref: 20559.001879
PF: Resource Sharing

Motlow State Community College
Adopt-A-School Program
Ann Simmons
Dean of Student Development, Tullahoma, TN
    37388
(615) 455-8511
Ref: 21237.006836
PF: Enrichment, Gifted

Motlow State Community College
Programs Providing College Courses to High
    School Students
Ed Kilgour
Dean of Admissions and Records, Tullahoma, TN
    37388
(615) 455-8511
Ref: 21238.006836
PF: College Courses for Students

▶ **Mount Holyoke College**   [170]
Partnership Advancing the Learning of
    Mathematics and Science (PALMS)
Marilyn Gass
Instructor, Psychology and Education, South
    Hadley, MA 01075
(413) 538-2844
mgass@mhc.mtholyoke.edu
Ref: 30004.002192
PF: Professional Development, Inservice

▶ **Mt. Hood Community College**   [265]
Mt. Hood Regional Cooperative Consortium
Jack D. Miller
Dean of Professional Technical Development,
    26000 S.E. Stark, Gresham, OR 97030
(503) 667-7313
Ref: 20500.003204
PF: Tech-Prep/2+2

▶ **Mount Mary College**   [68]
A Healthy Head Start
Alice R. Thomson
Instructor of Dietetics, 2900 N. Menomonee River
    Parkway, Milwaukee, WI 53222
(414) 475-7433
Ref: 31073.003869
PF: Minority, At-Risk

Mount Mary College
College Courses to High School Students
Laurie Becvar
Assoc. Academic Dean, 1105 W. 8th, Yankton,
    SD 57078
(605) 668-1584
Ref: 31132.003465
PF: College Courses for Students

Mount Mary College
Mount Mary College/Sixty-Fifth Street School
    Partnership
Kathleen M. Buse
Director of Career Development, 2900 N.
    Menomonee River Parkway, Milwaukee, WI
    53222-4597
(414) 258-4810
Ref: 31074.003869
PF: Minority, At-Risk

Mount Olive College
MORE (Math Out Reach Education)
Diane Joyner
Professor of Mathematics, 634 Henderson Street,
    Mount Olive, NC 28365
(919) 658-2502
Ref: 30747.002949
PF: Minority, At-Risk

▶ **Mount St. Mary's College**   [16]
STEP (Strides Toward Educational Proficiency)
Sr. J. Adele Edwards
Director, 10 Chester Place, Los Angeles, CA
    90049
(213) 746-0450
Ref: 21188.001243
PF: Minority, At-Risk

Mt. San Antonio College
Articulation Model for Vocational Education
Elizabeth L. Cipres
Director, School and College Relations, 1100 N. Grand Avenue, Walnut, CA 91789
(909) 594-5611
Ref: 21106.001245
PF: Tech-Prep/2+2

▶ **Mt. San Antonio College**   [16]
Links: Women in Math, Science & Technology
Kay Ragan
Dean, Student Services, 1100 N. Grand Avenue, Walnut, CA 91789-1397
(909) 594-5611
Ref: 31516.001245
PF: Minority, At-Risk

▶ **Murray State University**   [166]
West Kentucky Educational Cooperative
Jan Weaver
Dean, College of Education, Murray, KY 42071
(502) 762-3817
Ref: 30847.001977
PF: Professional Development, Inservice

▶ **Muskegon Community College**   [258]
Tech-Prep
Carol Maloney
Tech Prep Coordinator, 221 S. Quonterline Road, Muskegon, MI 49442
(616) 777-0418
Ref: 31033.002297
PF: Tech-Prep/2+2

Muskingum College
Foreign Language in the Elementary School
Helene Lowe-Dupas
Asst. Professor of French, New Concord, OH 43762
(614) 826-8252
helenel@muskingum.edu
Ref: 20796.003084
PF: Enrichment, Gifted

Muskingum College
Muskingum College Poetry Contests
William J. Schultz
Assoc. Professor of English, New Concord, OH 43762
(614) 826-8266
Ref: 21017.003084
PF: Enrichment, Gifted

Muskingum College
Standards in Mathematics: For the Present and the Future
James L. Smith
Emeritus Professor, New Concord, OH 43762
(614) 826-8306
Ref: 20415.003084
PF: Professional Development, Inservice

N

Nassau Community College
Liberty Partnership
Marilyn Faucette
Project Director, 1 Education Drive, Garden City, NY 11530
(516)572-7354
Ref: 30350.002873
PF: Minority, At-Risk, Retention, Continuing Education

▶ **Naugatuck Valley Community-Technical College**   [251]
Tech Prep (2+2) Program
Ann Palmieri
Coordinator, 750 Chase Parkway, Waterbury, CT 06708
(203) 575-8158
Ref: 20468.001423
PF: Tech-Prep/2+2

▶ **Nazareth College of Rochester**   [51]
D.D. Eisenhower Grant
Alean Rush
Director of Graduate Grant Programs, 4245 East Avenue, Rochester, NY 14618-3790
(716) 586-2525 x572
Ref: 30301.002779
PF: Minority, At-Risk

▶ **Nazareth College of Rochester**   [217]
Teacher Opportunity Corps
Alean Rush
Director of Graduate Grant Programs, 4245 East Avenue, Rochester, NY 14618-3790
(716) 586-2525 x572
Ref: 30300.002779
PF: Recruit, Preservice, Certification

▶ **Nebraska Wesleyan University**   [296]
Ventures in Partnership (VIP)
Rick Artman
Vice President for Student Affairs, 5000 St. Paul Avenue, Lincoln, NE 68504-2796
(402) 465-2153
rba@nebrwesleyan.edu
Ref: 31262.002555
PF: School-College-Business Partnerships

▶ **Neosho County Community College**   [255]
Tech Prep Program
Gordon Dyson
Asst. Vice President, Technical and Industrial Education, 1000 S. Allen, Chanute, KS 66720
(316) 431-2820
Ref: 31247.001936
PF: Tech-Prep/2+2

▶ **New England Network of Academic Alliances**   [279]
New England Network of Academic Alliances in Foreign Languages and Literatures
Mary Ellen Kiddle
Assoc. Professor of Spanish, Boston College, Chestnut Hill, MA 02167
(617) 552-3715
Ref: 30028.U00003
PF: Umbrella Programs

▶ **New Hampshire College**   [44]
Partnership for the 21st Century
Jacqueline Ribaudo
Director, Planning and Marketing, 2500 N. River Road, Manchester, NH 03106
(603) 645-9635
Ref: 30342.002580
PF: Minority, At-Risk

▶ **New Jersey Institute of Technology**   [45]
The Center for Pre-College Programs
Howard Kimmel
Assoc. Vice President for Academic Affairs, University Heights, Newark, NJ 07102
(201) 596-3550
kimmel@admin.njit.edu
Ref: 20980.002621
PF: Minority, At-Risk

New Mexico State University–Main Campus
Child Development Associate (CDA) Training
    Program
Sharon Wooden
College of Education, Curriculum and Instruction,
    Las Cruces, NM 88003
Ref: 31870.002657
PF: Recruit, Preservice, Certification

▶ **New Mexico State University–Main
Campus**   [101]
Citizen Bee
Greg Butler
Government Department, Las Cruces, NM 88003
Ref: 31866.002657
PF: Enrichment, Gifted

▶ **New Mexico State University–Main
Campus**   [216]
Dove Learning Center
Michael A. Morehead
Assoc. Dean, College of Education, Las Cruces,
    NM 88003
(505) 646-2498
Ref: 31869.002657
PF: Recruit, Preservice, Certification

New Mexico State University–Main Campus
Geographical Alliance
Robert J. Czerniak
Geography Department, Las Cruces, NM 88003
Ref: 31865.002657
PF: Professional Development, Inservice

▶ **New Mexico State University–Main
Campus**   [102]
High School Chemical Olympics
Dale Alexander
Chemistry and Biochemistry Department, Las
    Cruces, NM 88003
Ref: 31864.002657
PF: Enrichment, Gifted

▶ **New Mexico State University–Main
Campus**   [126]
Hispanic Student Mentorship Program
Josef Lapid
International Relations Department, Las Cruces,
    NM 88003
Ref: 31867.002657
PF: Tutoring, Counseling

▶ **New Mexico State University–Main
Campus**   [179]
Las Cruces Public Schools Bilingual Multicultural
    Teacher Education Institute
Herman S. Garcia
Director, Las Cruces, NM 88003
Ref: 31871.002657
PF: Professional Development, Inservice

▶ **New Mexico State University–Main
Campus**   [101]
Master Environmentalist Program
Jim Knight
Fishery and Wildlife Science, Las Cruces, NM
    88003
Ref: 31863.002657
PF: Enrichment, Gifted

New Mexico State University–Main Campus
MATHCOUNTS
Eldon Steelman
Assoc. Dean, Engineering College, Las Cruces,
    NM 88003
Ref: 31874.002657
PF: Enrichment, Gifted

New Mexico State University–Main Campus
Music Programs
William Clark
Music Department, Las Cruces, NM 88003
Ref: 31868.002657
PF: Enrichment, Gifted

▶ **New Mexico State University–Main
Campus**   [216]
New/Beginning Teacher Program (Agriculture
    Education)
Miley Gonzales
Agriculture and Home Economics Department,
    Las Cruces, NM 88003
Ref: 31862.002657
PF: Recruit, Preservice, Certification

▶ **New Mexico State University–Main
Campus**   [137]
New Pathways
Rod Merta
Counseling and Educational Psychology
    Department, Las Cruces, NM 88003
Ref: 31872.002657
PF: Career, Internships, Apprenticeships

New Mexico State University–Main Campus
Public School Enrichment Program
Edward Hensel
Mechanical Engineering, Las Cruces, NM 80033
Ref: 31876.002657
PF: Enrichment, Gifted

New Mexico State University–Main Campus
Special Education for the Economically
    Disadvantaged (SEED)
Stuart Munson-McGee
Chemical Engineering, Las Cruces, NM 80033
Ref: 31878.002657
PF: Career, Internships, Apprenticeships

▶ **New Mexico State University–Main
Campus**   [101]
Summer Sports Camp/Sport Education Institute
Department of Physical Education, Recreation
    and Dance, Las Cruces, NM 88003
Ref: 31873.002657
PF: Enrichment, Gifted

▶ **New Mexico State University–Main
Campus**   [179]
Systemic Initiative for Math and Science
    Education (SIMSE)
Elaine Hampton
College of Education, Las Cruces, NM 88003
Ref: 31877.002657
PF: Professional Development, Inservice

▶ **New Mexico State University–Main
Campus**   [239]
TV Earth
Barbara Powell
Engineering Technology, Las Cruces, NM 88003
Ref: 31875.002657
PF: Curriculum Development

**New York Institute of Technology, Main
    Campus-Old Westbury**
Strengthening Preparation of Future Teachers
Helen Greene
Dean, School of Education and Professional
    Services, Room B-17, Tower House, Old
    Westbury, NY 11568
(516) 686-7582
Ref: 30217.004804
PF: Recruit, Preservice, Certification

▶ **Newberry College**   [142]
Higher Education Awareness Program (HEAP)
Sandra P. Locan
Acting Vice President for Academic Affairs,
    Newberry, SC 29108
(803) 276-5010
Ref: 30759.003440
PF: Career, Internships, Apprenticeships

North Adams State College
Consortium for the Improvement of Math &
    Science Teaching
Augusta Leibowitz
Director, Box 9078, North Adams, MA 01247
(413) 664-4511
Ref: 20201.002187
PF: Professional Development, Inservice

▶ **North Arkansas Community Technical College**   [250]
North Arkansas Tech Prep Consortium
Rick Hinterthuer
Director, Pioneer Ridge, Harrison, AR 72601
(501) 743-6366
rhinter@comp.uark.edu
Ref: 31277.012261
PF: Tech-Prep/2+2

▶ **North Carolina Central University**   [297]
Central Carolina Consortium
Lawrence C. Walker
Executive Director, P.O. Box 19617, Durham, NC 27707
(919) 560-3222
Ref: 30727.002950
PF: School-College-Business Partnerships

North Carolina State University
Academic Enrichment Opportunities
George R. Dixon
Director of Admissions, Box 7103, Raleigh, NC 27695-7103
(919) 515-2434
Ref: 20805.002972
PF: College Courses for Students

North Carolina State University
Preparing School-Based Teacher Educators: A Collaborative Model
Alan J. Reiman
Clinical Asst. Professor, Department of Curriculum and Instruction, Box 7801, Raleigh, NC 27695-7801
(919) 515-1785
alan@poe.coe.ncsu.edu
Ref: 31624.002972
PF: Professional Development, Inservice

North Carolina State University
The Wake County Foreign Language Alliance
Susan Navey-Davis
Lecturer, Box 8106, Raleigh, NC 27695-8106
(919) 515-2475
navey-davis@social.chass.ncsu.edu
Ref: 21141.002972
PF: Professional Development, Inservice

North Harris Montgomery Community College District
Admissions Counseling
John Pickelman
Chancellor, 250 N. Sam Houston Parkway, Houston, TX 77060
(713) 591-3515
Ref: 31814.011145
PF: Tutoring, Counseling

North Harris Montgomery Community College District [
Business Professionals of America Contest
John Pickelman
Chancellor, 250 N. Sam Houston Parkway, Houston, TX 77060
(713) 591-3515
Ref: 31817.011145
PF: Enrichment, Gifted

▶ **North Harris Montgomery Community College District**   [276]
Montgomery College Partnerships
John Pickelman
Chancellor, 250 N. Sam Houston Parkway, Houston, TX 77060
(713) 591-3515
Ref: 31818.011145
PF: City/Regional Compacts

▶ **North Harris Montgomery Community College District**   [267]
NHCC/SISD Automotive Technology Program
Gail C. Phillips
Division Head, Applied Technology, 2700 W.W. Thorne Drive, Houston, TX 77073
(713) 443-5671
Ref: 20834.011145
PF: Tech-Prep/2+2

North Harris Montgomery Community College District
Tomball Partnership
John Pickelman
Chancellor, 250 N. Sam Houston Parkway, Houston, TX 77060
(713) 591-3515
Ref: 31815.011145
PF: Enrichment, Gifted

▶ **North Harris Montgomery Community College District**   [267]
Tech Prep
John Pickelman
Chancellor, 250 N. Sam Houston Parkway, Houston, TX 77060
(713) 591-3515
Ref: 31816.011145
PF: Tech-Prep/2+2

North Hennepin Community College
Concurrent Enrollment Program
Don McGuire
Assoc. Dean, 7411 85th Avenue N, Brooklyn Park, MN 55445
(612) 424-0885
Ref: 31123.002370
PF: College Courses for Students

North Hennepin Community College
Crestview-NIFCC Mentoring Program
John W. Dawson
Director, Cultural Diversity, 7411 85th Avenue N, Brooklyn Park, MN 55445
(612) 424-0939
Ref: 31687.002370
PF: Minority, At-Risk

North Hennepin Community College
Northwest Community Law Enforcement Project
John W. Dawson
Director for Cultural Diversity, 7411 85th Avenue N, Brooklyn Park, MN 55445
(612) 424-0939
Ref: 31125.002370
PF: Minority, At-Risk

▶ **North Hennepin Community College**   [258]
Tech-Prep Consortium
William Ardrum
Assoc. Dean of Instruction, 7411 85th Avenue N, Brooklyn Park, MN 55445
(612) 424-0752
Ref: 31124.002370
PF: Tech-Prep/2+2

North Hennepin Community College
Wright County Center of North Hennepin Community College
Connie Wahlstrom
Director, 214 N.E. 1st Avenue, Buffalo, MN 55313
(612) 682-5304
Ref: 31122.002370
PF: College Courses for Students

North Iowa Area Community College
Tech Prep
Michael C. Morrison
Vice President, Mason City, IA 50401
(515) 421-2410
Ref: 31038.001877
PF: Tech-Prep/2+2

Northeast Mississippi Community College
Tech Prep
Nelson Wall
Tech Prep Coordinator, Booneville, MS 38829
(601) 728-7751
Ref: 30700.002426
PF: Tech-Prep/2+2

▶ **Northeast Missouri State College**   [215]
Summer School
David E. Bethel
Assoc. Vice President for Academic Affairs, 203
    McClain Hall, Kirksville, MO 63501
(816) 785-5406
Ref: 31225.002495
PF: Recruit, Preservice, Certification

▶ **Northeast Texas Community College**   [63]
Communities In Schools/PASS (Positive
    Alternatives for SuccesS)
Paul K. Lane
Project Director, P.O. Box 1307, Mt. Pleasant, TX
    75455
(903) 572-1911
Ref: 20802.023154
PF: Minority, At-Risk

Northeast Texas Community College
Northeast Texas Communities In Schools
Judy G. Taylor
Dean of Adult and Developmental Education, P.O.
    Box 1307, Mt. Pleasant, TX 75456-1307
(903) 572-1911
Ref: 31316.023154
PF: Minority, At-Risk

▶ **Northeast Texas Community
College**   [242]
Quality Work Force Planning
Walter York
Director, P.O. Box 1307, Mt. Pleasant, TX
    75456-1307
(903) 572-1911
Ref: 20548.023154
PF: Curriculum Development

▶ **Northeastern Illinois University**   [122]
Bridges to the Future
Richard Rutschman
Director, Chicago Teachers' Center, 770 N.
    Halsted, Chicago, IL 60622
(312) 733-7330
Ref: 31173.001693
PF: Tutoring, Counseling

Northeastern Illinois University
Clustered Student Teaching Project
Janet T. Bercik
Coordinator, Clinical Experience, 5500 N. St.
    Louis Avenue, Chicago, IL 60625
(312) 583-4050
Ref: 31180.001693
PF: Recruit, Preservice, Certification

▶ **Northeastern Illinois University**   [272]
CUBE (Coalition of Universities and Businesses
    for Education)
Michael E. Carl
Dean, College of Education, 5500 N. St. Louis,
    Chicago, IL 60625
(312) 794-2813
Ref: 31726.001693
PF: City/Regional Compacts

▶ **Northeastern Illinois University**   [162]
Cultural Linguistic Approach/Follow Through
    Project
Naomi Millender
Project Director, Chicago Teachers' Center, 770
    N. Halsted Street, Chicago, IL 60622
(312) 733-7330
Ref: 31170.001693
PF: Professional Development, Inservice

▶ **Northeastern Illinois University**   [30]
Dropout Prevention Program/Chicago Teachers'
    Center
Alejandro Perez
Program Director, 770 N. Halsted, Room 420,
    Chicago, IL 60622
(312) 733-7330
Ref: 31174.001693
PF: Minority, At-Risk

Northeastern Illinois University
Educational Talent Search Program
Maxine Anderson-Moffett
Program Director, 770 N. Halsted Street, Fourth
    Floor, Chicago, IL 60625-4699
(312) 733-7330
Ref: 31164.001693
PF: Minority, At-Risk

▶ **Northeastern Illinois University**   [31]
Future Teachers of Chicago
Joan Macala
Co-Director, Chicago Teachers' Center, 770 N.
    Halsted, Suite 420, Chicago, IL 60622
(312) 733-7330
Ref: 31179.001693
PF: Minority, At-Risk

Northeastern Illinois University
Glen Grove/NEIU Field Experience
Janet T. Bercik
Coordinator, Clinical Experience, 5500 N. St.
    Louis Avenue, Chicago, IL 60625
(312) 583-4050
Ref: 31181.001693
PF: Recruit, Preservice, Certification

Northeastern Illinois University
Health, Physical Education, Recreation, and
    Athletics
Tony Schimpf
Chairperson, 5500 N. St. Louis, Chicago, IL
    60625
(312) 583-4050
Ref: 31700.001693
PF: Recruit, Preservice, Certification

Northeastern Illinois University
Interactive Science, Mathematics & Technology
Jerry B. Olson
Director, Chicago Teachers' Center, 770 N.
    Halsted Street, Chicago, IL 60625-4699
(312) 733-7330
Ref: 31730.001693
PF: Professional Development, Inservice

▶ **Northeastern Illinois University**   [31]
Neighborhood Arts Partnership
Jackie Murphy
Director, Chicago Teachers' Center, 770 N.
    Halsted, Chicago, IL 60622
(312) 733-7330
Ref: 31172.001693
PF: Minority, At-Risk

▶ **Northeastern Illinois University**   [162]
Professional Development Program
Wendy M. Stack
Director, 770 N. Halsted, Suite 420, Chicago, IL
    60622
(312) 733-7330
uwstack@uxa.ecn.bgu.edu
Ref: 31175.001693
PF: Professional Development, Inservice

Northeastern Illinois University
Project Co-Lead
Jean Baxter
Director, 5500 N. St. Louis, Chicago, IL
    60625-4699
(312) 794-2786
Ref: 31165.001693
PF: Professional Development, Inservice

Northeastern Illinois University
Project Upward Bound
Deon Brown
Director, 770 N. Halsted, Chicago, IL 60622
(312) 733-7330
Ref: 31176.001693
PF: Minority, At-Risk

▶ **Northeastern Illinois University**   [212]
Preparing Bilingual Teacher Aides as Special
    Educators: A Field-Based Project
Rita Brusca
Assoc. Professor, 5500 N. St. Louis, Chicago, IL
    60625
(312) 794-2823
Ref: 31168.001693
PF: Recruit, Preservice, Certification

Northeastern Illinois University
Reading Department Partnerships
Joyce Jennings
Chairperson, 5500 N. St. Louis, Chicago, IL
    60625
(312) 583-4050
Ref: 31167.001693
PF: Professional Development, Inservice

▶ **Northeastern Illinois University**   [212]
RAISE (Russian/American Initiative to Strengthen
    Education)
Salme H. Steinberg
Provost, 5500 N. St. Louis, Chicago, IL 60625
(312) 794-6675
Ref: 31725.001693
PF: Recruit, Preservice, Certification

Northeastern Illinois University
Scientific Literacy Partnership for the Urban
    Classroom
Jerry B. Olson
Director, Chicago Teachers' Center, 770 N.
    Halsted Street, Chicago, IL 60625-4699
(312) 733-7330
Ref: 31731.001693
PF: Professional Development, Inservice

Northeastern Illinois University
Summer Geography Institute Program
Barbara Winston
Professor, 5500 N. St. Louis, Chicago, IL 60625
(312) 794-2609
Ref: 31169.001693
PF: Professional Development, Inservice

▶ **Northeastern Illinois University**   [212]
Teachers for Chicago
Patricia Schutt
Chairperson, 5500 N. St. Louis, Chicago, IL
    60625
(312) 583-4050
upschutt@uxa.ecn.bgu.edu.
Ref: 31166.001693
PF: Recruit, Preservice, Certification

▶ **Northeastern Illinois University**   [31]
University Scholars Program
Evelyn Gray
Project Director, 770 N. Halsted Street, Suite 420,
    Chicago, IL 60622-5972
(312) 733-7330
Ref: 31171.001693
PF: Minority, At-Risk

Northeastern Illinois University
Urban Education Partnership
Anne Schultz
Program Director, 770 N. Halsted, Chicago, IL
    60622
(312) 733-7330
Ref: 31178.001693
PF: Minority, At-Risk

▶ **Northeastern Illinois University**   [31]
Writing From the Source
Anne Schultz
Program Director, 770 N. Halsted, Chicago, IL
    60622
(312) 733-7330
Ref: 31177.001693
PF: Minority, At-Risk

Northeastern University
History-Social Studies School-College Alliance
Gerald Herman
Asst. Professor, History Department, 249 Meserve
    Hall, Boston, MA 02115
(617) 373-2660
Ref: 30016.002199
PF: Professional Development, Inservice

▶ **Northern Arizona University**   [277]
Arizona Small and Rural School Association
Robert Fallows
Assoc. Professor, Educational Leadership, P.O.
    Box 5774, Flagstaff, AZ 86011
(602) 523-7108
fallows@nauvax.ucc.nau.edu
Ref: 31460.001082
PF: Regional Articulation

▶ **Northern Arizona University**   [207]
DeWitt-Wallace/NAU Peace Corps Fellows
    Program
Sam Minner
Professor, P.O. Box 5774, Flagstaff, AZ 86001
(602) 523-7114
Ref: 31454.001082
PF: Recruit, Preservice, Certification

▶ **Northern Arizona University**   [148]
Educational Personnel Training Program
    (USDOE, Title VII)
Gina P. Cantoni
Director, Center for Native Education & Cultural
    Diversity, P.O. Box 5774, Flagstaff, AZ 86011
(602) 523-4842
Ref: 31461.001082
PF: Professional Development, Inservice

▶ **Northern Arizona University**   [148]
EMPIRE (Exemplary Multicultural Practices in
    Rural Education) Partnership Project
Linda Shadiow
Professor, Educational Foundations, P.O. Box
    5774, Flagstaff, AZ 86011
(602) 523-7121
Ref: 31459.001082
PF: Professional Development, Inservice

Northern Arizona University
Flagstaff Elementary Block Program
Peggy Vervelde
Professor, Elementary Education, P.O. Box 5774,
    Flagstaff, AZ 86001
(602) 523-2198
Ref: 31463.001082
PF: Recruit, Preservice, Certification

Northern Arizona University
Flagstaff Professional Preparation Partnership
Peggy Vervelde
Professor, Elementary Education, P.O. Box 5774,
    Flagstaff, AZ 86011
(602) 523-2198
Ref: 31464.001082
PF: Recruit, Preservice, Certification

Key: "▶" denotes those partnerships abstracted in Parts 1-5; the corresponding page numbers are given in brackets. "PF:" denotes the partnership's "primary focus." "Ref:" denotes the partnership's assigned reference number in the National School-College Partnership Database (see Appendix B).

▶ **Northern Arizona University**   [207]
Ford Foundation/Navajo Nation Teacher Training
   Program
Gloria Johns
Project Director, P.O. Box 5774, Flagstaff, AZ
   86001
(602) 523-1003
Ref: 31462.001082
PF: Recruit, Preservice, Certification

Northern Arizona University
Integrating the Humanities in Spanish in Arizona
   Schools K-8
Manuel C. Rodriguez
NEH Project Co-Director, P.O. Box 5774,
   Flagstaff, AZ 86011
(602) 523-5857
Ref: 31458.001082
PF: Curriculum Development

Northern Arizona University
Navajo Teacher Preparation Partnership
Ray Vervelde
Assoc. Executive Director, Center for Excellence
   in Education, Flagstaff, AZ 86001
(602) 523-2641
Ref: 31455.001082
PF: Recruit, Preservice, Certification

Northern Arizona University
Program for Learning Competent Teaching
Ward Cockram
P.O. Box 5774, Flagstaff, AZ 86011
(602) 523-7142
Ref: 21064.001082
PF: Recruit, Preservice, Certification

▶ **Northern Arizona University**   [12]
Project ASSIST, Educational Psychology, Center
   for Excellence in Education
William E. Martin, Jr.
Chair and Assoc. Professor, Educational
   Psychology, P.O. Box 5774, Flagstaff, AZ
   86011
(602) 523-6757
bmartin@nauvax.ucc.nau.edu
Ref: 31465.001082
PF: Minority, At-Risk

Northern Arizona University
Rural Multicultural Training Collaborative
Patricia Peterson
Assoc. Professor, Special Education, P.O. Box
   5774, Flagstaff, AZ 86011
(602) 523-4007
Ref: 31456.001082
PF: Professional Development, Inservice

Northern Arizona University
Rural Special Education Project
Susan A. Miller
Assoc. Professor and Chair, Special Education
   Department, P.O. Box 5774, Flagstaff, AZ
   86001
(602) 523-3221
sam@nauvax.ucc.nau.edu
Ref: 31466.001082
PF: Recruit, Preservice, Certification

Northern Arizona University
Sedona Partnership Program
Emilie Rodger
Asst. Professor, P.O. Box 5774, Flagstaff, AZ
   86001
(602) 523-5863
Ref: 31453.001082
PF: Recruit, Preservice, Certification

▶ **Northern Arizona University**   [148]
Sedona Professional Preparation Partnership
   Program
Margaret Hatcher
Assoc. Executive Director, Center for Excellence
   in Education, P.O. Box 5774, Flagstaff, AZ
   86011
(602) 523-7101
Ref: 31457.001082
PF: Professional Development, Inservice

Northern Illinois University   [273]
Northern Illinois University/Harlem Clinical
   Schools
Diane Kinder
Undergraduate Coordinator/Special Education,
   Department EPCSE, DeKalb, IL 60115
(815) 753-8465
Ref: 31151.001737
PF: Professional Development, Inservice

Northern Kentucky University
Educational Partners
Tom Isherwood
Dean, College of Professional Studies, Highland
   Heights, KY 41099-6006
(606) 572-5666
isherwood@nkuvak.bitnet
Ref: 31728.009275
PF: Professional Development, Inservice

▶ **Northern Kentucky University**   [273]
Northern Kentucky Cooperative for Educational
   Services
Clifton L. McMahon
Director, Local School Services, Room 100, BEP
   Building, Highland Heights, KY 41076
(606) 572-5632
Ref: 20418.009275
PF: City/Regional Compacts

Northern Michigan University
The Glenn T. Seaborg Center for Teaching and
   Learning Science and Mathematics
Peggy A. House
Director, The Seaborg Center, Marquette, MI
   49855
(906) 227-2002
Ref: 31035.002301
PF: Teacher Education Centers

Northwest Missouri State University
Northwest Missouri State University–Washington
   Middle School Co-Op
Gary Bennerotte
Asst. Professor, 800 University Drive, Brown Hall
   210, Maryville, MO 64468
(816) 562-1768
Ref: 31239.002496
PF: City/Regional Compacts

▶ **Northwestern University**   [94]
Center For Talent Development
Paula Olszewski-Kubilius
Acting Director, 617 Dartmouth Place, Evanston,
   IL 60208
(708) 491-3728
pkubius@casbah.acns.nwu.edu
Ref: 31153.001739
PF: Enrichment, Gifted

▶ **Northwestern University**   [94]
Midwest Talent Search/Midwest Talent Search for
   Young Students
Paula Olszewski-Kubilius
Acting Director, 617 Dartmouth Place, Evanston,
   IL 60208-4175
(708) 491-3782
pkubius@casbah.acns.nwu.edu
Ref: 31152.001739
PF: Enrichment, Gifted

Norwich University
Norwich-Barre Partnership
James Catone
Professor of Education, Northfield, VT 05663
(802) 485-2000
Ref: 30140.003692
PF: Professional Development, Inservice

Notre Dame College
Cleveland Public Schools Partnership Program for
   Excellence in Education
Sr. M. Lien Novak, S.N.P.
Chair, Education Department, 4545 College Road,
   South Euclid, OH 44121
(216) 381-1680
Ref: 30862.003085
PF: School-College-Business Partnerships

▶ **Nova University** [159]
University Liaison Project
Richard Goldman
Dean, 3301 College Avenue, Fischler Center for
    the Advancement of Education, Fort
    Lauderdale, FL 33314
(305) 475-7458
Ref: 30653.001509
PF: Professional Development, Inservice

O

Oakland Community College
Oakland County Tech Prep Consortium
David Doidge
Academic Dean, 27055 Orchard Lake Road,
    Farmington Hills, MI 48334
(810) 471-7707
dadoidge@occ.bitnet
Ref: 31018.008760
PF: Tech-Prep/2+2

Oakland University
Brandon-Oxford Professional Development
    School
James Clatworthy
Assoc. Dean, School of Education and Human
    Services, Rochester, MI 48309-4401
(810) 370-3052
Ref: 31009.002307
PF: School-College-Business Partnerships

▶ **Oakland University** [172]
K.B. White Professional Development School
Sandra Alber
Asst. Professor of Education, School of Education
    and Human Services, Rochester, MI
    48309-4401
(810) 370-3080
Ref: 31010.002307
PF: Professional Development, Inservice

Oakland University
Longfellow Professional Development School
Angie Melhado
Coordinator, Longfellow Elementary School, 31 N.
    Astor Street, Pontiac, MI 48342
(810) 253-0370
Ref: 31012.002307
PF: School-College-Business Partnerships

Oakland University
Meadow Brook Leadership Academy
Gerald J. Pine
Dean, School of Education and Human Services,
    Rochester, MI 48309-4401
(810) 370-3050
Ref: 20406.002307
PF: Professional Development, Inservice

▶ **Oakland University** [172]
National Career Development Training Institute
Howard H. Splete
Professor of Education, 522 O'Dowd Hall,
    Rochester, MI 48309-4401
(810) 370-4173
Ref: 31014.002307
PF: Professional Development, Inservice

Oakland University
Oakland Counselor Academy
Howard H. Splete
Professor of Education, School of Education and
    Human Services, 522 O'Dowd Hall, Rochester,
    MI 48309-4401
(810) 370-4173
Ref: 20408.002307
PF: Professional Development, Inservice

Oakland University
Oakland-Macomb Writing Project
Wilma Garcia
Professor of Rhetoric, College of Arts and
    Sciences, Rochester, MI 48309-4401
(810) 370-4118
Ref: 31015.002307
PF: Professional Development, Inservice

▶ **Oakland University** [172]
Oakland University Early Childhood Collaborative
Donald M. Miller
Co-Director, Institute for Action Research and
    Professional Development, Rochester, MI
    48309-4401
(810) 370-4233
Ref: 31013.002307
PF: Professional Development, Inservice

Oakland University
Pontiac Central Professional Development School
James Clatworthy
Assoc. Dean, School of Education and Human
    Services, Rochester, MI 48309-4401
(810) 370-3052
Ref: 31011.002307
PF: School-College-Business Partnerships

▶ **Oakland University** [41]
Preprimary Impaired Program
Gerald G. Freeman
Professor of Education, School of Education and
    Human Services, Rochester, MI 48309-4401
(810) 370-4164
Ref: 31017.002307
PF: Minority, At-Risk

Oakland University
Reading Recovery
Robert Schwartz
Professor of Education, School of Education and
    Human Services, Rochester, MI 48309-4401
(810) 370-3075
Ref: 31016.002307
PF: Professional Development, Inservice

Oakton Community College
Accounting
Paul Grosso
Professor of Accounting, 1600 E. Golf Road, Des
    Plaines, IL 60016
(708) 635-1979
Ref: 31150.009896
PF: Career, Internships, Apprenticeships

Oakton Community College
Drafting
Les Jacobs
Professor of Architecture, 1600 E. Golf Road, Des
    Plaines, IL 60016
(708) 635-1851
Ref: 31149.009896
PF: Career, Internships, Apprenticeships

Oakwood College
Oakwood College-Academy Partnership
John Blake
Chairman, Math and Computer Science
    Department, Huntsville, AL 35896
(205) 726-7266
Ref: 30679.001033
PF: College Courses for Students

▶ **Occidental College** [151]
Keck Foundation Curriculum Project
Don Goldberg
Assoc. Professor of Mathematics, Los Angeles,
    CA 90041
(213) 259-2524
don@oxy.edu
Ref: 31641.001249
PF: Professional Development, Inservice

▶ **Occidental College** [87]
OPTIMO
Don Goldberg
Assoc. Professor of Mathematics, Los Angeles,
    CA 90041
(213) 259-2524
don@oxy.edu
Ref: 31640.001249
PF: Enrichment, Gifted

▶ **Occidental College** [151]
TOPS (Teachers + Occidental = Partnership in
    Science)
April Mazzeo
Program Coordinator, 1600 Campus Road, Los
    Angeles, CA 90041
(213) 259-2892
Ref: 31642.001249
PF: Professional Development, Inservice

Ohio Northern University
Business & Education Together Council
    Internship Program
Terry L. Maris
Dean, College of Business Administration, Ada,
    OH 45810
(419) 772-2070
t-maris@onu.edu
Ref: 30938.003089
PF: Career, Internships, Apprenticeships

Ohio Northern University
Collaboration Between Ohio Northern University
    and Hardin County Schools
Mary Haynes
Director of Teacher Education, Ada, OH 45810
(419) 772-2122
Ref: 30937.003089
PF: City/Regional Compacts

▶ **Ohio Northern University** [141]
Jets Teams Competition
Robert Ward
Assoc. Professor, Civil Engineering Department,
    Ada, OH 45810
(419) 772-2399
bward@newton.onu.edu
Ref: 30932.003089
PF: Career, Internships, Apprenticeships

Ohio Northern University
Minority Recruitment Project
Patricia Freeman
Asst. Professor, Ada, OH 45810
(419) 772-2129
Ref: 30936.003089
PF: Recruit, Preservice, Certification

Ohio Northern University
Ohio Northern Foreign Language Alliance
Patricia S. Dickson
Assoc. Professor of French, 2035 Huntington
    Drive, Lima, OH 45806
(419) 645-4225
Ref: 30933.003089
PF: Professional Development, Inservice

Ohio Northern University
Secondary School English Teachers Colloquium
Thomas Baules
Professor of English, Ada, OH 45810
(419) 722-2102
Ref: 30935.003089
PF: Professional Development, Inservice

▶ **Ohio Northern University** [106]
Street Law
Sherry Young
Director and Assoc. Professor of Law, Ada, OH
    45810
(419) 772-2217
syoung@crassus.onu.edu
Ref: 30934.003089
PF: Enrichment, Gifted

The Ohio State University–Main Campus
Biological and Earth Systems Education
    Professional Development Site
Victor J. Mayer
Professor, 1945 N. High Street, Columbus, OH
    43210
(614) 392-7888
vmayer@magnus.acs.ohio-state.edu
Ref: 31796.006883
PF: Recruit, Preservice, Certification

The Ohio State University–Main Campus
Educators for Collaborative Change
Marilyn Johnston
PDS Co-Coordinator, 1945 N. High Street, 203
    Arps Hall, Columbus, OH 43201-1172
(614) 292-8020
mjohnsto@magnus.acs.ohio-state.edu
Ref: 31810.006883
PF: Teacher Education Centers

▶ **The Ohio State University–Main
Campus** [241]
ESEP (Earth Systems Education Program)
Victor J. Mayer
Professor, 1945 N. High Street, Columbus, OH
    43210
(614) 292-7888
vmayer@magnus.acs.ohio-state.edu
Ref: 31797.006883
PF: Curriculum Development

▶ **The Ohio State University–Main
Campus** [189]
Professional Development School (PDS) Network
    in Social Studies and Global Education
Merry Merryfull
Assoc. Professor, 249 N. High Street, Columbus,
    OH 43210
(614) 292-5341
mmerryfu@magnus.acs.ohio-state.edu
Ref: 31799.006883
PF: Professional Development, Inservice

The Ohio State University–Main Campus
Professional Development Schools (PDS) &
    Professional Partnership Schools
George E. Newell
Assoc. Professor, 1945 N. High Street, 249 Arps
    Hall, Columbus, OH 43210
(614) 292-1844
gnewell@magnus.acs.ohio-state.edu
Ref: 31798.006883
PF: Professional Development, Inservice

▶ **The Ohio State University–Main
Campus** [280]
Project Learn: Closing the Gap
Barbara S. Thomson
Assoc. Professor of Science Education, 1945 N.
    High Street, 249 Arps Hall, Columbus, OH
    43210
(614) 292-5381
Ref: 31800.006883
PF: Regional Articulation

▶ **The Ohio State University–Main
Campus** [190]
Reynoldsburg Professional Development Site
Anna O. Soter
Assoc. Professor, 1945 N. High Street, 249 Arps
    Hall, Columbus, OH 43210
(614) 292-5381
asoter@magnus.acs.ohio-state.edu
Ref: 31845.006883
PF: Professional Development, Inservice

The Ohio State University–Main Campus
The Urban Professional Partnership School
Theresa Rogers
Coordinator, College of Education, 1945 N. High
    Street, 253 Arps Hall, Columbus, OH 43210
(614) 292-8324
throgers@magnus.acs.ohio-state.edu
Ref: 31846.006883
PF: Recruit, Preservice, Certification

The Ohio State University–Mansfield Campus
Local Schools and University Professional
  Partnership
Lynn G. Johnson
Assoc. Professor, 1680 University Drive,
  Mansfield, OH 44906
(419) 755-4271
Ref: 30915.003093
PF: School-College-Business Partnerships

▶ **The Ohio State University–Mansfield
Campus**   [56]
The Richland County Collaborative Integrated
  Preschool
Lynn G. Johnson
Assoc. Professor, 1680 University Drive,
  Mansfield, OH 44906
(419) 755-4271
Ref: 30916.003093
PF: Minority, At-Risk

Ohio University
Ohio Valley Foreign Language Alliance
Lois Vines
Professor of French, Department of Modern
  Languages, Ellis Hall, Athens, OH 45701
(614) 593-2765
Ref: 21268.003100
PF: Professional Development, Inservice

Oklahoma Baptist University
North Rock Creek School Intersession
Joseph D. Brown
Chair, Division of Teacher Education, Box 61771,
  Shawnee, OK 74801
(405) 878-2244
Ref: 31294.003164
PF: Recruit, Preservice, Certification

**Oklahoma Christian University of Science &
  Arts**
Oklahoma District V-National History Day
John T. Maple
Professor of History, P.O. Box 11000, Oklahoma
  City, OK 73136-1100
(405) 425-5456
Ref: 31282.003165
PF: Enrichment, Gifted

Oklahoma City Community College
Applications in Mathematics for High Schools in
  Oklahoma (AIM-HI Oklahoma)
Ann Ackerman
Dean of Science and Mathematics, 777 S. May
  Avenue, Oklahoma City, OK 73159
(405) 682-7508
Ref: 31283.010391
PF: Enrichment, Gifted

▶ **Oklahoma State University**   [241]
Early Placement Evaluation in Mathematics
John Wolfe
Professor of Mathematics, Stillwater, OK 74078
(405) 744-5781
wolfe@math.okstate.edu
Ref: 21031.003170
PF: Curriculum Development

Oklahoma State University
High School Financial Planning Program
Glennis M. Couchman
Family and Consumer Economics Specialist, 336
  HES, Stillwater, OK 74078-0337
(405) 744-6282
Ref: 31285.003170
PF: School-College-Business Partnerships

▶ **Oklahoma State University**   [220]
Educational Alliance
Karen S. Cockrell
Director, 101 Gunderson Hall, Stillwater, OK
  74078-0146
(405) 744-6252
Ref: 31284.003170
PF: Recruit, Preservice, Certification

▶ **Onondaga Community College**   [104]
College for Kids
Barbara Van Siclen
Director, Lifelong Learning, EXCELL, Syracuse,
  NY 13215
(315) 492-6078
Ref: 30247.002875
PF: Enrichment, Gifted

▶ **Onondaga Community College**   [182]
Elementary Science Mentor Network
Nancy Leo
Director, Chemistry Department, Syracuse, NY
  13215
(315) 469-2433
Ref: 30248.002875
PF: Professional Development, Inservice

Onondaga Community College
Health Career Project
Larry Reader
Dean, Health and Community Professions,
  Syracuse, NY 13215
(315) 469-2540
Ref: 20870.002875
PF: Tech-Prep/2+2

▶ **Onondaga Community College**   [104]
Leaders of Tomorrow
Patricia Pirro
Dean, Community Education, EXCELL, Syracuse,
  NY 13215
(315) 469-6090
Ref: 20873.002875
PF: Enrichment, Gifted

Onondaga Community College
Liberty Partnership Program
Carol Cowles
Assistant to the President, Syracuse, NY 13215
(315) 469-8695
Ref: 20871.002875
PF: Minority, At-Risk

Onondaga Community College
Minority Access to the Licensed Professions
Vivian E. Moore
Director, Multicultural Resources and Diversity
  Awareness, Syracuse, NY 13215
(315) 469-2536
Ref: 20876.002875
PF: Minority, At-Risk

Onondaga Community College
Programs at Secondary Schools (PASS)
Nancy C. Speck
Registrar, Syracuse, NY 13215
(315) 469-2350
Ref: 20872.002875
PF: College Courses for Students

Onondaga Community College
Regional Summer School
Patricia Pirro
Dean, Community Education, EXCELL, Syracuse,
  NY 13215
(315) 492-6090
Ref: 30246.002875
PF: Tutoring, Counseling

Onondaga Community College
Tech Prep
Suzy Tankersley
Director, Route 173, Syracuse, NY 13215
(315) 469-2503
Ref: 20901.002875
PF: Tech-Prep/2+2

▶ **Orange Coast College** [151]
California Institute for Career Development
Pat Stanley
Administrative Dean, Career Education, P.O. Box
5005, Costa Mesa, CA 92628-5005
(714) 432-6528
Ref: 31526.001250
PF: Professional Development, Inservice

Orange Coast College
College-To-Career Transition Model for California
Community Colleges
Pat Stanley
Administrative Dean, Career Education, 2701
Fairview Road, Costa Mesa, CA 92626
(714) 432-5628
Ref: 31524.001250
PF: Curriculum Development

Orange Coast College
Cooperative Work Experience Model: Internships
Training Opportunity for Special Populations
Pat Stanley
Administrative Dean, Career Education, 2701
Fairview Road, Costa Mesa, CA 92626
(714) 432-5628
Ref: 31525.001250
PF: School-College-Business Partnerships

Orange County Community College
Gender Equity Program
Lynne Sheren
Gender Equity Coordinator, 115 South Street,
Middletown, NY 10940
(914) 341-4585
Ref: 30346.002876
PF: Career, Internships, Apprenticeships

Orange County Community College
High School/College Partnership
James Tarvin
Assoc. Dean for Curriculum, 115 South Street,
Middletown, NY 10940
(914) 341-4590
Ref: 30349.002876
PF: College Courses for Students

Orange County Community College
Jointly Registered Teacher Education Program
Barbara Greenwald
Teacher Education Coordinator, 115 South Street,
Middletown, NY 10940
(914) 341-4007
Ref: 30347.002876
PF: Recruit, Preservice, Certification

Orange County Community College
Tech Prep
John Hoffman
Tech Prep Coordinator, 115 South Street,
Middletown, NY 10940
(914) 341-4712
Ref: 30348.002876
PF: Tech-Prep/2+2

▶ **Orangeburg-Calhoun Technical
College** [281]
Articulation Agreements
June Cole
Department Head, 3250 St. Matthews Road,
Orangeburg, SC 29115
(803) 535-1307
Ref: 30760.006815
PF: Regional Articulation

Oregon Institute of Technology
Advance Credit Program
Jo Anne M. Ogborn
Director, Continuing Education and Summer
Session, 3201 Campus Drive, Klamath Falls,
OR 97601
(503) 885-1340
Ref: 31578.003211
PF: College Courses for Students

Our Lady of the Lake University
CEDE (Center for Educational Development and
Excellence)
Denise Staudt
Chair, Department of Education, 411 S.W. 24th
Street, San Antonio, TX 78207
(210) 434-6711
Ref: 31349.003598
PF: Professional Development, Inservice

Our Lady of the Lake University
San Antonio Education Partnership
Loretta Schlegel
Dean, Enrollment Management, 411 S.W. 24th
Street, San Antonio, TX 78207
(210) 434-6711
Ref: 20829.003598
PF: Minority, At-Risk

Owens Technical College
Northwest Ohio Tech Prep Consortium
Paul V. Unger
Vice President for Academic Affairs, P.O. Box
10000, Toledo, OH 43699
(419) 661-7250
Ref: 30855.005753
PF: Tech-Prep/2+2

P

▶ **Pacific Lutheran University** [130]
Center for Public Service
Oney Crandall
Director, Tacoma, WA 98447
(206) 535-7173
Ref: 20773.003785
PF: Tutoring, Counseling

Pacific Lutheran University
Middle College
Judith W. Carr
Dean, Special Academic Programs/Summer
Sessions, Tacoma, WA 98447
(206) 535-7130
Ref: 31887.003785
PF: Middle/Early Colleges

Pacific Lutheran University
Summer Scholars Program
Judith Carr
Dean, Special Academic Programs/Summer
Sessions, Tacoma, WA 98447
(206) 535-7130
Ref: 20772.003780
PF: Enrichment, Gifted

Parkland College
Illinois Prairie Higher Education Consortium
Sandra M. Boileau
Dean of Continuing Education, 2400 W. Bradley
Avenue, Champaign, IL 61821
(217) 351-2274
Ref: 31196.007118
PF: Minority, At-Risk

**The Pennsylvania State University–Altoona
Campus**
Southern Alleghenies Tech Prep Consortium
Robert E. Loeb
Asst. Director of Academic Affairs, Altoona, PA
16601-3760
(814) 949-5282
rxl5@psuadmin.psu.edu
Ref: 30416.003331
PF: Tech-Prep/2+2

▶ **The Pennsylvania State University–Beaver Campus** [193]
Communication Skills Consortium
Stacy Koutoulakis
Consortium Coordinator, Brodhead Road, Monaca, PA 15061
(412) 775-1682
Ref: 20284.003332
PF: Professional Development, Inservice

▶ **The Pennsylvania State University–DuBois Campus** [266]
Tech Prep For Tomorrow
David L. Welton
Coordinator, College Place, DuBois, PA 15801
(814) 375-4708
kmn2@psuvm.psu.edu
Ref: 30401.003335
PF: Tech-Prep/2+2

The Pennsylvania State University at Erie-Behrend College
The Penn State Educational Partnership Program
Diane Daniels
Director, 2931 Harvard Road, Erie, PA 16508
(814) 871-6463
Ref: 30415.003333
PF: Minority, At-Risk

▶ **The Pennsylvania State University–Main Campus** [193]
Center for Total Quality Schools
William T. Hartman
Director, 308 Rackley Building, University Park, PA 16802
(814) 865-2318
Ref: 30422.006965
PF: Professional Development, Inservice

The Pennsylvania State University–Main Campus
PEPP (Penn State Educational Partnership Program)
Robert F. Nicely, Jr.
Assoc. Dean, College of Education, Outreach and Faculty Development, University Park, PA 16802
(814) 865-2525
Ref: 30420.006965
PF: Minority, At-Risk

The Pennsylvania State University–Main Campus
Schools for Success Network
Robert F. Nicely, Jr.
Assoc. Dean, College of Education, Outreach and Faculty Development, 227 Chambers Building, University Park, PA 16802
(814) 865-2525
Ref: 30421.006965
PF: Professional Development, Inservice

▶ **The Pennsylvania State University–McKeesport Campus** [57]
PEPP (Penn State Educational Partnership Program)
Darrell G. Thomas
Director, University Drive, McKeesport, PA 15132
(412) 675-9032
Ref: 20915.003339
PF: Minority, At-Risk

The Pennsylvania State University–Wilkes-Barre Campus
Wilkes-Barre Area School District Partnership
William A. Penman
Campus Executive Offices, P.O. Box PSU, Lehman, PA 18627
(717) 675-9221
Ref: 30441.003346
PF: Minority, At-Risk

▶ **Peru State College** [77]
Early Entry
James Thomas
Dean of Continuing Education, Peru, NE 68421
(402) 872-2241
Ref: 20644.002559
PF: College Courses for Students

Phillips County Community College
Lee High-PCCC Advanced Placement
James Brasel
Dean of Admissions, Helena, AR 72342
(501) 338-6474
Ref: 20623.001104
PF: College Courses for Students

▶ **Phoenix College** [148]
Maricopa English Teachers' Network (METNET)
Camilla A.H. Westenberg
English Instructor, 1202 W. Thomas Road, Phoenix, AZ 85013
(602) 285-7365
Ref: 21271.001078
PF: Professional Development, Inservice

Piedmont College
Partners in Education
Nancy L. Singer
Director, Annual Fund and Special Events, P.O. Box 429, Demorest, GA 30535
(706) 778-3000
Ref: 31625.001588
PF: Resource Sharing

Pikes Peak Community College
Post Secondary Enrollment Option
Beth A. Lebsock
Director of Articulation and Transfer, 5675 S. Academy Boulevard, Box 6, Colorado Springs, CO 80906
(719) 540-7217
lebsock@ppcc.colorado.edu
Ref: 31425.008896
PF: College Courses for Students

Pikeville College
American College Testing Workshop
John Sanders
Dean of Admissions/Financial Aid, Sycamore Street, Pikeville, KY 41501
(606) 432-9322
Ref: 30840.001980
PF: Enrichment, Gifted

Pikeville College
College/Community Partnership
Elgin Ward
Instructor/Director of Tutoring, 214 Sycamore Street, Pikeville, KY 41501
(606) 432-9337
Ref: 30845.001980
PF: Minority, At-Risk

Pikeville College
Destination Graduation
Ron Damron
Program Coordinator, Pikeville, KY 41501
(606) 432-9200
Ref: 30844.001980
PF: Minority, At-Risk

Pikeville College
Educational Talent Search
Russell McIntosh
Coordinator, C.P.O. Box 26, Pikeville, KY 41501
(606) 432-9314
Ref: 30842.001980
PF: Minority, At-Risk

Key: "▶" denotes those partnerships abstracted in Parts 1-5; the corresponding page numbers are given in brackets. "PF:" denotes the partnership's "primary focus." "Ref:" denotes the partnership's assigned reference number in the National School-College Partnership Database (see Appendix B).

▶ **Pikeville College**   [166]
Pikeville College Math & Science Resource
   Center
Jack Wells
Professor of Physics, 214 Sycamore Street,
   Pikeville, KY 41501
(606) 432-9300
Ref: 30841.001980
PF: Professional Development, Inservice

Pikeville College
Pikeville College Upward Bound Program
Russell McIntosh
Director, C.P.O. Box 26, Pikeville, KY 41501
Ref: 30843.001980
PF: Minority, At-Risk

▶ **Pima County Community College**
District   [249]
Pima County Tech Prep Consortium
John Merren
Director of Occupational Education, 4907 E.
   Broadway Boulevard, Tucson, AZ 85709-1080
(602) 748-4901
jmerren@pimacc.pima.edu
Ref: 20512.007266
PF: Tech-Prep/2+2

Pine Manor College
Greater Boston Foreign Language Collaborative
Brian Thompson
Professor of French, Department of Modern
   Languages, Boston, MA 02125
(617) 287-7569
Ref: 31808.002201
PF: Professional Development, Inservice

Pitzer College
Early Academic Outreach Program
David A. Perez, Jr.
Director, 1050 N. Mills Avenue, Claremont, CA
   91711
(909) 621-8437
Ref: 31514.001172
PF: Minority, At-Risk

Polk Community College
Dual Enrollment/ Early Admissions
William R. Swinford
Dean of Instruction, 999 Avenue H NE, Winter
   Haven, FL 33881
(813) 297-1096
Ref: 30663.001514
PF: Minority, At-Risk

▶ **Polk Community College**   [252]
Polk County Tech Prep Consortium
David H. Buckley
Director of Career and Special Programs, 999
   Avenue H NE, Winter Haven, FL 33881
(813) 297-1026
Ref: 30662.001514
PF: Tech-Prep/2+2

Pontifical College Josephinum
I Know I Can Special Scholarships
Rev. Blase J. Cupich
President, Higher Education Council of Columbus,
   7626 N. High Street, Columbus, OH
   43235-1498
(614) 885-5585
Ref: 30853.003113
PF: Minority, At-Risk

▶ **Portland Community College**   [265]
PAVTEC Education Consortium
Helen Gabriel
Dean, P.O. Box 19000-RI-B5, Portland, OR
   97280-0990
(503) 244-6111
Ref: 31650.003213
PF: Tech-Prep/2+2

▶ **Portland State University**   [82]
Challenge Program
Karen Tosi
Program Director, P.O. Box 751, 349 Cramer Hall,
   Portland, OR 97207
(503) 725-3430
Ref: 20636.003216
PF: College Courses for Students

▶ **Portland State University**   [82]
LINK Program
Karen Tosi
Program Director, P.O. Box 751, 349 Cramer Hall,
   Portland, OR 97207
(503) 725-3430
Ref: 31571.003216
PF: College Courses for Students

▶ **Portland State University**   [274]
PEN (Portland Education Network)
Samuel D. Henry
Executive Director, P.O. Box 751, Portland, OR
   97207
(503) 725-5565
Ref: 31572.003216
PF: City/Regional Compacts

Portland State University
Portland-MESA
H. Chik Erzurumlu
Dean, School of Engineering and Applied
   Science, P.O. Box 751, Portland, OR 97207
(503) 725-4631
bfhe@eas.pdx.edu
Ref: 20026.003216
PF: Minority, At-Risk

▶ **Portland State University**   [221]
Portland Teachers' Program
Joycelyn McKenna
Coordinator, UMASP/PTP, P.O. Box 751,
   Portland, OR 97207-0751
(503) 725-4457
Ref: 31573.003216
PF: Recruit, Preservice, Certification

Portland State University
Project PLUS/Educational Talent Search
Peggy Adams
Director, P.O. Box 751, Portland, OR 97207-0751
(503) 725-4458
Ref: 31574.003216
PF: Minority, At-Risk

▶ **Portland State University**   [190]
PSU Center for Science Education
William G. Becker
Director, P.O. Box 751, Portland, OR 97207
(503) 725-4243
i8wb@odin.cc.pdx.edu
Ref: 20421.003216
PF: Professional Development, Inservice

Portland State University
Upward Bound Program
Peggy Adams
Director, P.O. Box 751, Portland, OR 97207-0751
(503) 725-4010
Ref: 20024.003216
PF: Minority, At-Risk

Prairie View A & M University
Texas Education Collaborative (TEC)
M. Paul Mehta
Dean, College of Education, P.O. Box 4049,
   Prairie View, TX 77446
(409) 857-3820
Ref: 31338.003630
PF: Professional Development, Inservice

Presbyterian College
Joint Enrollees Program
Ron Dempsey
Asst. Academic Dean, Clinton, SC 29325
(803) 833-8224
Ref: 31747.003445
PF: College Courses for Students

Princeton University
BEST/TIMES 1993-94
Ruth Wilson
Assoc. Director, Teacher Preparation Program,
    228 W. College, Princeton, NJ 08544
(609) 258-3336
Ref: 30115.002627
PF: Professional Development, Inservice

Princeton University
Cotsen Seminars
Ruth Wilson
Assoc. Director, Teacher Preparation Program,
    228 W. College, Princeton, NJ 08544
(609) 258-3336
Ref: 30117.002627
PF: Professional Development, Inservice

▣ **Princeton University**   [177]
History Institute for Secondary School Teachers
Marue Walizer
Director, Teacher Preparation Program, 228 W.
    College, Princeton, NJ 08544
(609) 258-3336
Ref: 30114.002627
PF: Professional Development, Inservice

▣ **Princeton University**   [177]
Institute for Secondary School Teachers
Edward Cox
Professor, Molecular Biology Department, 333
    Moffett Labs, Princeton, NJ 08544
(609) 258-3856
ecox@pucc.princeton.edu
Ref: 30118.002627
PF: Professional Development, Inservice

Princeton University
Project Quest
Carole Stearns
Program Director, 228 W. College, Princeton, NJ
    08544
(609) 258-6796
Ref: 30116.002627
PF: Professional Development, Inservice

Purdue University–Calumet
Dual Credit Agreement
Sandra Singer
Vice Chancellor for Academic Affairs, Hammond,
    IN 46323
(219) 989-2446
Ref: 30962.001827
PF: College Courses for Students

▣ **Purdue University–Main Campus**   [244]
High School Testing Program-School of Science
Dennis H. Sorge
Director, Academic Services, School of Science
1390 MATH Building, Room 242, West Lafayette,
    IN 47907-1390
(317) 494-1990
pox@vm.cc.purdue.edu
Ref: 20841.001825
PF: Instructional Research

Purdue University–Main Campus
Professional Development School
Brenda F. Sands
Director, Office of Field Experience, and
    Coordinator, Professional Development School,
    1443 LAEB, Room 3229, West Lafayette, IN
    47907-1443
(317) 494-7990
Ref: 30985.001825
PF: Professional Development, Inservice

Purdue University–North Central
Tech Prep
J. Jeffrey Jones
Director of Continuing Education, Westville, IN
    46391-9528
(219) 785-5343
Ref: 30968.001826
PF: Tech-Prep/2+2

Q

Quincy College
Southeast Massachusetts Tech Prep Consortium
Stephen Kenney
Director, Grant Services, 34 Coddington Street,
    Quincy, MA 02169
(617) 984-1755
Ref: 30029.002206
PF: Tech-Prep/2+2

R

Ramapo College of New Jersey
Academic Alliance for Excellence in Science
    Education
Angela Cristini
Professor, Biology Department, 505 Ramapo
    Valley Road, Mahwah, NJ 07430
(201) 529-7724
Ref: 31690.009344
PF: Professional Development, Inservice

Ramapo College of New Jersey
Northern New Jersey Chemistry Alliance
Theodore Michelfeld
Professor of Chemistry, 505 Ramapo Valley
    Road, Mahwah, NJ 07430
(201) 529-7744
Ref: 31611.009344
PF: Professional Development, Inservice

▣ **Ramapo College of New Jersey**   [177]
Project SPACE (Stars, Planets, Asteroids,
    Constellations for Educators)
Helen R. Burchell
Director of Special Projects, 505 Ramapo Valley
    Road, Mahwah, NJ 07430
(201) 529-7475
Ref: 31610.009344
PF: Professional Development, Inservice

▣ **Ramapo College of New Jersey**   [101]
THE RECORD Debate Classic
Helen R. Burchell
Director of Special Projects, 505 Ramapo Valley
    Road, Mahwah, NJ 07430
(201) 529-7475
Ref: 31613.009344
PF: Enrichment, Gifted

Ramapo College of New Jersey
Youth Forum
Helen R. Burchell
Director of Special Projects, 505 Ramapo Valley
    Road, Mahwah, NJ 07430
(201) 529-7475
Ref: 31612.009344
PF: Enrichment, Gifted

▶ **Rancho Santiago College**   [17]
Networks
Sara Lundquist
Executive Dean, 1530 W. 17th Street, Santa Ana,
    CA 92706
(714) 564-6085
Ref: 31884.001284
PF: Minority, At-Risk

▶ **Reading Area Community College**   [55]
Even Start Family Literacy Program
Barbara Gill
Coordinator, P.O. Box 1706, Reading, PA 19603
(610) 372-4721
Ref: 30460.010388
PF: Minority, At-Risk

Reading Area Community College
Talent Search
Sandra F. Sorrels
Project Director, P.O. Box 1706, Reading, PA
    19603
(610) 372-4721
Ref: 30459.010388
PF: Minority, At-Risk

Reading Area Community College
Tech Prep
John DeVere
Assoc. Dean for Instruction, P.O. Box 1706,
    Reading, PA 19603
(610) 372-4721
Ref: 30461.010388
PF: Tech-Prep/2+2

▶ **Reed College**   [128]
Community Services Tutoring Program
L. Allen Poole
Community Service Coordinator, 3203 S.E.
    Woodstock Boulevard, Portland, OR 97202
(503) 777-7563
apoole@reed.edu
Ref: 31580.003217
PF: Tutoring, Counseling

▶ **Reed College**   [57]
HHMI Summer Science Program for
    Under-Represented High School Students
Steve Black
Program Director, 3202 S.E. Woodstock
    Boulevard, Portland, OR 97202-8199
(503) 771-1112 x644
sblack@reed.edu
Ref: 31584.003217
PF: Minority, At-Risk

▶ **Reed College**   [191]
Partners in Science
Eileen Trudehn
Director, Corporate/Foundation Support, Portland,
    OR 97208
(503) 777-7560
Ref: 31581.003217
PF: Professional Development, Inservice

Reed College
Reed College/Oregon I Have a Dream Foundation
    Computer Workshop
Marty Ringle
Director, Computing and Information Systems,
    3203 S.E. Woodstock Boulevard, Portland, OR
    97808
(503) 777-7254
ringle@reed.edu
Ref: 31579.003217
PF: Minority, At-Risk

▶ **Reed College**   [107]
Super Quest
Marty Ringle
Director, Computing and Information Systems,
    3203 S.E. Woodstock Boulevard, Portland, OR
    97202
(503) 777-7254
ringle@reed.edu
Ref: 31582.003217
PF: Enrichment, Gifted

▶ **Reed College**   [129]
Take Charge
David Roth
Asst. Dean of Admissions, Portland, OR 97202
(503) 777-7511
Ref: 31583.003217
PF: Tutoring, Counseling

▶ **Reed College**   [82]
Young Scholars
Toinette Menashe
Director of Special Programs, 3203 S.E.
    Woodstock Boulevard, Portland, OR
    97202-8199
(503) 777-7259
Ref: 20954.003217
PF: College Courses for Students

Regis University
Cascade Project
Jaimie Birge
Coordinator, Center for Service Learning, 3333
    Regis Boulevard, Denver, CO 80221
(303) 458-3550 x3550
montrose@regis.edu
Ref: 31418.001363
PF: Minority, At-Risk

▶ **Regis University**   [154]
Regis Institute of Chemical Education
James Giulianelti
Professor of Chemistry, 3333 Regis Boulevard,
    Denver, CO 80221
(303) 458-4045
Ref: 31419.001363
PF: Professional Development, Inservice

▶ **Rensselaer Polytechnic Institute**   [140]
Capital District Science and Technology Entry
    Program (STEP)
Debra Nazon
Coordinator, Troy, NY 12180-3590
(518) 276-6272
Ref: 31820.002803
PF: Career, Internships, Apprenticeships

Rhode Island College
Grove Avenue Elementary Governor's School
    Partnership for Academic Excellence: A
    Teaching/Learning Community
Susan J. Schenck
Director, Clinical Experiences in Teacher
    Education, SEHD, Providence, RI 02908
(401) 456-8114
Ref: 30049.003407
PF: Professional Development, Inservice

Rhode Island College
Mt. Pleasant High School Teacher Academy
Susan Schenck
Director, Clinical Experiences in Teacher
    Education, SEHD, Providence, RI 02908
(401) 456-8114
Ref: 30050.003407
PF: Professional Development, Inservice

▶ **Rice University**   [198]
Center for Education
Ron Sass
P. O. Box 1892, Houston, TX 77251
(713) 527-4066/4827
cened@rice.edu
Ref: 31337.003604
PF: Professional Development, Inservice

Richard Stockton College of New Jersey
Admissions Ambassador Program
Melvin L. Gregory
Asst. Director, Admissions, Pomona, NJ
    08240-9988
(609) 652-4832
siprod37@vax003.stockton.edu
Ref: 20861.009345
PF: Minority, At-Risk

Richard Stockton College of New Jersey
G.O.A.L. (Go On And Learn)
Harvey Kesselman
Vice President for Student Services, Pomona, NJ
08240
(609) 652-4225
iaprod89@vax003.stockton.edu
Ref: 31794.009345
PF: College Courses for Students

▶ **Richmond Community College** [264]
Tech Prep
Joseph W. Grimsley
President, P.O. Box 1187, Hamlet, NC 28345
(979) 582-7007
Ref: 30746.005464
PF: Tech-Prep/2+2

▶ **Ringling School of Art and Design** [72]
Pre-College Perspective
Sandra MacDonald
Director, Office of Continuing and Professional
Education, 2700 N. Tamiami Trail, Sarasota, FL
34234
(813) 359-7577
Ref: 30664.012574
PF: College Courses for Students

Ripon College
Advance College Experience
Douglas A. Northrop
Dean of Faculty, P.O. Box 248, Ripon, WI
54971-0248
(414) 748-8109
northropd@mac.ripon.edu
Ref: 20077.003884
PF: Enrichment, Gifted

Ripon College
Eisenhower Mathematics and Science
Enrichment
Mary Williams-Norton
Chair, Department of Physics, P.O. Box 248,
Ripon, WI 54971
(414) 748-8132
Ref: 31120.003884
PF: Professional Development, Inservice

Ripon College
Extended Opportunity Program
Douglas A. Northrop
Dean of Faculty, P.O. Box 248, Ripon, WI
54971-0248
(414) 748-8109
northropd@mac.ripon.edu
Ref: 20075.003884
PF: College Courses for Students

Rivier College
Challenge Program
Nancy Riley
Director, Education Department, 420 S. Main
Street, Nashua, NH 03060
(603) 888-1311 x8539
Ref: 20129.002586
PF: Enrichment, Gifted

Rivier College
Sunset Heights Elementary School/Rivier College
Adopt-A-School Program
Jane Deneault
Program Coordinator, 420 Main Street, Nashua,
NH 03060-5086
(603) 888-1311 x8225
Ref: 20598.002586
PF: School-College-Business Partnerships

Roane State Community College
Tech Prep
Sharon Cordell
Tech Prep Coordinator, Patton Lane, Route 8,
Box 69, Harriman, TN 37748
(615) 354-3000
Ref: 30689.009914
PF: Tech-Prep/2+2

Roberts Wesleyan College
Success Project
Deborah Mott-Lundgren
Interim Chair, 2302 Westside Drive, Rochester,
NY 14624
(716) 594-6610
Ref: 30308.002805
PF: Minority, At-Risk

▶ **Rochester Community College** [295]
Manufacturing Electronics Youth Apprenticeship
Kathleen Schatzberg
Dean of Instruction, 851 30th Avenue SE,
Rochester, MN 55904
(507) 285-7256
Ref: 31127.002373
PF: School-College-Business Partnerships

▶ **Rochester Community College** [76]
Post Secondary Enrollment Options Program
Dale Amy
Student Services Assistant, 851 30th Avenue SE,
Rochester, MN 55904
(507) 285-7332
Ref: 21221.002373
PF: College Courses for Students

▶ **Rochester Community College** [258]
Rochester Area Tech Prep Consortium
Kathleen Schatzberg
Dean of Instruction, 851 30th Avenue SE,
Rochester, MN 55904
(507) 285-7256
Ref: 31128.002373
PF: Tech-Prep/2+2

▶ **Rochester Institute of Technology** [51]
Edison Tech/RIT Enrichment Program
James M. Papero
Director, 1 Lomb Memorial Drive, Rochester, NY
14623
(716) 475-2065
Ref: 30392.002806
PF: Minority, At-Risk

▶ **Rochester Institute of Technology** [80]
Key Program
Marion French
Coordinator, ETC Partnership Programs, 91 Lomb
Memorial Drive, Rochester, NY 14623
(716) 475-7215
mlfetc@ritvax.isc.rit.edu
Ref: 30393.002806
PF: College Courses for Students

Rochester Institute of Technology
Learning Development Center Project
Barbara S. Allardice
Clinical Supervisor, 30 Fairwood Drive,
Rochester, NY 14623
(716) 475-2281
Ref: 20671.002806
PF: Tutoring, Counseling

▶ **Rochester Institute of Technology** [51]
Partnership-School #4
Elaine Spaull
Assoc. Vice President, Student Affairs, 1 Lomb
Memorial Drive, Rochester, NY 14623
(716) 475-2268
exs3574@ritvax.isc.rit.edu
Ref: 21135.002806
PF: Minority, At-Risk

▶ **Rochester Institute of Technology** [288]
Rochester Area Interactive Telecommunications
  Network
Carol O'Leary
Coordinator, Partnership Programs, 91 Lomb
  Memorial Drive, Rochester, NY 14623
(716) 475-5089
ctoetc@ritvax.isc.rit.edu
Ref: 30389.002806
PF: Technology Application

▶ **Rochester Institute of Technology** [127]
Teen Health Issues Network
Carol O'Leary
Coordinator, Partnership Programs, 91 Lomb
  Memorial Drive, Rochester, NY 14623
(716) 475-5089
ctoetc@ritvax.isc.rit.edu
Ref: 30390.002806
PF: Tutoring, Counseling

▶ **Rochester Institute of Technology** [127]
Women in Science, Engineering, and Math
  Mentoring Program
Carol O'Leary
Coordinator, Partnership Programs, 91 Lomb
  Memorial Drive, Rochester, NY 14623
(716) 475-5089
ctoetc@ritvax.isc.rit.edu
Ref: 30391.002806
PF: Tutoring, Counseling

▶ **Rock Valley College** [254]
Youth Apprenticeship
Gary Schoot
Director, Tech Prep, 5279 28th Avenue, Rockford,
  IL 61109
(815) 397-4275
Ref: 31190.001747
PF: Tech-Prep/2+2

▶ **Rockhurst College** [174]
Center for the Advancement of Reform in
  Education
Joan Caulfield
Coordinator of College-School Relations, 1100
  Rockhurst Road, Kansas City, MO 64110-2561
(816) 926-4140
Ref: 31231.002499
PF: Professional Development, Inservice

▶ **Rockhurst College** [295]
Science Alliance
Joan Caulfield
Coordinator of College-School Relations, 1100
  Rockhurst Road, Kansas City, MO 64110
(816) 926-4651
Ref: 20066.002499
PF: School-College-Business Partnerships

Rockland Community College
Liberty Partnerships Program
Lorraine J. Glynn
Director, 145 College Road, Suffern, NY 10901
(914) 574-4294
Ref: 30193.002877
PF: Minority, At-Risk

Roger Williams University
Bridge to Success
Karen Haskell
Dean of Students, Bristol, RI 02809
(401) 254-3093
Ref: 30047.004917
PF: Minority, At-Risk

▶ **Rollins College** [72]
Florida Interacademic Consortium (FLIC)
Udeth A. Lugo
Asst. Dean, 1000 Holt Avenue, #2758, Winter
  Park, FL 32789
(407) 646-2230
udeth@rollins.edu
Ref: 20784.001515
PF: College Courses for Students

Rollins College
Talent Search Program
Udeth A. Lugo
Asst. Dean, 1000 Holt Avenue, #2758, Winter
  Park, FL 32789
(407) 646-1558
udeth@rollins.edu
Ref: 30641.001515
PF: Minority, At-Risk

Rollins College
Upward Bound Program
Udeth A. Lugo
Asst. Dean, 1000 Holt Avenue, #2758, Winter
  Park, FL 32789
(407) 646-2230
udeth@rollins.edu
Ref: 30642.001515
PF: Minority, At-Risk

▶ **Rose-Hulman Institute of
Technology** [123]
Homework Hotline
Susan L. Smith
Learning Center Director, 5500 Wabash Avenue,
  Terre Haute, IN 47803
(812) 877-8319
susan.smith@rose-hulman.edu
Ref: 30983.001830
PF: Tutoring, Counseling

▶ **Rowan College of New Jersey** [178]
Cooper's Poynt Professional Development Family
  School of Excellence
Carol Sharp
Assoc. Professor, Education Department,
  Glassboro, NJ 08021-1701
(609) 863-5241
Ref: 30143.002609
PF: Professional Development, Inservice

Rust College
College Discovery Program
Norma J. Strickland
Chair, Division of Education, Holly Springs, MS
  38635
(601) 252-8000 x4410
Ref: 30698.002433
PF: Professional Development, Inservice

▶ **Rust College** [98]
John Lennon Pre-College Summer Arts Award
  Program
Benedict C. Njoku
Vice President and Chair, Humanities Division,
  Holly Springs, MS 38635-2328
(601) 252-8000
Ref: 30699.002433
PF: Enrichment, Gifted

▶ **Rutgers, The State University of New
Jersey–New Brunswick Campus** [178]
MAPS (Mathematics Projects with Schools)
Carolyn A. Maher
Professor of Mathematics Education, 10 Seminary
  Place, New Brunswick, NJ 08903
(908) 932-7971
cmaher@math.rutgers.edu
Ref: 21166.006964
PF: Professional Development, Inservice

▶ **Rutgers, The State University of New
Jersey–New Brunswick Campus** [178]
Rutgers Literacy Curriculum Network
Dorothy S Strickland
Professor, Graduate School of Education, 10
  Seminary Place, New Brunswick, NJ 08903
(908) 932-7496
Ref: 20205.006964
PF: Professional Development, Inservice

**Rutgers, The State University of New
  Jersey–Newark Campus**
Saturday Academy
Freda McClean
Director, Center for Pre-College Education, 175
  University Avenue, Conklin 425, Newark, NJ
  07102
(201) 648-5416
Ref: 20133.002631
PF: Tutoring, Counseling

S

Saginaw Valley State University
Greater Saginaw Valley Regional Education
   Cooperative (GSVREC)
Ralph K. Coppola
Executive Director, 7400 Bay Road, University
   Center, MI 48710
(517) 790-4295
Ref: 20704.002314
PF: Professional Development, Inservice

▶ **St. Ambrose University**   [123]
Teens Teaching Youth
Robert S. Risbow
Director, Graduate Special Education Programs,
   Davenport, IA 52803
(319) 383-8743
Ref: 31064.001889
PF: Tutoring, Counseling

Saint Anselm College
Trinity High School/Saint Anselm College
   Cooperative Partnership
Todd C. Emmons
Asst. Treasurer, Manchester, NH 03102
(603) 641-7102
Ref: 30053.002587
PF: Retention, Continuing Education

▶ **St. Charles County Community
College**   [259]
Mid Rivers Tech Prep Consortium
Carol Ballantyne
Dean of Instruction, 4601 Mid Rivers Mall Drive,
   St. Peters, MO 63376
(314) 922-8000 x4321
Ref: 31223.025306
PF: Tech-Prep/2+2

▶ **St. Charles County Community
College**   [43]
Project YES (Youth Experiencing Success)
Daisy Vulovich-Carp
Assoc. Dean, Continuing Education, 4601 Mid
   Rivers Mall Drive, St. Peters, MO 63376
(314) 922-8316
Ref: 31222.025306
PF: Minority, At-Risk

▶ **St. Cloud State University**   [76]
Postsecondary Option Program
Harlan Jensen
Assoc. Professor, 729 Fourth Avenue S, 2 RS, St.
   Cloud, MN 56301-4498
(612) 255-3083
Ref: 31130.002377
PF: College Courses for Students

▶ **St. Cloud State University**   [288]
Rural/Urban Link
J. M. Nelson
Professor, 720 Fourth Avenue S, St. Cloud, MN
   56301-4498
(612) 255-2022
jmnelson@tigger.stcloud.msus.edu
Ref: 31129.002377
PF: Technology Application

St. Edward's University
Community Mentor Program
Donna Braun Hagey
Project Director, 3001 S. Congress Avenue,
   Austin, TX 78704-6489
(512) 448-8594
donnah@admin.stedwards.edu
Ref: 31374.003621
PF: Minority, At-Risk

▶ **St. Edward's University**   [64]
State Migrant Program
Robert A. Montgomery
Director, 3001 S. Congress Avenue, Box 1038,
   Austin, TX 78704
(512) 448-8628
Ref: 20929.003621
PF: Minority, At-Risk

St. Edward's University
Teachers as Agents of Change
Barbara Fiandsen
Assoc. Professor, 3001 S. Congress Avenue,
   Austin, TX 78704
(512) 448-8616
Ref: 31375.003621
PF: Professional Development, Inservice

Saint Francis College
Southern Alleghenies Tech Prep Consortium
Colleen M. Neely
Asst. Director, P.O. Box 600, Loretto, PA 15940
(814) 472-3248
Ref: 30402.003366
PF: Tech-Prep/2+2

St. John Fisher College
St. John Fisher College-Jefferson Middle School
   Partnership
Mary Pat Seurkamp
Vice President for Academic Affairs/Dean of
   Students, 3690 East Avenue, Rochester, NY
   14618
(716) 385-8000
Ref: 21243.002821
PF: Minority, At-Risk

Saint John's University
College Bound: Liberty Partnerships Program
Laura M. Arvin
Director, 8000 Utopia Parkway, Jamaica, NY
   11439
(718) 990-1374
Ref: 30213.002823
PF: Minority, At-Risk

Saint John's University
The Collaborative Project Between St. John's
   University and St. John the Baptist School
Margret Fitzpatrick
Senior Vice President, 81-50 Utopia Parkway,
   Perboyre Hall, Jamaica, NY 11439
(718) 990-1680
Ref: 30212.002823
PF: Professional Development, Inservice

Saint John's University
Project SUMS
Jamaica, NY 11439
(718) 990-6161
Ref: 31617.002823
PF: Professional Development, Inservice

▶ **Saint Joseph College**   [24]
Adventures in Science
Peter Markow
Assoc. Professor of Chemistry, West Hartford, CT
   06117
(203) 232-4571
Ref: 30175.001409
PF: Minority, At-Risk

▶ **Saint Joseph College**   [210]
Compensatory Education Internships
Dolores Peters
Professor, Education Department, West Hartford,
   CT 06117
(203) 232-4571
Ref: 30070.001409
PF: Recruit, Preservice, Certification

▶ **Saint Joseph College**   [156]
Project Construct
Claire Markham, R.S.M.
Director, Institutional Research, West Hartford, CT
    06117
(203) 232-4571
Ref: 30069.001409
PF: Professional Development, Inservice

Saint Joseph's College
College Articulation Program (CAP)
Sr. Mary Ellen Murphy
Dean of the College, White Bridge Road,
    Windham, ME 04062
(207) 892-6766
Ref: 31699.002051
PF: College Courses for Students

Saint Joseph's College-Suffolk Campus
Bridge Program
Sr. Jean M. Amore
Academic Dean, 155 W. Roe Boulevard,
    Patchogue, NY 11772
(516) 447-3200
Ref: 20956.029081
PF: College Courses for Students

▶ **St. Lawrence University**   [80]
Modern Language Collaborative
Rita Goldberg
Dana Professor of Modern Languages and
    Literatures, Canton, NY 13617
(315) 379-5156
rgol@slumus.bitnet
Ref: 30269.002829
PF: College Courses for Students

St. Lawrence University
Pre-Collegiate Opportunity Program
Theodore C. Linn
Director, 20 Romoda Drive, Canton, NY 13617
(315) 379-5256
Ref: 30268.002829
PF: Minority, At-Risk

St. Lawrence University
Talented Juniors
Betsy Cogger Rezdman
Assoc. Dean for Faculty Affairs, 104 Vilas Hall,
    Canton, NY 13617
(315) 379-5998
brez@slumus.bitnet
Ref: 30270.002829
PF: Enrichment, Gifted

St. Lawrence University
Upward Bound
Brenda Mattice-Thurman
Director, Hepburn Hall, Canton, NY 13617
(315) 379-5749
Ref: 30267.002829
PF: Minority, At-Risk

▶ **St. Louis Community College at
Meramec**   [239]
Landmarks
Rosemary Hyde Thomas
Director, English Department, 11333 Big Bend,
    Kirkwood, MO 63122
(314) 984-7556
srcthom@umsl.vma.umsl.edu.
Ref: 31214.002472
PF: Curriculum Development

Saint Mary College
PRESTO (Pre-Service for Significant Teaching
    Outcomes)
Sr. Marie Brinkman
Chair, Department of Language and Literature,
    4100 S. 4th Street, Leavenworth, KS 66048
(913) 758-6147
Ref: 31246.001943
PF: Minority, At-Risk

▶ **Saint Mary College**   [232]
River Valley English Alliance
Sr. Marie Brinkman
Chair, Department of Language and Literature,
    Leavenworth, KS 66048
(913) 758-6147
Ref: 31245.001943
PF: Faculty Exchanges

▶ **Saint Mary's College of California**   [209]
Beginning Teacher Support and Assessment
    Program
Katherine D. Perez
Asst. Dean, School of Education, P.O. Box 4350,
    Moraga, CA 94575
(510) 631-4292
Ref: 31711.001302
PF: Recruit, Preservice, Certification

▶ **St. Mary's College of Maryland**   [76]
Charlotte Hall Fellows Program
J. Roy Hopkins
Head, Human Development Division, St. Mary's
    City, MD 20686
(301) 862-0337
hopkins_r@vaxa.smcm.edu
Ref: 21146.002095
PF: College Courses for Students

Saint Michael's College
HHS/SMC: Holyoke High School-Saint Michael's
    College Partnership
Daniel Bean
Professor, Biology Department, Colchester, VT
    05439
(802) 654-2622
bean@smcvax.smcvt.edu
Ref: 30063.003694
PF: Minority, At-Risk

▶ **Saint Michael's College**   [201]
Vermont River Teacher Enhancement Project
Arthur C. Hesster
Professor, Biology Department, Colchester, VT
    05439
(802) 654-2626
hesster@smcvax.smcvt.edu
Ref: 30062.003694
PF: Professional Development, Inservice

Saint Norbert College
Adaptive Education Program
Charles Peterson
Director, 100 Grant Street, De Pere, WI 54115
(414) 337-3076
Ref: 31086.003892
PF: Professional Development, Inservice

▶ **Saint Norbert College**   [68]
AISES-St. Norbert College American Indian
    Summer Math Camp
Bonnie Berken
Instructor, Mathematics, De Pere, WI 54115
(414) 337-3191
berkba@sncac.snc.edu
Ref: 31091.003892
PF: Minority, At-Risk

▶ **Saint Norbert College**   [204]
Assistive Technology Project
Charles Peterson
Director, 100 Grant Street, De Pere, WI 54115
(414) 337-3076
Ref: 31087.003892
PF: Professional Development, Inservice

Saint Norbert College
Early Childhood Conference
Mary Alyce Lach, S.S.N.D.
Assoc. Professor, Director of Early Childhood
    Programs, 100 Grant Street, De Pere, WI
    54115
(414) 337-3063
Ref: 31084.003892
PF: Curriculum Development

▶ **Saint Norbert College**   [230]
Menominee/Oneida Teacher Preparation Program
Robert A. Rutter
Director of Teacher Education, 219 Boyle Hall, De
   Pere, WI 54115
(414) 337-3090
Ref: 31090.003892
PF: Teacher Education Centers

Saint Norbert College
Parkview Collaboration
Reid R. Riggle
Asst. Professor, College of Education, 100 Grant
   Street, De Pere, WI 54115
(414) 337-3065
Ref: 31092.003892
PF: Professional Development, Inservice

Saint Norbert College
Professional Growth Seminars for Cooperating
   Teachers
Jerald Hauser
Assoc. Professor, De Pere, WI 54115
(414) 337-3365
Ref: 31085.003892
PF: Professional Development, Inservice

Saint Norbert College
The Reading Clinic
Yvonne Murnane
Asst. Professor, De Pere, WI 54115
(414) 337-3363
murnyv@sncac.snc.edu
Ref: 31088.003892
PF: Teacher Education Centers

▶ **Saint Norbert College**   [85]
St. Norbert College Credit Program
Jeanne Lucier
Director, De Pere, WI 54115
(414) 337-3060
Ref: 21181.003892
PF: College Courses for Students

Saint Norbert College
The St. Norbert Precollege Education Power
   Workshop
Jerald Hauser
Assoc. Professor, De Pere, WI 54115
(414) 337-3365
Ref: 31083.003892
PF: Minority, At-Risk

▶ **Saint Norbert College**   [111]
Young Artist Workshops
Charles Peterson
Director, 100 Grant Street, De Pere, WI 54115
(414) 337-3176
Ref: 31089.003892
PF: Enrichment, Gifted

Saint Peter's College
Special Program for Credit
Virginia Bender
Director, High School and College Relations, 2641
   Kennedy Boulevard, Jersey City, NJ 07306
(201) 437-1293
Ref: 20844.002638
PF: College Courses for Students

▶ **Salem State College**   [170]
Collaborative Project for Math and Science
   Education
Kenneth D. Laser
Executive Director, Biology Department, 352
   Lafayette, Salem, MA 01970
(508) 741-6068
klaser@rcn.mass.edu
Ref: 30014.002188
PF: Professional Development, Inservice

▶ **Salt Lake Community College**   [84]
Applied Technology Center for Secondary
   Students
Rand A. Johnson
Director, Advanced Technology Center, P.O. Box
   30808, Salt Lake City, UT 84130
(801) 967-4215
Ref: 31435.005220
PF: College Courses for Students

▶ **Salt Lake Community College**   [84]
Concurrent Enrollment
Maria Lee
Coordinator, 4600 S. Redwood Road, Salt Lake
   City, UT 84130
(801) 964-4668
Ref: 31434.005220
PF: College Courses for Students

Salt Lake Community College
Kids on Campus
Rosemary Johnson
Workshops Coordinator, 1575 S. State Street,
   Salt Lake City, UT 84115
(801) 461-3430
Ref: 31436.005220
PF: Enrichment, Gifted

Salt Lake Community College
Project Cooperation/Business Skills and/or
   Beginning Carpentry
Paco Salazar
Director, Skills Center, 1575 S. State, Salt Lake
   City, UT 84115
(801) 468-4231
Ref: 31433.005220
PF: Minority, At-Risk

Samford University
Greystone Plan
Ruth Ash
Dean, Orlean Bullard Beeson School of
   Education, Birmingham, AL 35229-2312
(205) 870-2745
Ref: 30675.001036
PF: Professional Development, Inservice

▶ **Samford University**   [206]
Hoover Elementary School Program
Jean Ann Box
Chair, Teacher Education, Birmingham, AL 35229
(205) 870-2559
Ref: 30674.001036
PF: Recruit, Preservice, Certification

San Bernardino Valley College
Inland/Desert Tech Prep Consortium
Tom Clark
Dean, Occupational Education, 701 S. Mt. Vernon
   Avenue, San Bernardino, CA 92410
(909) 888-6511
Ref: 31520.001272
PF: Tech-Prep/2+2

▶ **San Diego State University**   [17]
Auditory Discrimination in Depth Project
Li-Rong Lilly Cheng
Professor of Communicative Disorders, San
   Diego, CA 92182-0409
(619) 594-6898
lcheng@sciences.sdsu.edu
Ref: 20337.001151
PF: Minority, At-Risk

▶ **San Diego State University**   [17]
College of Professional Studies & Fine
   Arts/National City Middle School
Carol A. Robasciotti
Asst. Dean for Student Affairs, College of
   Professional Studies and Fine Arts, San Diego,
   CA 92182
(619) 594-5124
crobasciotti@sciences.sdsu.edu
Ref: 20588.001151
PF: Minority, At-Risk

San Diego State University
Granger Junior High School/Adopt-A-School
Kathleen H. Ross
Scholarship Director, San Diego, CA 92182
(619) 594-6180
Ref: 20619.001151
PF: Minority, At-Risk

San Diego State University
International Studies Education Project of San
   Diego (ISTEP)
Elsie Begler
Director, Center for Latin American Studies, San
   Diego, CA 92182
(619) 594-2412
Ref: 20347.001151
PF: Professional Development, Inservice

San Diego State University
La Mesa Middle School Partnership
Clifford P. Bee
Professor of Education, 5300 Campanile Drive,
   San Diego, CA 92182
(619) 594-6086
Ref: 20520.001151
PF: Teacher Education Centers

San Diego State University
MESA (Mathematics, Engineering, Science
   Achievement)
Robert W. Goode II
Assoc. Director, College of Engineering, Room
   403L, San Diego, CA 92182
(619) 594-4197
Ref: 20892.001151
PF: Minority, At-Risk

▶ **San Diego State University**   [225]
Model Education Center
Marlowe Berg
Professor, School of Teacher Education, San
   Diego, CA 92182
(619) 594-1378
Ref: 20349.001151
PF: Teacher Education Centers

▶ **San Diego State University**   [152]
San Diego Mathematics Enhancement Project
Nadine Bezuk
Project Director, 6475 Alvarado Road, Suite 104,
   San Diego, CA 92120
(619) 594-6526
Ref: 20888.001151
PF: Professional Development, Inservice

▶ **San Francisco State University**   [88]
Alexander String Quartet Outreach Program
Patricia Taylor Lee
Chair, Music Department, 1600 Hollowly Avenue,
   San Francisco, CA 94132
(415) 338-1344
Ref: 31554.001154
PF: Enrichment, Gifted

San Francisco State University
Arts Bridge to College
Jim Davis
Assoc. Dean, School of Creative Arts, 1600
   Hollowly Avenue, San Francisco, CA 94132
(415) 338-1478
Ref: 31555.001154
PF: College Courses for Students

▶ **San Francisco State University**   [18]
Graduate Program in Physical Therapy Outreach
   Program to Grade Schools
Ann Hallum, P.T.
Assoc. Professor, 1600 Hollowly Avenue, San
   Francisco, CA 94132
(415) 338-2001
Ref: 31557.001154
PF: Minority, At-Risk

San Francisco State University
Mathematics, Engineering, Science Achievement
   (MESA)
Harold Bannerman
Director, 1600 Hollowly Avenue, San Francisco,
   CA 94132
(415) 338-1989
Ref: 31550.001154
PF: Minority, At-Risk

▶ **San Francisco State University**   [18]
NASA SHARP PLUS
Harold Bannerman
Director, 1600 Hollowly Avenue, San Francisco,
   CA 94132
(415) 338-1989
Ref: 31552.001154
PF: Minority, At-Risk

▶ **San Francisco State University**   [18]
On the Right Track
Susan Sung
Chair, Women Studies Department, and
   Professor, Social Work Education, 1600
   Hollowly Avenue, San Francisco, CA 94132
(415) 338-1052
ssung@sfsuvax.edu
Ref: 31558.001154
PF: Minority, At-Risk

San Francisco State University
SFSU/Rooftop Collaboration
Luz Cruz
Asst. Professor of Kinesiology, 1600 Hollowly
   Avenue, San Francisco, CA 94132
(415) 338-1671
lcruz@sfsu.edu
Ref: 31556.001154
PF: Recruit, Preservice, Certification

▶ **San Francisco State University**   [17]
Women and Girls in Science, Engineering, and
   Mathematics (WGSEM)
Harold Bannerman
Director, 1600 Hollowly Avenue, San Francisco,
   CA 94132
(415) 338-1989
Ref: 31549.001154
PF: Minority, At-Risk

▶ **San Francisco State University**   [88]
Young Engineers and Scientists (YES)
Harold Bannerman
Director, 1600 Hollowly Avenue, San Francisco,
   CA 94132
(415) 338-1989
Ref: 31551.001154
PF: Enrichment, Gifted

▶ **San Jacinto College**   [64]
Middle School Math and Science Project [(MS)^2]
Sharon Sledge
Chairman, P.O. Box 2007, Pasadena, TX
   77501-2007
(713) 476-1804
Ref: 31339.003609
PF: Minority, At-Risk

San Joaquin Delta College
EOPS (Extended Opportunities, Programs and
   Services)
Elliott R. Chambers
Director, 5151 Pacific Avenue, Stockton, CA
   95207
(209) 474-5682
Ref: 31533.001280
PF: Minority, At-Risk

San Joaquin Delta College
Math Articulation
James J. Thome, Sr.
Chair, Science and Math Division, 5151 Pacific
   Avenue, Stockton, CA 95209
(209) 474-5354
Ref: 31754.001280
PF: College Courses for Students

▶ **Santa Barbara City College**   [250]
Santa Barbara Articulation Council
John Romo
Vice President for Academic Affairs, 721 Cliff
   Drive, Santa Barbara, CA 93109
(805) 965-0581
Ref: 20454.001285
PF: Tech-Prep/2+2

Santa Fe Community College
High School Dual Enrollment Program
Linda Lanza-Kaduce
Coordinator, 3000 N.W. 83rd Street, Gainsville,
   FL 32606
(904) 395-5490
Ref: 20826.001519
PF: College Courses for Students

Santa Rosa Junior College
Tech Prep
Lu Ann C. Ponken
Dean, Science and Technology, 1501 Mendocino
   Avenue, Santa Rosa, CA 95405
(707) 524-1506
Ref: 31560.001287
PF: Tech-Prep/2+2

Schenectady County Community College
Schenectady Collaborative Mathematics and
   Science Project
Nancy Begg
Grants Coordinator, 78 Washington Avenue,
   Schenectady, NY 12305
(518) 346-6211 x116
Ref: 30239.006785
PF: Minority, At-Risk

▶ **School of the Art Institute of
Chicago**   [163]
Basic Art Support in the Curriculum (BASIC)
Angela G. Paterakis
Director, 112 S. Michigan Avenue, Chicago, IL
   60603
(312) 345-3514
Ref: 21059.001753
PF: Professional Development, Inservice

Schreiner College
Program for Accelerated College Enrollment,
   Early and Co-Enrollment (P.A.C.E.)
Darlene Bannister
Registrar, Kerrville, TX 78028
(210) 896-5411
Ref: 20836.003610
PF: College Courses for Students

▶ **Seattle Central Community College**   [116]
Middle College High School
Mildred Ollee
Vice President, Student Services, 1701
   Broadway, Seattle, WA 98122
(206) 587-5480
Ref: 31585.009705
PF: Middle/Early Colleges

Seattle Community College District Office
College in the High School
Julie Hungar
Vice Chancellor, Education and Planning, 1500
   Harvard Avenue, Seattle, WA 98122
(206) 587-4101
Ref: 20028.010106
PF: College Courses for Students

Seattle Community College District Office
Seattle Coalition for Educational Equity
Julie Hungar
Vice Chancellor, Education and Planning, 1500
   Harvard Avenue, Seattle, WA 98122
(206) 587-4101
Ref: 31885.010106
PF: Minority, At-Risk

▶ **Seattle University**   [116]
Matteo Ricci College
Bernard M. Steckler
Dean, Broadway and Madison, Seattle, WA 98122
(206) 296-5405
bsteck@seattleu.edu
Ref: 21102.003790
PF: Middle/Early Colleges

▶ **Seattle University**   [85]
Matteo Ricci College Consortium
Bernard M. Steckler
Dean, Matteo Ricci College, Broadway and
   Madison, Seattle, WA 98122
(206) 296-5405
bsteck@seattleu.edu
Ref: 31586.003790
PF: College Courses for Students

Seminole Community College
Dual Enrollment Program
Elaine A. Greenwood
Director of Arts and Sciences Services, 100
   Weldon Boulevard, Sanford, FL 32773
(407) 323-1450
Ref: 20718.001520
PF: College Courses for Students

▶ **Seminole Community College**   [252]
Tech Prep Consortium
Pamela Peláez
Tech Prep Coordinator, 100 Weldon Boulevard,
   Sanford, FL 32773
(407) 323-1450 x393
Ref: 31627.001520
PF: Tech-Prep/2+2

Seton Hall University
Project Acceleration
William A. Smith
Coordinator, South Orange, NJ 07079
(201) 761-9430
Ref: 30085.002632
PF: College Courses for Students

Seton Hill College
Tutoring for Success
Terrance DePasquale
Chair, Education Department, Greensburg, PA
   15601
(412) 834-2200
Ref: 30399.003362
PF: Minority, At-Risk

Shawnee State University
Cultural Enrichment Programs: Teaching Spanish
   in the Elementary School
Marlene Domo
Assoc. Professor, 213 Massie Hall, Portsmouth,
   OH 45662
(614) 354-3205
Ref: 30929.012748
PF: Enrichment, Gifted

Shawnee State University
Project Discovery-South Region
David Todt
Director, South Region, Portsmouth, OH
   45662-4303
(614) 355-2239
dtodt@shawnee.edu
Ref: 30931.012748
PF: Professional Development, Inservice

Key: "▶" denotes those partnerships abstracted in Parts 1-5; the corresponding page numbers are given in brackets. "PF:" denotes the partnership's "primary focus." "Ref:" denotes the partnership's assigned reference number in the National School-College Partnership Database (see Appendix B).

▶ **Shawnee State University**   [106]
Scioto River Water Quality Project
David Todt
Project Director, Portsmouth, OH 45662-4303
(614) 355-2239
dtodt@shawnee.edu
Ref: 30928.012748
PF: Enrichment, Gifted

Shawnee State University
Shawnee District-Ohio Junior Academy of
  Science
David Todt
Co-Director, Portsmouth, OH 45662-4303
(614) 355-2239
dtodt@shawnee.edu
Ref: 30930.012748
PF: Enrichment, Gifted

Shoreline Community College
Tech Prep
David A. Starr
Professor, 16101 Greenwood Avenue N, Seattle,
  WA 98133
(206) 546-4725
Ref: 31587.003791
PF: Tech-Prep/2+2

▶ **Siena Heights College**   [295]
Payback for Education
Robert Gordon
Dean/Provost, Adrian, MI 49221
(517) 263-0731
Ref: 31030.002316
PF: School-College-Business Partnerships

▶ **Sierra Nevada College**   [100]
DOE Pre-Freshman Enrichment Program
Sue Welsch
Chair, Science Department, Box 4269, Incline
  Village, NV 89450
(702) 831-1314
Ref: 31471.009192
PF: Enrichment, Gifted

▶ **Sierra Nevada College**   [176]
Eisenhower Grants In Math & Science
Sue Welsch
Chair, Science Department, Box 4269, Incline
  Village, NV 89450
(702) 831-1314
Ref: 31470.009192
PF: Professional Development, Inservice

▶ **Sierra Nevada College**   [176]
EPA Grant
Sue Welsch
Chair, Science Department, Box 4269, Incline
  Village, NV 89450
(702) 831-1314
Ref: 31472.009192
PF: Professional Development, Inservice

▶ **Simon's Rock College of Bard**   [114]
Early College Partnership
Brian R. Hopewell
Director of Admissions, 84 Alford Road, Great
  Barrington, MA 01230
(800) 235-7186
Ref: 20121.009645
PF: Middle/Early Colleges

▶ **Sinclair Community College**   [189]
Breakfast Forums
Sara Smith
Director of Admissions, 444 W. Third Street,
  Dayton, OH 45402
(513) 226-3060
ssmith@midas.sinclair.edu
Ref: 30923.003119
PF: Professional Development, Inservice

Sinclair Community College
Career Days/Nights at High Schools
Sara Smith
Director of Admissions, 444 W. Third Street,
  Dayton, OH 45402
(513) 226-3060
ssmith@midas.sinclair.edu
Ref: 30920.003119
PF: Career, Internships, Apprenticeships

Sinclair Community College
Career Dimensions
Veronica R. Watkins
Admissions Officer, Minority Student
  Recruitment/Retention, 444 W. Third Street,
  Dayton, OH 45402
(513) 226-3060
Ref: 30924.003119
PF: Career, Internships, Apprenticeships

Sinclair Community College
Post Secondary Enrollment Options Program
Sara Smith
Director of Admissions, 444 W. Third Street,
  Dayton, OH 45402-1460
(513) 226-3060
ssmith@midas.sinclair.edu
Ref: 30922.003119
PF: College Courses for Students

Sinclair Community College
Trotwood Madison High School Career Day
Veronica R. Watkins
Admissions Officer, 444 W. Third Street, Dayton,
  OH 45402
(513) 226-3060
Ref: 30921.003119
PF: Career, Internships, Apprenticeships

Sinclair Community College
Young Scholars Program
Veronica R. Watkins
Admissions Officer, Minority Student
  Recruitment/Retention, 444 W. Third Street,
  Dayton, OH 45402
(513) 226-3060
Ref: 30925.003119
PF: Minority, At-Risk

Skagit Valley College
Running Start
Jim Sorenson
Dean of Admissions/Registration, 2405 E. College
  Way, Mt. Vernon, WA 98273
(206) 428-1227
Ref: 31592.003792
PF: College Courses for Students

▶ **Slippery Rock University of
Pennsylvania**   [58]
Head Start
Thomas L. Gordon
Early Childhood Education, Slippery Rock, PA
  16057
(412) 738-2298
Ref: 31685.003327
PF: Minority, At-Risk

▶ **Slippery Rock University of
Pennsylvania**   [221]
Partnership in a Laboratory School for Exceptional
  Children
Catherine Morsink
Special Education, Slippery Rock, PA 16057
(412) 738-0512
Ref: 31682.003227
PF: Recruit, Preservice, Certification

Slippery Rock University of Pennsylvania
Slippery Rock U-Seneca Valley School District
  Partnership
Jack L. Burtch
Elementary Education, Early Childhood
  Department, Slippery Rock, PA 16057
(412) 738-0512
Ref: 31683.003327
PF: Professional Development, Inservice

Slippery Rock University of Pennsylvania
Triad Partnership for Quality Education
Catherine Morsink
Dean, Secondary Education/Foundations of
   Education, Slippery Rock, PA 16057
(412) 738-2007
Ref: 31684.003327
PF: Resource Sharing

▶ **Smith College**   [294]
Secondary Math and Science Outreach Program
Casey Clark
Science Outreach Program Coordinator, Clark
   Science Center, Northampton, MA 01063
(413) 585-3804
cclark@science.smith.edu
Ref: 31879.002209
PF: School-College-Business Partnerships

▶ **Smith College**   [97]
Smith Summer Science Program
Gail E. Scordilis
Director, Clark Science Center, Northampton, MA
   01063
(413) 585-3879
gscordilis@smith.smith.edu
Ref: 30003.002209
PF: Enrichment, Gifted

▶ **Sonoma State University**   [231]
Jack London Award for Educational Excellence
David Stoloff
Coordinator, East Cotati Avenue, Rohnert Park,
   CA 94928
(707) 664-2315
david.stoloff@sonoma.edu
Ref: 31548.001156
PF: Teaching Awards

▶ **South Dakota School of Mines and
Technology**   [62]
Scientific Knowledge for Indian Learning and
   Leadership (SKILL)
Sara J. McCulloh
Program Director, 501 E. St. Joseph Street, Rapid
   City, SD 57701
(605) 394-1828
smccullo@silver.sdsmt.edu
Ref: 31133.003470
PF: Minority, At-Risk

▶ **South Dakota State University**   [83]
Teaching Russian in Rural America
Gary Sheeley
Head of Instructional Media, Instructional Media
   Center, Pugsley, Brookings, SD 57007
(605) 688-5512
Ref: 31131.003471
PF: College Courses for Students

South Plains College
Tech Prep
Allen F. Meriwether
Director, 1302 Main Street, Lubbock, TX 79401
(806) 744-6477
Ref: 31377.003611
PF: Tech-Prep/2+2

South Puget Sound Community College
Tech Prep-Thurston County Tech Prep
   Consortium
Dorna Bullpitt
Assoc. Dean of Instruction, 2011 Mottman Road
   SW, Olympia, WA 98512
(206) 754-7711 x207
Ref: 31593.005372
PF: Tech-Prep/2+2

▶ **South Seattle Community College**   [267]
Tech Prep Consortium
Marie Coon
Director, 6000 16th Avenue SW, Seattle, WA
   98106
(206) 764-5300
Ref: 31651.009706
PF: Tech-Prep/2+2

▶ **Southeastern Louisiana University**   [256]
Tangipahoa Tech Prep Partnership
Patsy M. Causey
Dean, College of Basic Studies, SLU 672,
   Hammond, LA 70402
(504) 549-3755
Ref: 31267.002024
PF: Tech-Prep/2+2

Southeastern Oklahoma State University
Children's Opera
Andrew Seigrist
Instructor of Music, Station A, Box 4126, Durant,
   OK 74701
(405) 924-0121
Ref: 31287.003179
PF: Enrichment, Gifted

▶ **Southeastern Oklahoma State
University**   [107]
Children's Theatre
Molly Risso
Assoc. Professor of Communications and
   Theatre, Station A, Box 4209, Durant, OK
   74701
(405) 924-0121
Ref: 31291.003179
PF: Enrichment, Gifted

Southeastern Oklahoma State University
Honor Band
Paul Garrison
Asst. Professor of Music, Station A, Box 4047,
   Durant, OK 74701
(405) 924-0121
Ref: 31288.003179
PF: Enrichment, Gifted

Southeastern Oklahoma State University
Honor Show Choir
Mary Ann Craige
Asst. Professor of Music, Station A, Box 4094,
   Durant, OK 74701
(405) 924-0121
Ref: 31289.003179
PF: Enrichment, Gifted

Southeastern Oklahoma State University
Professional Mentor Program
Cheryl Jackson
Director, Teacher Education Services, Box 4135,
   Durant, OK 74701
(405) 924-0121
Ref: 31292.003179
PF: Recruit, Preservice, Certification

Southeastern Oklahoma State University
Southeastern Oklahoma Council for Public School
   Improvement (SOCPSI)
Charles S. Weiner
Executive Director, Box 4145, Durant, OK
   74701-0609
(405) 924-0121 x2943
Ref: 31293.003179
PF: City/Regional Compacts

Southeastern Oklahoma State University
Teen Theatre
Molly Risso
Assoc. Professor of Communications and
    Theatre, Station A, Box 4209, Durant, OK
    74701
(405) 924-0121
Ref: 31290.003179
PF: Enrichment, Gifted

Southern California College
Master of Science in Education
Ray White
Chair, Department of Education, 55 Fair Drive,
    Costa Mesa, CA 92626
(714) 556-3610
Ref: 31719.001293
PF: Recruit, Preservice, Certification

Southern College of Seventh-Day Adventists
Extension Classes
Floyd Greenleaf
Vice President for Academic Administration, P.O.
    Box 370, Collegedale, TN 37315-0370
(615) 238-2804
Ref: 31848.003518
PF: College Courses for Students

▶ **Southern Illinois University at**
Carbondale   [226]
Aviation Technology Program
Charles Rodriguez
Asst. Professor, Department of Aviation
    Technologies, Carbondale, IL 62901-6816
(618) 536-3371
Ref: 31202.001758
PF: Teacher Education Centers

▶ **Southern Illinois University at**
Carbondale   [134]
Careers in Aviation
David A. NewMyer
Chairperson, Aviation Management and Flight,
    Carbondale, IL 62901
(618) 453-8898
Ref: 31203.001758
PF: Career, Internships, Apprenticeships

Southern Illinois University at Carbondale
Foreign Languages in the Elementary Schools
Thomas Keller
Chair, Department of Foreign Languages and
    Literature, Carbondale, IL 62901
(618) 549-4018
ga3598@siucvmb.siu.edu
Ref: 31199.001758
PF: Enrichment, Gifted

▶ **Southern Illinois University at**
Carbondale   [286]
Southern Illinois Instructional Technology
    Association
Candis Isberner
Director, Office of TV Learning Services, 1069
    Communications Building, Carbondale, IL
    62901-6612
(618) 453-6174
Ref: 31204.001758
PF: Technology Application

▶ **Southern Illinois University at**
Carbondale   [232]
Southern Illinois School-College Collaboration
    Committee
Lisa J. McClure
Director, General Education in English,
    Department of English, Carbondale, IL
    62901-4503
(618) 453-6811
Ref: 31201.001758
PF: Faculty Exchanges

▶ **Southern Illinois University at**
Edwardsville   [32]
Project CARING (Children at Risk: Initiating New
    Gateways)
Donald Baden
Assoc. Dean, School of Education, Edwardsville,
    IL 62026
(618) 692-2328
Ref: 31197.001759
PF: Minority, At-Risk

▶ **Southern Maine Technical College**   [36]
Students of the 21st Century
Penny Cary
Assistant to the President, South Portland, ME
    04106
(207) 767-9507
Ref: 31880.005525
PF: Minority, At-Risk

Southern University at New Orleans
Southern University at New Orleans and New
    Orleans Public Schools Partnership
Deborah B. Smith
Coordinator, 6400 Press Drive, New Orleans, LA
    70126
(504) 286-5351
Ref: 31266.002026
PF: Minority, At-Risk

Southwest Missouri State University
Coalition of Essential Schools
Candice Fisk
Coordinator, Greenwood Lab, 901 S. National,
    Springfield, MO 65804
(417) 836-5124
Ref: 31244.002503
PF: City/Regional Compacts

Southwest State University
Enrollment Options Project
John M. Bowden
Dean of Graduate Studies, N. Highway 23,
    Marshall, MN 56258
(507) 537-6108
Ref: 20070.002375
PF: College Courses for Students

Southwest Texas Junior College
Tech Prep
Dick Whipple
Director, 2401 Garner Field Road, Uvalde, TX
    78801
(210) 278-4401
rwhipple@tenet.edu
Ref: 31376.003614
PF: Tech-Prep/2+2

Southwest Texas State University
Annual Staff Development Conference of the
    Texas Association for the Gifted and Talented
John J. Edgell, Jr.
Professor, Department of Mathematics, 601
    University Drive, San Marcos, TX 78666-4616
(512) 245-2551
Ref: 31724.003615
PF: Professional Development, Inservice

Southwest Texas State University
National Council of Teachers of Mathematics
    Regional and National Conferences
John J. Edgell, Jr.
Professor, Department of Mathematics, 601
    University Drive, San Marcos, TX 78666-4616
(512) 245-2551
Ref: 31366.003615
PF: Professional Development, Inservice

▶ **Southwest Texas State University**   [64]
Southwest Texas Summer Science Camp
Julius R. Kroschewsky
Asst. Director, Edwards Aquifer Research Data
    Center, San Marcos, TX 78666
(512) 245-2329
Ref: 31364.003615
PF: Minority, At-Risk

▶ **Southwest Texas State University** [64]
Spruce Cluster Partnership
Margaret E. Dunn
Director, 1002 Education Building, San Marcos,
    TX 78666
(512) 245-2438
Ref: 31365.003615
PF: Minority, At-Risk

▶ **Southwest Texas State University** [222]
SWT Center for Professional Development and
    Technology
Patrice Werner
Assoc. Professor, 601 University Drive, 3047
    Education Building, San Marcos, TX 78666
(512) 245-2310
Ref: 31371.003615
PF: Recruit, Preservice, Certification

Southwest Texas State University
Texas Alliance for Geographic Education
Richard G. Boehm
Chair, Department of Geography and Planning,
    San Marcos, TX 78666
(512) 245-2170
Ref: 31372.003615
PF: Professional Development, Inservice

Southwest Texas State University
Uplift Geography
Richard G. Boehm
Chair, Department of Geography and Planning,
    San Marcos, TX 78666
(512) 245-2170
Ref: 31373.003615
PF: Professional Development, Inservice

Southwest Texas State University
Wonderland School Collaboration
John J. Edgell, Jr.
Professor, Department of Mathematics, 601
    University Drive, San Marcos, TX 78666-4616
(512) 245-2551
Ref: 31370.003615
PF: Instructional Research

Southwestern Community College
Tech Prep
Al Phillips
Coordinator, S.C.C., P.O. Box 151, Whiteville, NC
    28472
(910) 642-7141
Ref: 30750.002964
PF: Tech-Prep/2+2

Southwestern University
Southwestern University/Georgetown
    Independent School District Partners in
    Education
Jim Hunt
Assoc. Professor, Department of Education, P.O.
    Box 770, Georgetown, TX 78627
(512) 863-1391
Ref: 20832.003620
PF: Minority, At-Risk

Spartanburg Technical College
Area Vocational/Technical Center Articulations
    (Health Occupations)
Karen Atkins
Dean, Health Sciences Technologies, P.O. Box
    4386, Spartanburg, SC 29305
(803) 591-3835
Ref: 30787.003994
PF: Career, Internships, Apprenticeships

▶ **Spartanburg Technical College** [266]
Area Vocational-Technical Center in Engineering
    Technologies
Kemp I. Sigmon
Dean, Industrial/Engineering Technologies,
    Spartanburg, SC 29305
(803) 591-3723
Ref: 30788.003994
PF: Tech-Prep/2+2

▶ **Spartanburg Technical College** [195]
Math TRANSIT (Technology Reform and Network
    Specialist Inservice Training)
Sue Stokley
Assoc. Professor of Education, P.O. Box 4386,
    Spartanburg, SC 29305-4386
(803) 591-3852
Ref: 30789.003994
PF: Professional Development, Inservice

▶ **Spring Arbor College** [173]
Learning Environments for the 21st Century
Diane Orchard
Assoc. Professor of Education, 106 N. Main,
    Spring Arbor, MI 49283
(517) 750-6416
Ref: 31031.002318
PF: Professional Development, Inservice

▶ **Springfield College** [294]
Springfield College/DeBerry School Partnership
Linda C. Delano
Coordinator, Teacher Preparation and
    Certification, 263 Alden Street, Springfield, MA
    01109
(413) 748-3155
Ref: 30006.002211
PF: School-College-Business Partnerships

▶ **Springfield Technical Community
College** [39]
METRICS Program (Mentorship, Experimentation
    and Tutoring Resources for Increasing
    Competence in Science)
Sheila Blair
Coordinator, One Armory Square, Springfield, MA
    01101-9000
(413) 781-7822
Ref: 30008.008078
PF: Minority, At-Risk

▶ **Stanford University** [152] [243]
Stanford Educational Cooperative
Beverly Carter
Director, School of Education, Stanford, CA
    94305-3096
(415) 723-1483
kp.bcc@forsythe.stanford.edu
Ref: 20695.001305
PF: Professional Development, Inservice;
    Instructional Research

Stark Technical College
Early College Admission Program
Kelly Mullane
Counselor, Admissions Coordinator, 6200 Frank
    Avenue NW, Canton, OH 44720
(216) 494-6170
Ref: 30897.010881
PF: College Courses for Students

Stark Technical College
Tech Prep
Robert Kollin
Vice President for Instruction, 6200 Frank Avenue
    NW, Canton, OH 44720
(216) 494-6170
Ref: 30908.010881
PF: Tech-Prep/2+2

Stark Technical College
Two Plus Two Articulation
Wallace C. Hoffer
Assoc. Dean of Admissions and Records, 6200
   Frank Avenue NW, Canton, OH 44720
(216) 499-6170
Ref: 30896.010881
PF: College Courses for Students

▶ **State University of New York at
Albany** [128]
Camp Liberty
Alda Walker
Director, Professor, Development Center, 135
   Western Avenue, Albany, NY 12222
(518) 442-5700
Ref: 30238.002835
PF: Tutoring, Counseling

▶ **State University of New York at
Albany** [183]
Capital Area School Development Association
   (CASDA)
Richard Bamberger
Executive Director, Husted 211, Albany, NY
   12222
(518) 442-3796
Ref: 20293.002835
PF: Professional Development, Inservice

▶ **State University of New York at
Albany** [297]
Capital Area Science Advisory Council
Dan Wulff
Professor of Biological Sciences, Biology 108,
   Albany, NY 12222
(518) 442-4290
Ref: 30237.002835
PF: School-College-Business Partnerships

State University of New York at Albany
Capital District Writing Project
Lil Brannon
Director, Humanities 367, Albany, NY 12222
(518) 442-4051
Ref: 30235.002835
PF: Professional Development, Inservice

State University of New York at Albany
Center for Computing and Disability (CCD)
Richard Read
Executive Director, Lecture Center 13, Albany, NY
   12222
(518) 442-3874
readrf@granite.albany.edu
Ref: 30233.002835
PF: Technology Application

State University of New York at Albany
Community and Public Service Program
Neil Cervera
Director, Ten Broeck #102, Dutch Quad, Albany,
   NY 12222
(518) 442-5683
Ref: 30230.002835
PF: Tutoring, Counseling

State University of New York at Albany
Exchanging Information With School
   Superintendents
Mark Berger
Department Chair, Education Administration and
   Policy Studies, Ed 320, Albany, NY 12222
(518) 442-5080
Ref: 30236.002835
PF: Professional Development, Inservice

▶ **State University of New York at
Albany** [104]
Geography and the Capital Region
Floyd Henderson
Professor of Geography and Planning, Social
   Sciences 328, Albany, NY 12222
(518) 442-3912
Ref: 30228.002835
PF: Enrichment, Gifted

▶ **State University of New York at
Albany** [182]
Institute for the Arts in Education
Marlinda Menashe
Administrative Director, Ten Broeck #107, Dutch
   Quad, Albany, NY 12222
(518) 442-4239
Ref: 30232.002835
PF: Professional Development, Inservice

▶ **State University of New York at
Albany** [183]
Laboratory Research Opportunities
Richard Cunningham
Professor of Biological Sciences, Albany, NY
   12222
(518) 442-4290
Ref: 30226.002835
PF: Professional Development, Inservice

▶ **State University of New York at
Albany** [52]
Model for Social Work Intervention in Schools
William Reid
Professor, School of Social Welfare, Richardson
   112, Albany, NY 12222
(518) 442-5331
Ref: 30231.002835
PF: Minority, At-Risk

State University of New York at Albany
Partnership With the Bronx High School of
   Science
Sung Bok Kim
Dean of Undergraduate Studies, Library 0094C,
   Albany, NY 12222
(518) 442-5180
Ref: 30227.002835
PF: Enrichment, Gifted

▶ **State University of New York at
Albany** [183]
Recombinant DNA Courses for High School
   Teachers/Students
Dan Wulff
Professor of Biological Sciences, Biology 108,
   Albany, NY 12222
(518) 442-4290
Ref: 30234.002835
PF: Professional Development, Inservice

▶ **State University of New York at
Albany** [81]
University in the High School Program
Greg Stevens
Director, Social Science 363, Albany, NY 12222
(518) 442-4292
Ref: 20863.002835
PF: College Courses for Students

State University of New York at Albany
Upstate New York Junior Science & Humanities
   Symposium
Dan Wulff
Professor of Biological Sciences, Biology 108,
   Albany, NY 12222
(518) 442-4290
Ref: 30229.002835
PF: Enrichment, Gifted

▶ **State University of New York at
Buffalo** [217]
BRIET (Buffalo Research Institute on Education
   for Teaching)
Catherine Cornbleth
Director and Professor, 208 Baldy, Buffalo, NY
   14260
(716) 636-2461
Ref: 20387.009554
PF: Recruit, Preservice, Certification

State University of New York at Buffalo
University at Buffalo Gifted Math Program
Gerald R. Rising
Director, 560 Baldy, Buffalo, NY 14260-1000
(716) 645-3175
Ref: 21125.009554
PF: Enrichment, Gifted

▶ **State University of New York–College of Agriculture and Technology at Cobleskill** [262]
Agri-Tech Prep
Terry Hughes
Project Coordinator, Cobleskill, NY 2043
(518) 234-5571
hughestr@scobva.cobleskill.edu
Ref: 30363.002856
PF: Tech-Prep/2+2

State University of New York–College of Agriculture and Technology at Cobleskill
College in High School
Chester J Burton
Dean of Business, Cobleskill, NY 12043
(518) 234-5427
burtoncj@scobva.cobleskill.edu
Ref: 30359.002856
PF: College Courses for Students

▶ **State University of New York–College of Agriculture and Technology at Cobleskill** [52]
Project Quest
Marsha Foster
Project Coordinator, Center for Lifelong Learning, Cobleskill, NY 12043
(518) 234-5520
fosterm@scobva.cobleskill.edu
Ref: 30360.002856
PF: Minority, At-Risk

State University of New York–College of Agriculture and Technology at Cobleskill
Schoharie County Business and Education Partnership Project
W. Clifton Collins
Project Director, Knapp Hall, Cobleskill, NY 12043
(518) 234-5528
Ref: 30362.002856
PF: Career, Internships, Apprenticeships

State University of New York–College of Agriculture and Technology at Cobleskill
Schoharie County Tech Prep Associate Degree (Tech Prep)
Charles Macick
Tech Prep Coordinator, Box 98 Knapp Hall, Cobleskill, NY 12043
(518) 234-5353
Ref: 30358.002856
PF: Tech-Prep/2+2

State University of New York–College of Agriculture and Technology at Cobleskill
SUNY-Cobleskill Liberty Partnership Program
Patricia A. Graney
Program Director, Cobleskill, NY 12043
(518) 234-2114
Ref: 30361.002856
PF: Minority, At-Risk

State University of New York–College of Agriculture and Technology at Morrisville
Aristotle Program
Arthur Haber
Assoc. Professor, Chemistry, Morrisville, NY 13408
(315) 684-6184
habera@snymorva.cs.snymor.edu
Ref: 20900.002859
PF: Enrichment, Gifted

▶ **State University of New York–College at Brockport** [217]
Teacher Opportunity Corps (TOC)
Betsy Balzano
Professor of Education, Education and Human Development, Brockport, NY 14420
(716) 395-5549
Ref: 20232.002841
PF: Recruit, Preservice, Certification

State University of New York–College at Buffalo
Project RICE (Response Inner City Education)
Rudy Mattai
Professor of Education, Buffalo, NY 14222
(716) 878-4101
Ref: 31619.002842
PF: Professional Development, Inservice

State University of New York–College at Cortland
Access to College Education Initiative
Cindy Reed
Coordinator, B-127 Van Hoesen Hall, Cortland, NY 13045
(607) 753-5663
reedc@syncorva.cortland.edu
Ref: 30379.002843
PF: Retention, Continuing Education

State University of New York–College at Cortland
Celebration of Teaching
Mary Connery
Director, Center for Educational Exchange, Box 2000, Cortland, NY 13045
(607) 753-4704
connerym@snycorva.cortland.edu
Ref: 30374.002843
PF: Professional Development, Inservice

▶ **State University of New York–College at Cortland** [184]
Center for Educational Exchange
Mary A. Connery
Director, Center for Educational Exchange, Box 2000, Cortland, NY 13045
(607) 753-4704
connerym@snycorva.cortland.edu
Ref: 30375.002843
PF: Professional Development, Inservice

▶ **State University of New York–College at Cortland** [240]
Cortland Curriculum Confab
Richard Castello
Coordinator, Educational Administration, Box 2000, Cortland, NY 13045
(607) 753-5684
castellor@snycorva.cortland.edu
Ref: 30377.002843
PF: Curriculum Development

▶ **State University of New York–College at Cortland** [217]
Elementary Reading Clinic
Larry Bell
Chair, Education Department, Box 2000, Cortland, NY 13045
(607) 753-2705
Ref: 30376.002843
PF: Recruit, Preservice, Certification

State University of New York–College at Cortland
FL Teach (Foreign Language Teaching Forum)
Jean LeLoup
Asst. Professor, ICC Department, P.O. Box 2000, Cortland, NY 13045
(607) 753-4303
flteach@syncorva.cortland.edu
Ref: 30381.002843
PF: Professional Development, Inservice

State University of New York–College at Cortland
High School/College Course Partnership
Mary Connery
Director, Center for Educational Exchange, Box 2000, Cortland, NY 13045
(607) 753-4704
connerym@snycorva.cortland.edu
Ref: 30371.002843
PF: College Courses for Students

▶ **State University of New York–College at Cortland**   [104]
High School Leadership Conference
Mary Connery
Director, Center for Educational Exchange, Box 2000, Cortland, NY 13045
(607) 753-4704
connerym@snycorva.cortland.edu
Ref: 30370.002843
PF: Enrichment, Gifted

▶ **State University of New York–College at Cortland**   [183]
IBM/NYS Education Department Partnership
C. Jane Snell
Dean, School of Education, Box 2000, Cortland, NY 13045
(607) 753-2701
snell@syncorva.cortland.edu
Ref: 30382.002843
PF: Professional Development, Inservice

State University of New York–College at Cortland
Liberty Partnership Program
Cindy Reed
Project Director, B-127 Van Hoesen Hall, Cortland, NY 13045
(607) 753-5663
reedc@syncorva.cortland.edu
Ref: 30380.002843
PF: Minority, At-Risk

State University of New York–College at Cortland
Non-Credit Coaching
Mary Connery
Director, Center for Educational Exchange, Box 2000, Cortland, NY 13045
(607) 753-4704
connerym@snycorva.cortland.edu
Ref: 30369.002843
PF: Professional Development, Inservice

State University of New York–College at Cortland
Teacher Center Affiliation
Mary Connery
Director, Center for Educational Exchange, Box 2000, Cortland, NY 13045
(607) 753-4704
connerym@snycorva.cortland.edu
Ref: 30373.002843
PF: Professional Development, Inservice

State University of New York–College at Cortland
Teachers for the 21st Century
Larry Bell
Chair, Education Department, Box 2000, Cortland, NY 13045
(607) 753-2705
Ref: 30378.002843
PF: Recruit, Preservice, Certification

State University of New York–College at Cortland
Teachers in Training Conference
Mary Connery
Director, Center for Educational Exchange, Box 2000, Cortland, NY 13045
(607) 753-4704
connerym@snycorva.cortland.edu
Ref: 30372.002843
PF: Recruit, Preservice, Certification

▶ **State University of New York–College at Fredonia**   [228]
Fredonia-Hamburg Teacher Education Center
Matthew J. Ludes
Chairperson, Department of Education, Fredonia, NY 14063
(716) 673-3311
Ref: 21075.002844
PF: Teacher Education Centers

State University of New York–College at New Paltz
Curriculum Materials Center
Phil Schmidt
Dean, Faculty of Education, Old Main Building, New Paltz, NY 12561
(914) 257-2800
Ref: 20316.002846
PF: Professional Development, Inservice

▶ **State University of New York–College at New Paltz**   [233]
Dean's Award for Excellence in Teaching
Philip A. Schmidt
Dean, School of Education, Old Main Building, New Paltz, NY 12561
(914) 257-2800
Ref: 21076.002846
PF: Teaching Awards

State University of New York–College at New Paltz
Science and Technology Entry Program (STEP)
Cornelia D'Alessandro
Project Staff Assistant, Education Studies, OMB 112, New Paltz, NY 12561
(914) 257-2836
Ref: 21089.002846
PF: Minority, At-Risk

State University of New York–College at Old Westbury
Creative Problem-Solving Workshop Series & Inservice Retraining Program
Jong Pil Lee
Distinguished Service Professor, Mathematics Department, Old Westbury, NY 11568
(516) 876-3126
Ref: 30218.007109
PF: Professional Development, Inservice

▶ **State University of New York–College at Old Westbury**   [52]
Dwight D. Eisenhower Title IIA Cooperative Demonstration Program
Henry Teoh
Program Director, P.O. Box 210, Old Westbury, NY 11568
(516) 876-2706
Ref: 30219.007109
PF: Minority, At-Risk

State University of New York–College at Old Westbury
Institute of Creative Problem-Solving for Gifted & Talented Students
Jong Pil Lee
Distinguished Service Professor, Mathematics Department, Old Westbury, NY 11568
(516) 876-3126
Ref: 30223.007109
PF: Enrichment, Gifted

State University of New York–College at Old Westbury
NIMH-High School Honors Research Program
George B. Stefano
Project Director, P.O. Box 210, Science Building, Old Westbury, NY 11568
(516) 876-2732
Ref: 31744.007109
PF: Minority, At-Risk

State University of New York–College at Old Westbury
Science and Technology Entry Program (STEP)
Henry Teoh
Program Director, P.O. Box 210, Old Westbury, NY 11568
(516) 876-2706
Ref: 30221.007109
PF: Minority, At-Risk

State University of New York–College at Old Westbury
Science Educators Enhancement & Development Program
Stephen C. Pryor
Assoc. Professor of Biology, Science Building, Old Westbury, NY 11568
(516) 876-2736
Ref: 30222.007109
PF: Professional Development, Inservice

State University of New York–College at Old Westbury
Summer Science Camp
Henry Teoh
Program Director, P.O. Box 210, Old Westbury, NY 11568
(516) 876-2706
Ref: 30220.007109
PF: Minority, At-Risk

▶ State University of New York–College at Oneonta [140]
SUNY's Best Academic Alliance
Dennis Banks
Asst. Professor and Campus Liaison, 334 Fitzelle Hall, Oneonta, NY 13820
(607) 436-3391
Ref: 30289.002847
PF: Career, Internships, Apprenticeships

State University of New York–College at Oswego
Foreign Language Immersion Program (FLIP)
Linda A. Syrell
Dean, Continuing Education, Public Service and Summer Sessions, 43 Swetman Hall, Oswego, NY 13126
(315) 341-2270
Ref: 20765.002848
PF: Enrichment, Gifted

▶ State University of New York–College at Oswego [184]
Project SMART (Science/Mathematics Applied Resources for Teaching)
C. Thomas Gooding
Dean of Graduate Studies and Research, Oswego, NY 13126
(315) 341-3152
gooding@oswego.oswego.edu
Ref: 21212.002848
PF: Professional Development, Inservice

State University of New York–College at Oswego
Teach America Project
Stephen L. Weber
President, Oswego, NY 13126
(315) 341-2211
Ref: 30245.002848
PF: School-College-Business Partnerships

▶ State University of New York–College at Potsdam [218]
Akwesasne Potsdam College Teacher Education Partnership
William J. Doody
Assoc. Professor of Science Education, Potsdam, NY 13676
(315) 267-2530
doodywj@potsdam.edu
Ref: 30281.002850
PF: Recruit, Preservice, Certification

State University of New York–College at Potsdam
Clinical Observation Program
Carol Ann Kissam
Instructor, Project Future, c/o 238 Sisson Hall Potsdam, NY 13676
(315) 267-2623
kissamca@potsdam.edu
Ref: 30283.002850
PF: Recruit, Preservice, Certification

▶ State University of New York–College at Potsdam [105]
County-Wide Science Fair
Mimi Moulton
Senior Staff Assistant, Graduate and Continuing Education Office, 206 Raymond Hall, Potsdam, NY 13676
(315) 267-2166
Ref: 30279.002850
PF: Enrichment, Gifted

State University of New York–College at Potsdam
French Immersion Weekend
Mimi Moulton
Senior Staff Assistant, Graduate and Continuing Education Office, 206 Raymond Hall, Potsdam, NY 13676
(315) 267-2166
Ref: 30273.002850
PF: Enrichment, Gifted

State University of New York–College at Potsdam
High School Science Lab Day
William Kirchgasser
Chairperson, Geology Department, Timmerman Hall, Potsdam, NY 13676
(315) 267-2286
Ref: 30274.002850
PF: Enrichment, Gifted

State University of New York–College at Potsdam
High School Speech Tournament
Nancy Belodoff
Coordinator, Non-Credit Programs, 206 Raymond Hall, Potsdam, NY 13676
(315) 267-2167
Ref: 30276.002850
PF: Enrichment, Gifted

State University of New York–College at Potsdam
Model UN
Nancy Belodoff
Coordinator, Non-Credit Programs, 206 Raymond Hall, Potsdam, NY 13676
(315) 267-2167
Ref: 30277.002850
PF: Enrichment, Gifted

▶ **State University of New York–College at Potsdam** [184]
North Country School Study Council
Constance G. Zelinski
Director of Continuing Education, 206 Raymond Hall, Potsdam, NY 13676
(315) 267-2166
zelinscg@snypotvx.bitnet
Ref: 30272.002850
PF: Professional Development, Inservice

State University of New York–College at Potsdam
North Country School/College Partnership for Elementary Teacher Education
Leslie Crawford
Dean, Satterlee Hall, Potsdam, NY 13676
(315) 267-2515
crawfolw@potsdam.edu
Ref: 30280.002850
PF: Recruit, Preservice, Certification

State University of New York–College at Potsdam
NSF Model Middle School Mathematics and Science Teacher Preparation Program
Timothy J. Schwob
Assoc. Professor, Teacher Education, 304 Satterlee Hall, Potsdam, NY 13676
(315) 267-2474
schwobtj@potsdam.edu
Ref: 30282.002850
PF: Recruit, Preservice, Certification

▶ **State University of New York–College at Potsdam** [52]
Very Special Arts Festival
Leona Ghostlaw
Stenographer, Graduate and Continuing Education Office, 206 Raymond Hall, Potsdam, NY 13676
(315) 267-2166
Ref: 30275.002850
PF: Minority, At-Risk

▶ **State University of New York–College at Purchase** [273]
SUNY-Purchase/Westchester School Partnership
Mary Beth Anderson
Director, 735 Anderson Hill Road, Purchase, NY 10577-1400
(914) 251-6870
Ref: 20288.006791
PF: City/Regional Compacts

State University of New York–College of Technology at Delhi
Tech Prep of South Central New York
Kevin Hodne
Coordinator, 171 Bush Hall, Delhi, NY 13753
(607) 746-4159
Ref: 30288.002857
PF: Tech-Prep/2+2

State University of New York–College of Technology at Farmingdale
Nassau Tech Prep Consortium
Morton P. Seitelman
Director of Learning Technologies, Ward Hall, Farmingdale, NY 11735
(516) 420-2222
Ref: 30353.002858
PF: Tech-Prep/2+2

State University of New York–College of Technology at Farmingdale
Project CARE
Veronica Henry
Professor, Nursing Department, Gleeson Hall, Farmingdale, NY 11735
(516) 420-2032
Ref: 30355.002858
PF: Minority, At-Risk

State University of New York–College of Technology at Farmingdale
Project SAM (Science & Mathematics)
Morton P. Seitelman
Director of Learning Technologies, Ward Hall, Farmingdale, NY 11735
(516) 420-2222
Ref: 30357.002858
PF: Minority, At-Risk

State University of New York–College of Technology at Farmingdale
Science & Technology Entry Program (STEP)
Morton P. Seitelman
Director of Learning Technologies, Ward Hall, Farmingdale, NY 11735
(516) 420-2222
Ref: 30356.002858
PF: Minority, At-Risk

State University of New York–College of Technology at Farmingdale
SUNY-Farmingdale Partnership
Michael J. Vinciguerra
Provost, Melville Road, Farmingdale, NY 11735
(516) 420-2239
Ref: 30351.002858
PF: Professional Development, Inservice

▶ **State University of New York–College of Technology at Farmingdale** [262]
SUNY-Farmingdale's Liberty Partnerships Program
Ruth Redlener
Project Director, 129 Thompson, Farmingdale, NY 11735
(516) 420-2418/2353
Ref: 30352.002858
PF: Tech-Prep/2+2

State University of New York–College of Technology at Farmingdale
Tech Prep-A Partnership Between BOCES III & SUNY-Farmingdale
Morton P. Seitelman
Director of Learning Technologies, Ward Hall, Farmingdale, NY 11735
(516) 420-2222
Ref: 30354.002858
PF: Tech-Prep/2+2

▶ **State University of New York–Institute of Technology at Utica-Rome** [53]
Today's Women in Science and Technology (TWIST)
Betty Klauk
Assistant to the President, Box 3050, Utica, NY 13504-3050
(315) 792-7302
Ref: 30264.006792
PF: Minority, At-Risk

▶ **Stevens Institute of Technology** [178]
Center for Improved Engineering and Science Education (CIESE)
Beth Callihan
Deputy Director, Castle Point on the Hudson, Hoboken, NJ 07030
(201) 216-5037
bcalliha@vaxc.stevens-tech.edu
Ref: 21094.002639
PF: Professional Development, Inservice

▶ **Stonehill College** [125]
Brockton High School Access Center
Rita E. Smith
Director, Stonehill Education Project, 320 Washington Street, North Easton, MA 02357
(508) 230-1056
Ref: 30043.002217
PF: Tutoring, Counseling

Stonehill College
Catholic Educators Collaborative at Stonehill
   College
Rita E. Smith
Director, Stonehill Education Project, 320
   Washington Street, North Easton, MA 02357
(508) 230-1056
Ref: 30044.002217
PF: Professional Development, Inservice

▶ **Stonehill College**   [125]
Helping Each Other Reach Out
Rita E. Smith
Director, Stonehill Education Project, 320
   Washington Street, North Easton, MA 02357
(508) 230-1056
Ref: 30041.002217
PF: Tutoring, Counseling

Stonehill College
Mentor/Tutor Program
Fr. Dan Issing
Director of Campus Ministry, 320 Washington
   Street, North Easton, MA 02357
(508) 230-3732
Ref: 20869.002217
PF: Minority, At-Risk

Stonehill College
Staff Development Academy
Rita E. Smith
Director, Stonehill Education Project, 320
   Washington Street, North Easton, MA 02357
(508) 230-1056
Ref: 20328.002217
PF: Professional Development, Inservice

▶ **Stonehill College**   [170]
Superintendents' Center for Leadership,
   Advocacy and Collaboration, Inc.
Rita E. Smith
Director, Stonehill Education Project, 320
   Washington Street, North Easton, MA 02357
(508) 230-1056
Ref: 20329.002217
PF: Professional Development, Inservice

Stonehill College
Teacher on Tour
Rita E. Smith
Director, Stonehill Education Project, 320
   Washington Street, North Easton, MA 02357
(508) 230-1056
Ref: 20591.002217
PF: Professional Development, Inservice

▶ **Stonehill College**   [125]
Wednesday Academic Club for Kids
Rita E. Smith
Director. Stonehill Education Project, 320
   Washington Street. North Easton, MA 02357
(508) 230-1056
Ref: 30042.002217
PF: Tutoring, Counseling

Sul Ross State University
Big Bend Educational Consortium
Kip Sullivan
Director, Teacher Education, Box C-115, Alpine,
   TX 79832
(915) 837-8170
Ref: 31384.003625
PF: Professional Development, Inservice

Sul Ross State University
Tech Prep
David Cockrum
Vice President for Academic and Student Affairs,
   Alpine, TX 79832
(915) 837-8036
Ref: 31383.003625
PF: Tech-Prep/2+2

Sullivan County Community College
College Courses for High School Students
Paul D. Goldstein
Assoc. Dean of Faculty, P.O. Box 4002,
Loch Sheldrake, NY 12759
(914) 434-5750
Ref: 30241.002879
PF: College Courses for Students

Surry Community College
Tech Prep Program
Robert B. Holder
Coordinator, Dobson, NC 27017
(910) 386-8121
Ref: 31713.002970
PF: Tech-Prep/2+2

▶ **Susquehanna University**   [234]
Susquehanna University/Liberty Valley Project
Peggy Holdren
Instructor/Advisor, R.D. 9, Box 291, Bloomsburg,
   PA 17815
(717) 372-4236
holdren@einstein.susqu.edu.
Ref: 30431.003369
PF: New Faculty Roles

Sussex County Community College
Multicultural Alliance on Intercultural and Gender
   Issues
Anita Ulesky
Dean, Academic Affairs, College Hill, Newton, NJ
   07860
(201) 300-2130
Ref: 30105.025688
PF: Curriculum Development

Sussex County Community College
Northwestern New Jersey Academic Collaborative
Eleanor Carducci
Asst. Professor, English Department, Newton, NJ
   07860
(201) 300-2169
Ref: 30107.025688
PF: Professional Development, Inservice

Sussex County Community College
Partnership in Education
Janice P. Cullinane
Science/Health Division Coordinator, College Hill,
   Newton, NJ 07860
(201) 300-2170
Ref: 30106.025688
PF: Enrichment, Gifted

Sussex County Community College
Sussex County Learning Connection
Eleanor Carducci
Asst. Professor, English Department, Newton, NJ
   07860
(201) 300-2169
Ref: 30108.025688
PF: Professional Development, Inservice

Syracuse University
Jamesville-Dewitt/Syracuse University Teaching
   Center
Gerald M. Mager
Chair, Teaching and Leadership, 150 Marshall
   Street, 150 Huntington Hall, Syracuse, NY
   13244-2340
(315) 443-2684
mager@sued.syr.edu
Ref: 30254.002882
PF: Teacher Education Centers

▶ **Syracuse University** [53]
Maxwell School/High School for Leadership and
    Public Service
William D. Coplin
Director, Public Affairs Program, 105 Maxwell
    Hall, Syracuse, NY 13244
(315) 443-2348
Ref: 30252.002882
PF: Minority, At-Risk

▶ **Syracuse University** [228]
Physics-Teacher Workshops
Allen Miller
Assoc. Professor of Physics, Physics Department,
    Syracuse, NY 13244-1130
(315) 443-5962
Ref: 30249.002882
PF: Teacher Education Centers

▶ **Syracuse University** [228]
Professional Development School
Gerald M. Mager
Chair, Teaching and Leadership, 150 Marshall
    Street, 150 Huntington Hall, Syracuse, NY
    13244-2340
(315) 443-2684
mager@sued.syr.edu
Ref: 30253.002882
PF: Teacher Education Centers

▶ **Syracuse University** [81]
Project Advance®
Franklin P. Wilbur
Director, 111 Waverly Avenue, Suite 200,
    Syracuse, NY 13244-2320
(315) 443-2404
fpwilbur@advance.syr.edu
Ref: 21143.002882
PF: College Courses for Students

▶ **Syracuse University** [184]
SUPER (Schools and University Partnership for
    Educational Responsibility)
Jack Graver
Program Director, Mathematics Department, 215
    Carnegie Hall, Syracuse, NY 13244-1100
(315) 443-1576
jegraver@suadmin.syr.edu
Ref: 21142.002882
PF: Professional Development, Inservice

▶ **Syracuse University** [53]
TechReach®
Cynthia S. Hirtzel
Director, Department of Chemical Engineering,
    Syracuse, NY 13244
(315) 443-3622
chirtzel@suvm.syr.edu
Ref: 30255.002882
PF: Minority, At-Risk

Syracuse University
TRANSIT Onondaga County Project
Joanna O. Masingila
Asst. Professor of Mathematics Education, 215
    Carnegie Hall, Syracuse, NY 13244-1150
(315) 443-1471
jomasing@sued.syr.edu
Ref: 30251.002882
PF: Professional Development, Inservice

▶ **Syracuse University** [53]
University Reach
William D. Coplin
Director, Public Affairs Program, 105 Maxwell
    Hall, Syracuse, NY 13244
(315) 443-2348
Ref: 30250.002882
PF: Minority, At-Risk

Syracuse University
West Genesee/Syracuse University Teaching
    Center
Gerald M. Mager
Chair, Teaching and Leadership, 150 Marshall
    Street, 150 Huntington Hall, Syracuse, NY
    13244-2340
(315) 443-2684
mager@sued.syr.edu
Ref: 21124.002882
PF: Teacher Education Centers

T

Tallahassee Community College
Dual Enrollment/Early Admission
Terry Cox
Counselor, 444 Appleyard Drive, Tallahassee, FL
    32304
(904) 922-8128
Ref: 21092.001533
PF: College Courses for Students

▶ **Tallahassee Community College** [28]
Panhandle College Reach-Out Program (CROP)
    Consortium
Craig Fletcher
Administrator, 444 Appleyard Drive, Tallahassee,
    FL 32304
(904) 922-3668
Ref: 20823.001533
PF: Minority, At-Risk

Tarrant County Junior College
Adopt-A-School
Eva Williams
Asst. Director, Nursing, 5301 Campus Drive,Fort
    Worth, TX 76119
(817) 534-4861
Ref: 31328.008898
PF: Minority, At-Risk

▶ **Technical College of the
Lowcountry** [142]
Career and Choices Exploration Program
Carolyn Banner
Director of Student Services, P.O. Box 1288, 100
    S. Ribaut Road, Beaufort, SC 29901-1288
(803) 525-8218
Ref: 20684.009910
PF: Career, Internships, Apprenticeships

Technical College of the Lowcountry
Dwight D. Eisenhower Mathematics and Science
    Education Programs
Martha Sette
Environmental Technology Instructor, P.O. Box
    1288, Beaufort, SC 29901-1288
(803) 525-8225
Ref: 30829.009910
PF: Professional Development, Inservice

Technical College of the Lowcountry
Educational Talent Search
Beverly Stark
Director, P.O. Box 1288, Beaufort, SC
    29901-1288
(803) 525-8243
Ref: 20682.009910
PF: Minority, At-Risk

▶ **Technical College of the
Lowcountry** [196]
Lowcountry HUB
Anne S. McNutt
President, P.O. Box 1288, Beaufort, SC 29901-
    1288
(803) 525-8246
Ref: 30830.009910
PF: Professional Development, Inservice

Technical College of the Lowcountry
Lowcountry Tech Prep Consortium
Fred Seitz
Curriculum Development, P.O. Box 1288,
    Beaufort, SC 29901-1288
(803) 525-8204
Ref: 30828.009910
PF: Tech-Prep/2+2

▶ **Technical College of the Lowcountry**   [60]
TCL Black Male Mentor Program
Frances McCollough
Director, P.O. Box 1288, Beaufort, SC
    29901-1288
(803) 525-8228
Ref: 30827.009910
PF: Minority, At-Risk

Technical College of the Lowcountry
Upward Bound
Frances McCollough
Director, P.O. Box 1288, Beaufort, SC
    29901-1288
(803) 525-8228
Ref: 20683.009910
PF: Minority, At-Risk

Teikyo Marycrest University
ECHO (Early College Credit Hour Option)
Tim McDonough
Assist. Vice President for Enrollment
    Management, 1607 W. 12th Street, Davenport,
    IA 52804
(319) 326-9251
Ref: 31066.001876
PF: College Courses for Students

▶ **Teikyo Marycrest University**   [301]
Quad-LINC (Quad City Libraries IN Cooperation)
Sr. Joan Sheil
Director of Library Services, 1607 W. 12th Street,
    Davenport, IA 52804
(319) 326-9255
joantmui.mcrest.edu
Ref: 31067.001876
PF: Resource Sharing

▶ **Teikyo Marycrest University**   [164]
TIP (Teacher Incentive Program)
Michelle Schiffgens
Professor, Education Department, 1607 W. 12th
    Street, Davenport, IA 52804
(319) 326-9241
Ref: 31065.001876
PF: Professional Development, Inservice

▶ **Teikyo Post University**   [24]
Proyecto METAS
Dolores M. Riollano
Director, General Studies/Special Programs, P.O.
    Box 2540, Waterbury, CT 06723-2540
(203) 596-4622
Ref: 31819.001401
PF: Minority, At-Risk

Teikyo Westmar University
Post Secondary Enrollment Options Act (Chapter
    261C, Iowa Code)
Leon E. Scott
Assoc. Dean, Le Mars, IA 51031
(712) 546-2003
Ref: 31825.001899
PF: College Courses for Students

Temple University
21st Century Mathematics Center for Urban
    Schools
John C. Chen
Program Director, College of Education, 460 Ritter
    Hall, Philadelphia, PA 19122
(215) 204-6086
Ref: 20757.003371
PF: Enrichment, Gifted

Temple University
Comprehensive Approach to Schooling Success
    (CASS) Program
Margaret C. Wang
Professor and Director, Center for Research in
    Human Development and Education, 13th
    Street and Cecil B. Moore Avenue, 933 Ritter
    Hall Annex, Philadelphia, PA 19122
(215) 204-3001
crhde1@vm.temple.edu
Ref: 20754.003371
PF: Student Health, Welfare

▶ **Temple University**   [275]
The Learning City Program
Margaret C. Wang
Professor and Director, Center for Research in
    Human Development and Education, 13th
    Street and Cecil B. Moore Avenue, 933 Ritter
    Hall Annex, Philadelphia, PA 19122
(215) 204-3001
crhde1@vm.temple.edu
Ref: 30453.003371
PF: City/Regional Compacts

Temple University
PRIME Saturday Tutorial and Enrichment
    Program
F. Stanton Woerth
College of Engineering, Computer Science and
    Architecture, CE Building, Philadelphia, PA
    19122
(215) 204-7805
Ref: 20759.003371
PF: Minority, At-Risk

▶ **Temple University**   [107]
PRIME Universities Program (PUP)
F. Stanton Woerth
College of Engineering, CE Building, Philadelphia,
    PA 19122
(215) 204-7805
Ref: 20758.003371
PF: Enrichment, Gifted

Temple University
Professional Development Schools
Jayminn Sanford
Asst. Professor, 339 Ritter Hall, Philadelphia, PA
    19122
(215) 204-5205
Ref: 30454.003371
PF: Professional Development, Inservice

Temple University
Russel Conwell Educational Services
    Center/Upward Bound
Norma Arnold
Director, Broad and Cecil B. Moore Avenue,
    Seltzer Hall, Room 202, Philadelphia, PA
    19122
(215) 204-5544
Ref: 30456.00337
PF: Minority, At-Risk

▶ **Temple University**   [58]
Teaching Opportunities Program for Students
    (TOPS)
Lynne M. Roberts
Special Assistant to the Dean, Broad and Cecil B.
    Moore Avenue, 12th Floor-Anderson,
    Philadelphia, PA 19122
(215) 204-5198
Ref: 30455.003371
PF: Minority, At-Risk

▶ **Temple University**   [193]
Temple LEAP (Law, Education and Participation)
David Keller Trevaskis, Esq.
Executive Director, 1719 N. Broad Street,
    Philadelphia, PA 19122
(215) 204-8954
Ref: 20238.003371
PF: Professional Development, Inservice

▶ **Temple University**   [241]
Temple University–School District of Philadelphia
   Exemplary Schools Project
Margaret C. Wang
Director, Center for Research in Human
   Development and Education, 933 Ritter Hall
   Annex, Philadelphia, PA 19122
(215) 204-3001
crhde1@vm.temple.edu
Ref: 20425.003371
PF: Curriculum Development

▶ **Terra State Community College**   [264]
Workforce Development Council
Leslie Mack Evans
Tech Prep Director, 2830 Napoleon Road,
   Fremont, OH 43420
(419) 334-8400
Ref: 31843.008278
PF: Tech-Prep/2+2

▶ **Texas A & M University**   [199]
Principals' Center
David Erlandson
Director, Department of Educational
   Administration, College Station, TX 77840
(409) 845-2766
dae2215@zeus.tamu.edu
Ref: 20219.010366
PF: Professional Development, Inservice

Texas A & M University at Galveston
Science Fair
Gerald E. Hite
Assoc. Professor, Oceanography,
   TAMUG-MARS, Galveston, TX 77553-1675
(409) 766-5700
Ref: 20801.010298
PF: Enrichment, Gifted

Texas A & M University–Kingsville
Learning and Teaching Mathematics
Dwight Goode
Professor of Mathematics, Department of
   Mathematics, Campus Box 172, Kingsville, TX
   78363
(512) 595-3189
Ref: 31360.003639
PF: Professional Development, Inservice

Texas Christian University
Professional Development School Project
Jo Ann Houston
Project Co-Director, School of Education, P.O.
   Box 32925, Fort Worth, TX 76129
(817) 921-7698
Ref: 31329.003636
PF: Professional Development, Inservice

Texas Lutheran College
Academic Decathlon
Jennifer Ehlers
Director of Admissions, Seguin, TX 78155
(210) 372-8050
Ref: 31345.003641
PF: Enrichment, Gifted

Texas Lutheran College
Dual Participation
Josie Herrera
Assoc. Director of Admissions, Seguin, TX 78155
(210) 372-8050
Ref: 31346.003641
PF: College Courses for Students

▶ **Texas Lutheran College**   [302]
Facilities Sharing
Pat Patterson
Seguin, TX 78155
(210) 372-8000
Ref: 31348.003641
PF: Resource Sharing

Texas Lutheran College
Honor Band Participation
Doug Bakenhus
Director, Seguin, TX 78155
(210) 372-8000
Ref: 31347.003641
PF: Enrichment, Gifted

▶ **Texas State Technical College-
Sweetwater**   [267]
West Central Texas Tech Prep Consortium
Bill Daugherty
Director, 300 College Drive, Sweetwater, TX
   79556
(915) 235-7485
Ref: 31380.009932
PF: Tech-Prep/2+2

Texas Tech University
Adopt-A-Classroom
John Nevius
Interim Dean, College of Education, Box 4560,
   Lubbock, TX 79409
(806) 742-2377
Ref: 20566.003644
PF: Faculty Exchanges

Texas Tech University
Panhandle-South Plains Center for Professional
   Developmental Technology
Cathy Morton
Director, ESC/17, 1111 W. Loop 289, Lubbock,
   TX 79416
(806) 792-1801
Ref: 31379.003644
PF: Technology Application

▶ **Texas Tech University**   [276]
Professional Development School Collaborative
Charles Reavis
Director, College of Education, Lubbock, TX
   79409
(806) 742-1956
Ref: 31378.003644
PF: City/Regional Compacts

Texas Wesleyan University
Kuumba Project
Allen Henderson
Dean, School of Education, 1201 Wesleyan, Fort
   Worth, TX 76105
(817) 531-4945
Ref: 31327.003645
PF: Minority, At-Risk

▶ **Texas Woman's University**   [229]
College of Education and Human Ecology C^5
   Program
Michael Wiebe
Dean, College of Education and Human Ecology,
   P.O. Box 23029, Denton, TX 76204-1029
(817) 898-2202
Ref: 31330.003646
PF: Teacher Education Centers

Thiel College
Education: TEAM (Thiel Education Affiliation
   Model)
Georgina Rettinger
Chair, Education Department, 75 College Avenue,
   Greenville, PA 16125
(412) 589-2083
Ref: 30404.003376
PF: Recruit, Preservice, Certification

▶ **Thiel College**   [298]
Mercer County School/Business Partnership
Joanne Schell
Director, Career Services, 75 College Avenue,
   Greenville, PA 16125
(412) 589-2014
Ref: 30403.003376
PF: School-College-Business Partnerships

▶ **Thiel College**   [82]
Thiel Scholars Program
Joy Miller
Coordinator, 75 College Avenue, Greenville, PA
   16125
(412) 589-2015
Ref: 30405.003376
PF: College Courses for Students

▶ **Thomas Nelson Community College**   [144]
Project FOCUS (Future Oriented Choices for
    Undecided Students)
Lorraine Hall
Coordinator, P.O. Box 9407, Hampton, VA 23670
(804) 727-1023
Ref: 30575.006871
PF: Career, Internships, Apprenticeships

Three Rivers Community College
Educational Talent Search
Janice Duffy
Project Director, 2080 Three Rivers Boulevard,
    Poplar Bluff, MO 63901
(314) 686-4128
Ref: 31226.004713
PF: Minority, At-Risk

**Three Rivers Community-Technical College,
Thames Campus**
Tech Prep
Ann Gaulin
Coordinator, 574 New London Turnpike, Norwich,
    CT 06360
(203) 886-0177
Ref: 30080.001413
PF: Tech-Prep/2+2

Tompkins-Cortland Community College
Tech Prep
Peggy McKernan
Director, P.O. Box 139, Dryden, NY 13053
(607) 844-8211
Ref: 30383.006788
PF: Tech-Prep/2+2

▶ **Towson State University**   [168]
Baltimore County Public Schools/Towson State
    University PreKindergarten Collaboration
Frances T. Bond
Assoc. Dean, Hawkins Hall-301, Towson, MD
    21204
(410) 839-3998
Ref: 30543.002099
PF: Professional Development, Inservice

▶ **Towson State University**   [38]
Kenwood Adolescent Parenting Project
Frances T. Bond
Assoc. Dean, Hawkins Hall-301, Towson, MD
    21204
(410) 830-3998
Ref: 30542.002099
PF: Minority, At-Risk

Towson State University
Maryland Writing Project (MWP)
Elyse Eidman-Aadahl
Director, Hawkins Hall, Towson, MD 21204
(410) 830-3593
Ref: 20161.002099
PF: Professional Development, Inservice

▶ **Towson State University**   [304]
Parkville Magnet High School
Laurence J. Boucher
Dean, College Natural and Mathematical
    Sciences, Towson, MD 21204
(410) 830-2121
dtpns2@toa.towson.edu
Ref: 30541.002099
PF: Magnet Schools

Tri-County Technical College
Partnership for Academic and Career Education
    (PACE)
Diana M. Walter
Executive Director, P.O. Box 587, Highway 76,
    Pendleton, SC 29670
(803) 646-8361
Ref: 20516.004926
PF: Tech-Prep/2+2

▶ **Tri-County Technical College**   [299]
Anderson County Business and Education
    Partnership
Amy Fendley
P.O. Box 587, Pendleton, SC 29670
(803) 646-8361
Ref: 30807.004926
PF: School-College-Business Partnerships

Tri-County Technical College
Partnership for Lifelong Learning
James H. Williams
Asst. Dean of Instruction, P.O. Box 587,
    Pendleton, SC 29670
(803) 859-7033
Ref: 30810.004926
PF: Retention, Continuing Education

Tri-County Technical College
Partnership in Quality Education
Karen R. Shobe
Coordinator, P.O. Box 587, Pendleton, SC 29670
(803) 646-8361
Ref: 30809.004926
PF: Resource Sharing

Tri-County Technical College
Pathway Partnership
R. H. Mitchell
Access and Equity Coordinator, P.O. Box 587,
    Pendleton, SC 29670
(803) 646-8361
Ref: 30808.004926
PF: Minority, At-Risk

Trinity College (CT)
Bulkeley Connection
Ivan A. Backer
Director, SINA, 300 Summit Street, Hartford, CT
    06106
(203) 297-2278
Ref: 30067.001414
PF: Tutoring, Counseling

▶ **Trinity College (CT)**   [118]
Career Beginnings
Eddie Perez
Director, Community Relations, 300 Summit
    Street, Hartford, CT 06106
(203) 297-2479
eddie.perez@mail.trincoll.edu
Ref: 21194.001414
PF: Tutoring, Counseling

▶ **Trinity College (CT)** [118]
Community Outreach Youth-At-Risk
Tara Gill
Community Service Coordinator, 300 Summit
    Street, #3024, Hartford, CT 06106
(203) 297-2383
tara.gill@mail.trincoll.edu
Ref: 21192.001414
PF: Tutoring, Counseling

▶ **Trinity College (CT)**   [25]
Connecticut Pre-Engineering Program (CPEP)
Naomi Amos
Director of Faculty Grants, 300 Summit Street,
    Hartford, CT 06106
(203) 297-2010
naomi.amos@mail.trincoll.edu
Ref: 21191.001414
PF: Minority, At-Risk

▶ **Trinity College (CT)** [118]
I Have A Dream
Eddie Perez
Director, Community Relations, 300 Summit
   Street, Hartford, CT 06106
(203) 297-2383
eddie.perez@mail.trincoll.edu
Ref: 21200.001414
PF: Tutoring, Counseling

▶ **Trinity College (CT)** [25]
National Youth Sports Program (NYSP)
Rick Hazelton
Director of Athletics, 300 Summit Street, Hartford,
   CT 06106
(203) 297-2055
Ref: 21196.001414
PF: Minority, At-Risk

▶ **Trinity College (CT)** [89]
Poet-in-Residence
Ronald R. Thomas
Chairman, Department of English, Hartford, CT
   06106
(203) 297-2455
Ref: 21198.001414
PF: Enrichment, Gifted

Trinity College (CT)
Ramon E. Betances School
Ivan A. Backer
Director, SINA, 300 Summit Street, Hartford, CT
   06106
(203) 297-2278
Ref: 21201.001414
PF: Tutoring, Counseling

Trinity College (CT)
Scholar of the Month
Ivan A. Backer
Director, SINA, 300 Summit Street, Hartford, CT
   06106
(203) 297-2278
Ref: 21199.001414
PF: Enrichment, Gifted

▶ **Trinity College (VT)** [201]
Summer Math/Science Teacher Institute
Tim Whiteford
Professor, 208 Colchester Avenue, Burlington, VT
   05401
(802) 658-0337
timwhiteford@wintermute.uvm.edu
Ref: 30156.003695
PF: Professional Development, Inservice

Trinity University
Alliance for Better Schools
John H. Moore
Chair, Education, San Antonio, TX 78212
(210) 736-7501
Ref: 21117.003647
PF: Teacher Education Centers

Trinity University
Upward Bound Program
Joyce McQueen
Director, Education Department, 715 Stadium
   Drive, San Antonio, TX 78212
(210) 736-7590
Ref: 21087.003647
PF: Minority, At-Risk

Trocaire College
Articulation Agreement-Trocaire College and Erie
   BOCES I
Mary Jo O'Sullivan
Executive Vice President, 110 Red Jacket
   Parkway, Buffalo, NY 14220
(716) 826-1200
Ref: 30384.002812
PF: College Courses for Students

Trocaire College
Early Admissions Program with Bishop Timon/St.
   Jude High School
Mary Jo O'Sullivan
Executive Vice President, 110 Red Jacket
   Parkway, Buffalo, NY 14220
(716) 826-1200
Ref: 30387.002812
PF: College Courses for Students

Trocaire College
Early Admissions Program with Mount Mercy
   Academy
Mary Jo O'Sullivan
Executive Vice President, 110 Red Jacket
   Parkway, Buffalo, NY 14220
(716) 826-1200
Ref: 30386.002812
PF: College Courses for Students

Trocaire College
Early Admissions Program With North Collins
   High School
Mary Jo O'Sullivan
Executive Vice President, 110 Red Jacket
   Parkway, Buffalo, NY 14220
(716) 826-1200
Ref: 30385.002812
PF: College Courses for Students

▶ **Troy State University at Dothan** [206]
Learning Coalitions/Professional Development
   Schools
Betty J. Kennedy
Dean, School of Education, Dothan, AL 36304
(205) 983-6556
Ref: 30681.001048
PF: Recruit, Preservice, Certification

▶ **Truckee Meadows Community
College** [280]
Joint Occupational Council
Elsie Doser
Dean of Instruction, Reno, NV 89512
(702) 673-7134
Ref: 21255.021077
PF: Regional Articulation

Tulane University
Pathways to Teaching
Diane Manning
Chair, Department of Education, New Orleans, LA
   70005
(504) 865-5341
Ref: 31265.002029
PF: Recruit, Preservice, Certification

▶ **Tulsa Junior College** [265]
Planning for High School and Beyond
Bill Wells
Dean, 6111 E. Skelly Drive, Tulsa, OK 74135
(918) 631-7840
Ref: 21224.009763
PF: Tech-Prep/2+2

▶ **Tyler Junior College** [303]
Forest Trail Library Consortium
Mickey Slimp
Dean, Learning Resources, P.O. Box 9020, Tyler,
   TX 75711
(903) 510-2591
Ref: 31722.003648
PF: Resource Sharing

Tyler Junior College
High School to College Articulation
Richard T. Minter
Dean, P.O. Box 9020, Tyler, TX 75711
(903) 510-2328
Ref: 20428.003648
PF: Tech-Prep/2+2

Tyler Junior College
Partnership for Accelerated Education (PACE)
Aubrey Sharpe
Director, TJC/RTDC, 1530 S.S.W. Loop 323,
   Tyler, TX 75701
(903) 510-2900
Ref: 31319.003648
PF: Minority, At-Risk

Tyler Junior College
Reaching Out: College Mentoring for At-Risk
    Youth
Frankie E. Muffoletto
Dean, P.O. Box 9020, Tyler, TX 75711
(903) 510-2525
Ref: 31320.003648
PF: Minority, At-Risk

U

▶ **Union College**   [54]
G.E. Scholars
Patrick Allen
Director, Educational Studies, 27 N. College,
    Schenectady, NY 12308
(518) 388-6561
Ref: 31801.002889
PF: Minority, At-Risk

▶ **Union College**   [185]
Principles of Engineering Leadership Group
Cherrice Traver
Asst. Professor of Electrical Engineering, EE/CS
    Department, Schenectady, NY 12308
(518) 388-6326
traverc@doc.union.edu
Ref: 30368.002889
PF: Professional Development, Inservice

Union County College
Union County 2+2 Tech Prep
Ivan Rubin
Tech Prep Coordinator, 12-24 W. Jersey Street,
    Elizabeth, NJ 07202
(908) 965-2999
Ref: 30048.002643
PF: Tech-Prep/2+2

▶ **United States Naval Academy**   [96]
Anne Arundel County/USNA Gifted/Talented
    Program
J. D'Archangelo
Mathematics Department, Annapolis, MD
    21402-5002
(410) 293-2795
jmd@sma.usna.navy.mil
Ref: 30565.002101
PF: Enrichment, Gifted

▶ **Universidad del Turabo**   [108]
Pre-Engineering Preparatory Program
Maria de Los Angeles Ortiz
Vice President for Academic Affairs, Sistema
    Educativo Ana G. Mendez, APDO. 21345 Rio
    Piedras, Puerto Rico, PR 00928
(809) 751-0178
Ref: 31742.012841
PF: Enrichment, Gifted

Universidad del Turabo
Upward Bound
Myriam Cintron Riera
Asst. Director, P.O. Box 3030, Gurabo, PR 00778
(809) 743-7979 x4141
Ref: 30002.012841
PF: Minority, At-Risk

University of Akron, Main Campus
AAMP (Akron Achieving Math Proficiency)
A. Quesada
Project Director, Department of
    Math/Development, Programs, Akron, OH
    44325
(216) 972-7192
r1quesa@vm.uakron.edu
Ref: 30891.003123
PF: Professional Development, Inservice

▶ **University of Akron, Main Campus**   [220]
Adapted Physical Education Lab
Thomas A. Eidson
Asst. Professor
Department of Physical and Health Education,
    Akron, OH 44325
(216) 972-7475
r1tae@vm1.cc.uakron.edu
Ref: 30883.003123
PF: Recruit, Preservice, Certification

University of Akron, Main Campus
Adopt-A-School
Michele L Watral
Coordinator of Fraternity and Sorority Life, Akron,
    OH 44325
(216) 972-7909
Ref: 30892.003123
PF: Tutoring, Counseling

University of Akron, Main Campus
Business Education Alliance Reaches Schools
    (BEARS)
Pealmarie W. Goddard
Academic Advisor, Akron, OH 44325-6206
(216) 972-7430
d2pwg@vm1.cc.uakron.edu
Ref: 30890.003123
PF: Minority, At-Risk

University of Akron, Main Campus
Children's Concert Society
Elizabeth Butler
Director, E J Thomas Hall, Akron, OH 44325
(216) 253-6868
Ref: 30889.003123
PF: Enrichment, Gifted

University of Akron, Main Campus
Collaboration Between Coventry Schools and
    College of Education
Lynne Pachnowski
Asst. Professor, Zook 135, Akron, OH
    44325-4202
(216) 972-7115
r1lmp@vm1.cc.uakron.edu
Ref: 30888.003123
PF: Tutoring, Counseling

University of Akron, Main Campus
Drafting & Computer Drafting Technology
Paul John
Coordinator, Akron, OH 44325-6104
(216) 972-6040
Ref: 30894.003123
PF: College Courses for Students

University of Akron, Main Campus
East Regional Professional Development Center
Larry G. Bradley
Assoc. Dean, College of Education, Akron, OH
    44325
(216) 974-6400
Ref: 30882.003123
PF: Professional Development, Inservice

University of Akron, Main Campus
Educational Technology Program
Harriet Herskowitz
Coordinator, Polsky 165C, Akron, OH 44325
(216) 972-7796
Ref: 30873.003123
PF: College Courses for Students

Key: "▶" denotes those partnerships abstracted in Parts 1-5; the corresponding page numbers are given in brackets. "PF:" denotes the partnership's "primary focus." "Ref:" denotes the partnership's assigned reference number in the National School-College Partnership Database (see Appendix B).

University of Akron, Main Campus
Educational Talent Search
Bradley McClain
Director, Pre College Programs, Gallucci Hall,
 Akron, OH 44325
(216) 972-6804
Ref: 30893.003123
PF: Minority, At-Risk

University of Akron, Main Campus
Financial Aid Outreach Programs for Local High
 Schools
Robert D. Hahn
Director, Akron, OH 44325-6211
(216) 972-7032
Ref: 30884.003123
PF: Retention, Continuing Education

University of Akron, Main Campus
Harris Elementary School
Claire Tessier
Asst. Professor, KNEL 204, Akron, OH 44325
(216) 972-5304
Ref: 30876.003123
PF: Resource Sharing

University of Akron, Main Campus
Health and Safety Services, American Red Cross
Lynn M. Leon
Instructor, College of Nursing, Mary Gladwin Hall
 3703, Akron, OH 44325
(216) 972-7865
Ref: 30879.003123
PF: Minority, At-Risk

University of Akron, Main Campus
Informal Collaborative Between Brecksville
 Schools and College of Education
Lynne Pachnowski
Asst. Professor, Zook 135, Akron, OH
 44325-4202
(216) 972-7115
r1lmp@vm1.cc.uakron.edu
Ref: 30872.003123
PF: Professional Development, Inservice

University of Akron, Main Campus
K-16 Council
D. Wright
Director of Higher Education and Special Projects,
 Department of Educational Foundations and
 Leadership, Akron, OH 44325
(216) 972-8253
Ref: 30875.003123
PF: City/Regional Compacts

▶ **University of Akron, Main Campus**   [190]
Magnet Schools Assistance Project-Akron Public
 Schools
Larry G. Bradley
Assoc. Dean, College of Education, Akron, OH
 44325
(216) 974-6400
Ref: 30880.003123
PF: Professional Development, Inservice

▶ **University of Akron, Main Campus**   [264]
Mechanical Engineering Technology
Harold Belofsky
Engineering and Science Technology, SHS 117D,
 Akron, OH 44325
(216) 972-7111
Ref: 30887.003123
PF: Tech-Prep/2+2

University of Akron, Main Campus
Multicultural Communities Akron Public Schools
W. Neal Holmes
Director, African American Studies, 201 F&G
 Leigh Hall, Akron, OH 44325-6234
(216) 972-7143
Ref: 30885.003123
PF: Professional Development, Inservice

University of Akron, Main Campus
Post Secondary Enrollment Options Program
Barbara Bucey
Academic Advisor, 302 E. Buchtel Avenue, Akron,
 OH 44325-6206
(216) 972-7431
r1bab@vm1.cc.uakron.edu
Ref: 30182.003123
PF: College Courses for Students

University of Akron, Main Campus
Pre College Programs, Upward Bound
 Math/Science
David L. Jamison
Interim Senior Vice President and Provost, 102
 Buchtel Hall, Akron, OH 44325-4703
(216) 972-7593
jamison@provost.uakron.edu
Ref: 30881.003123
PF: Minority, At-Risk

University of Akron, Main Campus
Pre Nursing Club: A Recruitment Program for
 Minority and Disadvantaged School Age
 Children
Susan J. Stearns
Assoc. Professor, College of Nursing, Mary
 Gladwin Hall 3703, Akron, OH 44325
(216) 972-7539
Ref: 30878.003123
PF: Minority, At-Risk

▶ **University of Akron, Main Campus**   [220]
Professional Development
Pat Edwards
Assoc. Professor, 127 Carroll Hall, Akron, OH
 44325-5007
(216) 972-8152
r1ple@vm1.cc.uakron.edu
Ref: 30886.003123
PF: Recruit, Preservice, Certification

University of Akron, Main Campus
Recruitment to Nursing
Phyllis A. Fitzgerald
Asst. Dean, Nursing, 555 Hampton Ridge Drive,
 Akron, OH 44313
(216) 836-6165
Ref: 30877.003123
PF: Career, Internships, Apprenticeships

▶ **University of Akron, Main Campus**   [219]
University–Urban School Collaboration
Harold M. Foster
Professor of English Education, 134 Zook Hall,
 Akron, OH 44325-4202
(216) 972-7765
r1hmf@akronvm.edu
Ref: 21053.003123
PF: Recruit, Preservice, Certification

▶ **University of Alabama at
Birmingham**   [270]
The Birmingham Compact
Barbara A. Lewis
Assoc. Professor, 204-A Education Building,
 Birmingham, AL 35294-1250
(205) 934-9154
edu5045@uabdpo.dpo.uab.edu
Ref: 31881.001052
PF: City/Regional Compacts

University of Alabama at Birmingham
High School Articulation Conference
John J. Haggerty
Chair, Department of English, 216 Humanities
 Building, Birmingham, AL 35294-1260
(205) 934-4250
Ref: 30676.001052
PF: Curriculum Development

▶ **University of Alabama at Birmingham**   [87]
Theatre Touring to Elementary and Secondary
 Schools
Lang Reynolds
Chair, Department of Theatre and Dance, 101 Bell
 Building, Birmingham, AL 35294-3340
(205) 934-3236
Ref: 30677.001052
PF: Enrichment, Gifted

▶ **University of Alaska–Fairbanks** [12]
Rural Alaska Honors Institute
Gorden O. Hedahl
Dean, College of Liberal Arts, 405 Gruening,
 Fairbanks, AK 99775
(907) 474-7231
Ref: 20735.001063
PF: Minority, At-Risk

▶ **University of Arizona** [13]
Educational and Community Change Project
Paul E. Heckman
Asst. Professor and Principal Investigator, 1415
 N. Fremont, Tucson, AZ 85719
(602) 622-5719
Ref: 31452.001083
PF: Minority, At-Risk

University of Arizona
Secondary Education Cohort Program
Janice Streitmatter
Interim Assoc. Dean, College of Education,
 Tucson, AZ 85721
(602) 621-1463
jstreitmatter@ccit.arizona.edu
Ref: 31451.001083
PF: Teacher Education Centers

▶ **University of Arkansas at Pine Bluff** [207]
Arkansas Coalition for Diversity in Education
Jacqueline Pryor
Program Coordinator, School of Education, 1200
 N. University Drive, Box 93, Pine Bluff, AR
 71601
(501) 543-8243
Ref: 31849.001086
PF: Recruit, Preservice, Certification

▶ **University of Arkansas–Main
Campus** [149]
Moore Center for Economic Education
Thomas McKinnon
Director, BADM 118, Fayetteville, AR 72701
(501) 575-2855
Ref: 31278.001108
PF: Professional Development, Inservice

▶ **University of Baltimore** [168]
UB/Southwestern High School Partnership
James S. Paige
Assoc. Provost, 1420 N. Charles Street,
 Baltimore, MD 21201-5779
(410) 837-5243
Ref: 20162.002102
PF: Professional Development, Inservice

University of California–Davis
CAL-SOAP-Solano University and Community
 College Educational Support Services
 (SUCCESS) Consortium
Michele Butler
Assoc. Director, Undergraduate Admissions, 175
 Mrak Hall, Davis, CA 95616
(510) 233-3201
Ref: 31566.001313
PF: Minority, At-Risk

University of California–Davis
Capitol Center MESA
James F. Shackelford
Assoc. Dean for Undergraduate Students, College
 of Engineering, Davis, CA 95616
(916) 752-0556
jfshackelford@ucdavis.edu
Ref: 20634.001313
PF: Minority, At-Risk

▶ **University of California–Davis** [236]
College Preparatory Mathematics: Change From
 Within
Judith Kysh
Co-Director, Cress Center, Davis, CA 95616-8729
(916) 752-8467
fzkysh@bullwinkle.ucdavis.edu
Ref: 31565.001313
PF: Curriculum Development

▶ **University of California–Davis** [243]
CRESS (Cooperative Research and Extension
 Services for Schools) Center
Sandra Murphy
Director, Davis, CA 95616-8729
(916) 752-0281
Ref: 21026.001313
PF: Instructional Research

▶ **University of California–Davis** [19]
Engineering Summer Residency Program
Mary C. Ramirez
Coordinator, Special Programs, College of
 Engineering, Davis, CA 95616
(916) 752-3316
mcramirez@ucdavis.edu
Ref: 20635.001313
PF: Minority, At-Risk

▶ **University of California–Davis** [117]
Mathematics Diagnostic Testing Program
Daniel D. Roy
Director, Student Special Services, Davis, CA
 95616-8714
(916) 752-2007
Ref: 20699.001313
PF: Tutoring, Counseling

▶ **University of California–Davis** [152]
Northern California Mathematics Project
Nancy Aaberg
Project Director, Cress Center, Davis, CA
 95616-8729
(916) 752-8784
Ref: 20395.001313
PF: Professional Development, Inservice

▶ **University of California–Davis** [152]
Summer Agriscience Institute
James Leising
Supervisor of Teacher Education, Department of
 Agronomy and Range Science, Agricultural
 Education Program, Davis, CA 95616
(916) 752-1808
jgleising@ucdavis.edu
Ref: 20393.001313
PF: Professional Development, Inservice

University of California–Davis
Teacher Education
Barbara Goldman
Assoc. Director, Teacher Education, Division of
 Education, Davis, CA 95616
(916) 752-5395
bggoldman@ucdavis.edu
Ref: 31649.001313
PF: Teacher Education Centers

▶ **University of California–Davis** [18]
The UC-Davis Early Academic Outreach Program
Gary Tudor
Director, Undergraduate Admissions and
 Outreach Services, Mrak Hall, Davis, CA 95616
(916) 752-3924
Ref: 31567.001313
PF: Minority, At-Risk

University of California–Davis
Upward Bound Program
Ping Chan
Director, 2828 Cowell Boulevard, Davis, CA
    95616
(916) 757-3101
ijchan@ucdavis.edu
Ref: 31564.001313
PF: Minority, At-Risk

▶ **University of California–Irvine**   [19]
KIDS (Kids Investigating and Discovering
    Science)
Luis Villarreal
Professor, Developmental and Cell Biology,
    Irvine, CA 92717-2300
(714) 856-6105
Ref: 31792.001314
PF: Minority, At-Risk

▶ **University of California–Irvine**   [19]
PRISM (Partnership for Reform in Science and
    Mathematics)
Robin Casselman
Assoc. Director, EOP/SAA Outreach, 160
    Administration Building, Irvine, CA 92717-2505
(714) 856-7481
rncassel@uci.edu
Ref: 31527.001314
PF: Minority, At-Risk

▶ **University of California–Irvine**   [153]
STEP (Student/Teacher Educational Partnership)
Robin Casselman
Assoc. Director, EOP/SAA Outreach, 160
    Administration Building, Irvine, CA 92717-2505
(714) 856-7481
rncassel@uci.edu
Ref: 21272.001314
PF: Professional Development, Inservice

University of California–Irvine
UCI Professional Development Schools
Dennis Evans
Assoc. Director, Department of Education,
    Berkeley Place, Suite 245, Irvine, CA 92717
(714) 856-5117
devans@olympia.gse.uci.edu
Ref: 31528.001314
PF: Recruit, Preservice, Certification

▶ **University of California–Los
Angeles**   [153]
Center for Academic Interinstitutional Programs
    (CAIP)
Eugene Tucker
Executive Director, 405 Hilgard Avenue, 304
    Gayley Center, Los Angeles, CA 90024
(310) 825-2531
Ref: 20379.001315
PF: Professional Development, Inservice

▶ **University of California–Riverside**   [244]
California Educational Research Cooperative
    (CERC)
Douglas Mitchell
Professor of Education, Riverside, CA 92521
(909) 787-3026
Ref: 21202.001316
PF: Instructional Research

University of California–Riverside
Comprehensive Teacher Education Institute
Judith H. Sandholtz
Director, School of Education, 1200 University
    Avenue, Riverside, CA 92521
(909) 787-5798
sandholtz@ucrac1.ucr.edu
Ref: 21203.001316
PF: Teacher Education Centers

University of California–Riverside
Inland Area Mathematics Project
Linda Rankin
Project Coordinator, 1200 University Avenue,
    Suite 347, Riverside, CA 92507-4596
(909) 787-4371
edoffice@ucx.ucr.edu
Ref: 21206.001316
PF: Professional Development, Inservice

University of California–Riverside
Inland Area Science Project
Linda Rankin
Project Coordinator, 1200 University Avenue,
    Suite 347, Riverside, CA 92507
(909) 787-4361
edoffice@ucx.ucr.edu
Ref: 31523.001316
PF: Professional Development, Inservice

▶ **University of California–Riverside**   [209]
Project TEAMS (Teacher Excellence and
    Authorization in Math and Science)
Linda Rankin
Project Coordinator, 1200 University Avenue,
    Suite 347, Riverside, CA 92507
(909) 787-4361
edoffice@ucx.ucr.edu
Ref: 31522.001316
PF: Recruit, Preservice, Certification

▶ **University of California–San
Francisco**   [153]
Science and Health Education Partnership
Margaret R. Clark
Director and Professor, 100 Medical Center Way,
    Woods Building, San Francisco, CA
    94143-0905
(415) 476-0300/0337
clarke@jekyll.ucsf.edu
Ref: 21207.001319
PF: Professional Development, Inservice

▶ **University of California–Santa
Barbara**   [244]
UCSB/Schools/SBCC Partnership
Jules M. Zimmer
Acting Dean, Graduate School of Education,
    Santa Barbara, CA 93106-9490
(805) 893-3917
jules@edstar.gse.ucsb.edu
Ref: 21023.001320
PF: Instructional Research

University of Central Arkansas
Arkansas Education Renewal Consortium
Joe Hundley
Director, Center for Academic Excellence,
    Conway, AR 72032
(501) 450-5491
Ref: 21107.001092
PF: School-College-Business Partnerships

▶ **University of Central Arkansas**   [270]
Center for Academic Excellence
Dick B. Clough
Assoc. Professor, Department of Administration
    and Secondary Education, 201 Donaghey
    Street, Conway, AR 72035
(501) 450-3174
Ref: 31275.001092
PF: City/Regional Compacts

▶ **University of Charleston**   [85]
Community Alliance to Support Education (CASE)
Robert L. Frey
Vice President for Academic Life, 2300 MacCorkle
    Avenue SE, Charleston, WV 25304-1099
(304) 357-4875
Ref: 20599.003818
PF: College Courses for Students

▶ **University of Chicago**   [163]
Summer Seminars for Chicago Teachers
Laura Bornholdt
Director, Office of University-School Relations,
    5801 Ellis Avenue, Room 501, Chicago, IL
    60637
(312) 702-8135
l-bornholdt@uchicago.edu
Ref: 31806.001774
PF: Professional Development, Inservice

University of Cincinnati-Raymond Walters College
Access/Success
Sharon R. Wilson
Asst. Dean, Student Services, 9555 Plairfield
    Road, Cincinnati, OH 45014
(513) 745-5737
Ref: 20108.004868
PF: Minority, At-Risk

▶ **University of Colorado at Boulder**   [155]
Colorado Geographic Alliance
A. David Hill
Professor, Geography Department, CB 260,
    Boulder, CO 80309-0260
(303) 492-6760
hill_ad@cubldr.colorado.edu
Ref: 21265.001370
PF: Professional Development, Inservice

University of Colorado at Denver
Career Development Research Project
Andrew Helwig
P.O. Box 173364, Denver, CO 80217
(303) 556-3374
Ref: 31410.006740
PF: Instructional Research

▶ **University of Colorado at Denver**   [155]
Collaborative Network for School Quality
    Teaching and Research
Maurice Holt
P.O. Box 173364, Denver, CO 80217
(303) 556-4373
Ref: 31398.006740
PF: Professional Development, Inservice

▶ **University of Colorado at Denver**   [209]
Collaborative Special Education Teacher Training
    (C-SETT)
Nancy French
P.O. Box 173364, Denver, CO 80217
(303) 556-4380
Ref: 31405.006740
PF: Recruit, Preservice, Certification

▶ **University of Colorado at Denver**   [244]
Colorado Literacy Project
Alan Davis
P.O. Box 173364, Denver, CO 80217
(303) 556-4858
Ref: 31416.006740
PF: Instructional Research

University of Colorado at Denver
Colorado State Systemic Initiative (PEAKS)
Bill Juraschek
P.O. Box 173364, Denver, CO 80217
(303) 556-4355
Ref: 31400.006740
PF: New Achievement, Assessment Standards

▶ **University of Colorado at Denver**   [282]
Columbia Area Writing Project
Nancy Shanklin
P.O. Box 173364, Denver, CO 80217
(303) 556-8446
Ref: 31415.006740
PF: New Achievement, Assessment Standards

University of Colorado at Denver
Comprehensive Intervention Specialists
Elizabeth Kozleski
P.O. Box 173364, Denver, CO 80217
(303) 556-8449
Ref: 31401.006740
PF: Recruit, Preservice, Certification

University of Colorado at Denver
Denver Academy for School Leadership
Paul Bauman
P.O. Box 173364, Denver, CO 80217
(303) 556-4849
Ref: 31402.006740
PF: Instructional Research

University of Colorado at Denver
Developmentally Appropriate Practice in Early
    Childhood Education
Donna Wittmer
P.O. Box 173364, Denver, CO 80217
(303) 556-4367
Ref: 31413.006740
PF: Professional Development, Inservice

University of Colorado at Denver
Evaluating the Outcomes of Preschool Programs
Donna Wittmer
P.O. Box 173364, Denver, CO 80217
(303) 556-4367
Ref: 31414.006740
PF: Instructional Research

University of Colorado at Denver
Innovative Special Education Preparation (ISEP)
Elizabeth Kozleski
P.O. Box 173364, Denver, CO 80217
(303) 556-8449
Ref: 31406.006740
PF: Recruit, Preservice, Certification

University of Colorado at Denver
Jobs Newsletter
Stacy Kalamaros
P.O. Box 173364, Denver, CO 80217
(303) 556-3359
Ref: 31407.006740
PF: Recruit, Preservice, Certification

University of Colorado at Denver
Los Padres Unidosen Accion
Sheila Shannon
P.O. Box 173364, Denver, CO 80217
(303) 556-4356
Ref: 31399.006740
PF: Minority, At-Risk

▶ **University of Colorado at Denver**   [155]
Northern Colorado School Leadership Academy
Rodney Muth
P.O. Box 173364, Denver, CO 80217
(303) 556-4657
Ref: 31408.006740
PF: Professional Development, Inservice

University of Colorado at Denver
Partner Schools
Lynn Rhodes
P.O. Box 173364, Denver, CO 80217
(303) 556-3336
Ref: 31411.006740
PF: Recruit, Preservice, Certification

University of Colorado at Denver
School Leadership Ph.D.
Rodney Muth
P.O. Box 173364, Denver, CO 80217
(303) 556-4657
Ref: 31409.006740
PF: Professional Development, Inservice

University of Colorado at Denver
Social Inclusion Facilitator/Collaborator Training in
    Early Childhood Special Education
Donna Wittmer
P.O. Box 173364, Denver, CO 80217
(303) 556-4367
Ref: 31412.006740
PF: Recruit, Preservice, Certification

▶ **University of Colorado at Denver**   [210]
Stanley British Primary School Alternative
    Teacher Certification Program
William Goodwin
P.O. Box 173364, Denver, CO 80217
(303) 556-3355
Ref: 31417.006740
PF: Recruit, Preservice, Certification

University of Colorado at Denver
Teaching Self Advocacy to Students With
    Disabilities
Beth Doll
P.O. Box 173364, Denver, CO 80217
(303) 556-8448
Ref: 31403.006740
PF: Instructional Research

▶ **University of Colorado at Denver**   [210]
Urban Partnership
Nancy French
P.O. Box 173364, Denver, CO 80217
(303) 556-4380
Ref: 31404.006740
PF: Recruit, Preservice, Certification

▶ **University of Colorado System**   [23]
CU Systemwide Precollegiate Development
    Program
Ron Gallegos
Assistant to the Vice President, Offices of the
    President, Academic Affairs, C Box 51,
    Boulder, CO 80309
(303) 492-6209
Ref: 20072.007996
PF: Minority, At-Risk

▶ **University of Connecticut**   [156]
Connecticut Academy for English, Geography and
    History
Lawrence Goodheart
Professor, History Department, U-103, Storrs, CT
    06269
(203) 455-0305
Ref: 30076.001417
PF: Professional Development, Inservice

University of Connecticut
Connecticut Geographic Alliance
Judith W. Meyer
Assoc. Provost, Storrs, CT 06269
(203) 486-0374
meyer@uconnvm.uconn.edu
Ref: 30077.001417
PF: Professional Development, Inservice

▶ **University of Connecticut**   [156]
Connecticut Writing Project
Mary T. Mackley
Director, English Department, Storrs, CT 06269
(203) 486-5772
Ref: 20446.001417
PF: Professional Development, Inservice

University of Connecticut
Coventry Professional Development Center
Mary Weinland
Coordinator, Education Department, Storrs, CT
    06269
(203) 486-3813
Ref: 30071.001417
PF: Teacher Education Centers

▶ **University of Connecticut**   [156]
Hartford Professional Development Center
Charles W. Case
Dean, School of Education, U-64, 249 Glenbrook
    Road, Storrs, CT 06269-2064
(203) 486-3813
cwcase@uconnvm.uconn.edu
Ref: 30078.001417
PF: Professional Development, Inservice

University of Connecticut
Mansfield Professional Development Center
Mary Weinland
Coordinator, Education Department, Storrs, CT
    06269
(203) 486-3813
Ref: 30072.001417
PF: Teacher Education Centers

University of Connecticut
Minority Engineering, Pre-Engineering Program
Simeon Ochi
Professor, Engineering Department, Storrs, CT
    06269
(203) 486-5536
Ref: 30075.001417
PF: Minority, At-Risk

▶ **University of Connecticut**   [225]
Windham Professional Development Center
Pam Campbell
Professor, School of Education, Storrs, CT 06269
(203) 486-0200
Ref: 30073.001417
PF: Teacher Education Centers

University of Connecticut
Young Scholars Program
Martin Fox
Professor, Engineering Department, Storrs, CT
    06269
(203) 486-3494
Ref: 30074.001417
PF: Enrichment, Gifted

University of Delaware
Delaware Geographic Alliance
Peter W. Rees
Assoc. Professor, Department of Geography,
    Newark, DE 19716
(302) 831-2294
rees@gog.udel.edu
Ref: 30466.001431
PF: Professional Development, Inservice

▶ **University of Delaware**   [237]
Delaware Teacher Enhancement Project
Ronald Wenger (DTEP)
Director, Mathematical Sciences Teaching and
    Learning Center, Newark, DE 19716
(302) 831-2140
ronald.wenger@mvs.del.edu
Ref: 30465.001431
PF: Curriculum Development

▶ **University of Delaware**   [158]
Delmarva Power Energy Education Program
Betty Wier
Assistant to the Dean, College of Education,
    Newark, DE 19716-2901
(302) 831-2311
elizabeth.wier@mvs.udel.edu
Ref: 30470.001431
PF: Professional Development, Inservice

▶ **University of Delaware**   [157]
Literacy Connections
Carol Vukelich
Director, College of Education, Inservice
    Education, Newark, DE 19716
(302) 831-1657
Ref: 30469.001431
PF: Professional Development, Inservice

University of Delaware
Professional Development School: Thurgood
    Marshall Elementary School
Elizabeth Wier
Assistant to the Dean, College of Education,
    Newark, DE 19716
(302) 831-2311
elizabeth.wier@mvs.udel.edu
Ref: 30468.001431
PF: Professional Development, Inservice

▶ **University of Delaware**   [237]
Project 21
Paul LeMahieu
Principal Investigator, College of Education, 105
  Willard Hall, Newark, DE 19716
(302) 831-4433
Ref: 30464.001431
PF: Curriculum Development

▶ **University of Delaware**   [292]
Science Alliance
Elizabeth Wier
Assistant to the Dean, College of Education,
  Newark, DE 19716
(302) 831-2311
elizabeth.wier@mvs.udel.edu
Ref: 30467.001431
PF: School-College-Business Partnerships

▶ **University of Delaware**   [70]
Summer College
Martha Collins-Owens
Coordinator, Honors Program, Newark, DE 19716
(302) 831-6560
martha.collins-owens@mvs.udel.edu
Ref: 20679.001431
PF: College Courses for Students

University of Delaware
Summer Institute for Foreign-Language Teachers
Theodore Braun
Professor, Foreign Language and Literatures,
  Newark, DE 19716
(302) 451-2852
braun@bach.udel.edu
Ref: 20217.001431
PF: Professional Development, Inservice

▶ **University of Denver**   [89]
Odyssey of the Mind
Margie Kelley
Coordinator, 2135 E. Wesley Avenue, Denver, CO
  80208
(303) 871-2531
Ref: 31388.001371
PF: Enrichment, Gifted

▶ **University of Denver**   [89]
Rocky Mountain Talent Search Program
Rich Radcliffe
Coordinator, 2135 E. Wesley, Denver, CO 80208
(303) 871-2533
Ref: 31390.001371
PF: Enrichment, Gifted

▶ **University of Denver**   [88]
University of Youth
Rich Radcliffe
Coordinator, 2135 E. Wesley, Denver, CO 80208
(303) 871-2533
Ref: 31391.001371
PF: Enrichment, Gifted

▶ **University of Denver**   [23]
VIP Program
Elinor Katz
Dean, School of Education, 2450-60 S. Vine
  Street, Denver, CO 80208
(303) 871-2496
Ref: 31389.001371
PF: Minority, At-Risk

University of Detroit Mercy
Detroit Public Schools Professional Development
  School Collaboration
Karen Shirilla
Asst. Dean of Education, P.O. Box 19900, Detroit,
  MI 48219-1900
(313) 993-6308
Ref: 31008.002323
PF: Professional Development, Inservice

University of Evansville
High School Bridge Program
Lynn R. Penland
Program Director, Center for Continuing
  Education, 1800 Lincoln Avenue, Evansville, IN
  47722
(812) 479-2981
Ref: 20054.001795
PF: College Courses for Students

▶ **University of Evansville**   [232]
Outstanding Educator Award
Cathy L. Barlow
 Dean, College of Education and Health Science,
  1800 Lincoln Avenue, Evansville, IN 47722
(812) 479-2360
barlow@evansville.edu
Ref: 30981.001795
PF: Teaching Awards

University of Evansville
Quality Teacher Recruitment Program
Cathy L. Barlow
Dean, College of Education and Health Sciences,
  1800 Lincoln Avenue, Evansville, IN 47722
(812) 479-2360
Ref: 30980.001795
PF: Recruit, Preservice, Certification

▶ **University of Evansville**   [74]
University of Evansville-Evansville Day School
  Alliance
William F. Pollard
Assoc. Vice President for Academic Affairs,
  Evansville, IN 47722
(812) 479-2278
Ref: 30982.001795
PF: College Courses for Students

▶ **The University of Findlay**   [107]
Mazza School Extension Program
Jerry J. Mallett
Director of Mazza Collection Galleria, 1000 N.
  Main Street, Findlay, OH 45840
(419) 424-4777
Ref: 21187.003045
PF: Enrichment, Gifted

▶ **University of Georgia**   [272]
Program for School Improvement
Lewis Allen
Director of Outreach, 124 Aderhold Hall, Athens,
  GA 30602
(706) 542-2523
LPs@uga.cc.uga.edu
Ref: 20231.001598
PF: City/Regional Compacts

▶ **University of Hartford**   [25]
Aetna/Ward Career Ladder Scholarship Program
Anita E. Marchant
Assistant to the Dean, 200 Bloomfield Avenue,
  West Hartford, CT 06117
(203) 768-4795
Ref: 20137.001422
PF: Minority, At-Risk

▶ **University of Hartford**   [25]
Hartford Urban Education Network
Donn Weinholtz
Dean, College of Education, Nursing and Health
  Department, 200 Bloomfield Avenue, West
  Hartford, CT 06117
(203) 768-4648
Ref: 30068.001422
PF: Minority, At-Risk

University of Hawaii–Hawaii Community College
Credit-by-Articulation Program
Joni Onishi
Articulation Coordinator, Business Education Division, 200 W. Kawili Street, Hilo, HI 96720-4091
(808) 933-3327
Ref: 20501.005258
PF: Tech-Prep/2+2

▶ **University of Hawaii–Kapiolani Community College** [133]
RESHAPE
Cynthia N. Kimura
Coordinator, Enrollment Services, 4303 Diamond Head Road, Honolulu, HI 96816
(808) 734-9559
Ref: 21111.001613
PF: Career, Internships, Apprenticeships

▶ **University of Hawaii at Manoa** [211]
Hawaii School University Partnership
Antonette Port
Executive Director, 1776 University Avenue, Castle Memorial Hall, Honolulu, HI 96822
(808) 956-7709
Ref: 20320.001610
PF: Recruit, Preservice, Certification

▶ **University of Hawaii at Manoa** [161]
Philosophy in the Schools
Thomas Jackson
Director, Department of Philosophy, 2530 Dole Street, Honolulu, HI 96822
(808) 956-7824
tjackson@uhunix.uhcc.hawaii.edu
Ref: 20283.001610
PF: Professional Development, Inservice

University of Hawaii at Manoa
Rainbow Connection
Jan Tamiguchi
Coordinator, School and College Services, 1630 Bachman Place, BA 10, Honolulu, HI 96822
(808) 956-7137
score@uhccvx.uhcc.hawaii.edu
Ref: 21021.001610
PF: Retention, Continuing Education

University of Hawaii at Manoa
University of Hawaii Center for Economic Education
Gail A. Tamaribuchi
Director, 2424 Maile Way, Porteus 540, Honolulu, HI 96822
(808) 956-7009
tamaribu@uhunix.uhcc.hawaii.edu-inter
Ref: 21170.001610
PF: Teacher Education Centers

▶ **University of Houston-Clear Lake** [222]
BAER[2] (Bay Area Education Recruitment & Retention)
Anne Baronitis
Coordinator of Advising, 2700 Bay Area Boulevard, Houston, TX 77058
(713) 283-3615
Ref: 31333.011711
PF: Recruit, Preservice, Certification

University of Houston-Clear Lake
Reading Recovery™
Margaret Hill
Asst. Professor, Reading and Language Arts, 2700 Bay Area Boulevard, Box 162, Houston, TX 77058
(713) 283-3533
Ref: 31335.011711
PF: Professional Development, Inservice

University of Houston-Clear Lake
Teacher Education Advancing Academic Achievement Collaborative (TEA|M)
Nolie B. Mayo
Project Director and Principal Investigator, Box 245, 2700 Bay Area Boulevard, Houston, TX 77058
(713) 283-3567
mayo@uhcl4.cl.vh.edu
Ref: 31336.011711
PF: Teacher Education Centers

▶ **University of Houston-Clear Lake** [199]
University of Houston-Clear Lake Teacher Center
Jackie Raspberry
Center Director, 2700 Bay Area Boulevard, Box 30, Houston, TX 77058
(713) 283-3612
Ref: 31334.011711
PF: Professional Development, Inservice

▶ **University of Illinois at Chicago** [32]
Early Outreach Health/Science Enrichment Program (H/SEP)
Ethel L. Caldwell
Director, 1919 W. Taylor, Room 107, M/C 969, Chicago, IL 60612
(312) 996-2549
Ref: 31161.001776
PF: Minority, At-Risk

▶ **University of Illinois at Chicago** [32]
Early Outreach Saturday College Program
Ethel L. Caldwell
Director, 1919 W. Taylor, Room 107, M/C 969, Chicago, IL 60612
(312) 996-2549
Ref: 31162.001776
PF: Minority, At-Risk

▶ **University of Illinois at Chicago** [32]
Summer Enrichment Program for Sixth Graders Attending Project CANAL Schools
Ethel L. Caldwell
Director, 1919 W. Taylor, Room 107, M/C 969, Chicago, IL 60612
(312) 996-2549
Ref: 31163.001776
PF: Minority, At-Risk

▶ **University of Illinois at Urbana-Champaign** [33]
Principal's Scholars Program
Lynette O'Neal
Director, 302 E. John Street, 1909 University Inn, Champaign, IL 61820
(217) 333-0234
Ref: 20064.001775
PF: Minority, At-Risk

▶ **University of Illinois at Urbana-Champaign** [134]
Research Apprentice Program in Applied Sciences (RAP)
Jesse C. Thompson, Jr.
Assistant to the Dean, College of Agriculture, 1301 W. Gregory Drive, Room 104, Urbana, IL 61801
(217) 333-3380
Ref: 20063.001775
PF: Career, Internships, Apprenticeships

▶ **University of Illinois at Urbana-Champaign** [33]
Young Scholars in Agriculture Program
Jesse C. Thompson, Jr.
Assistant to the Dean, College of Agriculture, 1301 W. Gregory Drive, Room 104, Urbana, IL 61801
(217) 333-3380
Ref: 31195.001775
PF: Minority, At-Risk

▶ **University of Iowa** [164]
Iowa Writing Project
Cleo Martin
Asst. Professor Emeritus, Rhetoric and English, 405 Ciustview Avenue, Iowa City, IA 52245
(319) 338-3154
Ref: 21050.001892
PF: Professional Development, Inservice

University of Kentucky
Homework Pals
Ann Garrity
Assistant to the Chancellor, 111 Administration Building, Lexington, KY 40506
(606) 257-1961
Ref: 30846.001989
PF: Minority, At-Risk

▶ **University of Kentucky** [213]
Teacher Opportunity Program
Sharon Brennan
Director of Field Experiences and School
  Collaboration, 104 Taylor Education Building,
  Lexington, KY 40506
(606) 257-1857
cpd434@ukcc.uky.edu
Ref: 31795.001989
PF: Recruit, Preservice, Certification

▶ **University of Louisville** [245]
Center for Collaborative Advancement of the
  Teaching Profession
Ric A. Hovda
Assoc. Director, School of Education, Room 127,
  Dean's Office, Louisville, KY 40292
(502) 852-6471
Ref: 20419.001999
PF: Instructional Research

▶ **University of Louisville** [75]
College School Cooperative Program
John R. Hale
Assistant to the Dean, College of Arts and
  Sciences, Louisville, KY 40292
(502) 852-6490
Ref: 30835.001999
PF: College Courses for Students

▶ **University of Louisville** [75]
International Academy
John R. Hale
Assistant to the Dean, College of Arts and
  Sciences, Louisville, KY 40292
(502) 852-6490
Ref: 30834.001999
PF: College Courses for Students

University of Louisville
Ohio Valley Educational Cooperative/University of
  Louisville Partnership for Professional
  Development
Ken Jones
Partnership Coordinator, School of Education,
  Louisville, KY 40292
(502) 852-0566
Ref: 30831.001999
PF: Professional Development, Inservice

▶ **University of Louisville** [166]
Summer Institute for Teachers
John R. Hale
Assistant to the Dean, College of Arts and
  Sciences, Louisville, KY 40292
(502) 852-6490
Ref: 30833.001999
PF: Professional Development, Inservice

▶ **University of Louisville** [35]
Young Minority Scholars Program
John R. Hale
Assistant to the Dean, College of Arts and
  Sciences, Louisville, KY 40292
(502) 852-6490
Ref: 30832.001999
PF: Minority, At-Risk

▶ **University of Maine at Farmington** [238]
Institute on the Common Core of Learning
Nancy Hensel
Dean, College of Education, Farmington, ME
  04938
(207) 778-7154
Ref: 30138.002040
PF: Curriculum Development

▶ **University of Maine at Farmington** [167]
Western Maine Partnership
Margaret Arbuckle
Director, 104 Main Street, Farmington, ME 04938
(207) 778-7185
Ref: 30139.002040
PF: Professional Development, Inservice

▶ **University of Maine at Machias** [36]
Mawioyne Partnership
Art McEatee
Chair, Education Division, 9 O'Brien Avenue,
  Kimball Hall, Machias, ME 04654
(207) 255-3313
Ref: 30060.002055
PF: Minority, At-Risk

University of Maryland at Baltimore
Booker T. Washington Middle School/UMAB
  Partnership
Neil McCabe
Director of Community Relations, 511 W.
  Lombard Street, Baltimore, MD 21201-1691
(410) 706-4384
neilm@oia-2.ab.umd.edu
Ref: 30536.002104
PF: Minority, At-Risk

▶ **University of Maryland at Baltimore** [38]
Lexington Terrace Elementary School/UMAB
  Partnership
Neil McCabe
Director of Community Relations, 511 W.
  Lombard Street, Baltimore, MD 21204-1691
(410) 706-4384
neilm@oia-2.ab.umd.edu
Ref: 30539.002104
PF: Minority, At-Risk

University of Maryland at Baltimore
Paquin High School/UMAB Partnership
Neil McCabe
Director of Community Relations, 511 W.
  Lombard Street, Baltimore, MD 21201-1691
(410) 706-4384
neilm@oia-2.ab.umd.edu
Ref: 30540.002104
PF: Minority, At-Risk

University of Maryland at Baltimore
Samuel Coleridge Taylor Elementary
  School/UMAB Partnership
Neil McCabe
Director of Community Relations, 511 W.
  Lombard Street, Baltimore, MD 21201-1691
(410) 706-4384
neilm@oia-2.ab.umd.edu
Ref: 30537.002104
PF: Minority, At-Risk

University of Maryland at Baltimore
Steuart Hill Elementary School/UMAB Partnership
Neil McCabe
Director of Community Relations, 511 W.
  Lombard Street, Baltimore, MD 21201-1691
(410) 706-4384
neilm@oia-2.ab.umd.edu
Ref: 30538.002104
PF: Minority, At-Risk

▶ **University of Maryland–Baltimore
County** [124]
Choice Middle Schools Program
Leigh Curtis Higgins
Asst. Director, 5401 Wilkens Avenue, Shriver
  Center, Baltimore, MD 21228-5398
(410) 455-2806
Ref: 30561.002105
PF: Tutoring, Counseling

University of Maryland–Baltimore County
Elementary Science Integration Project
E. Wendy Saul
Assoc. Professor of Education, 5401 Wilkens
    Avenue, Baltimore, MD 21228
(410) 455-2377
saul@umbc2.umbc.edu
Ref: 30559.002105
PF: Professional Development, Inservice

University of Maryland–Baltimore County
The Choice Program
Monica Buccheit
Asst. Director, 971 Seagull Avenue, Baltimore,
    MD 21225
(410) 354-5511
Ref: 30560.002105
PF: Minority, At-Risk

▶ **University of Maryland–Baltimore
County** [124]
Shriver Center Student Literacy Corps
John S. Martello
Executive Director, 5401 Wilkens Avenue, Shriver
    Center, Baltimore, MD 21228
(410) 455-2493
Ref: 30562.002105
PF: Tutoring, Counseling

University of Maryland–Baltimore County
UMBC-West Baltimore Middle School Partnership
Jose Barata
Director, Academic Outreach, 5401 Wilkens
    Avenue, Baltimore, MD 21228
(410) 455-2680
jose-barata@umbcadmin.bitnet
Ref: 30563.002105
PF: Minority, At-Risk

▶ **University of Maryland–College Park** [168]
Center Alliance for Secondary School Teachers
    and Texts (CAST)
Kathleen L. Carroll
Program Director, 1120 Francis Scott Key Hall,
    College Park, MD 20742
(301) 405-6834
kc3@umail.umd.edu
Ref: 30512.002103
PF: Professional Development, Inservice

University of Maryland–College Park
Center for Urban Special Education
Margaret J. McLaughlin
Assoc. Director, Institute for the Study of the
    Exceptional, Department of Special Education,
    College Park, MD 20742
(301) 405-6495
mm28@umail.umd.edu
Ref: 30522.002103
PF: Professional Development, Inservice

▶ **University of Maryland–College Park** [97]
Chemathon
Howard DeVoe
Assoc. Professor, Department of Chemistry and
    Bio-Chemistry, College Park, MD 20742
(301) 405-1833
hd5@umail.umd.edu
Ref: 30523.002103
PF: Enrichment, Gifted

University of Maryland–College Park
Creative Initiative in Teacher Education (CITE)
Bessie C. Howard
Coordinator, College of Education, Benjamin
    Building, College Park, MD 20742
(301) 405-3139
Ref: 30516.002103
PF: Recruit, Preservice, Certification

▶ **University of Maryland–College Park** [246]
Drug Use Survey in Prince George's County
    Public Schools
Raymond P. Lorion
Professor, Department of Psychology, College
    Park, MD 20742
(301) 405-5891
lorion@b553.umd.edu
Ref: 30527.002103
PF: Instructional Research

▶ **University of Maryland–College Park**
Empowering Schools and Families
Raymond P. Lorion
Professor, Department of Psychology, College
    Park, MD 20742
(301) 405-5891
lorion@b553.umd.edu
Ref: 30529.002103
PF: Minority, At-Risk

▶ **University of Maryland–College Park** [38]
Equity 2000
Joan Rosenburg
School/University Programs Coordinator, 3238
    Benjamin Building, College Park, MD 20742
(301) 405-6828
jr106@umail.umd.edu
Ref: 30521.002103
PF: Minority, At-Risk

University of Maryland–College Park
Gymkana
Joseph F. Murray
Director, College of HLHP, College Park, MD
    20742
(301) 405-2566
Ref: 30520.002103
PF: Enrichment, Gifted

▶ **University of Maryland–College Park** [96]
High School Programming Contest
Satish K. Tripathi
Professor and Chair, Department of Computer
    Science, College Park, MD 20742
(301) 405-2662
tripathi@cs.umd.edu
Ref: 30513.002103
PF: Enrichment, Gifted

▶ **University of Maryland–College Park** [287]
ICONS (International Communication and
    Negotiation Simulations)
Patricia Landis
Simulation Director, College Park, MD 20742
(301) 405-4171
plandis@bss2.umd.edu
Ref: 30519.002103
PF: Technology Application

▶ **University of Maryland–College Park** [169]
Joint Education Initiative
Robert W. Ridky
Director, 3433 AV Williams, College Park, MD
    20742
(301) 405-4090
rr23@umail.umd.edu
Ref: 30510.002103
PF: Professional Development, Inservice

▶ **University of Maryland–College Park** [96]
Latin Day
Gregory A. Staley
Assoc. Professor of Classics, 2407 Marie Mount
    Hall, College Park, MD 20742
(301) 405-2016
gs32@umail.umd.edu
Ref: 30515.002103
PF: Enrichment, Gifted

▶ **University of Maryland–College Park** [124]
Literacy Internship Program
Billie Follensbee
Coordinator, 1111 Francis Scott Key Hall, College
    Park, MD 20742
(301) 405-2115
bfollens@arhu.umd.edu
Ref: 20615.002103
PF: Tutoring, Counseling

University of Maryland–College Park
MARY/EMPT
James Alexander
Professor, Department of Mathematics, College
    Park, MD 20742
(301) 415-5114
jca@anna.umd.edu
Ref: 30518.002103
PF: Retention, Continuing Education

▶ **University of Maryland–College Park**   [227]
Mid-Atlantic Region Japan-in-the-Schools
   (MARJiS) Program
Tracey Callahan Mahoney
Assoc. Director, Benjamin Building, Room 3113,
   College Park, MD 20742
(301) 405-3595
Ref: 30524.002103
PF: Teacher Education Centers

University of Maryland–College Park
National History Day
Billy Joe Davis
Professor, Department of History, Northeastern
   State University, Tahlequah, OK 74464
(918) 456-5511 x3516
Ref: 30526.002103
PF: Enrichment, Gifted

University of Maryland–College Park
Physics Summer Outreach Program for Middle
   School Girls
Angelo Bardasis
Professor of Physics, Department of Physics,
   College Park, MD 20742
(301) 405-5958
ab8@umail.umd.edu
Ref: 30525.002103
PF: Minority, At-Risk

▶ **University of Maryland–College Park**   [39]
Rising Stars Leadership Conference
Effie L. Lewis
Program Coordinator, 1126 Taliaferro Hall,
   College Park, MD 20742
(301) 405-5751
effiellewis@umail.umd.edu
Ref: 30517.002103
PF: Minority, At-Risk

University of Maryland–College Park
School/University Cooperative Programs
Thomas D. Weible
Acting Director, 3119 Benjamin Building, College
   Park, MD 20742
(301) 405-2336
tw@umail.umd.edu
Ref: 20709.002103
PF: Professional Development, Inservice

▶ **University of Maryland–College Park**   [169]
Study Abroad: Multicultural Education in the
   Netherlands, Belgium & Germany
Richard L. Hopkins
Assoc. Professor, College of Education,
   Department of Education Policy, Planning and
   Administration, College Park, MD 20742
(301) 405-3568
Ref: 30514.002103
PF: Professional Development, Inservice

University of Maryland–College Park
Summer Study Program in Engineering for High
   School Women
Marilyn R. Berman
Assoc. Dean, College of Engineering, College
   Park, MD 20742
(301) 405-5387
mberman@deans.umd.edu
Ref: 20969.002103
PF: Minority, At-Risk

University of Maryland–College Park
Talent Search Program
Shirley Morman
Director, Room 0112, Chemistry Building, College
   Park, MD 20742
(301) 314-7763
Ref: 30528.002103
PF: Minority, At-Risk

▶ **University of Maryland–College Park**   [38]
Team Maryland
Matthew Haas
Director, 1126 Taliferro Hall, College Park, MD
   20742
(301) 405-7954
Ref: 30511.002103
PF: Minority, At-Risk

▶ **University of Massachusetts at
Amherst**   [214]
MESTEP (The Math/English/Science/Technology
   Project)
Richard J. Clark
Director, Teacher Education, School of Education,
   Amherst, MA 01003
(413) 545-1574
rclark@educ.umass.edu
Ref: 20192.002221
PF: Recruit, Preservice, Certification

▶ **University of Massachusetts at
Amherst**   [40]
The TEAMS Project
Robert Maloy
Continuing Education Manager and Adjunct
   Assoc. Professor, 110 Furcolo Hall, Amherst,
   MA 01003
(413) 545-0945
rmaloy@educ.umass.edu
Ref: 20122.002221
PF: Minority, At-Risk

University of Massachusetts at Boston
Urban Scholars
Joan Becker
Director, 100 Morrissey Boulevard, Boston, MA
   02125-3393
(617) 287-5830
Ref: 30040.002222
PF: Minority, At-Risk

▶ **University of Massachusetts–
Dartmouth**   [97]
Projects for High Learning Potential (PHLP)
Robert L. Piper
Director, Political Science Department, North
   Dartmouth, MA 02740
(508) 999-8899/8036
Ref: 30046.002210
PF: Enrichment, Gifted

▶ **University of Massachusetts–Lowell**   [40]
College Prep Program
Eduardo B. Carballo
Assoc. Professor, College of Education, One
   University Avenue, Lowell, MA 01854
(508) 934-4657
Ref: 30013.002161
PF: Minority, At-Risk

University of Massachusetts Medical Center
High School Health Careers Program
Gladys Rodriguez-Parker
Office of Minority Affairs, 55 Lake Avenue N,
   Room S1-855, Worcester, MA 01655
(508) 856-5541
Ref: 20978.009756
PF: Minority, At-Risk

▶ **University of Medicine and Dentistry of New Jersey–New Jersey Medical School** [137]
Hispanic Center of Excellence Summer Youth Program
Julia Zabala
Program Coordinator, 185 S. Orange Avenue, MSB C-661, Newark, NJ 07103
(201) 982-3762
Ref: 30089.024507
PF: Career, Internships, Apprenticeships

▶ **University of Medicine and Dentistry of New Jersey–New Jersey Medical School**
Minority High School Research Apprentice Program
Ophelia Gona
Assoc. Professor of Anatomy, 185 S. Orange Avenue, Newark, NJ 07103
(201) 982-5245
gona@njms.edu
Ref: 30090.024507
PF: Minority, At-Risk

▶ **University of Medicine and Dentistry of New Jersey–New Jersey Medical School** [45]
Project 3000 by 2000
Frances J. Dunston, M.D.
Assoc. Dean for Special Programs, 185 S. Orange Avenue, Newark, NJ 07103-2714
(201) 982-3854
Ref: 30091.024507
PF: Minority, At-Risk

▶ **University of Memphis** [63]
Memphis Center for Urban Partnerships (MCUP)
George W. Etheridge
Director of Graduate Studies, College of Education, Memphis, TN 38152
(901) 678-2352
etheridge.george@coe.memst.edu
Ref: 30696.003509
PF: Minority, At-Risk

▶ **University of Memphis** [197]
Professional Development Schools
Cindi Chance
Director, College of Education, Undergraduate Curriculum, Ball 200, Memphis, TN 38152
(901) 678-4177
Ref: 31630.003509
PF: Professional Development, Inservice

University of Miami
Medical Magnet Partnership
Kenneth Goodman
Director, Science Outreach Programs, Medical School, P.O. Box 016189, Miami, FL 33101
(305) 547-5723
Ref: 30648.001536
PF: Enrichment, Gifted

▶ **University of Miami** [28]
Restructuring Education for All Learners (REAL)
Linda Saumell
Project Coordinator, P.O. Box 248065, Coral Gables, FL 33124
(305) 284-3141
Ref: 30647.001536
PF: Minority, At-Risk

University of Michigan–Ann Arbor
Detroit Compact
Felton Rogers
Program Associate, 1042 Fleming Building, Ann Arbor, MI 48109-1340
(313) 936-1055
felton.rogers@um.cc.umich.edu
Ref: 30989.009092
PF: Minority, At-Risk

▶ **University of Michigan–Ann Arbor** [42]
Martin Luther King/Cesar Chavez/Rosa Parks–Career Exploration Program
Felton Rogers
Program Associate, 1042 Fleming Building, Ann Arbor, MI 48109-1340
(313) 936-1055
Ref: 30992.009092
PF: Minority, At-Risk

University of Michigan–Ann Arbor
Martin Luther King/Cesar Chavez/Rosa Parks–College Club Program
Onis Elizabeth Cheathams
Program Associate, 503 Thompson Street, 1042 Fleming Building, Ann Arbor, MI 48109
(313) 936-1055
onis-cheathams@um.cc.umich.edu
Ref: 30990.009092
PF: Minority, At-Risk

University of Michigan–Ann Arbor
Martin Luther King/Cesar Chavez/Rosa Parks–College Day Program
Felton Rogers
Program Associate, 1042 Fleming Building, Ann Arbor, MI 48109-1340
(313) 936-1055
felton.rogers@um.cc.umich.edu
Ref: 30991.009092
PF: Minority, At-Risk

University of Michigan–Ann Arbor
Peace Corps Fellows Program
Stuart C. Rankin
Professor, 610 E. University, Ann Arbor, MI 48109-1259
(313) 747-4723
Ref: 30988.009092
PF: Recruit, Preservice, Certification

University of Michigan–Ann Arbor
Professional Development Schools
Stuart C. Rankins
Professor, 610 E. University, Ann Arbor, MI 48109-1259
(313) 747-4723
stuart.c.rankin@um.cc.umich.edu
Ref: 30987.009092
PF: Professional Development, Inservice

▶ **University of Michigan–Ann Arbor** [41]
Wade H. McCree, Jr. Incentive Scholarship Program
Onis Elizabeth Cheathams
Program Associate, 503 Thompson Street, 1042 Fleming Building, Ann Arbor, MI 48109
(313) 936-1055
onis-cheathams@um.cc.umich.edu
Ref: 31851.009092
PF: Minority, At-Risk

University of Michigan–Dearborn
Catherine B. White School
Rosalyn Saltz
Professor, School of Education, 4901 Evergreen Road, 242 FOB, Dearborn, MI 48128-1491
(313) 593-5090
Ref: 31859.002326
PF: Teacher Education Centers

University of Michigan–Dearborn
Detroit Area Pre-College Engineering Program (DAPCEP)
Keshav Varde
Assoc. Dean, School of Engineering, 4901 Evergreen Road, 222 ELB, Dearborn, MI 48128-1491
(313) 593-5117
Ref: 31855.002326
PF: Minority, At-Risk

University of Michigan–Dearborn
Engineering Career Day
Reinaldo Perez
Director, Student Records, School of Engineering, 4901 Evergreen Road, Dearborn, MI 48128-1491
(313) 593-5510
Ref: 31853.002326
PF: Minority, At-Risk

University of Michigan–Dearborn
High School Partnerships-General Programs
Reinaldo Perez
Director, Student Records, School of Engineering,
4901 Evergreen Road, Dearborn, MI
48128-1491
(313) 593-5510
Ref: 31852.002326
PF: Professional Development, Inservice

University of Michigan–Dearborn
Math/Science Institute
Kathy Evans
Admissions Counselor, 4901 Evergreen Road,
220 SSC, Dearborn, MI 48128-1491
(313) 595-0049
Ref: 31861.002326
PF: Minority, At-Risk

University of Michigan–Dearborn
Melvindale/North Allen Park School Consultant
Jerry Lapides
Lecturer, School of Education, 4901 Evergreen
Road, Dearborn, MI 48128-1491
(313) 593-5133
Ref: 31856.002326
PF: Instructional Research

University of Michigan–Dearborn
Southfield Education Committee
John Poster
Dean, School of Education, 4901 Evergreen
Road, 217 FOB, Dearborn, MI 48128-1491
(313) 593-5093
Ref: 31857.002326
PF: Professional Development, Inservice

▶ **University of Michigan–Dearborn**   [136]
Summer Internship Program
Reinaldo Perez
Director, Student Records, School of Engineering,
4901 Evergreen Road, Dearborn, MI
48128-1491
(313) 593-5510
Ref: 31850.002326
PF: Career, Internships, Apprenticeships

University of Michigan–Dearborn
Super Science Saturday
Richard Moyer
Professor, School of Education, 4901 Evergreen
Road, 238 FOB, Dearborn, MI 48128-1491
(313) 593-5099
Ref: 31860.002326
PF: Minority, At-Risk

University of Michigan–Dearborn
Vision 2000 Program
Keshav Varde
Assoc. Dean, School of Engineering, 4901
Evergreen Road, 222 ELB, Dearborn, MI
48128-1491
(313) 593-5117
Ref: 31854.002326
PF: Minority, At-Risk

University of Michigan–Dearborn
Woodward Elementary School Adoption
Donna McKinley
Vice-Chancellor for Student Affairs, 4901
Evergreen Road, 1060 AB, Dearborn, MI
48128-1491
(313) 593-5151
Ref: 31858.002326
PF: Minority, At-Risk

University of Michigan–Dearborn
Wade H. McCree Jr. Incentive Scholarship
Program
Kathy Evans
Admissions Counselor, 4901 Evergreen Road,
220 SSC, Dearborn, MI 48128-1491
(313)595-0049
Ref: 21119.002326
PF: Minority, At-Risk

University of Michigan–Flint
Math Field Day
Ricardo Alfaro
Asst. Professor, Mathematics Department, Flint,
MI 48502
(810) 762-3247
ralfaro@umich.edu
Ref: 20942.002327
PF: Enrichment, Gifted

University of Minnesota–Duluth
College in the Schools
Teri L. Williams
Director, Continuing Education and Extension, 10
University Drive, 403 Darland Administration
Building, Duluth, MN 55812
(218) 726-8835
Ref: 20959.002388
PF: College Courses for Students

▶ **University of Minnesota–Duluth**   [77]
Postsecondary Enrollment Options Act
Karen Heikel
Program Director, Continuing Education and
Extension, 10 University Drive, 403 Darland
Administration Building, Duluth, MN 55812
(218) 726-8835
Ref: 20958.002388
PF: College Courses for Students

▶ **University of Minnesota–Morris**   [214]
Teacher Education
Craig Kissock
Chair, Division of Education, Morris, MN 56267
(612) 589-6402
kissockc@caa.mrs.umn.edu
Ref: 31686.002389
PF: Recruit, Preservice, Certification

▶ **University of Minnesota–Twin Cities**   [246]
Center for Applied Research and Educational
Improvement
Geoffrey Maruyama
Director, 178 Pillsbury Drive SE, 105 Burton,
Minneapolis, MN 55455
(612) 624-3315
geofmar@vx.cis.umn.edu
Ref: 31126.003969
PF: Instructional Research

▶ **University of Missouri–Columbia**   [239]
Instructional Materials Laboratory
Bob R. Stewart
Professor and Chair, 323 Townsend Hall,
Columbia, MO 65211
(314) 882-8391
pavtbob@mizzou1
Ref: 31688.002516
PF: Curriculum Development

▶ **University of Missouri–Columbia**   [43]
Mid-Missouri Diagnostic and Prescriptive Clinic
James R. Koller
Professor, Department of Education and
Counseling Psychology, 16 Hill Hall, Columbia,
MO 65211
(314) 882-5092
Ref: 31847.002516
PF: Minority, At-Risk

Key: "▶" denotes those partnerships abstracted in Parts 1-5; the corresponding page numbers are given in brackets. "PF:" denotes the partnership's "primary focus." "Ref:" denotes the partnership's assigned reference number in the National School-College Partnership Database (see Appendix B).

University of Missouri–Columbia
Memorandum of Understanding
Sharon L. Huntze
Assoc. Dean, College of Education, 102 Hill Hall,
    Columbia, MO 65211
(314) 882-7831
spedslh@mizzou1
Ref: 20556.002516
PF: Recruit, Preservice, Certification

▶ **University of Missouri–Columbia**   [215]
Minority Intern Program
Sharon L. Huntze
Assoc. Dean, College of Education, 102 Hill Hall,
    Columbia, MO 65211
(314) 882-7831
Ref: 20554.002516
PF: Recruit, Preservice, Certification

University of Missouri–Columbia
Special Education
Sharon L. Huntze
Assoc. Dean, College of Education, 102 Hill Hall,
    Columbia, MO 65211
(314) 882-5068
Ref: 31243.002516
PF: Recruit, Preservice, Certification

University of Missouri–Kansas City
High School/College Program
Anna M. Larkin
Director, Outreach Program, 5100 Rockhill Road,
    Kansas City, MO 64110-2499
(816) 235-1165
Ref: 31886.002518
PF: College Courses for Students

▶ **University of Missouri–Kansas City**   [174]
Metropolitan Area Schools Project
Lora Smith
Coordinator, 5100 Rockhill Road, SASS #210,
    Kansas City, MO 64110
(816) 235-1174
lorasmith@vax1.umkc.edu
Ref: 20076.002518
PF: Professional Development, Inservice

▶ **University of Missouri–Kansas City**   [227]
Teacher Education
Don Knight
Professor, School of Education, 309 5100 Rockhill
    Road, Kansas City, MO 64110
(816) 235-2469
Ref: 31230.002518
PF: Teacher Education Centers

▶ **University of Missouri–St. Louis**   [43]
Access to Success
Doris A. Trojcak
Professor, Elementary and Early Childhood
    Education, 8001 Natural Bridge Road, 202
    Education Library, St. Louis, MO 63121
(314) 553-6741
Ref: 20645.002519
PF: Minority, At-Risk

▶ **University of Missouri–St. Louis**   [77]
Advanced Credit Program
Nan Kammann
Director of Special Programs, 8001 Natural Bridge
    Road, 318 Lucas Hall, St. Louis, MO 63121
(314) 553-5036
snlkamm@umslvma.umsl.edu
Ref: 20040.002519
PF: College Courses for Students

University of Missouri–St. Louis
Center for Economic Education
Sarapage McCorkle
Director, 8001 Natural Bridge Road, St. Louis, MO
    63121-4499
(314) 553-5248
ssmccor@umslvma.umsl.edu
Ref: 20397.002519
PF: Teacher Education Centers

▶ **University of Missouri–St. Louis**   [174]
Gateway Writing Project
Leslie Handley
Program Director, 8001 Natural Bridge Road, St.
    Louis, MO 63121
(314) 553-5578
Ref: 21220.002519
PF: Professional Development, Inservice

▶ **University of Missouri–St. Louis**   [99]
George Engelmann Mathematics and Science
    Institute
Charles R. Granger
Director, Engelmann Institute, 8001 Natural
    Bridge Road, St. Louis, MO 63121
(314) 553-6226
Ref: 31212.002519
PF: Enrichment, Gifted

University of Missouri–St. Louis
Professional Development School
Thomas R. Schnell
Assoc. Dean, 8001 Natural Bridge Road, St.
    Louis, MO 63121
(314) 553-5791
Ref: 31213.002519
PF: Professional Development, Inservice

▶ **University of Missouri–St. Louis**   [43]
Regional Science and Technology Career Access
    Center
Melva Ware
Project Director for Administration, 7952 Natural
    Bridge Road, St. Louis, MO 63121
(314) 553-5153
Ref: 31211.002519
PF: Minority, At-Risk

University of Missouri–St. Louis
St. Louis Storytelling Festival
Nan Kammann
Director of Special Programs, 8001 Natural Bridge
    Road, 318 Lucas Hall, St. Louis, MO
    63121-4499
(314) 553-5036
snlkamm@umslvma.umsl.edu
Ref: 21139.002519
PF: Technology Application

University of Montevallo
Collaborative Effort With Public Schools
Elaine W. Hughes
Director, Academic Program Initiatives, Station
    6501, Montevallo, AL 35115
(205) 665-6501
Ref: 20792.001004
PF: Enrichment, Gifted

University of Nebraska-Lincoln
University of Nebraska-Lincoln Independent Study
    High School
James E. Sherwood
Assoc. Director, College Independent Study, 269
    NCCE, Lincoln, NE 68583-9800
(402) 472-1926
sherwood@unl.edu
Ref: 20650.002565
PF: Retention, Continuing Education

University of Nebraska Medical Center
Adopt-A-School Program
Ann Carlson
Community Relations Assistant, P.O. Box
    985230, Omaha, NE 68198-5230
(402) 559-4689
Ref: 31261.006895
PF: Career, Internships, Apprenticeships

University of Nebraska at Omaha
Metropolitan Omaha Educational Consortium
Jill Russell
Coordinator, Kayser Hall 332, Omaha, NE 68182
(402) 554-3386
jrussell@unomaha.edu
Ref: 20540.002554
PF: City/Regional Compacts

▶ **University of Nevada-Las Vegas** [215]
Cultural Diversity Bridge to Academic Success
Elaine Jarchow
Assoc. Dean and Director of Teacher Education,
4505 Maryland Parkway, Las Vegas, NV
89154-3001
(702) 895-4851
jarchow@pioneer.nevada.edu
Ref: 31469.002569
PF: Recruit, Preservice, Certification

University of New England
Maine Learning Technologies for Educators
Partnership
Karen Kortecamp
11 Hills Beach Road, Biddeford, ME 04005
(207) 283-0171
Ref: 30055.002050
PF: Professional Development, Inservice

University of New England
University of New England-Biddeford Primary
Mentoring Collaborative
Jane Freedman
Coordinator of Teacher Education Programs, 11
Hills Beach Road, Biddeford, ME 04005
(207) 283-0171
Ref: 30056.002050
PF: Recruit, Preservice, Certification

▶ **University of New Hampshire** [176]
Center for Educational Field Services (CEFS)
Richard Goodman
Executive Director, #11 Morrill Hall, Durham, NH
03824
(603) 862-1384
Ref: 21223.002589
PF: Professional Development, Inservice

▶ **University of New Mexico, Main
Campus** [179]
Albuquerque Public Schools-University of New
Mexico Collaborative Programs
Keith Auger
Professor, College of Education, Albuquerque,
NM 87131
(505) 277-9126
Ref: 20423.010313
PF: Professional Development, Inservice

▶ **University of New Orleans** [167]
Portal School Project
Joan P. Gipe
Professor, Department of Curriculum and
Instruction, New Orleans, LA 70148
(504) 286-6607
jpgci@uno.edu
Ref: 20356.002015
PF: Professional Development, Inservice

▶ **University of North Alabama** [147]
Center for Economic Education
Veronica Free
Director, Box 5079, Florence, AL 35632
(205) 760-4675
Ref: 31629.001016
PF: Professional Development, Inservice

University of North Alabama
Geography: Alabama Geographic Alliance
William R. Strong
Professor and Chair, Department of Geography,
Box 5064, Florence, AL 35632
(205) 760-4218
bstrong@aol.com
Ref: 30678.001016
PF: Professional Development, Inservice

University of North Carolina at Charlotte
Area Local Physics Alliance
E. S. Oberhofer
Assoc. Professor of Physics, Physics Department,
Charlotte, NC 28223
(704) 547-2505
Ref: 20281.002975
PF: Faculty Exchanges

University of North Carolina at Charlotte
Buncombe County Partnership for Gifted and
Talented Professional Development
Ken Burrows
Director, Extension Programs for Schools,
Charlotte, NC 28223
(704) 547-4446
Ref: 20274.002975
PF: Professional Development, Inservice

University of North Carolina at Charlotte
Lincoln County Schools Partnership for Curricular
and Instructional Improvement
Ken Bumour
Director of Extension Programs for Schools,
Charlotte, NC 28223
(704) 547-4446
Ref: 20276.002975
PF: Professional Development, Inservice

▶ **University of North Carolina at
Charlotte** [240]
Mathematics and Science Education Center
Josephine D. Wallace
Director, Charlotte, NC 28223
(704) 547-4838
jdwallac@unccvm.uncc.edu
Ref: 30741.002975
PF: Curriculum Development

▶ **University of North Carolina at
Charlotte** [218]
Project REACH (Reaching Every At-Risk Child)
Melba Spooner
Coordinator, Office of Field Experiences, College
of Education and Allied Professions, Charlotte,
NC 28223
(704) 547-2886
mcspooner@unccvm.uncc.edu
Ref: 30743.002975
PF: Recruit, Preservice, Certification

▶ **University of North Carolina at
Charlotte** [185]
Project Supervisor: A Model Clinical Teaching
Program
Melba Spooner
Coordinator of Field Experiences, Office of Field
Experiences, College of Education and Allied
Professions, Charlotte, NC 28223
(704) 547-2886
mcspooner@unccvm.uncc.edu
Ref: 20282.002975
PF: Professional Development, Inservice

▶ **University of North Carolina at
Charlotte** [185]
UNC Charlotte/Charlotte Mecklenburg Schools
Cooperative Program for Middle Grades
Training
Ken Burrows
Director of Extension Program for Schools,
Charlotte, NC 28223
(704) 547-4446
Ref: 30740.002975
PF: Professional Development, Inservice

Key: "▶" denotes those partnerships abstracted in Parts 1-5; the corresponding page numbers are given in brackets. "PF:" denotes the partnership's "primary focus." "Ref:" denotes the partnership's assigned reference number in the National School-College Partnership Database (see Appendix B).

University of North Carolina at Charlotte
University Meadows Elementary School-UNCC Partnership
Melba Spooner
Coordinator of Field Experiences, Office of Field Experiences, College of Education and Allied Professions, Charlotte, NC 28223
(704) 547-2886
mcspooner@unccvm.uncc.edu
Ref: 30742.002975
PF: Recruit, Preservice, Certification

▶ **University of North Carolina at Greensboro** [298]
Invitational Education and Next Century Schools
William Watson Purkey
Professor, Greensboro, NC 27412
(910) 334-3431
Ref: 30724.002976
PF: School-College-Business Partnerships

▶ **University of North Carolina at Greensboro** [186]
Piedmont Triad Horizons Education Consortium
Frances F. Jones
Executive Director, School of Education, Greensboro, NC 27412
(910) 334-5100
Ref: 30725.002976
PF: Professional Development, Inservice

University of North Carolina at Greensboro
UNCG Professional Development Schools
Mary Olson
Assoc. Dean, School of Education, Greensboro, NC 27412
(910) 344-5100
Ref: 30726.002976
PF: Professional Development, Inservice

▶ **University of North Dakota-Main Campus** [187]
Lake Agassiz Professional Development School
Mary McDonnell Harris
Dean, Center for Teaching and Learning, Box 7189, Grand Forks, ND 58202
(701) 111-2674
maharris@vml.nodak.edu
Ref: 31137.003005
PF: Professional Development, Inservice

University of North Dakota-Main Campus
North Dakota LEAD Center
Donald L. Piper
Professor of Educational Administration, Box 7189, Grand Forks, ND 58202-7189
(701) 777-4255
Ref: 31139.003005
PF: Professional Development, Inservice

University of North Dakota-Main Campus
North Dakota Teacher Center Network
Mary McDonnell Harris
Dean, Center for Teaching and Learning, Box 7189, Grand Forks, ND 58202
(701) 777-2675
maharris@vml.nodak.edu
Ref: 31138.003005
PF: Teacher Education Centers

▶ **University of North Dakota-Main Campus** [105]
Suitcase Shakespeare
Sandra Lindberg
Asst. Professor, UND Theatre Arts, Box 8136, University Station, Grand Forks, ND 58201
(701) 777-2853
Ref: 31136.003005
PF: Enrichment, Gifted

▶ **University of North Dakota-Main Campus** [219]
UND/North Dakota School for the Blind
Myrna R. Olson
Professor and Graduate Coordinator/Special Education, Box 7189 University Station, Grand Forks, ND 58202
(701) 777-3188
Ref: 31141.003005
PF: Recruit, Preservice, Certification

▶ **University of North Dakota-Main Campus** [187]
Walsh-Pembina Consortium
Donald L. Piper
Education Ad/Facilitator and Professor of Educational Administration, Box 7189, Grand Forks, ND 58202-7189
(701) 777-4255
Ref: 31140.003005
PF: Professional Development, Inservice

University of North Texas
North Texas Center for Professional Development & Technology Network
Kaaren Day
Director, College of Education, Denton, TX 76203
(817) 565-4377
Ref: 31753.003594
PF: Professional Development, Inservice

▶ **University of Northern Colorado** [155]
Greeley Strategic Planning Initiative
Gary Galluzzo
Dean, College of Education, Greeley, CO 80639
(303) 351-2817
Ref: 21022.001349
PF: Professional Development, Inservice

▶ **University of Northern Colorado** [231]
Partnership for Professional Renewal of Master Teachers
Sandra Simmons
Asst. Dean, College of Education, Greeley, CO 80639
(303) 351-2430
Ref: 20348.001349
PF: Faculty Exchanges

▶ **University of Northern Colorado** [271]
Project SPAN (Standards and Performance Based Academic Networking)
Francis A. (Jerry) Griffith
Coordinator, University Assessment Program, Academic Affairs, Carter Hall, Greeley, CO 80639
(303) 351-2823
Ref: 31424.001349
PF: City/Regional Compacts

▶ **University of Northern Iowa** [165]
Janesville Project
Mary J. Selke
Coordinator, PLS 116, Cedar Falls, IA 50614
(319) 273-2202
selke@uni.edu
Ref: 31046.001980
PF: Comprehensive Systemic Restructuring

▶ **University of Northern Iowa** [35]
Minorities in Teaching (MIT)
Janet E. McClain
Director, 184 Schindler Education Center, Cedar Falls, IA 50614-0606
(319) 273-2924
Ref: 31048.001980
PF: Minority, At-Risk

▶ **University of Northern Iowa** [165]
Office of Student Field Experiences Network
Roger A. Kueter
Professor, Department of Teaching, Cedar Falls, IA 50613-3593
(319) 273-2202
kueter@uni.edu
Ref: 31047.001980
PF: Professional Development, Inservice

University of Notre Dame
Educational Talent Search
Warren G. Outlaw
Director, P.O. Box 458, Notre Dame, IN 46556
(219) 631-5670
Ref: 30969.001840
PF: Minority, At-Risk

▶ **University of Notre Dame**   [95]
Linkup
Roland B. Smith, Jr.
Executive Assistant to the President, 306 Main
    Building, Notre Dame, IN 46556
(219) 631-6798
Ref: 30971.001840
PF: Enrichment, Gifted

University of Notre Dame
Project Upward Bound
Dorine Blake-Smith
Director, P.O. Box 458, Notre Dame, IN 46556
(219) 631-5669
Ref: 30970.001840
PF: Minority, At-Risk

University of Oklahoma–Norman Campus
Oklahoma Public School Consortium
Fred H. Wood
Dean, College of Education, Collings Hall,
    Norman, OK 73019
(405) 325-1081
Ref: 31280.003184
PF: Technology Application

▶ **University of Oklahoma–Norman
Campus**   [220]
Responsive Leaders for All Children
Frank O. McQuarrie, Jr.
Director, Office of Field Experiences, College of
    Education, Norman, OK 73019
(405) 325-4844
Ref: 31281.003184
PF: Recruit, Preservice, Certification

▶ **University of Oregon**   [141]
Career Information System Consortium
Michael J. Neill
Director, 1177 Pearl Street, Suite 200, Eugene,
    OR 97401
(503) 346-3872
mneill@oregon.uoregon.edu
Ref: 21226.003223
PF: Career, Internships, Apprenticeships

▶ **University of Oregon**   [191]
Oregon Writing Project
Nathaniel Teich
Project Director, Department of English, Eugene,
    OR 97403
(503) 686-3911
Ref: 21045.003223
PF: Professional Development, Inservice

▶ **University of Pennsylvania**   [141]
Adopt-a-School
Carole Hawkins
Training Coordinator, 1050 Steinberg Hall-Dietrich
    Hall, Philadelphia, PA 19140-6373
(215) 898-5039
hawkins@wharton.upenn.edu
Ref: 20914.003378
PF: Career, Internships, Apprenticeships

▶ **University of Pennsylvania**   [193]
Center for School Study Councils
Harris J. Sokoloff
Executive Director, Graduate School of
    Education, Center for School Study Councils,
    3700 Walnut Street, Philadelphia, PA
    19104-6216
(215) 898-7371
harriss@nwfs.gse.upenn.edu
Ref: 20292.003378
PF: Professional Development, Inservice

University of Pennsylvania
The Philadelphia Writing Project
Susan L. Lytle
Director, Graduate School of Education, 3700
    Walnut Street, Philadelphia, PA 19104-6216
(215) 898-1919
lytle@literacy.upenn.edu
Ref: 20515.003378
PF: Professional Development, Inservice

▶ **University of Pennsylvania**   [58]
Say Yes To Education
Norman Newburg
Executive Director, Graduate School of
    Education, 3700 Walnut Street, Philadelphia,
    PA 19104-6216
(215) 898-1819
Ref: 20123.003378
PF: Minority, At-Risk

University of Pennsylvania
Teen Parent Education & Employability Skills
    Program
Ann O'Sullivan, F.A.A.N.
Assoc. Professor, 420 Guardian Drive,
    Philadelphia, PA 19104
(215) 898-4272
o'sull@son.nursing.upenn.edu
Ref: 30451.003378
PF: Minority, At-Risk

▶ **University of Pennsylvania**   [275]
West Philadelphia Improvement Corps (WEPIC)
Ira Harkavy
Director, Center for Community Partnerships, 133
    S. 36th Street, Suite 519, Philadelphia, PA
    19104-3246
(215) 898-5351
harkavy@pobox.upenn.edu
Ref: 30452.003378
PF: City/Regional Compacts

▶ **University of Pittsburgh**   [83]
College in High School
Susan Harkins
Director, 140 Thackeray, Pittsburgh, PA 15260
(412) 624-6789
sharkins@vms.cis.pitt.edu
Ref: 20878.003379
PF: College Courses for Students

**University of Puerto Rico–Humacao University
College**
Saturday Academy for Mathematical Research
Alberto Caceres
Program Director, Department of Mathematics,
    Humacao, PR 00971
(809) 850-9386
a_caceres@cuhac.upr.clu.edu
Ref: 30340.003943
PF: Enrichment, Gifted

**University of Puerto Rico–Humacao University
College**
School Adoption and Collaborative Program with
    other Region Schools
Cecilia Alvarez Melendez
Administrative Official, P.O. Box CUH Station,
    Humacao, PR 00971
(809) 852-8580
Ref: 30341.003943
PF: Resource Sharing

▶ **University of Puerto Rico–Humacao
University College**   [194]
Workshops on Problem Solving Based on the
    NCTM Standards
Alberto Caceres
Program Director, Department of Mathematics,
    Humacao, PR 00791
(809) 850-9386
a_caceres@cuhac.upr.clu.edu
Ref: 30339.003943
PF: Professional Development, Inservice

Key: "▶" denotes those partnerships abstracted in Parts 1-5; the corresponding page numbers are given in brackets. "PF:" denotes the partnership's "primary focus." "Ref:" denotes the partnership's assigned reference number in the National School-College Partnership Database (see Appendix B).

▶ **University of Redlands**   [236]
Implementing "It's Elementary!" Through
    Collaborative Arrangements
June Canty Lemke
Chair, Education Department, 1200 E. Colton
    Avenue, Redlands, CA 92373
(909) 335-4010
lemke@ultrix.uor.edu
Ref: 31518.001322
PF: Curriculum Development

▶ **University of Redlands**   [231]
University of Redlands/Franklin Elementary
    School Partnership
June Canty Lemke
Chair, Education Department, 1200 E. Colton
    Avenue, Redlands, CA 92373
(909) 335-4010
lemke@ultrix.uor.edu
Ref: 31519.001322
PF: Faculty Exchanges

University of Rhode Island
URI/Providence School Department Partnership
Marcia Marker Feld
Executive Director, URI Urban Field Center, 22
    Hayes Street, Providence, RI 02908
(401) 277-3982
Ref: 21088.003414
PF: City/Regional Compacts

University of Rochester
Martin Luther King School Day
Judy Abelman
Assoc. Director, University and Community
    Affairs, 108 Todd Union, Rochester, NY 14627
(716) 275-7211
Ref: 30310.002894
PF: Enrichment, Gifted

▶ **University of Rochester**   [54]
School #37
Judy Abelman
Assoc. Director, University and Community
    Affairs, 108 Todd Union, Rochester, NY 14627
(716) 275-7211
Ref: 30309.002894
PF: Minority, At-Risk

▶ **University of San Diego**   [88]
Partnership in Education
Judy Rauner
Director of Volunteer Resources, Alcala Park, San
    Diego, CA 92110-2492
(619) 260-4798
Ref: 20725.010395
PF: Enrichment, Gifted

University of Scranton
Education Department
David A. Wiley
Director, Secondary Education, Education
    Department, Scranton, PA 18510-4603
(717) 941-4032
daw315@jaguar.uofs.edu
Ref: 30440.003384
PF: Tutoring, Counseling

University of Scranton
Teachers Talking With Teachers
Shirley M. Adams
Dean, Scranton, PA 18510
(717) 941-7580
Ref: 30439.003384
PF: Professional Development, Inservice

University of Scranton
Teenage Mothers Program
Mary Muscari
Asst. Professor, Scranton, PA 18510
(717) 941-7647
Ref: 30438.003384
PF: Minority, At-Risk

University of South Alabama
SECME (Southeast Consortium for Minorities in
    Engineering)
David T. Hayhurst
Dean, College of Engineering, Mobile, AL 36688
(205) 460-6140
Ref: 31749.001057
PF: Minority, At-Risk

▶ **University of South Alabama**   [147]
South Alabama Research's Inservice Center
Phillip Feldman
Professor, College of Education, Mobile, AL
    36688
(205) 460-6119
pfeldman@jaguar.usouthal.edu
Ref: 20289.001057
PF: Professional Development, Inservice

▶ **University of South Carolina–Aiken**   [299]
Partner Schools
Margaret Corboy
Head, School of Education, 171 University
    Parkway, Aiken, SC 29801
(803) 648-6851
Ref: 30821.003449
PF: School-College-Business Partnerships

University of South Carolina–Aiken
Ruth Patrick Science Education Center
Jeffrey M. Priest
Director, Aiken, SC 29801
(803) 648-6851
jpriest@univscvm.csd.scarolina.edu
Ref: 20385.003449
PF: Professional Development, Inservice

▶ **University of South Carolina–Aiken**   [143]
Teacher Cadet Program
Audrey Skrupskelis
College Partner, 171 University Parkway, Aiken,
    SC 29801
(803) 648-6851
Ref: 20094.003449
PF: Career, Internships, Apprenticeships

▶ **University of South Carolina–
Columbia**   [109]
Adventures in Creativity
James L. Stiver
Assoc. Dean, South Carolina Honors College,
    Columbia, SC 29208
(803) 777-8102
Ref: 30774.003448
PF: Enrichment, Gifted

▶ **University of South Carolina–
Columbia**   [109]
Benjamin E. Mays Academy for Leadership
    Development
John McFadden
The Benjamin E. Mays Professor, Department of
    Educational Psychology, Columbia, SC 29208
(803) 777-7797
Ref: 30777.003448
PF: Enrichment, Gifted

▶ **University of South Carolina–
Columbia**   [109]
Carolina Journalism Institute (CJI)
Andrew Bosman
Director, College of Journalism and Mass
    Communications, Columbia, SC 29208
(803) 777-6284
Ref: 30784.003448
PF: Enrichment, Gifted

University of South Carolina–Columbia
Criminal Justice 101 for High School Students
Danny E. Baker
Interim Dean, College of Criminal Justice, Carrell
    College, Columbia, SC 29208
(803) 777-7097
Ref: 30773.003448
PF: College Courses for Students

▶ **University of South Carolina–Columbia** [196]
Educators In Industry
Margaret Z. Burggraf
Assoc. Professor, College of Education, Columbia, SC 29208
(803) 777-3053
Ref: 30780.003448
PF: Professional Development, Inservice

University of South Carolina–Columbia
Give Yourself Some Credit
William A. Mould
Dean, South Carolina Honors College, 202 Harper, Columbia, SC 29208
(803) 777-8102
Ref: 30775.003448
PF: College Courses for Students

University of South Carolina–Columbia
Graduate Regional Studies
John J. Duffy
Vice Provost for Regional Campuses and Continuing Education, Carolina Plaza, Columbia, SC 29208
(803) 777-7695
Ref: 30776.003448
PF: Professional Development, Inservice

▶ **University of South Carolina–Columbia** [108]
Odyssey of the Mind State Competition
Reenea Harrison-Cook
Director of Academic Affairs, Columbia, SC 29208
(803) 777-8102
Ref: 30779.003448
PF: Enrichment, Gifted

▶ **University of South Carolina–Columbia** [196]
Professional Development Schools
Sandra Winecoff
Co-Chair, College of Education, Columbia, SC 29208
(803) 777-4265
Ref: 30778.003448
PF: Professional Development, Inservice

▶ **University of South Carolina–Columbia** [242]
South Carolina Comprehensive School Health Education Coalition
Ruth P. Saunders
Research Asst. Professor, Department of Health Promotion and Education, Columbia, SC 29208
(803) 777-2871
Ref: 30782.003448
PF: Curriculum Development

▶ **University of South Carolina–Columbia** [281]
South Carolina Health Education Partnership
Ruth P. Saunders
Research Asst. Professor, Department of Health Promotion and Education, Columbia, SC 29208
(803) 777-2871
Ref: 30781.003448
PF: Regional Articulation

University of South Carolina–Columbia
South Carolina Scholastic Broadcasters Association
John Lopiccolo
Director, College of Journalism and Mass Communications, Columbia, SC 29208
(803) 777-3324
Ref: 30783.003448
PF: Enrichment, Gifted

University of South Carolina–Columbia
South Carolina Scholastic Press Association
Bruce E. Konkle
Director, College of Journalism/Mass Communications, Columbia, SC 29208
(803) 777-6284
Ref: 31789.003448
PF: Enrichment, Gifted

▶ **University of South Carolina–Columbia** [109]
Southern Interscholastic Press Association
Beth Dickey
Assoc. Director, College of Journalism and Mass Communications, Columbia, SC 29208
(803) 777-6284
Ref: 31788.003448
PF: Enrichment, Gifted

University of South Carolina at Lancaster
Program Offering College Classes to Talented & Gifted High School Students
Peter N. Barry
Academic Dean, P.O. Box 889, Lancaster, SC 29720
(803) 285-7471
Ref: 20681.003453
PF: College Courses for Students

University of South Carolina–Salkehatchie
High School Program
Frank Shelton
Assoc. Dean, Academic Affairs, Box 617, Allendale, SC 29810
(803) 584-3446
Ref: 30826.003454
PF: College Courses for Students

University of South Carolina–Salkehatchie
Salkehatchie Consortium
Bess M. Lawton
Assoc. Dean, Box 617, Allendale, SC 29810
(803) 584-3446
Ref: 30825.003454
PF: Professional Development, Inservice

▶ **University of South Carolina–Salkehatchie** [196]
Teachers' Aides Program
Frank Shelton
Assoc. Dean, Academic Affairs, Box 617, Allendale, SC 29810
(803) 584-3446
Ref: 30824.003454
PF: Professional Development, Inservice

University of South Carolina–Spartanburg
The Saturday Academy
Jimmie E. Cook
Dean, School of Education, 800 University Way, Spartanburg, SC 29303
(803) 599-2577
Ref: 31200.006951
PF: Minority, At-Risk

University of South Carolina–Sumter
Academic Center (Sumter School District #2)
Thomas Lisk
Assoc. Dean for Academic Affairs, Sumter, SC 29150
(803) 775-6341
toml@uscsumter.uscsu.scarolina.edu
Ref: 30761.012112
PF: Enrichment, Gifted

Key: "▶" denotes those partnerships abstracted in Parts 1-5; the corresponding page numbers are given in brackets. "PF:" denotes the partnership's "primary focus." "Ref:" denotes the partnership's assigned reference number in the National School-College Partnership Database (see Appendix B).

University of South Florida
Job Shadowing Experience
Patricia Crumbley, R.N.
Educator, Department of Education, 12902
    Magnolia Drive, H. Lee Moffitt Cancer Center,
    Tampa, FL 33612-9497
(813) 972-4673
Ref: 30654.001537
PF: Career, Internships, Apprenticeships

▶ **University of South Florida** [283]
Centennial Elementary Professional Development
    School
Susan Homan
Professor, College of Education, EDU 208B, 4202
    Fowler Avenue, Tampa, FL 33620
(813) 974-3460
Ref: 30655.001537
PF: New Achievement, Assessment Standards

University of South Florida
USF/ Cypress Creek Collaboration
Kathryn Laframboise
Asst. Professor, College of Education, EDU 208B,
    4202 Fowler Avenue, Tampa, FL 33620
(813) 974-3460
Ref: 30656.001537
PF: Professional Development, Inservice

▶ **University of South Florida–St. Petersburg
Campus** [28]
Accelerated Literacy Learning
Ruth A. Short
Project Coordinator, College of Education, 208B,
    140 7th Avenue S, St. Petersburg, FL 33701
(813) 893-9524
Ref: 30657.001537
PF: Minority, At-Risk

**University of South Florida–St. Petersburg
Campus**
BRIDGE Program
Kim Stoddard
Asst. Professor, 140 7th Avenue S, St.
    Petersburg, FL 33701
(813) 813-9573
Ref: 30658.001537
PF: Professional Development, Inservice

**University of South Florida–St. Petersburg
Campus**
Palm Harbor University High School-USF
    Collaborative Project
Herb Kare
Professor, 140 7th Avenue S, St. Petersburg, FL
    33701
(813) 893-9155
Ref: 30661.001537
PF: Professional Development, Inservice

▶ **University of South Florida–St. Petersburg
Campus** [237]
Rawlings Elementary School Developmental
    Writing Program
Barbara Frye
Asst. Professor, 140 7th Avenue S, St.
    Petersburg, FL 33701
(813) 893-9574
Ref: 30659.001537
PF: Curriculum Development

University of South Florida–Sarasota Campus
Moody Elementary Manatee County, Florida
Wendy Kastin
Assoc. Professor, 5700 N. Tamiami Trail, PMC
    210, Sarasota, FL 34243
(813) 359-4342
Ref: 31736.001537
PF: Curriculum Development

▶ **University of Southern California** [225]
Center To Advance Precollege Science Education
Lois Slavkin
Executive Director, 2250 Alcazar Street, Los
    Angeles, CA 90033
(213) 342-3169
Ref: 31496.001328
PF: Teacher Education Centers

▶ **University of Southern California** [271]
Coalition of Essential Schools
Juli Quinn
Director, PH 702, Los Angeles, CA 90740
(213) 740-9340
Ref: 31503.001328
PF: City/Regional Compacts

▶ **University of Southern California** [20]
Education Consortium of Central Los Angeles
    (ECCLA)
Samuel Mark
Asst. Vice President, Civic and Community
    Relations, 835 W. 34th Street, Suite 102, Los
    Angeles, CA 90089-0751
(213) 740-5480
Ref: 21253.001328
PF: Minority, At-Risk

▶ **University of Southern California** [19]
Educational Talent Search Program
Jeffrey L. Clayton
Director, E.O.P.C., 3708 S. Figueroa Street, Los
    Angeles, CA 90007
(213) 743-6395
Ref: 31474.001328
PF: Minority, At-Risk

▶ **University of Southern California** [21]
EEXCEL (Educational Excellence for Children
    With Environmental Limitations)
Julie Barber
Educational Director, 12010 S. Vermont Avenue,
    Los Angeles, CA 90044
(213) 200-1131
Ref: 31497.001328
PF: Minority, At-Risk

▶ **University of Southern California** [20]
Joint Educational Project
Richard Cone
Director, 801 W. 34th Street, Los Angeles, CA
    90089-0471
(213) 740-1837
Ref: 21136.001328
PF: Minority, At-Risk

▶ **University of Southern California** [21]
MESA (Mathematics, Engineering, Science
    Achievement)
Larry Lim
Director, Minority Programs, School of
    Engineering, Los Angeles, CA 90089-1455
(213) 740-1999
llim@mizar.usc.edu
Ref: 21078.001428
PF: Minority, At-Risk

▶ **University of Southern California** [21]
National Youth Sports Program (NYSP)
Dave Koch
Project Administrator, Lyon University Center, Los
    Angeles, CA 90089-2500
(213) 740-5127
d.koch@spiff.usc.edu
Ref: 31499.001328
PF: Minority, At-Risk

▶ **University of Southern California** [20]
Peer Counseling Program
Jeffrey L. Clayton
Director, E.O.P.C., 3708 S. Figueroa Street, Los
    Angeles, CA 90007
(213) 743-6395
Ref: 31476.001328
PF: Minority, At-Risk

▶ **University of Southern California** [22]
Precollege Summer Art Program
Penelope Jones
Director of Admissions, School of Fine Arts, Watt
    Hall 104, Los Angeles, CA 90089-0292
(213) 740-9153
Ref: 31502.001328
PF: Minority, At-Risk

▶ **University of Southern California**   [304]
Science Museum School Collaborative
William F. McComts
Director, Science Education Programs, School of
    Education, WPH 1001E, Los Angeles, CA
    90089-0031
(213) 740-3470
mccomas@usc.edu
Ref: 31500.001328
PF: Magnet Schools

University of Southern California
Student Speakers Bureau
Jeffrey L. Clayton
Director, E.O.P.C., 3708 S. Figueroa Street, Los
    Angeles, CA 90007
(213) 743-6395
Ref: 31475.001328
PF: Minority, At-Risk

University of Southern California
Troy Camp
David Crandall
Director, Student Activities, Student Union 202,
    Los Angeles, CA 90089-0890
(213) 740-5693
dcrandal@mizar.usc.edu
Ref: 31501.001328
PF: Minority, At-Risk

University of Southern California
Upward Bound Math/Science Program
Jeffrey L. Clayton
Director, E.O.P.C., 3708 S. Figueroa Street, Los
    Angeles, CA 90007
(213) 743-6395
Ref: 31473.001328
PF: Minority, At-Risk

▶ **University of Southern California**   [20]
Upward Bound Project
Jeffrey L. Clayton
Director, E.O.P.C., 3708 S. Figueroa Street, Los
    Angeles, CA 90007
(213) 743-6395
Ref: 20637.001328
PF: Minority, At-Risk

▶ **University of Southern California**   [303]
U.S.C./Bravo Science Partnership
Cynthia Rogers
Project Coordinator, 1975 Zonal Avenue, KAM
    B-33, Los Angeles, CA 90033
(213) 342-3265
Ref: 31495.001328
PF: Magnet Schools

▶ **University of Southern California**   [153]
USC Inter-Professional Initiative
Stephanie Taylor-Dinwiddie
Executive Director, University Park, WPH 1004B,
    Los Angeles, CA 90089-0031
(213) 740-3279
Ref: 31498.001328
PF: Professional Development, Inservice

University of Southern California
USC Med-COR Program
John A. Davis
Director, 1420 N. San Pablo, PMB C-301, Los
    Angeles, CA 90033
(213) 342-1882
Ref: 20633.001328
PF: Minority, At-Risk

▶ **University of Southern California**   [21]
USC Mobile Dental Clinic
Charles M. Goldstein
Chair, Community Dentistry and Public Health,
    School of Dentistry, 925 W. 34th, Los Angeles,
    CA 90080-0641
(213) 740-1423
Ref: 31643.001328
PF: Minority, At-Risk

▶ **University of Southern Colorado**   [271]
Educational Alliance of Pueblo
Sally McGill-Eagan
Director of Community Services, 2200 Bonforte
    Boulevard, Pueblo, CO 81001-4901
(719) 549-2219
freeman@starburst.uscolo.edu
Ref: 31426.001365
PF: City/Regional Compacts

University of Southern Indiana
College Achievement Program
Ginger Ramsden
Coordinator, 8600 University Boulevard,
    Evansville, IN 47712
(812) 464-1863
Ref: 30979.001808
PF: College Courses for Students

▶ **University of Southern Maine**   [283]
Southern Maine Partnership
Lynne Miller
Executive Director, 117 Bailey Hall, Gorham, ME
    04038
(207) 780-5479
lynnem@maine.edu
Ref: 30057.009762
PF: New Achievement, Assessment Standards

▶ **University of Southern Mississippi**   [99]
Foreign Language Exploratory Program
Sam L. Slick
Chairman, Foreign Languages, Box 5038,
    Hattiesburg, MS 39406
(601) 266-4964
Ref: 30706.002441
PF: Enrichment, Gifted

University of Southern Mississippi
Southern Mississippi Writing Project
James R. Ezell
Director, Southern Station Box 10021,
    Hattiesburg, MS 39406-0021
(601) 266-5066
Ref: 30707.002441
PF: Professional Development, Inservice

University of Southern Mississippi
University of Southern Mississippi/Twenty-Eighth
    Street Elementary School Literacy Partnership
Janet C. Richards
Asst. Professor, Division of Ed/Psychology, 730
    E. Beach Boulevard, Long Beach, MS 39560
(601) 865-4547
Ref: 30705.002441
PF: Recruit, Preservice, Certification

▶ **University of Tampa**   [121]
Project SERVE
Ed Cloutier
Assoc. Professor, Department of Education, 401
    W. Kennedy, Tampa, FL 33606
(813) 253-6224
Ref: 20616.001538
PF: Tutoring, Counseling

▶ **University of Tennessee at Martin**   [197]
21st Century Partner Schools
Don Kellogg
Director, Center of Excellence for Science and
    Math Education, Martin, TN 38238
(901) 587-7163
dkellogg@utm.edu
Ref: 30697.003531
PF: Professional Development, Inservice

▶ **University of Texas at Arlington**   [199]
CREST (Collaborative Redesign of Education
    Systems in Texas)
Ranae Stetson
Director, Box 19227, Arlington, TX 76019
(817) 273-2849
stetson@albert.uta.edu
Ref: 31326.003656
PF: Professional Development, Inservice

Key: "▶" denotes those partnerships abstracted in Parts 1-5; the corresponding page numbers are given in brackets. "PF:" denotes the partnership's "primary focus." "Ref:" denotes the partnership's assigned reference number in the National School-College Partnership Database (see Appendix B).

University of Texas at Dallas
Adopt-A-School
Gloria Williams
Coordinator of Special Services, P.O. Box
   830688, Richardson, TX 75083-0688
(214) 690-2098
Ref: 31298.009741
PF: Minority, At-Risk

University of Texas at Dallas
Developing Reasoning Skills in Mathematics
George W. Fair
Director, Communication and Learning Center,
   P.O. Box 830688, Richardson, TX 75083-0688
(214) 690-2057
Ref: 31306.009741
PF: Professional Development, Inservice

University of Texas at Dallas
Ecology
Fred Fifer
Professor, Natural Sciences and Mathematics,
   P.O. Box 830688, Richardson, TX 75083-0688
(214) 690-2496
Ref: 31304.009741
PF: Professional Development, Inservice

University of Texas at Dallas
Expanding Your Horizons
Jackie Beitler
Administrative Assistant, P.O. Box 830688,
   Richardson, TX 75083-0688
(214)690-2563
Ref: 31311.009741
PF: Minority, At-Risk

University of Texas at Dallas
Financial Aid for Higher Education
Mike O'Rear
Director of Financial Aid, P.O. Box 830688,
   Richardson, TX 75083-0688
(214) 690-2941
Ref: 31302.009741
PF: Tutoring, Counseling

▶ **University of Texas at Dallas**   [65]
Hispanic Mother Daughter Program
Teresa Cruz-Lynd
Program Manager, P.O. Box 830688, Richardson,
   TX 75083-0688
(214) 690-2270
Ref: 31299.009741
PF: Minority, At-Risk

University of Texas at Dallas
Life Science for Elementary Teachers
Cynthia Ledbetter
Instructor, P.O. Box 830688, Richardson, TX
   75083-0688
(214) 690-2496
Ref: 31303.009741
PF: Professional Development, Inservice

University of Texas at Dallas
Mathcounts
Bernard List
Assoc. Dean, School of Engineering, P.O. Box
   830688, Richardson, TX 75083-0688
(214) 690-2977
Ref: 31313.009741
PF: Enrichment, Gifted

University of Texas at Dallas
Minority Mathematics & Science Education
   Cooperative
George W. Fair
Director, Communication and Learning Center,
   P.O. Box 830688, Richardson, TX 75083-0688
(214) 690-2057
Ref: 31309.009741
PF: Professional Development, Inservice

University of Texas at Dallas
Minority Mathematics & Science Education
   Cooperative
George Fair
Professor, P.O. Box 830688, Richardson, TX
   75083-0688
(214) 690-2323
Ref: 31305.009741
PF: Professional Development, Inservice

University of Texas at Dallas
Minority Student Leadership Conference
Gloria C. Williams
Coordinator of Special Services, P.O. Box
   830688, Richardson, TX 75083-0688
(214) 690-2098
Ref: 31297.009741
PF: Minority, At-Risk

University of Texas at Dallas
National Engineers Week Future City Competition
Jackie Beitler
Administrative Assistant, P.O. Box 830688,
   Richardson, TX 75083-0688
(214) 690-2563
Ref: 31312.009741
PF: Technology Application

University of Texas at Dallas
Reading One-One
George Farkas
Professor, P.O. Box 830688, Richardson, TX
   75083-0688
(214) 690-2937
Ref: 31310.009741
PF: Minority, At-Risk

▶ **University of Texas at Dallas**   [65]
Region 10 Consortium for Education of Homeless
   Children and Youth
George W. Fair
Director, Communication and Learning Center,
   P.O. Box 830688, Richardson, TX 75083-0688
(214) 690-2057
Ref: 31307.009741
PF: Minority, At-Risk

University of Texas at Dallas
Student to Student Cultural Awareness
Virginia Salazar-LeBlanc
Student Development Specialist, P.O. Box
   830688, Richardson, TX 75083-0688
(214) 690-2070
Ref: 31301.009741
PF: Minority, At-Risk

University of Texas at Dallas
Taking It On the Road — Bridging the Gap
   Between African and African-American History
Gloria Williams
Coordinator of Special Services, P.O. Box
   830688, Richardson, TX 75083-0688
(214) 690-2098
Ref: 31296.009741
PF: Enrichment, Gifted

University of Texas at Dallas
TEAMS
Jackie Beitler
Administrative Assistant, P.O. Box 830688,
   Richardson, TX 75083-0688
(214) 690-2563
Ref: 31295.009741
PF: Enrichment, Gifted

University of Texas at Dallas
University Crossroads
Barry Samsula
Director of Admissions, P.O. Box 830688,
   Richardson, TX 75083-0688
(214) 690-2270
Ref: 31300.009741
PF: Minority, At-Risk

University of Texas at Dallas
Using Algebra to Develop Reasoning Skills
George W. Fair
Director, Communication and Learning Center,
  P.O. Box 830688, Richardson, TX 75083-0688
(214) 690-2057
Ref: 31308.009741
PF: Professional Development, Inservice

▶ **University of Texas at El Paso** [277]
El Paso Collaborative for Academic Excellence
Arturo Pacheco
Dean of Education, Education Building, Room
  414, El Paso, TX 79968-0001
(915) 747-5572
Ref: 31888.003661
PF: City/Regional Compacts

▶ **University of Texas at San**
Antonio [65]
Texas Prefreshman Engineering Program
  (TexPREP)
Manuel P. Berriozabal
Coordinator, 6900 North Loop, 1604 West, San
  Antonio, TX 78249-0661
(210) 691-5530
mberrioz@lonestar.utsa.edu
Ref: 31883.010115
PF: Minority, At-Risk

University of Texas at Tyler
Center for Innovation in Teacher Education
Chip Fischer
Professor, School of Education, 3900 University
  Boulevard, Tyler, TX 75799
(903) 566-7448
Ref: 31324.011163
PF: Recruit, Preservice, Certification

University of Texas at Tyler
The East Texas Tech Prep Consortium
Doris Sharp
Director, 3900 University Boulevard, Tyler, TX
  75799
(903) 566-7353
Ref: 31323.011163
PF: Tech-Prep/2+2

▶ **University of Texas at Tyler** [299]
Quality Work Force Planning Committee
John N. Fabac
Assoc. Professor, 3900 University Boulevard,
  Tyler, TX 75799
(903) 566-7315
Ref: 31325.011163
PF: School-College-Business Partnerships

▶ **University of Texas Health Science Center**
at San Antonio [143]
The Biomedical Program
Miguel A. Medina
Assoc. Dean for Student Affairs, Graduate School
  of Biomedical Sciences, 7703 Floyd Curl Drive,
  San Antonio, TX 78284-7945
(207) 567-2671
Ref: 31352.003659
PF: Career, Internships, Apprenticeships

▶ **University of Texas Health Science Center**
at San Antonio [242]
MESS (Modules for the Exploration of Science in
  Schools)
Joel B. Baseman
Department of Microbiology, 7703 Floyd Curl
  Drive, San Antonio, TX 78284-7945
(210) 567-3939
Ref: 31351.003659
PF: Curriculum Development

University of Texas Health Science Center at
San Antonio
Community Health Nursing Program
Delight Tillotson, MS.N., R.N.
Director of Special Programs/Nursing Programs,
  7703 Floyd Curl Drive, San Antonio, TX 78284
(210) 567-5810
Ref: 31733.003659
PF: Student Health, Welfare

University of Texas Health Science Center at
San Antonio
Discovering Science/Exploring UTHSCSA
Sylvia P. Fernandez
Director, Office of Special Programs, 7703 Floyd
  Curl Drive, San Antonio, TX 78284-7945
(210) 567-2654
Ref: 31359.003659
PF: Enrichment, Gifted

University of Texas Health Science Center at
San Antonio
Educational Experiences for Occupational
  Therapy Students Concerning Public School
  Settings
Karin Barnes
Assoc. Professor, 7703 Floyd Curl Drive, San
  Antonio, TX 78284-7945
(210) 567-3118
Ref: 31354.003659
PF: Recruit, Preservice, Certification

University of Texas Health Science Center at
San Antonio
Med Prep Program
Miguel A. Medina
Assoc. Dean for Student Affairs, 7703 Floyd Curl
  Drive, San Antonio, TX 78284-7945
(210) 567-2671
Ref: 31358.003659
PF: Minority, At-Risk

University of Texas Health Science Center at
San Antonio
Northside Health Careers High School Learning
  Lab Experience
Barbara L. Lust, R.N.
Assoc. Dean for Student Affairs, 7703 Floyd Curl
  Drive, San Antonio, TX 78284-7945
(210) 567-7000
Ref: 31353.003659
PF: Career, Internships, Apprenticeships

University of Texas Health Science Center at
San Antonio
Occupational Therapy Consultation to Rural
  School Districts
Marc Willey
7703 Floyd Curl Drive, San Antonio, TX
  78284-7945
(210) 567-3119
Ref: 31356.003659
PF: Minority, At-Risk

University of Texas Health Science Center at
San Antonio
Office of Special Programs Speaker's Bureau
Sylvia P. Fernandez
Director, Office of Special Programs, 7703 Floyd
  Curl Drive, San Antonio, TX 78284-7945
(201) 567-2654
Ref: 31350.003659
PF: Career, Internships, Apprenticeships

▶ **University of Texas Health Science Center**
at San Antonio [290]
Texas Math and Science Hotline
Molly Greene
7703 Floyd Curl Drive, San Antonio, TX
  78284-7945
(210) 567-3717
greene@uthscsa.edu
Ref: 31355.003659
PF: Technology Application

Key: "▶" denotes those partnerships abstracted in Parts 1-5; the corresponding page numbers are given in brackets. "PF:" denotes the partnership's "primary focus." "Ref:" denotes the partnership's assigned reference number in the National School-College Partnership Database (see Appendix B).

University of Texas Health Science Center at San Antonio
Volunteer Mentoring Program
Marilyn Alexander
Assistant to the Dental Dean, 7703 Floyd Curl Drive, San Antonio, TX 78284-7945
(210) 567-3166
Ref: 31357.003659
PF: Minority, At-Risk

University of Texas Medical Branch at Galveston
East Texas Area Health Education Center Health Professions Career Promotion Program
Steven R. Shelton
Assoc. Director, 301 University Boulevard, Route 1056, Galveston, TX 77555-1056
(409) 772-7884
Ref: 31341.004952
PF: Career, Internships, Apprenticeships

▶ **University of Texas Medical Branch at Galveston** [65]
Saturday Biomedical Sciences Forum
Sandra L. Williams
Director for Medical Student Recruitment, 301 University Boulevard, Galveston, TX 77550
(409) 772-3256
Ref: 31340.004952
PF: Minority, At-Risk

▶ **University of Texas Medical Branch at Galveston** [110]
Science Education
Marsha Ricks
Program Director, Route J-19, 3.158 Medical Research Building, Galveston, TX 77555-1019
(409) 772-0134
Ref: 31342.004952
PF: Enrichment, Gifted

▶ **University of Texas–Pan American** [199]
UTPA and Hidalgo County School Districts Teaming Initiative Partnership
Hilda Medrano
Assoc. Professor, 1201 W. University Drive, Edinburg, TX 78539
(210) 381-3627
Ref: 31363.003599
PF: Professional Development, Inservice

▶ **University of the South** [84]
Sewanee Summer Scholars Program
Frederick H. Croom
Provost, Sewanee, TN 37383
(615) 598-1101
Ref: 31631.003534
PF: College Courses for Students

▶ **University of Utah** [200]
Utah Education Consortium
Nedra A. Crow
Director, Graduate School of Education, 225 MBH, Salt Lake City, UT 84221
(801) 581-8221
Ref: 31444.003675
PF: Professional Development, Inservice

▶ **University of Virginia** [202]
Center for the Liberal Arts
Marjorie P. Balge
Asst. Director, P.O. Box 3697, Charlottesville, VA 22903
(804) 982-5204
mpb@virginia.edu
Ref: 20295.006968
PF: Professional Development, Inservice

▶ **University of Virginia** [202]
Virginia School-University Partnership
Ronald E. Comfort
Assoc. Dean, Ruffner Hall, Charlottesville, VA 22903
(804) 924-3335
Ref: 20196.006968
PF: Professional Development, Inservice

▶ **University of Washington** [130]
Early Scholars Outreach Program
Millie L. Russell
Director, Office of Minority Affairs, PC-45, Seattle, WA 98195
(206) 685-3637
Ref: 20767.003798
PF: Tutoring, Counseling

University of Washington
Puget Sound Educational Consortium
Richard C. Williams
Executive Director, 202 Miller Hall, DQ-12, Seattle, WA 98195
(206) 543-7267
rwill@u.washington.edu
Ref: 31588.003798
PF: New Achievement, Assessment Standards

▶ **University of Washington** [67]
Washington MESA (Mathematics, Engineering, Science Achievement)
Patricia MacGowan
State Director, College of Engineering, 353 Loew FH-18, Seattle, WA 98195
(206) 543-0562
macgowan@rio.engr.washington.edu
Ref: 20926.003798
PF: Minority, At-Risk

University of West Florida
Center for Economic Education
Parks B. Dimsdale
Dean, College of Business, 11000 University Parkway, Pensacola, FL 32514-2716
(904) 474-2348
Ref: 20881.003955
PF: Professional Development, Inservice

▶ **University of West Florida** [160]
Physics Alliance of Northwest Florida
M. C. George
Chairman, Department of Physics, Pensacola, FL 32514
(904) 474-2271
Ref: 30640.003955
PF: Professional Development, Inservice

▶ **University of Wisconsin Centers** [291]
Distance Learning
Diane Pillard
Director, Continuing Education, 2909 Kellog Avenue, Janesville, WI 53546
(608) 758-6541
Ref: 31635.003897
PF: Technology Application

University of Wisconsin Centers
History Teaching Alliance
James J. Lorence
Professor of History, 518 S. 7th Avenue, Wausau, WI 54401
(715) 845-9602
jlorence@uwmcmail.uwc.edu
Ref: 20315.003897
PF: Professional Development, Inservice

▶ **University of Wisconsin Centers** [68]
University Camp/Math-Science Project
Janet Brown
Director, Learning Lab, 1500 University Drive, Waukesha, WI 53188
(414) 521-5475
jbrown@uwmcmail.uwc.edu
Ref: 31069.003897
PF: Minority, At-Risk

▶ **University of Wisconsin–Eau Claire** [204]
Cray Academy
Charles Larson
Asst. Dean of Education Outreach, Brewer Hall 55, Eau Claire, WI 54702-4004
(715) 836-5843
Ref: 31105.003917
PF: Professional Development, Inservice

University of Wisconsin–Eau Claire
CUBE Science Institute
William P. Dunlap
Dean, School of Education, Eau Claire, WI 54702
(715) 836-3671
dunlapwp@uwec.edu
Ref: 31099.003917
PF: Professional Development, Inservice

▶ **University of Wisconsin–Eau Claire** [112]
Distance Education and Gifted/Talented Project
Nancy Schuster
Program Manager, Brewer Hall 55, Eau Claire, WI 54702-4004
(715) 836-5843
schustnb@uwec.edu
Ref: 31103.003917
PF: Enrichment, Gifted

▶ **University of Wisconsin–Eau Claire** [86]
Introduction to College Writing
Charles Larson
Asst. Dean, Educational Outreach, Brewer Hall 55, Eau Claire, WI 54702-4004
(715) 836-5843
larsonco@uwec.edu
Ref: 31107.003917
PF: College Courses for Students

▶ **University of Wisconsin–Eau Claire** [112]
Math Talent Development Project
Nancy Schuster
Program Manager, Brewer Hall 55, Eau Claire, WI 54702-4004
(715) 836-5843
Ref: 31102.003917
PF: Enrichment, Gifted

▶ **University of Wisconsin–Eau Claire** [204]
Microcomputer and Technology Fair
Charles Larson
Asst. Dean, Educational Outreach, Brewer Hall 55, Eau Claire, WI 54702-4004
(715) 836-5843
larsonco@uwec.edu
Ref: 31106.003917
PF: Professional Development, Inservice

University of Wisconsin–Eau Claire
Northwest Wisconsin Leadership Academy
Charles Larson
Asst. Dean of Education Outreach, Brewer Hall 55, Eau Claire, WI 54702-4004
(715) 836-5843
larsonco@uwec.edu
Ref: 31104.003917
PF: Professional Development, Inservice

▶ **University of Wisconsin–Eau Claire** [112]
Summer Institute for High-Potential Students
Nancy Schuster
Program Manager, Brewer Hall 55, Eau Claire, WI 54702-4004
(715) 836-5843
schustnb@uwec.edu
Ref: 31101.003917
PF: Enrichment, Gifted

▶ **University of Wisconsin–Eau Claire** [112]
WCATY (Wisconsin Center for Academically Talented Youth) Summer Program
Nancy Schuster
Program Manager, Brewer Hall 55, Eau Claire, WI 54702
(715) 836-5843
schustnb@uwec.edu
Ref: 31100.003917
PF: Enrichment, Gifted

▶ **University of Wisconsin–Eau Claire** [248]
Wisconsin Consortium for School Improvement
Michael Herrick
Evaluation Consultant, Brewer Hall, Room 55, Eau Claire, WI 54701
(715) 836-5843
Ref: 31098.003917
PF: Instructional Research

University of Wisconsin–La Crosse
Master of Education-Professional Development
John E. Castek
Director, 102C Morris Hall, La Crosse, WI 54601
(608) 785-8142
Ref: 31095.003919
PF: Professional Development, Inservice

▶ **University of Wisconsin–La Crosse** [68]
Milwaukee South Division High School/College of HPER Partnership
Garth Tymeson
Assoc. Dean, College of HPER, 124 Mitchell Hall, La Crosse, WI 54601
(608) 785-8155
tymeson@uwlax.bitnet
Ref: 31096.003919
PF: Minority, At-Risk

University of Wisconsin–La Crosse
Upper Mississippi Cooperative Rural Center
Theresa Faulkner
Director, La Crosse, WI 54601
(608) 785-8125
Ref: 31097.003919
PF: School-College-Business Partnerships

University of Wisconsin–Milwaukee
Milwaukee Area Academic Alliance in English
Jessica R. Wirth
Assoc. Dean, College of Letters and Science, P.O. Box 413, Milwaukee, WI 53201
(414) 229-5891
jwirth@convex.csd.uwm.edu
Ref: 21269.003896
PF: Professional Development, Inservice

University of Wisconsin–Oshkosh
A Learning Community of Preservice and Inservice Teachers Study Teaching
Joyce Boettcher
Chair, Department of Reading Education, Oshkosh, WI 54901
(414) 424-2478
boettchj@vaxa.cis.uwosh.edu
Ref: 31111.006930
PF: Recruit, Preservice, Certification

University of Wisconsin–Oshkosh
College of Nursing Health Place
Joan Johnson
Directory, Nursing Center, 800 Algoma Boulevard, Oshkosh, WI 54901
(414) 424-7219
Ref: 31115.009630
PF: Student Health, Welfare

University of Wisconsin–Oshkosh
Contract Courses
Patricia J. Koll
Asst. Vice Chancellor, Dempsey 335J, Oshkosh,
    WI 54901
(414) 424-1410
Ref: 31109.009630
PF: Professional Development, Inservice

▶ **University of Wisconsin–Oshkosh** [86]
Cooperative Academic Partnership Program
    (CAPP)
William J. Leffin
Co-Director, N/E 101, L and S Dean's Office,
    Oshkosh, WI 54901-8661
(414) 424-3003
Ref: 31117.009630
PF: College Courses for Students

University of Wisconsin–Oshkosh
Division of HPER Partnership
Darrel Lang
Professor and Chair, Division of HPER, Oshkosh,
    WI 54901
(414) 424-1248
Ref: 31108.009630
PF: Professional Development, Inservice

▶ **University of Wisconsin–Oshkosh** [230]
Educational Service Center
Wanda Stafford
Coordinator, Oshkosh, WI 54901
(414) 424-1032
Ref: 31116.009630
PF: Teacher Education Centers

University of Wisconsin–Oshkosh
Inservice Arrangements
Patricia J. Koll
Asst. Vice Chancellor, Dempsey 355J, Oshkosh,
    WI 54901
(414) 424-1410
Ref: 31110.009630
PF: Professional Development, Inservice

▶ **University of Wisconsin–Oshkosh** [113]
NEWACE Social Action Theatre for Children &
    Youth
Marsha Rossiter
Program Manager, Division of Continuing
    Education and Extension, 800 Algoma
    Boulevard, Oshkosh, WI 54901
(414) 424-1131
Ref: 31112.009630
PF: Enrichment, Gifted

▶ **University of Wisconsin–Oshkosh** [300]
Partnerships for School Improvement
W. Sam Adams
CQI Coordinator, 800 Algoma Boulevard,
    Oshkosh, WI 54901
(414) 424-7074
Ref: 31636.009630
PF: School-College-Business Partnerships

▶ **University of Wisconsin–Oshkosh** [204]
School Based Peer Mediation
Pat Nichols
Trainer, CCDET, Oshkosh, WI 54901
(414) 424-3034
Ref: 31114.009630
PF: Professional Development, Inservice

University of Wisconsin–Oshkosh
Science Outreach
Kenneth J. Hughes
Coordinator, Oshkosh, WI 54901
(414) 424-0287
hughes@vaxa.cis.uwosh.edu
Ref: 31113.009630
PF: Professional Development, Inservice

University of Wisconsin–Parkside
Discovering Research
Ann Scholz
Reference/Instruction Librarian, Library/Learning
    Center, Box 2000, Kenosha, WI 53141-2000
(414) 595-2143
Ref: 21132.005015
PF: Enrichment, Gifted

▶ **University of Wisconsin–Parkside** [205]
Regional Staff Development Center
Esther Letven
Director, Box 2000, Kenosha, WI 53141-2000
(414) 595-2002
Ref: 21057.005015
PF: Professional Development, Inservice

▶ **University of Wisconsin–River Falls** [205]
St. Croix Valley Association of Teacher Educators
Larry M. Albertson
Dean, College of Education, Ames Teacher
    Education Center, River Falls, WI 54022
(715) 425-3774
larry.m.albertson.@uwrf.edu
Ref: 31082.003923
PF: Professional Development, Inservice

University of Wisconsin–Stevens Point
Adopted Physical Education – K-12
John Munson
Head, HPERA, Stevens Point, WI 54481
(715) 346-2351
Ref: 31094.003924
PF: Minority, At-Risk

▶ **University of Wisconsin–Stevens
Point** [205]
CO-STAR (Collaboration: Starting Teachers
    Achieving Results)
Joan North
Dean, College of Professional Studies, Stevens
    Point, WI 54481
(715) 346-2947
Ref: 20272.003924
PF: Professional Development, Inservice

University of Wisconsin–Stevens Point
Joint Program in Communicative Disorders
Derrick Nash
Head, School of Communicative Disorders,
    Stevens Point, WI 54467
(715) 346-2351
Ref: 31093.003924
PF: Student Health, Welfare

▶ **University of Wisconsin–Whitewater** [291]
Ameritech-Whitewater Curriculum Integration
    Project
Jeffrey C. Barnett
Dean, College of Education, 2030 Winther Hall,
    Whitewater, WI 53190
(414) 472-1101
Ref: 31072.003926
PF: Technology Application

▶ **University of Wisconsin–Whitewater** [224]
Beginning Teacher Assistance Program
Tom Ganser
Director, Office of Field Experiences, Whitewater,
    WI 53190-1790
(414) 472-1123
gansert@uwwvax.uww.edu
Ref: 21120.003926
PF: Recruit, Preservice, Certification

▶ **University of Wisconsin–Whitewater** [113]
Family Fun Math Nights
Judy Knapp
Lecturer, Department of Math and Computer
    Science, Whitewater, WI 53190
(414) 472-2764
knappr@uwwvax.uww.edu
Ref: 31071.003926
PF: Enrichment, Gifted

University of Wisconsin–Whitewater
Read to Me!
Raj Millorna
Principal, 242 S. Prince Street, Whitewater, WI
    53190
(414) 472-4855
Ref: 31070.003926
PF: Enrichment, Gifted

▶ **Ursinus College** [59]
Ursinus College Partnership Scholarships
Richard DiFeliciantonio
Director of Admissions, Collegeville, PA 19426
(215) 489-4111
Ref: 30457.003385
PF: Minority, At-Risk

▶ **Utica College of Syracuse University** [54]
Young Scholars Program
Ruth Barwick
Administrative Assistant to the President, Utica,
   NY 13502
(315) 792-3364
rbb@ucl.ucsu.edu
Ref: 30263.002883
PF: Minority, At-Risk

V

Valencia Community College
Assessment in High Schools
Carol Riles
Assessment Coordinator, 1800 S. Kirkman Road,
   Orlando, FL 32811
(407) 299-5000
Ref: 30646.006750
PF: College Courses for Students

▶ **Valencia Community College** [72]
Dual Enrollment
Carolyn Allen
Vice-President for Student Affairs, P.O. Box 3028,
   Orlando, FL 32802
(407) 299-5000 x2253
Ref: 30645.006750
PF: College Courses for Students

▶ **Valencia Community College** [160]
Evans High School Liaison Project
Roberta Vandermast
Coordinator of Interdisciplinary Studies, Orlando,
   FL 32802
(407) 299-5000 x1300
Ref: 30643.006750
PF: Professional Development, Inservice

▶ **Valencia Community College** [132]
Nontraditional Careers Program
DeLaine Priest
Coordinator, P.O. Box 3028, Orlando, FL 32802
(407) 628-3511
Ref: 30644.006750
PF: Career, Internships, Apprenticeships

Valley City State University
Center for Innovation in Instruction
Dan Pullen
Director, 101 College Street SE, Valley City, ND
   58072
(701) 845-7434
pullen@sendit.nodak.edu
Ref: 31135.003008
PF: Technology Application

▶ **Valley City State University** [274]
Curriculum Leadership Institute-North Dakota
Ann T. Clapper
Project Director, Valley City, ND 58072
(701) 845-7195
Ref: 31134.003008
PF: City/Regional Compacts

▶ **Valparaiso University** [135]
Da Vinci & Me: Exploring Engineering
John Steffen
Professor, Mechanical Engineering Department,
   Valparaiso, IN 46383
(219) 464-5184
jsteffen@exodus.valpo.edu
Ref: 30967.001842
PF: Career, Internships, Apprenticeships

▶ **Valparaiso University** [34]
PRISMS (Precollege Research in the Sciences for
   Minorities Students)
A. Gilbert Cook
Professor, Department of Chemistry, Valparaiso,
   IN 46383
(219) 464-5389
Ref: 30965.001842
PF: Minority, At-Risk

▶ **Valparaiso University** [163]
Professional Development Coordinating Council
Sandra S. Michelsen
Miller Hall, Valparaiso, IN 46383
(219) 464-5079
smichelsen@exodus.valpo.edu
Ref: 30964.001842
PF: Professional Development, Inservice

Valparaiso University
Train the Trainers
Gerhard Auer
Asst. Professor of German, 108 Meier Hall,
   Valparaiso, IN 46383
(219) 464-5097
Ref: 30966.001842
PF: Professional Development, Inservice

Valparaiso University
VALCO
Fred Condos
Assoc. Professor of Education, Valparaiso, IN
   46383
(219) 464-5470
Ref: 30963.001842
PF: Resource Sharing

▶ **Vanderbilt University** [129]
PENCIL Foundation (Public Education: Nashville
   Citizens Involved in Leadership)
Malcolm Getz
Assoc. Provost, 419 21st Avenue S, Nashville, TN
   37240-0007
(615) 322-7120
getz@ctrvax.vanderbilt.edu
Ref: 20553.003535
PF: Tutoring, Counseling

▶ **Vermont Technical College** [66]
Women In Technology (WIT) Project
Amy Emler-Shaffer
Director, Randolph Center, VT 05061
(802) 728-3391
Ref: 30061.003698
PF: Minority, At-Risk

▶ **Virginia Commonwealth University** [223]
Project BEST (Basic Educational Skills &
   Training)
Diane Simon
Asst. Dean, School of Education, 1015 W. Main
   Street, Box 2020, Richmond, VA 23284-2020
(804) 367-1308
dsimon@cabell.vcu.edu
Ref: 20602.003735
PF: Recruit, Preservice, Certification

Virginia Highlands Community College
Highlands Consortium
Edwin Hardison
Dean of Instruction and Student Services, P.O.
   Box 828, Arlington, VA 24210
(703) 628-6094
Ref: 30577.007099
PF: Tech-Prep/2+2

▶ **Virginia Polytechnic Institute and State University** [223]
Tomorrow's Teachers Program (TTP)
Sidney E. Crumwell, Jr.
Executive Director, 225 War Memorial Hall, Blacksburg, VA 24061-0335
(703) 231-5920
Ref: 20445.003754
PF: Recruit, Preservice, Certification

Virginia Wesleyan College
Adopt-A-School
Lin Logan
Asst. Professor of Education, Wesleyan Drive, Norfolk, VA 23502
(804) 455-3382
Ref: 20132.003767
PF: Tutoring, Counseling

Virginia Wesleyan University
Rising Stars Program
Rita E. Frank
Asst. Professor of Psychology, Norfolk, VA 23502-5599
(804) 455-3200
Ref: 21274.003767
PF: Minority, At-Risk

W

Wabash College
Wabash-Washington Bridge Program
Jamie Watson
Program Director, P.O. Box 352, Crawfordsville, IN 47933
(317) 364-4301
Ref: 30986.001844
PF: Minority, At-Risk

Wake Forest University
Athletics Care Team (ACT)
Charles L. Davis
Director of Community Programs, Athletics Department, Box 7423 Reynolda Station, Winston-Salem, NC 27109
(910)759-6164
Ref: 30712.002978
PF: Tutoring, Counseling

▶ **Wake Forest University** [186]
Center for Research and Development in Law-Related Education
Julia P. Hardin
Executive Director, Law School, Box 7266 Reynolda Station, Winston-Salem, NC 27109
(910) 721-3355
Ref: 31714.002978
PF: Professional Development, Inservice

Wake Forest University
Kaleidoscope
Ernest Wade
Director of Minority Affairs, Box 7352 Reynolda Station, Winston-Salem, NC 27109
(910) 759-5864
Ref: 30709.002978
PF: Minority, At-Risk

▶ **Wake Forest University** [240]
LEGACY (Linking Educators and the Gifted With Attorneys for Civics: Yes!)
Julia P. Hardin
Executive Director, Center for Research and Development in Law-Related Education, Box 7206 Reynolda Station, Winston-Salem, NC 27109
(910) 721-3355
Ref: 30718.002978
PF: Curriculum Development

▶ **Wake Forest University** [186]
LIME (Logo-Integrated Mathematics Environment) Project
Leah P. McCoy
Assoc. Professor of Education, Box 7266 Reynolda Station, Winston-Salem, NC 27109
(910) 759-5498
Ref: 30715.002978
PF: Professional Development, Inservice

▶ **Wake Forest University** [289]
LREnet (Law-Related Education Network)
Julia P. Hardin
Executive Director, Center for Research and Development in Law-Related Education, Box 7206 Reynolda Station, Winston-Salem, NC 27109
(910) 721-3355
Ref: 30719.002978
PF: Technology Application

▶ **Wake Forest University** [105]
North Carolina Writing Awards Program
Rebecca Brown
Co-Director, 1304 Polo Road, Winston-Salem, NC 27106
(910) 727-0979
Ref: 30714.002978
PF: Enrichment, Gifted

Wake Forest University
Partners-In-Education
Susan Faust
Office of Special Projects, Box 7269 Reynolda Station, Winston-Salem, NC 27109
(910) 759-5891
Ref: 30717.002978
PF: School-College-Business Partnerships

Wake Forest University
School Tech
Nancy Crouch
Executive Director, Western Triad Science and Math Alliance, Box 7598 Reynolda Station, Winston-Salem, NC 27109
(910) 759-4642
Ref: 30710.002978
PF: Technology Application

Wake Forest University
Teaching Foreign Languages
Mary Lynn Redmond
Asst. Professor of Education, Box 7266 Reynolda Station, Winston-Salem, NC 27109
(910) 759-5347
Ref: 30716.002978
PF: Curriculum Development

Wake Forest University
Using the Outdoors to Teach Experimental Science (UTOTES)
Nancy Crouch
Executive Director, Western Triad Science and Math Alliance, Box 7598 Reynolda Station, Winston-Salem, NC 27109
(910) 759-4642
Ref: 30708.002978
PF: Professional Development, Inservice

▶ **Wake Forest University** [298]
Western Triad Science and Mathematics Alliance
Nancy Crouch
Executive Director, Box 7598 Reynolda Station, Winston-Salem, NC 27109
(910) 759-4642
Ref: 30711.002978
PF: School-College-Business Partnerships

Wake Forest University
Whole Language and the Teaching of Reading/Writing Skills in a Second Language
Mary Lynn Redmond
Asst. Professor of Education, Box 7266 Reynolda Station, Winston-Salem, NC 27109
(910) 759-5347
Ref: 30713.002978
PF: Curriculum Development

▶ **Wake Forest University**   [186]
Writing to Learn Math and Science
Joseph O. Milner
Chair, Department of Education, Box 7266
    Reynolda Station, Winston-Salem, NC 27109
(910) 759-5341
Ref: 31715.002978
PF: Professional Development, Inservice

Wake Technical Community College
Tech Prep
Vincent Revels
Vice President, Curriculum Education Services,
    9101 Fayetteville Road, Raleigh, NC 27603
(919) 662-3305
Ref: 31755.004844
PF: Tech-Prep/2+2

▶ **Warren County Community College**   [260]
Transitions
Janet Black
Dean, Academic Services, Route 57 W,
    Washington, NJ 07882-9605
(908) 689-7612
Ref: 30109.025039
PF: Tech-Prep/2+2

Washburn University of Topeka
High School/College Partnership
Robert D. Stein
Chair, English Department, Topeka, KS 66621
(913) 231-1010 x1441
Ref: 20649.001949
PF: College Courses for Students

Washington University
Art Major Career Planning Conference
Sarah Spurr
Assoc. Professor and Asst. Dean, One Brookings
    Drive, St. Louis, MO 63130
(314) 935-8402
Ref: 31219.002520
PF: Career, Internships, Apprenticeships

▶ **Washington University**   [100]
High School Art Competition
Libby Reuter
Asst. Dean, One Brookings Drive, St. Louis, MO
    63130
(314) 935-6597
Ref: 31217.002520
PF: Enrichment, Gifted

▶ **Washington University**   [100]
Magnet School-Art School Experience
Libby Reuter
Asst. Dean, One Brookings Drive, St. Louis, MO
    63130
(314) 935-6597
Ref: 31218.002520
PF: Enrichment, Gifted

▶ **Washington University**   [174]
Washington University/Soldan International
    Studies High School Collaborative
Anne Hetlage
Assoc. Dean, Campus Box 1064, St. Louis, MO
    63130
(314) 935-6778
Ref: 31216.002520
PF: Professional Development, Inservice

Washington University
Washington University/University City Science
    Education Partnership
Sarah C. R. Elgin
Professor of Biology, Biology Department,
    Campus Box 1229, St. Louis, MO 63130
(314) 935-5348
Ref: 31215.002520
PF: Professional Development, Inservice

Waukesha County Technical College
Tech Prep
Judy Jorgensen
Dean, 800 Main Street, Pewaukee, WI 53072
(414) 691-5392
Ref: 31068.009258
PF: Tech-Prep/2+2

Wayne Community College
Tech Prep-Associate Degree
Curtis Shivar
Assoc. Vice President for Academic Affairs, Caller
    Box 8002, Goldsboro, NC 27530
(919) 735-5151
Ref: 20477.002980
PF: Tech-Prep/2+2

▶ **Wayne State University**   [98]
Advanced Studies
James E. Facen
Asst. Provost, Detroit, MI 48202
(313) 577-2254
Ref: 20004.002329
PF: Enrichment, Gifted

Wayne State University
DAPCEP (Detroit Area Pre-College Engineering
    Program)
Donny Smith
College of Engineering, 1174 Engineering
    Building, Detroit, MI 48202
(313) 577-3812
Ref: 31000.002329
PF: Tutoring, Counseling

Wayne State University
Detroit Compact Initial Project
JoAnn Snyder
Teacher Education, College of Education, Detroit,
    MI 48202
(313) 577-2254
Ref: 20037.002329
PF: City/Regional Compacts

Wayne State University
Dual Enrollment
James E. Facen
Asst. Provost, Detroit, MI 48202
(313) 577-2254
Ref: 20005.002329
PF: College Courses for Students

▶ **Wayne State University**   [304]
Golightly Elementary School
Paula Wood
College of Education, Detroit, MI 48202
(313) 577-1620
Ref: 31004.002329
PF: Magnet Schools

▶ **Wayne State University**   [173]
Institute for Enhancement of Mathematics
    Teaching
Joella Gipson
College of Education, Detroit, MI 48202
(313) 577-1691/577-1728
Ref: 31005.002329
PF: Professional Development, Inservice

Wayne State University
Junior Science and Humanities Symposium
    Program
Rudi Alec
College of Education, Detroit, MI 48202
(313) 577-0953
Ref: 31003.002329
PF: Enrichment, Gifted

Key: "▶" denotes those partnerships abstracted in Parts 1-5; the corresponding page numbers are given in brackets. "PF:" denotes the partnership's "primary focus." "Ref:" denotes the partnership's assigned reference number in the National School-College Partnership Database (see Appendix B).

Wayne State University
The Martin Luther King, Jr./Cesar Chavez/Rosa
   Parks College Day Program
William Robinson, Jr.
345 Manoogian Hall, Detroit, MI 48202
(313) 577-3085
Ref: 31002.002329
PF: Tutoring, Counseling

Wayne State University
Project 1993 and Robotics
Creigs C. Beverly
Professor of Social Work, Detroit, MI 48202
(313) 577-5252
Ref: 20081.002329
PF: Minority, At-Risk

Wayne State University
Project SEED
Ronald R. Schroeder
College of Science, Chemistry Department,
   Detroit, MI 48202
(313) 577-2604
Ref: 31006.002329
PF: Enrichment, Gifted

▶ **Wayne State University**   [246]
University Public School
Paula Wood
College of Education, Detroit, MI 48202
(313) 577-1620
Ref: 31007.002329
PF: Instructional Research

Wayne State University
Upward Bound
Philip H. Berns
701 W. Warren Avenue, Detroit, MI 48202
(313) 577-1943
Ref: 31001.002329
PF: Minority, At-Risk

Wayne State University
Wade McCree Incentive Scholarship Program
Ronald Hughes
Admissions Office, 3 East HNJ Student Services
   Building, Detroit, MI 48202
(313) 577-3581
Ref: 20529.002329
PF: Tutoring, Counseling

Waynesburg College
Summer Challenge
Nancy Ferrari
Director, Waynesburg, PA 15370
(412) 852-3317
Ref: 20674.003391
PF: Enrichment, Gifted

▶ **Weber State University**   [143]
Center for Science Education
Richard Vineyard
Director, Ogden, UT 84408-2509
(801) 626-6160
Ref: 20304.003680
PF: Career, Internships, Apprenticeships

▶ **Weber State University**   [229]
Center for Social Science Education
LaRae Larkin
Director, Ogden, UT 84408-1216
(801) 626-7463
Ref: 31437.003680
PF: Teacher Education Centers

▶ **Weber State University**   [110]
Consortium for Academic Excellence
Carol A. Smith
Programs Coordinator, Ogden, UT 84408-2904
(801) 626-7336
Ref: 31440.003680
PF: Enrichment, Gifted

Weber State University
Early College
Linda Ward
Director, Ogden, UT 84408
(801) 626-6091
Ref: 20009.003680
PF: College Courses for Students

▶ **Weber State University**   [223]
Educational Technology Initiative
Al Forsyth
Assoc. Professor, Teacher Education, Ogden, UT
   84408-1304
(801) 626-7426
aforsyth@cc.weber.edu
Ref: 31439.003680
PF: Recruit, Preservice, Certification

Weber State University
Golden Spike Empire Language Association
Tony Spanos
Assoc. Professor, Ogden, UT 84408-1403
(801) 626-6996
Ref: 20302.003680
PF: Professional Development, Inservice

▶ **Weber State University**   [110]
Northern Utah Arts Consortium
Mary Dave Blackman
3750 Harrison Boulevard, Ogden, UT 84408
(801) 626-7181
Ref: 20010.003680
PF: Enrichment, Gifted

▶ **Weber State University** [200]
Ogden Area History Teaching Alliance
LaRae Larkin
Director, Center for Social Science Education,
   Ogden, UT 84408-1216
(801) 626-7463
Ref: 20306.003680
PF: Professional Development, Inservice

▶ **Weber State University**   [200]
Teacher Academy
Richard Sadler
Dean, Social Science, Ogden, UT 84408-1204
(801) 626-6232
Ref: 31442.003680
PF: Professional Development, Inservice

Weber State University
Tech Prep
Craig J. Smith
Director, Continuing Education, Ogden, UT
   84408-4012
(801) 626-6575
Ref: 31443.003680
PF: Tech-Prep/2+2

▶ **Weber State University**   [230]
Utah Geographic Alliance
Wayne Wahlquist
Professor, Ogden, UT 84408-2510
(801) 626-6943
wswwahlquist@cc.weber.edu
Ref: 20303.003680
PF: Teacher Education Centers

Weber State University
Weber School-Based Teacher Training
Shannon Butler
Assoc. Professor, Ogden, UT 84408-1304
(801) 626-6623
Ref: 31438.003680
PF: Recruit, Preservice, Certification

Weber State University
Weber State English Alliance
Gary Dohrer
Assoc. Professor, Ogden, UT 84408-1201
(801) 626-7318
Ref: 31441.003680
PF: Professional Development, Inservice

▶ **Weber State University**   [290]
WEMATH
Pat Henry
Professor, Ogden, UT 84408-1702
(801) 626-6098
Ref: 20305.003680
PF: Technology Application

Webster University
ARCH Service Grant
Jeri Levesque
Assoc. Professor, 470 E. Lockwood, WH 232, St.
    Louis, MO 63119
(314) 968-7479
Ref: 31210.002521
PF: Minority, At-Risk

Webster University
The Education Coalition for Urban Families
John L. Quigley, Jr.
Project Director, 470 E. Lockwood Avenue, St.
    Louis, MO 63119
(314) 968-7429
Ref: 31207.002521
PF: Minority, At-Risk

▶ **Webster University**   [239]
For the Love of Mathematics
Roy Tamashiro
Project Director, 470 E. Lockwood, St. Louis, MO
    63119
(314) 968-7098
Ref: 31208.002521
PF: Curriculum Development

▶ **Webster University**   [126]
Student Literacy Corps
Theresa Prosser
Asst. Professor, 470 E. Lockwood, St. Louis, MO
    63119
(314) 961-2660
Ref: 31209.002521
PF: Tutoring, Counseling

▶ **Wesleyan University**   [89]
Center for Creative Youth (CCY)
B. Joan Hickey
Director, Middletown, CT 06459
(203) 347-9411 x2684
Ref: 20919.001424
PF: Enrichment, Gifted

▶ **Wesleyan University**   [157]
Project to Increase Mastery of Math and Science
    (PIMMS)
Robert A. Rosenbaum
Director, A110 Butterfield, Middletown, CT
    06459-0200
(203) 347-9411 x2481
Ref: 21159.001424
PF: Professional Development, Inservice

▶ **Wesleyan University**   [26]
Upward Bound/Conncap
Peter Budryk
Adjunct Lecturer in Education, 212 College Street,
    Middletown, CT 06457
(203) 347-9411
Ref: 31746.001424
PF: Minority, At-Risk

West Virginia State College
Tech Prep Associate Degree Program
George Bilicic
Dean, Community College Division, P.O. Box
    1000, Institute, WV 25112
(304) 766-3118
Ref: 30589.003826
PF: Tech-Prep/2+2

▶ **West Virginia University**   [203]
Professional Development Schools
Sarah Steel
Assoc. Director, P.O. Box 6122, 601 Allen Hall,
    Morgantown, WV 26506-6122
(304) 293-6762
LNESTOR@WVNVM.edu
Ref: 20285.003827
PF: Professional Development, Inservice

▶ **Western Carolina University**   [187]
Administrator Academy
Casey Hurley
Asst. Professor, 250 Killian Building, Cullowhee,
    NC 28723
(704) 227-7415
Ref: 30755.002981
PF: Professional Development, Inservice

Western Carolina University
Alliance of Business Leaders and Educators
Margaret Studenc
Coordinator, 227 Killian Building, Cullowhee, NC
    28723
(704) 227-7312
Ref: 30754.002981
PF: School-College-Business Partnerships

▶ **Western Carolina University**   [234]
Model Clinical Teaching Program
Ruth A. McCreary
Coordinator, College of Education and
    Psychology, Cullowhee, NC 28723
(704) 227-7295
Ref: 30757.002981
PF: Faculty Exchanges

Western Carolina University
Strengthening Teacher Education Through a
    Partnership of Equals (STEPE)
Don Chalker
Head, Department of Administration, Curriculum
    and Instruction, 250 Killian Building, Cullowhee,
    NC 28723
(704) 227-7415
Ref: 30756.002981
PF: Professional Development, Inservice

▶ **Western Connecticut State
University**   [157]
Professional Practices Program
Janet Burke
Elementary Education Coordinator, 181 White
    Street, Danbury, CT 06810
(203) 837-8510
Ref: 30141.001380
PF: Professional Development, Inservice

▶ **Western Illinois University**   [163]
CommTech Curriculum Integration Project
David R. Taylor
Dean, College of Education, Macomb, IL 61455
(309) 298-1690
Ref: 31192.001780
PF: Professional Development, Inservice

▶ **Western Illinois University**   [73]
Satellite-Delivered Interactive AP Calculus
Michael Dickson
Executive Director, College of Education,
    Macomb, IL 61455
(309) 298-1811
Ref: 31191.001780
PF: College Courses for Students

▶ **Western Illinois University**   [287]
Science Alive Scientific Literacy Program
John Beaver
Professor, Elementary Education, Macomb, IL
    61455
(309) 298-2065
Ref: 31193.001780
PF: Technology Application

Western Iowa Tech Community College
Even Start Family Literacy
Christine Case
Adult Basic Education Coordinator, 4647 Stone
    Avenue, P.O. Box 265, Sioux City, IA
    51102-0265
(712) 274-6400
Ref: 31049.007316
PF: Student Health, Welfare

Key: "▶" denotes those partnerships abstracted in Parts 1-5; the corresponding page numbers are given in brackets. "PF:" denotes the partnership's "primary focus." "Ref:" denotes the partnership's assigned reference number in the National School-College Partnership Database (see Appendix B).

Western Iowa Tech Community College
Individualized Learning Center
Gary Swaney
Dean of Community and Continuing Education,
4647 Stone Avenue, P.O. Box 265, Sioux City,
IA 51102-0265
(712) 274-6400
Ref: 31050.007316
PF: Minority, At-Risk

▶ **Western Kentucky University** [166]
Professional Development Center Network
Jack Neel
Director, College of Education Building, Suite 427,
Bowling Green, KY 42101
(502) 745-2451
Ref: 21052.002002
PF: Professional Development, Inservice

▶ **Western Montana College** [227]
Butte/Western Partnership
W. Oldendorf
Assoc. Dean, 710 S. Atlantic Street, Dillon, MT
59725
(406) 683-7011
Ref: 31145.002537
PF: Teacher Education Centers

▶ **Western Nebraska Community
College** [296]
Adopt-a-School
Debbi Potts
Executive Director, Allied Health and Community
Education, 1601 E. 27th, Scottsbluff, NE 69361
(308) 632-6030
Ref: 31263.002560
PF: School-College-Business Partnerships

▶ **Western Nebraska Community
College** [259]
Western Nebraska Tech Prep
Nori Cannell
Tech Prep Coordinator, 1601 E. 27th Street,
Scottsbluff, NE 69361
(308) 635-6139
ncannell@nde.unl.edu
Ref: 31264.002560
PF: Tech-Prep/2+2

▶ **Western New York Consortium of Higher
Education** [280]
King Urban Life Center
Stephen C. Halpern
Assoc. Professor, Department of Political
Science, SUNY-Buffalo, Park Hall, Buffalo, NY
14260
(716) 645-2251
Ref: 30298.U00005
PF: Umbrella Programs

Western Washington University
Adventures in Science and Arts
Debbie Young
Program Coordinator, University Extended
Programs, Bellingham, WA 98225-9042
(206) 650-6820
debbieyy@henson.cc.wwu.edu
Ref: 31589.003802
PF: Enrichment, Gifted

Western Washington University
College/High School Courses
Lisa Marrs
Assistant to the Vice Provost, Continuing
Education, OM 400/MS 9042, Bellingham, WA
98225-9042
(206) 650-2850
lisa@henson.cc.wwu.edu
Ref: 31591.003802
PF: College Courses for Students

▶ **Western Washington University** [144]
Program for the Advancement of Science
Education
Thomas A. Storch
Director, Institute for Watershed Studies,
Bellingham, WA 98225
(206) 650-3385
Ref: 31590.003802
PF: Career, Internships, Apprenticeships

Westmoreland County Community College
Keep the Options Open Program
Sandra L. Montemurro
Director, Student Development, Youngwood, PA
15697
(412) 925-4050
Ref: 20576.010176
PF: Minority, At-Risk

Wheeling Jesuit College
Partnership in Education
Karen A. Bland, O.S.B.
Assoc. Academic Dean, 316 Washington Avenue,
Wheeling, WV 26003
(304) 243-2484
Ref: 30595.003831
PF: Resource Sharing

▶ **Wheelock College** [170]
Cambridgeport Partnership
Susan Swap
Director, Center on College-School-Community
Partnerships, 200 The Riverway, Boston, MA
02215
(617)734-5200
Ref: 30032.002228
PF: Professional Development, Inservice

Wheelock College
The Learning and Teaching Collaborative
Susan Swap
Director, Center on College-School-Community
Partnerships, 200 The Riverway, Boston, MA
02215
(617) 734-5200
Ref: 30030.002228
PF: Professional Development, Inservice

▶ **Wheelock College** [214]
Wheelock-Boston-Walker School Partnership
Susan Swap
Director, Center on College-School-Community
Partnerships, 200 The Riverway, Boston, MA
02215
(617) 734-5200
Ref: 30031.002228
PF: Recruit, Preservice, Certification

Whitman College
Blue Ridge Tutoring Program
Dannelle D. Stevens
Director of Teacher Education, 349 Boyer Street,
Walla Walla, WA 99362
(509) 527-5187
stevensd@whitman.edu
Ref: 31608.003803
PF: Minority, At-Risk

Whitman College
Campfire Boys and Girls Program
Dannelle D. Stevens
Director of Teacher Education, 349 Boyer Street,
Walla Walla, WA 99362
(509) 527-5187
stevensd@whitman.edu
Ref: 31701.003803
PF: Minority, At-Risk

Whitman College
Readiness to Learn Consortium
Dannelle D. Stevens
Director of Teacher Education, 349 Boyer Street,
Walla Walla, WA 99362
(509) 527-5187
stevensd@whitman.edu
Ref: 31607.003803
PF: Minority, At-Risk

Wichita State University
Grow Your Own Teachers
Marcus Ballenger
Assoc. Dean, Box 28, Wichita, KS 67208
(316) 689-3301
Ref: 31254.001950
PF: Recruit, Preservice, Certification

Wichita State University
Partnerships Assisting Student Success
Marsha Gladhart
Project Director, Box 28, Wichita, KS 67208
(316) 689-3322
Ref: 31256.001950
PF: Tutoring, Counseling

▶ **Wichita State University**   [213]
Peace Corps Fellow/USA Program
Robert Alley
Program Director, Box 28, Wichita, KS 67208
(316) 689-3322
Ref: 31255.001950
PF: Recruit, Preservice, Certification

Wilkes Community College
Tech Prep
Tony C. Randall
Dean of Instruction, Box 120, Wilkesboro, NC
   28697
(910) 651-8645
Ref: 30753.002983
PF: Tech-Prep/2+2

▶ **Wilkes University**   [194]
Project LEARN (Local Educational Action
   Resource Network)
Douglas J. Lynch
Chair, Education Department, P.O. Box 111,
   Wilkes-Barre, PA 18766
(716) 831-4684
dlynch@wilkes1.wilkes.edu
Ref: 30443.003394
PF: Professional Development, Inservice

▶ **Wilkes University**   [83]
Wilkes Young Scholars Program
Bing K. Wong
Assoc. Dean, School of Science and Engineering,
   Wilkes-Barre, PA 18766
(717) 831-4803
bwong@wilkes1.wilkes.edu
Ref: 30442.003394
PF: College Courses for Students

William Jewell College
WJC Concurrent Enrollment Program
Larry Stone
Vice President, Enrollment Management, 500
   College Hill, Liberty, MO 64068
(816) 781-7700
Ref: 31227.002524
PF: College Courses for Students

▶ **William Paterson College**   [179]
Northern New Jersey Writing Consortium
James Hauser
Professor of English, Wayne, NJ 07470
(201) 595-3063
Ref: 21169.002625
PF: Professional Development, Inservice

William Paterson College
WPC/Paterson Public Schools Professional
   Development School
300 Pompton Road, Wayne, NJ 07470
(201) 595-2000
Ref: 31614.002625
PF: Professional Development, Inservice

Wilmington College
Mentoring First Year Teachers in Rural
   Communities
Susan Hersh
Chair, Education Department, Pyle Center, Box
   1293, Wilmington, OH 45177
(513) 382-6661
Ref: 30918.003142
PF: Recruit, Preservice, Certification

▶ **Winona State University**   [214]
WSU/ISD 535 Graduate Induction Program
Lora Knutson
Director, Rochester Center, Highway 14 East,
   Rochester, MN 55904
(507) 287-2199
Ref: 20249.002394
PF: Recruit, Preservice, Certification

▶ **Winthrop University**   [61]
Child Abuse Prevention and Awareness Project
Susan J. Smith
Director, School of Education, Rock Hill, SC
   29733
(803) 323-4740
Ref: 20968.003456
PF: Minority, At-Risk

▶ **Winthrop University**   [61]
Governor's Remediation Initiative
John R. Rumford
Director, School of Education, Rock Hill, SC
   29733
(803) 323-2120
Ref: 21085.003456
PF: Minority, At-Risk

▶ **Winthrop University**   [61]
Phone Friend
Susan J. Smith
Director, School of Education, Rock Hill, SC
   29733
(803) 323-4740
Ref: 20600.003456
PF: Minority, At-Risk

▶ **Winthrop University**   [197]
Project PRISM
Everett Stallings
Project Director, School of Education, Rock Hill,
   SC 29733
(803) 323-2151
Ref: 30819.003456
PF: Professional Development, Inservice

Winthrop University
South Carolina Center for the Advancement of
   Teaching and School Leadership
Barbara Gottesman
Director, 139 Withers/WTS, Rock Hill, SC 29733
(803) 323-4772
Ref: 30820.003456
PF: Recruit, Preservice, Certification

▶ **Winthrop University**   [222]
South Carolina Center for Teacher Recruitment
Janice Poda
Director, Canterbury House, Rock Hill, SC 29733
(803) 323-4032
Ref: 30817.003456
PF: Recruit, Preservice, Certification

▶ **Winthrop University**   [110]
Summer ST-ARTS Program (Summer Program
   for Special Students in the Arts)
Donald M. Rogers
Director, Rock Hill, SC 29733
(803) 323-2255
Ref: 20093.003456
PF: Enrichment, Gifted

▶ **Winthrop University**   [60]
WINGS (Winthrop's Involvement in Nurturing and
   Graduating Students)
Susan J. Smith
Director, School of Education, Rock Hill, SC
   29733
(803) 323-4740
Ref: 30816.003456
PF: Minority, At-Risk

Key: "▶" denotes those partnerships abstracted in Parts 1-5; the corresponding page numbers are given in brackets. "PF:" denotes the partnership's "primary focus." "Ref:" denotes the partnership's assigned reference number in the National School-College Partnership Database (see Appendix B).

Winthrop University
Winthrop Olde English Consortium
Benny Coxton
Director, 204D Withers/WTS, Rock Hill, SC 29733
(803) 323-4737
Ref: 20173.003456
PF: Professional Development, Inservice

Winthrop University
Winthrop University Friends Program
Susan J. Smith
Director, School of Education, Rock Hill, SC
    29733
(803) 323-4740
Ref: 20973.003456
PF: Minority, At-Risk

▶ **Winthrop University**   [229]
Winthrop University/Public School Partnership
Patricia L. Graham
Assoc. Dean, 106 Withers/WTS, Rock Hill, SC
    29733
(803) 323-2115
Ref: 30818.003456
PF: Teacher Education Centers

Wittenberg University
Partners-In-Education: Franklin Middle School
    and Wittenberg
Deborah J. Dillon
Director of Community Services, P.O. Box 720,
    Springfield, OH 45501
(513) 327-7523
Ref: 20531.003143
PF: Tutoring, Counseling

▶ **Wofford College**   [143]
Spartanburg County Partnership
Meri Lynch
Director of Summer Programs, 429 N. Church
    Street, Spartanburg, SC 29303-3663
(803) 597-4516
Ref: 30786.003457
PF: Career, Internships, Apprenticeships

Wofford College
Summer Program for Academically Talented
    Students (SPATS)
Meri Lynch
Director of Summer Programs, 429 N. Church
    Street, Spartanburg, SC 29303-3663
(803) 597-4516
Ref: 30785.003457
PF: Enrichment, Gifted

Woodbury University
Academy of Finance
Marvin J. Richman
Dean, School of Business, 7500 Glenoaks
    Boulevard, Burbank, CA 91510
(818) 767-0888
Ref: 31513.001343
PF: Career, Internships, Apprenticeships

▶ **Woodbury University**   [291]
Verdugo Intensive Partnership
Peter Anderson
Asst. Professor, 7500 Glenoaks Boulevard,
    Burbank, CA 90027
(818) 767-0888
peander@eis.calstate.edu
Ref: 31477.001343
PF: School-College-Business Partnerships

▶ **Woods Hole Oceanographic
Institution**   [279]
Woods Hole Science and Technology Education
    Partnership (WHSTEP)
Lawrence Peirson
Education Office, Woods Hole, MA 02543
(508) 548-1400 x2219
Ref: 30045.U00009
PF: Umbrella Programs

▶ **Worcester Polytechnic Institute**   [238]
WPI School-College Collaborative
Francis Trainor
Director, 100 Institute Road, Worcester, MA
    01609
(508) 831-5707
Ref: 31809.002233
PF: Curriculum Development

Worcester State College
College to School Reporting Project
James R. Alberque
Assoc. Director, School/College Collaboratives,
    486 Chandler Street, Worcester, MA 01602
(508) 793-8000
Ref: 30010.002190
PF: Faculty Exchanges

Worcester State College
Kids to College
James R. Alberque
Assoc. Director, School/College Collaboratives,
    486 Chandler Street, Worcester, MA 01602
(508) 793-8000
Ref: 30012.002190
PF: Enrichment, Gifted

Worcester State College
Project PALMS
James R. Alberque
Assoc. Director, School/College Collaboratives,
    486 Chandler Street, Worcester, MA 01602
(508) 793-8000
Ref: 30009.002190
PF: Curriculum Development

Worcester State College
South Central Alliance of Middle Schools
James R. Alberque
Assoc. Director, School/College Collaboratives,
    486 Chandler Street, Worcester, MA 01602
(508) 793-8000
Ref: 31698.002190
PF: Instructional Research

Worcester State College
Turning Points/Worcester Public Schools
    Partnership
James R. Alberque
Assoc. Director, School/College Collaboratives,
    486 Chandler Street, Worcester, MA 01602
(508) 793-8000
Ref: 31697.002190
PF: Recruit, Preservice, Certification

▶ **Worcester State College**   [135]
Worcester Career Beginnings
James R. Alberque
Assoc. Director, School/College Collaboratives,
    486 Chandler Street, Worcester, MA 01602
(508) 793-8000
Ref: 30011.002190
PF: Career, Internships, Apprenticeships

▶ **Worcester State College**   [135]
Worcester Future Teachers Academy
James R. Alberque
Assoc. Director, School/College Collaboratives,
    486 Chandler Street, Worcester, MA 01602
(508) 793-8000
Ref: 31720.002190
PF: Career, Internships, Apprenticeships

Wright State University
ED LINK-12
James S. Trent
Director, Division of Professional Practice and
    Research, 228 Millett Hall, Dayton, OH 45435
(513) 873-2635
Ref: 20340.009168
PF: Professional Development, Inservice

Wright State University
Partners Transforming Education:
    School/University/Community
Dixie Barnhart
Asst. Dean, Partner and Program Development,
    228 Millett Hall, Dayton, OH 45435
(513) 873-3411
Ref: 30926.009168
PF: City/Regional Compacts

Wright State University
Wright STEPP
Giorgio M. McBeath
Assist. Dean and Director, Russ Engineering
    Center, #405, Dayton, OH 45435
(513) 873-5005
gmcbeath@matrix.cs.wright.edu
Ref: 30927.009168
PF: Minority, At-Risk

Wytheville Community College
Dual Credit Program
David N. Johnson
Director of Continuing Education, 1000 E. Main,
    Wytheville, VA 24382
(703) 228-5541
Ref: 20955.003761
PF: College Courses for Students

Y

Yakima Valley Community College
Adopt-an-Elementary School Program
Peggy Keller
Radiologic Technology Instructor, P.O. Box 1647,
    Yakima, WA 98907
(509) 575-2438
Ref: 31596.003805
PF: Minority, At-Risk

Yakima Valley Community College
YVCC and Perry Technical Institute Cooperative
    Degree Program
Paul Killpatrick
Dean, Professional and Career Education, P.O.
    Box 1647, Yakima, WA 98907
(509) 575-2429
Ref: 31597.003805
PF: Tech-Prep/2+2

▶ **Yale University**   [157]
Yale-New Haven Teachers Institute
James R. Vivian
Director, 53 Wall Street, New Haven, CT 06520
(203) 432-1080
Ref: 21046.001426
PF: Professional Development, Inservice

▶ **York College of Pennsylvania**   [129]
Adopt-a-School
Dominic J. Macri
Director of Student Activities, York, PA 17405
(717) 846-7788
Ref: 30427.003399
PF: Tutoring, Counseling

York College of Pennsylvania
York Opportunity Program
Dominic J. Macri
Director of Student Activities, York, PA 17405
(717) 846-7788
Ref: 30428.003399
PF: Minority, At-Risk

York Technical College
Educational Talent Search
Edward Duffy
Vice President for Development, 452 S. Anderson
    Road, Rock Hill, SC 29730
(803) 327-8012
Ref: 30814.003996
PF: Minority, At-Risk

▶ **York Technical College**   [61]
Learning Enhanced Achievement Program
    (LEAP)
Deborah L. Gladden
Director, 452 S. Anderson Road, Rock Hill, SC
    29730
(803) 327-8000
Ref: 30812.003996
PF: Minority, At-Risk

York Technical College
Summer Transition Enrichment Program (STEP)
Larry Erwin
Vice President for Student Affairs, 425 S.
    Anderson Road, Rock Hill, SC 29730
(803) 327-8016
Ref: 30815.003996
PF: College Courses for Students

▶ **York Technical College**   [62]
The Women's Center
Donna Wooldridge-Smith
Director, 452 S. Anderson Road, Rock Hill, SC
    29730
(803) 327-8004
Ref: 30813.003996
PF: Minority, At-Risk

Youngstown State University
Tech Prep
James Lewellan
Tech Prep Coordinator, Youngstown, OH 44555
(216) 742-2333
Ref: 30895.003145
PF: Tech-Prep/2+2

Youngstown State University
Youngstown State University/Youngstown Public
    Schools Partnership
James J. Scanlon
Provost, Youngstown, OH 44555
(216) 742-3103
Ref: 31156.003145
PF: City/Regional Compacts

□ □ □

APPENDIX A

Instructions for Participating in
The National Survey of School-College Partnerships

Readers are invited to photocopy and complete the National Survey of School-College Partnerships form on the following pages to have their partnerships included in the National School-College Partnership Database or to update previously submitted survey information. Inclusion in the database of up-to-date information about partnerships will facilitate future national surveys and ensure that those partnerships will receive information about upcoming publications and conferences.

Instructions

1. Use a **separate** survey form to describe each major partnership in which your institution is involved. One survey form may be returned for partnerships that coordinate multiple activities under a **single** program title or rubric.

2. Complete all four pages of the survey form that follows. If your partnership involves more than one precollege institution, you may include additional school contact information on a separate sheet(s). Also please note in identifying your program's **primary** classification that only **one** of the 33 options listed is to be selected.

3. Be sure to include a brief, carefully written annotation (100 words or fewer) describing your program activities. **Surveys returned without annotations cannot be included in the database** (see question 10 of the survey form for detailed instructions).

4. Do not use acronyms in program titles or your annotation without first providing full names or titles (e.g., "Board of Cooperative Educational Services," then "BOCES").

5. Feel free to enclose program brochures or other descriptive materials with your survey to be added to the files of the Center for Research and Information on School-College Partnerships.

Return Completed Surveys and Annotations to:

Center for Research and Information on School-College Partnerships
Syracuse University
111 Waverly Avenue, Suite 200
Syracuse, NY 13244-2320

Telephone: (315) 443-2404 ● Fax: (315) 443-1524
E-mail: partners@advance.syr.edu

THE NATIONAL SURVEY
OF SCHOOL-COLLEGE PARTNERSHIPS©

Coordinated by
Center for Research and Information on School-College Partnerships
Syracuse University

In cooperation with
American Association for Higher Education

Photocopy this form as needed. Use a separate form for each partnership submitted.

1. **Name of College/University:** _____

    a. Institution's location: ☐ Urban   ☐ Suburban   ☐ Rural

    b. Institution's status: ☐ Public   ☐ Independent

2. **Name of Program:** _____

    a. Year partnership was established: _____

    b. Number of schools served by this partnership: _____

    c. Is this program funded by agencies or organizations external to the educational institutions participating in the partnership?   ☐ Yes   ☐ No

    If yes, please name the agencies or organizations providing the support (e.g., foundation, government office, business, civic organization):

    _____

    _____

3. **Program Contacts:** (representatives who could be contacted for additional information):

College/University Contact

School Contact(s) *(Select a representative contact from each participating precollege institution, e.g., principal, teacher, coordinator.)*

College/University Contact	School Contact(s)
_____ Name	_____ Name
_____ Title	_____ Title
_____ Address	_____ Address
(____)_____ (____)_____ Phone Fax	(____)_____ (____)_____ Phone Fax
E-mail address: _____	E-mail address: _____

4. **Grade Levels:** Please check the school grade level(s) served by the partnership. *(Check all that apply.)*

☐ Elementary School ☐ Middle School ☐ High School

5. **Type/location of school(s)** served by this partnership: *(Check all that apply.)*

☐ Public ☐ Private

☐ Urban ☐ Suburban ☐ Rural

6. **Scope**: Please indicate the scope or affiliation of your partnership model. *(Check only one.)*

☐ National   Allied with a prominent national model (e.g., National Geographic Education Projects, AAHE's Community Compact for Student Success, National Writing Project, National Center for Urban Partnerships, Knight Foundation Collaborations).

Specify national affiliation: _____

☐ Regional/ Statewide   Serving schools throughout a state, region, or section of the country and *not* affiliated with a prominent national model.

Indicate region/state served: _____

☐ Local   Providing assistance or services to schools close to the sponsoring college or university (including citywide programs) and *not* affiliated with a prominent national model.

Indicate city/county/local area served: _____

7. **Content Orientation**: If your partnership has a particular discipline or content orientation, please check the appropriate codes below. *(Check all that apply.)*

Social Sciences
☐ Civics/Citizenship
☐ Economics
☐ Geography
☐ Global Education/ International Studies
☐ Government
☐ History
☐ Law
☐ Psychology
☐ Sociology
☐ Other _____

Humanities and Arts
☐ English
☐ ESL/Bilingual
☐ Foreign Language
☐ Music
☐ Reading/Language Arts
☐ Speech
☐ Studio Arts

☐ Theater/Drama
☐ Writing
☐ Other _____

Applied Sciences
☐ Business
☐ Computer Science
☐ Engineering/Technology
☐ Health Professions
☐ Occupational Education
☐ Other _____

Mathematics and Sciences
☐ Astronomy
☐ Biology
☐ Chemistry
☐ Earth Science
☐ EnvironmentalStudies/Ecology
☐ Mathematics
☐ Physics
☐ Other _____

Education
☐ Early Childhood Education
☐ Health and Wellness Education
☐ Physical/Sports Education
☐ Special/Inclusive Education
☐ Other _____

Miscellaneous
☐ Basic Skills/Study Skills
☐ Critical Thinking/ Problem Solving
☐ Cultural Pluralism
☐ Leadership Skills Development
☐ Library
☐ Literacy
☐ Parental and Community Involvement in Schools
☐ Research
☐ Scholarships/Financial Aid
☐ TQM/Strategic Planning
☐ Other _____

8. **Classification:** Please identify (P) the primary classification of your partnership and (F) the areas in which it focuses.
   IMPORTANT: Check only **ONE** box in the **(P) primary classification** column; check as many **(F) secondary focus codes** in the second column as apply.

(P)	(F)	Codes	Major Areas
		Serving Underrepresented, Minority, At-Risk Populations	Programs and Services for Students
		College Courses for High School Students	
		Enrichment and Gifted-and-Talented Programs	
		Middle Colleges and Early Colleges	
		Tutoring, Mentoring, and Counseling Programs	
		Career Exploration, Internships, or Apprenticeships	
		Student Health and Welfare	
		Retention, Continuing Education & Promotion, and Recruitment for Higher Education	
		Other:	
		Professional Development and Inservice Training, including Academic Alliances (School and College Faculty, Administrators, Counselors, and Staff)	Programs and Services for Educators
		Recruitment and Retention, Preservice Programs, Early Career Support, and Alternative Certification Programs	
		Teacher Education Centers	
		Teaching Excellence Awards, Rewards, and Recognitions	
		School-College Faculty Exchanges	
		Other:	
		Curriculum and Instructional Materials Development	Articulation, Development, and Evaluation of Curriculum and Instruction
		Instructional Research, Evaluation, and Testing	
		Tech-Prep 2+2 and Coordinated Vocational-Technical Programs	
		Regional and Statewide Interinstitutional Articulation Councils and Agreements	
		Comprehensive Systemic Restructuring	
		Other:	
		Citywide or Regional Compacts	Restructuring
		Joint Governance Responsibility	
		Shared Faculty/Staff Appointments	
		New Roles for Faculty	
		New Achievement Standards/Assessment Mechanisms	
		Coordinating Agencies and Umbrella Programs	
		Other:	
		Resource-Sharing Agreements	Other Partnerships, Cooperative Arrangements, and Collaborative Activities
		Magnet Schools	
		Innovative Uses of Learning/Communication Technologies	
		School-College-Business Partnerships	
		Other:	

9. **Systemic Reform**: While many collaborative efforts have a specific programmatic emphasis, others have been created to **broadly affect K-12 <u>and</u> postsecondary reform**.

> ### Example
>
> *The El Paso Collaborative for Academic Excellence involves the University of Texas at El Paso, El Paso Community College, and three urban school districts in a broad-ranging effort to improve student academic success and the quality of teaching, as well as to produce greater involvement of the larger community in support of education reform. Among many specific initiatives supporting the El Paso Collaborative are: a regular series of week-long institutes for teachers and principals to develop, at the building level, higher achievement standards and more effective teaching approaches; grass-roots organizations to involve parents and others in the community more effectively in local schools; and the development of more effective transfer agreements and mechanisms to help students move from two-year to four-year academic programs.*

With the goal of <u>systemic</u> reform at their heart, such efforts are often locally controlled and jointly administered, stress regular assessment and reporting, critically examine reward structures, and offer a variety of support services for teachers, administrators, and staff.

Do you feel that your collaborative effort is aimed at systemic reform? ☐ Yes ☐ No

10. **Annotation:** Please include a brief **annotation** (100 words or fewer) highlighting some of your program's primary objectives, population served, and major activities. To facilitate optical scanning, please write your annotation on a sheet of 8½" x 11" plain white paper. An annotation *must* be attached to this survey to be included in the database. As we build a "Yellow Pages" directory section for our next national publication, we would like to include just enough information about a large number of programs from throughout the nation for people to make decisions regarding whom they should contact for more complete information. To supplement your annotation, feel free to enclose brochures or other descriptive materials, which will then be added to our research center files. Surveys returned without annotations cannot be considered for inclusion in the National School-College Partnership Database or in any future publications.

> ### Sample Annotation
>
> *Syracuse University Project Advance is a partnership program linking the University and secondary schools. Its primary mission is to offer qualified high school students the opportunity to enroll in challenging Syracuse University freshman courses during their senior year of high school. Project Advance also provides several other important services in working with the high schools: inservice training for high school instructors; a continuing forum for communication between educators from both school and University settings; and an extensive research and evaluation effort to systematically improve instruction. (85 words)*

Return completed survey and annotation to:

Center for Research and Information on School-College Partnerships ● Syracuse University
111 Waverly Avenue, Suite 200 ● Syracuse, NY 13244-2320

Telephone: (315) 443-2404 ● Fax: (315) 443-1524 ● E-mail: partners@advance.syr.edu

Thank you for your assistance!

APPENDIX B

Instructions for Requesting a Search of
The National School-College Partnership Database

Information collected in the 1994 National Survey of School-College Partnerships has been used to compile this publication and to construct a national computer database of school-college partnerships. The database contains not only the data about each program found in the National Directory section of this publication, but also all other responses to the survey questions (see Appendix A). They include demographic information on the participating schools, colleges, and universities; the school contact(s), where available; founding date, number of participating schools, geographic scope, and funding information for the partnership; grade levels of students directly served; content orientation; all of the indicated focus codes; relationship to systemic reform; and the program annotation. In addition, information on programs responding to the National Survey after publication of this volume is being added on an ongoing basis. All of the survey response information fields, except for the program annotation and list of external funding agencies, can be used to include or exclude programs from a search of the database.

The database can be searched in a number of ways, and multiple styles of reports can be generated. It can be useful to educators for a variety of purposes, such as to locate specific types of programs serving particular groups in a defined geographic area (e.g., enrichment and gifted-and-talented programs dealing with mathematics involving public colleges and universities in New York, New Jersey, and Pennsylvania). Frequent users of the database include individuals interested in initiating partnerships in their region, graduate students writing theses and dissertations, state and federal officials planning legislation, foundations and other agencies developing funding guidelines, and organizations planning conferences. In addition to the standard report formats and mailing labels outlined below, custom reports can also be generated if necessary.

The Center for Research and Information on School-College Partnerships at Syracuse University reserves the right to deny access to the National School-College Partnership Database for purposes that it judges to be inappropriate.

Guidelines for Describing Your Request

The following guidelines are intended to assist you in preparing a database search request that will clearly communicate the inclusion and exclusion parameters you wish us to use in searching the database, as well as your desired output format(s). While this sequence will not necessarily be the best for all searches, it works well for most requests. In the absence of any stated search parameters for any of the categorizations discussed below, we will assume that **no** programs are to be **excluded** based on those categories.

Determine the Classification and Focus Codes Desired   (Appendix A, question 8)
If you wish to include only programs that emphasize particular populations or activities, request the appropriate categories from the database as shown on page 3 of the **National Survey of School-College Partnerships** form (Appendix A). Categories are listed either as the Primary Classification (P), of which each partnership has one and only one, or as Focus Codes (F), of which each partnership might have as many as 32. You may select programs that have any of the listed categories alone or in combination as either the Primary Classification, Focus Code(s), or both. You may wish to narrow the focus of your search by using the "and"/"or" operators — e.g., Resource-Sharing Agreements (as P) **and** New Roles for Faculty (as F) **or** School-

College Faculty Exchanges (as F). Please note that since each program can have only one P response, constructing a request with Ps on both sides of an "and" operator will **exclude all** programs. Finally, to simplify your request, if you wish to include *all* of the partnerships within one of the Major Areas as shown on page 3 of the survey form, you may indicate this by requesting that Major Area in lieu of requesting all its components.

Determine Content Orientation   (Appendix A, question 7)

If you are interested in programs that are explicitly involved with particular disciplines or content orientations, request the appropriate orientations from the list shown in question 7 of the **National Survey of School-College Partnerships** form (Appendix A). Although not all partnerships in the database have indicated specific orientations, approximately 90% have indicated at least one. As discussed above, the selections can be used to either widen or narrow the search. As with the Primary Classification and Focus Codes, if you wish to include *all* of the orientations in one of the indicated groupings (e.g., all those in Social Sciences, or in Education) you may select that group heading only.

Determine Other Desired Search Parameters

College/university partner characteristics   (Appendix A, question 1)
Searches can be defined by the college/university's *location* (Urban, Suburban, Rural); *status* (Public, Independent); or *Carnegie classification*. An additional classification, "U," has been added to the Carnegie listing to reflect programs, such as the California Academic Partnership Program and the Boston Higher Education Partnership, that have responded as umbrella entities covering partnership programs of a number of colleges and universities. With the exception of the umbrella programs, all programs have entries in the database for both location and status.

School partner characteristics   (Appendix A, questions 4 and 5)
The database also includes information concerning the *grade levels* (Elementary, Middle, or High School) served by the partnership. More than 74% of partnerships in the database have responded to this question. The school partners have also been categorized by *type* and *location*. As each partnership is likely to have more than one school partner, there can be more than one response in each of these categories. Approximately 75% of the partnerships in the database have indicated at least one *location* for school partners; 93% have indicted the *type* of school partners.

Program scope   (Appendix A, question 6)
Programs in the database have been categorized as National, Regional, or Local in *scope*. "National" scope has been defined as either affiliation with a prominent national partnership model or involving a national (or in some cases international) constituency. "Regional" programs are those involving institutions and individuals from an entire state or all or a significant portion of a number of states. All other programs are classified as "Local."

Systemic reform   (Appendix A, question 9)
Respondents to the survey were asked to respond to the question: Do you feel that your collaborative effort is aimed at systemic reform? About 60% of respondents answered this question.

Determine Geographic Constraints

If you wish to restrict your search to partnerships from a particular geographic area(s), you may do so by specifying a list of either states or zip codes to be included. Otherwise, your search will include all database programs nationwide.

Charges for Services and Report Selection

Four standard report formats, plus custom reports, are available as described below. The charges listed cover the cost of a comprehensive search of the database using the search parameters you request, production of the selected report, and shipping and handling.

Short report Includes the college/university name; the program name; and the name, telephone and fax numbers, and e-mail address of the college contact person. The report is printed nine records per page (see Figure B.1). The charge for a search producing the short report is $50.00.

Extended report: Includes all of the information in the short report, plus the program annotation and a grid showing the program's focus codes. It is printed two records per page (see Figure B.2). The charge for a search producing the extended report is $65.00.

Complete report: Includes all of the program information contained in the database. Although the survey form requests only one school contact person, in many instances multiple contacts are provided. These additional names are available as an option on the complete report for a small additional charge. This report is printed one record per page (see Figure B.3). The charge for the complete report is $90.00; the additional names option charge is $15.00.

Mailing labels: Labels are available for both the college and school contact persons. College contact labels are available in a two-across laser-printed format; each address label is 1⅓ x 4 inches. School contact labels come in three-across laser-printed format; each school contact label is 1 x 2¾ inches. All labels are pressure-sensitive. The charge for labels is $15.00 per 100 labels (minimum charge $30.00).

Custom reports: Custom reports to meet your specific requirements can be produced upon request. Please call to discuss your needs.

Once you have refined your search parameters to meet your needs and determined your desired report output format, please complete the request form that follows, including shipping information, the search description, and desired output format. Please include an approved institutional purchase order, check, or money order payable to **Syracuse University** for each request. Send orders (mail or fax) to:

Center for Research and Information on School-College Partnerships
Syracuse University
111 Waverly Avenue, Suite 200
Syracuse, NY 13244-2320

Telephone: (315) 443-2404 ● Fax: (315) 443-1524 ● E-mail: partners@advance.syr.edu

We will make every attempt to process and ship your request within 10 working days of receipt. If you have any questions regarding your order, call the Center at (315) 443-2404 between 9:00 AM and 4:00 PM EST, Monday through Friday. Fax requests or inquiries can be received anytime. The above rates for searches, report generation, and mailing labels were set for 1995; beyond 1995, prices are subject to change without notice.

Figure B.1.

Page 1   *Short Report*

University of California-Irvine
Project STEP (Student/Teacher
Educational Partnership)

College Contact:

Robin Casselman
Associate Director, EOP/SAA Outreach
Project STEP (Student/Teacher Educational
Partnership)
University of California-Irvine
160 Administration Building
Irvine, CA 92717-2505
Phone: (714) 856-7481
Fax: (714) 856-8219
Email: rncassel@uci.edu

University of Southern Maine
Southern Maine Partnership

College Contact:

Lynne Miller
Executive Director
Southern Maine Partnership
University of Southern Maine
117 Bailey Hall
Gorham, ME 04038
Phone: (207) 780-5479
Fax: (207) 780-5315
Email: lynnem@maine.edu

Mt. Hood Community College
Successful 2+2 Tech Prep Development

College Contact:

Jack D. Miller
Dean of Professional Technical Development
Successful 2+2 Tech Prep Development
Mt. Hood Community College
26000 S.E. Stark
Gresham, OR 97030
Phone: (503) 667-7313
Fax: (503) 667-7389
Email: NA

Gallaudet University
Summer Science Program

College Contact:

Dr. Richard W. Meisegeier
Director, Honors Program
Summer Science Program
Gallaudet University
800 Florida Avenue, NE
Washington, DC 20002
Phone: (202) 651-5550
Fax: (202) 651-5759
Email: rwmeisegeier@gallua.bitnet

Five Colleges Inc.
Five College/Public School Partnership

College Contact:

Mary Alice B. Wilson
Coordinator
Five College/Public School Partnership
Five Colleges Inc.
P.O. 740
Amherst, MA 01004
Phone: (413) 256-8316
Fax: (413) 256-0249
Email: mwilson@titan.ucs.umass.edu

University of Texas at San Antonio
Texas Prefreshman Engineering Program

College Contact:

Manuel P. Berriozabal
Coordinator
Texas Prefreshman Engineering Program
University of Texas at San Antonio
6900 North Loop 1604 West
San Antonio, TX 78249-0661
Phone: (210) 691-5530
Fax: (210) 691-4500
Email: mberrioz@lonestar.utsa.edu

University of Tampa
Project SERVE

College Contact:

Dr. Ed Cloutier
Associate Professor
Project SERVE
Dept. of Education
University of Tampa
401 W. Kennedy
Tampa, FL 33606
Phone: (813) 253-6224
Fax: (813) 258-7404
Email: NA

City University of New York LaGuardia
Community College
Middle College High School

College Contact:

Dr. Janet Lieberman
Special Asst. to the President
Middle College High School
City University of New York LaGuardia
Community College
31-10 Thomson Avenue
Long Island City, NY 11101
Phone: (718) 482-5049
Fax: (718) 482-5443
Email: NA

University of Wisconsin-La Crosse
Milwaukee South Division High
School/College of HPER Partnership

College Contact:

Garth Tymeson
Associate Dean
Milwaukee South Division High
School/Collegeof HPER Partnership
College of HPER
University of Wisconsin-La Crosse
124 Mitchell Hall
LaCrosse, WI 54601
Phone: (608) 785-8155
Fax: (608) 785-6520
Email: tymeson@uwlax.bitnet

Figure B.2.

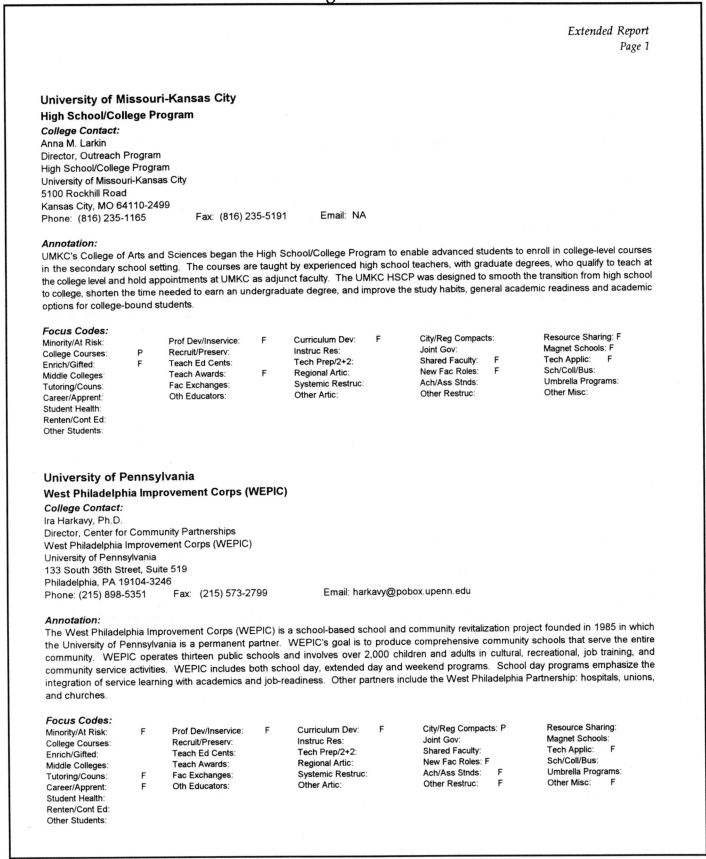

University of Missouri-Kansas City

High School/College Program

College Contact:

Anna M. Larkin
Director, Outreach Program
High School/College Program
University of Missouri-Kansas City
5100 Rockhill Road
Kansas City, MO 64110-2499
Phone: (816) 235-1165   Fax: (816) 235-5191   Email: NA

Annotation:

UMKC's College of Arts and Sciences began the High School/College Program to enable advanced students to enroll in college-level courses in the secondary school setting. The courses are taught by experienced high school teachers, with graduate degrees, who qualify to teach at the college level and hold appointments at UMKC as adjunct faculty. The UMKC HSCP was designed to smooth the transition from high school to college, shorten the time needed to earn an undergraduate degree, and improve the study habits, general academic readiness and academic options for college-bound students.

Focus Codes:

Minority/At Risk:		Prof Dev/Inservice:	F	Curriculum Dev:	F	City/Reg Compacts:		Resource Sharing: F
College Courses:	P	Recruit/Preserv:		Instruc Res:		Joint Gov:		Magnet Schools: F
Enrich/Gifted:	F	Teach Ed Cents:		Tech Prep/2+2:		Shared Faculty:	F	Tech Applic: F
Middle Colleges:		Teach Awards:	F	Regional Artic:		New Fac Roles:	F	Sch/Coll/Bus:
Tutoring/Couns:		Fac Exchanges:		Systemic Restruc:		Ach/Ass Stnds:		Umbrella Programs:
Career/Apprent:		Oth Educators:		Other Artic:		Other Restruc:		Other Misc:
Student Health:								
Renten/Cont Ed:								
Other Students:								

University of Pennsylvania

West Philadelphia Improvement Corps (WEPIC)

College Contact:

Ira Harkavy, Ph.D.
Director, Center for Community Partnerships
West Philadelphia Improvement Corps (WEPIC)
University of Pennsylvania
133 South 36th Street, Suite 519
Philadelphia, PA 19104-3246
Phone: (215) 898-5351   Fax: (215) 573-2799   Email: harkavy@pobox.upenn.edu

Annotation:

The West Philadelphia Improvement Corps (WEPIC) is a school-based school and community revitalization project founded in 1985 in which the University of Pennsylvania is a permanent partner. WEPIC's goal is to produce comprehensive community schools that serve the entire community. WEPIC operates thirteen public schools and involves over 2,000 children and adults in cultural, recreational, job training, and community service activities. WEPIC includes both school day, extended day and weekend programs. School day programs emphasize the integration of service learning with academics and job-readiness. Other partners include the West Philadelphia Partnership: hospitals, unions, and churches.

Focus Codes:

Minority/At Risk:	F	Prof Dev/Inservice:	F	Curriculum Dev:	F	City/Reg Compacts: P		Resource Sharing:
College Courses:		Recruit/Preserv:		Instruc Res:		Joint Gov:		Magnet Schools:
Enrich/Gifted:		Teach Ed Cents:		Tech Prep/2+2:		Shared Faculty:		Tech Applic: F
Middle Colleges:		Teach Awards:		Regional Artic:		New Fac Roles: F		Sch/Coll/Bus:
Tutoring/Couns:	F	Fac Exchanges:		Systemic Restruc:		Ach/Ass Stnds:	F	Umbrella Programs:
Career/Apprent:	F	Oth Educators:		Other Artic:		Other Restruc:	F	Other Misc: F
Student Health:								
Renten/Cont Ed:								
Other Students:								

Figure B.3.

Syracuse University

Location: ☒ Urban ☐ Suburban ☐ Rural *Status:* ☐ Public ☒ Independent *Carnegie Class:* RES II

Partnership Name: Project Advance®

Year established: 1973   *Number of schools served:* 102

Grade level(s) served: ☐ Elementary ☐ Middle ☒ High

Types of schools served: ☒ Public   ☒ Pr ivate   ☒ Urban ☒ Suburban   ☒ Rural

Scope of partnership: ☐ National   ☒ Regional   ☐ Local

Area, Region, or Affiliation: Northeast (MA, ME, NJ, NY) and Michigan

Is partnership aimed at systemic reform? No

Annotation:

Syracuse University Project Advance® is a partnership program linking Syracuse University and secondary schools. Its primary mission is to offer qualified high school students the opportunity to enroll in challenging Syracuse University freshman courses during their senior year of high school. Project Advance also provides several other important services in working with the high schools: in-service training for high school instructors; a continuing forum for communication between educators from both school and University settings; and an extensive research and evaluation effort to systematically improve instruction.

Focus Codes: *(P = Primary Focus, F = Secondary Focus)*

Minority/At Risk:	Prof Dev/Inservice: F	Curriculum Dev: F	City/Reg Compacts:	Resource Sharing:
College Courses: P	Recruit/Preserv:	Instruc Res: F	Joint Gov:	Magnet Schools:
Enrich/Gifted: F	Teach Ed Cents:	Tech Prep/2+2:	Shared Faculty: F	Tech Applic: F
Middle Colleges:	Teach Awards:	Regional Artic:	New Fac Roles:	Sch/Coll/Bus:
Tutoring/Couns:	Fac Exchanges:	Systemic Restruc:	Ach/Ass Stnds:	Umbrella Programs:
Career/Apprent:	Oth Educators:	Other Artic:	Other Restruc:	Other Misc:
Student Health:				
Renten/Cont Ed:				
Other Students:				

Content Orientation or Particular Discipline:

SOCIAL SCIENCES
- ☐ Civics/Citizenship
- ☒ Economics
- ☐ Geography
- ☐ Global Educ./Intnl. Studies
- ☒ Government
- ☐ History
- ☐ Law
- ☒ Psychology
- ☒ Sociology
- ☐ Other

EDUCATION
- ☐ Early Childhood Educ.
- ☐ Health/Wellness Educ.
- ☐ Physical/Sports Educ.
- ☐ Special/Inclusive Educ.
- ☐ Other

HUMANITIES AND ARTS
- ☒ English
- ☐ ESL/Bilingual
- ☐ Foreign Language
- ☐ Music
- ☐ Reading/Language Art
- ☐ Speech
- ☐ Studio Arts
- ☐ Theater/Drama
- ☒ Writing
- ☐ Other

APPLIED SCIENCES
- ☐ Business
- ☐ Computer Science
- ☒ Engineering/Technology
- ☐ Health Professions
- ☐ Occupational Education
- ☐ Other

MATHEMATICS AND SCIENCES
- ☐ Astronomy
- ☒ Biology
- ☒ Chemistry
- ☐ Earth Science
- ☐ Envir. Studies/Ecology
- ☒ Mathematics
- ☐ Physics
- ☐ Other

MISCELLANEOUS
- ☐ Basic Skills/Study Skills
- ☐ Crit. Thinking/Prob. Solv.
- ☐ CulturalPluralism
- ☐ Leadership Skills Dev.
- ☐ Library
- ☐ Literacy
- ☐ Parent/Comm. Involvement
- ☐ Research
- ☐ Scholarships/Financial Aid
- ☐ TQM/Strategic Planning
- ☐ Other

College Contact:

Dr. Franklin P. Wilbur
Director
Project Advance
Syracuse University
111 Waverly Ave., Suite 200
Syracuse, NY 13244-2320
Phone: (315) 443-2404   Fax: (315) 443-1524   Email: fpwilbur@advance.syr.edu

National School-College Partnership Database
Search Request Form

_____

Name   Title

_____

Institution

_____

Address

_____

_____

City   State   Zip

Note: Search reports will be **shipped** to the name and address above unless otherwise instructed.

Search Description:

_____

_____

_____

_____

_____

_____

Output Format Options/Charges:

☐ Short Report: $50.00   _____

☐ Extended Report: $65.00   _____

☐ Complete Report: $90.00   _____

   ☐ school contacts option: *addl* $15.00   _____

☐ Mailing Labels: $15.00 per 100, $30.00 minimum   _____

                        Total   =====================

For descriptions of each option, see p. 461.

For examples of report output formats, see Figures B.1, B.2, and B.3.

Important: Please attach an approved institutional purchase order, check, or money order to this request form.

NOTE: If you are ordering mailing labels, the number of labels to be produced will not be known until after the requested search has been completed. For label orders, include the minimum charge of $30 with your search request; you will be billed at $15/hundred for any labels produced in excess of 200.